A LIGHT
THAT NEVER
GOES OUT

A LIGHT THAT NEVER GOES OUT

THE ENDURING SAGA OF THE SMITHS

TONY FLETCHER

WILLIAM HEINEMANN: LONDON

Published by William Heinemann 2012

2 4 6 8 10 9 7 5 3 1

Copyright © Tony Fletcher 2012

Falkirk Council		
BN		
Askews & Holts		
B-SM 1	£20.00	
781.660922		

www.randomhouse.co.uk

Addresses for companies within The Random House Group Limited can be found at:
www.randomhouse.co.uk/offices.htm

The Random House Group Limited Reg. No. 954009

A CIP catalogue record for this book
is available from the British Library

ISBN 9780434020669 (Hardback)
ISBN 9780434022182 (Trade Paperback)

The Random House Group Limited supports The Forest Stewardship
Council (FSC®), the leading international forest certification organisation.
Our books carrying the FSC label are printed on FSC® certified paper.
FSC is the only forest certification scheme endorsed by the leading
environmental organisations, including Greenpeace.
Our paper procurement policy can be found at
www.randomhouse.co.uk/environment

Typeset in Goudy by Palimpsest Book Production Limited,
Falkirk, Stirlingshire

Printed and bound in Great Britain by Clays Ltd, St Ives plc

To everyone who survived the '80s

INTRODUCTION:
A LIGHT THAT NEVER GOES OUT

It takes a particular confidence for one unknown musician to pronounce to another that their first meeting has the hallmarks of legend. But then Johnny Marr, eighteen years old when he arrived uninvited at the Stretford home of Steven Patrick Morrissey one afternoon in May of 1982, had such confidence in abundance; what he did not have, and it was the reason he had come knocking on the door of the nondescript semidetached council house at 384 Kings Road that day, was a partner for his singular talent on the guitar.

Steven Morrissey, a writer of speculative merit and a singer of absolutely no repute whatsoever, managed but sporadic bursts of self-assurance. Though he had been a figure about town since punk rock had exploded in Manchester with a special vigour back in 1976, and was respected, even liked, for his quick wit and bookish intellect, he frequently retreated into a shyness that, as he later penned with devastating certitude, was 'criminally vulgar.' Unlike Marr, who seemed to be on first-name terms with almost everyone involved in Manchester street culture, Morrissey could count his friends on the fingers of one hand.

1

He lived on Kings Road with his divorced mother. He was unemployed – by choice, for sure, but unemployed all the same. He was turning twenty-three that month. By any standard measurement, time appeared to be passing him by.

Aware of Morrissey's shyness, Marr did not show up alone. He was accompanied on his mission by Stephen Pomfret, a mutual guitar-playing acquaintance whose presence was perhaps justified by the painfully long time it took Morrissey to descend from his bedroom to the front door. But once Pomfret had made the introductions, then Marr, not known to waste his time on trivialities, announced that he was on a quest for a singer and lyricist, and Morrissey, not previously known to accept strangers into his life at first glance, promptly invited the visitors in.

The trio ascended to Morrissey's bedroom, where, amidst a life-size cut-out of James Dean and shelves laden with books on feminism, film criticism, and crime, there stood the requisite record player and a collection of neatly filed 45s. Marr, whose encyclopedic knowledge of popular music was arguably unrivaled among Mancunians his age, immediately gravitated to the vinyl, and Morrissey, whose own outspoken opinions on the form had seen him ascend from letter writer to concert reviewer with the weekly music papers over the years, invited his guest to play something. If it was a test of taste, Marr was thrilled to take it: the singles were heavy on the 1960s girl pop that he himself had been busy accumulating on recent trips to secondhand stores, the sort of music he hadn't dare assume anyone else in his vicinity followed with quite such a passion. Bypassing Sandie Shaw and the Shangri-Las, much though he liked the British pop star and, especially, the New York girl group, he instead pulled out a rare 1966 flop single by the Marvelettes on Tamla Motown. It was an American jukebox copy, with the centre hole punched out, and it didn't specify the A-side. So rather than play 'Paper Boy', which had the traditional uptempo Motown feel, Marr put on its flip, 'You're the One', a slower Smokey Robinson composition, and then sang along to prove that he knew the song, that this was more than just a cute gesture. Morrissey was impressed; Marr later said that he felt that was the moment that initiated their friendship.

The pair talked excitedly for the next couple of hours, Pomfret fading into the background, aware that for all the talk of him as a second guitarist in their future band, he was already superfluous to requirements. Morrissey and Marr, so different in age, dress sense, social skills, and various other interests, quickly bonded over that which they had in common: music – a journey that took them from the present day back to Patti Smith and the New York Dolls, then to David Bowie and T. Rex, to the Stooges and the Velvet Underground, and on through '60s girl pop, to a love for rockabilly advertised by their matching retro 'quiff' haircuts. As they sat there in Morrissey's bedroom, they spoke of seeing their own names on a record label – not just as artists but as composers. That Morrissey had but a handful of half-formed lyrics currently to his name, or that Marr had never completed a song to his own satisfaction mattered little; they could sense in each other a shared sense of purpose and dedication, of craftsmanship and intellect. To borrow a phrase from more of their influences – Lou Reed describing his and Andy Warhol's work ethic with the Velvet Underground – neither of them was kidding around.

Johnny Marr had a reference point all his own for their meeting. He had recently watched a documentary that detailed how, way back in 1950, a sixteen-year-old lyricist had knocked on the door of a fellow teenage pianist with a view to forming a songwriting partnership; the pair had gone on to become one of the most successful in popular music. It was the account of this unscripted meeting that had given Marr the inspiration to visit the mysterious Morrissey in the first place. And so he couldn't help himself.

'Hey,' said Johnny, 'this is just how Leiber and Stoller met!'

* * *

3

LEIBER AND STOLLER. Not Lennon and McCartney or Jagger and Richards, though in years to come the names 'Morrissey and Marr' would frequently be spoken of in the same reverential terms – just as the band that they formed out of their meeting that day, the Smiths, would similarly be hailed as Britain's greatest since the Beatles and the Rolling Stones. No, when they first met, Morrissey and Marr looked instead to America for inspiration, where Leiber and Stoller, composers and/or producers of 'Hound Dog', 'Jailhouse Rock', 'Stand By Me', and so many more, helped turn a nation of white teenagers on to black rhythm & blues, playing a crucial part in the explosion of rock 'n' roll and the phenomenon that was Elvis Presley. Three decades since that fateful first encounter, Leiber and Stoller were still self-confessed soul mates. Marr's desire to emulate such an introduction was entirely understandable.

Sadly, his relationship with Morrissey would not last nearly as long. Barely five years later, the camaraderie would dissolve beneath the weight of subtle acrimonies, mutual exhaustion, and implacable musical differences. But during the time they spent together fronting the Smiths, Morrissey and Marr proved themselves every bit the contemporary rivals of Leiber and Stoller, affecting their own followers as significantly as Elvis Presley had affected his. Together, they carved out a unique place for themselves in popular music, an exposed position at the very centre of mid-'80s cool, from where they proceeded to challenge expectations of what constituted an acceptable vocal, a recognisable song title, a typical chord pattern, a traditional lyric, a familiar record sleeve, a standard interview, or, to the extent that they made them at all, a normal promotional video.

Along the way, Morrissey emerged from his cocoon to become one of the late twentieth century's unlikeliest of sex idols, and one of its greatest lyricist-poets. Alongside him, Johnny Marr became revered as perhaps his generation's most gifted guitarist and certainly one of its finest arrangers, as well as an icon of fashion-conscious band leadership in his own right. And in Andy Rourke and Mike Joyce, the Smiths employed a heavyweight rhythm section that not only looked the part – the description of them as 'lads' was typically meant as a compliment – but that could wipe the floor with the best of them. 'The feeling of power onstage,' reflected Morrissey after the band's breakup, with a characteristically prosaic choice of words, 'was just like having a vacuum cleaner shoved up your . . . blazer!'

And yet for all these attributes, the Smiths' success – and their enduring popularity – ultimately comes down to that intrinsic intangible that lies at the very heart of pop culture's pull on us all: their relationship with their audience. Put in the most straightforward of terms, the Smiths expressed the hopes – and just as relevantly, the *fears* – of a generation in a manner unmatched by any other band of their era. That they did so with such a remarkable combination of sexual ambiguity, political panache, collective confidence, and, especially, savage humour not only gained them immortality among their contemporaries but helped win them subsequent generations of equally loyal fans, for whom the long-defunct Smiths exist on a pedestal typically reserved for saints and gods.

Fortunately, the Smiths left behind a sufficiently glorious body of music to justify this quasi-religious devotion: four studio albums, as many compilations, and seventeen singles, for a total of seventy original compositions recorded in the space of just fifty-two months, an output unrivalled since the heyday of mid-'60s creativity, and a catalogue that has cast an impressively long cultural shadow over the subsequent quarter century.[1] Morrissey's exquisite song titles, for example, have been used as titles for novels (Douglas Coupland's *Girlfriend in a Coma*, Marian Keyes's *This Charming Man*), memoirs (Andrew Collins's *Heaven Knows I'm Miserable Now*), off-Broadway plays (a 2009 production entitled *How Soon Is Now?*), cartoons (Andre Jordan's *Heaven Knows I'm Miserable Now*), and a collection of short stories (*Paint a Vulgar Picture*). Their songs have been covered by dance, rock, folk, and pop acts alike, some of them (most notably 'Please, Please, Please Let Me Get What I Want') many times over. The Smiths even provided the inciting incident for a Hollywood movie: in the 2009 American romantic comedy *(500) Days of Summer,* the film's young protagonists bond for the first time in an office elevator when the female lead, listening in on her male workmate's headphones, recognises 'There Is A Light That Never Goes Out,' and proclaims 'I *love* the Smiths!' then promptly sings along to the chorus:

To die by your side, is such a heavenly way to die.

This brief exchange – which duly inspires a love affair that drives the remainder of the movie – acknowledges the band's continued appeal with an audience that was not alive during the Smiths' heyday while simultaneously accepting the 'insider' nature of that following. As for the choice of song, 'There Is a Light That Never Goes Out' is not only among the most popular of Smiths numbers, but it is also (as the Hollywood producers clearly understood) the most romantic: for all of Morrissey's self-proclaimed celibacy, an attribute that distinguished him from almost every other pop idol or rock star through the ages, it's a love song of such perfect devotion that it could only have been written by someone who had himself experienced the boundless yearning of one human heart for another.[2] Curiously, it was never a single. Neither, for that matter (at least not originally or intentionally), was 'How Soon Is Now?' – the other primary candidate for most memorable or identifiable Smiths song, on which Morrissey, more to the public perception of his personality, expressed the pain of the unloved (and unlovable?) with a precision that made it an immediate – and permanent – anthem for anyone who had ever gone to a club on their own, left on their own, gone home, cried, and wanted to die.

But words alone do not guarantee a classic. 'There Is a Light That Never Goes Out' and 'How Soon Is Now?' were each impeccably arranged in the studio by Johnny Marr – one with sampled strings in the chorus tugging tearfully at the heart like the best of Leiber and Stoller's productions for the Drifters, the other expressing its disarmingly simple statement of alienation atop a painstakingly constructed wall of guitars. Though the two songs are so distinctly different in scope, style, and sonics, the end result in each case remains impeccably and unquestionably the sound of the Smiths: as with all the most enduring of musical icons, these songs are instantly recognisable – even when heard through someone else's headphones in an elevator.

This is not to say that the general public at large shares a mutual love and respect for the Smiths. Due to Morrissey's untrained and limited vocal range, which he compensated for in early days with the addition of yodelling, yelping, and the occasional grunt; abetted by the politically personal stance of his lyrics, which sought to tease, amuse, comfort, and confront (though were too often dismissed by ill-informed critics as being merely self-medicating); aided by such a determined collective refusal to compromise that the Smiths were often misconstrued as awkward or arrogant, confirmed by the manner in which they stood musically and visually at direct odds to the mainstream soundtrack of the mid-1980s, to all those now painfully anachronistic booming snare drums and cheap digital keyboards, to the ludicrous fashion statements immortalised in comically ambitious (yet, in hindsight, awkwardly primitive) promotional videos . . . For all these reasons the Smiths were either loved or hated. There was no room for mild acceptance in between.

As such, the Smiths can be considered an archetype, perhaps even the apotheosis, of the 'cult' group. That term certainly seems relevant in the States, where they experienced a form of audience hysteria on their two sold-out tours greater than anything back in Britain, and yet hardly charted. While working on this biography in America, where I moved from my UK homeland shortly after the Smiths broke up, I was occasionally surprised by how few of my neighbours, in what is considered a musical community, had ever heard of the Smiths. But that was just the older folk. Those my own age, most of us parents now, some even with angst-ridden teenagers of our own, mostly greeted a mention of the Smiths as if I were speaking of a former lover. And it's true: the Smiths helped many an American youth of the 1980s through the growing pains of high school and college in lieu of (and occasionally, for those lucky couples who bonded over the band, in the company of) a boyfriend or girlfriend. Crucially, they continue to do so. There is not a 'retro' or 'alternative' dance floor in America that doesn't resonate approximately once an hour to the Smiths; the irony that 'How Soon Is Now?' has become an evergreen dance-club anthem is hopefully not lost on those who lose themselves in it.

Back in the UK, the legacy is a much more public affair. The Smiths were massive then. They are massive now. In 2002, the *New Musical Express* (*NME*) named them its Most Influential Artist ever. In 2006, Morrissey was voted by viewers of BBC2's *The Culture Show* as Britain's second greatest living icon, behind Sir David Attenborough but ahead of Sir Paul McCartney, David Bowie, and Michael Caine. And in 2011, rumours that both Marr and Morrissey were penning their autobiographies were considered significantly newsworthy as to make the national press. Yet perhaps the most extreme example of the Smiths' cultural heritage in their homeland has been the political battle for their affections. The Smiths' four-year chart reign – 1983–87 – coincided with the second of Margaret Thatcher's three consecutive stints as the British Conservative Party's iron-fisted prime minister, an eventual eleven-year tenure marked by strikes, riots, wars, mass unemployment, government clampdowns, and frequently violent confrontations best typified by a year-long miners' strike through 1984–85 that resembled a regional civil war. Beyond Morrissey's unapologetically political lyrics (from both a personal and collective standpoint), the Smiths put their profile where their beliefs lay, playing concerts on behalf of London and Liverpool's embattled Labour city councils, and showing up on the Labour-friendly Red Wedge tour in 1986.

And in a career full of outrageous quotes frequently designed to inflame first and address the interviewer's question later, few were more infamous than Morrissey's opining that 'the sorrow of the Brighton bombing [by the IRA] is that Margaret Thatcher escaped unscathed.'

So when a subsequent Conservative Party leader, David Cameron, chose 'This Charming Man' as one of his 'Desert Island Discs' on the BBC radio show of the same name in 2006, it raised not just eyebrows but questions. Was Cameron, whose party had been in opposition at this point for almost a decade, to a Labour Government led by Prime Minister Tony Blair, disingenuously seeking credibility with wavering left-wingers? Or, given his age – seventeen at the time that 'This Charming Man' became a hit – was he merely paying honest tribute to his youthful allegiances? The politician pleaded the latter, and when the pendulum swung back to the right and he became prime minister in 2010, he continued to bait the media with his avowed love of the Smiths. The media readily bit, especially once his government's early proposal to triple the cost of student tuition was met by angry protests, with some 50,000 descending on London in November 2010, storming and turning over the Conservative Party campaign headquarters in the process. Left-wing columnists instantly resurrected the music of the Smiths, especially *The Queen Is Dead*, as a suitable soundtrack for what seemed like an overnight return to Thatcherite class war.

As the protests (and their attendant violence) continued, Johnny Marr used his Twitter account to demand of the prime minister: 'David Cameron, stop saying that you like the Smiths . . . I forbid you.' In the instantly inflammable age of the Internet, the somewhat flippant tweet became a widely distributed rallying call, with the unexpected result, a few days later, that Morrissey himself took to the web, publishing a letter supporting and expounding upon his former partner's point of view – a rare sign of public affection in what has otherwise become a terminally tense relationship. If it was a mark of the Smiths' exalted stature that, more than two decades after their breakup, the founding members' online musings should become national news, it was a mark of even greater status (and opportunism) when, on the eve of the parliamentary vote over the tuition-fee increase, a Labour MP goaded Cameron over his taste in music during Question Time, leading to a positively surreal bantering of Smiths song titles back and forth across the House of Commons floor.

The following day, students marched to the scene of the impending vote, at Parliament Square. There, a female protester who looked too young to have been alive when the Smiths were first active, scaled the barricades, her hair died blond and cropped short in retro '80s fashion and wearing Dr Martens boots and workmanlike jeans as had been the style back then for a certain segment of the female public. A photographer on the front lines captured her at that instant, looming over a line of nervous riot police with the instantly recognisable phallic symbol of Big Ben looming large in the background; the writer Jon Savage subsequently compared the image to that of the Delacroix painting *Liberty Leading the People*.

It was, truly, a stirring picture. But the reason it ended up being discussed by rock critics, used for the cover of a *Mojo* magazine compilation CD itself named for the Smiths single 'Panic', and forming the welcome image to Johnny Marr's website was due to the girl's crowning choice of fashion statement: a T-shirt depicting the Smiths' *Hatful of Hollow* LP sleeve. Back in the 1980s, the Smiths T-shirt came to serve as something more powerful than a concert souvenir or promotional device: it became the fans' common denominator, their mark of affiliation with other self-proclaimed outsiders. At Parliament Square that day in December 2010, and in particular thanks to the widely distributed photograph in question, the Smiths were once again positioned as outsiders – or, at least, as belonging to the protesters, not the system. The prime minister was careful not to celebrate them again.[3]

*　*　*

I RECALL THIS anecdote in such detail not only because it demonstrates the immense influence of a group that existed for such a short time but because part of my personal remit with this biography is to place the saga of the Smiths in a social context. This is one reason you will find that, rather than starting the book proper with the band's formation and then making repeated forages into the past to explain their musical and lyrical influences, I take the opposite approach. I begin with a historical journey through Manchester and take time to detail the group members' childhoods there through the 1960s and '70s – especially the musical developments that turned Manchester into England's Second (some would say First) Musical City – to explain why the Smiths arrived on the scene fully formed, so complete in their thought process, already so musically and lyrically accomplished that they became Britain's best band within mere months of their first gig.

There is, after all, already something of an extensive library on this most literary of bands. Several of these books fulfill their goals admirably. Simon Goddard's meticulously researched *The Smiths: Songs That Saved Your Life* explores the songwriting process and recording details behind each Smiths composition with almost impeccable exactness; it is partly because of this work that I don't attack the individual songs and sessions in my biography with quite the same ferocity, but rather, focus on the larger narrative surrounding them. Mark Simpson's *Saint Morrissey*, for all the arch grandeur of its title, is a concise, witty, yet constantly well-reasoned armchair psychoanalysis of the singer by a self-confessed obsessive. *Why Pamper Life's Complexities: Essays on the Smiths*, the result of an academic symposium (itself no small mark of respect), is heavy going for those of us who are not fans of the written thesis, but it nonetheless reveals many a home truth amidst the convoluted writing. At the opposite end of the spectrum, *All Men Have Secrets* enabled fans to offer personal memories of the Smiths songs that most greatly affected them.

In the vast expanse in between these extremes, the reader can decipher the Smiths' story through books on the history of the Manchester music scene or that of their record label, Rough Trade; they can garner tidbits from memoirs by such diverse singers as Sandie Shaw and James Maker; they can read visual chronologies and sizable magazine tributes, cultivate yet more fiction and memoir inspired by or related to the group, and even purchase a self-guided tour of the Smiths' Manchester roots.

And yet despite this apparent cottage industry, there has only been one solid biography of the Smiths until now: that by Johnny Rogan, twenty years old at the time of my writing. It is partly the lack of a subsequent study of similar length and depth that inspired me to take on the task for myself. (That and my own love for, empathy with, and contemporaneous experience of the band's music, which will hopefully prove evident throughout, and which is explained anecdotally in some of the endnotes.) Rogan's detective work on Morrissey's family background and adolescence was impressive, and he wrote with comfortable expertise about the music business. But he could only write of what he knew, and at the time that he set about his book, the dust had yet to settle from the Smiths' breakup to provide any kind of clear picture as to their long-term reputation. Two decades' subsequent passing of time hopefully affords me that perspective.[4]

There are plenty of other reasons for my taking on this subject matter. The aforementioned (and other, unmentioned) books all have something in common in that they were written in Britain and published initially or exclusively in Britain, and as a result there is often a parochial quality to them that can find them mired in an analysis of British chart positions, album reviews, and BBC airplay (or lack thereof) as if every act of the group's brief drama were played out only on the British stage. (Interestingly, the exceptions, Marc Spitz's *How Soon Is Never?* and Joe Pernice's *Meat Is Murder* contribution to the 33 1/3 series on classic albums, both of which capture the Smiths' appeal to wayward American youth of the 1980s, are each works of fiction.) There is, as such, a perceived notion of the Smiths as archetypally British.

To be fair, the Smiths embodied a definite view of their (dis) United Kingdom. They launched one album, named (perhaps) for the royal family, with the chorus from a World War I patriotic song, 'Take Me Back to Dear Old Blighty'; they titled another after Manchester's Strangeways Prison. They sung of how 'England is mine, it owes me a living,' and part of what made the single 'Panic' so triumphant was how it rendered temporary gravitas on the decidedly provincial Dundee and Humberside. But in each case, Morrissey was merely flexing his literary muscles, demonstrating the importance of detail to a good story. (Bruce Springsteen routinely does the same thing.) This explains why Smiths fans who couldn't find the locale on a Manchester map still instantly understood the connotations of the 'rented room in Whalley Range' as referenced in the early Smiths song 'Miserable Lie'. Morrissey may have written mostly about what he knew – which was England – but the group he fronted was international through and through.

Finally, crucially, almost every book published about the Smiths has leaned towards the cult of Morrissey. Simpson's *Saint Morrissey*, Len Brown's *Meetings with Morrissey,* and Gavin Hopps's *Morrissey: The Pageant of His Bleeding Heart* make no excuses or apologies for doing so, and given their titles, nor should they. But even Rogan's biography, *Morrissey and Marr: The Severed Alliance,* neglected to mention the band in its title, and depicted only the singer on its cover. Only Goddard's studio analysis could claim neutrality in this regard, and yet he subsequently used much of his research, which of all the Smiths' studio personnel lacked only the cooperation of the singer, into the self-explanatory *Mozipedia*.

One can sympathise. Any biography devoted purely to Johnny Marr, as Richard Carman's *The Smiths and the Art of Gun-Slinging* reveals all too readily, is notably short on the high drama, sexual intrigue, outrageous sound bites, and overwhelming (indeed, domineering) force of character that makes up so much of Morrissey's life story. But as mentioned at the beginning of this introduction, that life was going nowhere (and in no sort of a hurry, either) until the day Johnny Marr came knocking on his door. The beauty of the Smiths, something that most true fans appreciate and which will hopefully become apparent to the more casual reader over the coming pages, is that each of the two geniuses – and I don't use the term lightly – needed the other to complete each other, to realise each other's potential. For the devotion that they afforded each other during their years of creativity, for the extent to which they inspired each other to brilliance, for the solidarity they provided for each other in the face of considerable animosity and extreme pressure, theirs is one of the great love stories of our musical age. And that's where the references to Lennon and McCartney, and especially to Jagger and Richards, come back into play. Morrissey and Marr exist on an equal plane to those greatest of Great British songwriters and bandleaders, and this book will attempt to demonstrate how that came to be, and, in the process, why it couldn't last.

And what, then, of Andy Rourke and Mike Joyce? It's to the Smiths' lasting shame that in a group that continually pitched itself as a band, a gang, a group of 'lads' and 'mates', some members turned out to be more equal than others. It's all the more disappointing given that Rourke and Marr had been best friends since secondary school, and that their musical and personal comradeship formed the heart and soul of the Smiths. Of course, few groups of merit survive into history without some sort of lawsuit over ownership or distribution of their valuable back catalogue, but we typically expect the accused figure(s) to be the corrupt manager, the fraudulent accountant, or the unscrupulous record label, not the band members themselves. Because it was never my intent to write much beyond the group's breakup, the details of the High Court case that embarrassed the Smiths both collectively and individually in 1996 are not examined in any more detail than on this page, but in telling the band's story, I attempt to lay out the paper trail (or, more precisely, the lack of it) that ultimately led Joyce to sue Morrissey and Marr. (Rourke, penniless at the time and with no inclination to face his former best friend across the dock, settled out of court.) I also attempt to provide the background for why such a knowledgeable student of Oscar Wilde's downfall as Morrissey should have attempted to verbally spar with the High Court judge as if he were but a cub reporter for a regional newspaper. The end result was not only the judge's irreparable description of Morrissey's evidence as 'devious, truculent, and unreliable where his own interests were at stake,' but a finding in Joyce's favour (worth more than a million pounds at the time, and with considerable additional royalties in the decades since) that the singer still refuses to publicly acknowledge. It is, I suspect, no coincidence that the two members of the Smiths who offered their cooperation with this book were those who have made their peace with the group's financial failings. (A full list of those who participated in interviews and otherwise helped out extensively with research can be found in the Acknowledgements.)

The Smiths' inability to properly account for themselves in the monetary sense can be largely explained by their lack of ongoing representation. Following the departure of their original mentor and manager, Joe Moss, Morrissey and Marr proved unable between them to agree on, appoint, and then, crucially, to *trust* a band manager. Almost unprecedented among groups of their stature, the band was, therefore, (in)effectively self-managed at the very height of their popularity, in 1986 – at which point, not coincidentally, they signed to EMI, Britain's oldest establishment major label, despite still being contractually bound to Rough Trade, Britain's leading post-punk independent.

This battle for rights to the Smiths' music provides an intriguing subplot, a fascinating insight into both the machinations of the music business and the motivations of its

15

performers. Personally, I doubt very much that the Smiths would have enjoyed equal creative freedom – while simultaneously experiencing uninterrupted critical acclaim *and* commercial success – on any other label than Rough Trade, which became something of a household name as a result of successfully breaking the Smiths. And yet Morrissey saw it the other way: that it was the Smiths who took Rough Trade into the mainstream, that the label would have gone under without them, and that, in turn, the group would have been that much 'bigger' in more traditionally corporate hands. It's a hypothetical debate, perhaps, but the fact remains that because Rough Trade was known as a pioneering record store and major distribution centre as well as an imprint, the saga of the Smiths has become something of a cipher for the larger independent scene that produced and nurtured them. Indeed, there is a strong argument to be made that the concept of 'indie music' as a sound and a style (as opposed to a mere descriptor of the mode of distribution) began with the success of the Smiths, and that the Britpop successes of the post-Smiths 'Madchester' era – when the likes of Blur and Manchester's own Oasis sold millions upon millions of albums (on major labels) – would not have occurred without the Smiths helping pave the way on Rough Trade. The fact, then, that the Smiths broke up before EMI could even get them into the studio offers a rather vicious sting in their tale of wanderlust.

As such, there were times during the telling of this story, when stories of the (dis)organisational machinations threatened to overwhelm those of the musical brilliance, that I felt tempted to subtitle the book *How Not to Succeed in the Music Business* . . . Except that, of course, the Smiths did succeed. And how. Out of the chaos, confusion, and high drama that passed for everyday normality in the Smiths came some of the most magical and enduring music of their generation. In other words, had the Smiths run a tight business ship, with an experienced managerial figure at the helm, perhaps on an established record label, subscribing to traditional industry values regarding the aural quality of their recordings, the timing of their releases, and the methods of their promotion, then the musical part of the story would likely have been so very, very different. And with it, the cultural impact would not possibly have been the same. That would have been their loss, for sure. And ours, for certain.

CHAPTER ONE

I don't really feel any kinship with the place. It's just somewhere that I just so happen to live. It doesn't mean a great deal to me. And I'm sure I'll leave very soon – when I'm rich.

 – MORRISSEY, the David Jensen show,
July 1983

We felt like every little town was our hometown. And I think that the people in Inverness and Brighton and St Austell and Norwich all felt that way when they came out to see us.

 – JOHNNY MARR, May 2011

The story of the Smiths is intrinsically entwined with that of Manchester. And yet the group proved curiously conflicted in their loyalties to the city that birthed them – and which has subsequently claimed them as one of its most successful exports and biggest tourist attractions. It's not just that the Smiths concluded their first album with the disparaging refrain, 'Manchester, so much to answer for,' or opened their second one with the equally negative line, 'Belligerent ghouls run Manchester schools.' It's not only that they packed their bags and moved to the British capital at more or less the first sign of success (though the fact that they returned to Manchester a year later suggests that they may have gained a new appreciation for their hometown in their absence). It's also that the Smiths played in Manchester less often in *the entire four years* of their performing career than they played in London during their first twelve months alone.

Such ambivalence can partly be excused and justified as ambition, a determination to escape the relative confines of their semidetached, semiurban surroundings and spread their musical wings across a national, and then an international, stage. From the beginning, the Smiths sensed greatness, and to realise that greatness meant a refusal to accept confinement to the margins. They were never going to content themselves with being anything as trifling as a mere *Manchester band*.

And yet, more deeply conflicted feelings about their origins are readily understandable. As children, Steven Morrissey and Johnny Marr were ejected from their inner-city childhood homes, in the overlapping neighbourhood of Hulme and Moss Side, and Ardwick, respectively, as part of a sweeping programme of 'slum clearance' that provided them with better housing, but at the cost of community upheaval. All four members of the band were subject to the city's arcane and draconian (in their case, Catholic) school system, which failed miserably to provide them with a quality education, let alone a means to pursue their artistic talents. And they came together at a time when Manchester was declining more precipitously than any other British city under the weight of poverty, unemployment, and attendant social ills – and yet, during the early days of the Smiths' unanimous acclaim from the London music media, it often seemed as if they had to fight for every last drop of local civic respect. What, in a sense, was there to be loyal *towards*?

This, in a more general sense, has long been Manchester's dilemma. A city that launched the Industrial Revolution, that contributed so enormously to Britain's wealth, that to a large extent financed and furnished the Victorian empire, did so on the backs of its underpaid, malnourished, mistreated workers. Its inhabitants therefore mix an instinctive pride for their city's copious achievements (including its ongoing sporting and cultural successes) with a necessary prejudice against their own bosses and municipal leaders who have often sold them out without a second thought. The result is a somewhat cheerful cynicism; Mancunians remain among Britain's most outgoing and welcoming people despite their history of hardships. The occasional good-natured ribbing aside, there is rarely any genuine antagonism exhibited towards residents of the 'soft south.'

As for the Smiths, however, perhaps the main reason they never waved a Manchester flag was because, for three of them at least, their recent family histories lay not in Lancashire but in Ireland. 'With so much Irishness around us, my sister and I growing up never really felt we were Mancunians,' said Morrissey in 1999, five years before he released a solo song describing himself as being of 'Irish Blood, English Heart'. Johnny Marr put it another way: 'I don't think of myself as being English and I don't think of myself as being Irish. I think of myself as being Mancunian Irish.' If one or both of these viewpoints was true too of the other Smiths, so it was of so many Mancunians down the course of history, because a significant part of Manchester's wealth – or at least the wealth of its industrialists, who were not readily predisposed to share it – was built upon Irish blood.

BEFORE ITS TRANSFORMATION in the eighteenth century, Manchester served as but a respectable agricultural centre, with an additional reputation for textile production thanks to an influx of Flemish weavers exiled there in the 1300s; it was Liverpool, thirty miles west along the River Mersey, that stood radiant as the 'Gateway to the British Empire'. Liverpool's fortunes were built in part on the export of Manchester textiles, and on guns made in Birmingham, but they were especially enhanced by the exchange of such goods on the west coast of Africa for human cargo, which was then transported for sale into slavery in the West Indies or along the American Atlantic coast before returning from the New World laden with raw goods. Come the year 1800, and Liverpool was considered the second wealthiest city in all of Europe.

By then, however, the harnessing of steam power, and the successive inventions, mostly in the British Midlands and northwest, of a series of jennies, looms, frames, and mules that exponentially increased the production capabilities in the cotton industry, were already serving to shift that balance of regional power. Manchester benefited from these inventions in part due to its existent foothold in textiles, but also because it had the attributes required by the new large-scale industries – natural high humidity, heavy rainfall, a copious supply of soft water, and, thanks to the pioneering Bridgewater Canal that connected a private regional coal mine to the owner's warehouse in Manchester, easy access to coal and a burgeoning system of further arterial canals. The world's first water-powered mill was built in Royton, in the east of modern Manchester, in 1764; the city's first steam-driven mill opened in Shudehill, in the heart of modern Manchester, in 1782. From there, the mills expanded by the dozen, many of them built on the banks of the Rochdale Canal in Ancoats, the border of modern Manchester's fashionable Northern Quarter. Mills were also constructed on the northern edges of Chorlton-on-Medlock, through which ran the Oxford Road south from the city, and on which was later built the University of Manchester, the city's most populous seat of higher learning and one that, studies have frequently shown, now attracts students as much for Manchester's musical reputation as any educational one.

Britain abolished slavery in 1807, and Liverpool's position at the core of its global trade suffered accordingly; the 'Middle Passage' having been eliminated, ships arrived at the Mersey port increasingly laden with raw cotton from India or the Americas, and departed with finished cotton textiles from Manchester for sale around the globe. In 1830, when the world's first passenger railway line opened, connecting the two great northwestern English cities, there was little doubt which of them held the key to Britain's future prosperity: 'Cottonopolis', as Manchester had come to be known, the engine room of the Industrial Revolution.

By this point in time, fully one-fifth of Manchester's population was Irish.[1] They had come in part because of the poverty in their homeland, where, especially since the Acts of Union at the start of the nineteenth century, they had been subjugated by absentee British landlords to the point that the greater part of their food production ended up on English dinner tables. They came to Manchester especially for the promise of jobs in the vast new cotton mills, as well as the iron foundries, machinery plants, and glass works that were built in large part to service this industry. And yet they arrived to find themselves shunned by the English, who viewed them not only with the religious prejudice of a Protestant nation, and not just as a threat to employment but, with their foreign tongue (for many of the immigrants spoke Gaelic) and equally distant ways, as a different and inferior race entirely.

As a result, the Irish had been cast into ghettoes, where they lived in quite possibly the worst conditions yet witnessed in a (then) modern society. Details of their hardships were eventually publicised by Dr James Phillips Kay in his 1832 study entitled *The Moral and Physical Condition of the Working Classes Employed in the Cotton Manufacture in Manchester*. Kay served as physician to the Ardwick and Ancoats Dispensary, neighbourhoods that, along with New Town (or Irish Town), served as the main residential areas for the Irish immigrants and were, not by coincidence, the core of the city's squalor. In these areas, entire families of sixteen or more could be found cohabiting in single, sublevel, damp, pestilent rooms barely one hundred square feet in size, crowded in with pigs and other animals. Such was the lack of basic sanitation that on Parliament Street, some 380 people shared a single 'privy', from which the human waste not surprisingly ran over into adjacent houses. (In whole swathes of inner Manchester, there were a greater number of beer houses, taverns, and gin shops than there were toilets.) Allowing too that the city's rivers were poisoned any number of odorous colours by chemical dumping, and that the air was thickened with polluting soot to the point that the houses were coated black with the stuff, it was no wonder that cholera epidemics often swept the city – and that fully half the city's infants died before the age of five.

Those children who survived found themselves called to

work in the factories and mills; it was a mark of just how deeply they were enslaved in such premises that an 1819 Cotton Factories Regulation Act had been required to restrict their labour even to twelve hours a day. Still, partly because there was no enforcement of these laws until a new act of Parliament in 1833, children as young as five – many of them orphans provided by local parish authorities – continued to be freely beaten, easily injured, otherwise mistreated and abused, and disciplined violently, often dipped headfirst into water cisterns when they inevitably became drowsy from overwork. Men, women, and children alike worked in a machinery-driven din of such volume that the French philosopher Alexis de Tocqueville wrote of the Manchester of this time that he heard it before he saw it, using appropriately rhythmic language to bemoan the 'crunching wheels of machinery, the shriek of steam from boilers, the regular beat of the looms.'

Likewise, in his groundbreaking report, Dr Kay rightly compared 'The dull routine of a ceaseless drudgery' in the mills to 'the torment of Sisyphus – the toil, like the rock, recoils perpetually on the wearied operative'. Yet Kay could not hide an underlying contempt for the unskilled Irish among these toilers. With free use of the term 'savage,' he cited their 'contagious example of ignorance and a barbarous disregard of forethought and economy,' and concluded that 'such a race is useful only as a mass of animal organisation, which consumes the smallest amount of wages.'

By the end of the 1830s, cotton accounted for fully half of Britain's export earnings, but there had been little change in living standards. When the German-born Friedrich Engels came to town in 1842, sent by his father to oversee the family's cotton spinning mill in the hope that the experience would temper the young man's radical beliefs, his exposure to the effects of large-scale industry encouraged him instead to formulate his own vision of society alongside his political partner, Karl Marx, with whom he would meet and devour economic theories at Chetham's public library (the oldest in Britain) during the latter's visits to Manchester. Engels and Marx would later pen *The Communist Manifesto*, but first, in 1845, Engels was to publish *The Conditions of the Working Class in England*, at the age of just twenty-four. In it, Engels – suspecting that it was more by design than accident – astutely noted of Manchester how its city centre was filled with impressive offices and warehouses, and the main roads out of town were lined with well-kept shops. As such, a businessman 'commuting' from his suburban village, or a visitor whom he might wish to impress, could make the journey in and out of the city centre without exposure to the destitution of the working-class residences that lay hidden behind the main roads in a vast, unmapped configuration of alleys and terraces and jerry-built cottages – out of sight and, to many, out of mind.

Detailing the conditions of the slum people and the factories that employed them as a powder keg ready to explode, Engels framed his study not just as an indictment of the Industrial Revolution but as a warning of an inevitable *Workers* Revolution. 'The fighting proletariat *will help itself*,' he believed. Yet Engels, like Kay before him, seemed to simultaneously believe that self-emancipation was beyond the Irish. In a special section of his 'Conditions' devoted to Irish Immigration, he stooped to every caricature ever identified with the nationality:

'The worst dwellings are good enough for them; their clothing causes them little trouble, so long as it holds together by a single thread; shoes they know not; their food consists of potatoes and potatoes only; whatever they earn beyond these needs they spend upon drink. What does such a race want with high wages?'

It has sometimes been suggested by Engels apologists that these comments were a form of bitter sarcasm, perhaps intended to reflect the views of the Industrial barons, but his conclusions still made for awkward reading: 'Even if the Irish, who have forced their way into other occupations, should become more civilised, enough of the old habits would cling to them to have a strong degrading influence upon their English companions in toil, especially in view of the general effect of being surrounded by the Irish.' Engels's theory was to be immediately put to the test, as potato crops repeatedly failed across Ireland in the 1840s, leading to famine and the mass emigration of up to a million young Irish in less than a decade, many of whom followed a now familiar journey – to the mills, works and slums of inner Manchester.

MANCHESTER GAINED RENOWN as more than just the birthplace of modern capitalism *and* communism. In 1801, the Church of England Sunday Schools in Manchester, proud of their part in helping to educate the poorest of factory children, paraded them to the Collegiate Church on Whit Monday to hear a special holiday sermon. The practice soon spread across the country, while growing more popular in Manchester so that by the middle of the century, a minimum of 10,000 'scholars' could be found marching behind church banners; in time, the children would come to anticipate the Whit Walks as an alternate Christmas, a day for new clothes and financial gifts from relatives and friends. Other events carried a heavier weight of history. In 1819, years of worker unrest following the Napoleonic Wars culminated in an astonishingly large crowd of 60,000 gathering in the city's St Peter's Field from all across Lancashire to hear the top orators of the day call for parliamentary reform. (Despite its size and economic importance, Manchester still did not have representation in Parliament.) Though the crowd had been urged to come in peace, local magistrates feared the worst, sending in sabre-wielding cavalry and yeomanry to arrest the speakers. The result was fifteen fatalities, women and children among them, and several hundred more injuries. Among those arrested on the podium was the reporter from the (London) *Times*; the subsequent media outcry at the treatment of speakers, journalists, and unarmed civilians alike led quickly to the creation of the (Manchester) *Guardian*, to this day considered the most consistently informative liberal newspaper in the world. Yet the 'Peterloo' massacre served as such a stain on Manchester's reputation that it has been largely swept under the carpet of history; only in 2010 did a plaque at the site finally acknowledge the civilian deaths. That plaque is affixed to the former Free Trade Hall, best known among classical music fans as the home of the Hallé Orchestra; widely revered by some rock historians as the venue at which Bob Dylan was declared a Judas for playing the electric guitar in 1966; and known by many more as the place where the Sex Pistols performed twice, in close succession, in 1976, kick-starting the now-venerable local punk scene. Steven Patrick Morrissey was among a highly select band of Mancunians to attend both shows.

The Free Trade Hall was itself built on behalf of the Anti-Corn Law League, established in Manchester in 1838 by industrialists who believed that unfettered trade would result in greater wealth for all. Reformers who sided closer with the plight of the workers aligned themselves instead with the Chartist movement, also launched in 1838, which called for annual elections and universal suffrage, and gained public credence with a rally on the Moors just north of Manchester that same year that attracted 200,000 people. In the summer of 1842, a mass movement of angry workers, influenced by the Chartists, responded to a long-term economic depression by refusing the familiar imposition of hefty wage reductions and by going on strike, 'pulling the plug' from factory steam engines across industrial England. Come early August of that year, as the unrest spread to inner Manchester, a volatile crowd of up to 15,000 was to be found roaming Ancoats, fighting police, looting shops, and even torching factories. Read the Riot Act by frightened authorities, the protesters were eventually dispersed with the help of cannons and five hundred newly sworn-in special constables. By the end of the month, with cavalry patrolling the streets, the city had the feel of an occupied territory – and the management of Ermen & Engels Cotton

Mill, just weeks before young Friedrich arrived, took out an advertisement on the front page of the *Guardian* to thank the police for putting down the 'Plug Riots'.

Not all industrialists were interested in suppressing their workers with brute force. Running parallel to the protests of the Chartist era in Manchester was an invigorating cooperative movement, influenced by the philosophy of Robert Owen, a former Manchester mill owner and reformer who had moved his business to Scotland to establish a more munificent factory environment, including a free village school. In 1840, he returned some of his profits to Manchester by replacing the oversubscribed Social Institute in Manchester's adjoining city of Salford with a Hall of Science, just off Deansgate in the heart of the city's squalor. Engels, who frequented the Hall of Science as part of his cavalier flitting between Manchester's various races and classes, remarked on how its working-class members devoured not only the political theories of Voltaire and Paine but also the British romantic poets. As well they might, for the poets at least spoke to their existence. After travelling through Manchester in 1807, for example, Robert Southey had concluded that, 'a place more destitute than Manchester is not easy to conceive.' And Percy Shelley wrote his 'Masque of Anarchy' – the poem that called on the English to 'rise like lions after slumber in unvanquishable number' – upon hearing of the Peterloo massacre. Almost 150 years after that poem's belated British publication, a burgeoning Manchester musician, Pete McNeish, would change his last name to Shelley, and as lead singer and songwriter with the Buzzcocks go on to write some of the most enduring – albeit brief – romantic poems in the modern British canon. And so the wheel turns.

Over the course of the nineteenth century, the plight of Manchester's working poor slowly, incrementally improved. A series of Factory Acts restricted child labour, enforced mandatory education, and reduced adult shifts to a point where workers could develop (and spend their) leisure time. The newly embodied Manchester City Council passed its first construction bylaws in 1868, the same year that the Trades Union Congress (TUC) was formed at the invitation of the Manchester and Salford Trades Council. There were still cyclical busts as the new global markets learned to deal with the repercussions of bank collapses and wars; the lack of raw cotton imports during the American Civil War led to famine and riots even as the Manchester workers officially supported the American Union in its opposition to slavery (which explains the statue of Abraham Lincoln in Manchester's Lincoln Square). At such times of hardship, the Irish often became easy targets for resentment and prejudice; the failed Fenian Rising in the late 1860s, in particular, inspired regional outbursts of anti-Irish mob violence. But as the city's biggest minority, the Irish in Manchester were increasingly emboldened to express their cultural heritage through branches of the Gaelic Athletic Association, the Gaelic League, St Patrick's Day celebrations, Catholic Whit Walks held on the Friday of the Whit Week, literary and debating clubs – and, of course, through music. Ultimately, though, nothing declared their Irishness as much as their faith; not only were a number of Catholic churches built in Manchester in the nineteenth century but, significantly to the future story of the Smiths, an equally large number of Catholic schools.

By 1914, Manchester's commercial dominance appeared uncontested: the opening of the Manchester Ship Canal twenty years earlier had opened up a direct route to the Irish Sea that bypassed Liverpool entirely, helping Manchester claim processing rights to an astonishing two-thirds of the world's cotton. But a decline in manufacturing subsequently took hold during World War I, as Britain's access to its foreign markets became greatly restricted; it accelerated again when the war ended though other nations soon began producing equivalent goods at a cheaper price (often, ironically, on machinery made in Manchester). The Great Depression hit Manchester especially hard, with mills falling like dominoes, forcing a permanent decline in its population from its 1931 peak of 766,000, and although World War II saw much of the workforce gainfully employed in the manufacture of munitions, it was the United States, not Great Britain, that emerged from global battle as the prevalent economic empire. The balance of power that had shifted over the nineteenth century from Liverpool to Manchester had now emigrated entirely.

But no city of any merit takes defeat lying down, and Manchester in the immediate aftermath of World War II had reason to still believe in itself. It had been spared the excessive bombing runs of the Nazi Luftwaffe that had flattened entire sections of Liverpool, and thanks to the Manchester Ship Canal, its port was still the country's third largest. The city had two of England's finest and best-supported football teams (Manchester United and Manchester City), a reputation for music and nightlife, and a pronounced love of jazz and blues. And the Labour Party, born of a TUC conference held in 1900, had come to power at the end of the war and embarked on an immediate and exhausting programme of welfare reforms and nationalisation of industries that promised a fairer distribution of industrial wealth. Not only had Engels's vision of a workers' revolution come about in precisely the manner he had considered impossible – in small steps, without armed insurrection – but his fears of Irish savages corrupting English mores had been proven hopelessly ill informed: the 'civilisation' of the Irish in Manchester in fact helped improve conditions for everyone.

CHAPTER TWO

I was very aware of being Irish and we were told that we were quite separate from the scruffy kids around us – we were different to them. In many ways, though, I think I had the best of both places and the best of both countries. I'm 'one of us' on both sides.

Morrissey, *Irish Times*, November 1999

One of my first ever memories is of seeing two young Irish women who were not long over here from a tiny Irish village, skint but better off than they were back home, entirely liberated by this new life. Needing to live within feet of each other as a support system.

Johnny Marr, March 2011

The new wave of Irish immigrants were not fleeing famine, and neither were they living under British rule anymore. Ireland had gained independence in 1922 and officially became a Republic – Éire – in 1948, even though the decision by the six counties of the mostly Protestant north to stay part of the United Kingdom meant that the issue of full Irish unity and independence would remain frustratingly unresolved. But for the time being, there was peace. Indeed, under the leadership of President Éamon de Valera, Ireland had successfully sat out World War II entirely – referring to it instead as 'The Emergency'. And in a reversal of mid-nineteenth-century (mis)fortunes, a protectionist policy had ensured that the Irish had plenty of meat on their plates throughout and beyond the war years, while the British endured continual rationing. But isolation had come at a price: Éire was denied membership of the United Nations until 1955 as a result of its neutrality, and the economy barely limped along as a result, its agricultural base no match for the (re)building boom that was taking place across war-ravaged Europe. Great Britain, embarking on an ambitious plan to construct a million new homes, had even taken to advertising for immigrant workers in its colonies. It was all too tempting for the youth of Éire to travel across the Irish Sea and pick up some of these jobs in the big British cities. Through the first half of the 1950s, some 200,000 left Ireland, and once again, a significant percentage settled in Manchester.

Among them were a majority of seven Morrissey siblings who had been raised in a central Dublin tenement until they were moved into the new housing estates of Crumlin, south of the city, in a process of enforced 'slum clearance' that would become a constant refrain in the life of the second youngest, Peter Aloysius Morrissey, but a week old at the time of the family's relocation in November 1935. The Irish nation under de Valera was to be applauded for addressing the housing needs of its urban poor, but it skimped on the social amenities necessary to establish true community bonds: with a lack of good schools, playing fields, and jobs, Crumlin could not contain the postwar ambitions of this new generation.

Mary Bridget Morrissey emigrated first, opening up a pet shop in the solidly Irish part of South Manchester's Moss Side neighbourhood with her husband, Leo Corrigan. Cathryn Patricia followed, marrying in London in 1952 and relocating with her husband, Richard Corrigan – Leo's brother – to Moss Side's Stockton Street, one of several roads laid out on a north-south pattern leading from Moss Lane down towards Alexandra Park. The two- and three-storey terraced houses of this enclosed residential area opened onto the street as was typical in working-class England, but several of the larger ones had cellars, gabled windows and tiny front yards; they were not by any means the slums of the nineteenth-century Irish immigrants. Distinct from the new West Indian community of Moss Side that lay to the east of the Princess Street jazz clubs, the neighbourhood provided a base for the ever-growing number of Manchester Morrisseys. Around the same time that another sister, Ellen, married there in 1955, Peter Morrissey, still a teenager, was enticed to join them, staying with Richard and Patricia Corrigan on Stockton Street while he found a job and made plans for his girlfriend to follow suit.

That girl, Elizabeth Ann Dwyer, known to all as Betty, was the second oldest in a family that, like the Morrisseys, consisted of five girls and two boys and had likewise lived in the very heart of Dublin, on Pearse Street, until being moved out to the corporation houses in Crumlin. Further back on the Dwyer family line there was reputedly some serious wealth – considerable land ownership around the tourist village of Cashel – but that was hardly evident when Betty Dwyer left school at fourteen to take a job at one of the Crumlin factories, sewing buttons. It was there she had met Peter Morrissey, himself employed making ashtrays and lampshades; they started courting, and by the time they made their respective moves to Manchester, where Betty settled into digs around the corner from Stockton Street with an elderly couple who looked after her like she was their own, they were a firm couple.

And a fine-looking one at that. Betty was nothing less than beautiful in her youth, whether photographed standing next to Peter's mother outside the Stockton Street house in an everyday cardigan, her evident Irish features accentuated by her broad smile, or dressed to the nines, likewise beaming for the camera, during a day out in Alexandra Park. Peter had broad shoulders, a comparatively stout build, and typically met the camera with an air of quiet determination and resilience; he became quickly known in Manchester for his positive attitude, his reliability as a friend and worker, his cheerful demeanour, and especially his love of football, a sport that was officially frowned on in Éire, which promoted the Gaelic version of the game instead. Peter had been among many of his hometown's youth to have taken a pledge of temperance during the time of their confirmation into the Church, and reached adulthood without developing a taste for alcohol. When he arrived in Manchester, he was more interested in the freedom to play Association Football than the opportunity to knock back the booze; over subsequent years, he developed a parallel reputation as a devoted, exceptionally talented amateur player and a reluctant, equally amateur drinker.

Peter Morrissey quickly got a job as a forklift truck driver in the Trafford Park warehouse of the venerable Manchester company Richard Johnson, Clapham and Morris (JCM); Betty gained employment as a packer for a firm of blanket makers. On the surface, neither job appeared much more attractive than those they had left behind in Crumlin, and to be sure, the new Irish immigrants still experienced their share of discrimination. But by this point they were too well established in Manchester, and conditions sufficiently improved for the working class as a whole, to accept themselves as scapegoats or to be manipulated as scabs. There were jobs for all, on building sites and roads, in hospitals and factories, at shops and schools, with a fair day's pay for any who could commit to a hard day's work. And when work was done, there were Irish pubs and social clubs to gather at, Catholic churches to attend on Sundays, and Catholic schools for the children when they came along. There was a *life*, and all things considered, it was a good one. On 16 March 1957, Peter Morrissey and Betty Dwyer, twenty-one and nineteen years old respectively, wed at the Church of Our Lady of Perpetual Succour in Moss Side. The service was followed by a party back on Stockton Street that raged all night and all the way through the subsequent St Patrick's Day, with several of Betty's siblings, visiting from Dublin – and her parents, too – enjoying themselves so much that they immediately hatched their own plans to move to Manchester.

Less than six months later, Betty gave birth to a girl, Jacqueline Mary. The daughter arrived in the midst of a transition for the British so vivid that many who lived through it saw it as if the world had switched in front of them from black-and-white to colour. The arrival of rock 'n' roll music from America, and the simultaneous explosion of its simplistic British sibling, skiffle, came at a point when food rationing had finally ended and the abolition of national service loomed enticingly on the horizon, inviting the nation's youth to rediscover themselves as something brand-new: teenagers. They did so in a growing economy, with a disposable income on which to buy the 45 rpm singles of the newly hip hit parade, as well as to indulge in fresh fashions that experienced a tabloid-enhanced heyday with the drape jackets of the 'teddy boys', but were more generally enjoyed for the novel freedom to express oneself as something other than merely a working person. For the musically minded, the concept of hire purchase – payment on installment plans – presented the opportunity to own guitars and drums, to form rock 'n' roll or skiffle bands, to explore career opportunities beyond the familiar office apprenticeship and factory line. Hastening this dream process down in London, a thoroughly British entrepreneur by the name of Larry Parnes set up a personal assembly line by which he transformed teenage boys of faultless physicality and dubious talent into singing sensations with vaguely risqué stage names: Tommy Steele, Marty Wilde, Billy Fury and the like. None was to be confused with Elvis Presley, Little Richard, or even Buddy Holly, but given that by the end of the 1950s, those three had, respectively, gone into the Army, found religion, and been killed in a plane crash, the Brits took what Parnes and his ilk could produce – and with gratitude.

Peter and Betty Morrissey were just the wrong side of the newly delineated teenage line to enjoy all of this; it would be not them but their children who would benefit from the changed society. Shortly after the arrival of Jacqueline, the family moved from temporary rented digs on Moss Side's Henrietta Street to a more permanent home at 17 Harper Street, part of the same neighbourhood but, crucially, just to the west of the City of Manchester lines and inside the Municipal Borough of Stretford. Peter Morrissey took an improved job at the JCM factory and continued to play football religiously. There were, it was suggested, opportunities to swap the one profession for the other, especially after February

1958, when eight of the Manchester United first team, which had just won the English league two years in a row, died as their charter plane crashed on takeoff following a European Cup quarter-final in Munich. As the star striker both of a league-topping pub team *and* works team, Peter Morrissey was routinely urged by his fellow amateurs to take trials for United, whose Old Trafford ground was close by the JCM warehouse; the thought was that he might at least make a now-depleted reserves team. But Morrissey had been through the process before, passing a trial at neighbouring Bury then turning down further invitations due to a clash with his overtime schedules. Morrissey was a risk taker on the football field only; when it came to work and family, he erred on the side of caution. The arrival of a son, in spring 1959, put paid to any last hopes – more on the part of his friends by now than his own – to meet a professional calling outside of the factory.

The boy was born at the Park Hospital in Davyhulme, on 22 May, Whit Friday – which made the Morrisseys among the few Mancunian Irish not to spend the day alongside 50,000 of their fellow Roman Catholics, some of whom marched through the city streets to the sound of pipes, fife, drums, and brass bands, others of whom broke through barriers to rush the American-born Archbishop Gerald Patrick O'Hara. It was the kind of religious hysteria that would later befall the newborn Morrissey on a nightly basis – not, of course, that anyone had great expectations of such worship as he lay on the hospital bed.

When it came to naming the boy, Peter and Betty looked to tradition. As was not uncommon for inner-city Dublin of the 1930s, Peter Morrissey had seen two younger siblings die in infancy, one of them named Patrick Steven; with the slightly different spelling of Patrick Stephen, this had also been the name of Betty's father. Patrick, however, was *too* Irish a name to go up front; it was bad enough knowing their son might be called a Paddy for his Irish roots without, literally, calling him Paddy. For his part, the child would later claim he had been named for the American actor Steve Cochran, a former on-screen tough guy and ongoing off-screen Romeo who, at the time of the Morrissey boy's birth, was about to hit his nadir as the lead in a schlock movie that promised to lift the lid off 'the wild, weird world of the Beatniks!' That movie, *The Beat Generation*, opened in July 1959, the same month Peter and Betty got around to officially registering their son's name – as Steven Patrick Morrissey.

IF *THE BEAT GENERATION* represented some scraping of the Hollywood barrel, British cinema was going through a far more fertile period the year of Steven Morrissey's birth. January saw the release of the movie *Room at the Top*, based on a recent John Braine novel in which the narrator moves to a prosperous West Yorkshire market town from his desperate Lancashire mill town outside Manchester; in September followed an adaptation of the highly acclaimed John Osborne play *Look Back in Anger*, set largely in an attic apartment in a smoky Midlands city. Between them, the two films announced a 'new wave' of British cinema: powerfully earnest movies that depicted, in stark black-and-white film and equally plain, even vulgar language, the stymied, hampered, claustrophobic lives of the contemporary working class and their often frustrated attempts at upward mobility.

The literary and theatrical movement that led to these films had initially been heralded as one of 'Angry Young Men', as in the Osborne play, but that title had been rendered almost instantly obsolete when, in 1958, *A Taste of Honey* introduced a new and unsettling version of femininity onto the London stage. A savagely hilarious and brutally amoral tale of a northern teenage working-class girl, Jo; her pregnancy by a black soldier who promptly vanishes from her life; her subsequent friendship with a protective gay student; and, throughout, her troubled relationship with a semi-whoring mother, Helen, and Helen's latest alcoholic playboy partner, *A Taste of Honey* managed to break almost every taboo that existed across British social mores. (Homosexuality being illegal, that character's sexual orientation was never actually stated, though it was certainly implied by the familiar, flowery insults hurled his way by Helen's lover.) The breakthrough was rendered all the more astonishing by the fact that A *Taste of Honey*'s author, Shelagh Delaney, was just seventeen years old when she wrote it and not part of any perceived theatrical 'set'; a working-class girl determined that the theatre should be a place 'where the audience has contact with real people, who are alive,' she had set the play in her native Salford.

In a BBC profile on Delaney broadcast in 1960, at which point her second play, *The Lion in Love*, had just been launched and a superb cinematic rendition of A *Taste of Honey* was in production, Salford was described, in the clipped tones of the Queen's English, as a 'grey industrial town near Manchester.' This was typical patronising southern ignorance, for Salford was a city in its own right. Divided from Manchester to the east (and Stretford to the south) only by the meandering flow of the River Irwell, Salford had played its own pivotal role in the Industrial Revolution. It was home to the quays and warehouses of the Manchester Ship Canal, and the base for numerous factories and mills – including those of Ermen & Engels. The cooperative movement had been born here in the 1830s, when Salford's population had already reached 50,000; the Salford Working Men's College had been founded as far back as 1858; the Salford Lads Club had been opened to provide additional opportunities to the city's working boys in 1903. L. S. Lowry, though born and raised in Stretford, one road over from Stockton Street, had studied at the Salford School of Art for ten years and located many of his most famous paintings there. Salford was home to Britain's first unconditionally free public library and to its first gaslit street; the gas works themselves were immortalised by Salford's native songwriter Ewan MacColl in his 1949 song 'Dirty Old Town'.[1]

Salford would come to greater prominence in the months after the BBC's brief profile on Delaney, due in large part to the cinematic adaptation of *A Taste of Honey*, though it did not go unnoticed that the city had also birthed Albert Finney – whose starring role in the 1961 movie adaptation of the novel *Saturday Night and Sunday Morning* was perhaps the greatest of all working-class performances of this era. But Salford's most famous contribution to British popular culture was to introduce itself not at the movie houses but on the small screen, at the very end of 1960, when Manchester's independent television network, Granada, launched a new twice-weekly drama series. *Coronation Street* was officially set in a fictional town called Weatherfield, but the programme was named for the street in Salford on which stood the Lads Club, and most viewers never imagined it otherwise. *Coronation Street* championed recognisable working-class characters speaking in regional dialect, and focused on the terraced streets and corner pubs, the social gossip and failed romances and broken dreams that were the very stuff of life for the vast majority of British people – and, as with *A Taste of Honey*, it focused less on the 'angry young man' than the domineering northern woman. Quickly defying its early critics to become the most popular (and eventually the longest running) soap opera on British television, *Coronation Street* represented nothing less than a seismic shift in British viewing values.

This 'kitchen-sink realism', to use the most appropriate umbrella term for the groundbreaking plays, novels, movies and TV shows of the very late 1950s and early 1960s, was to have a vigorous effect on Steven Morrissey. In 1986, he proclaimed 'I've never made any secret of the fact that at least fifty per cent of my reason for writing can be blamed on Shelagh Delaney,' a comment only partly prompted by the fact that so many of his early lyrics had by then been traced back to specific lines from *A Taste of Honey*. As the Smiths' lyricist, certainly, Morrissey set out to incorporate and revive the imagery, the plots, and often the direct words of Delaney

41

and her fellow playwrights and screenwriters, rightly seeing their cultural contribution as equal to the revolution that took place in the popular music of the era: 'For the very first time people were allowed regional dialects, were allowed to be truthful and honest about their situation,' he explained along the way. 'And regardless of what colour the truth is, it's always gratifying to have it.'

As the Smiths' artistic director, Morrissey celebrated the stars of these plays, TV shows and movies, as well as other musical entertainers and figureheads that had come to prominence in (or before) his very early childhood, by placing them on the front of Smiths record sleeves in lieu of the traditional band shot. Delaney, of course, received the honour. So too did Rita Tushingham, who played Jo in *A Taste of Honey* with phenomenal vigour for an unknown seventeen-year-old; Tushingham's fellow Liverpudlian Ronald Wycherley, himself just eighteen when Larry Parnes transformed him into Billy Fury; Pat Phoenix, who became famous as *Coronation Street*'s Elsie Tanner; and, twice, Viv Nicholson, who was but a struggling young Yorkshire miner's wife when she won the football 'pools' in 1961 and famously proclaimed her intent to 'Spend, spend, spend,' sadly succeeding in this ambition in record time and confirming the firmly held belief – by some – that wealth was wasted on the working classes.[2] And although Albert Finney never made it onto a record sleeve, it was not for lack of trying; the group eventually settled for a photo session outside the Salford bookmaker's shop founded by his father, also named Albert. Morrissey said later that he was 'completely handcuffed to' *Saturday Night and Sunday Morning*, citing, in particular, Finney's role as the philandering, bruising, and ultimately self-loathing young lathe operator Arthur Seaton. 'I can't describe the poetry the film has for me.'

'It was part of our aesthetic,' confirmed Morrissey's future partner, Johnny Marr, years later, of this glorious period in British cinema. 'I liked the camera shots, and the clothes, and the dialogue. I loved all of that. But for me, only as entertainment and art. I, having lived through that, didn't want for life to go back to that. *Really* wouldn't want to go back there. It was a world that me and my family had managed to work our way out of.'

JOHNNY MARR'S PARENTS, John Joseph Maher and Frances Patricia Doyle, hailed not from the big city of Dublin or its new-town suburbs, but Athy, a small town in County Kildare known for its British garrison, forty-five miles southwest of the Éire capital.* John was one of five children, Frances one of fourteen, and like the Morrisseys and Dwyers, when they felt the call of emigration, their families heeded it as if a clan, all the Mahers and many of the Doyles settling at once into what was left of Ardwick, not a mile southeast of Manchester city centre and due south of Ancoats – the area right at the heart of Dr Kay's depressing reports about Irish living and working conditions back in the 1830s.

John and Frances married upon arrival in Manchester in 1962 and set up their first home at 12 Hayfield Street, one of several tightly interlocking rows of narrow terraced houses separated only by back alleys, situated just north of the major Hyde Road. All around stood the shadowy ghosts and bustling legacies of the Industrial Revolution: to the west a car works and bus depot; to the northeast an electric substation and the old Ardwick Works; to the east, into Gorton, an old ironworks; to the north the remains of Galloway's Boiler Works; and spreading farther all across the northern and western landscape the railway lines extending out from Manchester Piccadilly

---

* In his teens, Johnny Marr changed the spelling of his last name to avoid confusion with the Buzzcocks drummer John Maher, also from Manchester. For the sake of consistency, the Smiths guitarist is referred to as Marr throughout.

Station, and an extensive crisscrossing network of tracks that formed the train yards.

It was on the edge of these yards that Manchester City Football Club had been formed, out of the more localised Ardwick AFC, at the Hyde Road Hotel in 1894. The Hyde Road ground had grown, piecemeal, to accommodate crowds of more than 40,000, but shortly after a fire burned down the main stand in 1923, the club moved to a new, purpose-built ground on Maine Road, in Moss Side. All that was left come the 1960s were ruins. Still, the proximity to the original ground helped explain the Maher family's loyalties to what they considered the 'true' Manchester club. (United, as City fans know instinctively, had been born farther out in Newton Heath, and did not adopt the Manchester prefix until 1904.)

Farther south down Hyde Road, where the railway line passed over it, stood the Fenian Arch, named for the site of a mass ambush of a police wagon in 1867 carrying two Irish nationalist leaders arrested in the wake of the failed Fenian Rising. The shooting death of a Manchester policeman in the ambush (the first to die on duty) had led to the rapid trial and executions of three Manchester Irishmen whose role in the attacks was never properly identified; to this day, the arch serves as a gathering point for intermittent 'Martyrs Marches', a reminder that Irish immigration in Manchester is sometimes inseparable from the larger, more potent issue of Irish nationalism.

The menfolk among the immigrants from Athy took manual-labour jobs, happily exchanging the prospect of working in fields for farmers for that of digging up roads for the council, as in John Maher's case, or working on building sites for Irish contractors. The last generation to wear suits as they went about this work, they had money in their pockets and they knew how to spend it. Short-term enjoyment of the city life took precedence over any long-term planning: the families operated an open door policy that extended long into the nights, filled with laughter, conversation and the clinking of glasses to the sound of music.

The same way that the families had emigrated as a unit, so too did they have kids en masse – a whole number of Maher and Doyle cousins born at more or less the same time. John Martin Maher arrived on 31 October 1963, at the end of a month in which a new phenomenon had swept across the British front pages. The story had been building throughout the year: that of a Liverpool beat group of largely (Protestant) Irish descent, formed in the short-lived skiffle and rock 'n' roll boom of the late '50s, toughened up by multiple residencies in the red-light district of Hamburg, popularised in lunchtime sessions at the Liverpool Cavern and nighttime gigs around the dance halls of the Mersey, and yet considered so unlikely to succeed that they signed, as a last resort, to what was for all intents and purposes the comedy-label outpost (Parlophone) of what was otherwise Britain's most esteemed major label (EMI). That group, the Beatles, broke with convention in almost every respect: a guitar band at the point that it was considered passé, they were named not for a lead singer and his backing band but as if an inviolable unit. All four members could sing, all played an instrument, and each had a distinct personality, at least as far as the fans were concerned. More important, the Beatles wrote their own songs, and by the time of Johnny Marr's birth, several had reached number one – the most recent of them, 'She Loves You', as the fastest-selling British record of all time. When they appeared on *Sunday Night at the London Palladium* on 13 October 1963, their devoted young fans' hysterical reaction on the surrounding central London streets inspired the media to coin a new word: Beatlemania. It stuck.

Not surprisingly, the success of the Beatles had brought with it a craze for the sound of the band's home city: Merseybeat. From August 1963 through the start of the following year, all but one of Britain's seven chart-topping singles (and both the number-one albums) was by a Liverpool act; the week of Maher's birth, it was the turn of Gerry and the Pacemakers, for the third time in as many singles, with the song that would be taken up by fans of Liverpool Football Club as their official anthem, 'You'll Never Walk Alone'.

Manchester followed close behind Liverpool in the beat boom. Like its rival, it had played host to thousands of American servicemen during the war, had developed its own system of importing records from the USA, had launched its own late-night jazz clubs, its own skiffle and rock 'n' roll bands, had its own coffee bars, and had a particular reputation for its knowledge and love of the blues. And there were areas in which it had taken the cultural lead. In 1957, the city centre's Plaza Ballroom had launched a lunchtime 'hop' to the sound not of live bands (per Liverpool's Cavern Club) but a disc jockey – the shamelessly flamboyant transplanted Yorkshireman Jimmy Savile, who played Pied Piper to thousands of schoolkids who should otherwise have been in class. Still, it said plenty about the antiquated, London-based music business that the first Manchester 'beat' band to succeed in the wake of the Beatles was Freddie and the Dreamers, whose lead singer, Freddie Garrity, was less of a rock 'n' roll performer than a career actor and comedian, best remembered for his trademark dance, a lateral flailing of legs and arms often copied by his backing band behind him. The Manchester beat scene was more authentically represented by Wayne Fontana and the Mindbenders, who would go on to have some memorable hits (though none of their own authorship), but it was, perhaps unfairly, best remembered for Herman's Hermits, a group of teenagers from Davyhulme who would sweep the charts with such simplistic songs and such a wholesome image that Freddie and the Dreamers looked positively mature and risqué by comparison.

The only Manchester beat band that truly reflected the Beatles' influence, down to type of name and eventual songwriting acclaim, was the Hollies. In October 1963, the month of Johnny Marr's birth, the Hollies were enjoying their first run in the top 20 with a cover of an older American R&B hit. The song was called 'Searchin'', and it had been written by the partnership of Jerry Leiber and Mike Stoller. The Hollies' calling card at this point was less the jangly guitar sound for which they would later become renowned (and with which the Smiths would be compared) and more the depth, range, and sheer sweetness of their harmonies. In this, it was often said, they were like the Everly Brothers, and for that reason the Hollies readily appealed to John and Frances Maher, who fairly *worshipped* the Everlys. For, more so than the Morrisseys and Dwyers, the Mahers and Doyles were obsessed with music. And not the traditional Gaelic sound of rural Kildare. 'Because they were young, they were rebelling against that,' Johnny Marr later noted. 'Like a lot of Irish people they were very enamoured with American culture.' The Everly Brothers represented that most American culture of all – rock 'n' roll – but with a country lilt that had clear antecedents in the Emerald Isle and leaned heavily on the minor keys that were to become the stock-in-trade of Johnny Marr's own future ballads. Indeed, country and western loomed large in the Maher household: their firstborn would recall growing up listening to the likes of Jim Reeves, Eddie Arnold, and 'the occasional Hank Williams.'

Irish enthusiasm for American rock 'n' roll and country music had, in the years between the Morrissey and Dwyer families' departure for Manchester and that of the Mahers and Doyles, led to the development of its own musical culture, the showband. A truncated form of the larger dance orchestra (the same way that skiffle emerged in Great Britain from the bigger trad jazz bands), the showband, whose prime intention was to get a new generation of young folk dancing until they dropped, was still typically large enough to include drums, guitars, keyboards, a couple of vocalists, and maybe the basics of a brass section. After gathering momentum in Ireland, showband culture predictably jumped across the Irish Sea and took off among the emigrants. So while the coffeehouses and dance halls of central Manchester reverberated to beat bands, the Irish public houses and private social clubs shook to a very Celtic interpretation of American rock 'n' roll and country: 'Joe Dolan doing Del Shannon,' as Johnny Marr later described it.

47

The future Smith even suspected that he was nicknamed Johnny for the famed Irish singer Johnny McEvoy.

Frances, on the other hand, was mad for all forms of pop music. She was young – still only nineteen even when her second child, Claire, was born in 1965 – and she exhibited what her son called an 'exuberant idealism' that he undoubtedly inherited. Frances loved the Beatles and the Hollies in particular, and took pride in Manchester's growing reputation as a cultural capital. On New Year's Day, 1964, the city further laid its claim to musical fame when Jimmy Savile introduced the initial airing of the television chart show *Top of the Pops* from a BBC-converted church in Rusholme. As it happens, the very first performance was by a new band from London who would become Johnny Marr's mainstay: the Rolling Stones. Twenty years later, by which time *Top of the Pops* had become perennially unfashionable (but remained popular and thereby powerful), the Smiths made a point of appearing on the show at every opportunity. By then, it had long since moved to London.

The Maher home in Ardwick was filled with mementoes of Catholicism: 'pictures of the Sacred Heart, harps, ornaments everywhere, crucifixes, little statues of the saints, all the iconography of Irish Catholicism and Irish culture,' recalled their older son. Prominent amongst them was a portrait of the thirty-fifth president of the United States of America: John F. Kennedy, whose youth and good looks meant nothing to the Irish in Britain as much as the fact that he was a Catholic. Years of prejudice and discrimination in Britain and America had failed to prevent one of their own from rising to become leader of the free world. In America, then, it was true: anyone could become president.

Johnny Marr was all of three weeks old when JFK was assassinated in Dallas. In the aftermath of the president's death, a mourning young American nation seeking some sort of positive distraction immersed itself in the British fad of Beatlemania – and the Liverpool group rose to the challenge of history, taking popular music into uncharted waters, in the process establishing the deep devotion among Americans for British music that the Smiths would successfully tap into some two decades later. Still, that first 'British Invasion' of America remained months away, and the deeply disputed circumstances behind JFK's assassination very much on the regional front pages as well as the international ones, when another story took hold in Manchester.

It transpired that the very day after JFK's assassination, a Saturday, a twelve-year-old boy, John Kilbride, had gone missing in Ashton-Under-Lyne on his way back from the cinema. Crime, both petty and violent, was common enough in Manchester, but the abduction of a child was unthinkable. As such, the finger was subtly pointed at those who did not fit in, the *Manchester Evening News* noting in its first report on the search that Kilbride 'was seen helping coloured stall-holders earlier in the day.' But that lead went nowhere, and by the end of the week, cadets had been brought in to comb the local moors, and frogmen to search the reservoirs and canals. No body was found, and the story eventually disappeared from the headlines.

Eight months later, another twelve-year-old boy, Keith Bennett, disappeared on his way to his grandmother's; he was last seen crossing the Stockport Road, one main street over from Hyde Road. His stepfather was considered the main suspect and a wider search was not undertaken; the body was never found (nor the stepfather ever prosecuted). Only with the disappearance, on Boxing Day, 1964, of ten-year-old Lesley Anne Downey, on her way back to her Ancoats council flat after spending the afternoon at the local fair, did it truly dawn on residents and police alike that a child killer might be living among them. The search for the missing child dominated the Manchester papers all the way into the New Year. And then, as with Kilbride and Bennett before her, the disappearance of Downey itself disappeared from the front pages. She had vanished into thin air, and after a while, that stopped being news.

We know now that Kilbride, Bennett and Downey, along with sixteen-year-old Pauline Reade before them, had been enticed from the city streets by Ian Brady and his girlfriend, Myra Hindley, sexually assaulted, and brutally murdered, the bodies buried in shallow graves on nearby Saddleworth Moor. We know because in October 1965, seventeen-year-old Edward Evans, who lived just off the Oxford Road, was picked up outside Central Station after a night on the beer, invited to Hindley's home in the overspill suburb of Hattersley, and there, in front of David Smith, Hindley's brother-in-law, beaten with an axe and then strangled with an electrical cord. Brady had intended for Smith, also just seventeen, to become an accomplice, but the teenager confided instead in his equally young wife, and the next morning the couple called the police. Within days, Brady and Hindley had taken on infamy, and a new identity, as the Moors Murderers.

At their trial in Chester in April 1966, Brady and Hindley were found guilty of murdering Kilbride, Downey, and Evans between them; the death penalty having only just been abolished, they were sentenced to life imprisonment. (Two decades later – at which point Morrissey and Marr's Smiths were at their peak, and no strangers to the controversy surrounding the Moors Murders – Brady confessed to the additional killings of Reade and Bennett; though the former's body was found on Saddleworth Moor, the latter's has never been recovered.) The horrific story cast a pall over Manchester arguably more damning than the Peterloo Massacre, the assembled ranks of childhood fatalities brought on by disease in the city's nineteenth-century slums, or the Munich Air Disaster. The Glasgow-born Brady was a career criminal and surely a psychopath, and Mancunians could readily disown him. But Hindley had been born and raised in Gorton, the neighbourhood that overlapped with the Mahers' own Ardwick; the abduction of Pauline Reade had taken place in a typical Gorton side street. The residents of Manchester so desperately wanted to believe that Brady and Hindley's awful deviance from basic human decency, their sickening betrayals of childish trust, and the appalling sexual abuse and murderous violence they cultivated were genuine aberrations of normal behaviour, and as such, that they could have happened anywhere. But the fact was, they had happened there, in the heart of Manchester, and no matter how much they tried to ignore the awful truth, the city had to answer to it.

CHAPTER THREE

We were quite happy to ghettoise ourselves as the Irish community in Manchester; the Irish stuck rigidly together and there'd always be a relation living two doors down, around the back or up the passage. It always struck me as quite odd that people who had lived 20 or 30 years in Manchester still spoke with the broadest and the sharpest Pearse Street accent.
— MORRISSEY, *Hot Press*, May 1984

It was very loving but quite a heavy, oppressive background. There was a lot of wild talk, a lot of wild behaviour, and a lot of drinking. But at the same time as being quite intimidated by a lot of wild, young Irish kick-ass guys, it wasn't half exciting for me and my sister.

— JOHNNY MARR, March 2011

Early in the 1960s, the Morrissey family moved out of Harper Street and into a terraced house on Queen's Square, at the eastern tip of Stretford.[1] This was a significant step up the social ladder: the two-storey houses were set somewhat grandly behind brick arches and opened onto small front yards, some of which boasted basic gardens. Better still, the 'square' in front of these gardens was a pedestrianised side street, vehicular traffic blocked by concrete bollards. At the eastern end of the square, over the line into Manchester proper, stood the famed Loreto College, founded back in 1851 by nuns from the Blessed Institute of the Virgin Mary to educate the city's then-underserved Irish Catholics. It stands there still, now proudly multi-ethnic as befits modern Manchester, but its mission no less steeped in firm Catholic values.

It was at Queen's Square that the Morrisseys – or, to be more precise, the Dwyers – came closer together than at any time since growing up in Crumlin. Betty's parents lived on one side, her sister Mary's family on the other. A number of Steven Morrissey's other aunts and uncles were dotted within walking distance all across Stretford and Trafford, Hulme and Moss Side. Primary school – St Wilfrid's, firmly Roman Catholic and fondly regarded by all who attended – was a short walk away, over the Stretford Road. No surprise, then, that Morrissey would later reflect how, 'It was a very strong community, and very tight. Very solid. And it was also quite happy.'

The use of the word 'quite' sounds like a deliberately Morrissey-esque downplay – as if, God forbid, he should ever admit to having been *very* happy. But there were good reasons for the adult Morrissey to qualify his Queen's Square childhood: In 1965, the year he turned six, his family was repeatedly ripped apart by tragedy. The first calamity came in March, when his paternal grandfather, also named Peter Morrissey, died suddenly, at age sixty-three, in Dublin. The second came in November, when his maternal grandfather, Patrick Stephen Dwyer, after whom he had been named and who lived next door, passed from a heart attack at the age of just fifty-two. And then, the following month, just a day after his grieving grandmother broke her leg at home and was admitted to the hospital, his uncle Ernie, one of Betty's siblings who had followed her to Manchester, was pronounced dead on arrival at Ancoats Hospital. A postmortem revealed atrophy of the liver. The curse of the drink, something with which the Irish were so closely associated and yet something that Steven Morrissey's father had so assiduously avoided, had taken one of the Dwyers at the ludicrously young age of twenty-four.

Six-year-olds sense the sadness of death but don't so readily register the permanence; it's part of our Darwinian survival instincts that, at such a young age, we find it relatively easy to shrug off the demise of those older than us and persist merrily along with what we assume to be our personally bright futures. But the morbid atmosphere that hung over the Morrissey and Dwyer households that Christmas coincided with the arrests of Brady and Hindley and the unearthing, all too literally, of their horrendous deeds; as the murder trial came to court the following spring, dominating the national news and local emotions, too, Steven came to imagine himself as 'a potential victim.' In truth, he was much younger than Brady and Hindley's victims (six at the time the couple were arrested for the killing of a seventeen-year-old), and those abductions that had taken place on the streets of south Manchester had occurred much closer to the Mahers' neighbourhood than that of the Morrisseys. He took the prospect of his own demise painfully seriously all the same, adopting the Moors Murders as something of a personal cause. In doing so, he found a way to vicariously share in the family deaths, too.

On a very basic level, the series of premature departures heralded a significant change in family dynamics. 'I came from a monstrously large family who were quite absurdly Catholic,' Morrissey explained to the Irish music magazine *Hot Press* in 1984, but 'when I was six there were two very serious tragedies within the family which caused everybody to turn away from the church, and quite rightly so, and from that period onwards there was just a total disregard for something that was really quite sacrosanct previous to the tragedies.'

The disregard was, in fact, far from total: Steven Morrissey still took his first communion at St Wilfrid's Church just a few months into 1966, would be prepared for confirmation later during his time there, and would go on to attend a strict Roman Catholic secondary school. But the seeds of disenchantment had been sown, the requirement for attendance at Sunday Mass was gradually relaxed, and the adult Morrissey would go on to become one of British pop's more articulate, and resentful, critics of Catholicism, railing in particular against the charge of original sin. 'It is probably the worst thing you can do to a child, to make it feel guilty,' he correctly observed in the *Guardian* in 1997, explaining his antagonism towards his religious upbringing. 'And guilt is astonishingly embedded in Catholic children without them knowing why. It is a ferocious burden to carry. How evil can children be?'

The loss for Peter and Betty of their fathers cut deeper than provoking mere doubts in their faith, however; it exposed cracks in their marriage, too. They had come to Manchester as not much more than kids; they were that much older now, and that much different from each other than they had been back in Crumlin. Peter's continued preference for the night shift made him something of a distant character to his son, and though he tried to impart his love of football by taking the child to matches at Old Trafford – Manchester United success-fully rebuilding their team to win the Football League again in 1967, with teenage sensation George Best at the fore – Steven never developed the devotion to the sport that was otherwise innate among British working-class kids. He preferred, instead, the books that his mother shared with him as she – a school leaver at fourteen, with no proper qualifications, no career expectations, and at a point before women's liberation had taken proper hold – determined to make more of her adult life than the caricature of the intellectually ignorant Irish home-maker.

His parents' domestic differences would be successfully swept under the carpet for the time being; well into his secondary school years, Steven Morrissey's friends would remark on his parents, with some envy, as a thoroughly modern and handsome couple, unaware of the extent to which the marriage was trou-bled. Once he became famous, Morrissey was less guarded about his childhood, telling *Sounds* that 'At the age of eight I became very isolated – we had a lot of family problems at that time – and that tends to orchestrate your life.'

Morrissey's inward turn was noticed by school friends and relatives alike. Perfectly likeable, clearly intelligent, and artfully witty when he wanted to be, he nonetheless started keeping himself to himself. In particular, he began to fixate on his own impermanence. Most kids struggle to get around the idea that they must die; Morrissey could not deal with Catholicism's promise of an alternative: 'It was impressed on you that you would go to heaven and live forever and ever and ever, and I always remember the very idea of living forever petrified me because I couldn't imagine *life without end!*'

He began, then, to consider the alternative. The fact that his comments on this aspect of his life came from the perspective of a (finally!) successful young adult should not be taken to denigrate the details of this childhood, which have always remained remarkably consistent. 'I can remember being obsessed with (death) from the age of eight,' he said, 'and I often wondered whether it was quite a natural inbuilt emotion for people who're destined to take their own lives, that they recognise it and begin to study it.' Another time, he put it yet more bluntly: 'The realisation that suicide was quite appealing and attractive happened when I was eight.'

It was a topic that Morrissey took up beyond the potentially self-aggrandising interview quote to address in song, and more than once; of the Smiths' many unique lyrical qualities, prominent among them was a willingness to address suicide as a credible, rather than a cowardly, option. There was never any doubt, throughout, that Steven Morrissey was 'saved' from following up on his darkest desires not by religion, but by pop music. Notably, it was Sandie Shaw on *Top of the Pops*, singing the Bacharach-David classic, '(There's) Always Something There to Remind Me', that he cited as his earliest musical experience, at the age of just five. Only a few months later, at the record store on nearby Alexandra Road, he made his binding betrothal to the world of vinyl when he picked up his first 7" single, 'Come and Stay with Me' by another girl singer of the era, Marianne Faithfull.

That choice could have been a one-off, a passing phase, a tentative dip into the cold waters of the shallow commercial tide before taking off for deeper and headier shores. But when it came to pop music, Morrissey's first love turned out to be his true love. The girl singers of the 1960s, especially the British ones, said everything the young boy needed to hear in a song. And they said it – verse, chorus, middle eight, and quite likely a modulation, too – in barely two minutes. Morrissey appeared to instinctively understand that this was an art form, no less worthy than great literature or movies, and he set about collecting it with a passion that would never cease. He was helped in his obsession by the fact that, unlike many of the American girl groups – even those he came to enjoy from the Motown stable – the British female singers each had an individual story and a particular look. Faithfull was the London high-society waiflike beauty discovered by (Marr's future hero) Andrew Loog Oldham and dragged into dangerous liaisons with the Rolling Stones; Cilla Black the Liverpudlian girl-next-door and future family entertainer found in the Cavern Club cloakroom and set up with songs by Lennon and McCartney. Lulu was the loud Glaswegian lass whose stunning rendition of 'Shout' made her a pop star at fifteen and every similarly aged boy's wet dream, Twinkle the upper-class suburban Tory councillor's daughter turned unlikely death-song composer of 'Terry'. As for Sandie Shaw, she was harder to define: the atypically casual, disarmingly forward, plaintively distinct and yet oddly distant Essex girl whose delivery of '(There's) Always Something There to Remind Me' sounded, as Morrissey delightfully described it years later, 'as if she'd just walked in off the street and begun to sing, and strolled back home and bought some chips.'

And they were not the only ones. Helen Shapiro, Petula Clark, Dusty Springfield . . . the list sometimes threatened to be endless, and if it was important to Morrissey's critical persona that he did not love them all equally (he worshipped Sandie Shaw's Eurovision Song Contest winner 'Puppet on a String' despite the singer disowning the song, but could not get his head around Dusty Springfield's acclaimed excursion into Memphis soul with 'Son of a Preacher Man'), it was vital nonetheless that he cherished the entire genre: 'They had the heart and soul and they were more willing to be open than, say, the groups.' That may have seemed an initially odd justification given that many of the 1960s 'groups' were writing their own songs and the girl singers were not, and even a little disloyal considering that, just as he was latching on to Marianne Faithfull, Manchester's own Freddie and the Dreamers, Herman's

Hermits, and Wayne Fontana and the Mindbenders were topping the American singles charts in successive order. But Morrissey intrinsically understood how the female singers, plucked from various social strata at a time when the swinging '60s hit factory was working overtime and there was no shortage of eager replacements lined up outside the company gates, approached the material they were given with a singular passion, throwing themselves into every song with the full knowledge that their careers depended on it. It's fair to say that their individual hits, and their equally unique personalities, have stood the test of time better than those of the Manchester bands that briefly threatened to replace Merseybeat.

Down the line, Morrissey came to a further understanding of what made these singers, whose songs he would cover with the Smiths, and in one special case, whose career he would help revive, so attractive: they were part of the same social revolution that had brought in Shelagh Delaney and Elsie Tanner. 'The grand dame gestures of the late '50s had gone,' he wrote in a feature on the subject for *Sounds* shortly after he had finally 'made it' himself, 'the overblown icky sentiment had gone, and in its place came a brashness and fortitude: girls with extreme youth and high spirits who were to boldly claim their patch in a business which was obviously a male domain.' Of course, as his later championing of Billy Fury, the Righteous Brothers and Elvis Presley served to confirm, the young Morrissey was devoted not so exclusively to the female voice as to 'any pop singer who sang, and didn't have an instrument, and just stood there, in front of the camera, with no musicians, nobody in the way, just you, your voice and there is the audience.' In this regard, he had already seen his vocation in the television screen. 'I took pop music very seriously. I thought it was the heart of everything. I thought it affected everybody and moved everybody. It started me as a person. As a child I would sing every single night – and the neighbours would complain – because I had this insane desire to sing.'

Steven Morrissey's musical tastes changed little throughout

his primary-school years. During his last term at St Wilfrid's, when the fourth-years were rewarded with an afternoon school disco, his classmates brought in Motown and Stax, ska and reggae – essentially, the music of the day. Morrissey was not immune to such rhythms (several black dance hits of the era would show up on his future hit lists), but for the school disco, he brought along his beloved Sandie Shaw and Twinkle singles, and even a one-off 1962 hit by Susan Maughan, the sexually submissive 'Bobby's Girl'.

He may have been waiting, patiently, for the right set of circumstances to come along and create a music he could (again) call his own. If so, he didn't have long to go. Only a year or so later, youthful British rock music combined with the grand tradition of British pop to reinvent itself in dramatically camp fashion, adorned in the glitter and the baubles of female divas, but performed almost exclusively by grown men with long hair playing electric guitars. The first proven proponent of the new sound was Marc Bolan's T. Rex, who, in the space of just sixteen months from early 1971, had four number-one singles, a run incomparable since the Beatles. The last of those singles, 'Metal Guru', had only just been dislodged from the top spot when Steven Morrissey, a few weeks into his teens, saw T. Rex play live at the Kings Hall in Belle Vue, on Hyde Road, on 16 July 1972. His memory of his first-ever concert suggested another comparison with the Beatles: he couldn't hear the music for the screaming. It was enough to (further) convince him that this – pop music, rapture, adulation, adrenaline – was everything that mattered.

By COINCIDENCE so perfect it could have been by design, Johnny Marr made his own entry into pop music obsession with the same act. He did so just a few months before Steven Morrissey saw T. Rex in concert, and from a mile or so up Hyde Road, where his family had moved, early in Johnny's life, from Hayfield

Street to Brierley Avenue, a short cul-de-sac of two dozen ancient, narrow 'two-up and two-down's' just off Higher Ardwick. Back in the early nineteenth century, nearby Ardwick Green had been the most desirable residential area in Manchester. It was home to the likes of 'merchant prince' John Ryland, considered the city's first multimillionaire, and George Wilson, chairman of the Lancashire and Yorkshire Railway and also, as chairman of the Anti-Corn Law League, partly responsible for the construction of the Free Trade Hall. The green itself had become the city's first public park in 1867, adorned with ponds, fountains and a bandstand, but by that point, as rows of terraced housing extended southward from the inner city to accommodate the ever-increasing number of factory workers, so the wealthy had already begun moving even farther south to escape them. Ardwick's population had peaked at the turn of the century and been in steady decline ever since. The area around the green became an entertainment centre instead, with four cinemas (the vast Apollo among them), billiard halls, music halls, and swimming pools attracting the ruffians from across the city. The old mansion houses were rundown or knocked down, and the terraced side streets, like Brierley Avenue, still lacked, even in the late 1960s, for indoor toilets, let alone telephones. But it was, in many ways, an improvement on Hayfield Street, especially because, as had been the case for the Morrisseys in Queen's Square, the Mahers and Doyles were now living more or less alongside each other.

Marr was eight years old when he was given permission – and money – to buy his first 7" single. Growing up surrounded by music – when she wasn't listening to it with him, his mother would stick him in front of the radio while she went about her cleaning – he already knew which hits were out there. So, when he found, languishing in the half-price box of his local record shop, a copy of the most recent T. Rex hit, 'Jeepster', it wasn't that he needed to hear it, because he already knew what it sounded like: it was that he couldn't stop *looking* at it. Singles generally came in paper sleeves, though occasionally they'd be deemed worthy of a coloured bag instead. Labels were almost always generic. Not this one though. One side of the label was artfully handwritten, with a massive hand-drawn fly up top – Fly being the name of Bolan's boutique label within EMI – and that was unusual enough. The other side was taken up by a soft-focus, full-colour picture of Bolan and his musical partner, Mickey Finn, almost effeminate in their flowing long hair, the neck and body of a guitar (a Gibson Les Paul) just about visible across the bottom. Johnny was sold. He left the store with that copy of 'Jeepster' in hand, knowing that he would not, could not be disappointed.

As with his future partner Morrissey, Marr immediately threw himself into the camp of Marc Bolan. It was futile to do otherwise; Bolan was omnipotent at the time, as popular with the boys as the girls, exuding sexuality in a way that even an eight-year-old could somehow sense. His electric boogie was almost impossibly simple – essentially, just a two- or three-chord riff repeated ad infinitum – and yet it was not necessarily simplistic; it aimed somewhere higher than the surface level of most pop music, and when it got there, it kept right on going. That would explain why, when 'Metal Guru' came out in the spring of '72, it was, for Marr, the greatest thing he had ever heard. Bar none. 'It was a feeling I'll never forget,' he told Martin Roach, 'a new sensation. I got on my bike and rode and rode, singing this song. It was a spiritual elevation, one of the best moments of my life.'

In 1986, when Marr and Morrissey decided to rehire their first proper producer for a new Smiths single, 'Panic', he asked if they had any reference points in mind. "'Metal Guru",' they said. In the spring of 1972, it had said everything to them about their lives.

IT IS STRIKING just how many similarities existed between Morrissey and Marr's respective upbringings. We know, already, the shared experiences of their parents' generation. But it's worth noting too how their classically large Irish Catholic families (Morrissey had a dozen bloodline aunts and uncles, Marr some seventeen) shrunk to a more 'Protestant' size once in Manchester: the Morrisseys had just the two children, the Mahers a grand total of three, Johnny's brother Ian born another seven years after Claire. Both Steven Morrissey and Johnny Marr, then, grew up in the company of a sister only two years apart in age, and each looked up to their youthful mothers in a similar fashion, as much as a friend, mentor and surrogate older sibling as a matriarch. At the same time, they were somewhat remote from their fathers, whose work and social lives kept them away from such constant engagement.

The two boys were each required to wear a uniform to their Roman Catholic primary schools, Johnny going to St Aloysius around the corner from Brierley Avenue five years after Steven started attending St Wilfrid's in Hulme. Despite – or perhaps because of – the insularity of their families, neighbourhood, and schooling environments, both boys recalled being subject to external racial slurs. 'I was called Paddy from an early age,' said Morrissey; 'In the early '70s, we were called Irish pigs quite a lot,' said Marr.

And both of them enjoyed frequent, pleasurable holidays in the Ireland of their parents' childhood. 'We'd go back to Crumlin,' said Morrissey, 'and of course I saw it with a child's vision, but the people seemed happier and more carefree and Crumlin seemed so open – certainly more so than the confines of Hulme.' Marr's trips to Kildare, which would sometimes take up the whole summer holiday, involved a greater exposure to country air, to live music (he talked of 'a very hip uncle who wore suede Beatle boots and played a Gibson acoustic'), to drinking, and to the wild behaviour that was a natural byproduct of all this. He recalled how, one time, 'very, very late after a party, a few of the men got in a couple of cars and went racing round the country roads with the lights off. And these were the adults!' (In 1903, partly because it had the straight, flat roads for it, Kildare had hosted the first ever international motor race in what was then still part of the United Kingdom; the Mahers were merely continuing a fine tradition.)

Each was, not surprisingly then, acutely attuned to his roots. 'My Irishness was never something I hid or camouflaged,' Morrissey told the *Irish Times*. Though this was equally true of the Maher children, they were also encouraged to embrace the land of their birth. 'It was a particular bug bear of my parents that they'd go out for a night and come back complaining that someone had been sitting there boozed up just slagging off England,' recalled Marr. 'And my mum's thing always was that "If it's so great back there, why don't you just go back home?" The message I was getting was: "It's great to be here. This is the greatest city in the world."'

But that city, even as it expanded geographically to incorporate any number of former satellite mill towns and modern suburbs, was going through enormous upheaval during Morrissey and Marr's childhoods, and it would affect each of them directly, leading to a major diversion in their previously parallel lives. The housing that had been built for the working classes during the Industrial Revolution, much of it of inferior quality to begin with, was now falling apart: in 1945, the City of Manchester's planning commission admitted that some 68,000 houses – slums, as they were commonly known – were officially unfit for human habitation, and that number was only set to increase. But a lack of funding meant that improvements on existing buildings were rare, and it wasn't until after a 1961 development plan that the decision was made to bulldoze the slums instead. From there, it was as if the city were intent on making up for lost time by wiping out as much of old Manchester as possible. St Wilfrid's, of which the pupils' only complaint was that part of the upstairs was haunted, was torn down in 1969 and a new, single-storey, modern glass building erected in its place. But at least there was still a St Wilfrid's. Much else of what used to be Hulme and Moss Side was simply obliterated. The quaintly pedestrianised Queen's Square, where three different groups of the Morrissey and Dwyer family lived contentedly side by side?

Wiped from the map. Harper Street, where Steven Morrissey spent his first few years of life? No longer exists. Stockton Street, where the marriage between Peter Morrissey and Betty Dwyer had been celebrated with that twenty-four-hour party? Reduced to the shortest of cul-de-sacs, the rest of the residential grid of side streets having completely vanished. The route that Steven Morrissey took to primary school would be impossible to follow now without wings, Upper and Lower Moss Lanes having been all but eradicated.

It was much the same story over in Ardwick. Hayfield Street, where the Mahers had first lived upon arrival in Manchester? Gone, along with many of its surrounding streets. Brierley Avenue, off of Ardwick Green? Disappeared. (The Mahers were among 199 families in five 'clearance areas' wiped off the Ardwick map by a single mark of the council pen in 1970. There were so many of these 'clearance areas' cited for destruction across Ardwick that the arrival of the bulldozers often followed years behind the official condemnation.) The terraced streets of Morrissey and Marr's childhood, with their corner shops and pubs, where kids were let loose to play outdoors, where everyone knew their neighbours' names and often even shared them, and families were in and out of one another's unlocked houses all day long, are all but memories.

Nobody was defending the old slums to the extent that that's what they were. What was truly indefensible was that the city replaced them with new slums. To rebuild the area between Steven Morrissey's Queen's Square home and his primary school, for example, the Manchester Corporation hired the same architects whose 'streets in the sky' concept had already proven such a failure in the Yorkshire steel city of Sheffield but who, clearly none the wiser, came along proposing another ludicrous euphemism: 'deck access'. By saving on the number of lifts in the building process, they forced tenants to routinely walk several hundred feet just to travel from apartment to street level; that they might be carrying children or heavy shopping did not appear to have been taken into consideration. In Hulme, four long blocks of six-storey housing (two floors per family) with shared 'deck access' were laid out in vast crescents in preposterous imitation of the famously fashionable (low-rise) Georgian terraces of Bath. With Manchester including its most troubled council tenants among the 13,000 people who were moved there, the Hulme Crescents quickly became what twenty-first-century Britain would refer to as 'sink estates', where one problem quickly begat another.[2] The police refused to recognise these crescents as 'streets', and so did not patrol them above ground level; unfortunately, nobody had thought to clear that one in advance. With no police presence, crime was effectively allowed to prosper, and the daily deliveries of milk, newspapers and the like soon dried up due to regular attacks on the merchants. Children no longer played freely on the streets because there were none; ball games were mostly forbidden on the grassy areas; there were no youth programme or social clubs. Drug deals and fights duly became the common daily interactions instead. A damning 1978 report by the TV show *World in Action* compared the crescents with apartheid South Africa, stating that 'Manchester's Hulme bares all the sociological characteristics of a Bantustan reservation.'

In Ardwick, on Hyde Road, smack in between the Maher family's two former homes, the city similarly built a 537-unit complex of 'deck access' homes using the cheapest available system, that of the LEGO-like 'Bison Wall Frame.' The city named it Coverdale Crescent, but with its jutting walkways that interconnected at sharp right angles and its sense of total social alienation, the residents quickly took to calling it Fort Ardwick instead. The roofs leaked at once, and as the steel fixings began corroding almost as quickly, so concrete started breaking away. Over in the Hulme Crescents, leaks compounded with an ineffective and expensive under-floor heating system meant that tenants had to decide either to go cold or live with perpetual condensation. The city spent emergency funds attempting to shore up the buildings, but the damage – to the tenants' morale as much as to the buildings themselves – had been done. Fort Ardwick was torn down in the mid-1980s, barely ten years after being erected. (The 'slums', by comparison, had lasted well over a hundred years.) The Hulme Crescents lasted into the mid-1990s before they, too, were demolished, a monumental tribute to the worst excesses of urban planning.

It's worth briefly considering what might (not) have become of Morrissey and Marr had they been rehoused into the crescents that all but swallowed up their old homes. Fortunately, because it was they who had to make way for the new buildings, and needed housing in the meantime, they were spared that social experiment. But that's not to say that Morrissey, in particular, ever bought into the validity of the slum clearance that forced his family out of Queen's Square. 'It was almost a political movement to squash this very, very strong body of people,' he said on the *South Bank Show* in 1987. Two years earlier, still enjoying the initial flush of stardom, he tried to go back to his old street for a short TV clip about his upbringing, but he couldn't find it – except in a photograph at a library. 'Everything has just vanished; it's just like the whole thing has been completely erased from the face of the earth,' he said as he paced the soulless concrete concourses of the modern Hulme and Moss Side tower-block estates that had taken its place. 'I feel great anger and I feel massive sadness. It's like a complete loss of childhood.'

It was more than that. It was a complete loss of Manchester, its roots, its traditions, its community and culture. As the old terraced streets were replaced by soaring tower blocks, deck-access crescents, and modern council estates, and as these replacements were proven to cause more problems than they solved, and as unemployment and crime and depression and drug abuse rose accordingly, the city that had given birth to the Industrial Revolution began to look very much like it was dying. Many believed that it was already dead.

CHAPTER FOUR

My education in St Mary's Secondary School in Manchester wasn't an education. It was all violence and brutality.

— MORRISSEY, *Irish Times*, 1999

The vast majority of council tenants in Hulme and Moss Side forcibly relocated by slum clearance were sent to estates in Wythenshawe, south of Manchester. But because the Morrisseys lived just outside the city line, their circumstance was different, and when Queen's Square was torn down, they were relocated westward within their native Stretford. The new family home at 384 Kings Road stood almost halfway along the street's two mile stretch, just before the council houses of the eastern end gave way to private property heading west. By the Morrisseys' previous standards, these new semidetached homes were sumptuous, backing and fronting onto private gardens, with bushes distinguishing property lines; there were side entrances, and space between the buildings for those who had motor cars – which came to include the Morrisseys. They had proper bathrooms, three bedrooms, and a downstairs living room looking out to the front garden. All in all, they were the very picture of respectability. Yet all this precise *niceness* came at a cost. Stockton Road, Harper Street and Queen's Square had all been of a terraced variety typical of working-class, industrial-era England north of the Home Counties; these new semidetached council houses, though, were prevalent in every city, town, and even many villages in England from the 1960s and '70s onward, and their heterogeneous architecture only emphasised Kings Road's existent anonymity. Neither side street nor busy main road, neither rich nor poor, not especially violent but never exactly safe, the council end of Kings Road was, by Steven Morrissey's own admission, 'bland,' and for a child already all too aware of life's stifling boundaries, to be relocated into such normality was an offence against his humanity. The effect of it seemed to permeate his subsequent personality.

But that was hardly the biggest crime perpetuated against his upbringing. As with every publicly educated child of his generation, at the end of his time at St Wilfrid's, Steven Morrissey sat for the exam known as the 11-plus, which determined which type of secondary school he would attend. Those who passed it had the perceived good fortune to attend their local grammar school, which received the lion's share of funding, attracted better teachers, and theoretically treated the students with some understanding of their basic intellectual capacity, endeavouring to ensure that they would leave, with O-Levels at the age of sixteen and hopefully A-Levels beyond that, to go on to solid, white-collar jobs. Those who failed the 11-plus, on the other hand, were sent to the local secondary modern, where they were viewed as little more than fodder for what was left of the factory floor and were rarely offered more than a course of CSEs (Certificates of Secondary Education that were only introduced in the late 1960s). Disenchantment with how this system had doomed three-quarters of British pupils to an education of low expectations, the Labour Government of the 1960s had been seeking to replace secondary moderns (and, eventually, grammar schools) with totally inclusive, properly funded 'comprehensive' schools. But in 1970, the year Steven Morrissey started secondary school, Labour was voted out, and the process of further educational change was promptly postponed.[1]

It appears inexplicable that someone of Steven Morrissey's evident intelligence could have failed his 11-plus. But that was the vagary of the system that reduced up to seven years of primary-school education to a single day's IQ test: catch kids on a bad morning, in the wrong environment, at a weak point in their educational development, or just ask them the wrong questions for their aptitude, and you potentially damned them for life. According to Johnny Rogan's biography *The Severed Alliance*, only three students from St Wilfrid's passed the exam and went on to grammar school, but at least the majority of the failures moved on together, to St Ignatius in Hulme. Being a resident of Stretford, however, Steven Morrissey (and two classmates from St Wilfrid's) was sent to St Mary's Roman Catholic Secondary Modern. The school lay on the other side of the railway tracks, literally, from the Morrisseys' Kings Road back garden – accessed via an iron footbridge just up the road, past the shops – and attracted, if that could be considered the right word given that they had no choice in the matter, the toughest Catholic kids in all of Stretford.

It had not always been that way. Until 1963, when the girls were farmed off to the newly built Cardinal Vaughan, St Mary's had enjoyed a mixed intake, which served to self-regulate some of the excesses of juvenile misbehaviour. The school had its share of success stories too, especially in sports. Come Morrissey's time, though, many of the pupils were, like him, recently displaced and relocated, Old Trafford having gone through its own slum clearance programme in the 1960s. The rootless boys of modern Stretford had no hunger for the school's demand for spirit, be it pride in St Mary's as a whole or in one of the four assigned 'houses' within the school intended to instill good-natured competition and team camaraderie. Their working-class parents, many of them immigrants from Ireland or other Catholic countries (Italy and Poland, for example), remained generally disconnected from the process, and St Mary's pointedly did nothing to encourage them, sending home only twice-yearly reports and hosting only annual parents' evenings that were sparsely attended.

Like all British secondary schools, St Mary's insisted its pupils wear uniforms, which included a blue blazer for the first three years, along with the nominal requirement of short trousers and a cap for the first years too. But in working-class areas like Stretford, this long-standing tradition had come up against the reality of the kids' own uniforms in the shape of their stylised youth culture; by the time Morrissey attended St Mary's, the enduring mod look of the mid-'60s had given way to the tougher, more pronounced imagery of the suedehead and skinhead, meaning that there were multiple dress codes competing with one another. In addition, the social upheavals and scientific discoveries of the 1960s had caused many to question, if not their religious background – one could no more deny being Catholic at St Mary's than deny one's skin colour – then certainly their religious *faith*, as per the Morrissey family. And yet St Mary's remained unapologetically strict in its Catholic doctrine. There was a monthly Friday Mass conducted by the local priest, regular prayers and religious lessons, frequent visual demonstrations on the sin of abortion, and what Morrissey recalled as a Monday-morning inquisition regarding one's attendance at church the previous day.

Rather than acknowledge the depth of these problems and seek an innovative way to solve them, the school's head-master, Vince 'Jet' Morgan, a former Army officer whose educational qualifications were held in low esteem by his teachers, opted for a programme of strict discipline designed to instill fear and respect. The routine started every morning with assembly, where, alongside the singing of hymns, Morgan would deliver a religious sermon, as likely as not about the saint of the day or one of the Catholic martyrs after which the four school houses had been named. Morrissey was assigned to Clitherow House, after Margaret Clitherow of York, a sixteenth-century convert to Catholicism who was executed for her religious beliefs by being crushed to death.[2]

In October 1970, just after Morrissey started at St Mary's, Margaret Clitherow was canonised by the pope, but her sainthood had little effect on the students, who typically recoiled in horror from the gruesome details of the morning sermon, taking away from it only the (intended) sense of Catholic persecution, a chip on their shoulder they could use and abuse when they ran into pupils from the local nondenominational secondary modern, Great Stone.

Assembly ended with the headmaster ritual, that which inspired the Smiths song of the same name, surely the most damning musical indictment of British public education ever composed by someone who failed their 11-plus. Each morning, Morgan selected a different item of the pupils' dress or cleanliness for inspection. It could be the shoes; were they of the formal kind and were they suitably polished? It might be the tie; was it properly knotted at the top button? But it could easily have been the fingernails; had they been duly clipped and cleaned? Those who failed to meet Morgan's exacting standards were sent down to his office to await his personal delivery of the 'strap' (which the pupils referred to as the 'whip') on their outstretched hand. And so the school day began.

Not that corporal punishment ceased there. While a focus on term grades and exam results might have seemed a loftier aspirational goal, St Mary's promoted a system of 'merits' and 'conduct marks'. The idea was that the four houses would compete for merits and seek to rein in those receiving conduct marks; the reality was that nobody cared much about their individual house to begin with and only marginally more about school in general. Conduct marks were therefore allocated disproportionately, noted with what the teacher considered the number of applicable 'straps', and the pupil sent down to receive them from the staff member on punishment duty.

All this was merely the *official* process by which the pupils were physically disciplined. Unofficially, the metalwork teacher had a two-foot-long piece of tapered wood that he nicknamed Charlie and administered freely on the boys' backsides; he was also given to pulling post-pubescent kids up by their fashionable sideburns, which many considered to be more harmful in the long run. A female teacher who struggled to control her pupils was given her own piece of wood by another teacher (assumed to be her lover), which she rapped viciously against the boys' calves. Another used the slipper; another still threw the blackboard duster directly at the boys' heads. The swimming teacher used a long bamboo pole to whack kids on the head to prevent them from hanging on to the edges of the pool over at Stretford Baths. In contrast, one of the physical education teachers kept kids hanging from the bars in the school gym until their fingers turned blue.

No wonder, then, that many of his fellow former pupils shared, and even applauded, Morrissey's subsequent condemnation of the place as 'a very sadistic school, very barbaric.' One of the boys in his year compared the routine of daily beatings and whippings to 'martial law'; another used the term 'scandalous.' A third, Steven Adshead, who went on to become a Labour councillor and mayor of modern Trafford, observed, in words not dissimilar to Morrissey's own, 'It is a shameful reflection of our society at that time that children could be beaten in this way, I really think society should apologise for it.' Arguably the greatest sadist on the staff was the main PE teacher, a Mr Sweeney, who took delight in having his class run around the gym while he took potshots at them with a medicine ball. Midweek on the playing fields, as Morrissey later referenced in 'The Headmaster Ritual', Sweeney had the boys run from school, over the iron bridge (the pupils called it the 'Monkey Bridge') to Kings Road, from where they turned away from Morrissey's home (no doubt to his relief), down a side street, and after a mile, onto the fields alongside Stretford Grammar School. The boy who came last was forced to bend over and get a ball kicked at his backside. (In summer, he would be whacked on the rear with a cricket bat.) Those who weren't then among the twenty-two selected to play team sports had to run instead all afternoon around the fields, frequently rendered a mud pit by the wet Manchester weather.

The likes of Sweeney were hardly unique to St Mary's. In fact, by 1969, his type was so familiar that it was caricatured in the movie *Kes*, in which the actor Brian Glover played a sports teacher whose (Manchester United and England centre forward) Bobby Charlton complex leads him to chop, push, punish and otherwise cheat his way through a football match that he shouldn't even be participating in other than as referee. By all accounts, Sweeney revelled in identical action. Morrissey himself later recalled how he once – and only once – had the temerity to 'take the ball' off Sweeney. 'His response to this was to ignore the game, ignore the ball, ignore the pupils – and just kick me.'

To the extent that it had one, St Mary's academic focus was evidenced by the fact that it offered metalwork, woodwork, technical drawing, and engineering drawing, but not music, drama or even foreign languages; that there was no school magazine, no orchestra, no instruments, no annual productions of plays or of music. For sure, there were some boys who benefited from this approach and who look back fondly on their time at St Mary's, even the beatings. Typically, they're the ones who excelled at competitive sports, respected the firm arm of authority, and were good with their hands. Steven Morrissey was not among them.

He hardly helped his case by showing up on the first day accompanied by his mother, and wearing, as he would throughout his first year, the optional shorts rather than the long trousers favoured by almost all the other new boys. Along with his decision to take the short journey home across the bridge for lunch every day, he was immediately marked as a 'mummy's boy', and even as 'posh'. And yet he was not victimised for it. Though bullying was certainly perpetrated by some of the boys (who were only copying the teachers, after all), it was nonetheless considered a sign of weakness by most of them. After all, if you wanted to fight, there was always another tough lad happy to oblige; you didn't need to pick on the effeminate kid or the token Pakistani to prove your mettle.

Morrissey inadvertently secured his safety by befriending one of the tougher kids in his year, Mike Foley, the pair discovering that they were more interested in fashion and music than were other kids, and that they each excelled at athletics. Morrissey described this as his 'saving grace at school,' noting that he got 'streams and streams of medals for running.' These sporting talents were inherited from his footballing father, no doubt, who would surely have loved the son to follow (further) in his footsteps, but Steven had learned the hard way, via Sweeney's boot, what became of people who dared to play team sports with any degree of passion. So while being 'a model athlete,' as he described it, afforded him important status with teachers and pupils alike, he chafed at the commitment it required, complaining later of being carted off to 'places very far away' under the threat of 'being beaten to death' if he failed to show.

Uninterested, then, in the camaraderie of sports, uninspired by the rote teaching, unconverted by the Catholic indoctrination, unimpressed with the relative unintelligence of many fellow pupils, at the same time he was unwilling to rebel and risk a daily thrashing. 'He wasn't being educated,' his classmate Mike Moore told Johnny Rogan. 'He was being manipulated by a system that was streamlining him to work in industry. The whole principle of the system was that you didn't buck it, but accepted. If you showed any individuality, they tried to wipe it out. They preferred to ignore him at school, and he ignored them because if you started to argue about the conditions, you were whipped.'

'He was too clever for us,' said Paul Whiting, who started off in Morrissey's class. (There were three classes in each year, totalling approximately 100 pupils, streamed according to each year's exam results into classes A, B and C.) 'We were all fucking dur-durs from the council estate fighting each other and robbing each other, and Steve Morrissey was above that. He shouldn't have been in that school.' Future head boy Barry

Finnegan, whose younger brother Terry became a good friend and frequently visited the Morrissey household on Kings Road, was forever catching him in the hallways during breaks, avoiding the machismo of the playground by 'walking round, looking at things, intently.' Morrissey, he quickly concluded, 'was either painfully shy or he purposefully blocked other people and didn't want other people in his life. It seemed like he had a shield around him.'

As befitted an insular and intelligent personality, Morrissey's personal passions were for the most part firmly askew of his classmates'. While comics were all the rage among adolescents of the time (many musicians and groups naming themselves for superheroes), Morrissey preferred monster magazines full of Boris Karloff and Christopher Lee. As his classmates tried their best to bunk into 'AA' (over fourteen) or 'X' (over eighteen) movies, Morrissey celebrated the camp theatrics of Britain's sexually titillating but cheerfully unrevealing *Carry On* series instead, developing a particular fascination with Charles Hawtrey and Kenneth Williams. In particular, whereas the fictional James Bond was viewed as the archetypal film hero, Morrissey preferred the deceased American actor James Dean, whom he had discovered back at primary school after watching *Rebel Without a Cause* 'quite by accident'; he became obsessed not so much with Dean's acting ability as with his life story, the way that the public image of the handsome young rebel masked a 'constant uneasiness with life.' That Dean was ambivalent about his sexuality certainly did not escape the attention of a bookish young boy who claimed, 'I did research about him and it was like unearthing Tutankhamen's tomb.'

In a culture that measured a family's success by the amount of meat on its Sunday dinner table, Morrissey became a vegetarian at the age of eleven after watching a TV documentary about farm animals: he found the image of 'pigs and cows still thrashing about after they'd been supposedly stunned' to be 'so violent, so horrendous,' that he gave up eating them there and then, never to return. Unusually for boys of his age, most of whom viewed it (if at all) as their parents' soap opera, he was so devoted to *Coronation Street* that at the age of twelve, he took to writing scripts for the show, sending them off to Granada Television and, by his own claims, entering into correspondence with the writer Leslie Duxbury during the process of having them routinely rejected.

All of this, clearly, helped formulate the adult Morrissey, along with the words, music and imagery of the Smiths, but arguably nothing proved as influential towards his future persona as when his mother, determined to cultivate her son's literary instincts, followed up an introduction to Thomas Hardy's novels by giving him the *Complete Works of Oscar Wilde* with the assurance that, as Steven quoted her, 'It's everything you need to know about life.' The gift was rendered, according to its recipient, before Morrissey started at St Mary's; he has cited the shortest of Wilde's fairy tales, 'The Nightingale and the Rose', as making a particularly strong first impression. In that story, a songbird sacrifices itself against a thorn to produce a red rose for a love-struck student; after the object of the student's desire returns the rose as hopelessly insufficient compared to another suitor's gift of jewels, the student casually throws the flower in the road (where it is crushed under oncoming wheels) before concluding, 'What a silly thing Love is! . . . It is always telling one of things that are not going to happen, and making one believe things that are not true.' During his first round of media scrutiny, in late 1983, attempting to explain his lack of a love life, Morrissey noted, 'In your formative years you're led to believe that lots of magical things will happen with other people – which doesn't actually happen.' 'The Nightingale and the Rose' was, then, in essence, his introduction to the 'Miserable Lie' of love.

From Wilde's fairy tales, it was a short step up to his plays, set in a world equally far removed from 1960s and '70s Stretford, that of the landed gentry of late Victorian England, where the lords and ladies of the manors sat or strolled around one another's drawing rooms and gardens, flinging devastatingly witty and occasionally barbed one-liners at one another, inevitably drawing themselves into complex personal and financial relationships until a dastardly clever denouement brought a happy ending for those who deserved it (and occasionally, those who did not). As was true for Morrissey in later life with the Smiths albums, Wilde's four 'society plays' were written in the space of four years – and represented the author's commercial peak, bringing Wilde both the popular acclaim that he desperately desired and the financial rewards he direly needed to maintain his flamboyant lifestyle. Despite the fact that the cream of British society flocked to Wilde's every new theatrical presentation in the early 1890s and craved his company at their dinner tables, they were always acutely aware that his comedies of errors barely disguised a contempt for their conceits, arrogance, hypocrisy and other defects; this would invite a powerful denouement of its own.

Certainly, Wilde the writer shied from neither provocation nor controversy. His first published work, a collected book of poems, was returned to the author by his former university debating society amidst claims that it was mired in plagiarism. His novel *The Picture of Dorian Gray* was castigated upon publication in serialised magazine form for its sexual, moral and violent decadence; in a rare sign of defensiveness, Wilde removed some of the more homoerotic passages for the subsequent book. And his play *Salome*, written in French just after *Dorian Gray* and just before his run of mainstream hits, was refused a licence for the London stage because it depicted biblical characters in salacious scenes.

As all this makes evident, it is impossible to read much of Oscar Wilde without reading an awful lot *about* Oscar Wilde, which is how the writer wanted it. After all, it was Wilde himself who stated, 'I put all my genius into my life, I put only my talent into my work.' As Morrissey read up on the amazing life story of Oscar Wilde, he could hardly have contemplated that they would ever be written of in the same sentence, for, other than their Irish heritage, their difference in backgrounds was almost impossibly pronounced. Wilde was born into a prestigious, intellectual family, his father a noted – indeed, knighted – surgeon, author, naturalist (and womaniser); his mother a poet, acclaimed translator and rabble-rouser (a Protestant one, at that) in the cause of Irish nationalism. (Morrissey would later take Lady Wilde's call to arms for a Smiths song title.) Wilde grew up in one of Dublin's most fashionable houses, furnished with six servants, a governess, and a maid, where dinner guests often numbered a dozen and afternoon parties sometimes a hundred. And he started his education at a renowned Irish private school (proclaimed 'the Eton of Ireland'), after which he attended Dublin's premier school of higher learning, Trinity College, then went on to Oxford, where he graduated with a 'double first'. The council houses and secondary moderns of Stretford this was not.

At Trinity and Oxford, Wilde embraced aestheticism, a fashionable reaction to strict Victorian morality that sought to promote beauty (often in the pursuit of decadence) in everything from furnishings to mannerisms. Making his entry in London society as the ultimate dandy, sporting colourful breeches and brocaded velvet suits completed by the personal touch of a green carnation in the buttonhole, Wilde quickly became such a stereotype of the aesthetic that he inspired not one but two characters in Gilbert and Sullivan's parody of the movement, *Patience*; when that operetta became a hit in the United States, Wilde toured America lecturing on the subject. Though Wilde married, and sired two sons (for whom he wrote his fairy tales), he was never shy about his fondness for what a Trinity professor euphemistically described as 'Greek love' (the aesthetics worshipped the ancient Greeks). Still, it was one thing to have crushes at college, conduct discreet affairs with other male literary types, or to engage in anonymous rough trade in the dark alleys of London and Paris, all of which was part of Wilde's rich life story; it was another thing entirely to parade a (much younger) member of the aristocracy on his arm about town, as he did with Lord Alfred Douglas, son of the Marquess of Queensbury, throughout the early 1890s – a time when the crime of homosexuality was subject to increased punishment under the moral Victorian establishment.

The affair caused Wilde's downfall: when the pugilistic, confrontational marquess left a calling card at Wilde's club accusing the writer of 'posing as a sodomite,' Wilde sued for libel, against the warnings of his lawyers. In court, perhaps inevitably, he was brought down by the rapaciousness of his own wit like a character in one of his society plays; when asked, directly, whether he had kissed a certain one of Lord Douglas's servants, he replied that he had not, because the boy 'was unfortunately ugly.' Upon such a facetious quip did his world turn. The prosecution instantly dropped its case, and Wilde was arrested at the Cadogan Hotel in Knightsbridge that same day and charged with 'gross indecency'. Both Wilde and Lord Douglas were ultimately found guilty and sentenced to two years hard labour. Wilde's plays were immediately withdrawn from the stage, his books recalled, his epigrams silenced. With but one or two exceptions, his friends disowned him rather than risk their own ruination. Wilde died of meningitis in a fleapit Paris hotel at the age of forty-six. Though his literary output survived his personal downfall – *The Importance of Being Earnest* was still taught in British secondary schools during the 1970s – his life story remained disgraced (except in gay circles, where it was celebrated) through much of the twentieth century.[3]

'It's a total disadvantage to care about Oscar Wilde, certainly when you come from a working-class background,' Morrissey later opined. But it didn't stop him: Wilde became more than one of his obsessions but rather his first true hero, indeed something of a role model and an inspiration. Everywhere he turned in the story of Wilde's life, there was something from which Steven Morrissey could learn and apply to his own artistic ambitions. From Wilde's writing structure, for example, he acquired the power of simplicity: 'He used the most basic language and said the most powerful things,' observed Morrissey, suggesting that his famous quotations surpassed even those of Shakespeare because Wilde's were more easily understood. From Wilde's demeanour, he learned the importance of the sartorial statement, best manifested in the Smiths via the gladioli in his back pocket. From his pen and conversation (Wilde was considered nothing less than 'the greatest natural talker of modern times') Morrissey learned and perfected the art of the precise epigram: the style of his wit and wisdom, delivered time and again through the Smiths' career not only in his lyrics but in those devastatingly perceptive, frequently hilarious and purposefully provocative interview quotations, was almost entirely based on that of Oscar Wilde.[5] And from Wilde's own maxim that 'talent borrows, genius steals,' he would offer no apologies for heisting entire phrases from beloved plays, movies and novels for his lyrics – though he appeared to know better all along than to claim Wilde's actual words as his own.

But in one area, he crucially differed. From Wilde's downfall, Morrissey learned that there are certain things society will countenance and certain things it will not, and to be on the safe side, he would endeavour, forever, to keep his own personal life entirely private. His fans would have to draw their own conclusions from the fact that so many of his childhood heroes – from Wilde to Dean, from Kenneth Williams to Charles Hawtrey – were homosexuals or bisexuals of variously, and arguably understandable, degrees of self-repression; Morrissey was not going to be any more forthcoming on the subject than that.

CHAPTER FIVE

They were my only friends. I firmly believed that.
– MORRISSEY on the New York Dolls, *Select*,
July 1991

Just before he saw T. Rex perform live in the summer of 1972, Steven Morrissey bought the single 'Starman', David Bowie's first hit since his number-one 'Space Oddity' back in 1969. Morrissey claimed he 'hadn't even seen a picture of' Bowie before then, though he was hardly alone in his conversion: 'Starman' caused something of an epiphany with a significant segment of British youth after a performance on *Top of the Pops* that June, when Bowie, his hair dyed orange and wearing a lurid jumpsuit, cuddled up to guitarist Mick Ronson, equally resplendent in a gold lamé two-piece. As a middle-aged Morrissey would acknowledge, 'There was no doubt that this was fantastically homosexual.'

The thirteen-year-old Morrissey of 1972 promptly went out and bought Bowie's last three albums. His enthusiastic commitment made perfect sense, for Bowie was the closest that the British glam rock scene – indeed, that British pop culture throughout the 1960s and '70s – came to an Oscar Wilde figure. Presenting his provocative output as his own inventions though much of it was borrowed from society's fringes, confronting conventional mores with his increasingly (and unapologetically) flamboyant changes in image, proving almost impossibly prolific now that he had the public's attention (he and Ronson, as producers and/or songwriters, revived the careers of both Britain's Mott the Hoople and America's Lou Reed in the space of a year), Bowie also turned musical society mildly on its head with his comment to *Melody Maker*, in January 1972, that 'I'm gay, and always have been.' Homosexuality had only been legal for five years; it was a mark of how far Britain had come that Bowie, despite being married with a child, could make such a claim as a quest for publicity, whereas Oscar Wilde had been brought to ruin for a similar yet unintended statement of sexual orientation.

As for so many kids in Britain, Morrissey's maturing musical tastes directly coincided with his immersion in the country's thriving music press; he saw his name in print for the first time when he won a copy of Bowie's latest LP, *The Rise and Fall of Ziggy Stardust and the Spiders from Mars*, in a competition in the weekly paper *Sounds*. In particular, Morrissey learned from Bowie's cult of personality and his powerful confidence in the face of potential adversity. 'He would roll into Doncaster or Bradford in 1972, looking as he did, and if you had a problem with it, then it was your problem – not his – he was the one who was always laughing or smiling. He wasn't persecuted by anything. It was the people who objected who were persecuted.'

Morrissey would often claim that his love of Bowie put him in the minority at school, but when the Ziggy Stardust tour came to Manchester in September 1972, Bowie was already popular enough to play two nights in the city. They took place at the Hardrock Concert Theatre, on Great Stone Road, which extended northward from the large roundabout (the 'Quadrant') close to Morrissey's Kings Road home; through the early 1970s, the venue was a major Manchester performance venue, one of the few saving graces of growing up in Stretford. Morrissey was at the second of Bowie's two Hardrock shows, and returned in November with Mike Foley to see Bowie's early partners in glam, Roxy Music. After that show, the pair ventured into town hoping to meet the band, only to be attacked outside the Midland Hotel for their appearance, which presumably showed the influence of a glam infatuation. Foley recalled that while he stood his ground against the 'queer bashers, or whatever they were,' Morrissey relied on his athletic skills to sprint through the hotel doors to safety.

The pair had arrived early at the Hardrock that November night to see the opening band, the New York Dolls; though they had yet to release a record, Morrissey knew about them already from their constant write-ups courtesy of *Melody Maker*'s New York correspondent. What he did not know was that just a few days earlier, the group's drummer had died from a totally preventable drugs-and-coffee accident at an exclusive house party in London. He only learned about the calamity when someone came onstage to announce that the New York Dolls would not be performing.

A full year would pass before Morrissey had the chance to see the (revamped) New York Dolls play live – and then only on television, when the quintet appeared on the BBC's late-night programme *The Old Grey Whistle Test* wearing, variously, frilly blouses, leather trousers, polka-dot shirts and gold bow ties, their curtains of long hair occasionally opening to reveal considerable layers of mascara and eyeliner. This presentation, along with the group's musical manifestation of a primitive, dirty rock 'n' roll, so inflamed the show's host, 'Whispering' Bob Harris, that he dismissed the band on air as 'mock rock.'

Not Morrissey, though. For him, the appearance of the New York Dolls on the *Old Grey Whistle Test* served as his 'private "Heartbreak Hotel"', in the sense that they were as important to me as Elvis Presley was important to the entire language of rock 'n' roll.' He loved the way that they embraced the gang ideal integral to all great rock groups – but that they did so in a deliberately juvenile, almost amateur manner, perfect for a musically untutored fourteen-year-old. He loved too that they appeared to be blue-collar/working-class street toughs, and yet that they were delightfully decadent, parading through the mean streets of 1970s New York City like peacocks. And if it was true that they were all firmly hetero at heart, there was nonetheless an element of gay pride – or at least gay solidarity – about the New York Dolls. That the four-month summer 1972 residency that brought them their initial acclaim took place in a room named for Oscar Wilde, within a downtown Manhattan Arts Centre, must have seemed beyond coincidence.

Steven Morrissey duly pledged himself to the New York Dolls with all the blind devotion of a teenager's first romantic infatuation, going so far as to get permission from the group's American office to establish a British fan club of sorts. The Dolls were to be almost as roundly ignored in the UK as in their homeland, and therefore his role, by his own account, 'wasn't very dramatic.' It consisted of little more than placing ads in the back of the music papers seeking other fans, and then endeavouring to keep them informed, hopefully cultivating a few pen-pal relationships in the process. His status as fan club president was perhaps more notable for the fact that he did not grow out of it, continuing to champion the group with unabashed devotion long after they broke up and well into his adulthood.

More so than any of his other many fanaticisms, this obsession with the New York Dolls seems confusing given the lack of reference points in the Smiths. The adult Morrissey never moved about onstage with the suave sexual confidence of Dolls singer David Johansen; he did not wear such colourful and effete costumes as anyone in the band; his lyrics did not venture into the Dolls' world of hard drugs and open transgression – although two lines from 'Lonely Planet Boy' *were* lifted for 'There Is a Light That Never Goes Out'. (Equally, despite Johnny Marr having his own youthful fixation on Dolls guitarist Johnny Thunders, little of that came across in either his playing or the Smiths' arrangements.) What the Dolls represented, for Morrissey, at the point when glam rock was becoming a watered-down commodity for the preteens, and when the 1960s rock bands had distanced themselves from their original audience as a result of their increasingly artistic pretentions, was rock 'n' roll as genuine rebellion, something that could still offend your parents (and Bob Harris). The fact that the Dolls released just two albums – the latter entitled, with inadvertent prescience, *Too Much Too Soon* – only added to Morrissey's sense of private ownership and public injustice. For while his love of Bowie and Reed, of Roxy Music and Mott the Hoople, and also of the duo Sparks (his first published letter in a British music paper effusively cited 1974's *Kimono My House* as 'the album of the year'), rendered him part of a significant cult, his devotion to the New York Dolls, at school at least, safely inoculated him within a church of one disciple. Revelling in this newly acquired role as prophet without honour, he wore homemade Dolls T-shirts on the St Mary's playing fields, adorned his schoolbooks with the group's photos, and somehow convinced a teacher to play one of their songs to the whole class. 'Everyone got to say how they felt afterwards,' he recalled of the occasion. 'And they didn't feel too well, I'm afraid.'

Morrissey also bought into the hype surrounding the New York glam rocker Jobriath, whose 1974 debut album had one of the most lavish publicity campaigns of all time. The first *truly* gay rock musician to put his heart on the line as such (unlike Bowie, who was only teasing), Jobriath appeared for his coming-out concert on American television in a pink leotard, grossly overestimating the public's willingness to support such overt sexual liberation. Musically, he was almost equally overdramatic, rooted in an impersonation of the 'cosmic jive' that his obvious role model, David Bowie, had long left behind. When his album flopped on a titanic scale, a European tour was cancelled; like the New York Dolls, Jobriath never played in Manchester. And like the New York Dolls, Morrissey's failure to see the act live only served to increase his lifelong passion.

Emboldened by his love of obscure New York glam acts, and

inspired by the brazen fashions of the era, Morrissey started dressing the part. When a large group of St Mary's pupils went to see Bowie at Manchester's Free Trade Hall in June 1973, he and Mike Foley cut and dyed their hair for the occasion, though the results were reputedly a disaster and Morrissey was sent home from school for his troubles. He also took to carrying a denim bag around with him – a relatively simple statement of individuality, but a brave one all the same, given his local environment. A neighbour, Ivor Perry, two years his junior, had a clear recollection of Morrissey 'walking down the road, having tight pants, pointy shoes, a quiffy hairstyle, and a man bag, which was outrageous in . . . 1974–75.' But while Perry acknowledged that Morrissey 'had a lot of courage to carry it off,' such individuality came at a cost. 'My friends' older brothers would mug him for his money. Nobody beat him up, they didn't hate him. They'd even leave him his bus fare. They'd just make him pay a fee for walking up the road!'

Morrissey's own recollections of attempts at social integration reflected that sense of persecution. He attended Old Trafford on his own once or twice, but after being robbed of his woollen souvenir hat (by a Manchester United fan, there being no honour among thieves), soon gave up. He went to the fair over at Stretford Raceway – drawn, admittedly, by the atmosphere of danger – but 'somebody just came up to me and head-butted me.' He knew better than to ask why. 'There never needed to be a reason.'

At school, he mostly managed to avoid such outright aggression (and though he claimed to have received the strap, it was not often), but his increasingly camp appearance only furthered the notion that he was, to use the word most frequently bandied about in retrospect, 'effeminate'. Coarser words were likely used at the time, and there may have been outright insinuations about Morrissey's sexuality – except that, not only was he *not* seen dating boys, but he was proven to be attractive to girls: the opposite sex recognised in Steven Morrissey a handsome, intelligent and, above all, a sensitive teenager, with a good line in conversation and a refreshing absence of sexual intent. His friends Mike Foley and Mike Ellis were both baffled by (and jealous of) the ease with which Morrissey could secure female company, which peaked with the news that he was hosting a regular group of girls in his bedroom each Sunday evening – to listen to the Radio 1 chart countdown.

Indeed, friends were always welcome to stop in at the Morrissey household – and regardless of the fact that Steven chose his company carefully, he had no small share of it. He attended the occasional school disco, camped out in the back garden with his neighbours, and even took vacations with other kids' families, going to North Wales with schoolmate Jim Verrechia, who was sufficiently impressed by Morrissey's musical knowledge as to try to teach him guitar. The effort proved no more successful than Morrissey's other attempts to learn an instrument; despite being a walking encyclopedia on pop, it remained evident that he had almost no natural musical affinity.

School itself, meanwhile – or rather, *the* school itself – was going from bad to worse. Morrissey's close friend Mike Foley was now moving in particularly troublesome circles, alongside Paul Whiting, Ian Campbell, and another lad who, said Whiting, had the rare ability to 'shit at will'; he would defecate into a class desk, place a firework 'banger' on top, light the touch paper, step back . . . and watch with delight as the explosion sent his faeces around the classroom. This boy's dubious talents were most infamously used when he defecated in a fire-bucket of sand that Foley then emptied into the school piano, the blockage only noticed during the following morning's assembly, when efforts to play 'Kumbaya' failed to elicit a recognisable sound but emitted a distinctive smell. According to the ringleaders, Morrissey was often on hand during such escapades, though never quite so close as to be accused of instigation.

The relentless beatings of the pupils evidently had no positive effect on their behaviour. 'Nobody showed us kids respect,' said Whiting; rather, the violence 'taught you how to fight and who to fight. If you know you can't beat 'em, go 'round the back and get 'em from behind.' The classrooms and playing fields of St Mary's increasingly became a battleground. There were incidents of pupils knocking out teachers, teachers flattening students, and kids arranging classroom distractions so they could rob unwitting teachers' handbags, taking the money to the Stretford Shopping Precinct, though they'd be as likely to shoplift the latest fashions from the Pakistani stall owners as buy them. Rare attempts at field trips usually ended in disgrace, the St Mary's pupils thrown out of a magistrates' court gallery for shouting their opinions on proceedings and awarded the rare distinction of having the police called on them when they visited an Army barracks, a search of the school bus revealing that they had attempted to steal grenades and bullets.

The breakdown in law and order, in mutual respect and honour, merely mirrored British society at large. With inflation riding high, a series of successful worker strikes for matching wage increases led to ever-greater inflation and ever more strikes in turn as the trade unions, largely established in the factories and mills of nineteenth-century Manchester, were seen by many to be taking control of the country. In an attempt to establish its authority, the Conservative government declared a state of emergency and a three-day workweek, with the result that pre-announced power cuts became a regular part of the evening 'entertainment' and lining up for petrol a national pastime. The government collapsed all the same, although it took two general elections in 1974 before Labour could secure a sufficient parliamentary majority of its own – at which the left-wing party duly assumed the role of adversary to the recalcitrant unions.

The situation in Northern Ireland, in the meantime, which had remained under British rule (and neglect) for the past half century, turned ugly as the Catholic minority, demanding civil rights, came under attack first from the Protestant-controlled police force and then from a British Army that had been sent in ostensibly to protect them. The unrest awoke the sectarian paramilitaries, and in the aftermath of the Bloody

Sunday of January 1972, wherein thirteen unarmed protestors were shot dead by the British Army, the Provisional IRA brought a bombing campaign to the British mainland. In February 1974, an IRA bomb exploded at the magistrates' court in Manchester, injuring a dozen people and leading to a new round of soul-searching amongst, and allegations about, the local immigrant Irish.

The football terraces were also turning into battlegrounds, with Manchester United fans – specifically those at Old Trafford's 'Stretford Road' end – garnering one of the fiercest reputations in the country, not unrelated to the fact that they also drew the biggest crowds: more than 50,000 a week routinely crammed onto crumbling terraces. And all the while, the factories and mills continued to retrench or shut down completely, forcing unemployment to levels not seen since the Depression; as a city built on manufacturing, Manchester suffered as severely from the nation's economic decline as anywhere in Britain. In such a climate, the small handful of teachers who attempted to cut through the mutual animosity and overriding apathy at St Mary's and deliver something approximating a valuable education were faced with an almost Herculean struggle. English teacher Graham Pink acknowledged that for all his attempts to bring in a wider range of relevant literature (for example, *Kes* and *Billy Liar*) he spent more time 'sitting on the loud-mouths' than attending to the likes of Morrissey, whom he saw, to the extent he paid attention to him at all, as being 'very retiring.' For his efforts Pink endured disdain from his school's more strident disciplinarians, and later went into nursing.[1]

One of the few who succeeded in getting through to the Stretford kids was a Mr Hopkins, who wore a Crombie coat fashionable with the skinheads, and conversed with the tougher boys on their level. In Morrissey's final year, Hopkins somehow circumvented Headmaster Morgan's aversion to drama and directed a production of the play *The Long and the Short and the Tall*, which had first come to the British stage in 1959, directed by Lindsay Anderson in the wake of *Look Back in*

Anger and *A Taste of Honey*. Hopkins secured the support of the troublemakers like Foley and Whiting by giving them leads (it helped that the parts were of embittered, working-class conscripts in World War II); secured a role for everyone who wanted to be involved, even if just as a stagehand or extra; and even let the boys smoke real cigarettes onstage instead of fakes. For those who had fought, stolen and truanted their way through school, it was a rare moment of consideration and collaboration.

For Morrissey, though, such efforts proved too little, too late. Taking as much time out from his latter years as he could get away with (rather than shoplift at the Stretford Shopping Precinct, he would generally just go on a walkabout), he left in the spring of 1975, right around his sixteenth birthday, with the barest of CSEs to his name. (He subsequently embarked on an additional year of schooling, at Stretford Tech, on a crash course to secure the handful of O-Levels that would gain him worthy employment.) Morrissey remained forever unforgiving about his treatment at St Mary's, to the point of celebrating Morgan's passing from the stage at the Old Trafford cricket ground during a homecoming solo show in 2004. In interviews, he was no less restrained. Talking to Manchester's own Paul Morley in 1988, a year after the Smiths split, it was evident that his time at St Mary's had left a deep scar of bitterness. 'The horror of it cannot be overemphasised,' he said. 'Every single day was a human nightmare. In every single way that you could possibly want to imagine. Worse . . . the total hatred. The fear and anguish of waking up, of having to get dressed, having to walk down the road, having to walk into assembly, having to do those lessons . . .' And more than a decade later, speaking to Brian Boyd of the *Irish Times*, he even floated the idea of formal retribution.

'It was so abysmal – and you may snigger, you may not, I'll chance it – that I've considered actually suing the Manchester Education Committee because the education I received was so basically evil and brutal. All I learnt was to have no self-esteem and to feel ashamed without knowing why. It's part of being working-class, this pathetic belief that somebody else, somewhere, knows better than you do and knows what's best for you.'

Due to dwindling class sizes, itself not unrelated to such an appalling reputation for corporal punishment that even the Department of Education and Science took note, St Mary's was closed in the early 1990s and demolished. A housing estate was built over its grounds. The iron bridge across the railway tracks to Kings Road remains as it was – except for extensive graffiti, added since the 1980s, almost every last word of which lovingly quotes a lyric by the most famous St Mary's 'old boy' of all.

CHAPTER SIX

It's something that's in me spiritually. And psychically.
Just as a being, this sort of absorption in music. Popular
culture is more of an intellectual thing, but that
connection with the sound is just something that is
in my DNA.

– Johnny Marr, March 2011

When it was the Maher family's turn to be moved out of their terraced street in the name of slum clearance, they were relocated, as were so many from Ardwick, Hulme and Moss Side alike, to a growing – indeed, overflowing – community eight miles south. The 'garden city' of Wythenshawe, to give what would later be damned as 'Europe's largest council estate' its true title, had first been envisioned back in the 1920s. A product both of necessity (the imperative to create new housing for an overpopulated Manchester), and idealism (the desire to do so in a positive manner), its planners took their lead from the original garden cities in the south of England: Letchworth, completed in 1904, and Welwyn, finished just after World War I. They set their sights on open lands around the ancient Cheshire villages of Northenden and Baguley, each referenced in the *Domesday Book* of 1086, and Wythenshawe ('Willow Wood') itself, a relative newcomer of a mere seven hundred years' existence. The River Mersey and its surrounding floodplains had long provided a psychological and physical barrier to such urban encroachment, allowing the lords of the

Cheshire manor houses to enjoy their fiefdoms in relative peace and quiet – although the decision by the Tattons of Wythenshawe Hall to stand with the Loyalists in the English Civil War had resulted in cannons being shipped from parliamentarian Manchester to encourage a rethink. Wythenshawe Hall survived that four-month siege almost intact, but was not able to halt the march of history. In 1926, the Tattons sold 2,600 acres to the City of Manchester, while locally born businessman Ernest Simon bought Wythenshawe Hall and its surrounding 250-acre estate to create Wythenshawe Park, which he then gifted 'as some return for all that we owe to Manchester.' More than a mere philanthropist, Simon pushed relentlessly for the garden-city project; at various times a Manchester city councillor, chairman of the housing committee, Lord Mayor and Liberal MP, he was in Parliament to vote on the 1930 bill that forcibly transferred the surrounding lands of the Cheshire villages to the City of Manchester for development. In addition, Simon was the author of *The Smokeless City*, *How to Abolish Slums*, and *The Rebuilding of Manchester*, among other books, and therefore considered primarily responsible for Wythenshawe becoming one of Britain's first smoke-controlled areas.[1]

Despite these best laid plans, the vision for a garden city that would preserve local woods and ponds, include ample amenities, and allow for a number of 'self-conscious' smaller communities of approximately 10,000 apiece, was hampered by fiscal and physical realities. The onset of the Depression, the interruption of World War II, and the rush to build substandard housing in the wake of that war, meant that by 1964 Wythenshawe's population had already reached its goal of nearly 100,000, but that shops, cinemas, performance spaces and the like languished desperately far behind. The local papers filled up with headlines about 'vandalism', and Mancunians who had never been there came to view Wythenshawe as a 'rough, rundown huge council estate where the kids were savages,' according to one of its inhabitants who came of age in the 1970s. But when the Mahers were moved, alongside a number of other Mancunian families – Irish, English, Indian and Caribbean among them – into the new Shady Lane estate, just off Altrincham Road, their elder boy, Johnny, took one look at his new surroundings and figured it for exactly what the garden-city planners had intended: Utopia.

Marr's excitement was understandable. Shady Lane was a cul-de-sac, which allowed kids the freedom to play without constant traffic, and though the houses on the Mahers' own terrace, Churchstone Walk, lacked the space and comfort of the Morrissey family's semidetached in Stretford, the mere existence of indoor toilets and phone lines seemed positively luxurious after Victorian Ardwick. The Mahers had arrived just as Wythenshawe was turning a corner; a long-overdue civic centre (with sports facilities) and accompanying forum (with concert capabilities) had been opened in 1971; a new hospital arrived in 1973. Wythenshawe had its trouble spots, for sure, but the worst of them – Benchill, Woodhouse Park and Peel Hall – were far off to the south and the east, over the new M56 motorway that extended from the city centre out to Manchester Airport. The Mahers were in Baguley, on the northern periphery, bordering Sale and Altrincham, which had original 1930s-era council houses of considerable high quality. On the other side of Altrincham Road from Shady Lane stood Brookway High School, which took in most of the local non-Catholic residents, girls included, not only from Baguley but from the estates of Brooklands, Northern Moor and Royal Oak, which were almost middle-class – or at the very least, what Johnny Marr would come to consider 'bohemian.' Just off to the east of the school was Wythenshawe Park itself, its ancient hall of less interest to the local youths than its multiple football pitches, or the prospect of the fair that set up every Easter weekend, where Johnny and his sister, Claire, soon learned to spend every waking hour soaking up the music that blared from the speakers day and night.

In Ardwick, by his own admission, Johnny had been 'a very quiet, introspective little fella,' overwhelmed by the wild behaviour of the young Irish immigrant community; at his primary school there, 'everyone was very uptight and aggressive and I was very intimidated.' But on his first day at Sacred Heart Roman Catholic Primary School, adjoined to the church of the same name, he recalled looking around and thinking, 'Everyone's really *nice*.' The kids didn't have to wear uniform, and Johnny could flaunt his fondness for high-street/football fashion, in the form of Oxford 'bags' (baggy trousers), V-neck 'star' jumpers, Budgie jackets (as worn by Adam Faith on the TV show of the same name), and black Brutus jeans. Wearing such clothes to primary school, said Johnny, 'I became aware that I was considered almost exotic.' He found that people were interested in him, perhaps even impressed by him. 'I saw at the age of eleven that I'd got out of an intimidating place and into this world, and a certain image was reflected back at me who I was, and it gave me confidence that I absolutely didn't have.'

It was, in short, precisely the opposite experience from that of Steven Morrissey in *his* new environment, and there remains the interesting hypothetical question of what would have become of Morrissey (and subsequently any band like the Smiths) had his own family followed the more common forced relocation path from Hulme and Moss Side into Wythenshawe. Some things, however, appeared consistent regardless of location. Though Johnny Marr passed his 11-plus, leaving Sacred Heart Primary in the early summer of 1975 (the same time Morrissey said good-bye to St Mary's Secondary), when he started the following school year at St Augustine's Grammar School, a Roman Catholic establishment three miles east along Altrincham Road towards Gatley, it proved a major disappointment. The headmaster at St Augustine's, Monsignor McGuiness, was an alcoholic, with the stink of gin noticeable on his breath; the teachers all wore mortar boards and gowns; uniforms were again compulsory, the striped school blazer making him a natural target of ridicule for the boys at Brookway High School; Latin was mandatory for the first two years;

discipline was harsh, the strap used constantly by any number of openly vicious teachers; music was restricted to its Catholic associations of choirs and orchestras; and there was constant religious indoctrination, down to morning sermons on the saint of the day. It was, as a grammar school, still a better seat of learning than Stretford's St Mary's, but the philosophy remained almost identical: drill the kids religiously in Catholicism, and beat them fearlessly if they step out of line. (As at St Mary's, the beatings were not restricted to officially recorded punishment. One former pupil recalled a math teacher 'meting out brutality which, I'm sure, would not have seemed out of place in a street brawl.')

Quickly frustrated by his school's rigidity, Marr preferred spending his evenings not on homework but at West Wythenshawe Youth Club, located in the college of the same name. Here he could mingle not only with friends from St Augustine's, but with lads from Brookway – and lasses, too. The youth club was all-embracing, offering chess and other activities, roller-skating, and rock-climbing excursions, and helping keep the kids further out of trouble with Wednesday-night discos, where the DJ played dance music a step beyond the chart-topping sounds of ABBA or Tina Charles, introducing Marr to the Fatback Band and Hamilton Bohannon, which would prove to be key influences on a boy who had otherwise followed his love of T. Rex onto a conventional path through prepubescent glitter: David Bowie, Roxy Music and Sparks. Other, more physical, introductions were also made at 'West Wythy': through his fellow Ardwick emigrants Marc Johnson and Chris Milne, older boys who attended Brookway, Marr fell quickly under the spell of a group of lads from that school, scattered in the (comparatively) upscale estates on the north side of Altrincham Road. More than mere fellow music obses-sives, most of them were accomplished guitar players too. The likes of Dave Clough, Robin Allman, Billy Duffy and Barry Spencer would all, and to varying degrees, exert an enormous influence over Marr's teenage years.

Marr was by now no slouch on the guitar himself. The potential had always been there, fostered by the perpetual sound of music back in Ardwick, by his mother's habit of leaving him not only alone in front of the radio as she went about her cleaning, but in front of the amplifiers at the guitar stores in central Manchester while doing her shopping. At a very young age, he'd been given a harmonica and had occasionally pitched in on drunken living-room jams with his extended family and neighbours. Over the course of multiple Christmases and birthdays, he had then asked for, and received, a steadily improving run of guitars, until 'the one I took with me from Ardwick I was able to restring and get chords out of.' In his new bedroom on Churchstone Walk, he had learned to play along to many of the hits of his childhood: specifically, with a classic such as 'All the Young Dudes', he would incorporate the melodies into the chord structures. At Sacred Heart, he had gained immediate kudos for this – 'I think what I brought from Ardwick with me was my identity as a guitar player' – but now, at secondary school, at an impressionable age, and with glam receding from the charts, he felt the need to emulate the musical tastes of the older guitar players from Brookway.

It wasn't that easy. He couldn't relate to Deep Purple 'because it was so organ-based,' couldn't identify with Led Zeppelin 'because it was groove-based,' and couldn't get down with Jimi Hendrix because 'I wasn't sophisticated enough to appreciate it.' What he *could* relate to was the Rolling Stones. His mother had always been a fan – she used to sing 'Get Off of My Cloud' at him when he got too pushy with her – and when Marr was sat down with a more extensive collection of the band's 45s by local guitar player Dave Clough, it proved something of a revelation. This was partly about the music, the fact that more than a decade into their career, the Stones continued to turn out hit singles as diverse as 'It's Only Rock 'n' Roll' and 'Fool to Cry'. But it was also about the *style*, especially that of Keith Richards, whom Marr thought 'just seemed to be the coolest man on two feet.' For some, that coolness was manifested in the reputation Richards had for staying up days and nights on end and taking the kind of drugs that weren't readily available in Wythenshawe. For Marr, it was about the way he played guitar – Keith could take the most simple riff and embellish it with inflections that made it distinctly, inimitably his own – and how he led the band without making a big statement about it. The general public might have thought that the Stones were run by their famous singer, Mick Jagger, but guitarists knew better; they saw Keith as what Marr called 'the engine.'

Recognising a Stones influence when they heard it, some of the older lads in Wythenshawe had also gotten into the New York Dolls, and as obsessive devotees of the British music press, they discovered that there was a lad in Stretford who shared their enthusiasm. In the Christmas 1975 edition of *Sounds*, a letter from Steve (no longer Steven) Morrissey of Kings Road credited the Dolls with influencing everyone from Bruce Springsteen, Kiss and Aerosmith (spurious claims at best), on to Wayne County, the Tubes and the Dictators – acts you could only know about if you read the music papers scrupulously, and which you could barely hear for yourself even if you made the effort. The Wythenshawe boys figured to keep an eye out for this Morrissey character.[2]

They got their chance in July 1976, when they made a trek up to the Free Trade Hall to see a local group perform in the city centre for the first time. Slaughter & the Dogs had been formed out of a friendship between vocalist Wayne Barrett, slum-cleared out of Moss Side, and guitarist Mick Rossi. Each had attended St Augustine's Grammar, a year apart, until they were expelled (long before Johnny Marr's time) and kicked down into Sharston Secondary Modern, where they became classic problem children of the '70s, hanging out on the streets of Benchill and Woodhouse Park looking for trouble, and finding it. 'It was fighting, mugging, stealing, that's all there was,' said Barrett, who recalled that the Wythenshawe of that neighbourhood and period 'was a dump. There was nothing.'

Barrett was part of a generally rare breed of that era that nonetheless had a strong presence in Wythenshawe. He described himself as 'a bootboy,' but that 'at the same time I was walking 'round with platform shoes and dyeing my hair. You'd be going to the football matches, going to see Man United on Saturdays, beating shit out of the other team's fans, and then Saturday night you'd be listening to *Ziggy Stardust* and taking acid pills and pyramids and uppers and downers, getting off your head and escaping from reality.' (Though too young to associate with them as yet, Marr identified upon moving to Wythenshawe with characters who were 'being working-class and going to the match but having ideas about David Bowie and being freethinking – and that was incredibly liberating for me.')

Barrett was saved from his worst tendencies by a music teacher at Sharston who recognised that his infatuation with Bowie and Roxy Music went beyond the norm, and encouraged him and Rossi to learn instruments. Picking up additional band members from school, including Johnny Marr's future friend Howard Bates on bass, they took their name from Mick Ronson's *Slaughter on 10th Avenue* and David Bowie's *Diamond Dogs*, and then financed the band by stealing water drains off the streets, weighing them in to illicit scrap metal merchants and using the cash to buy instruments and amps. Slowly, they built up a set based on Bowie, Velvet Underground, and New York Dolls covers and embarked on playing the local British Legion and Conservative Clubs, where their hardened teenage Wythenshawe following would strike such fear into the older regulars that they'd often be asked to leave before they'd started playing.

Having developed a local following, Slaughter & the Dogs called up a 'mad hippie' who had been advertising his home recording studio in nearby Didsbury. His name was Martin Hannett, and in early 1976, he produced a demo that included a song entitled 'Love Speed and Beer', which pretty much summed up the band's spheres of interest. ('Everyone was on pills half the time – because heroin was too expensive,' said Barrett.) Impressed, Hannett took it upon himself to cold-call the one person in the Manchester media he thought might be interested in the results, the presenter of the 'What's On' segment of local TV show *Granada Reports*: Tony Wilson. Of working-class Salford stock, Wilson had nonetheless made it to Cambridge University, where he picked up a plum BBC accent that aggravated as many Mancunians who watched him on TV as it fooled the guests he frequently took to task for their lack of social-political integrity. In the spring of 1976, Wilson was preparing to launch a music television show of his own, *So It Goes*, and at Hannett's recommendation, he journeyed to Stockport to see Slaughter & the Dogs in concert. The sheer energy of the band and their teenage following excited him, especially as, almost the same week, he received a note in the mail from one Howard Trafford, inviting him to come see a group called the Sex Pistols that Trafford and his friend Peter McNeish were bringing up from London to play the Lesser Free Trade Hall – a smaller room underneath the main hall – in June. Wilson didn't make it to that show; only fifty or so people did. But in July, Trafford and McNeish – now renamed Howard Devoto and Pete Shelley, respectively – announced that they would be bringing the Sex Pistols back to Manchester, and that this time their own band, Buzzcocks, would be opening. Headlining, according to posters that went up around town, were Wythenshawe's Slaughter & the Dogs.

The night of the show, Tuesday, 20 July, the massive contingent that came up from Wythenshawe to support their local heroes included various of the area's many budding guitarists, such as Billy Duffy, Steven Pomfret, Marc Riley and Craig Scanlon, and, among the nonmusicians, Phil Fletcher and Jimmy Walsh. Buzzcocks (absent the definitive article at the front of their name) opened the bill, the first band in the north of England ever to play a set directly influenced by the Sex Pistols. Slaughter & the Dogs went on next; it turned out that the posters declaring them top of the bill had been their own hopeful handiwork. Still, they generated no small amount of teenage testosterone, and at some point after the Sex Pistols came on, it exploded, as the Wythenshawe Man United crew got into a pitched battle with the Pistols fans who had come up from London. Partially as a result of this incident, but also because of their musical, visual and intellectual simplicity, Slaughter & the Dogs were to be largely ostracised by the artsy side of a Manchester punk scene that was otherwise promulgated into existence that night.

In the middle of it all, Phil Fletcher spotted someone off to the side, 'in a multicoloured cardigan, carrying the first New York Dolls album under his arm,' as he recalled. '"That must be that Steve Morrissey,"' Fletcher said to his friends. It was.

GIVE HIM CREDIT for knowing where to find the action, for Morrissey was among the select few who had also attended the *first* of the Sex Pistols' Lesser Free Trade Hall shows, in early June. He would have known that the band's manager, Malcolm McLaren, had only just given up trying to resurrect the career of his beloved New York Dolls, and he'd read about the Sex Pistols in the music papers, where they'd stirred up immediate (if wary) interest in their apparent preference for chaos over music. But he probably would have attended if he'd never heard of them, for the simple reason that the city was screaming out for activity. Manchester at the time, as he later recalled to author John Robb with his usual poetic sense of drama, was:

> . . . a maze of dirty streets. Street lighting was still a very dull yellow . . . Violence was everywhere – and accepted. There was a spiritual darkness as well as a literal darkness: still lots of tramps in demob suits, record shops in murky buildings, city squares

completely unlit, 70 per cent of city-centre buildings unused, and everything revolving around the last bus home. It was still very visibly post-war, and very industrial-ugly, discoloured with the dirt of 100 years, and rock music was a swarm of misery.

He was hardly alone in this thinking. Howard Devoto's old school friend Richard Boon came to Manchester from Reading to help put on the Sex Pistols concerts only to find that 'Manchester was structurally derelict, culturally derelict, musically derelict.' Boon took on part-time work compiling the music listings for the fortnightly *New Manchester Review*, but 'there was hardly anything to list. You got the sense that the tide had gone out.' Manchester had a major success story in 10cc, whose wryly intellectual pop music had made them one of the biggest bands in the country, and who owned a recording studio, Strawberry, in Stockport. But 10cc didn't represent anything other than themselves; it was perhaps indicative of Manchester's musical malaise that its most discussed act, Alberto y Lost Trios Paranoias, was viewed primarily as a comedy band.

As such, it's hard to overstate the influence of the Sex Pistols in Manchester that summer. Tapes of the first concert, at which the support group was comprised of local hippies, reveal a crowd boisterous enough to provoke Johnny Rotten into telling them to 'fuck off!' at least twice – and it was the very idea of a front man insulting his audience like this that helped make the Sex Pistols so revolutionary. Morrissey felt sufficiently inspired by the insider nature of the gig to write a review that he sent to the *NME* in his customary form of a reader's letter but, as is often the case when someone is subjected to something essentially new and unproven, he was guarded in his conclusions. He noted how 'the bumptious Pistols in jumble sale attire had those few that attended dancing in the aisles,' but used the opportunity primarily to reference instead what he considered their elders and betters: 'It's nice to see that the British have produced a band capable of producing atmosphere created by The New York Dolls and their many imitators, even though it may be too late.'

It was not. And there was considerably less dispute about the second Sex Pistols show, in no small part because the supporting bands seemed to reflect a similar desire for musical and social change. Wayne Barrett, for example, recalled how he heard 'meaning in the Sex Pistols' words' that didn't exist in his own. 'Just watching Rotten onstage . . . He went completely against everything. And the filth and the edge of the Pistols, the way they were playing, their arrogance towards everything . . .' After the show, Barrett and Rossi, despite the fight in the audience, sat down with the Pistols and discovered they were cut from the same cloth: disaffected teenagers abandoned by a crumbling British society, but determined to make something of their lives all the same. In a heartbeat, Barrett and Rossi realised they didn't have to imitate their superstar heroes anymore. They could do exactly what they wanted.

That feeling – that sense of complete artistic and personal freedom – took hold among almost everyone who attended the two shows. Steve Diggle, who'd left his secondary modern in Openshawe with the feeling that 'there was no hope,' happened on the first gig on his way to a pub; he left as a member of Buzzcocks. Bernard Sumner and Peter Hook, two twenty-year-olds from Salford, were so inspired by the June show that Hook bought a bass guitar the very next day to form a band; Ian Curtis, their future lead singer in that band, felt similarly motivated after attending the July gig. The same with Mark E. Smith, a Salford docker who figured that if the Pistols could get onstage with a singer who couldn't sing, so could he, and formed the Fall, in which Marc Riley and Craig Scanlon from Wythenshawe would each come to join him.

Others, like Billy Duffy, for whom attendance at the July show 'changed my life forever,' had to bide their time. For although it's convenient to believe that the Sex Pistols were capable of changing the world in one night, the revolution (to the extent that there was one) moved slowly. The first season of Tony Wilson's TV show *So It Goes* proved barely distinguishable from *The Old Grey Whistle Test* in its choice of established, respectable album-oriented studio guests, which would explain why Steve Morrissey sent Tony Wilson a cover of the New York Dolls LP (perhaps even the same one he'd been carrying around to gigs) with a note saying, 'Why can't you feature more bands like this?' (Wilson, stunned by what he saw at the Lesser Free Trade Hall, managed to bring the Sex Pistols into the studio for the final show of that series, for which he deserves eternal credit; their debut British television performance was nothing short of incendiary, and would likely have had a greater effect on British youth had its broadcast not been confined to the Granada catchment area.) Hair lengths continued to run long, and trouser legs remained fashionably wide. And few people, if any, threw out their old record collections, because other than the new music slowly emerging from New York, it wasn't like there was anything to replace them with.

And so, if you were a twelve-year-old bedroom guitarist in Wythenshawe named Johnny Marr, you could try to relate to this thing called 'punk' that had gotten some of your older friends so suddenly excited; you could join in the local mob scene that August at the Wythenshawe Forum, for one of your very first gigs, where Slaughter & the Dogs headlined above Wild Ram, a heavy local band that featured your schoolmate's big brother, and you could find it 'scary.'[3] You could laugh at the fact that Wild Ram promptly changed their name to Ed Banger and the Nosebleeds, and in an alternate world, maybe you could imagine yourself following suit. But you had been brought up to believe that practice made perfect and that talent won out. You certainly weren't about to give up all your self-taught guitar skills for a quick, tuneless thrash.

Eager to find artists he could call his own, Johnny Marr had been drawn to the blues-based guitarist Rory Gallagher: 'He seemed to have a lot of integrity, and there was just something about his Irishness that I connected with.' In 1975, Gallagher released an album *Against the Grain*, which, in the fashion of the era, featured the artist's guitar as the cover star. But Gallagher's Fender Stratocaster had been sanded down which, although it had been done primarily to improve the sound, gave Gallagher an additional anti-image. Marr was smitten. It helped his devotion that this new hero played the Free Trade Hall at least once a year, and it helped too that the bigger lads he'd latched on to promised they could get him in to the man's next Manchester concert – for free. (They had learned how to open the side doors of the building with an antenna conveniently snapped from a local parked car.)

The same crowd – including Billy Duffy before his epiphany with the Sex Pistols, and Robin Allman, who lived almost opposite Marr's estate, on Altrincham Road – had turned Marr on to the folk-rock group Pentangle, specifically the finger-picking guitar playing of Bert Jansch and how it interacted with second guitarist John Renbourn. This would exert an enormous, clearly audible influence on Marr's own future style: one of the future Smiths guitarist's most notable traits was his use of the plectrum to pick his way back and forth across individual strings, creating a melody in the process rather than simply strumming chords. At the time the Smiths came along, however, the likes of Pentangle were unfashionable; Marr would not talk publicly about Jansch in hallowed terms until many years later (enabling a sense of himself as a wunderkind in the meantime for those unaware of Pentangle's period of creative influence).

Marr proved marginally more vocal about his love of Neil Young and Nils Lofgren. Like Gallagher, Young oozed credibility and musicianship and yet was not, in Britain, a superstar, which made him an ideal mid-'70s cult hero. Lofgren, meanwhile, released a debut LP in 1975 acclaimed not only for his incredible guitar playing, the kind that Marr could only dream of emulating, but for the standout song, 'Keith Don't Go', a plea to the Stones guitarist to keep his drug abuse in check. To complete the circle, Lofgren also appeared on the record and accompanying 1975 tour for Young's *Tonight's the Night*. As a token of his good taste, Johnny got himself a *Tonight's the Night* button badge and wore it on his school blazer, uniform requirements be damned. Badges were large in those days, and hard to ignore. And it was for this reason that Johnny Marr came to the attention of Andy Rourke.[4]

CHAPTER SEVEN

All my life I had this feeling that I wasn't going to
live long. So I never really made any plans beyond
twenty-five, twenty-six. I didn't think I would still be
here. I just kind of wing it every day.
— ANDY ROURKE, December 2010

Of the four Smiths, Andrew Michael Rourke was in many ways the odd one out: the only one not of pure Irish stock, the only one raised even vaguely middle-class, the only one without a female sibling. He was also the youngest, born 17 January 1964. His father, Michael, came from a family that had emigrated from Ireland several generations back, and had remained sufficiently devoted to Catholicism as to have initially planned a career in the priesthood. But after Michael met his English wife Mary Stones and they married as teenagers, that plan was forgotten, and the couple had four children in less than ten years: Christopher, Phillip, Andrew and John. They settled into a four-bedroom house at the end of Hawthorn Lane in Ashton-upon-Mersey, between Stretford and Wythenshawe. Christopher and Phillip went on to the best of Catholic secondary schools, St Ambrose and De La Salle, but when it looked like Andy, as he was always known, was set for the nondenominational Stretford Grammar, his mother had the local priest put in a good word with Monsignor McGuinness at St Augustine's. Despite the fact that the journey required up to four buses over the course of a two-hour commute, Andrew started at the Wythenshawe-based Catholic school the same week as – but in a different class from – Johnny Marr.

Much like Marr, Rourke had proved quick in infancy to pick up on his mother's love of the Beatles and the Stones. He, too, then became a typical child of glam rock, in his case soaking up more populist acts like Wizzard and Slade and Suzi Quatro. And again like Marr, he sought to emulate his icons by asking for a musical instrument as his annual gift. A progression through plastic trumpet and electric organ culminated one year with the Christmas gift of a plastic guitar – and upon Andy's insistence that real guitars were made of wood, then with a birthday gift, three weeks later, of a proper classical model.

Lessons followed, somewhat begrudgingly, though Rourke later recognised that they taught him some of the 'dexterity' for which he would later be so admired. 'The revelation,' he recalled, 'was when I realised I could play along to a record.' He soon found that he could accompany every song on his mother's Beach Boys compilation – 'and then I just used to put the radio on and try and play along to whatever song came up.' With two older brothers, Andy was an easy sell for the rock music of the era – which is why he struck up a conversation at school with Johnny Marr over Neil Young. The fact that he was carrying his own guitar invited more than a passing response, although the initial exchange was guarded, Marr seemingly concerned that someone else his age should share anything like his own musical knowledge.

That first year Andy was at secondary school, the Rourke family was dealt a bombshell: Andy's mother Mary moved out, all the way to the Mediterranean island of Majorca, to work as nanny for an American millionaire with whom she eventually settled down. Her departure left an enormous void in the family structure, to put it mildly, one that was exacerbated by the fact that Michael Rourke, a trained architect, was employed by a Sale roofing company that had him overseeing projects across the country. He had little choice but to leave the boys home alone, up to four nights a week, where they learned to fend – and especially, to fight – for themselves. Andy tussled most regularly with his oldest brother, Christopher, who was in his late teens already and, as befitted vaguely middle-class suburban England in the mid-'70s, smoking cannabis regularly. Under the circumstances, it was inevitable that Andy would start experimenting with drugs himself at a young age. 'We started smoking weed,' said Rourke, 'and then we started selling weed,' using the side door intercom and a back window to circumvent their father's possible knowledge – which was limited, given how frequently Michael Rourke was away.[1]

The domestic dysfunction carried over into school. Andy fell in with the perceived troublemakers at St Augustine's, among them a boy named Phil Powell. Hoping to break up the gang before it took too deep a hold, the school switched Rourke and Powell out of their class at the end of the first year, and into one whose teacher, Adrian Jessett, was a renowned disciplinarian, unlikely to cut them any slack. Their new classmates happened to include Johnny Marr, and once Rourke and Marr got over their initial wariness of each other, the firmest of all the future Smiths' friendships, the bedrock of the band's music, was formed. With it, too, came the foundation of the band's touring organisation, for Phil Powell would remain not only Rourke's close friend but go on to become Johnny Marr's personal roadie, lodger and right-hand man.

Marr and Rourke took to playing in the music room together at lunchtime, and then with Marr's friend Marc Johnson on Churchstone Walk. The budding three-piece saw themselves, said Marr, as 'the junior version of Rob (Allman), Billy (Duffy) and Dave (Clough),' the local guitar heroes, who were themselves part of a band so heavily influenced by Crosby, Stills, Nash & Young that they had taken their name from the act's live album, 4 Way Street. The younger trio of Marr, Rourke and Johnson focused primarily on acoustic versions of Neil Young's songs. Johnson soon fell by the wayside; Rourke saw it as a falling-out with Marr, who preferred to observe instead that he and Andy 'had more tenacity.' Certainly, nobody who knew him had any doubt as to Marr's determination, or the speed at which his skills were now developing. 'When I first started playing guitar with Johnny, I was a bit more knowledgeable,' said Rourke. 'I would show him everything I knew. But then the next week he'd have taken it to a whole new level. He was just a really quick learner.' By the age of thirteen, said Rourke, 'we knew . . . what we wanted to do – be in a band.'

They talked themselves into one with two older boys, Kevin Kennedy and Bobby Durkin, part of the West Wythy youth club crowd. Marr and Kennedy were united by their passion for Manchester City in an area that was predominantly United, he and Durkin by family associations that extended back to Ardwick. Then again, *everyone* knew Bobby Durkin. 'Very eccentric, mad as a hatter, and good fun,' said Kennedy. 'If you had to portray a drummer, with all their idiosyncrasies, Bobby fitted the bill perfectly.' Crucially, Durkin had his own kit, while Kennedy had an amplifier as well as a bass. Naming themselves the Paris Valentinos on an inspired whim, the quartet initially rehearsed at the Durkins' house, until noise complaints from his mother led Bobby to lean instead on his father, who ran the social club that was part of Sacred Heart's adjoined church and primary school. A deal was struck with the priest: they could use the church hall if they would play guitar at the weekly Folk Mass. For the next few months, Rourke, Marr and Kennedy, natural-born Catholics but none of them especially devoted to religion, spent Sunday afternoons in church, trying to keep a straight face as they performed 'Kumbaya' and 'Peace Perfect Peace' on acoustic guitars while simultaneously endeavouring to distract the trio of more devoted female singers in front.

The Paris Valentinos drew on the kind of no-nonsense rock that appealed to their age group at this juncture, just before punk threw the marketplace wide open: 'Breakdown' by the new American band Tom Petty and the Heartbreakers, and 'The Boys Are Back in Town' by Ireland's Thin Lizzy, who were

considered honorary Mancunians by virtue of front man Phil
Lynott having spent his infancy years in Moss Side, the only
place his Irish Catholic mother felt comfortable raising a mixed-
race boy born out of wedlock. Marr also brought in Rory
Gallagher's 'Moonchild' and 'Shadowplay', and as he did so,
Kennedy was blown away by his friend's ability. 'He was superb.
He was very fast, his fingers were fast. Some of his riffs were
really beautiful and melodic and not as harsh as what was about
at the time.' Growing in confidence, observing his friends'
strengths and weaknesses, Marr then made a pivotal suggestion:
that Rourke and Kennedy swap instruments.

For Rourke, it initially felt like a demotion. He had not paid
much attention to the bass in the past. 'I knew that if you took
it away a song would be that much different. But I was so
focused on playing guitar that my ears would tune into a guitar
when I listened to a song.' Almost as soon as he picked up
Kennedy's instrument, however, he realised how much he liked
it and 'just immersed myself in it.' He began to study the parts
he heard on record; in particular, Rourke began to emulate
Rory Gallagher's bass player Gerry McAvoy, whose sound was
'very punchy, plectrum-oriented.' It helped that Andy's brother
Phil Rourke also joined a band at this time on bass. For a while,
they even shared an instrument. When Phil dropped his ambitions by the wayside, Andy persisted.

The relationship between Marr and Rourke has often been
viewed as one-way traffic, even among those who grew up with
them both. 'Andy followed Johnny,' said Bobby Durkin. 'Andy
wasn't going to make it without Johnny . . . not a chance.'[2]
But for all that Rourke looked up to Marr for leadership, so
Marr looked to Rourke for grounding. Marr already had a
reputation for flash: in fashion, on the football field, in musical
taste, in his gift of the gab, and now on the guitar as
well. Rourke, who sported long hair and sideburns at the time,
having gravitated from glam rock to folk rock and now to the
space rock of Gong and Hawkwind, was more taciturn and less
outwardly ambitious. But he was contagiously funny, had an

abundance of instinctive musical talent, and was unquestionably, almost uncommonly, loyal. No less so than with Morrissey later in life, Marr needed Rourke to help complete himself.

The same week of June 1977 that the Sex Pistols had the top-selling single in the country with the Monarchy-baiting 'God Save the Queen', the Paris Valentinos played their only gig, a Silver Jubilee Street Party in Benchill to honour the Queen's twenty-five-year reign. There was no particular incongruity to this: Johnny and Andy were only thirteen, too young to know about punk political correctness. Besides, the Paris Valentinos were more of a social group than a functioning band. Their rehearsals at Sacred Heart would often end with a raid on the church hall's stock cupboard (the key had come with that for the front door) of donated jumble-sale items, among them prized 1960s 7" singles and not a few outrageous costumes. Then it would be time to crack open some cider or beer. In such moments, while Durkin played the merry drummer role, Kennedy would explain how he *really* wanted to be an actor, and the others would laugh – until he left the group to pursue his eventual career. A few years later, he would become a national icon, as famous as Morrissey in his own right for a while, as 'Curly' Watts, the first truly 1980s character on *Coronation Street*.

IN BETWEEN THE Sex Pistols' two Manchester shows in the summer of 1976, while waiting for his O-Levels results, Morrissey fulfilled a dream by visiting New York and New Jersey, where his aunts Patti and Mary on his mother's side had relocated. Morrissey was infatuated now with Patti Smith, the former New Jersey factory worker turned downtown Manhattan poetess/music journalist/actress/shamanistic performer, whose debut album, *Horses*, had made the American top 40. After hearing it, he said, 'I was never the same again.' The New York City punk scene, though not routinely called by that name, was not only far ahead of that which was just gathering steam in Britain, but that much more diverse, and Morrissey already knew more about it than most British teenagers. He did his best to educate himself further about it while on the East Coast, venturing to CBGB on the Bowery, where he had his picture taken outside the club with one of his childhood heroes, Russell Mael of Sparks.[3] But if he was hoping to find a city infatuated with the New York Dolls, he was disappointed: the conversation that summer was all about the Ramones, with whom he was not greatly impressed.

Morrissey came back to England to find that he had passed three of his four O-Levels, just enough for acceptance into an entry-level job with the Civil Service. He quit after two weeks, horrified by its mundane nature (though he would soon return to government bureaucracy for a year-long stint at the local Inland Revenue office), and resumed his preferred, albeit unpaid occupation: firing off missives to the music press. Before the year was out, he scored the rare feat of having two letters published in the same issue of the same music paper – twice. The theme was relentlessly, almost depressingly familiar: praise for the New York Dolls and Patti Smith (whom he travelled to Birmingham to see in concert that October), and damnation of the Ramones and the Sex Pistols for, at least in the case of the Pistols, their 'infantile approach and nondescript music.' He made this latter observation in response to writer Jonh Ingham, who had dared criticise the Dolls in *Sounds*; it became something of a career habit to aggressively assail people by mail if their opinions did not gel with his own, and many a friendship was to be ended via the letter box. All the same, he was at the Electric Circus in early December when the Sex Pistols returned to Manchester on their Anarchy in the UK tour, primarily because the now-defunct Dolls' spin-off band the Heartbreakers (not to be confused with Tom Petty's band of the same name) were on the bill too, and he was not about to turn down the chance to finally see Johnny Thunders and Jerry Nolan in the flesh. Yet when he showed up at the soundcheck, they rebuffed him. Later, he tried to downplay the cold shoulder: 'They weren't friendly and why should they be? Who was I, anyway?' Who was he? Only their former band's UK fan club head, and more so, the biggest, most relentlessly persistent, and hopelessly single-minded fan they had ever had in the country. His encounter sounds suspiciously like the one that was recounted years later in the Smiths song 'Paint a Vulgar Picture', in which a fan shows up at the soundcheck and is rejected: 'To you I was faceless, I was fawning, I was boring.'

He fared better with a member of another support band that night, Mick Jones of the Clash, whom he had spoken to on the phone earlier in the year in response to a 'singer wanted' classified ad in the music papers, a position that had gone, instead, to Joe Strummer. And he struck up the courage to talk, however briefly, to Howard Devoto's girlfriend, Linder, the Manchester punk movement's most visible female intellectual and artist, and in the process begin perhaps his most lasting and mutually admiring cultural and personal friendship. Raised on the council estates of Wigan and Liverpool before attending Manchester Polytechnic to study art, Linda Sterling had met the Buzzcocks the night they opened for the Sex Pistols in July, an event that inspired her to complete personal transformation: 'Punk allowed you to rechristen yourself and be reborn,' she said of her subsequent decision to do away with her last name. 'Proclaiming Linderland then gave me a psychic territory, a home and a landscape.' The Sex Pistols must have done something right in Morrissey's eyes too at the Electric Circus, because his public criticism of the band ceased immediately. Still, when he placed an ad in *Sounds* for interest in forming a 'Manchester-based punk band,' he stressed that he was looking for 'Dolls/Patti fans,' with no mention of British influences. Nothing came of it.

Other events took precedence. Just two days before Christmas 1976, Peter Morrissey left his family, moving in with his sister Patricia. Family relations on Kings Road had become increasingly strained; the son claimed to have gone six months earlier that year without speaking to the father, who was hard put to explain the gap that had grown between them. 'I've never done anything against Steven,' said the man who was near enough idolised by his son's friends for his George Best-like looks and agreeable personality. 'I've never even raised my voice to him . . . Something happened to Steven and I can't explain it.' The son never set out to try. 'I was completely raised by my mother's family,' he stated firmly in 1999. 'My personal history is the Dwyer family, not actually the Morrissey family.' This would of course highlight the irony that while his mother duly reverted to her maiden name following her husband's departure, Steve Morrissey would end up dropping his Christian name to use solely his father's family name from which he claimed to be so disconnected.

In more positive future recollections, Morrissey would attempt to play down his parents' eventual breakup after so many years of underlying unhappiness, recognizing that in the big picture, it was neither the worst nor the most unique thing to happen to a teenager (although it was certainly less common among Catholic families). But the end result was nonetheless the same: he grew even closer to his mother, who would dutifully support him over the next several years of chronic underemployment and occasional depression, when many another parent of either sex would have kicked their grown son out of the house in a last-ditch attempt to make a man of him. In the biography *Saint Morrissey*, Mark Simpson suggests of Betty's indulgence that, having 'resigned herself to the failure of her marriage long before she and Peter finally divorced . . . she turned her spurned affections towards someone she could be more sure of, someone who needed them so much that he would never reject them.' It's a valid theory, especially given that the bond grew only stronger over subsequent years, with Morrissey buying a house for the pair of them once he acquired some wealth, and Betty duly casting a long and, for those on the opposite end, frustrating shadow as a quasi-managerial figure in her son's professional life. Regardless, it's not as if Morrissey ever shied away from acknowledging the particular closeness of their attachment, often joking about it at both his and her expense in interviews, and admitting to it in song: in 'The Queen Is Dead,' as a prominent example, he notes that 'when you're tied to your mother's apron, no one talks about castration.'

Indeed, in the wake of his father's departure, Steven Morrissey immersed himself in the politics of feminism – specifically acquiring such books as *The Facts of Rape*, *The Female Eunuch*, *Sex and Racism*, *Women and Madness*, and, interestingly, given his home setup, a book written by a prominent psychologist intended to help mothers communicate better with their children. None of this made for idle reading, even for a teenager already well versed in Oscar Wilde: the premise behind Susan Brownmiller's uncomfortable study *Against Our Will: Men, Women, and Rape*, for example, held that the male of the species had historically, categorically, and with deliberate prejudice, subjugated the female of the species as chattel, her virginity and motherhood to be bought and sold according to prevailing local customs. Despite the fact that 'women's suffrage' had gained its British foothold in nineteenth-century Manchester (yet again, the northern capital had been at the epicentre of political progression), the concept of actual 'Women's Liberation' was still relatively new in the mid-1970s, and the arguments presented by the feminist philosophers were not easily or readily accepted in the working-class, manual-labour households of the urban north.

If Morrissey's feminist leanings put him at odds with wider society, they fit in well with punk, a culture that initially embraced a challenge to gender stereotypes. In America it did so via icons like Patti Smith (who dressed in a purposefully masculine manner on the cover of *Horses*), the transvestite Wayne County (who eventually became the transsexual Jayne County), and the flamboyant dress sense and enthusiastic camping of the New York Dolls; in the UK, it did so with the provocative poses of Jordan, Siouxsie Sioux and Soo Catwoman, who struck fear in the heart of an establishment that had no idea how to react to such strong, beautiful women in control of their own sexuality. (This was most evident in the case of TV presenter Bill Grundy, whose drunken lechery in front of the Sex Pistols' female friends led to the band swearing live on camera and subsequently being banned from most venues on their Anarchy tour. Manchester, to its credit, was one of the few cities whose council did not seek to cancel the concert; in fact, the Anarchy package returned to the Electric Circus ten days after its initial show to fill up one of the sixteen cancelled concert dates, marking the fourth time the Sex Pistols played in Manchester within six months.) In Manchester, the influence of the London female punks was evident in local characters Joan and Denise, frequently photographed by Kevin Cummins; true feminist principles were most visible in the artwork of Linder, whose cover design for Buzzcocks' first major-label single in late 1977, *Orgasm Addict*, a photo-collage that replaced a naked woman's head with a clothing iron and her nipples with perfect teeth and lips, remains a classic of the format, the statement and the era.[4]

It was no coincidence that Morrissey's own immersion into feminism coincided with his growing friendship with Linder. 'She led me by the lapel,' he wrote in an essay accompanying a Linder career retrospective in 2006, citing the artist's influence as the direct reason, for example, that he acquired *Sex and Racism*. Linder, whose charismatic personality and forceful intellect were topped off with a fierce beauty, was hardly lacking for male attention; Pete Shelley reputedly wrote Buzzcocks' classic single 'What Do I Get?' about his unrequited love for her. (Shelley, who later came out as bisexual, was always careful never to specify gender in his love songs.) In spite of the fact there would be subsequent rumours about the extent of her physical contact with Morrissey, in 1977 the future Smiths singer was coming to terms, instead, with the fact that he wasn't desperately interested in the subject.

Asked bluntly about the loss of his virginity in an interview in 1987, Morrissey answered: 'It was in my early teens, twelve or thirteen,' spectacularly early even by 1970s inner-city standards. 'But it was an isolated incident, an accident. After that it was downhill. I've got no pleasant memories from it whatsoever.' At the age of sixteen, he had confided in writing that 'I don't have sex much, in fact I can count the number of times,' which suggested that, unlike many boys his age, at least he still *had* it. But two years later, at the height of his punk gig-going, just as his friendship with Linder solidified, he seemed to have reached an epiphany of sorts over the subsequent drought. 'I always thought that I was asexual, because I'm not really stimulated by either male or female. There was a period when I thought I could be gay, but then it suddenly dawned on me that I didn't like boys either.' His conclusion: 'I'm just not turned on by naked bodies.' These confessions may not have been intended for public consumption, but that only lent additional credence to the quotes Morrissey made at the start of the Smiths' career about his celibacy, such as in March 1984, that it was 'a series of very blunt and thankfully brief and horrendous experiences that made me decide upon abstaining, and it seemed quite an easy and natural decision.'

In the absence of conventional teenage dating, he continued to use the music papers as his personal pen-pal site. It wasn't so much that the British punk rock explosion energised him in any way; it was more that the rest of the country had caught up with his own tastes and so, as Xeroxed fanzines started to emerge by the plastic bag-load as an alternative to the weekly music papers, Morrissey contacted any and all that showed an interest or an understanding in the New York scene, offering to write articles about his favourite subjects. Both *Kids Stuff* in Surrey and *The Next Big Thing* in Scotland said yes to Dolls-related features, inspiring Morrissey to consider his own magazine-length fanzine on the band. Further letters to the weekly music papers on the same subject saw him gradually widen his network of pen pals: Brian Young in Belfast, a Thunders fanatic who played guitar in that city's leading punk band, Rudi, and who hooked Morrissey up with a local fanzine, *Alternative Ulster*; Tom Crossley, another budding guitarist, in

London; and also in London, a sixteen-year-old by the name of James Maker, who followed up the publication of Morrissey's full address in a letter in the summer of 1977 by calling up Directory Enquiries for his phone number and introducing himself.

Thrilled to encounter what he took to be a kindred spirit, Morrissey invited Maker to come up and stay for the weekend. Maker, who despite his youth had long come to terms with his own homosexuality, dressed for the occasion in a bowler hat and cork-heeled boots, which he considered relatively subtle accessories. Though a product of South London's tough dock-lands, around Bermondsey, and familiar with the parade of London punks on the Kings Road in Chelsea (not easily confused with Kings Road in Stretford) that occasionally ended in violent confrontations with reactionary teddy boys, Maker had not figured on the latent aggression and blatant homo-phobia of the northern cities. Having barely had time to make Morrissey's acquaintance in the flesh, Maker received a public beating in the middle of Piccadilly Gardens, and after being rescued (somewhat embarrassingly) by an elderly couple, he and Morrissey ran (according to Maker, Morrissey sprinted, his athletic prowess still quite evident) to board any bus that could outpace their attackers. When the driver insisted, with an undue lack of concern for their health, that the pair instead disembark, they took a look at the 'seven pairs of tattooed fists' banging against the window, and refused. Maker was impressed by Morrissey's calm obstinacy – 'Arms folded, unbudgeable' – correctly analysing the behaviour that day as another career-forming habit. 'Some people advance by fighting and struggling and pushing and scratching; others advance by simply not moving at all,' he noted in his memoir, *Autofellatio*. (Morrissey won that battle; the bus left with him and Maker on board.)

United by this experience, their acquaintanceship now blos-somed into a beautiful friendship. On trips to London, Morrissey would visit Maker; on one occasion the pair were insistent that they saw flying saucers 'hover low and slow over Bermondsey,' only about three hundred feet in front of them, and they reported the sighting to the UFO Society. ('At one point I stood on the balcony and stared directly into one hovering ship, and it STOPPED in mid-air above me,' Morrissey wrote to his friend Lindsay Hutton. 'Without a doubt, it was watching me!') On another occasion, they had their mutual friend Tom Crossley over and 'drank ourselves silly and sang Dolls songs (very badly) till the oily hours.' Maker would, despite his initial experience, continue to visit Manchester, even living there for a while himself in 1980; and the first time the Smiths ever stepped onto a stage, Maker stepped onto it with them.

IN EARLY 1977 Slaughter & the Dogs released a single, 'Cranked Up Really High', produced by Martin Hannett, on a local Manchester label set up especially for them, Rabid, only weeks after the Buzzcocks released an EP, *Spiral Scratch*, also produced by Hannett, on a label they and Richard Boon set up especially for *themselves*, New Hormones. The titles of the songs on that EP, like 'Breakdown' and 'Boredom', initially appeared to be imitating the Sex Pistols' seemingly nihilistic screed, but they emitted a highly visceral art-rock appeal that immediately distinguished them among Manchester punk bands; as Morrissey astutely noted, they were 'the only ones who possibly sat down beforehand and worked out what they intended to do.' In accordance with the values of these new times, Howard Devoto left the band the week the EP came out.

To the extent that any local record shop sold all the available punk records, from both near and far, and encouraged customers to pin up cards and fliers to find band mates and promote gigs, it was the Virgin Records store on Lever Street. Saturdays in particular, the place became a busy gathering ground. It was there that Phil Fletcher came across Morrissey again and decided this time to introduce himself. (He recalled that Morrissey was wearing a Dolls T-shirt while perusing the

New York Dolls section of the store.) Finding him perfectly pleasant to talk with, Fletcher invited Steve Morrissey to join the Wythenshawe crowd at a gig that week at the Electric Circus.

There were certainly enough shows to choose from. During that summer of 1977, the part-time hard-rock club, way out in Collyhurst, played host to the Clash, the Slits, Wayne County, the Ramones, the Talking Heads, the Buzzcocks, the Jam, Penetration *and* the debut gig by the Manchester band Warsaw, later to become Joy Division. Despite recalling pronounced antagonism from the council-estate kids across the road, whom he described as 'white working-class mutants of the most deranged cross-eyed variety,' Morrissey attended most of these shows as he did gigs at the Oaks Hotel in Chorlton, Rafters on Oxford Street and the Squat at the university.[5] And he was occasionally seen at the Ranch on Dale Street – a dimly lit, stageless, openly gay basement bar underneath Foo Foo's Palace that had been popular with the Bowie/Roxy kids in the mid-'70s and which was therefore an obvious venue for the occasional local punk gig.

As he became a permanent fixture on the scene, and perhaps even despite himself, Morrissey grew tight with the Wythenshawe crowd. 'He was quite gentle; very, very knowledgeable about music,' observed Fletcher. 'And because he was a New York Dolls fan, which we didn't think anyone else in the world was, he was accepted by us.' Morrissey had been close with the hard case Mike Foley back at school, but this new relationship was different: it offered him a chance to mingle with a whole gang of straight, masculine people off the council estates, Billy Duffy among them – people who chased women and rival football fans, people with whom he shared an interest in music but still struggled to form proper friendships. 'I don't think he was the most social animal at that age,' said Fletcher. 'He was quite a troubled young lad. Whereas we weren't.'

All the same, he saw in this new gang a potential for advancement, and promoted himself as a potential singer. He was invited to 'practise' with Duffy and Steve Pomfret at Pomfret's Wythenshawe home. He additionally answered a 'musicians wanted' ad in *NME* placed by a local sixteen-year-old girl, Quibilah Montsho. And he had the courage to bring them all together in the hope of stirring up something that might have been unique. It didn't happen, and the friendship with Montsho ended when she wrote and told him she was gay (which would have taken considerable courage in the UK at the time, additionally so given that she was 'coloured', which already marked her as a minority), and he responded, in what she described as a 'patronising and sarcastic' manner, by complaining that she hadn't shown interest in *his* sexuality.

His musical persistence finally paid off, however, at the end of 1977, when both the singer Ed Garrity, and guitarist, Vini Reilly, quit Wythenshawe's second most notorious punk group, Ed Banger and the Nosebleeds, leaving a rhythm section and a well-known local band name for the taking. That Billy Duffy seized one of the vacant spots was hardly surprising – he was a Wythenshawe punk guitarist, after all – but it was a shock to all when Steve Morrissey stepped up to replace Garrity, who tended to pogo relentlessly around the stage, and whose debut single, 'Ain't Bin to No Music School', laid out a cartoon punk manifesto at total odds with Morrissey's endless screeds to the music papers about British punk's frustrating lack of musicianship.[6] The process of auditioning for the role, being appointed to it, and then gradually writing some songs alongside Duffy was a slow one, but on 8 May 1978, Morrissey's dream of fronting a band took flight when the new Nosebleeds opened up for Howard Devoto's new group, Magazine, and John Cooper Clarke at the Ritz.[7]

The show went unrecorded, sadly. The Nosebleeds reportedly covered the Shangri-Las' 'Give Him a Great Big Kiss' in homage to the New York Dolls, plus a song by a Dolls spin-off project, and included Morrissey's first publicly performed lyrics, among them such unlikely Smiths candidates as '(I Think) I'm Ready for the Electric Chair' and 'Toytown Massacre'. Although it would not seem in retrospect like a particular portent of great-ness, music journalist Paul Morley, another local whose life had been changed at the Sex Pistols shows, was enthusiastic in the extreme in a concert-review roundup of four Manchester bands in *NME*. After cautiously citing Joy Division for their 'ambig-uous appeal', he put his stock instead in the Nosebleeds, giving them final billing. He referred to Steve Morrison [*sic*] as 'A Front Man With Charisma' and a 'minor local legend', who 'is at least aware that rock 'n' roll is about magic, and inspiration,' before concluding, with the kind of hyperbole by which music journalists secure their reputations: 'Only their name can prevent them being this year's surprise.'[8]

That . . . and the fact that they broke up the following month. It would be more than four years before Morrissey would appear onstage again fronting a band. Ironically, it would be at the same venue, the Ritz. That band, of course, would be the Smiths.

CHAPTER EIGHT

I was suicidal for years and years. It's really embarrassing to say that, but it's the truth. It really got to the point where I was so angry and yet I was really very ambitious and I was prepared to kick very, very hard.

        – MORRISSEY, *City Life*, Spring 1984

This gang of guitar players entered my life, and then I started to feel much more at ease, and those guys gave me a lot of confidence, because it was about whether you could play the guitar, and I had this natural ability that I didn't realise until then.

        – JOHNNY MARR, March 2011

In the wake of the Paris Valentinos, word of Johnny Marr's improved abilities spread among the Wythenshawe guitarists. He was invited to jam with David Clough one day, and 'it was significant,' he recalled. And Robin Allman brought him to see the Freshies front man, Chris Sievey, figuring that Marr was good enough to become the band's new guitarist, even at the age of fourteen. Sievey didn't disagree but, wary of the novelty factor, gave the job to another Wythenshawe local, Barry Spencer. Marr had once stood outside that lad's window, listening to Spencer play Thin Lizzy songs from his bedroom. That he was even moving in such circles was a sign of success.

'Johnny had something where he was accepted by the older guys because he knew his music,' said Phil Fletcher. 'I remember him coming up to me and saying, "Can I borrow four or five Rolling Stones albums off you?" and if any other fourteen-year-old had asked me that I'd probably have hit him. But I said no problem, lent him the albums, and he gave me them back a week later. He was a very engaging lad.'

Marr continued to crash concerts with these older friends, as in March 1977 at the Free Trade Hall for a Uriah Heep show where both the headliners and support act featured former members of the Spiders from Mars. Also along for the ride that night was Andrew Berry, who attended another Catholic grammar school, St Gregory's, and who recognised Marr from preteen evenings at the West Wythy youth club. The pair met again at the Ian Hunter show at the Free Trade Hall in June, when they both showed up at soundcheck hoping to meet Hunter and Bowie guitarist Earl Slick, and this time they truly bonded. At the time, recalled Marr, Berry sported 'red Bowie hair, a side parting with a flick, with a cap-sleeve Roxy T-shirt, with pegs,' which made him the very picture of the fashionable soul boy, or what in the 1960s mod culture would have been considered a 'face'. As important, said Marr, Berry was 'a notorious character and always very likeable.' The friendship the pair formed, like the ones Marr already had going with Rourke and Powell, was set to prove pivotal to the Smiths.

A week after the Uriah Heep show, the Wythenshawe crowd went to see an increasingly unfashionable T. Rex at the Manchester Apollo, on Ardwick Green, Marr's old stomping ground. The former cinema had only just started putting itself up as a concert venue, and was to prove so successful in its ambitions that it would soon replace the Free Trade Hall as the major Manchester stop on the tour circuit. Marr considered this ruinous, not only because 'the Free Trade Hall was just better,' but because 'the Apollo was much more difficult to sneak into.' Teenage loyalties can turn into lifelong grudges, and accordingly, the Smiths never played the Apollo; they did, however, twice play the Free Trade Hall.

As punk took hold across Manchester, Marr expressed interest in the new British bands (especially local heroes the Buzzcocks), but much like Morrissey, indeed much like Manchester in general, it could be argued, he was always more motivated by music from America. The older Wythenshawe crew turned him on to the New York Dolls, belatedly enough that he could only

express his enthusiasm for guitarist Johnny Thunders through
Thunders's new act, the Heartbreakers. (Unlike Morrissey, Marr
had long been a fan of Tom Petty's Heartbreakers, too, and he
hitchhiked to Knebworth in June '78, where Petty performed
in the middle of a typically bizarre festival bill, headlined by
Genesis, but which also featured Ohio New Wave futurists
Devo.) Billy Duffy, whom Marr considered his 'closest ally' and
'role model' at the time, additionally tutored him in Iggy Pop
and the Stooges, specifically the album *Raw Power*, and Stooges
guitarist James Williamson became yet another major influence.
('Me and my mates were obsessed with the Dolls and Iggy and
everything New York circa 1974,' recalled Duffy, who said of
himself and Marr that 'all we really wanted to be was rock stars
really; it's the old dream.') And he was awestruck by Patti
Smith. 'I was one of those rare people who loved *Radio Ethiopia*,'
Marr said of her generally derided second album. As a result,
he put aside his dislike of the Apollo and joined Duffy and
Slaughter bassist Howard Bates when Smith came to town in
August 1978.

He subsequently described it as a 'life-changing' concert,
despite the choice of venue. 'It was almost like the stage was
a window to another world, a world of real modern rock 'n'
roll, and these people were living it. It was like watching a
play. Like "I need to be in there; that's where I belong."' The
show should have been additionally notable for marking the
first occasion he met his future musical partner – except that
nothing came of it. Marr knew of Steve Morrissey as the Dolls
and Patti Smith fanatic who had dared to briefly front the
Nosebleeds, and perhaps imagined a character of Ed Garrity's
persuasive nature. But when Billy Duffy made the introductions,
Marr was disappointed. There was 'utter non-interest, disinterest, on Morrissey's part,' he recalled. And as for his own first
impressions, there was merely 'a reserved curiosity . . . because
he didn't look exactly as I'd pictured him.'

*   *   *

UNINTENTIONALLY, THE BUZZCOCKS having only pressed up the EP as a souvenir to hand out at gigs, *Spiral Scratch* started a revolution. Independent labels had always been a part of the British music industry, but with their familiar presence came an assumption, as proven by London pub/punk-rock upstarts Stiff, that they needed financing, a distribution contract, an office, and a staff with some kind of music business experience. New Hormones – which was nothing more than Richard Boon at the end of a phone – disproved this notion entirely. By the time he and the band ceased pressing *Spiral Scratch*, it had sold 16,000 copies.

A significant number of these were handled by the London record store Rough Trade, which had been opened on a Ladbroke Grove side street in 1976 by Geoff Travis, a Cambridge University graduate and, more important, an obsessive music fan of no fixed genre. Stocking punk from America, reggae from Jamaica, and Xeroxed fanzines from all across the UK, and encouraging both in-store browsing and politicking, Rough Trade quickly became *the* London one-stop for underground music fans, with a healthy mail-order business on the side. As the success of *Spiral Scratch* convinced any number of musicians, producers, hustlers, fellow record-store proprietors, or merely long-standing music fans of reasonable reputation that it was possible to record, press, design and sell a record without the permission, let alone the patronage, of the mainstream music business, Rough Trade was increasingly looked upon as a, if not *the*, major source of sales.

So while the Sex Pistols bounced around major labels, and the likes of the Clash, the Jam, and ultimately the Buzzcocks, too, signed on the old-fashioned corporate dotted line, a second generation decided to do it themselves. Most of the acts were lumped together as part of the 'New Wave', but it was evident that something more profound was being created in this world free of major-label manipulation – something that didn't subscribe to formulas of instrumentation, song structure, or production values; something that often reflected, additionally, the artist's geographic surroundings. Retroactively, it would come to be known as post-punk.

In Liverpool, where there was a thriving scene based around the club Eric's, Bill Drummond launched Zoo Records to promote his band, Big in Japan; he would soon put out the debut records by A Teardrop Explodes and Echo & the Bunnymen. Bob Last started Fast Product, introducing the sharp guitars and equally pointed politics of Leeds bands the Mekons and the Gang of Four, but also the simple synthesizer rhythms and oddball lyrics of Sheffield's the Human League. In London, a shy, twentysomething film editor by the name of Daniel Miller made a 45 *noir*, also on synthesizers, under the *nom de plume* the Normal; set up his own label, Mute Records; and, thanks to the Rough Trade staff's instinctive ear and eager sales push, saw 'TVOD'/'Warm Leatherette' become hugely successful on the independent circuit and massively influential on other bedroom musicians. Belfast's Terri Hooley launched a label named for his record store, Good Vibrations, to showcase local punk bands. He started with Rudi, as led by Morrissey's New York Dolls pen pal Brian Young, and came to prominence with a powerfully pop-oriented group from Derry, the Undertones, whose single 'Teenage Kicks' was championed with religious fervour by BBC's Radio 1 late-night DJ John Peel. Eventually Rough Trade itself got in on the act, though at first Travis seemed to have no more of a clear vision for the label than he'd had for his shop, given that initial releases featured both a French and an Irish punk band, a Jamaican reggae act, a Yorkshire electronic outfit, and a maverick London pop group, hugely influential on both Morrissey and Marr, called the Monochrome Set.

For all this explosion in creativity, the accepted wisdom remained that if a major label came sniffing, the independent would cut the band free or, better yet, license the group to profit from future sales. This was the process by which Manchester's Rabid Records became temporarily successful, selling off local punk poet John Cooper Clarke to CBS and licensing the highly entertaining eponymous punk single by

Jilted John to EMI, who took it into the top 10. Fast let the Gang of Four go to EMI as well; Zoo sold off the Bunnymen and Teardrop Explodes while staying involved in the management; Good Vibrations sold the Undertones to the American label Sire, whose founder, Seymour Stein, lionised in the UK for signing the Ramones and the Talking Heads, was now making frequent shopping trips to the British Isles; and Rough Trade, despite proving the power of its distribution abilities by taking its first LP, by Stiff Little Fingers, into the top 20, let the Belfast band sign to Chrysalis rather than be seen as holding them back on the more elusive hit single.

The same philosophy was initially applied by Factory Records, launched in late 1978 by Granada TV's Tony Wilson with Alan Erasmus, a Wythenshawe fly-by-nighter, and Peter Saville, a talented designer who had been turned on to punk at Manchester Polytechnic by fellow student Linder. Factory's formation followed several months' success with a club night of the same name at the Russel Club on Royce Road, in what the posters proclaimed was Moss Side though the location was within pissing distance of the notorious Hulme Crescents. From the beginning, Factory (its name a reference to Manchester's industrial history rather than that of New York's Andy Warhol) cultivated an artfully sophisticated and genially pretentious image, awarding catalogue numbers to posters, notepaper, movies, and even a menstrual egg-timer designed by Linder. Their first vinyl artifact, *A Factory Sample*, came wrapped in a Saville-designed, heat-sealed polyethylene sleeve, and featured four acts, the first and foremost of which was Joy Division, whose music had been stripped down in the studio by Martin Hannett to its bare, stark minimum before being built back up around Ian Curtis's oblique lyrics and urgent delivery. Joy Division wore old-men's clothes, sported crude haircuts courtesy of an ancient local barber, and were depicted by local lad Kevin Cummins in famous grainy black-and-white *NME* photographs against a snow-strewn Princess Highway or a dimly lit rehearsal studio. The musical and visual combination made Joy Division

135

the poster children for Manchester's postindustrial collapse — and not just with those outside the city looking in. 'Joy Division were definitive Manchester,' said Johnny Marr. 'They sounded like what it was like living up here.'

Factory soon followed up with a single by another local group, A Certain Ratio, which sounded nothing like its title, 'All Night Party', and one by a Liverpool synthesizer duo, Orchestral Manoeuvres in the Dark (OMD for short), which sounded everything likes *its* title, 'Electricity', and inspired Virgin Records to come knocking in pursuit of a possible hit act. Wilson and partners happily sold OMD to the major label and used the proceeds to set up office on Palatine Road in South Manchester's bohemian quarter of Didsbury. But when it came to Joy Division the band's manager, Rob Gretton, yet another product of the Wythenshawe council estates, suggested that they hold on to the act for themselves. And when the Hannett-produced LP *Unknown Pleasures* was released in the summer of 1979, both the music, which was as euphorically cathartic as it was (accused of being) dark and depressing, and artwork (an abstract silver astronomic image set small in the middle of black-grained paper) were rightly hailed as art. Best yet, this art found its way to the public: Rough Trade was now acting not only as a major retailer of the new independent music but as a wholesaler, supplying other, similarly-minded record stores. A new independent distribution network was growing by the day.

With it came a new, intentionally unrestrictive framework. Rough Trade kept its initial contracts to two paragraphs, Factory to two sentences; Mute did not even bother. At all three labels, royalties were eschewed in favour of a 50-50 profit split. With the acts effectively free agents, and the labels recognising one another as comrades-in-arms, there was considerable overlap: Rough Trade and Factory both released records by Sheffield's experimental electronic act Cabaret Voltaire, while Fast Products got an early look-in on Joy Division. Gradually, though, each of the independent labels created its own identity and accompanying philosophy. Rough Trade was the anything-goes, left-wing London collective. Mute became known as an electronic music label. As for Factory, it followed *Unknown Pleasures* with further local releases by the Distractions, Section 25, and former Nosebleeds guitarist Vini Reilly's new band, Durutti Column, but the label's genuine musical diversity was obfuscated by Saville's sleeve designs, which shunned pictures of the acts themselves in the name of art. The Buzzcocks had employed a similar tactic on a series of five romantic 45s that became a national teenage soundtrack in 1978, eventually leading them into the top 30, but those sleeves, designed by Malcolm Garrett (also a product of Manchester Poly), were (pop) artfully simplistic, to match the punk-pop (art) of the music. Besides, the band compensated by featuring themselves prominently on the album sleeves. The music on Factory was none so radio friendly, the designs that much more obtuse, and the album artwork no more likely to feature band photos than the singles. As the label grew more visible, it became apparent that Factory was being perceived across the country as 'representing' Manchester in a particularly stylised fashion – for better, in as much as it made the city a focal point, or, as Factory's influence grew and threatened to overshadow anything else happening on the scene, for worse.

STEVE MORRISSEY WAS almost nineteen when he performed with the Nosebleeds, the same age as Johnny Marr, Andy Rourke and Mike Joyce would be once the Smiths started gigging at the end of 1982. To a large extent, Morrissey's personality was formed already. Had he made it as a front man at that point in his life, it would not necessarily have been a surprise to those on the scene, nor would it have been unduly premature. What was lacking, though, in terms of completing his package, was the subsequent four years of his life before he met Johnny Marr (again): four years of

137

frustration and desperation that would further create the unique, singularly named Morrissey, the character who would prove so attractive (in so many ways) to myriad teenagers and young adults who were going through (or had occasionally emerged from) similarly disastrous periods of their lives. Without becoming a failure, in effect, Morrissey could never have become a success.

From one perspective, it was indeed a disastrous period. As a prominent example, he followed his short-lived, positively reviewed engagement with the Nosebleeds with an even shorter liaison in a similarly disintegrating Slaughter & the Dogs, whose Wayne Barrett had left behind the drudgery of his Wythenshawe council estate upbringing for a Parisian wife. Billy Duffy recommended Morrissey for the vocalist role, and he passed an audition with the band – but not with the record company on a sojourn to London. When the group renamed themselves the Studio Sweethearts and moved south, Duffy went with them; Morrissey was left behind.[1]

Increasingly desperate to find a way into the thriving Manchester music scene, and no longer certain that it would be as a singer, he started associating with A Certain Ratio, whose interest in 1970s German 'kraut rock' and funk initially suggested that it would set them apart from other Manchester bands. Morrissey helped out in something of a managerial capacity, which at this early point consisted of little more than collecting their gig money (though as with Slaughter & the Dogs, he also wrote about them quite generously in *The Next Big Thing*). But somewhere along the way, his relationship with the singer Simon Topping unravelled, over misinterpreted approaches, forcing Morrissey to write a nakedly – and painfully – honest letter, explaining that he was essentially non-sexual and that he chose his friends based on their personality alone. Though the sense of hurt was evident, so too was his capacity for humour, the acute balance between dark and light that would distinguish Morrissey as a lyricist, and he joked that he would be willing to discuss female anatomy with Topping in the hope of saving their friendship.

The appeal did not work, and given the general lack of forward motion in Morrissey's life, it may have seemed like time to leave Manchester behind entirely. Steven certainly thought so; in the summer of 1978, he wrote to tell a friend that in September he would be going to live in New York. His mother thought so too, and as preparation for what was touted as a brand-new start for the family in America, shepherded Steven and Jackie Morrissey off – not to New York but instead to Arvada, a suburb of Denver, Colorado, at the beginning of November, where they were to live with Betty's sister Mary. Jackie quickly got herself a job there; Steve did not, complaining instead, in a letter back home, 'It's dead here. Everyone walks like John Wayne, so starch and masculinist. I wore a pink tie and everyone thought I was a transvestite.' Rather than taking comfort in American music, he was evidently homesick for the British New Wave, noting that the latest singles by the Jam, X-Ray Spex and Public Image Ltd made his life worth living. It might not have been unrelated to his newly noted fondness for these London New Wave acts that he talked wistfully about moving to the British capital the following January. But when the New Year came around, he returned instead to the familiar, if cold, comforts of Kings Road, Stretford. Jackie stayed on in Colorado for the time being, but emigration for Steven was taken off the table.

Come May of 1979 and Morrissey's frustration with the stasis in his life was palpable in a letter he wrote to one of his closer pen pals, Lindsay Hutton of the Scottish magazine *The Next Big Thing*, who was busy publishing Morrissey's writings on the Dolls, Sparks, the Manchester scene, and even a poem about James Dean. Morrissey announced that he was working now in a local record shop for 'starvation wages and dungeon conditions.' (Like his other jobs, it wouldn't last.) He confessed to enormous disappointment in Patti Smith's new LP, *Wave*, that

Simple Minds bored him, and that he was happy to hear the Rezillos had broken up; even the fact that Johnny Thunders' Heartbreakers had reunited appeared of zero interest. That may have been because he couldn't find an affordable printer for his book-length fanzine on the New York Dolls. Throwing up his arms in despair, he announced that he was going to Paris the following month 'to be artistic.'

They were dark days all around. A week before this letter, the political pendulum in Britain had swung once more to the right. Following what was termed the 'winter of discontent' – crippling strikes in both the public and private sectors as the Trade Unions sought and won pay increases far beyond a government-imposed 5 per cent limitation, all while Britain endured its worst weather in sixteen years – Margaret Thatcher swept into Downing Street as the new Conservative (and Britain's first female) prime minister. She did so largely due to public frustration at Labour's inability to control the unions, but also on the back of a brilliantly simple campaign image: that of an unemployment line stretching off into the distance under the slogan 'Labour Isn't Working'. It was true that unemployment had reached 1,500,000 (out of a 50,000,000 population) by the time of her election. But it was equally true that this figure would double during her first period in office, to levels not seen since the Great Depression, as her unapologetically hardline programme of closing down loss-making factories and shipyards, privatising other state-owned industries, lowering taxes on the rich, and enacting laws to curb union powers, saw Britain enter a deep recession in which millions lost their jobs, with replacement work of any lasting value almost impossible to find. To those who came from a working Labour background – which included most residents of the industrial northern cities like Manchester – Thatcher's policies looked suspiciously like class war.

The same month Thatcher was elected, Morrissey endured an especially unhappy birthday. Understandably, he had 'found the prospect of turning twenty alarming . . . I hadn't a clue what was going to happen.' He tried to stave off the pending crisis with a two-week spate of movies on television, but it didn't help. 'When I'd go to bed at night I'd have terrible palpitations because I was so worried. I'd wake up at three o'clock and begin to pace the bedroom.' Other than his enthusiastic embrace of American psychobillies the Cramps, the rest of the year fairly passed him by. Around him, and despite – or quite arguably because of – Manchester's economy ruination, Factory Records was booming, Joy Division and the Fall were on the John Peel show almost every night, Tony Wilson was managing A Certain Ratio, Paul Morley was a permanent fixture at *NME*, and the Buzzcocks had released their third album in eighteen months. Steven Morrissey, meanwhile, had yet to get started. He rang in the 1980s at home, curled up with a copy of *Pride and Prejudice*.

CHAPTER NINE

Back then you couldn't go to University to do media studies or learn how to be in a band, like you can now, you had to just go and do it.

– JOHNNY MARR, 2011

On a Friday afternoon in early 1979, in the midst of the 'Winter of Discontent', with the mercury stuck at freezing, the snow deeper on the ground than it had been in sixteen years and the bus drivers on strike, Johnny Marr set off on foot to the part-time job he had landed for himself stacking shelves at the local Co-op supermarket, deep in the heart of Wythenshawe. When he got there, he was informed that he was being sacked, 'for being lazy and cocky and distracted' as he presumed after the event. This was bad enough, but the co-op workers had a ceremony for employees who were fired: 'At the end of that shift you had to go out the loading bay and you were greeted by all the adults with an endless supply of complimentary eggs. Literally. Pallets and pallets. And you're stuck like a trapped animal in the loading bay. And all the adults who think "This lad's had it coming" start pelting you.'

Within minutes, Marr had been turned into 'a human omelette'. As he set off on the long walk back through Wythenshawe, he realised he couldn't possibly make it the whole way home, let alone explain himself when he got in; he stopped off at a Brookway friend's house instead. That friend, Danny Patton, told Johnny about a house party that was taking place that same evening, that there would be 'a load of beautiful girls going.' Marr took a shower, borrowed a shirt and a jacket off Patton ('luckily, he had good dress sense') and accompanied his friend to the party. As soon as he walked in, a certain girl caught his eye. Her name was Angela Brown, a third-year pupil at Brookway who had been born, by coincidence, precisely one year to the day after Johnny. She was petite, like him, with brown eyes and a lively smile, and as far as Johnny was concerned, 'from the first minute I saw her I wanted to be with her all my life.'

He got his wish. 'She made me chase her around for six weeks while everybody observed it, which was her prerogative – quite rightly. And I completely complied. We started dating and I never let her out of my sight.'[1] The Browns were more middle-class than the Mahers, which caused some initial problems with her protective brothers, and she was a vegetarian, which appeared alien to the Maher household. But under Johnny's influence, her dress sense quickly gave way to classic-rock chic, the pair of them developing a mutual fondness for the eyeliner beloved by '60s mods and modettes – and 1970s Keith Richards. Before long, they were seen – inseparably – as a pair.

Marr was never in any doubt as to his good fortune: 'Her joints would knock you sideways like nothing else and in some people's eyes, that's why they had plenty of time for me, because I was with such an amazing person.' But that was only one reason to be grateful. As he and Angie settled into a permanent relationship, Johnny realised that 'the thing that takes up a lot of teenage boys' time – i.e., their hormones and trying to get a partner – was taken care of for me.' Having barely broken his stride in acquiring the love of his life, he could resume his musical ambitions – and without distractions, because Angie supported him every step of the way.

'The vibe was, I am a guitar player and that is what I am going to do for the rest of my life, and she was like, "OK, whatever that takes, I will do that with you.'" This was not to suggest that Angie lacked for her own personality – her energy and tenacity would often prove crucial to the Smiths' forward motion – as much as that she and Johnny could afford to share a similar goal because they shared similar music tastes. 'From the minute she heard *Raw Power*, she knew what she liked. She loved David Johansen, Iggy Pop, Jimi Hendrix, and not much else. And the great Stones records. And so it stopped me fucking around too much, musically.'

Perhaps most tellingly, Johnny and Angie were entirely, completely comfortable in each other's company. 'Those noises I was making on a guitar,' said Marr of the many evenings at home he played around with the shapes of chords both conventional and intuitive, honing his talent in the process, 'it wasn't some lonely kid sat in a bedroom on his own. I was sat there with a very beautiful fifteen-year-old girl, keeping quiet, flicking through magazines and looking at New York Dolls covers, sitting there two feet away listening to me doing it, her in her own world and me in mine.'

Marr understood the introduction of Brown in his life as a continuum of the close connection he had already with his mother and sister. 'My relationships with guys has always been very close but it's always been about work, and my relationships with women have always been about psychology,' he acknowledged years later. Perhaps because he and Rourke were already set on their musical path, they managed to avoid the usual consequence of a first serious teenage romance – the sacrifice of the best friend. 'It was the three of us,' said Marr. 'All the time. We were all into the same clothes. The same music.' Rourke concurred: 'We were all just really good friends. Every waking hour we'd spend together, the three of us.' Rourke would frequently host the couple over at his family house on Hawthorn Lane, and even lend them his father's bedroom when needed – an invitation that led to great embarrassment the time Michael Rourke came back early from a business trip and caught Marr running down the stairs wearing his dressing gown.

Around the middle of '79, Marr was asked to join the local band Sister Ray. Positioned musically on the fringes between Hawkwind and the Damned, they were, said Marr, 'much older, really hardcore guys, just speed freaks,' whose singer, Clive Robertson, had helped garner them a local reputation for the simple fact that he 'was crazy.'[2] Marr rehearsed with Sister Ray for a couple of weeks in a basement in Whalley Range before taking to the stage with them for his first-ever gig, a relatively prestigious slot opening for the Freshies at the Wythenshawe Forum, which subsequently saw him written up in the local paper. Because of musical, age and habit differences, he and the band were not meant to be, but Marr was grateful to bank the experience – and an ongoing friendship with the dreadlocked drummer, Bill Anstee.

The brief dalliance was effectively just a sabbatical from what looked like a more conventional progression into professional music. When the older Wythenshawe guitarists hit the age of eighteen, they largely went their separate ways, some giving up music for regular jobs, others – like Billy Duffy – setting off for London for the big-time. Robin Allman stuck at it on home turf, and Marr and Rourke found themselves sitting in with him and classically trained keyboard player Paul Whittall, practising multiple-part vocal harmonies and similarly complex picking guitars in the style of Pentangle. The next they knew, they had recruited Bobby Durkin and formed a new band, White Dice.

Allman's reputation was without compare in Wythenshawe. Marr called him 'about as talented as anyone I ever met.' Whittall said that Allman was 'a legend in South Manchester circles' and 'widely acknowledged as being a brilliant songwriter.' Rourke, whose home became the practice space, admitted, 'We used to look up to Rob,' that he was 'more knowledgeable about his music' and 'a very talented guy.' Allman's musical tastes, however, were almost painfully orthodox, and he set White Dice out on a path influenced not only by the familiar figures of Tom Petty, Rory Gallagher, and Neil Young, but by English folk group Fairport Convention and their approximate Irish equivalent, the Bothy Band. For Marr and, especially, Rourke, this was not of itself a great problem. They had grown up on many of these acts and were not ready to discard them for the sake of fashion; indeed, Marr was photographed in White Dice imitating Bruce Springsteen on the cover of *Born to Run*, while wearing a Tom Petty T-shirt. (Allman served as his Clarence Clemons.)

But as the 1970s came to a close, Marr and Rourke were increasingly taken by the music emerging out of the New Wave, especially given that the concept of musicianship – albeit of a less self-indulgent kind than in the pre-punk era – had returned. Rourke, now using a fretless bass that Marr had picked up 'on the cheap,' was naturally intrigued and subsequently influenced by the bass playing of Mick Karn in the group Japan, whose concert at the Manchester Apollo around that time he cited as 'one of the most amazing shows ever.' Rourke and Marr went to see the Cure together, twice, and Marr became a fan of Siouxsie and the Banshees, and even more so of the Only Ones, whom he followed religiously. This combination of the incredibly traditional and the highly experimental was, as Rourke admitted, 'schizophrenic,' but it was partly because 'we didn't want to follow trends.' Still, in White Dice, they were expected to keep their more modern interests at bay and follow the older bandleader. The result, said Rourke, was a 'very American soft rock.'

It was a perennially popular sound, as demonstrated by the fact that the biggest hit to come out of Manchester in 1979 was not by the Buzzcocks or Joy Division but 'Every Day Hurts' by the painfully mainstream group Sad Café. White Dice not only had the same kind of name, they used much the same instrumentation and arrangements. So when, in early 1980, they entered a demo contest hosted by F-Beat Records (started after Elvis Costello, Nick Lowe and label chief Jake Riviera peeled away from Stiff Records), for which they crowded around a cassette machine to record a single song complete with four-part harmony, it was perhaps not surprising that Riviera was sufficiently intrigued as to invite them to London to record at Lowe's home studio. White Dice did their utmost to prepare properly for the opportunity, rehearsing several more songs, for which Marr – despite his general disinterest in a lead vocal role – nonetheless insisted on a coauthorship credit with Allman for his contributions on guitar and arranging.

The trip to the capital, in April 1980, had its high points. Marr was invited to use Elvis Costello's Rickenbacker on the session; they all saw Nick Lowe's wife (and Johnny Cash's daughter) Carlene Carter in her negligee; they stayed in a hotel; and they reunited with Billy Duffy, who was living what looked like the rock-guitarist dream in a band called Lonesome No More. Six songs were recorded, and although their influences were overly betrayed by a cover of Tom Petty's 'American Girl', one of the self-composed numbers aroused significant interest from the engineer to focus on it above the others. Still, the demo was ultimately rejected, in a brief phone call to Allman from Riviera. 'We didn't have that spark or edge,' admitted Rourke. 'Something was missing.'

It needn't have been the end of White Dice – and in the short term, it was not. With the group essentially camped out in the Hawthorn Lane house, Chris Rourke took on a role as publicist, garnering local press and the prospect of gigs. But White Dice's progress was further constricted both by Rob Allman's fear of playing live and his tendency to mask that fear with alcohol. Since they were kids, Allman and Duffy had been into Special Brew, a particularly potent canned lager much favoured by street tramps and cost-conscious teenage drinkers. Duffy, though, could hold his drink; Allman could not. Two cans, said Whittall, and Allman 'was unrecognisable. He was one of those people who shouldn't probably have gone down that road.'

This made it all the more frustrating that when White Dice finally played a gig, at the Squat off Oxford Road a full year after forming, Allman got so drunk he could barely stand onstage. White Dice called it a day shortly afterward, in January 1981. That same month, Allman and Chris Rourke, perhaps predictably, had a fight, and Allman moved out.

Given Allman's high regard in Wythenshawe, the fact that he subsequently allowed the success of those around him to become a measure of his own sense of failure was upsetting to his friends. 'It was really hard for him, being top dog with all those people, Billy Duffy included,' observed Whittall, who continued playing with Allman for many years to come. 'In the South Manchester hierarchy, he was number one, and for Johnny to go ahead and beat him to it was a massive comedown.'

'It was an unfulfilled life that killed him,' said Marr of Allman, who died in 1993 of a brain haemorrhage brought on by alcoholism. (Marr, Duffy and Whittall were among the many former Wythenshawe musicians to attend his funeral.) 'He was a very clever middle-class kid, with a very, very loving and nurturing family, which, in a way, played a part in his psychology. Me and Billy, we just had to get out and do stuff. But Rob was almost too comfortable to make it, and he wasn't tough enough. He didn't have the "I will sleep on a couch" mentality. You need a sense of desperation to put up with a lot of stuff. You do need a certain kind of dissatisfaction.'

EARLY ON IN their friendship, Marr and Rourke had become particularly dissatisfied with St Augustine's. The pair frequently ran afoul of the school's variation on the St Mary's strap – in this case a three-pronged leather whip – though one of them more than the other. By the time he was thirteen, Rourke was receiving it almost on a daily basis – 'just because I couldn't hold my tongue.' (Unlike at St Mary's, where the number of whips was noted on a student's conduct card, a St Augustine's pupil sent to the headmaster's office often negotiated his own punishment.) Their interest in schooling had hardly been helped when the then-Labour government finally got its way in abolishing free grammar schools; in 1977 as Marr and Rourke went into their third year, St Augustine's was turned into a public high school and renamed St John Plessington, opening up its doors to what Rourke called 'renegades from Wythenshawe and Chorlton.' (Not, of course, that Rourke or Marr were angels.) This in turn led to a massive turnover in teachers. Monsignor McGuiness, who had become 'such a drunk,' said Rourke, that 'he used to wander around the corridors, banging off the walls,' was let go. But because he was living in a bungalow on the school property, he still made his presence felt – if only by leaning up against the school windows, crying, as Rourke recalled. (McGuiness died in early 1980, shortly before Marr and Rourke left school.)

As the pair's musical abilities increased in tandem with their ambitions, and given the regular beatings, the prospect of attending school at all became increasingly unattractive. Rourke's view was, 'Why do I need Latin or geography when I want to be a musician?' For Marr, the people he looked up to and hung out with were already out of school, spending their days working on their musicianship, making contacts and promoting themselves in town; he wanted to do likewise. By their final year, as White Dice looked like it might become a serious proposition, Marr and Rourke were barely going to class at all. Instead, they would meet at the bus stop opposite Marr's house (two bus journeys in for Rourke already), wait for the Mahers to go to work, then return to Churchstone Walk and work on their music. Marr had signed up to take music O-Level, but any initial enthusiasm disappeared once he became aware that it was largely about studying theory – which was math, and he hated math. Besides, the music teacher, Adrian Jessett, had served as his and Rourke's homeroom teacher earlier in their school days, and Marr had come to perceive him as a bully, in which he was not alone; another St Augustine's old boy called Jessett 'a sadistic opportunist.'

Jessett went on to found the acclaimed Manchester Boys Choir but was eventually disgraced after pleading guilty to repeated sexual assault on an underage male chorister. (Pupils from St Augustine's had their own memories of being sexually abused by other teachers, and while at the school.) Teachers aside, Marr was wary of knowing too much about how to make music properly: 'I *wanted* to be someone who learned from playing off records.'

STEVEN MORRISSEY HAD entered St Mary's in 1970; Marr and Rourke officially left St Augustine's in 1980. (Mike Joyce attended St Gregory's, the same Roman Catholic grammar school as Andrew Berry, from 1974–79.) To the extent, then, that the Smiths represented any British generation, it would be that of the 1970s secondary-school child; religious indoctrin-ation and physical beatings aside, their experiences were akin to those of grammar schools, secondary moderns and compre-hensives in other major cities through the 1970s. Like so many of their age group, they felt betrayed by this system; Morrissey fairly enough called his an 'education in reverse.' The sadism and the bullying and the general lack of personal compassion and progressive education had been bad enough, but it was made worse by the knowledge that the economy around them was failing, that the local industry was collapsing, and that the careers that they were once being trained for – the 'jobs for life' that previous generations had come to expect – didn't exist anymore. When Morrissey left school in 1975, inflation was at an astonishing 27 per cent, and unemployment at a million. When Marr and Rourke left in 1980, inflation was back down to 10 per cent but unemployment was at almost two million and still climbing. Did it make any *less* sense for them to blindly pursue their interest in music?

In Marr's case there had been an alternative. Throughout his early teens, despite the distractions of music, he had maintained his reputation on the football field. At school, he played for the first team. Locally he played for a Sunday team, Brooklands Athletic. Among those he trained with were future England international David Bardsley, and Gary Blissett, later of the Wimbledon 'Crazy Gang'; it was serious company. As befitted his eventual role in the Smiths and elsewhere, Marr's skill was as a winger, setting up goals for someone else to score. This was the type of player every team was looking for – and a scout from Whitehill, a feeder team for Manchester City, became a regular touchline presence, followed by one representing Nottingham Forest. At this time Forest was the best club in Europe; under the leadership of the inimitable Brian Clough and his (then) loyal assistant Peter Taylor, they'd won the English League in 1978, and were set to win the European Cup in both '79 and '80. The scout came around to Churchstone Walk after the Brooklands game, telling Johnny's parents that the boy would be good for a year's apprenticeship in Nottingham after he left school. But Marr wasn't interested. His memory of that morning was that 'I'd been out at a gig the night before with Andy and Angie, and I still had my eyeliner on. I just wanted to get the game over and done with, so me and Andy and Angie could go back to Andy's and do what we always did, which was kick back and listen to some records.'

The attitude appears cavalier but was in fact perfectly calculated. Marr knew how intensely he would have to work at football if he wanted to pursue it; he was perfectly aware that an equally low percentage of apprenticeship footballers made it to the big-time as did amateur musicians. He instinctively grasped that he could not possibly juggle two precarious (and contradictory) careers – and that if he moved away from Manchester right at the point that he was playing in bands with older, more respected musicians, he would be throwing away everything he had worked towards. The choice, for him, was therefore no choice at all. 'It was a long, long way from making records,' he said. Besides, 'I didn't really like being around professional footballers.' They were 'too macho.'

In the spring of 1980, then, Johnny Marr and Andy Rourke walked away from St Augustine's with, like Morrissey before them, the barest of qualifications. Rourke, as punishment for his constant truancy, had not even been allowed to sit for his exams in the end: 'They said "These cost the school money and you're a waste of money." I used to go in for my dinner and then go out again.' Determined to get himself a bass amp, he went into manual work at Snap-on Tools, stuck it out for the six or seven months it took to acquire the equipment, and then quit.

Like Morrissey, however, Marr felt compelled to go back to school and finish the job. It annoyed him that he had failed his O-Levels in English and art, although not half as much as it frustrated his father, who had come to despair of his son making anything of his life. Ironically, John Maher had moved into promoting live music in his spare time, and had been trying to get his son interested in the process, but the difference between the adult's country showbands and the teenager's rock 'n' roll was as distinct as that between football or music for a career. The younger Marr signed up to West Wythenshawe College of Further Education, in the same building where he had spent so much time at the youth club. He took a drama course, and to his surprise, thoroughly enjoyed it. He made friends with an eager student named Tony O'Connor, who had an interest of his own in the music business. And before he knew it, he was president of the student union. In addition, and just as important, Marr abandoned the local shelf-stocking jobs for those in city-centre clothing stores. And in the process, he went from being a Wythenshawe lad to a Manchester townie.

CHAPTER TEN

I am somewhat of a back-bedroom casualty. I spent a great deal of time sitting in the bedroom writing furiously and feeling that I was terribly important and feeling that everything I wrote would go down in the annals of history or whatever. And it's proved to be quite true.

    – MORRISSEY, *Oxford Road Show*, March 1985

On 18 May 1980, Ian Curtis, the singer for Joy Division, took his life, hanging himself at his house in Macclesfield, just outside Manchester, leaving behind a widowed wife, a fatherless baby daughter, and a distraught band and record company. The shockwaves did not cease there: Curtis's conscious decision to kill himself, at the age of twenty-three, reverberated all the way through his (post-punk) generation and beyond. Joy Division was on the brink of major success at the time. They had just completed their second album, *Closer,* and had a new, eminently commercial single, 'Love Will Tear Us Apart', scheduled for imminent release; indeed, the group was due to leave for an American tour the very *day* that Curtis took his life. On the face of it, Curtis had everything to live for.

There can be little doubt, given its subsequent longevity, that 'Love Will Tear Us Apart' would have been some sort of a hit regardless, but in the wake of Curtis's suicide, with media attention and radio airplay inspiring mass consumer sympathy, it became that much more of a hit, rising high into the British top 20 in July, matched then by the instant top 10 success of *Closer*. The record sales and chart positions provided bittersweet success for Factory and its main distributor, Rough Trade; satisfaction about market penetration dampened at record company meetings by the knowledge that they had on their hands a dead star. The surviving members of Joy Division decided to keep going under a different name, eventually recruiting drummer Stephen Morris's girlfriend Gillian Gilbert on keyboards, and with Bernard Sumner taking lead vocals, returning as New Order. They had known, amongst themselves, that Curtis suffered from epilepsy and that he was on a heavy cocktail of prescription pills, some of which seemed to be messing with his moods, but as working-class lads brought up in a culture that encouraged the masking of personal health problems, and which generally ignored psychiatric issues entirely, they had lacked the tools to recognise, let alone deal with, Curtis's suicidal tendency. The decision to continue as a band, they later admitted, was as much an act of anger as the change of name was one of professional courtesy.

Curiously, the death of Ian Curtis appeared not to have any effect on the life of Steven Morrissey; neither the music nor the personalities of Joy Division seemed to touch him at all. This was odd, not only because the group was so highly regarded within Manchester and beyond, and not just because Morrissey moved in Factory's circles but because Ian Curtis actually carried out Morrissey's long-standing threat: he took his life somewhere that Morrissey, for all that he talked so relentlessly about suicide, could only contemplate from a distance.

There was one regard in which Curtis's suicide impressed very deeply on the future Morrissey, however: the association it created with Manchester as a city so miserable and depressing that a talented young singer and lyricist with a happening young band would sooner kill himself than embrace the possibility of becoming a pop star. That was Ian

Curtis's legacy; Morrissey was determined it should not be his own.

THE WAY MORRISSEY subsequently talked about them, his lost years were a permanent period of introspection, solitude and soul-searching, marked by only the occasional glimmer of companionship or prospect of fulfilment. 'It is difficult to describe how really insular I was,' he said in one of many references to this period. 'Especially when I was twenty-one, twenty-two, twenty-three . . . I was entirely on my own. The very idea of me becoming what I have become was unthinkable. I found life unbearable at times.' Certainly, by the point at which Johnny Marr knocked on his door and 'rescued' him, Morrissey had drifted sufficiently far from a continually moving Manchester music scene that he had been largely written off as part of it even by those who genuinely liked him. Yet the sorry picture that he has painted of himself is at stark odds with the character who formed positive, active relationships with men and women alike, who continued to attend gigs on a regular basis, and who promoted himself, almost relentlessly, as a writer of merit.

The two perspectives are not mutually exclusive. The nature of many people who suffer from depression is that they can maintain what appears, on the surface, an active social life. In this regard, Morrissey's behaviour was near enough textbook. When his mood was positive, he came across to his friends, including his pen pals, as the witty, sociable, occasionally catty but ultimately rewarding companion they knew he could be. When life got him down, he retreated to his room on Kings Road, drew the curtains, likely sought prescriptions, and hid from the world at large.[1]

The downside explained the limitations to the upside. Morrissey had long tried all the obvious steps to get a band going – placing ads in music papers, responding to ads in music papers, suggesting himself to people he met at gigs, attending auditions, and even standing onstage. But he did not have the kind of resilience to find, corral and motivate the right band members for himself, to scare up equipment, secure a manager, book rehearsals, and find gigs. For the same reasons, he lacked the personality to manage a band (as his negative experience with A Certain Ratio revealed) or start a label, which required all the above *plus* a degree in bullshitting and putting up with other people's foibles. An incessant writer, his inability to publish his proposed New York Dolls book-zine demonstrated why he never got around to the obvious project for someone of such firm opinions, starting a fully-fledged fanzine. Though he could write (very well), type, and even lay it all out, he wasn't willing to part with the cash and endure the process of selling it into stores. He far preferred to find a paying patron for his literary talents.

The leading music papers did not welcome his appeals for employment. There was a separation of church and state between those who dictated what was hip and those who harangued the editorial pages to disagree, and Steven Morrissey had made enough of a nuisance of himself over the years for free that they were not predisposed to let him do so for money. Besides, the three major weeklies had all hired Manchester correspondents once it became apparent that it might be the second city of (post-)punk, back when Steve Morrissey still imagined himself as a singer. At one point, a staffer at *NME* even put the phone down on him mid-pitch.

He was left with *Record Mirror*, the smallest of the four weeklies in both circulation and credibility; in 1976, in a letter to the paper promoting his usual American idols, Morrissey had criticised its 'housewife image.' But in early 1980, with no other offers on the table, he accepted a humble role as its Manchester concert reviewer, the traditional point of entry into music journalism. Like any writer dealing with the realities of a paying gig for the first time, Morrissey fumed at his editors.

'They chop and change all my reviews, making me look trite and basic,' he complained. But the imposition of a deadline, a specific word count, and whatever editing took place in fact proved invigorating. Over eighteen months of sporadic concert reviews, his writing grew ever sharper and wittier. Of Wasted Youth, a London glam rock band with overly obvious influences, he wrote, with Wildean precision: 'The bassist appears from underneath what appears to be an abandoned ostrich's nest . . . The fab guitarist offers furtive sneers, and so would you if you had to apply your foundation with a shovel . . .' And of his former idol Iggy Pop, he wrote that he 'looks as fearsome as a well-laundered Klondike Annie . . . One would imagine that the next step for him would be the Golden Garter or, better still, retirement.'

The British music press has always been famously incestuous – as if, this being rock 'n' roll, the usual rules regarding professional conflicts and personal objectivity don't apply.[3] And so, as he had with his writings for various fanzines, Morrissey did not think twice about championing the bands he was already a fan or a friend of. He gave Billy Duffy's Lonesome No More an almost hysterically glowing appraisal as opening act for Wasted Youth. He referred to the Cramps as 'the most important American export since the New York Dolls,' neglecting to mention that he was in the midst of setting up their British fan club, Legion of the Cramped, with *The Next Big Thing* editor Lindsay Hutton, who had turned him onto the band in the first place. (He was so excited about it that he placed ads in *Sounds* before the club was properly organised, which resulted in letters complaining about a certain Steven Morrissey of Kings Road running off with the fans' money.) And he was positively relentless in trying to promote his best female friend.

Following her historic *Orgasm Addict* design, Linder had gone on to publish a provocative fanzine full of equally controversial (and in the eyes of those who did not understand art, equally pornographic) photocollages, *The Secret Public,* alongside writer Jon Savage; she had designed the album cover for Magazine's debut, *Real Life*; and she had formed the band Ludus, which she fronted as its only female member, taking to the Manchester live scene (and beyond) with a vengeance. If not quite famous, per se, Linder was certainly 'a name'. Morrissey, by comparison, having played just the one or two gigs with the Nosebleeds, was otherwise anonymous.[4] And yet the pair had nonetheless found themselves mutually compatible. 'Linder seemed to know something that I knew,' Morrissey wrote of their budding friendship in Manchester's post-punk years. 'We both spoke in cinematic language, and we both somehow knew that our own presence on earth was trouble enough for those around us.' Linder, who shared Morrissey's dry humour, has noted that what they most had in common was that each was 'totally unemployable.' (Linder insisted on living by her art. Morrissey continued to take short-term jobs, including, in 1980, a stint as a porter at the hospital where his father now worked – and this despite their apparent estrangement.)

Determined to grab the new decade by the horns, in early 1980 Morrissey moved into Linder's house at 35 Mayfield Road, adding to the eventual rumour that they were a couple. In fact, Morrissey's 'rented room in Whalley Range,' as he was to immortally describe it, was in Magazine guitarist Barry Adamson's former flat; Linder – indeed, pretty much everyone in Ludus – lived above him. All the same, the house had the bohemian air of a salon: 'It's an oasis of culture and free expression (in other words it's a dump but the rent is low),' he wrote to a friend. Morrissey was evidently infatuated with Linder as the complete package of brains *and* beauty – 'I did not know or hear anyone at all across human civilisation who was like Linder,' he later admitted – and in an interview conducted by Morrissey himself for *Interview* magazine in 2010, Linder waxed equally lyrical about their early friendship: 'The currency of ideas in the houses I shared – as you well know, given you were there – was, in retrospect, the most memorable education in intellectual imagination. Not that anyone would use those terms, but you and Howard Devoto and Pete Shelley and others were so very, very smart. All finding different ways of saying, "Yes, but . . ." It had less to do with talent than with genius – musicians and singers, but with the minds and eyes of novelists. Nowadays, boys with enormous . . . record collections describe me as the "muse" to this circle in Manchester. Perhaps, perhaps, perhaps . . . But you were my muses too.'

Away from the other central figures on this scene, Linder and Morrissey developed their devotion on long walks, Morrissey's preferred way to see the sights while simultaneously escaping from the world. Their visits to Southern Cemetery in Chorlton have become particularly legendary due to the song 'Cemetry Gates,' but the graveyards were far from their only destinations and distractions. 'We'd go wandering in Moss Side,' recalled Linder. 'Hours and days wandering, just the two of us together, but very alone at the same time, extremely intimate but very separate.'

Other than walking and talking, said Linder, 'we used to read obsessively, devouring book after book after book. It was a very essential ingredient in our lives.' Specifically, 'most of the books we read were by women, or about women.' This continual process of reading and talking (and walking) with such a strong feminist figure led Morrissey towards the concept of a 'fourth sex' that he would promote, once the Smiths got going, as part explanation for his proffered celibacy. In the meantime, however, Linder had her band, Ludus, and by 1980 they had started releasing records – on New Hormones, the label formerly associated with the Buzzcocks and now being run out of an office just off Manchester's Piccadilly by Richard Boon alongside band manager Peter Wright.

Ludus was not exactly commercial: Linder's lyrics took poetic license with traditional rhythmic formula, and the band's music was largely asymmetrical in response. When the two threads threatened to go off in entirely separate directions, she might scream or offer something very close to a yodel to mask the rip in the musical fabric. Songs were uneven in length, and titles like 'Anatomy Is Not Destiny' were clearly not designed for the daytime airwaves. (And yes, in all these regards, Linder's Ludus served as a blueprint for Morrissey's Smiths.) But in an era of thriving post-punk experimentation, Ludus fit in perfectly alongside the like minds of London's Slits and Raincoats, Leeds' Delta 5, and Birmingham's Au Pairs – all of them female-fronted/domi-nated groups releasing sexually political records on inde-pendent left-leaning labels. (Morrissey, not surprisingly, was a fan of Au Pairs, and DJ'd a gig for Delta 5, bringing along his Sandie Shaw records alongside those of Ludus.) But whether it was the good-natured disorganisation of New Hormones or, as Boon claimed, Linder's conscious resistance to popularity, her band never quite took off. Morrissey did his best to rectify this, reviewing them in *Record Mirror* not once, but twice.

The second of those occasions, a gig at which Ludus opened for Depeche Mode, turned out to be his final paid review. Neglecting to mention that he had lived with Ludus, written their most recent press release, asked New Hormones to send him to New York with the group, and, in fact, operated the lights for them at this particular show, he wrote instead how 'their music offers everything to everyone.' (Admittedly, he also noted that 'Ludus like to wallow in other people's deprav-ity.') Of course, as a pop magazine, *Record Mirror* was none so interested in Ludus as Depeche Mode. And Morrissey, not yet knowing that in a little over a year he would be leading a musical charge against the headlining band's form of synth-pop (and that a couple of years after that, they would share thousands of the same fans in America), manned the barricades for the time being from the critics' perspective. 'They resurrect every murderously monotonous cliché ever known to man,' he wrote, assailing their top 20 hit single 'New Life' as 'nothing more than a bland jelly-baby.'

He had a point in that Depeche Mode's early music revealed an old-fashioned pop sensibility wrapped in the sort of synthesizer bubblegum that veterans like Morrissey had grown out of around the time of Chicory Tip. But he also *missed* the point. For although Depeche Mode were poster boys for a new 'futurist' movement of synthesizer-favouring club-goers, they were also the inevitable result of the past three years of post-punk freedom, the love child of a musical orgy between (Rough Trade/Factory/Mute/Fast Products darlings) Cabaret Voltaire, the Human League, OMD, and the Normal. A self-functioning young group, much the same age as Morrissey and, like him, former Bowie and Roxy kids, they exhibited a do-it-yourself attitude; had a genuinely talented songwriter in Vince Clarke; and had been picked up by a proper independent label, Mute Records. And when, just a month after Morrissey's scathing but ultimately irrelevant review, they hit the top 10 with 'Just Can't Get Enough', it marked a further triumph for that label and its distributors, Rough Trade. As a revamped Human League, now signed to Virgin, swept the nation that Christmas with the omnipresent 'Don't You Want Me', and in a year that saw other independent label discoveries OMD and Soft Cell also scale the high peaks of the charts, the success of Depeche Mode – who remained loyal to Miller and Mute despite the allure of multimillion-pound advances – proved, without doubt, that the independent network could rival that of the major labels, and on a minuscule budget. The fact that it proved as much with a group who made guitars and drums look positively arcane seemed, at the time, just part of the apparent flow of history.

In October 1980, word emerged from Palatine Road that Factory was considering a publishing imprint, which made sense, given that Tony Wilson had studied literature at Cambridge and was vocal about his desire to maintain Factory as something other than a mere record label. In the end, nothing came of the idea, but Morrissey took up the rumour as an invitation to greatness. Before the announcement about Factory Books even hit the music papers, he was telling friends that they were publishing a play of his. Whatever assurances he might have been given by Tony Wilson to that effect turned out to be empty promises. After another lengthy sojourn to the States – Christmas 1980 in Colorado, and several weeks of the New Year on the East Coast in Philadelphia, New Jersey, and New York, where he fell in love this time with the vast secondhand book stores and the fact that they were open *on Sunday*, something that was, quite literally, sacrilegious at the time in Britain – he returned home eager to know the play's presumed good fortune. A letter to Wilson in March brought no response; in April, he wrote again, in what was now becoming his familiar, slightly spidery non-cursive handwriting: 'I feel it my juristic duty to remind you of my little play. Is it still to be printed?'

The lack of response should have convinced Morrissey that it was not, but he found he could not let the matter lie. In fact, what he perceived as Wilson's cold shoulder (which, as Morrissey would find out soon enough in the Smiths, was more the result of being overwhelmed by success) provoked him, two months later, to the typewriter for a more officious letter, 'concerning that little bit of hearth-fire hokum, my play. I wish you'd let me know what you're doing with it. But you won't.' Undeterred by this, and that Wilson had not returned the script either, he embarked on a separate plea on behalf of his friends in Ludus; the fact that they were already signed to New Hormones, and that Wilson was not likely to steal a band off his friend Richard Boon, appeared not to have occurred to him. He then followed with a further idea, suggesting that he viewed Tony Wilson's Factory as duty-bound to emulate the multi-media world of Andy Warhol's 1960s New York-based Factory: Wilson, he said, should find a theatre, create actors, and perform Morrissey's admittedly plotless plays. Though he was well-mannered and typically funny in his writing, Morrissey concluded with what could easily be construed as a challenge or provocation, using a line he would later work into a his lyrics, that 'I will write to you weekly until you either decide to speak to me, or spit right in my eye.' It appeared to be his last correspondence on the issue.

Years into the future, Wilson would talk positively about Morrissey's literary endeavours, even if the only thing he could recall about the script (before losing it, as he claimed) was that 'the characters lived on toast.' And he obviously saw enough potential in Morrissey that he kept the letters (though not, frustratingly, the play). But Morrissey's barrage of mail, especially the manner in which he appeared to turn from fan to foe in such a short time – that is, over the course of that one final letter – revealed a streak of jealousy, or something very similar. Morrissey, it appeared, wanted in with Factory; Wilson kept him out.

Morrissey's frustration was, perhaps, understandable – especially if he had neglected to make a Xerox of his play before entrusting it to Wilson. But his mood should have been buoyed by the fact that – finally! – his New York Dolls book-zine had seen print. Morrissey had offered his services to the publisher of a small local imprint, Babylon Books' John Muir, who, without the likes of Joy Division or New Order records to keep him busy, had positively leaped at the opportunity of an eager young author unlikely to press for royalty statements and printed it (eventually) in early 1981. That part of the forty-eight-page publication that was in Morrissey's own words revealed the sense of style, the poetic rhythm and ready wit that was only two years away from finding its true voice in the Smiths. But as further evidence that literature was less his obvious path than lyrics, the essay did not reveal a solid sense of construction. It began instead as a series of didactic potential opening sentences:

The New York Dolls were the first real sign that the Sixties were over. Their unmatched vulgarity dichotomised feelings of extravagant devotion or vile detestation. It was impossible to look upon the Dolls as adequately midstream, just as it was impossible to ignore them. Enough was written about the group to fill a library. They were the 'cause celebre' of New York's avant garde.

And it continued that way for several pages before giving in to exhaustion and quoting the group's own individual pen files instead. Still, at a point in time when quality music journalism was a relatively novel idea and had yet to extend into quality music biographies, the appearance on local record-shop (and some bookshop) shelves of a small book dedicated to a cult group proved sufficiently popular for reprints and eventual sales of around 3,000 copies. As an act of friendship, Morrissey dedicated the book to James Maker, 'Who lives it.'

His book on the New York Dolls turned out to be more or less Morrissey's last word on the subject for a number of years. Curiously, once the Smiths garnered the sort of attention that he had once thought the Dolls' birthright, he disowned his fandom as 'just a teenage fascination . . . I was laughably young at the time,' noting in other interviews that 'I hate the Dolls now' and that 'I could never possibly listen to one of their records.' Truth was, his 'fascination' had lasted a decade and would resume again in years to come; in fact, Morrissey would prove instrumental in the group's eventual reformation. A possible explanation for his bizarre volte-face was that the image of the New York Dolls contrasted too vividly with that of the Smiths in 1984 – and, more important, that he was happy to have become, at last, Morrissey the singer and no longer wanted to be identified as he had long been known around Manchester and throughout the music press, as Morrissey the oddly obsessed New York Dolls fanatic.

Not surprisingly, Muir asked Morrissey for a follow-up. This time, he indulged his fascination with James Dean, whose photocopied image accompanied any number of Morrissey's letters to friends and pen pals. Back in 1979, one such correspondent, Lindsay Hutton, had published Morrissey's poem, 'James Dean Is Not Dead' (which reworked the title of a François Truffaut essay), in *The Next Big Thing*. The poem offered the notion that Dean did not die in 1955 but rather, 'horribly maimed' by his car accident, was cast aside by 'bigwigs' who had no more use for him. Morrissey's poem imagined Dean seeing out his years in a 'robe worn and grey, well-worn slippers, spirit passed away,' and was, certainly by the standards of much teenage poetry of the era, nothing to be ashamed of. The subsequent book(let), also entitled *James Dean Is Not Dead*, relied more heavily on the kind of cut-and-paste journalism that would befall the likes of the Smiths in the 1980s. It was not actually published until 1983, by which point the Smiths were up and running, and Morrissey relatively keen to downplay it. Still, though weakly written, there was the occasional flexing of rhythmic humour – and eager discussion of sexual habits such as Morrissey would baulk at disclosing about his own life once he became the subject of equally prurient interest:

> In Hollywood, where young actors were picked, plucked and packed away, Dean was determined to make it on his own terms. When cross-examined by tell-all gossips of his bisexuality, he told them: 'Well I'm certainly not going through life with one hand tied behind my back!' It was rumoured far too frequently that he had worked his way up trousers down. Had Warners, on signing Dean, bought and destroyed the porn movies which showed their precious protege stripped for action?

A third book-length essay submitted to Babylon, *Exit Smiling*, was arguably the most interesting of the three, given that it focused not on a single band or actor but on a genre, 'some of the screen's also-rans.' Morrissey's fourteen (very) brief chapters, arranged again without apparent coordination or structure, homed in briefly on the talents of the relatively recognisable (future Smiths cover stars Terence Stamp and Rita Tushingham) and, for average British readers at least, the somewhat obscure (Pier Angeli and Mamie Van Doren). Far more than a collection of non-Hollywood Stars, *Exit Smiling* served also as an exploration of Morrissey's feminist tendencies, and was clearly influenced in that regard by Molly Haskell's groundbreaking 1974 book, *From Reverence to Rape: The Treatment of Women in the Movies*. Though Morrissey's brief canter around the edges of film criticism was hardly in Haskell's league, it was genuinely revealing of his lifelong interests and thought processes. If he was upset when Muir declined to publish it at the time, citing a lack of potential audience, he was understandably furious that it should eventually come out in 1998, in a strangely belated bout of obvious profiteering.[5]

A 'BACK-BEDROOM casualty' he may claim to have been, but Morrissey's communications with the outside world continued at a furious rate; he must at times have felt like he was single-handedly keeping the Royal Mail in business. (He did his best to shun the Royal part of it, refusing to use stamps celebrating the 1981 wedding of Prince Charles and Lady Di,.and good-naturedly castigated friends who dared to do so themselves.) Responding to a classified ad in *Sounds*, he began a pen-pal relationship with a Glaswegian teenager, Robert Mackie, almost unnerving in its combination of wicked wit, childlike enthusiasm, and patent condescension. The professional critic for *Record Mirror* and author for Babylon Books seemed far removed from the person who opened one of his missives with the sentences: 'So pleased that you enjoyed my last letter. Why don't you just admit that every word I write fascinates you? It would save so much time. The nicest thing I can say about your letter is that it exists.'

Early in the correspondence, which ran for fourteen months from October 1980, Morrissey set about convincing Mackie that he was American and that his early 1981 trip to the States would result in him living there. (He would, he insisted, miss *Coronation Street* and *Top of the Pops*, but that appeared to be all.) When he returned in March nonetheless, it was to enthuse instead about the group he was forming, Angels Are Genderless, for which he had written at least one song of which he was proud, entitled 'I'm Departed'. He pestered Mackie for a photograph, then trashed the results when he discovered his pen-pal sported a moustache, comparing it to a dead caterpillar. He nonetheless sought further personal details, teasing about his relationship with a girl he would later bring into the studio to sing backup on his first recordings with Johnny Marr: 'I have a girlfriend called Annalisa. We're both bisexual. Real hip, huh? I hate sex.' When Mackie replied that his sex life was nonexistent (he was eighteen at the time, Morrissey almost twenty-two), Morrissey offered a response somewhat at odds with his later proclamations: 'Oh yes, celibacy is real hip (sister), but, "no man is an island" so the saying goeth. And haven't you HEARD about sexual repression? You'll probably end up strangling your mother or becoming some deranged bisexual psychopatic (sic) child-murderer.'

At least Morrissey was to remain consistent in his disdain for employment; he appeared disappointed, if not entirely surprised, to discover that Mackie actually worked for a living. When it came to music, he noted that he had seen Bowie in concert some sixteen times, and that he had been able to elicit correspondence from Bryan Ferry because 'I tugged at his sleeve,' presumably back at the Midland Hotel in 1972. His name-dropping was relentless. 'Howard Devoto is staying with my friend Linder this week, so I'm going over tomorrow to chew the fat, as they say. Don't you think I'm an interesting person?' He (successfully) beseeched Mackie to listen not only to Ludus, but to the wryly intellectual pop group Monochrome Set, and felt compelled to note that he had received a letter from that band's lead singer too. To one of the pair's more mutual musical reference points, the Velvet Underground, he turned the subject around (repeatedly) to that of their debut album's headline singer, Nico: 'She's living nearby and can often be seen whirling about glamorous Manchester in a black cape humming "Le Pattite Chevalie."'

It was (partly) true: Nico *was* living in Manchester and, despite a well-known heroin addiction, being managed out of a room in the New Hormones office by local promoter Alan Wyse. Though very much in Factory's shadow, New Hormones maintained an interesting roster – Dislocation Dance, Diagram Brothers, Eric Random and, of course, Ludus – and its central location meant that the artists would stop by frequently. Richard Boon and Peter Wright grew familiar with a heavily stoned Nico sharing office space with a persistent Steven Morrissey, who would set himself up with a cup of tea and a desk on the basis that when he sat down to write it would typically be a review or letter in praise of Ludus. (Absent a phone at Mayfield Road through 1980, he availed himself of that utility whenever at New Hormones.) Wright thought of Morrissey at the time as 'somebody who had this crush on Linder. He was a smart guy but he was . . . kind of one of the crowd in Manchester. Didn't seem like anything was going to happen.'

Richard Boon had more faith. 'He hung around a lot and eavesdropped on conversations with people and picked stuff up. He had talent but hadn't found an outlet. Informally meeting him was always fascinating because he was aware of his interests and took them really seriously. And he was driven. You just knew this person would break through in some kind of cultural endeavour.' At one point, Boon said, Morrissey handed him a cassette of himself singing what he recalled as an old Bessie

Smith number: 'Wake Up Johnny', a choice of title that Boon, at least, subsequently found eerily prophetic.[6] Not surprisingly, Boon would prove somewhat dismissive of the notion of Morrissey as a perpetually depressed individual. 'Even though he was locked in his bedroom, looking in the mirror, he was actually looking out. And his magpie eyes were on the prize. I think there's been far too much melodrama attached to the bedroom.'

In the midst of this period, during which Morrissey went from mere fanzine contributor and pestering letter writer to published author and concert reviewer, he decided to write a book on Howard Devoto. This was a brave endeavour, given that Devoto was Linder's ex, and Morrissey's view of him appeared to vacillate according to access. Morrissey had rightly enthused about the Buzzcocks from their earliest days, citing Devoto as a large part of the group's appeal, but in the summer of 1978, shortly after opening for Devoto's new band Magazine at the Ritz, he wrote, 'I find Howard Devoto's voice very irritating and his lyrics are often plain bad.' By the start of the new decade, he had changed his mind again ('my recent discovery, Howard makes me proud to be a Mancunian,' he wrote to Hutton of how he was busy listening to 'all of Magazine's records'), and eventually cited *The Real Life of Soap* as his second favourite album of 1980 (the Monochrome Set's *The Strange Boutique* took first prize). The following March, he warned Tony Wilson, 'Watch for my book on poor Howard, who we all thought was bald enough to know better.' Yet within the month, he had heard that 'Lord Howard' would not consent to an interview, thereby scuppering the project, and Morrissey's opinion about the man's music changed once more: 'Magazine's new LP is – scoop! – "Pepsi-Cola". Dull, dull, dull. Thank God for the Associates!'

It remains uncertain whether Morrissey socialised at all with Devoto during this period: 'In 1976 or 1977 I remember Linder telling me about an "interesting" guy she'd met called Steven

Morrissey – but that's about it,' wrote Devoto to the author in response to his own interview request about these days in Manchester. 'I met him for the first time in 1985.'

Morrissey's correspondence with Robert Mackie continued throughout, the Glaswegian eventually taking up an offer to visit Manchester and stay on Kings Road. Morrissey announced that he could be recognised by his overcoat; his outer garment had become something of a fashion statement among certain northern bands and their followers and Morrissey would hardly be seen in anything else for the next couple of years. Having assured Mackie that they shouldn't expect anything of each other, Morrissey then humourously teased his visitor with the warning. 'After I've tied you to the rack, the bizarre Texan sexual ritual begins. You'll never believe what my sister can do with cotton wool and a tennis racket!'

As it turned out, the encounter proved tepid. 'Although he immediately made me feel very welcome,' said Mackie, 'I never felt as comfortable as I should have.' This was hardly surprising given the culture shock of the occasion for the younger, less-travelled of the pen-pals. After shopping for writing materials and going out for dinner (that was Betty Dwyer's suggestion, Mackie not being a vegetarian), Morrissey took Mackie to 'a bar hosted by a well-known Mancunian transvestite,' most likely Foo Foo's Palace. There, he grilled Mackie about his willingness to work a menial job, something he had already raised in writing. Back at Kings Road, where artwork for his James Dean book and the 'Orgasm Addict' sleeve was on display, Morrissey showed Mackie a collage of Bowie cuttings he had put together for a school art project, for which he was scored poorly due to the teacher's negative view of Bowie's 'bi-sexuality'. All in all, it was hardly surprising that Mackkie felt 'out of my depth'.

It would be several months after their visit before Mackie would dare resume the correspondence – at which Morrissey picked up right where it had left off. 'I'm sorry your visit here ended miserably, but that was your own fault. I will say that I did enjoy meeting you, but I often felt that you seemed to wish that you weren't here . . . But I never promised you that you'd have a good time, did I? Accept me for what I am – completely unacceptable.'

CHAPTER ELEVEN

Punk made me hungry and thirsty for experience and knowledge. Where was I going to get it? By working in a clothes shop and hanging out in a record shop.

— JOHNNY MARR, March 2011

The break-up of White Dice was probably the best thing that could have happened to Johnny Marr, in that it finally set him free from his neighbourhood mentors. At the age of fifteen, he had wanted to be seventeen; now that he was seventeen, he had no desire to be any older. 'I realised the power of my own age, and I was no longer looking upwards to the older guys that their lives were better. I looked around and thought, "This is our time."'

His sense of self-satisfaction was hardly unique; seventeen is typically a point of self-realisation amongst British youth. In Marr's case, though, this sense of self-realisation was propelled by an almost inordinate amount of personal and professional activity. As with Steven Morrissey at a similar age, relations with his father had reached a nadir – but in Marr's case, it was not the parents' marriage that was the problem. 'I thought he was from a different world to me and he probably was,' said Marr. 'And he thought I was this cocky, out-of-control law unto myself, which I probably was. We were both right.' Unable to talk through their differences, Johnny figured of his father 'that he wanted to see the back of me,' and packed his bags. (His mother, with whom he was so close, supported the break.) Only many years later, when the distance between them had narrowed again, did John Maher confess that the day his son moved out of Churchstone Walk was one of the saddest of his life.

A friend named Oliver May told Marr about an attic room available in the 'big funky Victorian house' he lodged at with Shelley Rohde and her four children in Bowdon, an upscale part of Altrincham, just west of Wythenshawe. Rohde was a local icon. Leaving (thirteen successive!) schools at age sixteen, she had become the first female correspondent in Moscow; had covered the Hungarian revolution; and, upon moving to Manchester in the 1960s as a divorcée, had served as a columnist for the *Daily Mail*, presented news on Granada alongside Tony Wilson, and published an authoritative biography on L. S. Lowry. She managed all this at a time when women were still not considered an equal presence in the newsroom, let alone in foreign war zones. Marr seized on the opportunity for a more bohemian home environment, and in the absence of Rohde herself, who was on a book-writing sabbatical ('It was probably several weeks before Shelley was even aware that some teenage oik hoi polloi was up in her attic'), successfully endeared himself to her three musically inclined sons, one of whom had even soundproofed a room, and the lone daughter, a ''60s flower child' just younger than Angie. Marr would maintain the attic apartment at Shelley Rohde's as his home base for a substantial period of time.

In the meantime, he and Angie took a Saturday job at Aladdin's Cave in the infamous Arndale Centre (the largest indoor shopping centre in Europe, and arguably the ugliest as well; no surprise that it was designed by the same architects as Hulme Crescents). What started out as 'a dodgy Goth shop' – a reference to the music and fashion movement that had its roots in post-punk Yorkshire – mutated into something more London-centric as the young couple began taking journeys down to Johnson's, the trend-setting rock 'n' roll store on London's King's Road – where, not coincidentally, Billy Duffy was now working behind the counter. Under its own name Johnson's was the modernist store of choice for the likes of the Jam and the Pretenders; a second label, the more retro La Rocka, was worn by the Stray Cats, Iggy Pop, and financially flush followers of a booming rockabilly revival. (This was, after all, the peak period of British youth style, with more fashion movements and revivals competing for teenage savings than probably at any point in history.) Johnny and Angie were careful, however, not to become the distinctive store's fashion victims; 'on the train on the way up' to Manchester, stressed Marr, the look 'got translated' into something more regional and personal.

Angie went on to work as receptionist and hair model at the salon Vidal Sassoon in the city centre (a poster of her was soon hanging in the store window), and Marr 'got poached' by the store Stolen from Ivor, where he joined his schoolmate, the Bowie/Roxy fanatic Phil Powell. Stolen from Ivor had enjoyed an impeccable reputation in the '70s for outfitting football fans in their Oxford bags and star jumpers, as preferred by a prepubescent Johnny Marr. But football fashions were moving on again, with the Liverpool Soul Boys and Manchester Perry Boys set to inspire a nationwide 'casuals' movement that placed high value on high-street fashion. Stolen from Ivor could not compete with the likes of Top Man; the owner took to sending Johnny and Angie to London instead, providing them with a blank cheque to buy clothes he told them he would resell. Lloyd Johnson took a liking to what he called the 'two little lovebirds', and began gifting them their outfits – something not even most of his rock-star customers could expect. Once it became apparent that Stolen from Ivor 'started to copy' Johnson's fashions, according to Marr, he and Brown kept the free clothes for themselves and used the owner's chequebook to buy 'crap.' And when Marr heard that a more reputable chain of street clothing from Yorkshire, X-Clothes, was opening up a Manchester store on Chapel Walks, he went for an interview and talked himself into a job.

As with the other staff, he was hired more for his own sense of style than any ability to fold clothes. The employee sent over from the store's Sheffield headquarters, for example, brought with him a Yorkshire Goth's interest in Clock DVA, Fad Gadget, and the Banshees, while the local assistant manager was into more esoteric indie music like the Fall and Australia's Birthday Party. They were all listening to the sounds coming out of Liverpool, where Echo & the Bunnymen in particular were proving that a northern rock band could develop a nationwide cult following centred on psychedelic guitar music and a charismatic lead singer. Then there was the new label from Edinburgh, Postcard, whose marquee acts Orange Juice, Josef K and Aztec Camera suggested that pop, if approached with sufficient élan, need not be a swear word. The Americans, meanwhile, continued to prove that they did dirty rock 'n' roll – from the Cramps to the Gun Club – better than anyone. It was, in short, a fascinating and fertile period for music, regardless of the gradual domination of the charts by synth-pop acts.

The band that Marr and Andy Rourke set about forming, however, now that White Dice had bit the dust, ignored most of these influences and aimed instead straight for the dance floor. In such a transformation they were hardly alone. Of the punk heavyweights, the Clash had gone off in a dozen different directions of groove on *London Calling* and *Sandinista!*, while the Jam were doing their level best to follow suit, and Johnny Rotten's post-Sex Pistols band, Public Image Ltd, had similarly immersed itself in the rhythms of the dance floor with 'Death Disco' and the album *Metal Box*. The migration was apparent too, across the Factory stable, with New Order, A Certain Ratio and Blackpool's Section 25 all placing increasing faith in programmed rhythms and 12" mixes. And it was reflected in the (newly established) independent charts, where probably the biggest record of 1981 was 'Papa's Got a Brand New Pigbag', a wild,

James Brown-influenced 12" instrumental by a band called Pigbag that had splintered off from the once-uncompromising Pop Group.[1]

As teenagers fresh out of school, with a wage packet in their pockets, Marr and Brown, often with Rourke in tow, were frequently to be found in 1981 dancing the night away at Legends disco in the town centre. They were soon joined by their new drummer, 'Funky' Si Wolstencroft. He and Rourke had met at a pub in Sale; invited back to Wolstencroft's house after closing time with the familiar explanation that the host's parents were out of town, Rourke had been followed by several dozen 'party-crashers' who trashed the place.[2] The bass player stuck around to help clean up in the morning, and a friendship was formed. He and Wolstencroft bonded musically, too, over their enthusiasm for a thriving British jazz-funk scene that included the acts Light of the World and Central Line but was most specifically focused on the band Level 42, whose front man, Mark King, played bass at considerable speed (and height). Catering to a section of the working class often disparaged as the 'Ford Cortina crowd', Level 42 managed to divide the British public in the early 1980s almost as much as the Smiths would just a couple of years later. Johnny Marr, certainly, was not part of that band's demographic, but the guitarist's own devotion to the dance floor saw him readily embrace the new rhythm section's love of slap bass, syncopated rhythms and pervasive hi-hat.

Freak Party, as the trio called themselves, secured a rehearsal space at Decibelle Studios, a former cotton mill on Jersey Street, in the heart of Industrial-era Ancoats, where they auditioned on an ongoing basis for a singer.[3] Yet the longer they played without one, the more complete – and complex – became their sound without, and therefore the harder for a would-be vocalist to pitch himself over it. (It can't have helped that they frequently set Public Image Ltd's 'Flowers of Romance' as an audition track.) Undeterred, at the end of 1981, and unbe-knownst to the studio's owner, Marr recruited Decibelle's resident engineer, Dale Hibbert, to record two instrumentals live to tape.[4]

Wolstencroft believed that Freak Party was aspiring towards the music of ABC. (A former lo-fi electronic act from Sheffield now fronted by Stockport's own Martin Fry, ABC's flaunting of gold lamé suits, along with their übercommercial producer, Trevor Horn, made them arguably the archetype of what was fast becoming the new decade's commercial shift from post-punk monochrome to preprogrammed colour.) The reality was less polished: one of the demo tracks had Marr providing a slashing rhythmic guitar not unlike that of the Gang of Four; the other sounded like the Jam covering Pigbag.[5] Throughout, Rourke and Wolstencroft held down the sophisticated rhythms with impeccable precision; that the overall sound was representative of what was then a prevailing Manchester mind-set can be demonstrated by the fact that Tony Wilson himself showed up at X-Clothes one day and invited Marr to join Section 25, whose guitarist had left suddenly due to fear of flying, jeopardising their European tour with New Order in the process. Section 25 encapsulated Marr's varied tastes in modern music as well as any northern act, but they were based in Blackpool, fifty miles away, and Marr was determined to no longer play second fiddle (or hired guitarist) in any one else's band.

Indeed, Wolstencroft noted how, throughout this period, and regardless of their shared love of dance music, 'Johnny was total guitar mad, always had a guitar, always looked cool, always dressed like a rock star, talked, acted like one.' Through his clothing-store earnings, and his connections in town – he was bringing his friends' business to one of the leading instrument stores – he had even acquired a secondhand Gibson Les Paul, the guitar of choice for Johnny Thunders among others. He was at Decibelle one evening, rehearsing with Freak Party, playing that Les Paul through his equally beloved Fender Twin Reverb amp, when the door was kicked down and four policemen rushed in; they identified Marr, threw him against

a wall, handcuffed him and arrested him. It was perhaps indicative of his personality during this period that he could claim,
'I didn't know what for at the time; it could have been
anything.'

It turned out to be for something very serious. Marr's reputation as someone who knew everyone had seen him pestered
by a Saturday workmate to find a 'fence' who would buy some
art – sketches that had been stolen from their display at a local
restaurant. They just happened to be by L. S. Lowry, Manchester
and Salford's most renowned artist. If Marr's instinct had been
to not get involved (especially because his landlady happened
to be Lowry's biographer), his personality as a compulsive Mr
Fix-It found him eventually suggesting to the thief an introductory visit to his local pot dealer. Though Marr stressed that he
wanted no further part of any transaction, including profits, he
had consciously interjected himself into a criminal enterprise
– and it had now caught up with him.

The case came before magistrates' court, and the prognosis
was not positive. On the eve of his appearance, he recalled, 'I
said good-bye to Angie and good-bye to Andy. And I had
people telling me that they knew people who would keep an
eye out for me [in prison]. I was told that I wouldn't be seeing
my girlfriend or my guitar for six, eight months. It was terri-
fying.' In court, custodial sentences were handed down to
everyone involved in the case except, said Marr, for himself.
'The judge . . . just sentenced me to embarrassment and
stupidity.' He was saved, as he understood it, because 'I had
done it without trying to make anything from it, I was just
trying to get this guy off my back.' It was both a close escape
and a valuable lesson; while Marr had relished his reputation
as a lad about town, he had no interest in becoming the sort
of 'wide boy' whose petty crimes led to a lifetime of increasing
jail sentences.

Ironically, it was for another form of criminal behaviour
that Freak Party eventually disbanded. With the father rarely
at home, the Rourke household on Hawthorn Lane had been

steadily descending into an ever-deeper pit of narcotics, the drug abuse so brazen that users from the local fire station would stop by in their truck to pick up supplies, thinking nothing of the attention they might be bringing to the house. More important, though, the drugs themselves had changed. 'We had gone from pot to smack,' admitted Andy Rourke, and 'the guy who was the dealer was now a lodger in the house.' As the second youngest of the four children, Andy was powerless to stop the dealing. And he found himself equally unable to keep from dabbling in heroin. He mostly just smoked it, very rarely snorted it, and was sufficiently scared of needles as to make sure that he never injected it, but it was a part of his attraction to the dark side, to the notion of 'scary', to the thought that he wasn't long for the world. In short, he liked it.

Marr did not. 'The scene at Andy's started off being very much about teenagers with guitars, and then other people started to come around who didn't have a musical bone in their body. The connection was drugs, and when it became nothing about music, then it was nothing about me.' Marr's fondness for weed, and his devotion to Keith Richards and Johnny Thunders, both of whom were closely associated with the allure of heroin (indeed, both of whom could be accused of glamorising it), suggests a degree of hypocrisy. But it also indicates an understanding of different drugs and their varying degrees of dependency and addiction. In addition, Marr had an opinion on the social causes behind the sudden flood of cheap heroin: 'It was a slow, insidious thing that was much less to do with rock-'n'-roll decadence than early '80s Manchester. And a lot to do with Thatcherism.'

Manchester's particular decline was evidenced in the release of the 1981 census, which revealed that it was one of the top three cities for percentage of single-parent households. Only Liverpool had a lower rate of car ownership. Fully 50 per cent of Manchester's housing stock was owned and rented out by the council. And the number of unemployed males (one in five, a figure that rocketed to one in three in Marr and Rourke's age group) was higher even than in the 1931 census, during the height of the Depression. Under the circumstances, it should have come as no surprise that uprisings occurred in Steven Morrissey's former home area of Moss Side in the summer of 1981, although, like those in London's Brixton and Liverpool's Toxteth that preceded them, they were predominantly the result of West Indian immigrant youth fighting police oppression and were conveniently labelled as 'race riots'.[6] The white working class seemed less willing to revolt, and Marr thought he understood why. 'If these kids are getting up in the morning and their main concern is nicking a hair dryer from Boots to get some heroin, it stops them from saying "Why have I got no job?" and "Why have I got no education?" I put that together. It was pretty sinister.'

But it didn't mean he was going to hang around heroin. The final straw occurred when Freak Party returned from a rehearsal, Johnny with Angie in tow as usual. Marr was staying at a (unnamed) friend's house for a few days. 'I went into the kitchen and one of my mates was shooting up another mate [neither of whom was Andy Rourke], and I did literally go get my bag, and I said to Angie, "We're out of here, we're not coming back, I'll tell you why when we get on the train."'

He and Andy Rourke would not speak again for several months. In fact, it was not certain at the time that they ever would.

IF THE BREAKUP of White Dice had served to push him out of the reactionary Wythenshawe rock scene and onto the dance floor, then the collapse of Freak Party propelled Johnny Marr further towards the heart of central Manchester's modern action. He and Angie continued to go out dancing at night; it was a mark of their fashionable status that they were even allowed entry into gay clubs like Devilles. When, at a new weekly night called the Exit, Marr heard the familiar sound of 'Let's Start the Dance' by Hamilton Bohannon, it brought him back to the good old days of the West Wythy Youth Club, and he went off to find the DJ – who turned out to be none other than Andrew Berry, his former West Wythy pal. Berry had followed through on his ambition to become a hairdresser, but had additionally partnered up with flamboyant promoter friend John Kennedy, who had launched the Exit out of an existing nightclub in an attempt to emulate London's futurist fashion culture of 'Blitz Kids'. Though this scene had grown out of but a small group of Central London dandies, its influence would prove quite profound across the new decade. It had first come to the fore in the November 1980 issue of the new monthly magazine *The Face*, in which author Robert Elms – attempting unsuccessfully to peg it as the Cult with No Name – noted that the scene had already spread to Liverpool, Birmingham, even Southend. If there was no mention of Manchester, it was because that same issue of *The Face* carried a separate story, by future Smiths biographer Mick Middlehurst, on 'Pip's' Disco, where the Bowie and Roxy kids had danced their way through the punk explosion and were now enjoying a return to fashionable status thanks to the success of electronic pop by the Human League, Gary Numan and the like. The Exit opened very much as an attempt to provide a home for the new, younger generation of Manchester Pip's/Blitz Kids. Essentially, where Berry and Kennedy went, the colourful night people – as opposed to the dour, grey Factory Records raincoat crowd – followed. This made it ironic that Berry was to be found living on Palatine Road, just down the road from Factory Records, where his own abode was considered the nearest that Manchester had to a proper New York, Warhol-like Factory scene.

Marr not only took to staying over on Palatine Road but to working alongside Berry (known by his middle name, Marc, at the time) in the Exit DJ booth. Berry was the more accomplished mixer, but he noticed that Marr looked after his records more carefully – and had that many more of them, including many of the disco and funk classics from the mid-'70s. Along with much of hip Manchester – white and black, straight and gay – they were both fascinated by the modern disco emerging from New York: labels like Ze and O, producers like Lovebug Starski and J. Walter Negro, and genres like 'electro' and 'hip-hop', which, they understood, were not mere novelties but style movements in their own right. This was the same sound and look that was proving highly influential on New Order, who were so impressed by the scene they had discovered upon playing New York that they had set about opening their own nightclub, the Haçienda, in conjunction with Factory, in a former boat showroom in central Manchester. The Haçienda's artistic director, Mike Pickering, even stopped in at X-Clothes one day to show Marr the floor plans.

Back in Altrincham, Marr had made friends with Pete Hunt, manager of the store Discount Records, who had encouraged the teenager to increase his musical knowledge even further via a growing (or renewed) love for 1960s girl pop, from Motown to the Shangri-Las, Sandie Shaw to Dusty Springfield. Hunt was an outgoing character in his own right and, following a social trip to London, invited Matt Johnson, who had just released the critically acclaimed album *Burning Blue Soul* on London's new esoteric independent 4AD Records, up to Manchester, suspecting he and Marr would hit it off. Johnson, always eager to widen his worldview, took Hunt up on the offer, and when introduced to Marr at X-Clothes, was duly impressed by 'how friendly, enthusiastic, and quick-witted he was' – and how closely Marr had been listening to *Burning Blue Soul*. That evening, Marr brought his guitar around to Hunt's house, eager to learn some of the songs. Instead, 'We opened some beers, snorted some lines of speed, picked up our guitars, and had a jam session,' recalled Johnson. 'We swapped riffs, stories about records, guitars, equipment and much else.' Then they went out to Legends 'to dance the night away.'

As this friendship developed, the twenty-year-old Johnson was bowled over by the younger guitarist's talents, noting that Marr 'had a natural fluency that only comes with much practice and a love of the instrument,' and that 'he was able to play lots of other people's songs,' whereas Johnson could only play his own. 'He had that young gunslinger vibe about him and seemed to see himself as naturally next in line of the great English guitarists: [Jeff] Beck, [Jimmy] Page, [Keith] Richards. He struck me as very confident yet not arrogant, with a real hunger to learn but with a deep-down certainty of who he was, where he was going, and how he was going to get there.'

For a while it seemed possible that Marr's journey would entail joining Johnson's band, to be called The The. But 'I was coming from a much more left-field area compared to where Johnny was at that point,' said Johnson, who had worked or performed live with such experimental and credible acts as This Heat, Wire and Cabaret Voltaire. 'It was quite a different place to where Johnny was musically at that point, which was more classic British and American pop songwriting.' The pair concluded that Marr 'was the right person at the wrong time' and vowed to remain friends.

JOE MOSS HAD come of age during the 1960s glory days (and all-nighters) of the Twisted Wheel, Manchester's immortal R&B club, where the resident DJ Roger Eagle had turned him on to soul music and he had witnessed several seminal live perform-ances at the peak of the British blues revival. Two decades later and Roger Eagle had moved to Liverpool, where he had proven equally (if unexpectedly) influential on that city's post-punk scene at the nightclub Eric's. For his own part, Moss had become extraordinarily successful in the clothing business. He had been one of the instigators of Manchester's pioneering store Eighth Day, launched in 1970 as a 'craft exchange' under the notion that 'on the seventh day God rested, on the eighth day He

(She or It) created something better.'[7] Noticing a gap in the market for fashionable but unavailable 'loon pants', Moss and a partner sewed a half-dozen pairs together, dropped them off at Eighth Day – and watched them sell in a single morning. Within a few months they were making several hundred pairs a week and had hired the staff and bought the equipment to do so. They named the business after a song by Moss's musical idol Van Morrison: 'Crazy Face'.

Through the 1970s, Moss lived an enviably profitable existence outside of the rat race. On Friday evenings, he would load a week's worth of newly manufactured clothing into his Citroën DS (the seats removed for extra cargo space), drive down to London, and deliver them to a prominent retail dealer at a house-cum-discotheque off Fulham Road. There his products would be immediately bundled into various black sacks for distribution to stores across the capital – and Moss paid in cash. By the dawn of the 1980s, he and his partner were renting several floors at 70 Portland Street in the heart of Manchester, where they employed as many as sixty people. They also owned two retail stores of their own. One was in Stockport; the other was on Chapel Walks, right next to X-Clothes.

In 1982, X-Clothes was the hipper of these two retail outfits. But Crazy Face had the credibility, a result not only of longevity but its manufacturing capabilities. (Owning a factory meant they could have a new line of clothing on the racks a week after formulating the idea.) As a sign that it was beyond the constant turnover in youth fashions, the Crazy Face store played music by Moss's preferred blues artists, and its walls were hung with high-quality photographs of rock, blues and jazz legends that he had picked up on his travels. Marr was now listening to more of this music, thanks in part to Pete Hunt entrusting him with Discount Records' entire stock when he packed up to travel around Europe. Marr's attic room in Bowdon was suddenly stacked to the rafters with vinyl from across the ages, affording him almost infinite access to vintage rock 'n' roll and '60s pop, which in turn led him to forage through secondhand record stores, searching out old Motown singles in particular. As he spent more time at Crazy Face during his lunch hour, soaking up the older music and perusing the photographs, he took to asking who owned them, whether he could talk to that person about them.

He eventually got the opportunity one such lunchtime when Moss came over to his satellite store. Introduced by the Crazy Face shop's manager, Marr held out his hand to Moss – a mark of respect for his elder in a city not widely given to formality – and said, 'My name is Johnny Marr, and I'm a frustrated musician.' Alerted by something in the teenager's direct approach, Moss invited Marr to take the short stroll over to Portland Street someday, where he kept a guitar of his own. (Moss was taking lessons from a former member of the Mindbenders, though he had no pretentions as to his ability; he was happy just hammering out a blues riff on the lower strings.) Marr took him up on the offer, and in response to Moss's request to be shown a Smokey Robinson riff, played 'Tracks of My Tears' – chords, arrangement, and vocal melody included. It was the same self-taught orchestration technique he had perfected in his Wythenshawe bedroom with 'All the Young Dudes'.

Moss was no neophyte. In the front rows at the Twisted Wheel, he'd stood almost nose-to-nose with some of the greatest blues guys in the world – including John Lee Hooker and Sonny Boy Williamson – and their many British imitators, such as Alexis Korner, Jack Bruce, Cyril Davis and Eric Clapton. As with Matt Johnson, with whom Moss had little else in common, something in what he heard put Marr straight into a similar league: 'This little kid, sat across the table from me, just blew me away completely,' he recalled.

The pair took to meeting most lunchtimes. Soon enough, Moss invited Johnny and Angie to dinner at his house in Heaton Chapel, where he lived with his second wife, Janet, and their baby son. Over the course of that evening, Moss found that 'my thoughts about this guy were pretty spot-on.

He seemed quite well sorted for someone who obviously wasn't a wealthy lad, who didn't have any spare money at all.' In addition, it was apparent 'from the word go [that] Angie was a great, intelligent woman, a real source of strength to him.'

Moss had an extensive record collection of his own, and could help steep Marr in the history of music, but he couldn't teach the teenager anything about musicianship itself. Likewise, Moss had a long-standing interest in 'the mechanics' of the music business from reading the music papers for twenty years, and was a highly successful entrepreneur, but he had never managed a band. For the time being, he took on what was, in the wake of Marr's exit from his family nest, an even more important role: that of the surrogate father – a supporting, nurturing and calming figure in the life of an eager if impatient young prodigy. Over the countless hours they spent together, at Chapel Walks, Portland Street or Halesden Road in Heaton Chapel, they learned to trust each other, implicitly.

MINUS A BAND, Marr's musical compositions changed dramatically during this period. As he described it, 'Because I was writing songs on my own, they became less riff-based, and much more about chords.' It was a crucial difference. As he began working up some of the progressions that would soon make their way into Smiths songs, and as he talked musical history with Moss, he became ever more interested in the 1950s and 1960s hit factories. Marr soon grasped that he had been going about the band process backward. He needed to first find himself a proper lyricist as a partner – hopefully someone who was a viable vocalist as well – and *then* worry about a rhythm section. The problem, as he already knew all too well, was that the field of prospective candidates was limited; Marr was so far ahead of the game that most people his age were simply not up to the task. That was one of the reasons that he came around to the idea of approaching the twenty-two-year-old Steven Morrissey. Back when Billy Duffy had been with the Nosebleeds, he had shown Marr some of Morrissey's lyrics, and Marr had been mildly impressed. That they had met – ever so briefly – at a Patti Smith show suggested an important shared reference point. (Marr went so far as to say of the Smith connection that it was 'one of the things that gave me the balls to go and knock on Morrissey's door.') But all he really knew that Morrissey had achieved in the years since was this locally distributed book on the New York Dolls, and although that meant that they shared another piece of common musical ground, it still wasn't an awful lot to go on. And yet something about Morrissey's reputed enigma, his supposed eccentricity, and his apparent literary talents, kept bringing the guitarist back to the same question: Might this be his man? He was either clutching at straws – or grasping for greatness. And he wouldn't know which until he tried it.

It was a fear he confided to Joe Moss, over a number of weeks, a matter that finally came to a head when they sat down in Heaton Chapel one night to watch a recent *South Bank Show* profile on Leiber and Stoller. Moss, who owned a coveted new VHS machine, had already seen it. So he knew to bring Marr's attention to the moment when the legends talked about how they met: the gregarious lyricist, Leiber, simply knocking on the door of the more taciturn musician, Stoller.[8]

Like Jerry Leiber before him, Johnny Marr was the walking antithesis of shyness. He had no qualms about knocking on anybody's door. (One of the better anecdotes of the period has the teenage Marr touting himself to Pete Shelley of the freshly disbanded Buzzcocks as a viable new guitar partner.) But something about Morrissey's reputation told him that in this particular case, the full-frontal assault would probably backfire. He approached Phil Fletcher for suggestions, as well as for confirmation that he wasn't heading up a dead end. Fletcher couldn't help him on the latter question – he hadn't spoken to Morrissey since they fell out over a Patti Smith concert review – and recommended Steve Pomfret as the best mutual contact. Marr duly pursued it all the way to Morrissey's door.[9]

Johnny Marr had a specific image at the time. It had a lot to do with Johnson's, and it was becoming increasingly influenced by the successful London punk-rock band Theatre of Hate, who were big on stylised quiffs and sleeveless jackets. (That Billy Duffy had just joined this group was beyond coincidence. From the Nosebleeds to Slaughter, Johnson's to Theatre of Hate, Duffy seemed to be living out the younger guitarist's fantasies; Marr even traded in his Les Paul for a Gretsch as favoured by Duffy in Theatre of Hate.) But the real inspiration was Stu Sutcliffe, the Beatles' original bass player, the one who looked so cool in leathers and shades and personalised haircut in his girlfriend Astrid Kirchherr's photographs, the one who stayed on in Hamburg to live with her and enrol in art school, the one who died of a brain haemorrhage before the Beatles made it. Stu Sutcliffe embodied a forgotten year in that musical period – 1961, when in theory, rock 'n' roll had died and pap ruled the pop charts. For those who truly knew what they were talking about, however – among them Joe Moss and now Johnny Marr – it was an era of new beginnings: not just the Beatles, but Tamla Motown, Phil Spector, the Beach Boys, the girl groups, the Brill Building, Leiber and Stoller, the British blues explosion, the subsequent beat boom, the British Invasion, and so on.

Knowing the importance of first impressions, Marr dressed in his finest to approach Morrissey. 'Wild One' biker boots. Vintage Levi's jeans 'rolled up exactly the right height.' A Johnson's sleeveless jacket and Johnson's shirt. A 'proper old American flying men's cap.' And, crucially, a 'tinted quiff' courtesy of hairdresser friend Andrew Berry.

Marr and Pomfret boarded a number 263 bus. It was lunch-time, and the sun was out, a rare treat in Manchester. It was May 1982. And when Steven Morrissey (eventually) descended the stairs, wearing his regulation cardigan and sporting a retro quiff of his own, he and Marr saw in each other, immediately, that their dreams just might be about to come true.

CHAPTER TWELVE

It was an event I'd always looked forward to and unconsciously been waiting for since my childhood. Time was passing – I was twenty-two – and Johnny was much younger, but it seemed that I'd hung around for a very long time waiting for this magical mystical event, which definitely occurred.

> – MORRISSEY, *Melody Maker*, September 1987

I think I thought he was waiting for the world to come to him. And it kind of did!

> – JOHNNY MARR, March 2011

The meeting at 384 Kings Road that May afternoon would turn out, as we know now, to be one of the great initial encounters of modern music. To quite some degree, both Morrissey and Marr recognised as much immediately, as evidenced by the extent to which Steve Pomfret's presence in the room was barely even acknowledged. Morrissey would prove more than capable of his familiar flippancy when it came to describing the occasion – 'I was just there, dying, and he rescued me,' he announced in an interview barely a year later, the fruits of the partnership apparent by the fact that he was appearing live on Radio 1 at the time – but generally speaking he sought to fully acknowledge the majesty, and indeed, the mystery, behind their seemingly unlikely attraction and how quickly it manifested into a collaboration of exceptional creativity and loyalty.

'I had no doubt that Johnny was *the moment*,' Morrissey explained to author-musician John Robb long after the event, 'and I was grateful that nothing had ever happened for me earlier on.' Certainly, Marr's carefully cultivated style that day had served its purpose in making a positive first impression. 'He looked a bit rockabilly, a bit wired and very witty, but also hard and indifferent. It was the exact opposite of the few rehearsals I'd had with Billy (Duffy) because with Johnny it was instantly right and we were instantly ready.'

This represented a crucial understanding on Morrissey's part. If he had developed a reputation for under-achievement on the musical front, it was because past experience had taught him not to get in too deep with the wrong partners. His gut instinct that day on Kings Road – that Marr was perfect for him in a way that Marr's neighbour and mentor Duffy was not – had him promise to call Marr within 24 hours. Being overly familiar with 'people who said they were going to do things and never did,' Marr could not be entirely sure that the call would come. But as it turned out, Morrissey's primary gripe with prospective partners was much the same as Marr's: 'So many people seem to enjoy talking about things and so few people seem to enjoy doing them,' as Morrissey put it upon release of the debut Smiths LP. ('And that's really been the history of the group, that we've got on with things,' he elaborated.) These mutual frustrations turned out to be one of many shared strengths and when Morrissey duly made the call to X-Clothes the following day, both of them knew that the partnership was on.

A few days later, Morrissey came over to Bowdon to work on songs. Stepping into Marr's abode, he could not have been anything but impressed. Morrissey, after all, had long dreamed of writing for *Coronation Street*, of finding some way into the entertainment world of Granada TV, and yet the teenage Marr was living inside that dream; his landlady was the great Shelley Rohde, and her living room walls were decorated with vast framed pictures of the *Corrie* stars. Upstairs, Marr's attic room offered, at least, a similar sense of obsession to that of Morrissey's bedroom back in Stretford: walls (and floors) of vinyl to match Morrissey's collection of books, guitars (and accompanying recording paraphernalia) for his typewriter and pens. But the pair had not met this second time to spin each other's 45s as much as to write them, to get to work and see if the initial spark of a few days earlier could light a fire.

The prospective lyricist and singer had already supplied the composer and guitarist with a cassette of himself singing a song entitled 'Don't Blow Your Own Horn', but despite having a few days to live with it, Marr had not been able to come up with a viable chord sequence, as evidenced by Morrissey's disappointed reaction. The musical partnership only took off when they moved on to work from a metaphorical blank sheet of paper: two sets of Morrissey words unconstrained by an existing melody. One of them was 'The Hand That Rocks the Cradle', and Marr saw something in its phrasing that reminded him of Patti Smith's 'Kimberly'. (Given Patti Smith's iconic influence on both Morrissey and Marr, and the fact that they had met so briefly at one of her concerts four years earlier, the use of the 'Kimberly' riff was as much an act of homage and tribute as theft. The similarities in the finished songs are minuscule.) The other was 'Suffer Little Children' and, in this case, *not* seeing a reference point from which he could similarly crib a riff, Marr came up with an arpeggio chord sequence on the spot. Morrissey expressed his enthusiasm in both cases, and the pair set about completing the songs there and then. Within a couple of hours, working in the same manner as the great 1960s songwriting partnerships that they so admired and to which they both aspired, the pair came up with the songs that would close out the two sides of their debut album. As auspicious starts go, this was one for the record books.

While much can and has been made of the music Marr composed that day, what was truly astonishing was that Morrissey turned up in Bowdon carrying a pair of poems of such emotional and literary depth. In comparison to his cut-and-paste biographies for Babylon, his hack gig reviews for *Record Mirror* . . . well, there simply *was* no comparison. Neither 'The Hand That Rocks the Cradle' nor 'Suffer Little Children' had any obvious reference points in the popular culture of the time, not even on the post-punk independent scene where, for the last three or four years, anything had been possible – including the recitation of poetry to whatever metre (or lack thereof) took the author's fancy. Morrissey, to his credit, knew as much. 'I was a bookworm,' he admitted readily in 1985. 'I was also an avid record collector and the two of them didn't seem to go together. But I always felt that they could, because the way I wrote, when I wrote words, it wasn't the traditional pop nonsense. It was quite literary.'

Indeed. 'The Hand That Rocks the Cradle' was anything *but* traditional pop nonsense. It appeared, on the surface of its title, to express the love of a parent for his or her infant child – an uncommon enough subject for a young working class lyricist, but one that turned out to be merely the bait before the switch. Reference to 'blood on the cleaver tonight' intimated something much more sinister, leading towards a gradual elaboration in the later verses, a veiled admittance by what was now clearly a male protagonist, of some form of unstated abuse on a male child, a child that may not even have been his own. And yet, as taboo subject matter goes, it was instantly outdone by 'Suffer Little Children', which dared detail that which was not discussable in Manchester: the Moors Murders. 'Fresh lilaced moorland fields/cannot hide the stolid stench of death,' Morrissey stated of the crimes and, in accordance with this couplet, he made no attempt to sugar coat his own lyrics. References were made to victims Lesley-Anne [Downey], John [Kilbride] and Edward [Evans] by name; and Morrissey quoted Myra Hindley directly, and thereby Ian Brady by association, as saying 'Whatever he has done, I have done,' and using poetic licence elsewhere to lightly alter Hindley's phrase. The fact that both the song title 'Suffer Little Children' and the lyrical couplet 'Hindley wakes' were chapter titles from *Beyond Belief*, Emlyn Williams' dramatically enhanced account of the Moors Murders (Marr recalled seeing a poster for the book on Morrissey's wall the day that they met), or that individual lines had similarities to specific expressions elsewhere in the book, really mattered very little. If only for having the courage to write the line 'Oh Manchester, so much to answer for,' a refrain that would inspire greater soul-searching in the Lancashire capital than any number of essays or editorials on the Moors Murders, Morrissey had already proven himself a poet beyond contemporary – or at least conventional – compare.

Both Morrissey and Marr have suggested that it was this second meeting that properly launched their relationship. And each has recalled that they laid out not so much a wish list that day as a game plan. They talked about the band they would form, and how they would dress alike, and stand close to each other in photographs, draped over each other if need be, like the New York Dolls. They decided that their first single would have a blue label, that it would be laid out like one of the 1960s hit factory releases rather than in any of the styles of the present day. They decided too, that they would like to be on Rough Trade – an understandable quest, especially given that the London label had recently added the Fall, the Monochrome Set and Aztec Camera to its roster, but a distant one, given that Morrissey and Marr didn't have a single contact at the company. And in confirming that they would write for other artists as well, per Leiber and Stoller and the '60s hit factories in general, they agreed immediately that Sandie Shaw would be their first choice. Years later, long after the split, long after the court case, and in an attempt to find some common ground and happy memories, Marr and Morrissey would meet up once more, and remind each other that everything they laid out that evening, they achieved.

OVER THOSE YEARS, Morrissey and Marr would frequently try and define the chemistry that lay at the heart of their partnership, while simultaneously acknowledging that it was ultimately intangible. (Or, as the Buzzcocks put it in one of their finest

197

recordings, presumably discussing love, 'Why Can't I Touch It?') Morrissey tended to the more matter-of-fact approach. 'We moved very very quickly,' he once recounted, acknowledging that while 'I thought of the name the Smiths . . . it was Johnny's venture. We both had an astonishingly solid sense of direction, and we very rarely disagreed which was unusual because we were opposites – he was full of excitement for everything and I was . . . *not*.'

Too much would be made over time of the pair as opposites – in geniality, exuberance, hedonism, sexuality; in hours kept, clothes worn and books read. In fact, as already noted, they had a phenomenal amount in common: Irish immigrant parents, working class roots, a single female sibling (within close age range), a strong relationship with mother and a distant one with father, the violent drudgery of the Manchester Catholic Schools system, and forced slum clearance from the inner city. Their musical tastes, too, while often defined by where they divulged – Morrissey's love for the Cilla Black of 1968 versus Marr's passion for the Rolling Stones of that year – were for the most part in stark alignment. Each was as fanatical about the New York Dolls and Patti Smith as they were turned on by T. Rex and Sparks. Each was devoted to the glamorous girl groups and solo female singers of the 1960s, and to the methodical workaday approach of the Brill era songwriters. And each came to the other at a time when the rockabilly revival was in full swing, and each a part of it according to his specific style. 'Johnny had his more modern approach, which was all the Hard Times/ripped jeans/La Rocka thing,' noted Andrew Berry. 'And Morrissey had that whole English thing after rock 'n' roll hit but before the Beatles.' The distance between Morrissey's fascination with the saga of Billy Fury and Marr's obsession with the look of Stu Sutcliffe was therefore no real distance at all – or, as Berry put it, 'Johnny's and Morrissey's styles merged . . . (They) influenced each other so two ideas came into one.'

Morrissey, for sure, was the more literate of the pair, and

Marr clearly the more musical, but of course that was merely the difference in their parts that added up to the sum of the Smiths, and the fact that both instantly recognised the abilities of the other was surpassed only by the fact that they tended not to interfere with or second-guess each other's contributions when writing and recording music together. Rather, they set to work on making the partnership visible. Or, as Marr told *Sounds* at the end of 1983, 'The whole idea of two people getting together with lots of common ground but with separate influences to bring out something we believe to be the best we've ever heard is something we feel has been missing since the Sixties. It's joyous the way we work together and if that's reminiscent of the Sixties that's fine.'

Almost thirty years later, Marr was able to elaborate upon the 'joyous' aspect of that collaboration. 'One thing that was never in doubt was my time and my dedication and the songs. But I met someone who was equally dedicated.' In the early days, Morrissey appeared no less driven to succeed than Marr; it was only after success hit in such a big way that the singer would develop a reputation for cancellations and disappearances. And so, said Marr, 'It was a fantastic thing to happen. If it was possible for me to be an even happier guy, it happened. Because I've got the most perfect relationship with the girl of my dreams. And then I met this guy I admire. And I'm able to share a side of me that he innately understands. Which is separate to "let's form a group." There's a thing inside him of what you can be. Without trying to sound too esoteric, it takes up half of your being. This desire to fulfil this . . . *knowing* about yourself as an artist. There's an unusual aspect to both our personalities that we both understand. It's about having a knowing of this vision of something that you can do and something that you can be, which is really a big part of you. I'm not just talking about success, it's about being *Johnny Marr*, or being *Morrissey*.'

Morrissey himself would frequently elaborate upon this sense of higher calling even as he avoided his partner's more spiritual observations. 'Though I always wanted to sing and I always wanted to make records, it was never really for the reasons that I felt most people did those kind of things,' he explained to MTV on the eve of playing the Royal Albert Hall, less than three years after he and Marr first met. 'I had no aspiration for stardom for the sake of stardom, for the sake of glamour, for the sake of money and elaborate clothing or lifestyle. It was never that. It was always for reasons that were much more serious – but not so serious I felt they were ungraspable for an audience.'

As such, both were adamant that they were driven by something much deeper than 'a relationship of convenience,' as Marr described the occasionally perceived notion that theirs was but merely a professional alliance. 'You can't need each other that intensely every day, on some convenient arrangement – it will not work. You can not need each other like that. And provide for each other. And be there for each other, if it's just about "here's a tune, here's some words." I'm not like that. I don't care about career enough to do that. I really don't.'

The fact was that the pair *did* need each other – and on a very deep, emotional level. There developed, undoubtedly, something much more than a friendship, but rather love between them such as can often be found on the battle field, occasionally on the sporting field, and which, when evident in a rock group too, inevitably fuels the flames of something erotic. Both Morrissey and Marr would occasionally invite such speculation, inadvertently or otherwise. 'I was so utterly impressed and infatuated,' said the singer of their initial encounter very shortly after the partnership dissolved, using a highly charged word, 'that even if he couldn't play it wouldn't have mattered because the seeds had been sown and from those seeds anything could sprout. He appeared at a time when I was deeper than the depths . . . he provided me with this massive energy boost. I could feel Johnny's energy just seething inside me.'

'From when we first met, we loved with each other,' said

Johnny Marr. 'We didn't fall in love *with* each other, because we respected that we both enjoyed having our own space and our own lives and we knew that was important. There was a very strong bond all the way through until the last couple of weeks of the band. And it was very very important. But we didn't fall in love *with* each other.'

'There was a love and it was mutual and equal,' confirmed Morrissey, 'but it wasn't physical or sexual.' From the singer's perspective, it would have been foolish to even dream of it being otherwise. The day that he went over to write songs with Marr for the first time, he was introduced to Angie Brown, who ferried him to the Altrincham train station in her VW Beetle. It was not a deliberate test of the prospective singer, not even a warning, but a mere confirmation of fact: 'You didn't get Johnny without Angie,' as Marr put it. Fortunately, Morrissey and Brown instantly warmed to each other, becoming close friends themselves, creating one of the many personality dynamics that would prove integral to the Smiths' ability to succeed as much – and to survive as long – as they did. So while it was true that Morrissey and Marr would spend considerable time travelling together and talking together, so it was likely that Brown would be in the driver's seat much of the time – and that Morrissey would often be the only passenger.

Besides, for all Morrissey's reputation as a loner, we already know that he was far from the suicidal figure he liked to paint himself as at the point that Marr arrived in his life. 'I think he was developing his own aesthetic,' said Marr of Morrissey up until that moment. 'And there's a lot to be said for cocooning oneself and doing research to make yourself who you want to be, intellectually and existentially.' Ultimately, 'I just went along with his explanation of it, really: Just sitting in his room. And I never saw any evidence that he was crushed by that activity.'

In fact, given Morrissey's intellect and his wit – in short, his way with words – Marr was not surprised to find that his new writing partner kept select but quality company. 'I didn't see him as someone who had zero friends,' said Marr, 'and the friends I met of his at that time,' citing James Maker, Richard Boon and Linder, 'I really liked, and I got along with. I had a tremendous amount of respect for all these people. His friends were cool. He never introduced me to anyone I didn't like.'

In turn, Marr took to introducing Morrissey to his own friends. Andrew Berry observed, as did so many at this point, before Morrissey truly found his voice (in the Smiths) that 'he was really quiet and private, especially when you were in the same room with him.' But Berry nonetheless sought to become Morrissey's friend – 'because if Johnny says he's cool then he obviously is.' And in this, Berry and his friends quickly grasped the great reality of the partnership: 'Johnny was very protective over him.'

'It's something I'll never regret, that relationship,' said Marr, 'because one day you get old – and hopefully very old – and you say, "Wow, I didn't see that relationship coming." Because it brought out something in me that maybe I didn't know I had, which was a very kind of prospective aspect. I just thought I was looking for a guy who was going to be a great lead singer.'

On Friday, 21 May 1982, towards the end of the same month, if not even the very same week, that Johnny Marr and Morrissey met for the first time, the Haçienda nightclub opened its doors on Whitworth Street in Manchester, the billing shared by ESG, the thrillingly contemporary all-girl New York electro/hip-hop trio, and Bernard Manning, the ageing, overweight, famously sexist, and decidedly unfashionable Manchester comedian. The club, also known early on by its catalogue number, FAC 51, was evidently trying at once to be both hip and ironic, and it would bounce uncertainly between these cultural extremes for several years to come. It did not help matters that Ben Kelly's industrial design turned out to be way ahead of its time, and that the acoustics bounced painfully about the vast club whenever it was less than half-full – which was most of the time

– or that the city only granted the alcohol license on condition of it being a members-only club. (Fortunately, members' guests were allowed entry too, or else the club would never have survived.)

History has suggested that the Smiths grew and operated in opposition to this perceived Haçienda aesthetic, that their performances at the club in 1983 represented an invasion of common sense and good taste, of a return to good-old uplifting guitar music in the midst of a Factory scene that had disappeared up its own sense of self-importance. 'The whole Haçienda thing,' Morrissey would reflect in the middle of that year, before even the second of their three shows at the club, and already using the past tense, 'seemed terribly antiseptic.'

The reality was that both Morrissey and Marr spent considerable time at the Haçienda when it opened. Indeed, it's of interest to the story of the Smiths' *own* aesthetic that through the early part of the group's development, both before and after the lineup was cemented, the two founding partners continued down their individual paths, accentuating in the process the marked differences between the two characters even as their friendship blossomed.

For his part, Johnny Marr remained firmly immersed in style culture; when Andrew Berry and John Kennedy organised a bus trip to the gay London nightclub Heaven (to see Animal Nightlife), in July 1982, he went along for the ride. And when Berry and Kennedy moved on to open a weekend night called Berlin, in a King Street basement club, Marr could be found there as well. So could Rob Gretton and Mike Pickering; despite the fact that the Haçienda was already booking the best of touring bands, it was struggling to pull people in for its dance nights, perhaps because the kind of kids they were looking for were over at Berlin instead. Berry was invited in for a meeting at the Haçienda and offered a role as a DJ. He agreed – on condition he could use the club as a hair salon during the day. He was duly given the use of a dressing room, and his new salon, Swing, assigned the catalogue number

FAC 98, was soon cutting hair for New Order as well as Morrissey and Marr and every visiting band that took advantage of the Haçienda's unlikely fashion opportunity. With Berry ensconced in the club six days and several nights a week, Marr, as his best friend, became an additional part of the Haçienda's inner circle, and though he never made a habit of spinning records there, he was frequently to be found hanging in the booth. In fact, when *The Face* commissioned a report on the Haçienda's progress at the end of 1982, amid the references to its 'bleak' landscape and half-filled dance floor was a quote from 'flat-top Johnny Marr' defending the Saturday night music policy: 'I schlepp to funk.'[1]

Contrary to his own subsequent dismissal of the place, Steven Morrissey could also be found hanging regularly at the Haçienda during its early days. That's where Cath Carroll and Liz Naylor first came across him, wearing his customary heavy overcoat on a typically quiet Saturday night shortly after the club opened; they got into a conversation with Linder there, and 'Steven came with Linder,' said Naylor. 'He was Linder's shadow.'

Carroll and Naylor were classic feminist children of punk, their desperately stifled teenage lives in the Manchester suburbs having been completely redirected at inner-city gigs by the Fall, and by moving into a council flat and surviving, as Carroll put it, 'single mothers who were drug addicts, and feral teenagers who would chase us.' With the support of Tony Wilson and others, they had gotten involved with the prominent local zine *City Fun*. They had also gotten involved with each other for a while, and their tendency to dress up in capes or anything else that caught their fancy ('it was so liberating just to be able to take off your polyester blouse and put on whatever you wanted to wear and go to a gig,' said Carroll) gained them almost as much notoriety on the scene as their band, Glass Animals. But by 1982, they were known (as the Crones, though good-naturedly so) for other reasons: in an act of wilful Stalinism against *City Fun*'s 'hippie, dope-smoking' editors, according to Naylor, they had 'hijacked the magazine on the way to the printers.' Their intent as *City Fun*'s new bosses was, said Carroll, to be 'irreverent' and 'oppositional.' 'We were just basically incredibly annoying. And people were amazingly indulgent.' No one proved more so than Richard Boon, who provided them with space at the New Hormones office on Newton Street. In accepting it, they had come into occasional contact with Linder, an obvious feminist icon, but were too intimidated by her reputation to converse with her: 'She was always in that fashionable atmosphere you don't ever think you're going to penetrate,' said Carroll. This made it all the more surprising when Boon said that Linder wanted them to manage Ludus; only after they accepted did they realise that 'as a daring lesbian duo,' in Naylor's words, they were being 'appointed managers as an art project.'

Following their introduction to Morrissey at the Haçienda, a four-way friendship quickly developed, an extension of the one that already existed between the two pairs of close friends. Typically, the relationship was conducted in person, by mail, and on foot. 'Everyone walked around Manchester at the time,' said Naylor. 'You were poor, you had to. Also, we didn't have a phone. Steven would write us letters. He would write letters, like, "We will meet at the gates of the cemetery," and that would be a jolly day out.'

Not that he always showed up for a proposed rendezvous. On one such occasion when they felt they had been stood up, the Crones decided to visit him on Kings Road to find out why. 'We were sure that he was in,' said Carroll, 'but he just didn't open the door. I wrote to him to say, "Where were you?" and he wrote back to say "I wasn't there. Give me proof that you were."' It was that sort of relationship. 'His truculence manifested itself [in that] if you sort of said the wrong thing, he would not communicate,' said Naylor. 'But communication was very slow in those days, so it was hard to tell if he was sulking or the post was late.'

The arrival of unemployment cheques would result in some pronounced attempt at upward mobility, 'ending up in these wine bars with hairdressers from Vidal Sassoon,' according to Naylor, an interesting if unintentional statement, given that Johnny Marr's best friend was a hairdresser and his girlfriend a Vidal Sassoon model. They might also celebrate the appearance of cash with tea at the historic Kendal Milne department store on Deansgate, where Linder, recalled Carroll, 'would produce something ridiculous from her handbag, some absurd sex toy, and she would put it on the table next to these tiny little chocolate cakes,' successfully frightening the ageing blue-rinse brigade on their genteel shopping trips.

It was, admitted Naylor, 'pretentious crap.' But 'they were pretentious times. We were all pretentious because we thought the world had ended. The world we knew *had* ended, in terms of technology, and cities, and the way we lived. It was unknown, the future.'

Pretentiousness, then, was matched by intellectual curiosity. The quartet would frequent the Equal Opportunities Library on Albert Square and study books on gynaecology and feminism. The issue of sexual politics, certainly, was always central to the relationship. 'As women, we had a lot more freedom because you could pretty much do whatever you wanted, because nothing much was expected of you,' said Carroll. 'Whereas for men, I think their role had been pretty well defined. So I think it was probably a lot harder for [Steven Morrissey] to find where he belonged. And there was also the possibility that he was someone who could not fit in with anything . . . He was someone who could not cope with an everyday existence. That part of his angst was absolutely genuine.'

Naylor, who wore her lesbianism as a badge of pride, believed that 'Steven was a lot more of an active gay man than he ever let on.' But she accepted that 'being gay in Manchester at that particular point was not really an option.' She saw Morrissey in much the same way as she saw herself and Carroll at the time: 'confused, frightened, unsure, lost between the modernist world and the postmodernist world we all inhabit now [in the twenty-first century], where we play with irony and identity. And at that point identity felt very serious.'

'There was a part of Steven that we never saw, a part of him that had personal relationships with people,' confirmed Carroll. 'He was never really interested in talking about that with us. He would make camp remarks or he would make remarks about things, but we never really knew what was going on with him when it came to his personal life . . . I think we got the sense that behind that wall was some stuff that wouldn't be quite so easy to deal with.'

It was noticeable that until the success of the Smiths – in which she would play an important promotional role – Carroll 'never had any doubt' that Morrissey's path to success in life would be literary. Ironically, at *City Fun*, she and Naylor had cast aside some of his contributions under the pen name Sheridan Whiteside (a character in *The Man Who Came to Dinner*) because they almost always promoted the New York Dolls, a band for whom the Crones had little time. Once they befriended him, they were more supportive of his literary endeavours, publishing a glowing retrospective of his on Sandie Shaw.

In the meantime, Naylor, Carroll and Morrissey alike remained unyielding in their support for Linder's musical career. On paper, things appeared to be going well for Ludus, who released three albums in 1982 and recorded a John Peel session replete with the wonderfully titled 'Vagina Gratitude'. (The title of a compilation released that year, *Riding The Rag*, was equally inspired.) But New Hormones could not do much more for a band that was determined to operate in the margins. In stepping up as Linder's unofficial PR person, Steven Morrissey acknowledged as much. 'Being the only sensible recipe for the culturally damaged,' he wrote in a press release for New Hormones that summer, 'Ludus are out to at least stretch their patience with the world to the very elastic limit.'

Of that he was not exaggerating. On 5 November 1982, Ludus headlined the Haçienda. Prior to the show, the Crones laid a red-stained tampon on every table. Linder then took to the stage wearing a dress made of meat, removing it for the last song to reveal a lengthy dildo strapped around her waist.[2] As the members of the audience recoiled – even in the experimental world of post-punk England, Linder's act was extreme – Naylor and Carroll wandered among them, distributing meat entrails wrapped in pornography.

The act infuriated the Haçienda's owners – and that was largely its intent. During its first six months, the club had been showing pornography, 'and they thought it was really cool,' recalled Linder. (It would have to have been 'soft' porn, given Britain's draconian indecency laws of the time.) By reducing herself to an object of meat, said Linder, 'I took my revenge.' But with such a confrontational act of performance art, she also brought herself to a crossroads. 'I thought, "That's it. Where do you go from here?"' That Haçienda show turned out to be her last in Manchester. She broke up Ludus the following year and moved to Belgium, gradually abandoning music entirely for visual art. Her feminist influence would live on in the rock world, not only in the many women musicians who took up her fight over subsequent years, but in Steven Patrick Morrissey – who, by the time of that last Ludus concert, had already played his first gig with the Smiths.

CHAPTER THIRTEEN

Because the years previous to the Smiths were quite dank for me, I could see this perhaps as my absolutely, perhaps sole key opportunity to do something constructive and something worthwhile, so therefore when the time came to actually mount the stage, it was almost as if this strange forceful character completely took over. I actually stayed in the wings almost.

— MORRISSEY, *The South Bank Show,*
October 1987

Early on in the process, Morrissey suggested, and Marr agreed, on the name for their band. The Smiths. Fans and critics alike have searched high and low over the years for explanations, and they are easy to come by, given that Smith is the most common last name in England. But that, really, is the only explanation that was ever needed. By calling themselves the Smiths, Morrissey and Marr asserted themselves as commoners, everyday working people. In doing so, they additionally disassociated themselves from the outlandish names that were so pervasive at the time – be it in their own musical world (Echo & the Bunnymen as the big northern rock band, Quando Quango as the latest Factory act, et cetera), or that of the New Romantic/Blitz Kids hit-makers (for example, Haircut 100, Duran Duran). And in the process of choosing a single-syllable, definitive-article name, they were subscribing to the lineage of British rock legends: the Who, the Stones (by common abbreviation), the Kinks, the Clash, the Jam, and so on, and the possibility that they might eventually be considered part of that rich tapestry. It was, in

short, a pronounced return to basics at a time when pomp-
ousness was dominant.

Having settled on a moniker, begun writing songs, and drawn
up something of a game plan, the next step was to solidify the
lineup. Stephen Pomfret, as acknowledged matchmaker between
Morrissey and Marr, was invited to early Smiths rehearsals in
Bowdon, but his presence, he felt, was requested more out of
duty than desire. 'Johnny never wanted another guitarist,' he
quickly concluded. 'If I'd been the greatest guitarist in the world
I wouldn't have been in the band.' He stepped back without
any evident bitterness, accepting his minor role in history with
grace.

That still left the need for a rhythm section. For a bassist,
Marr returned to Decibelle and recruited twenty-one-year-old
Dale Hibbert, who had engineered the Freak Party session.
Hibbert had never been in a band of which he wasn't the
leader, and he had one going at the time, the Adorables. It
speaks volumes for Johnny Marr's powers of persuasion that
Hibbert nonetheless allowed himself to be talked into quitting
this band before he had even met Steven Morrissey. Hibbert
considered Marr a good friend, knew him also as 'a really great
musician,' and knew even more so that Marr seemed to have
the connections to make a band happen, and when you'd been
in as many bands as Hibbert had, where *nothing* happened, that
was a strong selling point. When he came over to Bowdon to
meet Morrissey for the first time, Hibbert was pleased to find
that as vegetarians and Velvet Underground fans, they shared
common ground; over coming weeks and months, Hibbert
would frequently give Morrissey a ride home to Stretford on
the back of his motorbike. The relationship was pleasant but,
as so often the case with Morrissey and people who didn't fully
subscribe to his worldview, distant. 'I thought he was a reasonable guy,' said Hibbert, but 'there was nothing that stood out
about him.' If there was a surprise, it was that the first song
Hibbert was presented with – recorded, with just vocals and
guitar, to Marr's TEAC three-track Portastudio – was a cover

version, a long-forgotten single by early 1960s New York girl group the Cookies, 'I Want a Boy for My Birthday'.

Ostensibly, this was no more risqué than Ringo Starr singing the Shirelles' 'Boys' with a straight face on the Beatles' first album, a record that had also included their version of the Cookies' biggest hit, 'Chains'. (In their own choice of cover, therefore, deliberately or otherwise, Morrissey and Marr were paying *double* homage to the early Beatles.) And certainly, it was intended in part as a nod to the New York Dolls, who had incorporated the Shangri-Las into their own live set. The recording itself was none so upbeat as those reference points, however. Though Morrissey faithfully replicated the lead melody as he sang such traditionally romantic couplets as 'I want a boy to comfort me, and treat me tenderly,' his voice was no match for the Cookies' Earl-Jean McCrea. And though Marr laid out his template for the Smiths across his two guitar tracks – one softly playing the chords, the other offering a carefully picked arpeggio, and both of them drenched in reverb – neither was he on the level of Gerry Goffin, the original song's producer, nor Goffin's wife, Carole King, its arranger. At best, the Morrissey-Marr version of 'I Want a Boy for My Birthday' was a purposefully camp presentation of a classic piece of (very) early '60s sexual stereotyping, which is why it would have made some sense to Hibbert when he was duly informed that the Smiths 'were going to be a gay band.'

Interestingly, Marr claimed this idea as his own – a result of his, Andrew Berry's and John Kennedy's nocturnal habits. As Berry, who was straight, noted of Manchester's dire early '80s nightlife, 'We worked in the centre of town and the only bars that were open would be gay bars.' The notion of the Smiths as a gay band, then, said Marr, 'was just because a lot of my mates were gay guys who liked rock music. I liked the idea of us being a band that were . . . saying things for the gay community.' Gay imagery was becoming more prevalent in popular music for those who were searching for it – in the front men of the chart-topping acts Soft Cell and Culture

Club, for example – and yet the social climate was still suffi-ciently repressive that no pop act (including those two) was ready to risk its career by unequivocally coming out. Within the Smiths, Dale Hibbert already had a daughter by his girl-friend, and Marr was in a long-term relationship with Angie Brown; there was no way they *could* position themselves as a 'gay band' without putting the entire onus on Steven Morrissey – and in hindsight, Marr recognised that dilemma. 'I wasn't fronting the band, so it wasn't on my toes.' The idea was dropped. For the time being.

The quest for an image, though, remained paramount. With the new monthly style magazines proving so influential that the weekly music papers were now following their lead, a new band needed to have some sort of (inherently contrived) look to stand even the smallest chance of media attention. Hibbert was sent to the Army surplus store on London Road to acquire himself some bowling shirts (which were popular in the current rockabilly revival) and then to see Andrew Berry on Palatine Road for a flat-top haircut (ditto); the harder acquisition was a specific type of secondhand denim jeans, with a belt loop for a work tool. At some point over the next couple of months, the three-piece spent a day being photographed around Manchester in these clothes; the session never surfaced.

The decision to now record a demo tape before settling on a drummer was not a difficult one; it was part of their Brill Building-like plan that they should be seen as songsmiths, and besides, with Hibbert working at Decibelle, the session would cost them nothing. Si Wolstencroft, despite instant reservations about the name the Smiths, and Marr's warning that the band was 'totally different' from Freak Party (which Wolstencroft had loved), agreed to fill in and showed up at the beginning of August to record 'Suffer Little Children' and 'The Hand That Rocks the Cradle' without having previously heard the songs or met the singer.

The act as it existed was short on experience and practice all around. Morrissey, in particular, had not seen the inside of a studio in four years, and his natural singing style, at this point, was considerably lower in timbre, tone and especially pitch than it would need to be for the Smiths to become a success: both Smiths songs recorded that day would eventually be tuned up a full step to accommodate Morrissey's limited range. Similarly, Marr's guitar playing and arrangements reflected the windswept moors of the post-punk indie scene more than they did any form of elegiac pop for which he would become famous. And of course the production was inherently limited by time (an eight-hour overnight session) and space (Decibelle offered a mere eight tracks). This did not prevent Marr from singing backing vocals (on 'The Hand That Rocks the Cradle'), a contribution he would soon abandon, and neither did it prevent Morrissey from exercising a vibrato effect on his own vocals, clearly trying his best to demonstrate his capabilities as a fully fledged singer.

In addition, they engaged in some intriguing experimentation on 'Suffer Little Children'. As the song drew to a conclusion on a repeated minor chord, Morrissey's friend Annalisa Jablonska provided Hindley-like cackles, while someone else whistled along casually (playing the Ian Brady role?). A cassette recording of Marr playing piano in waltz rhythm at Bowdon (sounding much like a music box with his lilting time-keeping) was spliced in, along with a separate recording of local primary school children at play, which Marr had recorded through his open window at home. The overall effect was deliberately and understandably sinister, and showed an innate understanding of how found sound and small effects could contribute to musical atmosphere.[1]

The recordings showed definite signs of promise, but they were no more than an introductory statement, a mere hint at the band that the Smiths would soon become, with a different rhythm section. Yet as with almost any new, young band and its first demo, there were no such reservations from within. Marr took to playing it in X-Clothes as often as he could get away with. Morrissey lined up an appointment to play it for Tony Wilson. Wolstencroft, however, felt that his inherent

214

fears about Marr's new group had been confirmed upon meeting and working with the singer: quite simply, he said of Morrissey, 'I didn't like the cut of his jib.' The vocal mumblings and evident shyness, as far as the drummer was concerned, went hand-in-hand with his choice of long overcoat. 'There was a term for that kind of music at the time – the "raincoat brigade". Looking at your shoes. Ordinary. Not very flash.' Wolstencroft wanted no part of it. 'It wasn't jazz funk. I was Funky Si.'

Wolstencroft's objections were echoed throughout the subsequent long and arduous search for a permanent drummer. (It had become apparent by now that the songwriting partnership needed a band, and that a 'conventional set-up', as Marr described it to *Sounds* in late 1983, was now the right way to go.) Bill Anstee, who had been in bands alongside both Marr *and* Hibbert, came over to Bowdon, played along to some songs, and was asked his opinion. Upon comparing them to the Velvet Underground, he heard an exasperated Morrissey respond, 'Oh no, not another one.' Older than the others, the former Sister Ray drummer was losing the hunger for the various hassles that came with being in a gigging band at the bottom of the ladder, and he told Marr as much as he packed up his kit. Marr, clearly, was at the opposite end of the exuberance spectrum: 'He was just in love with the entertainment game and the people in it and oozed optimism for his new band.' Marr even showed Anstee the phone book belonging to Shelley Rohde, 'full of almost everybody you've ever heard of in the TV/record industry,' and the drummer was left thinking that 'To Johnny this was all he believed he needed to get where he was going.' But still Anstee refused to join the group. 'I would have had a total personality clash with Morrissey if I'd stayed around,' he said. 'I didn't like the music they were playing, especially the lyrics.'

Morrissey now suggested as drummer one of his neighbours and former St Mary's sufferers, Gary Farrell, who had just left a band with fellow Kings Road boys Ivor and Andy Perry; he had Marr call Farrell and ask him over for a meeting. If Farrell thought that process odd, given that he'd often walked home over the iron bridge from school with Steven Morrissey, he found the demo tape he was subsequently handed even more so. Unable to 'get anything out of it,' he declined further involvement. Despite living on the same road, he and Morrissey never talked again. 'I think he felt I'd insulted him.'

Hibbert brought in the drummer from the Adorables, but that didn't work out either. Through mutual friends in Altrincham, a drummer named Guy Ainsworth was invited along to the trio's new rehearsal space, at Spirit Studios on Tariff Street, just behind Piccadilly. (Hibbert had been promised an equal partnership in the setup and was busy bringing his clients over from Decibelle.) Ainsworth walked in to what he called 'a tense atmosphere.' Though he recognised Marr's talents immediately, he otherwise allowed himself to be scared off. 'There was a strange dynamic in the room. I couldn't put my finger on it.'

Even when the Smiths found their man – Mike Joyce, of course – it was not without initial trepidation on the drummer's part. Joyce recalled that when he showed up for an audition at Spirit, 'Morrissey said very little. He just kind of prowled round the room. Had a long tweed coat on. And just walked up and down. A couple of furtive glances over at me. I felt as though he just thought I was *stupid*. I just felt a bit intimidated by him.'

This could have been because, of the four people in the room, the drummer and the singer were the only ones who didn't already know each other. Joyce was acquainted with Marr from both X-Clothes and Legends; he lived in Chorlton with Pete Hunt's closest friend, which is how he'd been told about the vacant drum stool. And in his previous groups, Joyce had frequently shared the Manchester Musicians Collective stage(s) with Dale Hibbert. Any paranoia on Joyce's part might also have been due to digesting some magic mushrooms on the way to the studio; when he compensated for oncoming hallucinations by hammering the hell out of the drums to a new Morrissey-Marr song, written in the attic room in Bowdon, called 'What Difference Does It Make?' that was fortuitously heavy on a Keith Richards riff, the others were taken by his energy – as well as his 'balls' for daring to show up high. Over coming weeks, as it was ascertained that Joyce's parents were working-class Irish Catholic immigrants just like theirs; that he had attended St Gregory's Grammar School with Andrew Berry; that he was roughly their age; and that in addition to being an outgoing, effusive, enthusiastic sort of person, he was genuinely handsome and photographed well, Morrissey and Marr had every reason to believe they had found their man. History would, at least until Joyce sued them in high court in 1996, prove them right.

BORN IN FALLOWFIELD, South Manchester, on 1 June 1963, the youngest of four boys and a girl, Michael Adrian Joyce's path to joining the Smiths reflected the sense of stolid workmanship combined with irrepressible joie de vivre that he subsequently brought to the band. At a young age, he had convinced his mother (who, like Marr's parents, hailed from County Kildare; his father came from Galway) to invest in a drum kit after endlessly banging out rhythms on the school desk and the living-room couch. As a child of punk, he was subsequently taken by Manchester's own Buzzcocks (something else he had in common with his future Smiths), whose drummer, John Maher, was far ahead of his contemporaries in terms of ideas and the ability to realise them. Joyce was not yet in Maher's league, however. Shortly before his sixteenth birthday, he joined a local punk group, the Hoax, who, even in a scene that made cult heroes of Ed Banger and the Nosebleeds, struggled to be taken seriously. Whether by design or an inability to progress, the three-piece stayed resolutely true to their punk roots – as demonstrated by spiky haircuts, leather jackets, and song titles like 'Storm Trooper' and 'Rich Folk' across three EPs – before Joyce left the sinking ship in the summer of 1981, right around the time he received, according to Rogan's biography, 'substantial compensation for injuries sustained in a car accident some years before.'

Joyce took drumming lessons to improve his abilities, then joined another punk band, Victim, who had moved from Belfast to Manchester in 1979 when offered a deal by TJM, the label offshoot of the TJ Davidson's studios, where White Dice had occasionally rehearsed around that same time. Rootless as a result of their move, Victim never enjoyed the same popularity in Manchester as they had back in Belfast, and Joyce did not get to make a record with them.[2]

Given the limitations of these groups, it was no surprise that Joyce should have felt so enthused by his audition with the Smiths. 'Musicality was something that had passed me by in the other groups,' he said. 'Johnny's subtlety and his texture and playing guitar was radically different than any of the other players I'd worked with up to that point.' For their part, Morrissey and Marr were thrilled to have come to the end of their quest – except that for the next couple of months it wasn't entirely certain whether Joyce was on board; they could only assume that any ambivalence was a result of his loyalty to Victim – unless it was an attempt to confirm whether the Smiths were actually going somewhere.

THE SMITHS' FIRST gig took place on 4 October 1982, at the Ritz on Whitworth Street. If it was perhaps inevitable that it should be part of a John Kennedy/Andrew Berry promotion, it was advantageous, too. By appearing alongside a headlining act, DJs, a fashion show, a dance troupe, and more, all as part of 'An Evening of Pure Pleasure', the Smiths placed themselves instantly at the very centre of the city scene without making themselves the only focus of the evening's attention.

A month before the gig, *The Face* ran a story by Robert Elms entitled 'Hard Times', about the current look and sound

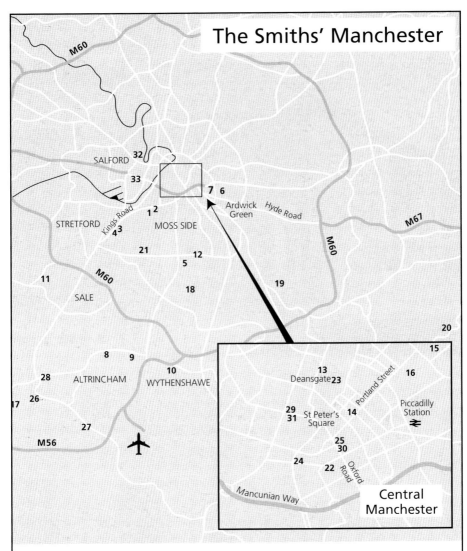

The Smiths' Manchester

M60

SALFORD **32**

33

STRETFORD Kings Road **1** **2** MOSS SIDE **7** **6** Ardwick Green Hyde Road M67

4 **3**

21 **12** **5**

11 M60 **18** **19** M60

SALE **20**

15

8 **9** **10** **13** Deansgate **23** Portland Street **16**

28 ALTRINCHAM WYTHENSHAWE St Peter's Square **14** Piccadilly Station

26 **29** **31**

17 **27** **25** **30**

M56 **24** **22** Oxford Road

Mancunian Way **Central Manchester**

1. Harper Street, Morrissey family home
2. Queen's Square, Morrissey family home
3. 384 Kings Road, Morrissey family home
4. St Mary's RC Secondary Modern
5. 35 Mayfield Road, Morrissey/Ludus flat
6. Hayfield Street, Marr family home
7. Brierley Avenue, Marr family home
8. Churchstone Walk, Marr family home
9. Sacred Heart RC Primary School
10. St Augustine's RC Grammar School
11. Hawthorn Lane, Rourke family home
12. Fallowfield, Joyce family home area
13. Chapel Walks: X-Clothes & Crazy Face
14. 70 Portland Street: Crazy Face/Smiths HQ
15. Decibelle Studios
16. Spirit Studios
17. Bowdon, Shelley Rohde/Marr home
18. Palatine Road: Factory Records, Berry/Marr part-time home
19. Moss family home, Marr/Rourke part-time home
20. Marple Bridge, Marr/Berry home
21. Drone Studios
22. The Ritz
23. Manhattan Sound
24. The Haçienda
25. Rafters
26. Marlborough Road, Marr adult home
27. Hale Barns, Morrissey family home
28. Springfield Road, Joyce adult home
29. Free Trade Hall
30. Palace Theatre
31. G-Mex Centre
32. University of Salford
33. Coronation Street/Salford Lads Club

Queen's Square, Hulme, the Morrissey family home, seen in 1964 (above), and
Brierley Avenue, Ardwick, the Maher family home, seen in 1969 (below).
Both were torn down for 'slum clearance'.

Kings Road, Stretford, where Steven Morrissey spent the rest
of his childhood and early adulthood. 'Quite bland, quite uneventful,'
said Morrissey. 'There's not really a great deal to say about Kings Road.'

Churchstone Walk, Wythenshawe, where Johnny Marr spent the rest of his
childhood until the age of sixteen. 'The estate was working class, but the people living
in Wythenshawe around our estate were to me incredibly bohemian...'

The Smiths, featuring James Maker as additional front man, at Manhattan Sound, 25 January 1983. 'We were all shitting ourselves,' said Andy Rourke, who made his debut at this show. 'But with that comes adrenaline and with that comes concentration and with that comes an amazing gig.'

The Smiths at Manchester Central Railway Station, May 1983. Johnny Marr:
'You can see the relationship in those photographs, not just because we're hugging each other,
but because we're so happy to be next to each other.' In 1986, the station was converted into the
G-Mex Centre, and the band performed there.

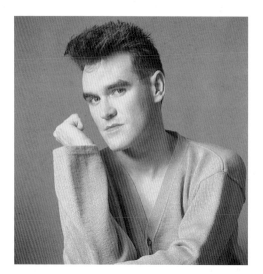

Morrissey and Johnny Marr. Photographs taken in London, 20 December 1983.
'I was just there, dying, and he rescued me,' said Morrissey of meeting Marr.
'It's something I'll never regret, that relationship,' said Marr of himself and Morrissey.

Andy Rourke ('the bass guitar') and Mike Joyce ('the drums').
In a group that continually pitched itself as a band, a gang, a group of 'lads' and 'mates',
some members turned out to be more equal than others.

'Without doubt we are incurable Sandie Shaw fans,' wrote Morrissey
and Marr to Shaw in 1983. By March 1984, she was recording their songs
and joining them onstage at the Hammersmith Palais.

Andy Rourke, Morrissey, Johnny Marr, Mike Joyce: The Smiths in concert, early 1984.

The Smiths in 1984, the year they had two top ten British albums.

Johnny Marr with Billy Bragg on the Red Wedge tour, January 1986. 'Johnny was the one I always thought understood the socio-political role of what we were doing,' said Bragg.

in the underground London clubs. When Johnny Marr read it, he was furious. 'Robert Elms killed off my scene', he said. 'He brought it overground and he spelled it out in a way that put us off.' Marr felt that the rambling analysis, which talked up specific warehouse parties and the currently hot electro-rap track from New York, 'Money's Too Tight to Mention,' ignored a large part of what Marr had been attracted to. 'There was no mention of all these little enclaves of people digging out vintage denim, Eddie Cochran original singles, listening to Vince Taylor, Gene Vincent, all these real specialists, kids my own age who got up early in the morning and were on a mission to look amazing.' It provoked a rethink in Marr's own vision for the band, and he no longer demanded that the Smiths try to outdo the London trendsetters at their own game. The decision to relax the group's image requirements proved a wise one when confronted with the headliners for their debut at the Ritz: Blue Rondo A La Turk, a perfectly tailored, jazz-influenced ten-piece who epitomised the London style bibles' sense of high fashion and who would go on to enjoy a couple of hit singles before shifting fashion rendered them yesterday's men.

The newly casual approach was also reflected in Morrissey's invitation to James Maker to come to Manchester and join the band for the evening – literally, by introducing them onstage (in French) to the music of (recently deceased, New York-based countertenor performance artist and gay icon) Klaus Nomi, and then dancing alongside the singer while playing maracas. For Morrissey, an inexperienced front man but intelligent music fan who knew all about the Velvet Underground's first shows as part of an 'Exploding Plastic Inevitable,' complete with projected films and dancers, the inclusion of Maker made perfect sense and needed no justification, and neither was he asked for one by a nonetheless bemused Johnny Marr.

The gig came up against unexpected competition when the Haçienda announced it was hosting the great American writers William Burroughs and John Giorno the very same night. Under normal circumstances, Steven Morrissey would certainly have attended that event, but circumstances were suddenly most *abnormal*. As it happened, the fact that the Factory crowd was otherwise engaged turned out to be a blessing, relieving him of any pressure to prove himself to those who considered themselves his betters.

Kennedy and Berry's promotion capabilities were hardly lacking, though, and the Ritz, a fine old theatre complete with sprung dance floor and balcony, was well attended. The Smiths played only four numbers – and one of those the Cookies cover – represented a careful calculation, a belief that it was better to offer a short, sharp, sweet set than conform to convention and include a half-dozen substantially unrehearsed songs just to make up the numbers. It also played into the style culture of the time; many of the New Romantic acts had signed deals based on equally brief showcases.

Alongside 'Suffer Little Children' and 'The Hand That Rocks the Cradle', the one other Morrissey-Marr composition unveiled at the Ritz was 'Handsome Devil'. Imbued with something of a rockabilly riff, a natural reflection of the pair's mutual interest in the genre, it was notably more exuberant than its antecedents. The lyrics, too, were more charged – and loaded with delightfully risqué couplets of both gay and straight connotations. The one that jumped out most readily from the microphone, 'Let me get my hands on your mammary glands,' was Morrissey's first act of popular lyrical (as opposed to poetic) genius, and also his first in a series of classic one-liners. A year later, he explained his intent. 'I felt there were so many long-winded songs in the history of popular music, and all that people wanted to say, all that New Order wanted to say, was "Let me get my hands on your mammary glands." And so I thought, Let's be very blunt.' It was therefore somewhat cruel that the song would become better known for another line, 'A boy in the hand is worth two in the bush,' which would stand accused of promoting paedophilia. A response to that argument might have been that the word 'boy' was the standard feminine

220

term for the male sex in pop lyrics, as proven by the Ritz gig's finale, 'I Want a Boy for My Birthday'.

Marr hadn't played a gig since the White Dice fiasco at the Squat almost two years earlier; he compensated for his nerves by coming across 'really threatening,' with 'heaps and heaps of attitude.' Morrissey, onstage for the first time in fully four years, was no doubt greatly relieved to have James Maker distract – or at least share in – some of the audience attention. But reactions to their live debut together were positive, especially from those that mattered. Joe Moss regarded it as 'a showcase for Johnny, [whose] guitar playing just soared over everything,' but similarly felt that 'Morrissey was just ten-foot-tall . . . you realised it was someone who was totally unique there in front of you.'

Mike Joyce, all agreed, also acquitted himself admirably. Dale Hibbert, apparently, did not. He danced onstage as was his habit, and perhaps more than usual to compensate for what he considered a 'rigid' Morrissey, and he sensed afterward that in doing so he had crossed a line. He had already become keenly aware that the Smiths were never going to be a band of equals. The way he saw things, 'It was totally irrelevant who played the bass and drums as long as (a) they were willing to be manipulated to some extent and (b) stayed in the background and did as they were told.' For someone used to leading his own band, 'the lack of control . . . wouldn't have worked out.'

His complaint, despite containing an important kernel of future dispute, was essentially irrelevant. Hibbert already had a baby daughter, which would have inhibited his ability to tour; and he was devoted to his prospects as a partner at Spirit Studios, where he found that, as an engineer, 'sitting there with a pile of tape was more fulfilling than playing bass.' When Marr gave him his marching orders on the stairs at Spirit Studios a few weeks after the Ritz show, there were initially no hard feelings.

The need to finalise the lineup proved paramount because, as a result of that single, carefully planned and expertly orchestrated show, the Smiths found themselves in the spotlight. *The Face* ran a paragraph about the Ritz gig that, though it didn't refer to them more than by name, observed that this was 'the kind of live music fashion show that the British don't attempt often enough.' Someone at *i-D* magazine proved sufficiently intrigued to arrange an interview. And Marr's friend from the West Wythenshawe student union, Tony O'Connor, having just landed a role as an A&R scout for EMI, took Morrissey – curiously, not Marr – to the major label's London headquarters to play the Decibelle demo to Hugh Stanley-Clarke, the head of A&R. To their surprise and delight, they came away with a budget to make another and, it was to be presumed all around, a much better recording.

(This was a considerably more positive reaction than Morrissey had received from Tony Wilson. The Factory front man later excused his rejection by saying that he'd passed the Decibelle tape on to New Order manager (and now Factory/Haçienda partner) Rob Gretton who, with customary bluntness, had come back with the opinion that it was 'shit.' Wilson presumably found a more polite turn of phrase to reject his relentless business suitor Morrissey.[5])

EMI was *the* major British record company, home to the Beatles, Pink Floyd and Queen, to name but three of the world's biggest UK-raised acts. In 1982, however, among those who considered themselves politically attuned in their musical tastes, it was reviled as much as it was admired; EMI, after all, was the label that had infamously dropped the Sex Pistols under pressure, and despite having signed its share of punk bands in the wake of that monstrous error, was making most of its money in the current marketplace from Duran Duran – for whom talk of 'the new Beatles' was accurate only insofar as it applied to their popularity with hysterical pubescent girls. As such, and as a matter of (re)course, EMI was commissioning inexpensive demo recordings by new bands at a furious rate, working on the familiar major-label theory that if it cast its net wide enough, it would surely reel in a few big fish alongside the many minnows. The common understanding with such demo sessions was that if a major 'passed' on the band, to use the terminology of record-company rejection, that group was then free to shop the recording to other labels.

Morrissey and Marr felt that they were ready for the challenge. Songs had been flowing freely from their guitars and pens ever since that first productive writing session back in May, and the fact that Dale Hibbert would only recall rehearsing the same three or four songs over and over, disappointed that he wasn't being invited to help compose new material by jamming together, was a clear indication of Morrissey and Marr's cautious approach to the band format. As it transpired, they already had several more compositions just about ready to go. In addition to the three that they had played at the Ritz, and 'What Difference Does It Make?', they were especially excited by 'Miserable Lie'. The lyrics reflected Morrissey's jaundiced view on romance, but also exhibited the humour that lay not so far beneath the surface. And though the reference to his 'rented room in Whalley Range,' where he had lived briefly in 1980, would become the song's most recognisable line, there were additionally treasurable couplets that suggested an approach to sex not far removed from the more coy characters in the *Carry On* movies. (E.g. 'I look at yours, you laugh at mine.') Marr approached the song musically with the familiar touch of the ambitious young songwriter – especially during that post-punk era, starting out in ballad form before increasing both speed and volume in the chorus. If played appropriately, it offered enormous potential as a set closer.

Among those songs that were not yet considered suitable for recording, the decidedly uptempo 'These Things Take Time' wore the influence of northern icons Echo & The Bunnymen, both in Morrissey's strained vocal at the end of each section, and in the dramatic slash of chords that Marr followed it with; the line 'the hills are alive with celibate cries' would come to have a lasting impact on the Smiths' audience, given that it was the only time Morrissey mentioned his oft-stated sexual preference in lyrics. 'What Do You See In Him?' (later to be re-titled 'Wonderful Woman') was slower and more methodical, darker all around, though Morrissey's subject matter was much the same: a female object of dubious merit but evident desire, the singer's lust unrequited. As an example of how the songs developed during the Smiths' early period, the only line to survive from the original composition into the song's eventual title was that of 'ice water for blood.'

Perhaps not surprisingly, Marr would look back on these songs and suggest that both the music and the words were coming 'from just before we met,' that they represented the still tentative marriage of Morrissey's existent poetry with riffs that Marr, likewise, had been carrying around with him. This might explain why neither 'These Things Take Time' nor 'Wonderful Woman' would end up on an album. Nor would 'Jeane', which Marr had originally envisaged in the style of the Drifters until Morrissey implored him to speed it up and the duo found themselves with an outright rocker to complement 'What Difference Does It Make?' – and arguably to succeed it as a fans' favourite. Though those Smiths fans would inevitably embark on a quest to unearth the source of Morrissey's muse in this song, it would be fair to assume that he fashioned it after the plays of Shelagh Delaney and co.: it was beyond coincidence that the line 'cash on the nail' was also used in Delaney's *The Lion In Love*. Ultimately, it was the refrain 'we tried and we failed' that would resonate most strongly with the Smiths audience, currently waiting in the wings for someone like Morrissey to echo their own history of romantic disappointments.

According to Marr's recollection of these early compositions, he and Morrissey had already set about another lengthy ballad, but this one more stark, more focused than the others. Supposedly influenced by listening to 1950s R&B vocal hits at Crazy Face (not that one could tell as much from the result), it had room to breathe, allowing Morrissey to pen his most intriguing and challenging sexual lyrics to date, and it would

224

help define the Smiths once it was introduced on stage. Indeed, it would eventually be chosen to open their debut album, and considered (and even pressed) as a single until external forces necessitated a rethink. That song was called 'Reel Around The Fountain'.

Clearly, it was time to finalise a bassist. Dale Hibbert had previously found himself giving Johnny Marr a ride on his motorbike to the lumberyard in Trafford Park, where Andy Rourke was now working. At the time, given that he often ferried Marr around town, Hibbert thought nothing of it. Nor was he chagrined when Rourke replaced him in the Smiths – 'Technically, he was a far better bass player than I was' – and even stopped into the subsequent session for EMI to see how the band was getting along. His complaint – and it was a major one – was the long-term implication that he had only ever been recruited to the Smiths because he could offer free studio time at Decibelle. As far as Hibbert was concerned, he had been busy touting himself as an engineer for free overnight sessions at the time; Marr, being a friend, only had to ask to receive. Besides, Hibbert was in the band for approximately four months, rehearsing way before and beyond the demo session, before and beyond the Ritz gig too. 'I can accept Johnny wanted me in the band as a bass player and then thought, "He's really shit" or, "He's not what we want and now we have to figure out a reason to get rid of him,"' he reflected. 'I would prefer that to the idea that I was completely manipulated to give him the studio time . . . I can't understand why Johnny would betray himself as treating a friend like that.'

The misunderstanding may well have come about because the bandleader was in some form of denial when it came to the bass-playing role. 'No one who was good who I liked as much [as Andy] ever came on my radar,' said Marr. 'And I think that I may have always known that I was going to go to Andy because I actually didn't try very hard to go for a bass player, and I was working very hard to get all the other pieces together.'

The call, when it came, was welcomed by Rourke. 'Even if

he didn't want me in the band,' said the bassist, who knew about Marr's new group through Wolstencroft, 'friendship-wise I wanted to hear from him.' As it turned out, though, Marr was on a mission. The Smiths were going into the studio imminently, for EMI; did Rourke want to play on the session and take it from there? He did, and he was driven to the session, at an 8-track studio called Drone in the basement of a Chorlton Victorian house, by Si Wolstencroft, who, like Hibbert, had no immediate regrets about watching someone else take his place in the studio.

Rourke's first impressions of Morrissey proved much the same as those of the long list of drummers. 'He just shook my hand and then stood in the corner in his long overcoat and didn't really say anything. I thought, "Hmmm, this is a bit strange, but let's see how this goes."' At least in Rourke's case, he had been forewarned that Morrissey's aloofness was largely due to shyness – and given the extent to which Marr had already talked up his new partner's lyrical talents, the fact that EMI was invested in the band, and that he didn't have anything else going on except the crushing manual work at the lumber-yard, Rourke was determined to prove himself. Besides, Mike Joyce was there, as drummer, and although 'there was still a little bit of the punk left in him,' not necessarily an advantage in Rourke's eyes, his easygoing nature put the bassist at ease.

Marr played through the three prospective songs a couple of times for Rourke's benefit, and then the tape rolled. The Smiths as we came to know them started playing together – and something special occurred, one of those rare moments in rock-music history when a great lineup comes together for the first time. 'It was like it wasn't me playing the bass, it was like I was possessed,' recalled Rourke. 'The energy was just there and it was right. And we were all looking at each other, just going, "Fucking hell."' Certainly, it was a positive reflection on Rourke's talent that many of the bass parts he came up with that day remained essentially unchanged throughout the Smiths' career. And where that proved not to be the case, where he and Marr engaged in some slapping bass and slashing guitars during a lengthy version of 'Miserable Lie', well, that was a fun throwback to Freak Party, the thrill of two old mates playing together after so long. Similarly, the session provided an opportunity to try out the addition of brass – as was all the rage at the time – on 'Handsome Devil', a doubled-up saxophone part opening the song with Stax-like embellishments. And even if the hired hand, Andy Gill, played a little too enthusiastically across the rest of the song, and despite the fact that his exuberance ultimately sounded incongruous, well, there was no harm in trying. To the same end, 'What Difference Does It Make?' was emboldened with Marr's backing 'oohs' and an odd outburst of applause in the middle of the song; there was a general sense of *reaching* in this recording session, of flexing musical muscles and instigating new ideas. If there was an evident overall weakness, it was Morrissey's vocals; they were still tentative, unassertive, pitched low in velocity and quiet in the mix. It might well have been for this reason that, after the tape was dispatched to London, EMI's Stanley-Clarke listened and, failing to hear 'What Difference Does It Make?' as the hit single it would turn out to be, or the other two songs as classics in their own right, told Tony O'Connor to keep an eye on the Smiths and let him know when they would be playing in London. It might also have been because that's just how the major labels worked at the time: Next.[4]

CHAPTER FOURTEEN

Each of us had the potential to feel invincible. But we needed the other's backup, belief and support.
— JOHNNY MARR, March 2011

So stay on my arm, you little charmer.
— MORRISSEY, 'Hand in Glove'

J oe Moss and Johnny Marr had been growing closer since the guitarist had put the Smiths together; it was evident already that the older man was set to be the band's manager. Not so much to facilitate that role as to get Marr away from another employer, enjoy the teenager's company on a daily basis and, in his own words, 'so he could run his band and still get paid,' Moss had opened a third Crazy Face store in the Portland Street basement and put Marr in charge of it. Now he provided a floor at Portland Street for the group to rehearse in and bought a PA for them to play through. More or less every weekday evening, at five p.m., Johnny Marr would shut up shop in the basement, ascend the work elevator to the fourth floor, and open up the gates for the arrival of the other three. Then they would rehearse through the evening, closing up only when it was time to get the last bus or train back to Stretford, Sale, Chorlton and Bowdon in the late-night cold and damp of their Manchester midwinter. The desire to push forward was self-evident. At the same time, they were careful not to get ahead of themselves; the debut gig having gained the band serious attention, Joe Moss insisted they hold off on another show until the new lineup was properly rehearsed and capable of a full set.

Moss's role as Marr's mentor and father figure took on even greater gravity when he invited Marr to move out of Shelley Rohde's house and into his own family home in Heaton Chapel. The official reasoning was to get Marr into work on time at Crazy Face in the mornings, but the net result was that the pair grew closer still, frequently commuting together, and discussing music, pop culture, and the future of the Smiths at pretty much all times when not otherwise engaged. If Morrissey had any reservations about the close bond between his musical partner and his manager, he did not express them.

In the meantime, Andy Rourke and Mike Joyce needed to acclimate themselves to the band in general and their lead singer in particular. It was not an easy process. 'I had a hundred per cent faith in the music,' said Rourke of his early impressions, 'but I had some doubts with Morrissey. I liked the lyrics. They were provocative, and going against the stream of what was going on at that time. I just knew that it was different.' Given that his listening pleasures these last couple of years had been in the lyrically uncomplicated if musically sophisticated world of jazz funk, it's understandable that he should recall his first six months as a 'strange' time.

Intrigued by his front man, Rourke desired 'to scratch the surface and go a little deeper,' but found that 'ultimately that's impossible, because Morrissey won't let you through the surface; he only lets you see what he wants you to see.' The pair would share the bus home from rehearsals in near silence. 'You started counting the lampposts,' Rourke recalled. 'This is a guy who lived in his bedroom. He was a recluse. And he's difficult to communicate with. To have a serious conversation of his choice – or my choice – was impossible. We had nothing in common.' The fact that there was a five-year age gap between the oldest and youngest members of the band surely played a part in this failure to connect, but

Rourke noticed something else in Morrissey that he was never able to shake off: 'He always had a little sense of superiority.'

Rourke had often served as the funny man in his relationship with Johnny Marr; his tendency to say the hilarious thing at the wrong time had earned them many a whipping at school. Recognising Morrissey's love of dry wit, Rourke played into and up to it as a way to connect, and 'I ended up being the clown. It was the only level I could meet him on.' In doing so, he realised that he was doing himself a long-term disservice. But if he suspected that Morrissey wasn't looking upon him as an equal, at least he could rely on his oldest friend to do so.

'I would elevate him, and he would ground me,' said Marr of Rourke. 'He could switch my intensity down. He was the one person who could do that. I don't think the other two were even aware of that importance, of that core chemistry in the band. So even aside from the fact that he's one of the most unique bass players of all time, his personality was really important to the band.'

At the same time, it was never Marr's intention to ignore the reasons he had walked away from his friendship with Rourke a year earlier. He had invited the bass player into the Smiths, he said, 'with the condition that he doesn't bring the drug habit back in.' Rourke, naturally, promised accordingly. But it proved easier said than done. 'Every time Johnny would see that look in my eyes, he'd sigh and say, "Fucking hell, are you still taking the smack?"' admitted Rourke. Faced with the prospect of sacking his friend already, right at the point that they *finally* had something going for themselves musically, Marr took a different stance; he confided in Joe Moss – who took immediate action, calling the bass player to say that he understood Rourke was having some 'problems,' and suggesting that he remove himself from the temptation. 'He took me into his house,' recalled Rourke. 'He had a basement apartment; he put me in there for two weeks to try and get me off the smack. It worked for a while.' And though it would not prove permanently effective, 'I'll never forget his generosity in doing that, and his concern,' said Rourke, who added, 'I loved Joe. Joe was a fucking saint. He was never in it for the money. He was like our dad. He was looking out for us.'

Rourke made his live debut at Manhattan Sound on 25 January 1983, followed ten days later by the Smiths' third gig, at the Haçienda, a show that was professionally filmed and recorded and therefore remains a permanent testimony to the Smiths' near-enough immaculate conception as a gigging four-piece. At both venues, the Smiths opened up for other Manchester acts as part of a local-band double bill, though there was little doubt that the Haçienda show, on a Friday night, alongside Factory's new signings 52nd Street – a primarily black Manchester act who were mixing Britain's jazz-funk sounds with those of the New York electro scene, essentially combining Rourke's dominant taste with one of Johnny Marr's – was the more prestigious of the two.

But that was not to belittle Manhattan Sound, a gay club on Spring Gardens that Marr and Moss, in particular, had often frequented for happy hour before the Smiths got going, and which had turned itself over to local promoter Rick Stonell for fortnightly local showcases. The Smiths played on the dance floor, nose-to-nose with the crowd, while 'porn' films were broadcast in a side room. 'We were all shitting ourselves,' said Rourke of the close contact. 'But with that comes adrenaline and with that comes concentration and with that comes an amazing gig.' The audience included not only their mates on the Manchester scene, but many of that scene's leading lights, including Richard Boon and Tony Wilson. The Factory boss later claimed, 'I was blown away, it was fantastic,' and that Morrissey, in particular, 'was amazing.'

Of that, there seemed to be little dispute. If Morrissey had still been partly ensconced in his shell at the Ritz, he left it behind at Manhattan Sound – for good. Morrissey the performer emerged in his place – and, it could be argued from the conven-ient perspective of history, pop music was destined never to be the same. As far as Marr was concerned, 'he was pretty much the finished article at the second show.' And when Morrissey concluded the set by throwing confetti in the air – something he'd neglected to mention to his band members – they understood, perhaps for the first time, the power of the personality in front of them. A 'masterstroke,' said Joyce; a 'magician,' thought Rourke.

The confetti did not make a return at the Haçienda. Instead, Morrissey came onstage clutching a bouquet of flowers, which he then slammed on the stage floor at the conclusion of the opening song, 'These Things Take Time'. Neither did James Maker return to dance alongside Morrissey. What had seemed like so much good-natured bonhomie over four songs at the Ritz had become something of an encumbrance over the longer set at Manhattan Sound, especially now that Morrissey appeared to have found his performing persona. It was Moss who insisted on the break, and that was fine by Maker, who had never intended anything more than to help out and have fun with one of his best friends, and who happily watched the subsequent Haçienda show from the audience. He retained a closer friendship with Morrissey than most, and would return to share the stage with the Smiths on tour three years later, fronting his own band, Raymonde.

Observing the footage of the Smiths at the Haçienda that February Friday night, it's worth noting that the concept of group image, which was important to Morrissey but more so to Marr, is evident in the band's perfectly coiffured quiffs (courtesy of Andrew Berry), but then pretty much gives up and gives way to the four individual personalities beneath. Marr has a white polo-neck underneath a jacket that's turned up at the collar, like an errant school pupil of the era (or James Dean); his rockabilly rebel revival look is given additional credence by the manner in which he rolls around his side of the stage with his Gretsch guitar, making enough noise for two, occasionally mouthing the lyrics, sometimes checking one of his friends out front, grinning throughout at the wonderful sensation of being onstage and feeling it *happening*, in a band of his own creation. Rourke has the sort of colourful sweater preferred by the jazz-funk crowd, and accordingly – and studiously – plays a borrowed Guild bass at a height that Level 42's Mark King would have approved of. Joyce, the only member with substantial gigging experience, performs in a workmanlike white T-shirt, which only serves to emphasise the drummer's naturally muscular physique and his spiky hair, a holdover from his punk days.

Of the four, only Morrissey seems to be close to the finished deal, a teasingly unbuttoned collarless work shirt exposing a white undershirt and love beads – an odd contradiction to his tightly belted 1950s office trousers. (Those would soon be replaced at Smiths shows by blue jeans.) Throughout the eight-song set he keeps the microphone in one hand, the other frequently clutching maracas or tambourine, and he stalks the stage and occasionally crouches on it, much as he had to Joyce and Rourke's consternation in the rehearsal and recording studios – except that at the Haçienda his movements are less those of a caged animal than one claiming its territory. And though his voice lacks for range, his confidence in it is apparent in its volume, the way he pronounces the lyrics meticulously, the occasional yelp for effect, and how for the last song, 'Miserable Lie', he breaks into the falsetto that would become his second vocal skin – and holds it through the finale for several riveting minutes.

Perhaps the most remarkable aspect of the Haçienda show is the set itself: of the eight songs, two would become hit singles, and those that did not join them on a bestselling debut LP would become equally celebrated as B-sides, one of them actually recorded from the mixing desk at that show. This simply does not happen in popular music; even those groups fortunate enough to formulate an immediately permanent and ultimately successful lineup are meant to write a set of songs, take them onstage, discard some, write a few more, rehearse them, try them out in public, discard a few more, and only gradually reach the point of no return. And yet, despite the fact that the Smiths had reason to be enthusiastic about all eight self-composed songs played at these first proper shows, one was already creating greater excitement than the others. The initial crop of Morrissey-Marr material, after all, was somewhat dark – a reflection, no doubt, of Morrissey's interminable bedroom years and Marr's own musical affinity with the moodier side of the post-punk period. There were a couple of exceptions – 'Handsome Devil' being the most obvious – but for the most part, the titles gave away the content: 'Miserable Lie' and 'What Do You See in Him?' on the face of it, appeared no more optimistic than 'Suffer Little Children'.

And then one Sunday evening in January 1983, Johnny was visiting his family in Wythenshawe with Angie when he picked up an acoustic guitar and found himself hammering out a riff. 'It was pure inspiration. I didn't have a concept before we played it. I didn't feel that "we need one that goes like this." I wasn't trying to make a chord change faster or slower or musing on it. I just had that exuberant riff that we had to turn into a song straightaway.' There was only one thing to do: drive to Stretford and trust that Morrissey would be home and happy to hear it. But as Brown's Beetle made its way up the A56 and Marr kept hammering out the chord structure, worried that he might forget it if he put it aside for more than five minutes, Angie implored him to 'make it more like Iggy!' Marr obliged – and so did Morrissey, by opening the door ('without an appointment!' as Marr later joked to Simon Goddard) and providing a cassette recorder. After Marr and Brown left, Morrissey wrote the lyrics to 'Hand in Glove' that same night.

His mission: to match the music with something 'searingly poetic and jubilant.' As was becoming customary, he stole from his idols in the process: the closing line, 'I'll probably never see you again,' was a direct lift from Shelagh Delaney's plays, while a Leonard Cohen lyric for Buffy Sainte-Marie, 'Everything depends how near you sleep to me,' was changed by only a word. But as was to prove equally common, such acts of artistic licence couldn't detract from the emotional effect of the assembled couplets when placed in Morrissey's order and alongside Marr's guitar. Most noticeably, the words in the opening verse 'No it's not like any other love, this one's different because it's us' were at once both eminently personal and equally universal. Any first-time listener, newly in love, could latch onto the line and sing it to his or her romantic partner, yet it could apply just as well to Morrissey and Marr's platonic relationship. The guitarist never asked; what mattered most to him was that 'the way [Morrissey] sang it and the words he sang had exactly the same spirit' as the riff Marr had taken to Stretford a few days earlier. As a result, he said, 'that song set us free. It felt like that the first time we ever played it. It felt like we were free.'

Morrissey felt much the same way. 'It was as if these four people *had* to play that song,' he said. 'Those words had to be sung.'

MOST GROUPS IN the Smiths' situation would, at this point, have considered other hometown gigs – a headliner, perhaps, at a respectable local club – to further tune and hone their set. They would have considered taking their most recent demo tape – in this case, generously financed by EMI – to various record companies. Had they been rejected, then down the line they might have considered a third recording session, taking what they had learned from the previous ones, hoping that this time they would get it right. And had all that failed, they might have considered releasing their own record – assuming that dejection had not yet set in.

But the Smiths, to paraphrase 'Hand in Glove', were not like any other group. (This one's different!) As far as the individual members were concerned, they had already paid their dues over multiple years in various gigging bands, rehearsal bands, half-considered bands and barely imagined bands. They'd sat in their various bedrooms and rehearsal studios and practised their craft, be it guitar or drums or lyric-writing, to the point where they had built up an entire catalogue of ideas and an inherent expertise on how to articulate them in a group format. They'd now come together as the Smiths and, by further developing that craft (both the songwriting and performing aspects) over several more workdays per week, were collectively convinced that they had something. Something very special. So, as much as it could be perceived as impatience, it was more a desire for perpetual forward motion that found the Smiths booking Strawberry Studios in Stockport on the last Sunday of February 1983, to record 'Hand in Glove' for the A-side of a single, barely a month after the song had been written and first performed.[1]

That this was the right course of events was proven by the master tape they emerged with at the end of that day, as recorded by Strawberry's resident engineer (and Martin Hannett's favoured right-hand man), Chris Nagle. Throughout the three-minute performance, the band played with a cohesion that made it sound like they'd been together for years, and though Morrissey was still not anybody's idea of a natural singer, and his vocals buried relatively deep behind Marr's multiple Gretsch guitar tracks, Joyce's cascading cymbals, and Rourke's punchy melodies, there was considerably more range and resonance to his voice than there had been up until that point (either onstage or in the studio), and greater character as well. As such, his attempts at the occasional tremolo and his ascension into a higher octave towards the end sounded less like the work of a freak than that of a genuine new voice.

Nagle, who hadn't heard of the group before, recalled that the Smiths were 'basically very keen, very energetic' and that the session went 'swimmingly well,' with Marr doing the talking for just about the whole band. 'Everyone was looking at the clock all the time. Can we do this? Have we got time? Can we do an overdub? Rush, rush, rush. It was a proper old-school recording.' At the end of the ten-hour session, the group then handed Nagle a cassette tape of 'Handsome Devil' as recorded live at the Haçienda. 'It gave me a real thrill that a band could be so keen to just say, "This is a B-side, this is what we sound like, let's just get it out,"' said Nagle, who spent a couple of additional, unpaid hours 'tarting it up' for potential release. 'It was lovely,' he said of the experience, 'and I was happy to do that.' (He was less happy to find, when the single was eventually released, that he was not mentioned, credit for production going to the Smiths instead.)

Two simple acts of brilliance that day at Strawberry took 'Hand in Glove' beyond the realm of the traditional introductory single. Just before the vocals came in for the first time, and immediately after they concluded for good, Johnny Marr added a simple harmonica line – which in addition to providing some instrumental warmth to the otherwise abrasive mix, resonated immediately as a reference and homage to the Beatles' debut single 'Love Me Do'. And though the choice to fade out on the 'Iggy' guitar riff was not unusual, the decision to fade *in* on it most certainly was. This was a bold statement of confidence, one that was rarely used in popular music because it distracted a disc jockey from his or her ability to talk over it. Few artists (other than the Beatles again, with 'Eight Days a Week') had ever used the fade-in and still garnered airplay. Fewer still had dared use it for their debut.

FOUR DAYS BEFORE the Strawberry session, the Smiths played their fourth gig, opening for Richard Hell, the original New York punk: it was *his* visual look, all torn T-shirts and spiky hair, from his time in the bands Television and the Voidoids, that Malcolm McLaren stole for the Sex Pistols; *his* song 'The Blank Generation' that had been heralded as the CBGB scene's first true anthem. For Morrissey especially, being such a devoted student of that scene, it must have seemed like a big deal. But Hell's time had long come and gone, and if the gig at Rafters on Oxford Street was noticeable for anything in the long term, it was the presence in the audience of the band James.

By any standards James were an odd bunch: their singer, Tim

Booth, was a frustrated former private-school boy who had come to Manchester to study drama and found himself, like so many others at the time, caught up instead in the music of the Fall and Joy Division. Living, surrounded by abject poverty and violence, in the Hulme Crescents, as did many band members on the Manchester scene, Booth befriended two feared members of Manchester City's terrace crew at a student disco. (While the Smiths would later title an album for the prison Strangeways, original members of the band James actually served time there.) This pair had a purposefully untutored band going and invited Booth in as a lyricist, dancer, and eventual front man. One of the founding pair, James Glennie, alongside Booth and their romantic partners, then took up meditation and vegetarianism as alternatives to the usual pressure valves for inner-city living, and by the time they came to see the Smiths perform, had cemented a semi-permanent lineup under their new moniker – that of Glennie's first name. This similarity between the Smiths and James was pure coincidence in as much as they didn't know each other, but signified a mutual determination to counter the considerable pretentiousness on both the independent and national music scene. Of the two groups, James had the greater pedigree; they played the Haçienda for the first time in November and again in January, at the Friday-night local band showcase, two weeks before the Smiths. There they had handed Mike Pickering and Rob Gretton a demo tape including the songs 'Hymn from a Village' and 'Stutter'. Both the Factory men were instantly excited by what they heard, and when Tony Wilson watched the footage of James at the Haçienda (filmed from stage right as per the Smiths at their show), Booth stalking that stage like a boyish and bearish Mark E. Smith, and the band members trembling at their instruments as if possessed by the Birthday Party, he too was convinced. After opening for New Order in March, James signed to Factory.

Yet Tim Booth recalled being bowled over by the Smiths at Rafters, by 'how big they looked onstage. The charisma. Morrissey and Marr I remember quite visually. Musically, I think we were quite a bit threatened, because it . . . it was like, "Oh shit, here's another band doing this thing." Although it seemed very different to us. We were so much wackier and weirder and so much more fucked-up in our music. Whereas the Smiths were, if not the finished article, definitely ready to go. We needed years to forge our way, learn our instruments, learn our trade. But they were ready.'

There was never going to be room for both James *and* the Smiths on Factory; it was quite enough for one new guitar band to come to the label with a sense of unease about Wilson and co.'s perceived elitism, and a demand for creative control that masqueraded, in James's case, as mischief when they became the first Factory band to refuse a Peter Saville-sanctioned sleeve, turning in a felt-tip drawing instead. Morrissey might well have desired the Smiths to be that band. But even had James not been on the scene, had Pickering and Wilson been quicker to react to what they saw at their first two Smiths shows, and had Gretton been not so (understandably) dismissive of the first Smiths tape, Johnny Marr was never going to let it happen.

Marr had nothing against Factory. He was, as we know, a regular at the Haçienda, friendly to various degrees of intensity with key figures Andrew Berry, Mike Pickering and Tony Wilson, and his musical tastes aligned with those of New Order, whose affinity for contemporary American dance music was about to manifest itself globally via 'Blue Monday', which would become the biggest selling 12" single of all time. Marr simply understood that the Smiths were capable of being *bigger* than Factory was willing to contemplate and encourage; that they didn't want to be so closely associated with Manchester as were other Factory acts; that, like James, they wanted to distinguish themselves from all the bands that had a Saville-sanctioned sleeve design. He knew, too, that Factory worked at its own pace, and it was not much faster than the major labels. (James would not release a single until November.) And he knew, musically, that it would never be a comfortable fit, that Factory would only constrain a band like the Smiths, who were interested in 7" pop singles at a point when Factory was moving increasingly, even exclusively, towards the extended mix on the 12" format.

Which is not to suggest that he and Morrissey had no interest in being on a Manchester label. Richard Boon recalled the pair bringing him the prospective single with a view to releasing it on New Hormones, which surely would have been an ideal home for Morrissey. They were unaware, however, that the label was about to close up shop – with Boon, not that he knew it yet, set to move to London and work at Rough Trade as production manager. 'They played it to me in my failing office and it was brilliant,' he recalled, 'but I couldn't help them. Because I just knew, hearing it, they really had it, whatever "it" is. It was substantial, it was fantastic, it had legs. But legs I couldn't walk with.'

Marr had another Manchester indie up his sleeve, and he was perfectly excited by the prospect: a 'Portland Street' imprint complete with a picture of Moss's premises at number 70 on its label, a Brill Building of their own. It would require manufacturing and promotion, but Joe Moss was an expert at the former and there were few better at the latter, at least in Manchester, than Marr himself. But before putting that plan into action, they needed to follow up on a London independent label that took priority: Rough Trade. In early March, shortly after recording 'Hand in Glove', and with the live version of 'Handsome Devil' appended to it on cassette, Marr and Andy Rourke – curiously, not Morrissey – took a train to London to present themselves in good, old-fashioned, Brill Building manner: by knocking on the door and asking to play their songs to the man in charge.

CHAPTER FIFTEEN

I was obsessed with fame, and I couldn't see anyone in the past in film or music who resembled me. So when I started to make records, I thought, well, rather than adopt the usual poses I should just be as natural as I possibly could, which of course wasn't very natural at all. For me to be making records at all was entirely unnatural, so really that was the only way I could be. Unnatural.

– Morrissey, *Blitz*, April 1988

B ack in 1981, Rough Trade had compiled a cassette tape
for free distribution through *NME*. *C81* reflected the independent music scene as it stood at the dawn of the new decade,
one of incredible vitality and variety. The track that got most
people talking, though, was the one placed, strategically, at the
beginning: 'The "Sweetest Girl"' by Rough Trade's own signing,
Scritti Politti. Incredulously, the former communist squatters
and scratchy reggae-rockers, infamous for listing the (cheap)
production costs of their records on their (broadsheet-style)
single sleeves, had turned in a svelte, luscious, romantic piece
of lovers rock set to sweetly programmed drums and keyboards.
It was the kind of dramatic shift that not only turned heads
but provoked arguments: was it the greatest pop song of all
time or a complete sell-out?

Geoff Travis leaned towards the former. For the thirty-year-old,
after several years on the front line of all things confrontational,
'The "Sweetest Girl"' represented a return to the soothing qualities of a divinely produced pop song. And for a moment – during
which a number of independent scene-watchers took a deep

breath and agreed that the new-look Scritti Politti (for there was an image change as drastic as the aural one) was better than the old one – he had the staff on board with him. It seemed 'The "Sweetest Girl"' was set to be Rough Trade's first hit single.

But then Travis second-guessed himself. Rather than release 'The "Sweetest Girl"' as it was, he encouraged the group (a group that was quickly being whittled down to just singer-songwriter Green Gartside) to tinker endlessly in the search for the perfect mix. By the time it was released as a single, at the *end* of 1981, it had cost the label a small fortune, and a song that had helped shape that year's pop music landscape on cassette now appeared to be chasing after it on vinyl. 'The "Sweetest Girl"' barely grazed the charts. Travis nonetheless persisted with Gartside through the expensive – and drawn-out – process of completing an album of similarly lavish new soul. Finally released late in 1982, *Songs to Remember* (such statements of grandeur were very much en vogue thanks to the peacock-strutting New Romantics) became Rough Trade's first top 20 album since Stiff Little Fingers, but it still failed to produce a proper hit. Unable to continue financing Gartside's musical ambitions, Travis set him free to sign with Virgin.

For Travis, the lack of a hit was becoming a proper thorn in his side. Rough Trade Distribution was now a powerhouse, and as part owner of the company, Travis could take pride and profit in its success. But that distribution side was effectively run by his partner, Richard Scott, for whom 'the process' was the all-important driving force. 'We were trying to set up an access structure for small labels and for people to have their fifteen minutes of fun – rather than fame,' said Scott, though in the case of a 'Love Will Tear Us Apart', 'Papa's Got a Brand New Pigbag', or, as he was about to discover, a 'Blue Monday', that fifteen minutes could go on for years.

Travis had gravitated towards precisely the opposite point of view: 'The music is ultimately the most important thing. The system is not more important than the content.' Scott's negative opinions about the nakedly commercial ambitions (and cost) of *Songs to Remember* had created a tense division between the partners, essentially opening up an ideological chasm at the very heart of the independent music scene. To make matters worse, in late 1982 it was revealed that Rough Trade had been ordering too much stock, diversifying into too many areas, signing too many artists, and spending too much money on them in the studio. In other words, it was insolvent. Only the forbearance of Daniel Miller, whose Mute Records was owed close to a million pounds, prevented Rough Trade from being declared bankrupt. The financial revelation had resulted in a night of the long knives, as it were: the record shop that started it all, as well as the booking agency and the publicity firm that emerged out of the growing enterprise, were restructured as stand-alone, employee-owned entities. The ongoing importance of Daniel Miller (and his hit act Depeche Mode) to Rough Trade's bottom line only served to spotlight Travis's primary problem: 'We were pioneers in setting up the distribution that enabled that system,' confessed Travis, 'but we weren't leading the way in commerciality.'

To rectify this, Travis replaced Scritti Politti at the label with Aztec Camera, whose records Rough Trade had previously distributed as part of the now floundering Postcard label. Like Scritti, Aztec Camera was a group based around one man, the teenage prodigy Roddy Frame, only seventeen when he had released his first single, and whose pop sensibilities were now indulged at Rough Trade as much as Gartside's had been. The end product was the album *High Land, Hard Rain*, set for release in April 1983, and preceded by a gorgeously cerebral single dominated by ringing acoustic guitars, 'Oblivious'. Travis's problem with Aztec Camera was clearly *not* the ability to make great music on a Rough Trade budget, but that Roddy Frame was just too young, too talented, and too handsome: the Warner Bros empire was dangling six-figure deals in front of the teenager and there was nothing that Travis could do about it – especially as his contract with Frame consisted of only a handwritten note of temporary acquiescence from the artist.

And so, that spring of 1983, even as 'Oblivious' hovered outside the top 40, and allowing that the label was enjoying ongoing kudos for typically diverse recent albums by Weekend, the Go-Betweens, and Robert Wyatt, Travis knew that for Rough Trade's long-term success – and his vindication as a music man – he needed to find his own Joy Division or Depeche Mode. He needed an act at the start of its career, without previous baggage, an act that would come with credibility but was also interested in commercial success, one that was willing to work hard and play live without costing a fortune in the studio, one with whom he could form a nurturing relationship as some kind of executive producer – and one that would agree to a long-term contract.

Enter the Smiths.

THE STORY HAS become as much a part of rock 'n' roll lore as Jerry Leiber showing up on Mike Stoller's doorstep – or Johnny Marr on Steven Morrissey's. It is, in fact, told in a very similar fashion. Johnny Marr and Andy Rourke took a train down to London on a Friday afternoon in March, and when they arrived at Rough Trade's West London offices late in the day, brandishing their cassette, they were introduced to Simon Edwards. Though he officially went without a job title, like everyone else at Rough Trade, where equal salaries were also the rule, Edwards was essentially the head of sales, and a vital liaison between Records and Distribution (in other words, the feuding partners Travis and Scott). He was a key figure in setting up the ironically named Cartel, the new national distribution network that fed records through six regional independent wholesalers, with Rough Trade in London as the largest and most influential. In a Blenheim Crescent building that often resembled a cross between a socialist republic and an insane asylum, he was also one of the few permanently composed individuals.

That Marr and Rourke were pointed towards Edwards may not have been mere coincidence. Richard Boon was certain that he told Morrissey and Marr when they came to see him with their tape, that 'if you want to do an indie thing, maybe you should talk to Simon Edwards at Rough Trade.' For his part, Edwards generally desired an introduction. 'They must have said something,' he recalled. 'They probably said "Richard Boon said we should come down." I knew Richard and liked Richard.' Indeed, from years of front-line involvement, Edwards had developed an instinct as to what would and would not sell in the independent marketplace, and it had been his own rapidly reducing orders for New Hormones product that had sounded the death knell for Boon's company. When Edwards played 'Hand in Glove' through the office's Tannoy speakers, however, he heard something he felt *would* sell. 'I thought it was excellent,' he recalled. 'The mouth organ sounded fresh and interesting. I said, "OK, I'm interested in distributing this if you like."'

Distribution was Plan B: the Portland Street label. And if that's as far as the meeting had gone, the plan would have been immediately put into operation: Joe Moss confirmed, 'I was really looking forward to doing our own label and putting it out ourselves if we hadn't have gotten [Rough Trade] interested.' But Marr was determined to push for Plan A: he asked to see Geoff Travis, with a view to putting it out on Rough Trade itself. And Edwards obliged. 'This was something that didn't sound like ninety-five per cent of the bands' that were coming through his door at that time, he recalled. 'When they said they wanted Geoff to hear it, I thought it was fair and true for him to listen to it. It was good enough as far as I was concerned.'

Whether Edwards, as he recalled it, took Marr and Rourke directly to Travis or just sent them back and told them to try their luck (which was how Marr recollected the event), the guitarist seized his opportunity once it finally arrived with both hands. Literally. 'I did actually grab Geoff and say, "You won't have heard anything like this before, we'd like for this to come out as a Rough Trade Records track" – and my knees were knocking – "but if not, we're going to put it out on our own label and put it out through Rough Trade." So he had two options. I didn't give him the option of not doing it at all.' Travis, like Edwards before him, instantly recognised something about Marr – 'the look of him; he was an interesting character' – that caused him to pay attention. He took the cassette and promised to listen to it over the weekend, and Marr and Rourke went off to stay (up) at Matt Johnson's flat for the night.

When he listened to 'Hand in Glove' as promised, Travis reacted much as had Edwards. 'I was just really intrigued by it. I loved the sound of it, I loved the guitar playing, I loved the springy beat.' And although he 'couldn't tell what the song was really about,' he grasped that 'the lyrics were really interesting.' But like Simon Edwards, what *really* caught him was that it sounded of itself. 'It wasn't obviously derivative of so many of the other demos that you would hear those days . . . I just loved it. And I just felt a little bit of a thrill.'[1]

Travis's reaction to 'Hand in Glove' revealed why he was known for having some of the finest ears in the business: he could hear, in a murky mix on a cassette tape, the essence of brilliance. His business reaction then confirmed why so many of the most important singles in history had been released on independent labels to begin with. He didn't take the tape into an A&R meeting, where it could be discussed, dissected, and perhaps dismissed; he didn't seek second opinions (although he had that of Edwards already, which counted for plenty). He didn't second-guess the quality of the recording, as he had, fatally, with 'The "Sweetest Girl",' and he didn't demand to see the band play live first, as had EMI. Instead, he did precisely what independent labels were meant to do, what they were famous for doing, what they had been doing to undermine the majors since the birth of the record industry.

On Monday morning, while Marr and Rourke were still recovering from their long weekend down South, Travis called the phone number on the cassette inlay and spoke to Joe Moss. He told the presumptive manager that he would like to put out 'Hand in Glove' on Rough Trade, and as soon as possible. Given that Marr had requested as much, he correctly assumed that he wouldn't need to make any sales pitch of his own.

THE SMITHS PLAYED their first London gig on Wednesday, 23 March. The booking at the Rock Garden, a basement club in Covent Garden popular with tourists, may have been made directly by Joe Moss; it was a comparatively easy venue to secure. It might also have been handled by All Trade Booking, the castoff Rough Trade booking agency still operating out of Blenheim Crescent. All Trade was the major player in the independent sector; its roster included just about every act that was on Rough Trade, and many of those that weren't, including the Birthday Party, Orange Juice, and the Sisters of Mercy. But having just been abruptly thrust onto their own financial feet, the agency's key figures, Mike Hinc and Nick Hobbs, were actively looking for their own Echo & the Bunnymen – 'a credible live act that could tour without that much support from a record company,' as Hinc put it.

It was a given that Travis would recommend the Smiths and All Trade Booking to each other – as he did on the group's first visit to London, when they came down to master 'Hand in Glove' just days after Travis first heard the recording. But both Hinc and Hobbs claimed to have already been aware of the band. Hinc, the primary British venue booker, was at some point sent a tape of the Haçienda desk mix by Mike Pickering, whom he knew well enough to consider a friend, and therefore took the recommendation seriously. To confirm his own enthusiasm (he had been raised on Chicago blues and was a big fan of guitar bands), 'I played it to Andrew Eldritch [singer with the Sisters of Mercy], who was sleeping on my floor, and Roddy Frame, who lived round the corner from me. And they both

249

liked it.' Figuring that these were two of the most diverse people on the scene, he sensed that the Smiths were an immediate winner.

In the meantime, Hobbs, ATB's European venue booker, had received an early demo tape from Ollie May, Johnny Marr's erstwhile roommate who was now a Smiths 'roadie' alongside Phil Powell, and a mutual acquaintance through May's brother Marcus, a club promoter in Zurich. 'I liked it enough to give it to Geoff Travis,' recalled Hobbs. 'Geoff obviously got lots of demos from lots of sources; we did too. And I normally wouldn't pass anything on to Geoff unless I thought it was appropriate for Rough Trade and that it was something that Geoff was going to like. It was a tip from Ollie and I followed up on it.'

That being the case, Travis had not found time to listen to it. 'The first I ever heard of the Smiths was when Johnny and Andy came into the warehouse,' he said, confirming Marr's insistence that 'Geoff Travis had no concept of who we were or might be when I went down there.' But later in 1983, the group did give an interview in which Morrissey explained about the group's path to Rough Trade: 'Some mysterious third party just sent a tape to Rough Trade and they got very excited, asked to see us, and we went to see them and we just embraced each other.'

Furthering the sense that this was a band with a buzz, on the very day the Smiths played the Rock Garden, the *NME* published a glowing review of their Haçienda show. Conveniently including three comparisons to Howard Devoto's Magazine (much to Morrissey's delight, no doubt), and one apiece to former Postcard acts Josef K and the Fire Engines (similarly good news to Marr), the review had the staunch feel of being written by a friend.[2] This was certainly the case with the review of the Manhattan Sound show that had just been published in Manchester's *City Fun*. In that latter, unsigned instance, Cath Carroll played up her personal acquaintanceship with Morrissey: she made comparisons to his heroes Iggy and the Dolls, called him 'a congenital show-off with a dreamily affected baritone,' and after praising his confetti finale, concluded that 'if the boy's head is anything to go by, the Smiths are going to be B-I-G.' Factor in the interview that had just come out in *i-D* – a surprisingly staid one that indicated the group's inexperience with the process – and it was evident that the Smiths were, by any measure, especially for a band that had only played four shows, a serious new noise. To that extent, Geoff Travis's quick response to 'Hand in Glove' was additionally fortuitous, as from here on in, several of London's A&R talent scouts would take to frequenting the band's shows. The assumption existed, as well it might, that any act on Rough Trade was free for the major-label picking.

That would no longer prove to be the case. What Geoff Travis saw at the Rock Garden he could only compare to that which he had *not* seen: the likes of the Stones or the Dolls or the Stooges in their early days. His sense of astonishment acknowledged the increasingly familiar truth about the Smiths: that they had arrived 'fully formed.' As for Morrissey in particular, what Travis called the 'transformation' between the 'intense, very serious' individual he had met on their business trip to London and 'the man that came out' onstage was nothing short of 'extraordinary.' Mike Hinc thought them 'equally fantastic,' taken by the 'perfect balance' onstage. But he was especially intrigued by his friend Travis's reaction. 'I could see from the smirk on Geoff's face that they blew him away. He was like the cat that got the cream.' With confirmation of their excellence from a handful of other Rough Trade staff among the very small crowd in attendance (a crowd bolstered slightly by some Manchester friends, including Andrew Berry), Travis returned to Joe Moss with a renewed proposition: he wanted to sign the Smiths to a long-term contract. It was the first time Rough Trade had ever offered one.

CHAPTER SIXTEEN

I live a saintly life. He lives a devilish life. And the combination is wonderful. Perfect.

> – MORRISSEY on Marr, *NME*, 1983

You can see that Morrissey means it and lives it. You can see that Johnny means it and lives it. You can't fake it. People can see that that individual means it.

> – JOHNNY MARR, March 2011

The same month that 'Hand in Glove' was released, May 1983, the Clash played their last-ever show with their founding partners of Strummer and Jones, at a massive American rock festival that signified their international success. Six months earlier, the only other superstar survivors from the British punk wars, the Jam, had announced their breakup at the peak of their own career, their front man Paul Weller collapsing under the weight of the 'spokesman-for-a-generation' mantle and deciding that, at the age of just twenty-three, he needed to break loose and relieve himself of the pressure. (He went on to form the Style Council.) The Jam left behind six studio albums in six years, four number-one singles, and a reputation as Britain's most fashion-conscious *and* most socially conscious band. The Jam also left behind a void – not so much among those who had been with them from near enough the beginning but among younger teenagers who had only come on board during the band's later, chart-topping years and had barely gotten to experience and enjoy them before they called it a day.

The Smiths had started out with their image rooted very much in Clash territory, as hard-times rockabilly rebels with flat-top haircuts, Gretsch guitars, turned-up blue denim jeans and cut-off shirts. Over the course of 1983, that look (and to a large extent the sound, too) changed considerably, to a very modern(ist) update of 1960s flower-power children, sporting love beads, polo necks, custom-made black denim jeans (courtesy of Crazy Face) and, in Marr's case, a mop-top haircut and a switch to the Rickenbacker 330, the guitar of choice for Paul Weller and, before him, George Harrison and Pete Townshend. The changes were entirely organic, but they served to make the Smiths that much more English, that much more *modern*, that much more appealing to an audience and an industry that was looking to fill the space left by the Jam – even if it had no idea it was looking for the Smiths. The fact that the Jam were so evidently influenced by the Who, and that the Smiths – Marr most evidently – were fans of the Rolling Stones, served as a subtle but important distinction: that while these two later bands' roots were each unquestionably English, they were travelling down different branches.

There were, to be fair, several existing candidates for the British rock crown at the time of the Smiths' arrival on the scene. In February and March of 1983, in the wake of the Jam's breakup, U2, Echo & the Bunnymen, Wah!, Big Country and Orange Juice all enjoyed (their first) British top 10 singles; New Order soon followed suit. All these acts were very much children of punk and representatives of post-punk, and their shared moment of mainstream success suggested a sea change of sorts. And yet the first two of these groups were already fully established; they were not something that teenagers looking for a new band could fully claim as their own. In addition, U2 was from Ireland, and the epic, grandiose manner of their musical and social statements sat uncomfortably within the independent sector; it always seemed as if their ambitions lay on the far side of the Atlantic Ocean.

Of the others, Wah! turned out to be a flash in the pan, and

Orange Juice, like their former Postcard label-mates Aztec Camera, could not transform their coy charm into a live reputation. New Order, despite representing a victory for bloody-minded independence, had wholeheartedly embraced dance music, and live performances had never been considered their strong point to begin with. As for Big Country, led by a former member of original post-punks the Skids, they were just that bit older, and openly epic, in a Celtic manner that was clearly indebted to U2.

There remained definite similarities to be drawn between Echo & the Bunnymen and the Smiths: the singers, for sure, with their long overcoats and their huge egos stroked through copious music press interviews, where incredulous boasts of self-worth were seemingly justified by savagely witty put-downs of the competition. Of the two, Ian McCulloch was by far the better vocalist, but his lyrics were oblique, poetic, contentedly clouded in metaphor. He was not interested in addressing teenage angst, let alone politics of either the personal or electoral kind. He was not looking for that kind of reputation – or responsibility. Steven Morrissey, on the other hand, most certainly was – and the evidence was apparent on the back cover sleeve of 'Hand in Glove', which confirmed, after weeks of telling friends and band members to address him accordingly, that the singer had chosen to do away with his Christian name. From here on, he would be forever known simply as Morrissey.

This was seen by those around him as a markedly deliberate reinvention. 'There's a pre-Smiths Steven and a post-Smiths Steven,' noted Liz Naylor, who, with Cath Carroll, continued the four-way friendship with Linder and Morrissey throughout 1983. 'Something happened. He constructs himself from the Smiths onwards.'

Carroll was now freelancing for NME (Naylor doing likewise for *Melody Maker*) and with that paper having already run a positive live review, she found it easy enough to sell her enthusiasm for 'Hand in Glove' into a short feature on the Smiths upon the single's release. ('It was like it fell out of the record speakers,' she recalled. 'That was the point where it seemed obvious that he knew what he was doing all along.') She found it harder to conduct and write it: 'It was difficult knowing Morrissey as much as I did, or liking him as much as I did, to write about his band without being sycophantic.' She compensated by keeping it to the Q&A format and including ample quotes from Johnny Marr, and one from Mike Joyce. Her editor sent her a note upon receipt, saying, 'This is a very grey article about four very grey boys.' It was an inauspicious debut to the world of the music weeklies, and one that Morrissey quickly learned from; Joyce, for his part, would rarely be offered the opportunity to speak again.

Perhaps Carroll should have focused more on the imagery surrounding the group and the lyrics to 'Handsome Devil' (which was inadvertently listed as the A-side in that introductory NME feature). After all, the front cover of 'Hand in Glove' portrayed the backside of a nude man, his close-cropped head facing a wall, his right hand reaching behind his back to cover – though definitely not obscure – his naked buttocks. Morrissey had found the image in Margaret Walters's book entitled The Nude Male, and his insistence that it form the group's initial visual image served as a clear statement of social intent as well as confirmation of his role as the group's artistic director. 'It blends with the record and it evokes both sorrow and passion,' he said of the photograph. 'It could be taken as a blunt, underhand statement against sexism, yet in using that picture I *am* being sexist. It's time the male body was exploited. Men need a better sense of their own bodies. Naked men should be splashed around the Co-Op, you know.'

This latter comment was again offered in an interview to Cath Carroll, but not in NME; it was proffered instead in a separate profile on Morrissey published in *Him* (aka *Gay Reporter*) magazine's August issue. The full-page story presented Morrissey as the 'Arthur Marshall of the new wave.' Marshall was a veteran writer known to the Smiths' generation as a genial old captain on the TV show *Call My Bluff*. Significantly, perhaps as a result of living through so many years of gay repression, Marshall never signed on to gay liberation. Neither would Morrissey. 'He was keen on using every possible mouthpiece to get the word out,' said Carroll of her friend's agreement to conduct the *Him* interview (at the editor's request, notably). 'But he never wanted to represent himself as a gay band or a gay man or even as a bisexual man or whatever he might have been . . . There was just something about him that whatever it was someone wanted to say about him, he would say, "Well no, it's not that."'

'I detest sexual segregation,' Morrissey duly confirmed (a comment he would repeat at every interview whenever the subject of gender or preference came up), and even launched into an attack on the contemporary gay scene for being 'so full of hate in all directions,' accusing the 'heterosexist behaviour of some gay men' as rendering them 'indistinguishable from Tetley Bittermen,' a term of the times for macho beer drinkers.

Yet as the Smiths' reputation spread over the second half of the year, Morrissey made a conscious decision to withdraw from the front lines of sexual identity. 'The gay connotation could well be harmful when it comes down to dealing with the press,' he told *Record Mirror* in November when asked about his presence in the gay media. 'I wouldn't like to be thought of as a gay spokesman . . . because it just isn't true.' The *Him* interview was quickly removed from the growing file of press cuttings.

THE SMITHS RETURNED to the capital on 6 May to play the University of London Union, opening for the Sisters of Mercy. The ULU gig, booked by Mike Hinc at All Trade as would be every Smiths concert in Europe from here on in, served as the launch for 'Hand in Glove', and word was put out throughout the label to invite anyone and everyone.

Key among those to do so was Scott Piering. A central part of the Rough Trade setup (one hesitates to call it an establishment) for four years already, Piering hailed from San Francisco, where he had made his name as an independent concert promoter in a city 'owned' by Bill Graham; famously, he had picked up and booked Bob Marley and the Wailers after they were thrown off a Sly Stone tour, earning Island Records boss Chris Blackwell's eternal gratitude. That led him to promote an entire tour by reggae band Third World when Richard Scott was managing that band, which eventually saw him invited to join Rough Trade by Scott, though not before he took a detour to New York to manage the Cramps. Piering enjoyed nothing more than to talk about music, which made him a born publicist, and in establishing that role for himself at Rough Trade, he helped take it out of its self-imposed ghetto (the label formerly insisted that journalists buy their own review copies of records) and into a more visible role at the vanguard of the post-punk maelstrom. If Piering didn't like a record, he freely admitted as much, which was not the way publicists traditionally operated, but when he did love something, he went above and beyond the call of duty to let the world know about it. Piering's passion for the music on and around Rough Trade had him visiting the music papers to hang out all afternoon and play new records, and then taking up a similar role at Radio 1 – at least within the offices that would admit him, essentially those of the evening and weekend shows.

Piering, like Mike Hinc, had been among the perceived 'victims' of Rough Trade's near-bankruptcy, forced out of the company's employ and told to set up on his own or vacate his office. He chose the former option, created the company Appearing PR – and very quickly emerged stronger as a result. Now he could not only charge Rough Trade a fee for his work even as he continued to operate out of their offices, he could charge other labels too. (Among them was Factory, whose 'Blue Monday' was gaining daytime airplay at the moment the Smiths signed to Rough Trade.) For all his eccentricities (long conversations on multiple phones intimated a glacial sense of progress, though the job always seemed to get done, usually at the expense of sleep), he was as beloved by record labels, editors, journalists, radio DJs and producers as he genuinely loved the music he promoted to them.

Impressed by the band's single and trusting the word of Travis and Hinc, Piering opened up his phonebook for the ULU gig. He scored two direct results: John Walters, the producer for John Peel's show and a respected music personality in his own right, attended, loved what he saw, and awarded the Smiths a much-coveted Peel session. It was recorded twelve days later and aired two weeks after that. And Dave McCulloch, a high-profile journalist at *Sounds*, reviewed the gig for the next week's paper and followed up with a major interview.

McCulloch's live review was enthusiastic in the extreme. Alongside the most evocative picture seen of Morrissey so far – leaning forward, eyes closed, love beads dangling, microphone in one hand, maracas in the other hand, looking every bit the 1966 San Francisco psychedelic love child – he struck all the right referential chords: Magazine, the Fall, Costello, Nietzsche. (Music journalists *loved* referencing Nietzsche.) He even prophesied, correctly, that 'one day Smiths could save [Rough Trade's] financial skin: *That's* how good they are.' But he also took what he could hear of Morrissey's lyrics and concluded that 'most are about child-molesting, and more mature sexual experimentation.' As for the use of the Al Jolson refrain 'Climb upon my knee, Sonny Boy' at the end of 'The Hand That Rocks the Cradle', he wrote, without any evidence, that 'it was used as a child molesting "come on" to a seven year old in a park.' One might have expected McCulloch to present this interpretation as a problem, but no: 'This kind of ultra-violent, ultra-funny grime is just what is needed to pull rock 'n' roll out of its current sloth,' he wrote. As another hyperbolic review of what could have been just another unrealised next big thing (other than the *NME* feature, McCulloch's was the only substantial piece of press that the Smiths received through the month of May), it seemed – at the time – like business as usual. And nobody – well, hardly anybody – paid the child-molesting reference much heed.

CHAPTER SEVENTEEN

Q: What is it that you do?
A: I'm not bad with words.
　　　　　　　– MORRISSEY to Paul Morley, *Blitz*, 1988

The Smiths' public onslaught began with the John Peel session, broadcast on 31 May 1983. As expertly recorded by BBC engineer Roger Pusey, the Smiths delivered four songs that revealed levels of texture and depth, clarity and contrast, that had not been evident in the claustrophobic mix of 'Hand in Glove'. The session ranged musically from the passive-aggressive ('Miserable Lie') to the relatively rockist ('What Difference Does It Make?'), to the pseudo rockabilly ('Handsome Devil') and the powerfully evocative ('Reel Around the Fountain', recently introduced into the live set). And yet, despite the fact that Johnny Marr's evident talents as a composer and musician shone brightly through all of this, it was Morrissey who truly stole the show. With every visit to the studio, he was improving. He no longer sounded strained or muffled; in fact, his voice now carried a resonance and warmth that afforded him the confidence to engage in the vocal tricks that would become his trademark: the falsetto, the yelp, the yodel.

On 'Handsome Devil' he petitioned, 'I'd like to help you get through your exams,' and for those Peel listeners busy studying for them while tuned into the radio between ten p.m. and midnight there at the end of the British school year, that was temptation enough to put aside the homework and hear what else Morrissey had to offer. It turned out to be an endless series of majestic one-liners about love and romance that covered every base (instinct): 'I look at yours, you laugh at mine' (from 'Miserable Lie'); 'I'd leap in front of a flying bullet for you' ('What Difference Does It Make?'); 'You can pin and mount me like a butterfly' ('Reel Around the Fountain'). Fifteen minutes with the Smiths? Who would say no?

Picking up the music papers the next day, that same Peel listener, intrigued by the Smiths for sure, perhaps even converted already, might have gravitated to Dave McCulloch's interview in *Sounds* under the (predictable) headline HAND-SOME DEVILS. It was only a page, and Johnny Marr shared the spotlight, but it was Morrissey's words that shone. Some of what he said was mere ego, the kind that would become a future trademark of so many Manchester bands: 'I tremble at the power we have, that's how I feel about the Smiths.' But most of it revealed a level of freethinking to back up the snatched couplets of the Peel session's lyrics: 'I feel I'm a kind of prophet for the fourth sex . . . It sounds trite in print but it's something close to men's liberation that I desire . . . I'm bored with men and I'm bored with women . . . I don't want to GO ON about feminism but it is an ideal state . . . This is a society that only likes women who faint and fawn and want to get married . . .'

Perhaps most profoundly, Morrissey also announced to McCulloch, 'I want a new movement of celibacy. I want people to abstain.' Celibacy? Abstention? Culture Club's Boy George had quipped about how he'd 'rather have a cup of tea' than sex, but nobody in the music world had ever come out and called for a celibate *movement*. It didn't exactly start a revolution, but for that teenage Peel fan, that teenage *Sounds* reader (the demographics of both leaning strongly towards the male) struggling to find and hold on to a lover or partner, the very hint from Morrissey that it might not be worth the effort – that Love was just a miserable lie – was indeed a moment of (men's) liberation.

And there was still more. 'Jobs reduce people to absolute stupidity, they forget to think about themselves. There's something so positive about unemployment. You won't get trapped into materialism, you won't buy things you don't really want.' Admittedly, this was coming from someone still living at home at the age of twenty-four, not from someone (like Marr alongside him) more or less kicked out of the house at the age of seventeen who worked in clothes stores to spend money on fashion. A similar observation could (and would) be made of Morrissey's calls for celibacy in a band whose other three members all had steady girlfriends. But that was both the point and not the point. The other three could represent the vast percentage of the 'normal' population if they wanted to. Morrissey was speaking to the others: the freaks, the loners, the depressives; the unemployable, the unlovable, and, as Morrissey put it in his last letter to Robert Mackie, the unacceptable. And he was so enjoying the opportunity to do this in print – finally, as a featured artist and not a signature on a letters page or a byline in a live review – that he allowed himself to state, accurately if fawningly, that 'the British music press is an art form.'

McCulloch played devil's advocate to that one and threw out the name of Garry Bushell, a fellow *Sounds* writer whose passion for working-class authenticity had led him to invent, champion and defend the Oi! movement of punk-skinhead bands, many of whom harboured far-right and racist beliefs. Morrissey replied, quick as a flash, 'There is always an exception to a rule, Dave,' and the conversation immediately returned to the word 'handsome' and Morrissey's assurance about his fans that 'in six months' time they'll be bringing flowers to our gigs.'

It would happen that much sooner. The Smiths had been booked back into the BBC for another session, this time for David 'Kid' Jensen, whose show went out directly before Peel's. As befitted the earlier time slot, Jensen's show was less eclectic, had a wider audience, and featured interviews and the occasional guest DJ. The few new bands that were granted one of the limited session slots were usually further rewarded with a phone interview from the Canadian-born DJ on the night of its broadcast, to introduce themselves on-air. The Smiths, however, had created *such* a buzz already that Morrissey was invited down to London to be interviewed live in the studio.

And so, on 4 July, Jensen's birthday, Morrissey pontificated at large from Broadcasting House to the rock-loving, radio-listening nation. (The nation? Yes. Other than sporadic late night shows on what passed for commercial local radio, there was no other place on the radio to hear rock music in Britain at the time; Radio 1 owned the medium.) He did so with the same casual self-confidence as had been evident in the *Sounds* interview: 'We planned a strategy and everything has worked and here we are,' he announced nonchalantly of the Smiths' rapid rise, as if it were preordained. 'We just followed nature and there you have it.' But he also ensured some self-deprecation as a balance: his life, he said, 'has been quite tragic, hence most of the words seem to be quite tragic and sorrowful.' Offering some background to 'You've Got Everything Now', he admitted, 'I sound such a mess,' but still went on to claim a modicum of revenge on his former St Mary's pupils: 'When I left school, it seemed like all these oafish clods from school were making tremendous progress and had wonderfully large cars and lots of money. And I seemed to be constantly waiting for a bus that never came. And it seemed as though I had the brains, I didn't have anything else.'

But now he did, which made it all the more beautiful that the refrain – 'What a terrible mess I've made of my life' – should resonate through the airwaves and into any number of bedrooms and bedsits, where listeners might well have experienced instant relief to hear that someone else, a singer in a pop band, no less, should have felt that way while confessing in the same song that he had no interest in rectifying that mess by taking up something as mundane as a job. Such pride in wilful unemployment sat perfectly alongside the reference in 'These Things Take Time' to 'the alcoholic afternoons where we sat in your room,' a line that caught the attention even of the former Buzzcocks guitarist Steve Diggle, who recalled himself sitting out society in early punk days by claiming quiet hours in the pub for philosophical, alcohol-fuelled debate.

The interview with Morrissey concluded with news that the group had been recording an album with Troy Tate – a former member of the Teardrop Explodes who had recently released a solo single of his own on Rough Trade. 'It's been quite a magical communion,' Morrissey assured listeners, promising that the album would be out 'within about six weeks,' suggesting, in reality, a September release. Jensen's producer immediately booked the band back in for another session that could air around that date. In the meantime, the Smiths followed up this high-profile broadcast with their first show in Manchester since February – at the Haçienda again, on 6 July. And this time, as headliners.

THE DECISION TO put the Smiths straight into the studio (Elephant Studios, in the London docklands area of Wapping) to record a full album reflected Geoff Travis's belief that they had the songs, the confidence, the dedication, and, judging by what he saw of them live as well, the skill to justify the immediate investment. With the music press and evening radio on board, he could safely assume that a Smiths album in the autumn would go some way towards compensating for the recent loss of Aztec Camera to WEA. Roddy Frame's group (which now included a Salford boy, Craig Gannon, on second guitar), had left with Travis's 'blessing', and Rough Trade would benefit financially from the major company's re-release of 'Oblivious', but the truth was, as he explained on a rare television appearance recorded around this time, he was 'sick of losing groups.'

'We were just living day to day – and that was part of the beauty and the beast of Rough Trade,' he said years later of the label's long-standing (lack of) approach to business. His decision to secure the Smiths to a long-term deal represented 'a moment when living day to day seemed less like a great philosophy than thinking a bit ahead. When you have something as good as the Smiths, you don't want to do all the work and see them go off elsewhere.'

The band had not been averse to Travis's long-term offer. In fact, they were ecstatic to be taken so seriously. 'Someone is going to promise that we are going to make an album, and then another one after it?' recalled Marr. 'And then another one after that? You are kidding me! It's what you've always dreamed of, that you're going to get a record contract.'

Contrary to widespread (and subsequently widely reported) belief, the Smiths had received only a modicum of interest from major record labels at this point. 'There were a couple of really dedicated young A&R scouts would have killed to sign the band,' said Joe Moss, but these scouts could not get their bosses on board. Tony O'Connor did not carry any weight at EMI. A likeable lad at Tamla Motown's London office named Alan Omokhoje was doing his best to revitalise the once-esteemed black American independent by trying to persuade them to sign white English rock bands, but without success. And Gordon Charlton at CBS was sufficiently enthused as to join in the stage invasions *and* invite the band along to his office in Soho Square. There, Marr noticed, just as Morrissey had over at EMI's Manchester Square offices a few months earlier, the only records on display were on the wall, framed in gold and platinum as tribute to the label's selling powers. Meanwhile, at Rough

Trade – as at Factory – 'you couldn't get in the door for records, it was chaos,' said Marr. The conclusion was self-evident. 'We'd already got a relationship with [Rough Trade] at that time. You were working with people you like. They were nice people. Who you respect.'

Morrissey's reasoning appeared very similar. 'At the end of the day,' he told David Jensen, 'we just thought, "Who would we really like to be with? Who would we like to work with once you put your calculator away and you forget about money and the rest of the world et cetera?" And the answer is Rough Trade. We really wanted to be with them. The majors were quite frightening. Most of the people we met there seemed like principally salespeople, and they really couldn't recognise anything unless it was immediately commercially viable or whatever, and it really didn't appeal to us too much to be harnessed by these kind of people.'

'We were always going to sign with Rough Trade,' said Joe Moss, whose principle of business was sufficiently straightforward: keep working with those you're working well with. Geoff Travis duly sent up a boilerplate contract dated 1 June. It was all of five pages long – more extensive, certainly, than the original two sentences Richard Scott had written up for early deals (split the profits 50-50; either party can end the deal if unhappy), but still laughably vague by major-label standards, where thirty-page contracts of convoluted legalese justifying multiple royalty deductions and complex option periods were the norm.

The original wording on this Rough Trade contract stipulated an initial period of one year, followed by four one-year options, but it was changed, in handwriting, to a period of three years with two one-year options. It was five years/albums either way, if seen to conclusion, but the difference was crucial: it meant that the label and group would be committed to each other for three years and/or albums, regardless. This was a sign of immense faith on Rough Trade's part; even the most lucrative major-label deals rarely committed to more than two albums, in case an act failed to live up to initial expectations and the label was left financing records that no one was going to buy.

As for the subsequent two one-year option periods, a hand-written note at the bottom of the clause, from the band's side, requested that 'the artists should have the same options.' It was the most familiar complaint in the music business: why should only the record company get to decide whether to renew the contract? The reality, however, was that Rough Trade had never actually worked this way: Travis had let both Scritti Politti and Aztec Camera move on rather than trap them in a negative relationship. Whether anyone around the Smiths knew as much, and then hoped that they might be allowed similar freedom of movement should the day arrive, was uncertain. Regardless, this particular contract had been intended to ensure that such previous acts of generosity on Rough Trade's part were a thing of the past. As the initial three-year period confirmed, Travis was not planning on letting the Smiths out of his sight anytime soon.

Elsewhere, the label did make a couple of concessions at the band's request. Rough Trade's right to final decision on producer was eliminated entirely; so was the clause that refused the group permission to release their Rough Trade material on any other label for five years after the contract's conclusion. The group additionally secured some control over promotional photos and press materials and were assured 'mutual consent' to appear on other artists' records. The split of 'net receipts' was set at 50–50 in the UK, and an extraordinarily generous 75–25, in favour of the artist, in the rest of the world. A list of pre-net 'expenses' (manufacturing, recording, promotion, etc.) was duly ticked off, one by one. Bizarrely, there was no reference to advance payments. (Typically, the list of ongoing advance payments would form part of a separate 'schedule' that would nonetheless be referenced in the primary contract.) All involved recalled the initial advance being approximately £4,000.

The biggest confusion on the contract was saved for the

highly pertinent question as to who they were each actually dealing with. On the boilerplate contract, 'The Company' was specified as 'Rough Trade Distribution', but the word 'Records' was subsequently written in above this, as if to clarify it for the band.[1] On 'The Artists' side, the contract allowed for any number of individual names to be listed as members of a band. That band was written in as 'The Smiths' and alongside the note, 'Check with manager', the individual names of 'John Marr' and 'Stephen Morrissey' [sic] were listed above. The fact that the manager did not add Andy Rourke and Mike Joyce was never a point of concern for a record label used to dealing with singularly fronted bands like Aztec Camera, the Fall, and Scritti Politti. 'I knew by then that Morrissey and Johnny were the ones that counted,' said Geoff Travis. 'In the nicest possible way.'

Many of these clarifications, crossed-out queries, deleted clauses and officious initiallings were handled on the day that Geoff Travis took a train to Manchester with the intention of closing the deal. He recalled, 'There was a lot of talking, lots of running 'round maypoles and chasing, hanging 'round in Joe's upstairs room, trying to get to talk to them, and lots of whispering in corridors.' But in the end, both parties clearly preferred to sign the deal in Manchester and get on with the act of making and selling records rather than have the lawyers type it up afresh for the avoidance of doubt. Johnny Marr and Morrissey (the latter using his spidery squiggle and leaving out his first name) signed as the Smiths, Geoff Travis for Rough Trade. The contract was duly witnessed and the date of execution written in: 24 June 1983.

For Rough Trade, the hasty process proved immediately beneficial. Only five days after the contract was signed, the Smiths played London's Ace club in Brixton, for the second time that month, opening for their now good friends the Sisters of Mercy. Thanks to the Peel session and increasing press, the buzz on the band was now out, and Hugh Stanley-Clarke of EMI, believing that commissioning the initial demo counted for something, and convinced that his scout Tony O'Connor was keeping the band abreast of the fact that he was now seriously interested in the band, brought a phalanx of staff (he recalled it being in the dozens) to see them in the flesh. It would have been hard for the major-label staff not to sense the spark of something very special by this point in time. But after the show, O'Connor emerged from the band's dressing room to tell the head of A&R, sheepishly, that the band had just signed a long-term deal with Rough Trade – 'much to my fucking fury,' said Stanley-Clarke, who insisted of O'Connor that 'his job was to report what was going on; that's what we'd paid him for.' The scout was let go soon after.

The very next night, the Smiths played at Warwick University, and this time it was CBS's head of A&R, Muff Winwood, finally responding to Gordon Charlton's cajoling, who showed up, excited to see the band. It was left to Joe Moss to inform him, too, that the train had already left the station.

ON 5 SEPTEMBER, the day that their second session for David Jensen was to be broadcast, the Smiths woke up to find that they were featured in Britain's biggest-selling newspaper, the *Sun* – albeit not in the way they had imagined when Morrissey had granted an interview to Britain's most notorious right-wing tabloid without considering their motives. Under the headline 'BAN CHILD-SEX POP SONG' PLEA TO BEEB, the paper's 'showbiz' columnist Nick Ferrari repeated one specific reference made by Dave McCulloch in his live review of the Smiths – that they performed '"Climb Upon My Knee, Sonny Boy" about picking up a seven-year-old in a park.' And he alleged another – that 'Handsome Devil' contained 'clear references to picking up kids for sexual kicks.' Morrissey was quoted (surely out of context), as saying 'I don't feel immoral singing about molesting children.' And Tory MP Geoffrey Dickens was called in to condemn the Smiths for their prurient subject matter and implore the BBC to ban the band. The result, crowed Ferrari, was that the BBC was holding an emergency meeting that day to decide whether 'a song about molesting' should be broadcast on the David Jensen show.

It was a setup, of course, and fingers were quickly pointed at Garry Bushell, who had just enacted some revenge of his own for Morrissey and McCulloch's put-down in *Sounds*, using a column in the same weekly to tie a homosexual attack on a young boy (as publicised on the front page of the *Sun*, not so coincidentally) to McCulloch's admittedly unsavoury justification of 'child-molesting' lyrics as 'the kind of ultra-violent grime rock 'n' roll needs.' 'Try telling *that* to the mother of the 6-year-old Brighton boy mob-raped by paedophiles,' wrote Bushell, who denied that he then fed the story to the *Sun*; as far as he was concerned, the band – and his nemesis McCulloch – had publicly dug its own grave.

To some extent, he was right. It was difficult to analyse the lyrics to 'Handsome Devil' or, as noted earlier, 'The Hand That Rocks the Cradle' or, to a lesser extent but to an extent all the same, 'Reel Around the Fountain' and not come away with a certain degree of unease. As a serious student of Oscar Wilde, Morrissey knew all about the aesthetic movement's endorsement of 'Greek love', and he may have been trying to express some of their sentiments in song. Then again, he may not have been. He had, after all, left the door open to multiple interpretations, let *Sounds* run away with some of them, and though he had tried to clarify himself in the subsequent interview ('We do not condone child molesting'), he had nonetheless allowed a Wilde-like glibness to muddy his sincerity ('We have never molested a child'). And so, if the *Sun*, in its familiar position as the self-appointed guardian of British morality, had taken McCulloch's conclusions and amplified them across its 4,000,000 print run, who was he to cry foul?[2]

It was nonetheless, on the immediate face of it, an awful interruption to the Smiths' inexorable upward rise. But unlikely though it seemed that morning, the *Sun*'s exposé did the Smiths multiple favours. The paper may have been taken as gospel by a significant percentage of the working-class population for its supposedly populist sympathies, but it was detested by just as many more for its pro-Thatcherite manipulation of the working class and for its malicious bloodlust. Following an incident during the previous year's Falklands War, when the *Sun* had printed the front-page headline GOTCHA! to celebrate the sinking of a retreating Argentinean warship with the loss of four hundred conscripted lives, there were many in Britain who would not, in good conscience, so much as open the paper, let alone buy it. In the wake of its attack on the Smiths, the *Sun*'s opponents – including the majority of the music press – instantly rallied to the band's defence, and those on the left who had barely noticed the group took them up as a worthy cause on the basis that 'the enemy of my enemy must be my friend.' Besides, how were the *Sun*'s readers going to protest against the Smiths anyway: by burning their records? 'Hand in Glove' had barely sold its initial 6,000 pressing.

The most damaging short-term effect of the *Sun* story turned out to be the band's greatest blessing. As threatened in the headline, 'Reel Around the Fountain' was withdrawn from broadcast on the BBC that evening. (The opening lines, 'It's time the tale were told, of how you took a child and you made him old,' were hardly going to sit well following the newspaper revelation.) This was hypocritical, given that the Smiths had recorded it for the John Peel session back in May and nobody had complained about it then, but it was more problematic in that the reason they had just recorded it again was because it was scheduled as their second single; test pressings had already been ordered and an advert stating 'out now' had been placed in the September issue of the fanzine-magazine *Jamming!* The furore in the *Sun* forced the Smiths to now reflect on this choice of single. After all, if the evening producers at Radio 1 already had cold feet about the song, the prospect of getting any daytime airplay – of moving into *Sun* readers' territory – was remote at best. This led to other considerations: 'Reel

Around the Fountain' was a ballad, some six minutes long; it was as if they were jumping straight into their 'True' moment (à la the chart-topping but credibility-sapping Spandau Ballet single from earlier that year) without having laid the two or three years of groundwork.

In the meantime, the Smiths were continuing to write material at a furious rate. And when John Walters, out of sympathy and solidarity (and as a reminder of who had found the band first) commissioned a second Peel session almost as soon as the *Sun* came out that September morning and forced 'Reel Around the Fountain' off the airwaves, the Smiths used the opportunity to unveil no fewer than four brand-new songs. One was a beautiful ballad, 'Back to the Old House'. It was the first of many that Johnny Marr, drawing on Irish traditions, wrote in a 6/8 time signature and that he performed with gorgeously precocious acoustic guitar flourishes, to which Morrissey applied some of his most yearning lyrics yet ('You never knew how much I really liked you . . .'). Another was the purposefully aggressive 'Still Ill', which reprised the harmonica-intro idea of 'Hand in Glove' and then took the unemployment sentiment of 'You've Got Everything Now' a step further: 'England is mine, and it owes me a living, but ask me why and I'll spit in your eye.'[3] A third, a 4/4 ballad entitled 'This Night Has Opened Your Eyes', returned to the troubled parenting that had haunted 'The Hand That Rocks the Cradle', but this time with a much clearer lyrical message – that of unplanned parenthood ('The dream has gone but the baby is real . . .'), another likely rewrite of *A Taste of Honey*.

And the fourth of the new songs was led by an upbeat, chiming guitar riff of the kind that Smiths songs, it could be fairly posited, had been lacking until now. That riff was a conscious tip of the guitar to Johnny Marr's new friend Roddy Frame, whose equally exuberant guitar lines were about to take Aztec Camera into the top 10 with WEA's re-release of 'Oblivious'. Marr was all too aware that Frame was one of the only successful musicians on the scene younger than him. 'This Charming Man', he admitted of the new Smiths song in question, 'was me pulling my finger out because Roddy got on the radio.' For his part, as with 'Hand in Glove', Morrissey had risen to the challenge of matching the musical mood. The title enabled him to reference a word that, like 'handsome', was part of a Romantic vocabulary he wanted to (re)introduce into the lexicon of a working-class British popular culture that generally frowned on such niceties.[4] After the furore over 'Handsome Devil', however, Morrissey was careful not to shout any homoeroticism from the song's (literal) hillside, but it was insinuated in the general perception of a male vocalist singing about a male suitor all the same, with lines like 'the leather runs smooth on the passenger seat' taking on a certain gravitas for those who were looking for it. Those who were not looking for it – which, *Sun* journalists and early Smiths obsessives aside, would have been the majority – could rejoice instead in the universal familiarity of the line 'I would go out tonight, but I haven't got a stitch to wear.' Ultimately, 'This Charming Man' lacked for an obvious meaning – Morrissey confessed that it was 'just a collection of lines that were very important' to him that he subsequently 'stitched together' – but that did not mean that it lacked for a feeling. With this song, more so than any of its predecessors (and many of its descendants), Morrissey mastered the great lyricists' skill of saying an awful lot to those who were listening, without actually saying anything in particular to those who were scrutinising.

Knowing that the Smiths were presenting four previously unheard songs for this fourth BBC session, Geoff Travis and Richard Boon had announced that they would stop in to hear them in progress. They happened to walk into the Maida Vale studio that 14 September at the precise moment the Smiths were recording 'This Charming Man' for the very first time. Travis took one listen and quickly voiced his instinct: 'That's a single.'

CHAPTER EIGHTEEN

It feels very comfortable – this waiting period. I'm ready to be accepted by everybody. I want to be heard and I want to be seen by as many people as possible.
MORRISSEY, *Melody Maker*, September 1983

In the Sixties records were actually *worth* something. People went out and bought a seven inch piece of plastic and they treasured it, which they don't seem to do any more. We're trying to bring back that precious element.
– JOHNNY MARR, *Sounds*, November 1983

As the buzz about the Smiths grew steadily greater, so the stakes rose higher, until it became evident that it would no longer suffice to release a relatively cheap and hastily recorded album in the autumn months. This was in large part because Smiths fans already had an album of sorts: as Peel and Jensen took to repeating the Smiths sessions due to popular demand, so fans started swapping the complete set around on cassette. The number of sessions, the fact they were spread evenly across the two influential shows, and the overwhelmingly positive reaction to them, was unprecedented for a band with just one, non-charting independent single under its belt, and for this reason the Peel and Jensen shows' role in 'breaking' the Smiths cannot possibly be underestimated. But if, from the late spring onward, the Smiths effectively 'owned' Radio 1's evening hours, so too was the pressure on them as a result. Nothing short of a classic debut album would now suffice. And after the 'playback' (the presentation of the final mix to the group in the studio), Morrissey – for all his previous hyperbole about the album to an increasingly attentive British media

– concluded that this was not it. 'He just decided he didn't like it,' said Marr. 'That was entirely his prerogative, and that was a big call to make on your first album.'

The 'Troy Tate' album, as it came to be known by Smiths fans (officially it was to be titled *The Hand That Rocks the Cradle*) was, for the most part, a fine record. Some of its fourteen songs sounded much better than the versions eventually released: 'Reel Around the Fountain' in particular, perhaps because it was mixed, mastered and even (test-)pressed onto vinyl, turned out to be the song's definitive version. Tate's version of 'Jeane' still came out as the second single's B-side, and was greatly loved for it; and the initially intended bonus track, 'Pretty Girls Make Graves', eventually made it to release and sounded perfectly fine, especially for the addition of Audrey Riley's cello. There is evidence in all this to suggest that if the other tracks had been taken through to the mastering process, they too might have been similarly revered.[1]

Certainly, these songs had their fans. 'I actually prefer those versions of the first album,' said Mike Joyce, while Joe Moss acknowledged, 'There is something brilliant about them because basically they captured how the band were live,' inadvertently pinpointing both their strength and their weakness. 'It was very much of its time,' confirmed Marr. The problem, then, was not with some of its parts, but the *sum* of its parts. Taken together, as a complete album, the fact that it reflected the Smiths as they had entered Elephant Studios that hot summer – untutored and inexperienced, or 'bleak' and 'northern' as Johnny Marr reflected on the final mix – was no longer good enough. The fact that the second Peel session had showcased four brand-new songs, pointing towards an entirely new level of musical sophistication, only made a rethink of the album more pertinent.

In the long run, Geoff Travis took the blame. 'That was way too impulsive a decision,' he said of appointing Tate. 'I learned a lot from that. Because recommending producers to bands is almost the most important thing you do as an A&R person apart from signing people.' For his part, Andy Rourke noted that much about the proceedings – the heat of the summer, the confinement of the basement studio, and especially the quality of the engineer (the Elephant Studios of the 1980s was never considered a top-grade facility) – contributed to the perceived drawbacks. Clearly, nobody wanted to make Troy Tate the fall guy, especially the band. 'He was a lovely guy,' said Marr; a 'talented musician,' observed Rourke. And yet the producer was all but destroyed by the album's rejection. 'Disappointment is not strong enough a word,' he said of the scrapped Smiths sessions while promoting his own subsequent solo release – which Morrissey generously and genuinely raved about when offered the chance to review the singles in *Melody Maker*. After two albums on Sire, Tate retired from the music business and refused to ever talk again about the Smiths on record.

In his place came John Porter, the former Roxy Music bass player and producer who, as an additional credential for the Smiths, had produced *Quiet Life* by Japan, a favourite of both Andy Rourke and Morrissey. The Smiths had met him on 25 August, when recording their second David Jensen session. According to Marr's recollections, he had not initially been assigned as their producer that day; rather, they met him in the canteen prior to the session and, said Marr, 'as soon as I found out that he was John Porter, we were all keen to get him in on the session.' (All the more so as they had felt a lack of interest on the part of the BBC's assigned producer at their first Jensen session.) Though this would have been a breach of the BBC's authoritarian bureaucracy, it would have been well within John Porter's impish nature to convince another producer to switch sessions based on positive first impressions with a group of effusive teenagers (and one reserved twenty-something).

Porter brought a new dimension to the group's sound at Maida Vale that day – especially to the guitars, layering acoustics and electrics in and around one another to the point that the four songs he recorded with them, in eight hours, sounded almost like finished masters. Thirty-five years old at the time, Porter was already a veteran at Maida Vale ('I must have done over a hundred bands there') and had gathered a reputation within the industry 'as a cleanup guy. I did a lot of records that had been started with other people and for whatever reason hadn't achieved a satisfactory result.' After the BBC session, as dissatisfactions emerged with the Troy Tate album, the Smiths recommended him for that role and Geoff Travis gave him a call to that effect.[2] But Porter recalled that after listening to the Troy Tate recordings, he returned to Travis saying, 'How much money have you got? Because I think it's going to cost more money in studio time to fix it than to do it all over again.' The decision to scrap the recordings entirely was not made immediately; as late as mid-September, weeks after they had worked together on the Jensen session, Morrissey appeared on BBC's Radio London and played the Troy Tate production of a song entitled 'I Don't Owe You Anything', which had first been unveiled two weeks earlier on the Porter-produced Jensen session. The album, Morrissey then said, was 'being remixed by John Porter. He has just waved his magic wand and it's very fruitful.'[3]

Certainly the Smiths – the playing members, at least – immediately bonded with Porter, who, likewise, saw them as kindred spirits. 'When I first went in the studio in London I was a clueless kid from the north,' he said of his entrance into the music business in the late 1960s, 'and I recognised, although they were very tied up in their own success even at that stage, they were clueless kids from the north too. And I . . . felt like a father figure. Particularly Johnny, I felt like he was a younger brother in many ways.'

Porter's relationship with Marr would prove pivotal to the group's progress. 'He was my mentor in the studio,' said the guitarist. 'I was like a sponge, and I had a lot of energy, and he had a lot of experience without really ever being given such an opportunity to teach. I couldn't have been with a better musician, because he's a master of recording guitars, and very, very patient. So every idea he threw at me, I would run with – and vice versa.' Porter quickly convinced Marr that it was a smarter idea to use a capo than to tune the guitars up a whole step or more, as they had been doing with the earlier songs to accommodate Morrissey's vocal range – and regularly breaking strings in the process. And it certainly didn't harm their instant friendship that Porter was married to Linda Keith, the former girlfriend of Keith Richards, and the woman responsible for seeing the talent in Jimi Hendrix at a Greenwich Village club in 1966 and not resting until she acquired him a manager. The fact that Porter smoked almost as much pot as Marr, and was not beyond countering it with 'uppers' when necessary, furthered that camaraderie.

With the future of the Tate album still up in the air, Porter was assigned to produce four songs for the second single, led by 'This Charming Man'. (The others were 'Accept Yourself', 'Still Ill', and 'Wonderful Woman'.) Allocated all of £500 to prove himself, he chose the studio Matrix near the British Museum because 'you could get a good sound in there and it was really cheap.' His first act of inspiration was to take the three-second guitar intro to 'This Charming Man' and append it with an additional section that had lain somewhat hidden under the verse on the Peel session. (While Marr was seen constantly with a Rickenbacker at this point, this particular guitar track, as with many other famous Smiths riffs, was recorded using Porter's own 1954 Fender Telecaster.) The elongated riff established a pattern of guitar intros to Smiths singles, a nod to the likes of Chuck Berry in that regard that simultaneously served to elevate Johnny Marr into the same category of greats. It also demonstrated that a good guitar intro could sell a whole song – something of a quaint notion that summer of 1983 when, to paraphrase Decca Records' famous rejection of the Beatles, guitar bands appeared to be on the way out.

Elsewhere in his arrangement, Porter re-structured Andy Rourke's bass line to give it more of a Motown punch and introduced a series of sudden stops for added dramatic effect. These were some of the oldest tricks in the production book, but it was the first time the Smiths had worked with someone who suggested them. 'It was quite a big change,' recalled Porter.

'And they were a bit put out by it, I think. But quickly they got into it and dug it and it was fine.' As they then dug deeper, Porter's initiatives took the form of the little audio tricks that help give a great production its polish (ones that Tate, for all his enthusiasm, did not have in his arsenal of effects). For the clanging guitar barely audible before the sudden stops on 'This Charming Man', Porter suggested taping down the guitar strings and dropping a knife or a screwdriver on them – and it worked. And for 'Wonderful Woman', one of the Smiths' earliest compositions, and one that the group could easily have run off as a live-performance B-side, Porter and Marr stayed behind at the end of the session working through the night on the song's final, ringing chord. 'He had the patience to do things like that,' said Marr. 'And if it didn't quite work right, he'd rewind the tape and do it again. And do it again. And again.' Marr realised how fortunate he was to find a thirty-five-year-old producer who was willing – and capable – to work so hard. 'I'd leave the studio at seven thirty in the morning, reeling, having forgotten ninety per cent of what I've just done. And then sleep and come back that afternoon. And then I'd listen to all these tiny little details and just think, "Wow, that was really worth it."'

Morrissey, by contrast, was resistant to delivering his vocals more than three or four times at most. This was in part his innate understanding that the emotional feel of an early 'take' was more important than the clinical perfection of a later one, but it also reflected a general disregard for the recording process, which quickly put him at odds with his new producer. 'I wanted everyone to feel at home in the studio, because if you feel good, you play good,' said Porter. 'So straightaway, I tried to explain the process to everybody. Mike and Andy, to a certain extent, were fine – "Just get on with it." Johnny was very interested. And basically if we were in the studio for eighteen hours, Johnny and I would be there for eighteen hours. It was a process that we both were into, every stage of the game. Straightaway with Morrissey, from the first session, I tried to do the same with him. It's like, "These are the fades, this does this, this is your voice on this fader, it goes to this, it's got these, this is the harmoniser, we've got echo, we've got delay." Morrissey wouldn't touch it. He just looked at me like, "Are you mad?"'

'He didn't click with Morrissey; they were like sandpaper together,' said Andy Rourke of Porter, who felt that the (lack of a) relationship had to be viewed with equal culpability, inasmuch as 'I think Morrissey felt shortchanged by the time that was invested for the vocals.' For his part, Rourke walked into the studio with 'massive respect for [Porter] anyway because he played bass with Bryan Ferry,' and came away equally impressed, citing him as being 'like everyone's favourite uncle.'

That feeling was mutual. 'Andy had good ears,' said Porter, noting that 'my reservations initially were stronger about Mike. I thought Johnny and Andy had more technique, if you will; they also had more, probably, in common in terms of music that we liked. My favourite music has always been R&B and black music – the JBs and the Meters and New Orleans music and funk – and the rhythm section was everything.' By comparison, Porter's experience as a producer was that 'English drummers were not very tight,' and that 'punk people couldn't play,' which put Joyce at a double disadvantage. 'You build a house on a strong foundation, and it's only as good as the drums,' said Porter. 'So my focus was very much "Let's get the drums tight." They don't have to be complicated at all, but we need to have a good feel. That was seventy-five per cent of it. Everything else came after that. So I was hugely concerned with the drums.' To compensate for what he saw as Joyce's inconsistencies, he had the drummer record to a metronomic 'click track'. Even then, there were enough imperfections that the Matrix Studio recording of 'This Charming Man' ultimately involved a lot of 'edits' – the splicing together of different taped sections – as opposed to the capturing of a genuine live performance.

It showed. When the results were presented to Rough Trade, Geoff Travis immediately announced that he did not hear what he had already pinpointed as a 'hit single.' His complaint, recalled Porter, was, 'It's all very fuzzy; you can't hear the snare drum.' When this version, what came to be known as the 'London' mix, was eventually released on a 12" single, Travis's doubts were proven entirely correct. Marr's reputed fifteen different guitar tracks dominated the mix, draped in reverb, to the exclusion of everything else – not just the vocals, which sounded far too pleasant, as if yearning for radio airplay, but also the rhythm section, which was buried way back in the mix, perhaps because it was weak to begin with.

Porter suggested a longer or 'proper' mix session.[4] Travis instead instructed him to record it all over again, and this time in Manchester, at Strawberry, where the Smiths had made 'Hand in Glove' and where they were reunited with engineer Chris Nagle. To ensure a solid rhythm, Porter painstakingly pre-programmed Joyce's entire multiple drum parts on an electronic LinnDrum and had the group record over the top of it. Some producers, especially those working for major labels at the time, might have left it like that: the sound of the LinnDrum haunted and came to date so many recordings from 1983. But that was never Porter's intent. Once all the other parts had been recorded – including Morrissey's vocals (assembled again from three separate takes that, according to Nagle, caused the singer to doubt his abilities and disappear from the studio on an hours-long walk as a result) and the multiple guitar overdubs – Porter brought Joyce in, who 'played it through in one take.' As far as Porter was concerned, in relieving the drummer of the pressure to establish the recording's foundation, he had set him free. Chris Nagle had never seen any producer employ this tactic before; he had considerable doubts that it would work, let alone that Joyce would pull it off in a single take. When it proved successful, he left the studio with what he described as 'full respect' for Porter.

The Strawberry version – 'This Charming Man (Manchester)' as it would occasionally be identified – achieved everything that the trial marriage of Porter and the Smiths had originally set out to accomplish. It built upon the commercial appeal that had been so evident in its initial Peel version, and it exuded the confidence within the band that was almost contagious at this point; indeed, said Marr of his partner Morrissey's contribution, 'it's the exuberance of his activity that is, in my mind, as caught up in that record as the sound of the guitar.' It had a shimmering production quality that sounded suitable for daytime radio; and it allowed Morrissey and Marr to shine equally as the band's evident stars even as the rhythm section's propulsive beat gave it a potential appeal on the dance floor.[5] Heard alongside 'Hand in Glove', it was almost hard to believe that this was in fact the same band, such was the progression in six short months. John Porter was duly handed the commission to re-record and produce the debut album from scratch, and Rough Trade set to work trying to achieve what may have seemed at the time if not entirely impossible, then certainly improbable: securing the label's first major hit in the midst of the Christmas market.

JOHN PORTER WAS not the only one who had doubts about Mike Joyce's abilities, and if the producer was unaware of this, that was only because the Smiths were already so adept at closing ranks. Negative comments had been ongoing since Joyce first joined the group and had peaked once already, in June, when the group started playing London on a regular basis. Si Wolstencroft, who had belatedly turned into a Smiths fan, witnessed such an occasion, at the Brixton Ace. 'Mike ended a song too soon, and there were some very important people there, and everybody was fuming about it, and I drove Andy home after the gig, and he said, "Well, I'm going to try and put you back in there, so you can get a second chance at it."' Being friends with the group, Wolstencroft was using Moss's Portland Street space to rehearse with the Colourfield (featuring Terry Hall, formerly of the Specials and Fun Boy Three), and Joyce feared the worst after seeing another drummer's kit in the room. In the end, said Wolstencroft, 'it never happened because Joe said it was too risky, didn't want to rock the boat.'

Marr backed Moss on this one. 'As is nearly always the case with young street rock bands, a producer and/or a record company will start saying, "The drummer isn't very good," and it's probably because . . . you can hide mistakes easier on the other instruments. And if the drummer isn't absolutely rock solid, then it can be criticised. The label can be straight onto it.' As far as he was concerned, 'Mike had to adapt his style somewhat. Before he played with us he was all-out bombast. There was discussion over the first eighteen months that he was maybe not as on it as me and Andy, but he shook that off. And it kind of fell on deaf ears, to be honest.'

With the band attracting a rapidly growing following, and with Joyce acquiring a strong reputation as a friendly face in the group, Porter had taken the right approach: find ways to improve the musicians' confidence and skills in tandem with each other, and then allow them to march onward together. This was crucial, because one of the things that the Smiths had going for them was the public's perception of them as a proper group. And so, even as they excluded the drummer and bass player from the process, Morrissey and Marr consistently talked them up in interviews. On Radio 1 in July, Morrissey had said, 'They are just the most capable musicians I ever came across in Manchester and it's a perfect little family.' And in a press interview conducted shortly before the Troy Tate album was abandoned, and leaving himself out of the equation only because he was assessing the group from the perspective of its leader, Johnny Marr said, with a little more clarity on how things would truly play out: 'There's Morrissey, the emotional vocalist and Andy the diligent, concentrating bass player who never misses a beat and the same with Mike. To me that's the way a band should be – the songwriters and the rhythm section.'

CHAPTER NINETEEN

I'm not a session player. I'm the drummer in the Smiths.

— MIKE JOYCE, 1999

When it became known that the money was going to be split that way, there was a very emotional meeting about it and then everybody just rolled with it for five years.

— JOHNNY MARR, March 2011

As part of his shifting attitude towards commercial success, Geoff Travis was increasingly taking appointments and forming liaisons with the major music business powers, especially those connected to Warner Bros. This would soon lead to his own partnership with another independent label's A&R man, Mike Alway of Cherry Red, in a Warner 'boutique' label called Blanco y Negro, from which Travis would draw a hefty salary – a sore point with the poorly paid staffers at Rough Trade, even though Travis claimed to have funnelled much of it back into his independent acts. With regard to the Smiths, these connections also led to him hinting at a likely licensing deal with Sire, the Warner-distributed American label, which offered the prospect not just of credibility and commercial opportunity but of additional funding for recordings and videos; and of a major publishing deal, which would help give the songwriters, and perhaps the band in the process, some immediate cash flow to compensate for Rough Trade's paltry advance.

Seymour Stein, Sire's founder, had come of age in the 1960s, working for Leiber and Stoller's label, Red Bird, in the Brill

Building, where the Shangri-Las and a veritable treasure trove of other mid-'60s girl groups resided, powered by the husband-and-wife songwriting team of Jeff Barry and Ellie Greenwich; such pedigree alone made him perfect for Morrissey and Marr. Stein and songwriter-producer Richard Gottehrer had then launched Sire at the end of the decade, trawling the European markets for major-label acts that had not been picked up by their American counterparts. They found both the Dutch group Focus and the British band Fleetwood Mac in this manner, giving the company the basis on which, as an established independent, it was able to sign the cream of New York's punk talent – the Ramones, Talking Heads, Richard Hell and the Voidoids – while the major labels prevaricated. When the punk boom in Britain then manifested itself in myriad independent releases, Stein resumed his transatlantic shopping trips. As early as 1978, Sire had signed the Normal, the Undertones and the Rezillos, all of which had been initially distributed by Rough Trade; by 1983 he had added other Rough Trade-distributed acts Depeche Mode, Yaz(oo), the Assembly, and the label's own signings Aztec Camera and Troy Tate. He had, in addition, taken on Echo & the Bunnymen and the Pretenders from the UK arm of Warner Bros; stolen Soft Cell from underneath Polygram's American nose and taken them into the top 10; and was busy making hit singles out of marginal British acts like Tin Tin and Modern English. He had also just signed a New York-based female singer and dancer who was part of the city's thriving electro/hip-hop club scene. She went by a single name, Madonna.

In short, a British act would need to have either a vastly better option on the table or be signed to a watertight world-wide deal with a non-Warner label to consider turning down Stein's approaches. The Smiths had neither, and fairly jumped when Stein indicated his enthusiasm. Although the Sire boss did not see the Smiths perform until he flew over for the show at London's ICA on the Mall in October 1983 – where, said

Moss, 'he just flipped' – Morrissey had actually announced the deal already, in an interview conducted at least a month earlier.[1] When they did finally meet then Stein, as was his fashion, regaled the duo with his celebrity stories. 'He told me that when Brian Jones first came to New York, he took him to get a guitar,' recalled Marr. 'I wasn't going to let that opportunity slip. So I said, "If we sign to you are you gonna get me a guitar?"' Stein said he would.

By this point in time, Sire was independent in name only. 'Seymour would sign bands and rely on a network of people within the company to help take care of the bands,' said Steven Baker of Warner Bros, who in 1983 was transitioning from an A&R position with the label in New York, where he had developed a close relationship with Stein, to working as right-hand man for label president Lenny Waronker in Burbank, California – an ideal position from which to champion Sire acts. Aware that Stein had just secured the Smiths for Sire, Baker went to see the group at one of their London college shows at the end of October. He was instantly impressed (both by the fact that 'Morrissey was an amazing front man' but also, from a vital American perspective, that 'the band was a good rock band') and joined Geoff Travis for a business lunch with the band a couple of days later – at a vegetarian café in Notting Hill, this being Rough Trade. From there, he quickly assumed the role of 'point person' for the group in the States.

Sire's arrival on the scene added to the pressure on the debut LP, and the decision to scrap the initial Troy Tate recordings. Equally, it was the injection of the label's capital that helped ensure the re-recording; John Porter noted that once the money arrived from America, it was instantly converted into studio time – at Pluto in Manchester.

While enticing Sire into the fold, Travis simultaneously talked up the Smiths to Peter Reichert, the newly promoted Managing Director of Warner Bros Music in the UK, as the group's possible song publisher. Songwriting was the lucrative side of the music business, that which, away from the glamour of the stage and the studio, offered guaranteed income from record sales, performances and airplay. A good publisher – and Warner Bros was among the very best in the UK – would ensure that every penny of royalties was claimed and duly distributed to the composers. While some music publishers chased after unsigned acts with the promise of helping secure them a record deal, Reichert, as a major player, tended to work the other way, enticing acts with generous publishing deals at the point when they cemented their record contracts. Publishing was, after all, essentially, a numbers game: without the risk of the recording and promotional budgets that record companies indebted, an advance could be calculated directly against the mechanical royalties from album sales.[2]

Reichert was already in the process of signing Travis's other major act of the moment, Aztec Camera. He took one look at Morrissey onstage, concluded, 'This guy's a total star,' and offered to sign the Smiths as well. As much as the singer attracted him, however – 'You couldn't take your eyes off him' – he loved that the band offered him some sort of alternative to most of the deals he was striking at the time. 'They were really against the grain. It was all Duran Duran and that polished '80s music, which I never liked. When I first saw the Smiths I felt "This is so real to me."'

When it came to offering Morrissey and Marr, as the sole songwriters, an advance, 'eighty thousand pounds sticks in my mind,' said Reichert – a figure he considered 'about normal for a hot band.' That translated, by his calculations, to a break-even of between 150,000–200,000 albums sold: double gold in the UK, but a relatively paltry amount for a global release. Additional mechanicals from single sales, and the performing-rights royalties that came from radio and TV airplay – that is, from hit records – would be considered 'icing on the cake.'

Joe Moss had set up a nominal publishing company (Glad Hips Music) for the debut pressing of the Rough Trade single, knowing well enough the horror stories of acts from the '50s and '60s who had signed away their songs – and effectively, their incomes. But by the 1980s, the business had changed considerably: there was more to lose by trying to collect the royalties oneself than by assigning the songs to a reputable publisher. And the deals had grown more generous: Morrissey and Marr were assured the reversion of their rights after ten years and would have been guaranteed at least 75 per cent of income, said Reichert. Plus, the advance payments were not inconsiderable to Morrissey and Marr. Even when split between the two of them, over the course of a year, and allowing for potential management commissions, it was a significant 'salary' for a pair of young men who had only previously worked in clothes and record shops, entry-level bureaucratic office jobs, and as hospital porters, if at all. A deal was duly struck.

When it came to signing, however, 'Geoff wasn't allowed to be there,' said Reichert. 'I think Morrissey particularly was a bit paranoid about the mighty Geoff Travis having too many influences over his career.' As Reichert recollected matters, Morrissey and Marr put aside the idea of continuing with Glad Hips or setting up a limited company to collect and distribute their income (there were tax incentives to support such a move, and an abundance of paperwork to counter it), and signed directly, as individuals. Reichert had made routine approaches about the rhythm section: 'I always liked to sign all members of the band just in case. It was very much pointed out, "They'll never write." I can remember saying, "Well, I would like to sign them anyway."' The response? '"No, they'll never write."'

THERE WAS NEVER any expectation that Rourke and Joyce *would* share in the songwriting credits. Marr had knocked on Morrissey's door with a definite view towards writing songs together, and the pair had completed several future Smiths classics before Joyce, and then Rourke, came on board. Even as the group slipped into a steady pattern of rehearsing, recording and playing live together, the songwriting process was always considered a private one between the lyricist and the musician, and most songs were composed in isolation from the rhythm section. Morrissey and Marr saw themselves in the grand tradition of Lennon and McCartney, Jagger and Richards, even Joe Strummer and Mick Jones. They were the band's acknowledged songwriters, and its leaders, and they expected not just the credit for it but the money, too.

There were, however, many groups who took a different approach, preferring to share the songwriting royalties on the understanding that everyone was in it together, and that each individual contributed in his own way to the band's overall success. This was the attitude of Britain's most highly visible, consistently successful post-punk groups: U2, Echo & the Bunnymen, and New Order. It was also the approach taken by the American group with whom the Smiths had most in common: R.E.M., who likewise had a magnetic front man of indiscernible lyrics and inscrutable personality, a Rickenbacker-playing guitarist with encyclopaedic musical knowledge, and a rhythm section entirely devoid of pretentions. R.E.M.'s debut album, *Murmur*, had proven a considerable success in 1983 in an American marketplace that was not just inherently conservative, but to the extent that it entertained what it still called 'New Wave', focused relentlessly on the 'British Invasion' of synth-pop and post-punk groups to the exclusion of its home-grown talent. It would prove eminently frustrating to R.E.M., who had been together since 1980, that when they embarked on their first visit to the UK right around the release date of 'This Charming Man', they found themselves hailed not so much for their individuality but for their similarities to British newcomers the Smiths.

When it came to *their* business setup, R.E.M. had decided on full equality. 'The songwriting money we share isn't necessarily for writing the songs,' Peter Buck, who would come to form a solid friendship with Johnny Marr, later explained. 'It's for sleeping on the floor for ten years while we toured, it's for the eight hours of rehearsal we used to do when we were making forty dollars a month.'

The problem with the Smiths – because this *would* become a problem – was that they had not been through a similar period of collective struggle. Morrissey and Marr had met, identified their potential as a songwriting partnership, worked to put together a group around those songs and their personas, and that group had taken off, all in less than a year. Given the speed of this process, there was no incentive to share the publishing – and neither was their complete and total ownership of the songs ever challenged by the rhythm section.[3]

But the same thinking was then applied to the lone signatures on the record deal. As Joe Moss later tried to justify the process, 'It couldn't be any other way, really. Two people were doing what Johnny and Morrissey were doing. For Mike and Andy to be able to have power of veto, to be able to say no to things, that's inconceivable. It's not *their* vision; they're part of Johnny and Morrissey's vision.'

The much-ballyhooed absence of Rourke's and Joyce's signature on the Rough Trade contract was a red herring of sorts. After all, there was nothing stopping Morrissey and Marr from signing the Rough Trade deal as the Smiths, thereby signifying their ownership of the name and effectively denying the rhythm section 'the power of veto' while still splitting recording proceeds evenly with Rourke and Joyce. (Similar deals are struck all the time in the music business.) This would have left the lion's share of income – the publishing – in their hands as songwriters, and presumably everybody would have been happy. But it didn't happen that way. With the record and publishing deals now signed, yet with Rourke's and Joyce's name absent from each, the rhythm section understandably sought to clarify their share of income; Morrissey, Marr and Moss likewise thought it prudent to establish an agreement. But when the conversation eventually took place, it was under less than ideal circumstances. The group was in the midst of re-recording its album at Pluto Studios in Manchester, in mid-October 1983, when a meeting was abruptly called. Either just before or after that announcement, Morrissey left the recording session, ostensibly to get food – and didn't come back.

'Before he moved on with the band he wanted to have it firmly established as to what each person was going to be earning out of it,' said Joe Moss in a BBC documentary, *The Rise and Fall of the Smiths,* in 2001. 'And as far as he was concerned, that was Johnny's job to do that with Mike and Andy. Johnny had brought them in. Morrissey doesn't want to be having to go doing that.'

'We didn't know where he was, couldn't find him,' said Johnny Marr of his partner on that same BBC documentary. 'And then later on that evening we got a phone call from Geoff Travis . . . saying, "He's in Rough Trade and he's not coming back until you sort out the business."' (Both John Porter and Geoff Travis recalled Morrissey leaving a recording session and taking a train to London to discuss business with Travis.) It fell to Moss and Marr to explain the proposed, and decidedly uneven, split of record royalties: 40 per cent for the bandleaders, 10 per cent each for the rhythm section.

To the BBC, Mike Joyce recalled the conversation as follows: 'Johnny Marr came in and said . . . "Morrissey wants me and him to get a higher percentage – or more money." And . . . um, Johnny said, "If you don't accept it, I'm going to leave the band."'

'All me and Mike were trying to do was stop Johnny leaving the band,' said Rourke on that documentary, presumably in defence of their apparent acquiescence. 'Which I hope he in hindsight realises was a good thing.' Another way of looking at it might well have been that both Joyce, whose drumming had been found wanting, and Rourke, whose drug habit was similarly troubling to those who knew about it, felt that their own positions in the group were precarious, that they were not in a position of strength (or knowledge) to argue the case that particular night. It didn't help that they were among the Smiths' biggest fans. 'It was stuff me and Johnny had dreamed about since kids, being in the recording studio,' said Rourke, who admitted to 'becoming obsessed' with listening to the latest Smiths recordings. 'And then we're in there almost every day. Living the dream and loving it.' The bassist had likened his previous job at the lumberyard to 'being on the chain gang. It was nasty work. It was manual labour.' Upon recently leaving that job, he'd told his boss ('[who] hated me anyway'), 'You'll see me on *Top of the Pops* in one year.' This was the kind of brash comment made by countless kids with dreams of making it as pop stars, but the nineteen-year-old could just about sense it coming true. He had no intentions of throwing that possibility away and returning to a life of drudgery.

So the rhythm section kept quiet. Rourke subsequently insisted that even though a conversation certainly took place at Pluto, 'nothing was ever worked out,' and Joyce ultimately went to court based on the same (mis)understanding: 'We didn't come to an agreement that we were going to get twenty-five per cent. There was no agreement that we were going to get less.'

Yet Joe Moss was absolutely adamant otherwise. 'It was agreed that Mike and Andy were going to get ten per cent,' he said in 2010. 'We agreed it in a room in a recording studio.' As to why the others might have 'forgotten', he offered his shorter period of tenure with the Smiths. 'Mine was, say, two years, so I've got less to remember . . . And these were very specific things that I had to do as manager.' But he never got it written down and signed. Rather, 'as soon as Geoff Travis was speaking to me [that day], I knew that that was it for me then,' he said on the BBC documentary. 'If Morrissey couldn't come to me to sort that out – which I would have sorted it out for him, without question, because that was the role – that there was too much of a division then for me to be able to stay. And I realised that if I stayed, that it was going to put a strain on Morrissey's relationship with Johnny.'

Marr was no longer living with Joe Moss and his wife, Janet, who were expecting a second baby any day. He had moved into a cottage owned by Janet, in Marple Bridge, outside Manchester's borders, taking Andrew Berry with him as roommate. (The rural surroundings belied a certain domestic chaos but proved productive, Marr writing several songs there, including 'This Charming Man' and 'Still Ill'; in fact, he was so busy at the time that he never even realised that Roddy Frame had retreated to the same village to write his own second album.) Marr had always told Joe Moss that he and Morrissey were equals, and the manager had operated on that understanding, determined to support the singer's wishes as much as those of the guitarist. Morrissey's decision that day to travel to London, to adopt Geoff Travis as some sort of surrogate manager (despite the apparent aversion to having Travis too closely involved in the publishing), was therefore taken by Joe Moss as a betrayal of trust. Moss would quit before the end of the year, without payment for his services – in fact, without repayment for the PA that he had bought the group – and no subsequent manager ever lasted long enough to properly discuss, let alone secure, a written understanding of the group's financial arrangements. In the meantime – meaning, over the course of subsequent years – the company Smithdom Ltd, established in May 1983 with Marr and Morrissey as sole, equal directors, wrote out what Rourke recalled as annual cheques to the band, of equal amounts. But the company's principal activities were listed only as 'that of live musical performances.' There was no reference to, and neither did the annual accounts reflect, the considerable income from recordings.

In hindsight, Johnny Marr tried to see the early group dynamic as more of a creative imbalance than anything else. 'It was one of those examples of actions speaking very much louder than words. The actions were that Morrissey went on the train to EMI, I found the other band members, I found Joe. I went and picked Mike's drum kit up: I went to this derelict house and got his kit from Victim and got the money together for rehearsals. Joe, who was my guy, got the PA. Morrissey went to see Tony

Wilson. These are just the bits that come to mind. The others might argue at the time, "Well you're doing that because you can. What can we do?" But unfortunately there's nothing I can say or do about that. If I have the dedication and the work ethic and the *nous* to do it, I will do it. Now what can you do? OK, you will turn up on time. Well, make sure you do. You will be great, fantastic, you will be a good vibe, you will be what is needed to be. I understand them saying, "Well, we want to help." So OK, then, do it. Let me see you do it. So, we didn't have a meeting and say, "You guys now have to sit on your hands and do nothing," we just did *more*.'

The bottom line, therefore, became whether 'doing more' justified more of the recording royalties. An experienced manager, knowing the importance of having a unified and contented band, and feeling equal responsibility to all four members, might have suggested that it did not, especially given the potentially lucrative proceeds from publishing that were already guaranteed the two songwriters. But Morrissey obviously thought that it did. And Moss, representing only the two founding members, had gone along with him.

Speaking about that evening at Pluto on television, Mike Joyce raised a highly valid hypothesis: 'If Johnny Marr would have come in and said "I'm going to leave the band because Morrissey wants some more money, [but] I'm going to stay if we all get equal amounts," it's a very important but slightly different way of looking at it . . .' One might well have thought that Marr *could* have called Morrissey's bluff; he had rescued the singer from 'dying,' after all. But Marr stated otherwise. 'I wasn't in the position to say it should be anything other than the way it was laid out,' he said in 2011. 'I wasn't in the position.'

The end result turned out to be much the same anyway, except that the Smiths' names and reputations were to be dragged through the courts, and – with the exception of Andy Rourke, who didn't have the stomach or resources for the fight – they would each be saddled with hefty legal bills that cut significantly into the ultimately more egalitarian division of recording royalties. And so, with the benefit of hindsight, and allowing that 'publishing is a different matter,' Marr eventually came to this conclusion: 'When bands form, they should agree right from the off to split everything equally. That's what should happen. Absolutely.'

CHAPTER TWENTY

We set off to take the world and we were winning. And we weren't bringing animosity and aggression to people: we were bringing joy.

                          – JOE MOSS, March 2010

On Friday, 4 November 1983, the Smiths appeared on British television for the first time. Launched the previous year by Tyne Tees Television, the regional independent station in the far northeast of England, *The Tube* was an attempt to replicate the excitement of the seminal 1960s show *Ready Steady Go!* and its famous tagline, 'The Weekend Starts Here'. Broadcasting entirely live across the new Channel 4 network, at 5:30 p.m., earlier than many adults were home from work but, in theory, perfect for teenagers, the ninety-minute show usually included three ten-minute live performances direct from the studio, along with interviews, comedy sketches, and previously filmed magazine pieces. In a British market limited to four television channels, where rock music was typically confined to late-night slots or patronising 'youth' shows, *The Tube*'s gleefully addictive chaos represented a major breakthrough.

To partly rectify a perception that its first season had nonetheless been in thrall to the major labels, the second show of the second season included a lengthy focus on two independent labels. One of them was Rough Trade, busy publicising its long-term deal with the Smiths and touting 'This Charming Man' as a possible hit. The other, which went by the name of Kitchenware, had emerged from Tyne Tees' home base of Newcastle, and was in the process of unapologetically licensing its hottest acts to major labels. The Kitchenware roster of four bands were each shown performing a partial song, captured in a variety of locations, including the windswept – but sunny – Tyne & Wear coastline, a nightclub and a terraced street. But despite the presence of genuine talent, including the Daintees and Prefab Sprout, the nature of their appearances and performances only confirmed for many viewers an impression of the independent music scene in general: that it was grey, insular and depressing. By comparison, the Smiths (significantly, for the Rough Trade segment, it was *only* the Smiths) were filmed lip-syncing to 'This Charming Man' at their Portland Street headquarters in Manchester – an environment that they could and most certainly did control. The floors were laden ankle-deep with brightly coloured flowers, which were additionally strewn over the drums and wedged into Marr's Rickenbacker; and the group dressed accordingly in their finest semi-psychedelic foppery, Morrissey wearing a shirt unbuttoned almost to the waist, exposing several rows of love beads, and waving a bouquet of gladioli like a trophy. Curiously, although his Keith Richards mop-top was seen from a distance and his Rickenbacker from close-up, Johnny Marr's face was never shown: the director was apparently convinced that Marr was on drugs at the time and refused to give him the exposure. (It was likely that *he* misinterpreted Marr's carefully cultivated 'wasted' image as the real thing.)

But no matter: it was Marr who had the honour of introducing the Smiths via his joyous guitar riff at the start of 'This Charming Man'. It was an electric moment, quite literally; by comparison with everything that Kitchenware had offered, the Smiths may as well have hailed from another planet. 'This Charming Man' – the London version, that being the only one completed at the point of *The Tube*'s commission – celebrated its pop sensibilities without apology, and what with the flowers, Morrissey's mild histrionics, and the pervasive sense of colour, there was no attempt by the Smiths to pay homage to their 'independence' as anything other than a state of mind.

This lengthy *Tube* segment, the manner in which the two record company heads talked openly about 'the inverted snobbery of independent labels' (Kitchenware) and 'competing with the charts' (Rough Trade), proved to be a watershed moment, a declaration *not* of countercultural ideals but a desire to share in mainstream spoils.[1] And it was a massively significant moment in the Smiths' rapidly advancing success story: a number of those who watched *The Tube* that night were sufficiently captivated by what they saw of the Smiths as to rush out and buy 'This Charming Man' the next day (a Saturday, the British shopping day), helping send it into the lower reaches of the charts. Another filmed performance of the song on the BBC2 TV show *Riverside*, just four days later – this one additionally shrouding the group in dry ice and including Morrissey lying on the stage floor, singing from behind a bouquet of flowers – was none so artful and less influential, but it maintained the single's upward momentum through the following chart week.

Rough Trade had ensured that there would be no failure to capitalise on these major promotional opportunities, hiring the sales force of major label London Records to push the single into the key record stores. After all, the telephone sales staff at Rough Trade could only achieve so much in this regard, whereas the London sales force had people on the ground, and the tools to aid them – which typically included free and bonus stock for chart stores, precisely the kind of chart-hyping process that the independent labels had long decried as unfair (and unethical if not often illegal) competition. As an added incentive, Rough Trade released 'This Charming Man' as a 7" and 12" single, each featuring different B-sides, ensuring that any determined new Smiths fan would have to buy both formats.

A year earlier, Rough Trade's actions would have been considered, in the eyes of most independent observers, an act of treason. But the sands had shifted, and multiple formats and major-label sales forces represented the difference between, as a good example, Aztec Camera's 'Oblivious' stalling outside the top 40 on Rough Trade and crashing into the top 10 on WEA. With 'This Charming Man' sweeping up music press accolades alongside its early TV exposure, and given its immediate entry into the chart's lower reaches, Scott Piering was able to secure all-important daytime airplay on Radio 1. Within three weeks of release, Rough Trade had finally scored its first ever top 30 single, which in turn generated an equally major milestone: the Smiths became the label's first act invited to appear on *Top of the Pops*.[2]

Even those who despised *Top of the Pops* for its inane DJs, its lip-synced performances, its unstated but clearly noted musical prejudices, and its incessant celebration of pop music as nothing but a happy-go-lucky form of mindless entertainment couldn't help but tune in for the Thursday evening ritual anyway, couldn't help hoping that the occasional act of note would sell enough records to justify an appearance or that a genuinely exciting new act might somehow slip into a slot typically reserved for those who played safe. For that particular audience, the appearance of the Smiths on Thursday, 24 November proved nothing short of a revelation; in fact, it has frequently been cited as one of Britain's most influential moments of music television. It is one that has to be (re)viewed in context. The Smiths were introduced by the blandest of daytime radio DJs, on a week when the top three chart positions were held by Billy Joel, Paul McCartney with Michael Jackson, and Shakin' Stevens; they were sandwiched in between Marilyn (a Boy George clone making the most of his brief patronage by the Culture Club star) and the Thompson Twins (who represented everything that the post-punk independent scene had ever sold out); and they performed on a stage lit in multiple hues from underneath and strewn on top with the show's endless barrage of balloons that reduced pop performance to the level of a child's birthday party, with a disco ball rotating above them. Yet the Smiths were somehow able to transcend this environment and present themselves as precisely what they were: a young four-piece guitar band steeped in musical tradition (Marr's rhythmic swaying to his red Rickenbacker recalling any number of 1960s acts on the same show), hip to their own sense of fashion (the three playing members mixed Crazy Face's exclusive black denim jeans with Marks & Spencer's high-street polo necks), unadorned of pretention and yet with a front man who instantly stood at odds to everyone else on *Top of the Pops* that night (or that month, or indeed that year). Morrissey's outfit, his movements, his flowers . . . all were essentially the same as on *The Tube* and *Riverside* – as was his unwillingness to stand before a microphone and pretend that this was anything but a lip-sync performance – but now it was all being viewed, quite literally, under the searing heat of the national spotlight. The Smiths appeared entirely comfortable, as if that stage had always been destined for them.

By one of those coincidences that help create a rock band's legend, the Smiths had a show booked for the same night as their appearance on *Top of the Pops* – at the Haçienda, no less. The Smiths had not performed live in Manchester since July (they'd played London eleven times in between), and so much had happened for them in the interim that they could have expected to pack the venue even without the TV exposure. But the excitement for Manchester music fans of having a hometown band in the top 30 and appearing on *Top of the Pops* just a couple of hours before playing a local gig turned what was already a triumphant homecoming into an *event*. Thousands showed up.

For the Smiths, excitement about performing that night was compounded by nervousness as to whether they would actually get there. They were still at the BBC studios well into the afternoon. Rough Trade, in an act of largesse quite out of character with the company's pre-hit history, booked a helicopter to ferry them the two hundred miles north, but no one had bothered to check whether the band would actually approve. Morrissey, whose abject fear of flying had not stopped him from visiting America so many times already, refused the transportation. The Smiths took a train to Manchester instead, arriving at the venue hours late, trusting that their crew, such as it was, would have everything set up for them and ready to go. The group James, who despite their head start on the Smiths had only just released their first single on Factory and were now playing the role of support act, had finished their set a long time ago. 'We had to be carried through the streets,' recalled Marr. 'And . . . there were people trying to touch you, and a couple of them are guys you went to school with. And suddenly they're your fans. That was surreal. Really surreal.' Adding to the madness, the Haçienda had a live camera feed, showing the group's eventual arrival in the dressing room as assurance to those on the inside that the band had made it north in time. For that night, it was like the mid-'60s – when Manchester had hosted *Top of the Pops* and put its bands on top of the American charts thrice in a row – all over again.

Inside, the Smiths were duly treated as the all-conquering heroes, enduring a series of stage invasions that trampled underfoot the flowers they had strewn across the place, like those in Oscar Wilde's 'The Nightingale and the Rose', returning for several encores to play their two singles a second time each, stretching the concert well past the British public's officially sanctioned bedtimes. Joe Moss was paid out on 2,400 people; the official capacity was 1,650. It was the biggest night in the eighteen-month-old club's history.

SIX MONTHS EARLIER, when he had first sat down with Mike Hinc to draw up some kind of game plan, Joe Moss had been clear about his vision for the band. 'He didn't want them growing up in public,' recalled Hinc, 'he wanted them to play the "toilets" as much as possible.' Given that All Trade Booking, laden as it was with independent acts at the start of their careers, 'had plenty [of] toilets,' Hinc readily set about booking the Smiths into them. Through the summer and early autumn of 1983, the group played its share of obscure venues in minor markets that were intended to allow the Smiths to develop their live show at a normal pace.

The problem – to the limited extent that it turned out to be one – was that the Smiths did not develop at a normal pace. They exploded at breakneck speed. The first true 'fans' were seen at the group's return to the Rock Garden in July: a couple named Josh and Anna 'stood there holding flowers,' as Marr recalled. They were quickly adopted to lead the stage invasions (which were 'as much a part of the plan as the flowers,' said Joe Moss) and rewarded with crash pads on the band's hotel-room floors when the budget extended to them. When it did not, the group would return to Manchester in the Renault 'splitter' van that Joe Moss had bought and paid for, its back seats removed to allow for the group's equipment and a couple of sleeping bags. On the way to and from their increasingly rambunctious shows, the group, along with Moss as manager and Ollie May and Phil Powell as roadies, and perhaps Angie Brown and Andrew Berry and some other friends if they didn't make the journey in another vehicle, would joke and smoke their way into oblivion.

'It was never just run-of-the-mill,' stressed Marr. 'Even if we were just in a car, driving down the motorway, it was always a big deal. Because it *was* a big deal: 99.5 per cent of the time it was a big deal in an upward direction. It was incredible.' The almost ecstatic sense of camraderie during 1983 was evident, said Marr, in the photographs by Paul Slattery that accompanied their first interview in *Sounds*, in May of that year. 'You can see the relationship in those photographs, not just because we're hugging each other, but because we're so happy to be next to each other. There's confidence growing there, there's a cockiness and an exuberance and there's so much affection.'

*   *   *

BY THE EARLY SUMMER, the numbers in the van included Grant Cunliffe, better known by his professional last name of Showbiz. A former member of the experimental hippie group Here & Now, co-owner of a studio called Street Level and a cassette label called Fuck Off Records, Showbiz, by his own admission 'a yappy, shouty, loudy kind of person' had also produced albums for the Fall and regularly worked as their sound engineer. He had been invited to the ULU show by Scott Piering with a view towards working with the Smiths in a similar capacity.

'It was a very weird combination,' Showbiz recalled of his first impressions of the Smiths. 'Mike was kicking seven shades of shit out of it – in a really nice way. And Andy was playing what appeared to be "another song" that was a countermelody to what Johnny was doing. And Johnny . . . literally was playing the eighteen parts that were in his head. And Morrissey was whooping charmingly over the top of it all.' Then again, for someone of his pedigree, the weirdness was but part of the attraction. 'Because I saw the Fall as pop music, the Smiths seemed to be . . . equally strange.' The difference, he concluded, was 'that it was done from proficiency. Certainly Andy and Johnny were incredibly proficient on their instruments, very skilled. And Morrissey and Mike were much more the raw kind of life force.'

When the Smiths returned to the capital a month later, at the Brixton Ace, Showbiz was there as sound engineer, which was (welcome) news to the band, who had not otherwise considered having their own man behind the mixing board. Only when introduced to the group did Showbiz discover that he had a fan among them. Andy Rourke, during his mid-teens space-rock stage, had been to see Here & Now in Manchester and raved at school the next day to Johnny Marr about 'this really cool guy, going 'round passing the bucket after the gig.' When Here & Now then split an album with punks-turned-hippies Alternative TV, the back cover showed the entourage of long-haired, bedraggled musicians and fellow travellers posing in front of their bus. Rourke had bought that album and pointed out Showbiz to Marr. As an oddball outsider hero, Showbiz was accordingly allowed inside the Smiths' inner circle – the first from outside Manchester to be afforded such status.

'They were *incredibly* welcoming,' said Showbiz, for whom the Smiths' sense of identity represented an almost complete reversal of his former hippie outfits. 'They were a total group. They all had the clothes, they all had the hair, they all had the jewellery, and then they all had the verbiage – a kind of slang that I couldn't really follow.'

'When Grant came along and couldn't understand us for a few weeks, it wasn't because of our accents, it was because of the language we used,' said Johnny Marr. 'This truncated conversation that came from sitting around watching the same films all day long. It was constantly quoting movies to make a point.' The group had latched on to phrases such as 'Them was rotten days' from the movie *Hobson's Choice*, and would similarly adopt lines from *A Taste of Honey* and *Saturday Night and Sunday Morning*, which had become permanent viewing fixtures. The inside banter, in which Morrissey was every bit as much a participant as anyone else in the van, may have provided a challenge to a newcomer like Showbiz, but it also indicated the depth of the Smiths' solidarity.

'It was a *band*,' confirmed Showbiz. 'No one was sending the bass player out to get fags. There wasn't any of that. And there was no disagreement within the band. It was like those legendary bands, like when you see those Beatles press conferences, where they're backing each other up and someone says something funny and someone spins off it . . . Everyone was into it. Everyone was laughing at the same jokes. And very quickly, I got my hair cut [by Andrew Berry] and started wearing the same clothes they were wearing.' To some, he became the fifth Smith.

In being hired, Showbiz was given one simple directive by Joe Moss: make Morrissey as loud as the rest of the band. And he was happy to act on it. 'It's a simple thing,' he explained. '*Let's hear what the singer is singing*. There are these great singers that you've been told are great singers and you go to the gig and you can't hear what they're singing.' But it was more than just that. 'What was very clear [with the Smiths] is that everything they were doing on every level was interesting, so you had to make everything audible. At the same time, if there were moments of hugeness, it didn't matter if you couldn't hear it all, it could just blend in. I believe in something called "psychoacoustics" – that you don't notice it's happening but it has some effect on you.' Showbiz's own effect on the Smiths' live presentation proved immediate, and he would maintain his presence behind the board for almost every single Smiths concert from June 1983 onward.

It was several months of further travelling in that 'upward direction' – opening for Howard Devoto and the Gang of Four on separate occasions at the London Lyceum, sharing the bill with Aztec Camera at Warwick University, topping a Rough Trade night over the Go-Betweens at London's the Venue, headlining Dingwalls in London (twice) and packing the place, sharing the bill with other Manchester bands at the ICA Rock Week in October – before they brought their next mainstay on board.[3] 'This Charming Man' had just been released and the group was on a patchwork tour of colleges and polytechnic venues, shows that were either turning into memorable madhouses or being rapidly rescheduled into larger rooms to meet the increasing demand. (The 'patchwork' aspect was due to the fact that the group was otherwise in the studio re-recording, overdubbing, and mixing its first album with John Porter.)

On 16 November, a week before the *Top of the Pops* performance, that tour rolled into Leicester Polytechnic, where the lighting was handled by an affable and intelligent nineteen-year-old named John Featherstone, who struck up a conversation with Marr at the soundcheck. He suggested to the guitarist that he light the stage without the usual dramatic effects and constant colour changes beloved by most bands on the throes of success – that he use 'just blues and greens' – and Marr agreed. That night, said Featherstone, 'it was immediately apparent just in the way they took the stage that there was something very different going on here.' As far as Featherstone saw it, 'So many of the bands that came through seemed like they were trying really hard to do the same thing that other bands were doing – and it seemed like the Smiths were trying to do something that no other bands were doing at the time. Obviously they were still very young and it was very rough around the edges. But [by the] second song I remember thinking, "This is something really quite remarkable."'

As much as he was impressed by what he saw onstage, though, Featherstone was, like Showbiz before him, taken by the personalities he encountered off of it. Things were clearly happening for the band – they were in the charts already – but 'they were trying very hard not to be rock stars. These were just four guys who . . . were still at that endearing stage where the band is delighted that people showed up and paid attention.'

Featherstone hit it off with Marr that night: it was like 'meeting a member of your lost tribe,' he recalled. The feeling must have been mutual, for a few days later, Joe Moss called to invite him to work a major show coming up at the beginning of December in Derby, where they were to be filmed in concert for a *Whistle Test* 'On the Road' special devoted entirely to the Smiths. (The show had dropped the 'Old Grey' prefix and hired new presenters, largely in response to the success of *The Tube*.) And so, at the age of nineteen, he stepped into the role of the Smiths' lighting designer; he would work alongside Showbiz as a fully fledged member of the inner circle until the bitter end.

Ironically, the Derby show was one of only two (and the other was also for TV) where Featherstone allowed himself to be talked into tracking Morrissey with a spotlight for the cameras' sake. Otherwise, it became a sacred point for the Smiths that they were not to be lit from the front. 'Most bands can't see for the lights in their eyes,' said Featherstone. 'They're oblivious to the audience. One of the reasons the Smiths responded to the audience the way they did was that Morrissey really could see the audience. When he looked out, he could see people and look in their eye and connect with them. And the band always had a really good sense of the *tone* of their audience.'

At the Derby Assembly Rooms concert, which was broadcast on the BBC just two nights later (while the Smiths were onstage at their first ever concert in Ireland, an important 'homecoming' of an entirely different kind), that connection with the audience was already apparent. The front rows all carried bouquets of flowers, which they threw at Morrissey during 'This Charming Man', and even if that was preplanned, the depth of something more than the usual audience adulation for a new chart band was evident throughout – especially when a teenage boy jumped onstage during 'Hand in Glove' and didn't just hug Morrissey but held on to him as if his life depended on it. Compared to the band that had played to a few dozen people at the start of the year, the most notable difference was not necessarily the professionalism – that had been remarkable all along – but the level of confidence. Johnny Marr no longer felt the need to run around and goon with the crowd; he was the epitome of calm control, hunched over his black Rickenbacker throughout, clearly concentrating on the job at hand. Morrissey, his quiff reaching almost as high as Johnny Marr's bowl cut hung low, had adopted the full idol persona, accentuating every one of his personal traits: the one-legged pirouette, the bouquet-as-weapon, and the shirt unbuttoned to the waist, revealing a torso and abdomen remarkable only for its everyday Anglo-Irish scrawniness. The concert culminated with a full-scale stage invasion, by boys and girls alike, during an encore of 'You've Got Everything Now' that forced Morrissey to the floor and an early fade-out by the BBC. The stage invasion itself was nothing new on the live scene – it had been a mainstay for the Jam and the Specials, equally energetic British live bands of recent years – but this audience seemed so uniformly (or uniquely) nonthreatening that there was something incredibly heartwarming about their presence onstage. It would be too much to suggest that they were all mini-Morrisseys, but they had seen a reflection of themselves in the Smiths' singer, even if it was just the recognition of their teenage angst masquerading as inadequacy, and they wanted to share in it. By jumping onstage, they were showing off, perhaps, claiming their little piece of the spotlight for sure, but as much as anything, they were claiming the Smiths as their own.

CHAPTER TWENTY-ONE

At the moment, it feels completely perfect. I feel that
if the Smiths were accepted by the entire universe
tomorrow, it wouldn't surprise me.

— Morrissey, *Jamming!*, January 1984

As 'This Charming Man' peaked in the British charts at number 25, Rough Trade released an additional 12" of 'New York' mixes: an extended vocal rendition on one side, an instrumental on the other. Though intended in part as an(other) incentive to maintain the single's chart run, the 12" was also designed to make an impact on American dance floors. In the States, new British bands such as the Smiths, despite being viewed as 'alternative' – in fact, in large part *because* they were viewed as alternative – had a distinct appeal in nightclubs, especially in the major music capitals like New York, that were actively mixing up hip-hop, electro, funk *and* New Wave. To this end, club remixes were an avenue by which several Sire artists – from Talking Heads to Madonna, Yaz(oo) to Tin Tin – had been staking out their claim to multidenominational appeal, and given that the likes of Echo & the Bunnymen and Elvis Costello had similarly surrendered to the 12" extended mix in 1983, it seemed almost inevitable that the Smiths follow suit. New York DJ Francois Kevorkian's remix of the Strawberry Studios multitracks (for which John Porter's use of LinnDrums

314

to ensure a precise rhythm must have been greatly appreciated) duly followed the formula for the period, allowing the song a straightforward run-through before accentuating various rhythmic elements as part of what could, at a stretch, be considered a 'dub' addendum. (By comparison, the instrumental version overly focused on these rhythmic elements to the detriment of the song's original melody.) These New York mixes were released by Rough Trade in multiple European and Antipodean territories and promptly imported into the States by Sire, to be provided to the growing number of 'alternative' DJs, via insider subscriber services like Rockpool, as an exclusive enticement to play their label's latest British signings. It was hardly coincidental that just as these mixes hit the turntables, it was announced that the Smiths would be playing Danceteria, New York's hottest cross-cultural club, on New Year's Eve 1984.

Unfortunately for Geoff Travis, no sooner were the mixes released than Smiths fans – the sort who had already laid claim to *their* band as guitar purists – reacted negatively, at which Morrissey publicly denounced the mixes as having been commissioned without the band's knowledge and as 'entirely against our principles.' (Travis was unlikely to have gone ahead with anything so potentially problematic without prior approval, though he allowed that when he sent them to the band upon completion, he might have taken silence to signify consent.) The issue of 'principles' was an important one: it signified that Morrissey saw the Smiths as distinguishable from their peers by their steadfast refusal to engage in the modern marketing methods of the era – which included not only the customary dance remix but, as Morrissey was busy telling the world by this point, the promotional video, too. The former stand made absolute sense to someone who had been raised on the pop music of the '50s, '60s and '70s, where the original version was the definitive version, and where a 7" single stood as a work of art, a souvenir of its time. The latter was a particularly brave position to take, and for the time being it won him many fans' further loyalty, especially among those who were rightly disgusted by the lavish budgets – frequently exceeding those of the recording studio – afforded the most insipid of pop acts in the pursuit of something called MTV. By what may not have been coincidence, the refusal to participate in either such endeavour also saved a considerable amount of marketing money that would otherwise be considered an 'expense' to be covered before profit-sharing.

In both cases, Johnny Marr stood by his partner. Even though, as a fan of the New York dance scene, he was flattered to have been remixed by Kevorkian, he was also aware that Smiths fans were perceiving Morrissey's fastidiousness as a positive. The belated complaints came in time to ensure that the New York mixes did not flood British record stores, but late enough that they established the group on the 'alternative' American dance floor all the same. In the meantime, the Smiths prepared to take New York in person.

Joe Moss accompanied the Smiths' entourage to the airport. He did not get on the plane. It turned out that he had already witnessed his last show as manager, a headliner at the Electric Ballroom in London shortly before Christmas that was almost as oversubscribed as the Haçienda. From there, he had gone back to Manchester, to his wife, Janet, and his newly born baby daughter. 'I got home for Christmas after spending most of the last six months away,' he said. 'And I saw this little girl . . . I saw her and I just realised I wasn't going anywhere again.'

The fact that Moss's first attempt at a family had ended badly made it imperative that he treat his new one with all due care and devotion, and he decided that spending time on it took priority over spending time with the family that was the Smiths. The decision was not made lightly; he had 'a *real* traumatic period' over it, he insisted. Neither was it impetuous. Moss had always seen himself as a mentor first, a manager second. He also believed that the fun part of managing a band was the early days: putting the team together, engaging the creative forces, and striking the initial deals. (And he had loved every moment of it; 'It was such a bloody joyous trip,' he said of his time with the band.) The nuts and bolts of subsequent recording and touring schedules didn't particularly excite him in the same way. That, at least, pursuant to the personal reasons, was part of his external justification for resigning.

Internally, it appeared that he could not put aside the notion that Morrissey saw him as Marr's man, as evidenced by the singer's defection to Geoff Travis over the four members' financial arrangements. It was a point of interminable frustration, given that 'I put more time into Morrissey and into what I considered protecting Morrissey and looking after Morrissey's interests than I did into Johnny, just because that was the way the job fell. I wasn't there as Johnny's mate, I was doing the job.'

'He understood both of them really well,' said Grant Showbiz, who had spent the last five months at every show with Moss and the band. 'And he, in a very effective way, had Morrissey's best interests at heart. He wanted the best for Morrissey and he knew how to get it and he went about getting it in a very intelligent way.' Unfortunately, said Showbiz, 'I don't know if Morrissey understood that.'

Moss had told Marr that he wouldn't be in it for the long haul, but Marr essentially ignored the warning, believing that as long as the band continued to move forward inexorably, Moss would never be crazy enough to jump ship. He was wrong. Shortly after the Electric Ballroom show, after returning to his family in Manchester, Moss had a conversation with Marr in his car. Moss had always insisted of his eventual departure that 'I wasn't going to go until they'd "made it", I wouldn't leave him in the lurch,' and he had reason to believe that he had lived up to his promise. The Smiths were in the top 30 with only their second single, all over the radio, the TV and the music papers (on the cover of *Sounds* and *Melody Maker* in consecutive weeks in November), selling out increasingly large venues, unanimously viewed as the most exciting and *important* new band of 1983. Moss had set them up with a rehearsal space, a PA, a van, even their clothes. He had financed their original recordings. He had structured the deals with Rough Trade, Warner Bros Music, Sire Records and All Trade Booking. He had overseen the hiring of Grant Showbiz and John Featherstone. He had helped put together a damned good team. What he had not been able to do, and it was to prove costly in all senses, was to leave the Smiths in the hands of an equally capable manager or get the group's internal finances down on paper. But had he stayed around to complete these goals, they might well have remained perpetually at arm's length; worse, given Morrissey's behaviour thus far, he may have found himself being fired. It is probably for these unstated, hypothetical explanations that Marr was later able to surmise that 'Maybe [Joe] saw something 'round the corner that I didn't see,' but at the time, when Moss told Marr he would not be coming to New York, the guitarist didn't believe him. In fact, for many years, he blocked out even the memory of the conversation. 'I didn't know that he really wasn't going to come on the American visit with us.'

'In truth I really, really *did* want to go,' said Moss. 'Oh God, there was nothing I ever wanted to do more, but I couldn't. I just couldn't do it.' That late December morning, the Smiths got on a plane to spend New Year's in New York. And Joe Moss got back in his car to spend it with his wife and two infants in Manchester.

MARR'S ANGUISH WAS compounded by the fact that he and Angie Brown had just broken up. Marr subsequently described it as 'one of those kids' bust-ups . . . that you have to have for ten days,' but it was unquestionably tied into the speed of the Smiths' ascendance. Marr and Brown had been together five years already, since they were schoolkids, had lived in each other's pockets almost that entire time, but now one of them had become a pop star. And something more than that: even at this early stage, Johnny Marr was being viewed by the record-buying public as a boy wonder, the first British antihero guitar hero in a generation, and a potential pinup in the process. It was his commitment to the Smiths that had gotten the group so far so quickly, but the same workaholic tendencies, his (lack of) diet and (lack of) sleep habits, and his sheer bloody-mindedness when it came to the group did not always make for easy companionship. And so, after an argument just before Christmas, Angie had decided to cool off and stay at home with her family for New Year's, when by rights she should have been enjoying a glamorous reward for her own support and devotion to the cause.

As a result, said Grant Showbiz of the guitarist during their stay in New York, 'Johnny was lost,' citing it as the lowest he saw Marr sink emotionally through the entire career of the Smiths (including the band's eventual breakup). But when Showbiz said of Marr that 'he was really down about Angie,' what he didn't realise, because the guitarist didn't yet want to admit it to himself, let alone to the others, was that he was more distraught about the breakup with Moss. Marr was on the phone every day with Brown, after all; he was certain that it was just 'some stupid kids' tiff,' as he put it. But the relationship with Moss was over.

'I understood Joe,' said Marr, ultimately, of his manager's decision. 'I was never angry with Joe, I was just frustrated by it. Because we were so close, and I trusted him. And it was a little like I'd already decided that I was going to be able to swim from Great Britain across the Atlantic and that was some kind of task, but then it felt like I was being asked to swim the Atlantic without Joe, without his help . . . I was really pretty devastated.'

The Smiths were met at JFK (after the first transatlantic flight for all of the group except Morrissey) in style, Danceteria promoter Ruth Polsky having hired a limousine. Polsky was a devoted Anglophile with the powerful presence of personality necessary to succeed in New York's high-risk nightclub stakes. Much like Seymour Stein, she specialised in acquiring the latest British buzz bands, crossing the Atlantic to witness and befriend them, then paying to bring them into the four-storey Danceteria (which had a restaurant and dance floor as well as live performance space) as one-off promotions, the exorbitant cost of such occasional promotions justified by how they maintained the club's reputation as market leader. For the Smiths' first night in New York, Polsky hosted a customary welcome dinner at her apartment, to which she invited Amanda Malone, her eighteen-year-old assistant. Malone had a British accent (she had been raised in Brighton before moving to New York to live with her gay, divorced father), shared a birthday with Morrissey, and had what she called an 'affectation' for all things 1960s and British, not just musical but cinematic as well. At Polsky's apartment, the two readily clicked.

'He had a great sense of humour,' Malone noted of Morrissey, as did so many. 'He made me laugh and I'd make him laugh.' In addition, they both 'had a very irreverent, naughty, smart-ass way' about them, she said, 'and I think he enjoyed that.' Over the course of the week in New York, the pair increasingly hung out together, Morrissey even coming over to Malone's apartment in Brooklyn Heights to watch old movies. Malone, extremely overweight at the time, harboured dreams of a musical career, and Morrissey, she was thrilled to discover, 'liked the sound of my voice' and did not consider her appearance a hindrance. By the end of the visit, the pair had developed such 'a really great complicity and connection,' as Malone described it, that Morrissey had invited her to England with the promise of singing on a Smiths record – or even recording one of her own.

Rough Trade had hired Peter Wright, the former New Hormones partner who had recently relocated to New York to set up his own publicity firm, to independently promote 'This Charming Man' to the New York press, and Wright, who failed to initially recognise the confident pop star Morrissey as the same retiring personality who had hung out at the Newton Street offices, additionally brought Morrissey over to see John Giorno, the poet and former Warhol lover. There was considerable business to be conducted as well, staff to meet from Warner Bros and opportunities to be wined and dined. Johnny Marr convinced Seymour Stein to live up to his earlier promise and was duly chaperoned to Forty-Eighth Street, home to the city's best instrument stores, and treated to a hollow-body Gibson 355. So enamoured was Marr by the acquisition that by the end of the visit, he had just about completed the complex composition of the Smiths' first post-album single.

Such examples of corporate largesse aside, the overall mood of the trip was not positive. As Grant Showbiz described it, 'On every level it should have been just the most fantastic thing, and on every level, it wasn't. It was a fucking nightmare.' The group and crew alike were shocked by the presence of cockroaches at their hotel, the Iroquois, where Showbiz also watched Rourke disappear on a mission with some people he met there and suspected that it was to score something other than pot.[1] The sub-freezing cold and deep snow of a New York New Year came as an additional shock to a group raised on damp but temperate British winters. And the attendant madness of performing on the biggest night of the year in the hottest nightclub of arguably the greatest city on earth got the best of them. At a pre-gig Indian meal, Morrissey was seen throwing back the wine to calm his nerves, while in the dressing room, the group's introduction to one of their 'support acts', Lovebug Starski – the DJ and producer who had been credited with inventing the term 'hip-hop' and was something of a hero to Johnny Marr – entailed the New York native introducing the crew in turn to the addictive, adrenaline-inducing and ego-enhancing powers of cocaine. For his part, Morrissey stayed solely on the wine, which might have explained why, shortly after taking the stage, he promptly fell off it. Though the distance was relatively benign, and the humbled new British sensation soon clambered back up to complete the show, Geoff Travis, who was in New York with the group, recalled that Morrissey's mother 'called me the next day complaining about Rough Trade's lack of security and ambulance men and proper medical care for her son.'

That turned out to be the least of their concerns. That same day, as his roommate Andy Rourke put it, Mike Joyce 'woke up a strange shade of green with red spots . . . ' Joyce was diagnosed with chickenpox (though it may well have been shingles), and remained bedridden in the cockroach-infested Iroquois; an apparently planned introductory concert in Boston was cancelled, adding to the sense of general disorder. (Indeed, while the Smiths were received with predictable enthusiasm at Danceteria, few people appeared to be in a sufficiently sober state as to properly recollect the concert.) If ever the calming presence of Joe Moss had been required, then surely this was the occasion. In the meantime, the absence of a managerial figure was duly noted by Ruth Polsky.

CHAPTER TWENTY-TWO

I get terribly embarrassed when I meet Smiths apostles – I hate the word fan. They seem to expect so much of me. Many of them see me as some kind of religious character who can solve all their problems with a wave of a syllable. It's daunting.

    – MORRISSEY, *Melody Maker*, November 1984

The release of *The Smiths*, as the debut album was re-titled with direct simplicity, was preceded in January 1984 by the single 'What Difference Does It Make?'. Led by Marr's guitar riff rooted in those blues chord progressions clearly indebted to the Rolling Stones, its sense of orthodoxy was amplified by Joyce's drums, which were transposed in the studio by John Porter from their tribal shuffle to a more direct two-four pounding, and Rourke's bass, which was simplified in the process. In terms of solidifying the Smiths' early success, these were proven correct decisions by the pace at which it rapidly rose up the charts, quickly achieving further multiple milestones that fed into one another: the band's (and Rough Trade's) first ever single sold by the high-street chains Woolworth's and WH Smith; their first top 20 hit; their second *and* third *Top of the Pops* appearance. Under these circumstances, Morrissey's subsequent denouncement of the single as 'absolutely awful' seems somewhat churlish, though it could be fairly noted that such an old composition revealed his voice at its most limited in range and among the lowest in register (even though it had been tuned up a tone to accommodate him along the way). Morrissey's criticisms of 'What Difference Does It Make?' were best expressed, perhaps, by a more nuanced remark he made later in 1984: 'I regret the production on that now.'[1]

Generally speaking, Morrissey had proclaimed the Smiths' virtues from the moment of their formation. The live show, for the most part, and the singles – most definitely 'This Charming Man' – had borne out his boasts, and he therefore started hyping up the John Porter-produced debut LP, just as he had already done with the now abandoned Troy Tate album. The New Year found Morrissey embarking on a new round of major publicity, loaded with bold assurances. 'I believe it's a signal post in music,' he said of the album on his first-ever television interview – a live outside broadcast by *The Tube*, from the Haçienda – on 27 January, not twenty-four hours after he had been seen on *Top of the Pops* sporting a hearing aid.[2]

By the time of the album's release a month later, the Smiths' profile was so pervasive, and the album so keenly anticipated, that *The Smiths* entered the British album charts at number 2 – a spectacular achievement given the lack of TV, radio, (most) print advertising and fly-postering, all of which Morrissey was proud to proclaim in the media as signifiers of Rough Trade's acumen and the Smiths' integrity. (Neither Mute nor Factory, let alone Rough Trade, had yet charted an album quite so high.) But as it made the journey from record shop to turntable, a percentage of fans and critics alike couldn't help but express some disappointment.

As Morrissey would later note, the album's primary fault, and that word had to be used, lay in its production. For those who had been paying attention (and collecting) the Radio 1 sessions, better – or, at least, more emotive – versions of most of the songs had already been recorded and aired; for those who had not, there was still something frustratingly restrained about the overall presentation. It didn't excite the fans that the LP's first two songs (a solid 'Reel Around the Fountain' followed by a weak 'You've Got Everything Now') featured a guest keyboard player, as if the original arrangements (and band members) were somehow insufficient, and it definitely didn't aid those fans' enjoyment of the package that of the ten songs (and only ten?), it was the first four that paled most evidently in comparison to their BBC renditions. Hearing the album come into its own on side two was scant consolation for those who had expected a religious experience from track one. John Porter's insistence that Mike Joyce restrict himself to metronomic twos and fours, combined with the decision to base every song around electric guitar arpeggios whether they were part of a song's original arrangement or not, served to create a homogenous atmosphere at the expense of the Smiths' naturally wide-ranging musical moods.

Not that Porter himself was the problem. By the time he was hired, most of the songs that would end up on *The Smiths* had been demoed, recorded for the BBC, and additionally recorded by Troy Tate, some of them twice over. The fifth go-round of any given song was rarely going to be the best. Porter had been additionally constrained by a limited studio budget, and especially hampered by the group's restricted availability. The sessions at Pluto, and a subsequent opportunity for overdubs at Eden in London (without which, he insisted, the album would have sounded no more polished than the Troy Tate version), had been in blocks of days, not weeks, the group forever packing up their equipment to play a gig here or a TV show there. Such a process might have worked for bands in the '60s; it quickly lost its charm for a producer who was given to making hit records, not quick ones.

John Porter had already proven with 'This Charming Man' (which, in classic British punk-ethical tradition, was left *off* the UK album) that he was capable of bringing the very best out of the band – in fact, with bringing something out of them that had otherwise remained latent and unexposed. He proved it again with another song from the most recent Peel session, 'Still Ill' (even though he removed the endearing harmonica riff). 'I Don't Owe You Anything', which he had previously produced at the Jensen session, came properly alive in his hands this second time around. And his production of 'The Hand That Rocks the Cradle' and, especially, 'Suffer Little Children', were surely the LP's most thrilling surprises for their emotional sincerity and musical clarity. (That they were also the ones that had been least recorded and performed onstage certainly helped Porter stamp his authority on them.) And throughout the album, he showcased Johnny Marr's natural guitar abilities in the most vivid light possible. If he hadn't achieved perfection with *The Smiths*, he could insist that it was not for lack of trying.

Other than sonic concerns, it may not have helped that *The Smiths* came packaged in a duotone sleeve that featured Joe Dallesandro's muscular torso in the Warhol movie *Flesh* at the expense of the Smiths' own colourful image; that the inner sleeve thumbnail pictures of the individual band members did nothing to display their collective camaraderie; or that the lyrics were laid out on the inner sleeve in minuscule type, masking their mirth and warmth beneath song titles like 'Still Ill'. Finally, the choice of material itself raised eyebrows: why, for example, did only one of the four spectacular songs unveiled on the second John Peel session – post-Troy Tate, and therefore not burdened by previous studio renditions – make it onto the album? Any group that could leave off its debut album the likes of 'Jeane', 'Handsome Devil', 'Accept Yourself', 'Back to the Old House', 'These Things Take Time', *and* 'This Charming Man' was either impossibly spoiled for choice or clinically insane when it came to commercial decisions. Or, quite possibly, both.

IN NOVEMBER 1983, Morrissey had been asked by *Melody Maker*, for its cover story on the Smiths, whether he'd 'ever thought about moving down to London.' He admitted, 'We did toy with the idea a while ago – but only for a second,' before confirming that, 'actually there's just no question of it. It's such an impersonal place.' By January 1984, he was showing *NME* (for *its* cover story coinciding with the annual readers poll, in which the Smiths were voted Best New Act) around his new rented flat in Kensington.

At the age of twenty-four, then, Morrissey had finally left home – possibly for good, and certainly in style: his new abode, on Campden Hill Road, was nestled comfortably between Notting Hill Gate to the north and Kensington High Street to the east, and his mansion-block neighbours included the actor Robert Powell and the newscaster Alistair Burnett. Previous assurances to the contrary notwithstanding, he had some justification for the sudden move south. Increased demands on his time from all manner of media and business interests in the capital had been turning him into a long-distance commuter, and the attractions of being driven back and forth to Manchester by Rough Trade's Dave Harper in a rented Mercedes diesel undertakers' limousine (that needed a screwdriver to start the engine) receded rapidly. Equally to the point, Joe Moss was out of the picture, nobody had yet replaced him, and with the apparent miscommunication over the New York mixes all too fresh in his mind, Morrissey felt the need to live close by Rough Trade to 'keep an eye on' them. Happy to accommodate this request, it was Geoff Travis who found Morrissey the flat; Richard Jobson, the former singer with the Skids, had just vacated it, and it was but a brief taxi ride away from Blenheim Crescent. Soon enough, albeit in significantly more stylish surroundings, Morrissey had it looking much like his room in Stretford, complete with the library of feminist and cinema literature, the framed James Dean photo, and with Morrissey as genial host, brewing cups of tea for visiting journalists and friends as he reflected on his apparent fortune.

Any concerns that Morrissey's relocation would create an (additional?) emotional distance from other band members were immediately squelched by the work schedule: the very week that 'What Difference Does It Make?' hit the charts, the

Smiths undertook their first major headlining tour of the UK. They were but three shows in when Ollie May quit, for good, telling tour manager Phil Cowie that he was 'disillusioned and disappointed with both the band and the direction that their career has been and is going.' (This was much to Johnny Marr's disappointment, the guitarist having hoped that if you gave your friends a job with a rock 'n' roll band, they'd stay with you for life.) The next night, the PA showed up to Loughborough University – but the band did not. Morrissey had apparently been taken ill, and as Cowie and Hinc struggled to ascertain the cause and the seriousness of his ailment, they were forced to cancel a whole string of shows. Morrissey was nonetheless roused from his sickbed for another *Top of the Pops* appearance, performing unshaven and without his usual élan, having lain horizontal in the green room all day. The rigours of rock 'n' roll – not so much the hedonistic lifestyle (Morrissey desired little more than some red wine) but simply the pressures of time, the demands for attention, the lack of proper meals (all the more so for a vegetarian who existed largely on chocolate and chips and cheese) – were already taking their toll. 'I never worried about him psychologically,' said his partner and protector, Marr. 'There were times that I worried about him physically when he was burned out, and you could see that, and he was going to be ill. And I think that happened because all of us had unhealthy lifestyles. But he had more on his plate, psychologically, in dealing with that pop world thing, and being that focal point. Us three lived off nicotine, amongst other things, and Morrissey needed to eat right, and none of us did. And I think it particularly affected him.' The lack of a manager to take control of the situation, to protect Morrissey's health and calm the agents and promoters, was again all too apparent. That made it somewhat understandable – if quite farcical – that when the tour resumed with a headlining show at the London Lyceum, Ruth Polsky showed up at the soundcheck, fresh from Manhattan, to announce that she had received Morrissey's personal blessing to assume the managerial reins.

'It wasn't as stupid as it seems,' said Grant Showbiz of her approach. 'Because she was the first to realise they were going to be massive. Other than Seymour Stein: maybe he just signed them because they were pretty young boys, I don't know. But Ruth was absolutely right. On a serious note, she was asking, "Why the fuck are you staying in such shit fucking hotels? Why are you getting paid so little money? Why are you on this crappy record label? Why are you getting these tiny advances?" And she was *right* on every single point.' All of which made her inherently unwelcome to those who were already invested in the band. 'She was the enemy to Rough Trade from day one.'

Showbiz, while admitting the diagnosis could apply to him, too, considered Polsky 'a crazy party lady who you felt had something missing in her that was completed by the band experience,' a viewpoint confirmed by Amanda Malone, her assistant at Danceteria, who had just moved over to London herself upon Morrissey's insistence that he was going to make her a star. 'You think about club culture: how many of these people would you really call winners?' said Malone. Polsky 'was a very spoiled, difficult person,' but on the other hand, 'she was very good to all the bands she represented.' At times too good: Malone had seen Polsky make a move on someone in the Smiths entourage when they were in New York, and how it had upset Morrissey. 'It meant that he couldn't take her seriously as a businessperson.'

Given Morrissey's noted fear of confrontation, it was entirely possible that Polsky had suggested herself as the band's manager – at the very least in America, where there was clearly great interest in the group – and that when Morrissey expressed cautious enthusiasm rather than a flat-out refusal, she promptly translated that into approval. All the same, said Malone, 'he was livid' when she announced as much to the industry. 'And the rest of them were even more livid.'

'I loved Ruth,' said Johnny Marr. 'But manager material she wasn't.' Though Morrissey quickly confirmed to his partner that he had not appointed her, Polsky was used to getting her way and surely felt that, given the chance to prove herself via her forceful personality, she would soon win over the group. The Smiths would certainly not have been the first or last band to find a manager muscling in on their vacant (or even occupied) territory and declaring control by fiat. The Polsky problem, which did not go away immediately, was compounded by the fact that the band already had two Americans operating on their behalf: Scott Piering and his assistant, Martha DeFoe. At the start of 1984, when it was evident that Joe Moss had vacated the premises, Piering did not so much ask to manage the Smiths as he began taking care of their business as a matter of course.

Eventually, Piering proposed that he be officially appointed – in large part, he insisted, to protect the Smiths. 'I wasn't sure whether I wanted the responsibility,' he told Johnny Rogan, 'but it seemed a good way of ensuring that Ruth would *not* become manager.' Curiously, despite his loyalties to Rough Trade, Piering did not disagree with some of Polsky's primary arguments. 'Ruth made every effort to basically point out how shabbily they were handled – which was, more or less, true! That psychology would attract Morrissey. His mother was constantly telling him the same.' Piering likewise believed that Morrissey needed to be treated like a star, and while the rest of the group were relatively comfortable fending for themselves, he frequently insisted that the singer be supplied not just with a taxi to a TV station, for example, but with a chauffeur; not just with the items on the backstage rider but his own dressing room too. If this ran counter to Rough Trade's long-standing socialist principles, and equally to those of the university social secretaries who still made up the majority of the first headlining tour's promoters, so be it.

From the perspective of Geoff Travis, or Mike Hinc, the fact that Piering was willing to take on the aggravation of being point person for the group was comforting; they knew him, after all, and as a comrade, if not always as a best friend. And from Morrissey and Marr's perspective, having Scott Piering fight for their cause was much more preferable than opening up a potential Pandora's box with Ruth Polsky. Piering may not have been as disciplined as a professional manager with the appropriate office staff and resources, but he was devoted, available and trustworthy. Besides, he was working for Rough Trade; no contract need be typed up, no commission paid out.

Or, as Johnny Marr put it in an interview that February, 'Everybody we meet wants to be our manager! But we're just organising ourselves at the moment and not listening to anybody.'

And so the tour rolled along, in its joyously chaotic manner. 'We were really making it up as we went along,' said John Featherstone. '"We're going on tour? How do we book a truck? How do we advance a show?" I didn't know that the band was supposed to have a manager. I hadn't gotten comfortable enough with Joe being around to know that this was a path fraught with peril.' Featherstone's subtle lighting, his refusal to drama-tise the band, came in for considerable early criticism, not least from Grant Showbiz, who himself was under constant attack from tour manager Phil Cowie, in part for acting more like a member of the band than one of the crew. And there lay the core of the group's intriguing dynamic. 'Even though we did not always see eye to eye, Grant and me,' said Featherstone, 'and there may have been a certain amount of insular fighting, we locked arms facing outwards as part of protecting the band whenever we were dealing with anyone outside of the organis-ation.' Cowie was considered one of those 'outsiders' and his days were quickly numbered. The PA crew, on the other hand, were very much viewed as insiders, and would work with the Smiths for years to come. 'They knew what they were doing; they were people who genuinely were part of the band gang,' said Featherstone of monitor engineer Eddie Hallam, and sound supervisors Diane Barton and Oz McCormick, whose company, OZ PA, also served New Order. 'It had that sense of being with the best bunch of mates at school.'

Central to the Smiths' touring sensibility was the fact that whatever else was going on around them – and on that first major tour, without personal management, and at odds with their tour manager, there were constant battles with security and promoters, multiple late arrivals for soundcheck and showtimes, and no small amount of debilitating hangovers – 'they checked their baggage at the stage door,' as Featherstone put it. 'They loved playing live.'

'The whole reason that I wanted to be a musician and be in a band was to go on tour and play onstage,' confirmed Andy Rourke. 'And when we were onstage it was perfect. Amazing. Every gig was amazing. And everybody gave one hundred per cent. One thousand per cent, if that exists.' The constant stage invasions, the routine late-show dance of mutual appreciation between Morrissey and Marr, the general level of hysteria, the fans who had started hanging around at soundcheck and whom the playing members of the Smiths readily welcomed backstage, all confirmed as much.

So did the peer approval that the group rapidly received from other artists. When *The Smiths* entered the national charts at number 2, held off the top spot only by the Thompson Twins, it simultaneously entered the 'independent charts' at number 1, replacing the debut mini-LP by Billy Bragg. (The Smiths also held the numbers 1, 2 and 3 positions in the singles chart – a first for any artist since the chart had been established in 1980.) A former punk musician and soldier with a thick cockney accent, Bragg had recently returned to the music scene as a solo artist, mixing the personal and the political in a format that might have been considered the domain of the folk singer but for the fact that he was wielding an electric guitar with considerable force. Bragg had already demonstrated his own songwriting ability with the opening track from *Life's a Riot with Spy Vs Spy*, 'A New England', which would later be taken into the top 10 by Kirsty MacColl, the daughter of the legendary Salford folk musician and writer Ewan MacColl. As such, he could afford to be initially wary of the buzz surrounding the Smiths, until he attended the Electric Ballroom show just before Christmas. 'I went with a fanzine writer who'd been telling me they were the new Beatles and I was saying, "Yeah, and I'm the new Bob Dylan." But then I saw them . . .'

Bragg had gained visibility in part because he was such an inexpensive, uncomplicated live act for promoters, and despite the fact that he'd had the number 1 indie album, he agreed to open for the Smiths at their London Lyceum show in February. A few days before, he had heard 'What Difference Does It Make?' at a soundcheck and asked the DJ to play the B-side as well: it was 'Back to the Old House'. 'I suddenly realised they weren't just a great live band, and they weren't just a great-sounding band. There was a real quality songwriting team there.' Until this point, Bragg had been, by his own admission, 'trying to compete with Elvis Costello, and you can't do that . . . I couldn't keep up with him. But with the Smiths, I understood where they were coming from, and the things they were riffing on. So it was much more feasible for me to measure myself against what they were doing: that kind of tough and tender thing that I was also trying to touch upon, the ability to be powerful but also personal in what you're writing about.' (If the Smiths were seen at this point to represent a northern sensibility, Bragg was already cursed by his accent to be viewed as representing a southern one, and so the deep and lasting friendship that quickly formed between the two acts helped serve as a unifying force.) In the meantime, Bragg took to covering the B-side to 'This Charming Man', 'Jeane'. Morrissey's tale of typically unsatisfied love was a two-chord rocker that gained extra poignancy from its sparse accompaniment. 'I loved the simplicity of it, the powerful imagery of it, and I just loved its whole velocity. There's a lot of stuff that Johnny played that can't be replicated, but '"Jeane" was four to the floor, and I can do that.'

The tour's original schedule (before the cancelled shows were tacked back onto the end of it) called for it to conclude with two triumphant statements. One was a headliner at the Free Trade Hall, the seat of so much cultural and political history in Manchester, not least those shows with the Sex Pistols and Buzzcocks; the other was a second London head-liner, a sold-out show at the 3,000-capacity Hammersmith Palais. That the Smiths had, already, achieved just about every ambition they had dared fix their gaze upon was confirmed when they brought out none other than Sandie Shaw to sing 'I Don't Owe You Anything' – which she had just recorded for a single, with the Smiths as her backing band.

SANDIE SHAW HAD not had a hit single in fifteen years, but contrary to the Smiths' subsequent suggestions, neither was she exactly in exile. In 1982, she had been coaxed back in to the studio by the British Electric Foundation to record 'Anyone Who Had a Heart', the Bacharach-David song, for an album on the Virgin label, whose cofounder, Nik Powell, she was dating. In the summer of 1983, it therefore proved relatively easy for Geoff Travis to meet with Powell, now Shaw's husband, and press upon him a letter from Morrissey and Marr, along with their home recording of the song they wanted her to consider. The fact that Marr had written the music to 'I Don't Owe You Anything' not only as 'something that Sandie Shaw could sing,' but in direct imitation of another Bacharach-David song 'Walk on By', would hopefully have come across on the demo. (Burt Bacharach and Hal David, after all, had also composed '(There's) Always Something There to Remind Me', the song that Shaw had taken to the top of the charts when she was all of seventeen.) But if not, then the title itself ought to have intimated a degree of obsessive knowledge; in 1967 Shaw had released an unsuccessful single entitled 'I Don't Need Anything', and the fact that Morrissey and Marr referenced its B-side in their letter to her demonstrated that at least one of them knew as much.

Indeed, the letter was almost extreme in its evident heroine worship. 'It is an absolute fact that your influence more than any other permeates all our music. Without doubt we are incurable Sandie Shaw fans . . . We have strong ideas about the musical backing which should accompany "I Don't Owe You Anything". . . We feel that your future needs an injection of high spirit and vengeance . . . We would be honoured to provide material for consideration.'

Shaw was honoured too, but also somewhat taken aback: the Smiths, after all, had only just released 'Hand in Glove' and were hardly household names. As such, it may not have been purely her desire to get acquainted with Morrissey and Marr that delayed any formal commitment until *after* the success of 'This Charming Man'. By that point Shaw would have been foolish to reject their approach, assuming that she had any desire to return to the charts. And she did. The collaboration was duly talked (and written) up – especially by Morrissey – over the last weeks of 1983 and into the New Year, at which point a recording session with John Porter at Matrix was shoehorned into the space created by the cancellation of the February live shows.

Once that session had concluded and the completed songs were played back, it was not 'I Don't Owe You Anything', but an exuberant reinterpretation of 'Hand in Glove' that was chosen as the A-side. Morrissey was not opposed to this decision; he had always believed that the song deserved to be a hit, and this was his best opportunity to be proven correct. But it could also be viewed as a missed opportunity of sorts: in this particular guise, afforded a production very much of its period, 'Hand in Glove' was reduced to a piece of ephemeral pop music. There is nothing wrong with that as a matter of course, and Shaw's distinction as a singer was highlighted by her remarkable ability to draw out the syllable at the end of each verse across several bars – but there was none of the youthful desperation of the Smiths' original version, nothing about the recording to confirm Morrissey's original belief that 'those words had to be sung.' (The fact that she insisted on changing 'you little charmer' to "cause you're my darling' did not, apparently, sit well with the original lyricist.)

On the other hand (and single side), 'I Don't Owe You Anything' sounded exactly as intended: as if it had been written for Shaw, and Shaw alone. She sang it with sincere tenderness (though her voice remained frustratingly low in the mix), and Porter and Marr surrounded her ample vibrato with an arrangement that positioned a Hammond organ against a distinct electric guitar twang. With Rourke's bass frequently rising an octave to demand attention and Joyce's refreshingly restrained drumming a sign of his increased confidence, it became the definitive version of the song. The need for a 'bonus' track saw Shaw stopping in on the next Smiths' session too, where she sang 'Jeane' – accompanied for the most part only by Marr's acoustic guitar (and the occasional background wail by Morrissey) – with such frightening sincerity that it quickly became a cult classic.

Upon release in April, Morrissey's long-standing faith in 'Hand in Glove' was vindicated by the new version's immediate airplay, and the Smiths had barely commenced their very first European tour when they were offered the opportunity to back Shaw on *Top of the Pops*. They didn't *have* to do it: the solo female singers of the 1960s were often depicted lip-syncing alone under the TV spotlight. And Morrissey was superfluous to official requirements: in theory, he could have converted any airfares home into a couple of nights at a five-star hotel and gone sightseeing around a European capital. But *Top of the Pops* was sacrosanct, and Morrissey wanted to be part of the celebration even if he was not to actually appear on the show with her. The three instrument-playing members of the Smiths duly accompanied Sandie Shaw on television that day in memorable fashion, performing barefoot in homage to Shaw's 1960s image. The singer kept her own shoes on but stole the entire show by collapsing on the floor and writhing suggestively. For those three minutes at least, Shaw was by far the coolest thirty-six-year-old mum in the nation, and the Smiths the coolest young band for fronting her comeback.

The next day, Dave Harper picked up various members of the group and brought them to Heathrow to resume the European tour. Morrissey, he noted immediately, 'was in this really dark mood.' Though the group checked in for their flight, they declined to go through to the departure lounge, sitting around instead, partaking in furtive private conversations. Harper's sinking feeling proved well founded when, he recalled, Morrissey turned to him and said, 'I'm not getting on the plane; I don't want to do the rest of the tour.' Morrissey's band mates appeared unable or unwilling to convince the singer otherwise (one is reminded of James Maker's memory of Morrissey, 'arms folded, unbudgeable') and all too aware that he lacked the authority to make any demands of his own, Harper retrieved their bags, drove them back into London, and returned to Rough Trade to deal with the fallout. (It was, he said, 'the first time I saw Scott [Piering] really angry.') Five shows were cancelled, four of them in Germany, where Rough Trade had its own division which had bankrolled the tour. 'They lost a lot of money on it,' said Mike Hinc, and the Smiths in turn lost considerable credibility with the German label and media (though they were coaxed back out a week later to play a full concert for a prestigious German television show and stop off in Paris for a scheduled concert on the way home). 'There was a failure of anybody at that stage to see the importance of Europe as a market equal in both cultural and commercial terms to the UK.'

This was true. So too was the fact that, coming off the hysteria of the UK tour, the number 2 album, the constant media attention and adulation, and lacking the level of touring organisation that a band of their calibre and popularity already required, the initial dates in Europe prior to the Sandie Shaw *Top of the Pops* appearance had been an enormous let down. 'I think we were feeling like they just didn't quite get it,' said Marr. 'It's not news that young British bands that are on top of the tree [in the UK] get quite a shock when they go to other countries who aren't on the same page – yet. I think we all just felt fucked. I can't speak for Mike and Andy.' (Harper recalled them being immensely 'frustrated.') 'I didn't feel disappointed. I felt like, "He's expressing what we all feel. We were trashed."'

THE SMITHS/SANDIE Shaw collaboration made for ready media fodder, and the two acts continued to do the rounds of press, radio and TV.[3] Ideally, the professional relationship would have continued as well, and even more so with patented compositions; the great shame of the Morrissey-Marr writing partnership is that they never gave material to another artist without releasing it in their own name first. When Morrissey finally brought Amanda Malone into the studio, in April 1984, it was as if he was trying to repeat the Sandie Shaw formula: he had Malone sing 'This Charming Man' and a new song that the Smiths had just recorded as a B-side, 'Girl Afraid'. While both songs would have taken on new light sung from a female perspective, the recording, at the Power Plant, with Geoff Travis nominally in the producer's chair, was something of a disaster. Amanda Malone had never been in a recording studio before; Sandie Shaw she was not. 'Geoff Travis, as soon as I met him, had animosity towards me,' she recalled, and while Marr, Joyce and Rourke were never anything but friendly toward her, they 'were not into it' either.

All concerned recognised the possibility of reversing what was otherwise a fairy-tale story of increasingly high chart success and critical acclaim; the fact that no less an icon than Paul Weller was engendering serious credibility issues for persisting with his own untutored female teenage protégée (Tracie) would have been very much on Travis's mind. The single was duly shelved, and Morrissey, afraid as always of confrontation, neglected to tell Malone until she pushed him on the matter during a visit to Campden Hill Road – at which point he admitted that 'Geoff Travis hates it.'

Malone, 'stressed at the idea' that the single might actually be released, assured Morrissey that if anything, she was relieved to hear that it had been canned. She had been living in England for three months already, in a bedsit in Battersea, while awaiting her studio appointment, and she decided to stay on in London. Malone developed a close friendship with Morrissey away from the day-to-day rigmarole of the Smiths, a female companion similar in some regards to those he had back in Manchester. Morrissey's sartorial sense of mischief had not been left in the north; on one occasion, he told Malone to dress up and meet him in Notting Hill for a formal lunch, at which, equally well attired, he walked them from his flat to the cafeteria at the British Home Stores on Kensington High Street – for a down-market version of the afternoon teas he'd once enjoyed at Kendal Milne. That he was constantly interrupted by fans appeared not to be a problem – yet. 'He was always charming and kind, no matter how many there were or how long they were there,' said Malone. 'He really got that he was lucky to be in that position, he really enjoyed it – and enjoyed being loved. Not just in a conceited way, but that to these people in some way he meant something. It wasn't like he was full of himself.'

Sandie Shaw had gamely promoted 'Hand in Glove' despite having only recently delivered a daughter, but she soon became pregnant again with a son. Still emotionally affected by her first bout of stardom as a teenager, she decided to focus on family over fame, and subsequently retreated from the spotlight for the next two years. In the meantime, she maintained her friendship with Morrissey, visiting him in Kensington and learning to circumvent his tendency of hiding from the door-bell by whatever means necessary. It was while they were still promoting the 'Hand in Glove' collaboration that Johnny Marr received a phone call from Scott Piering, with what was becoming a familiar cry for help. An important piece of publicity had been scheduled, requiring Morrissey and Shaw together, but the singer was nowhere to be found. Marr went to Campden Hill Road; he was the one person Morrissey would always open up for. Marr recalled his partner that day looking 'stubbly and wrecked, obviously not slept. Burned out.' (This would have been within weeks of the illness that caused the cancellations on the British tour.) It was on occasions such as these that Marr's presence was required to bring him around to the day's duties.

What was most surprising to Marr that day was not Morrissey's appearance but what he saw outside the kitchen window: their beloved 1960s teenage pinup, Morrissey's ultimate pop idol, no small heroine to Johnny Marr, the person they had once dreamed of writing a song for, was now standing on a fire escape, having taken the long way around to try and attract the singer's attention and get him going on the publicity jaunt.

'Oh, look,' said Marr to Morrissey, 'there's Sandie Shaw outside the window.' And they both waved to her. It was, he recognised later, 'one of the most amazing moments of my life.' As confirmation of how far they had come in such a short while, and what Morrissey's personality still had in store for them, it was also among the most surreal.

CHAPTER TWENTY-THREE

We'll never be a flavour of the month; I think we're just a little bit too clever for that.
                                    – MORRISSEY, *NME*, January 1984

In some scenarios, the story could have ended there. For despite the Smiths' exalted status within the independent world, still they would not have been the first group to generate incredible initial interest, sign quickly to a label, have their first single create a buzz, their second become a hit, their third capitalise on the second, and then their debut album storm the charts only for it to gradually seep in as a disappointment – at which, suddenly forced to write a second album as quickly as the first, they either deliberate over the follow-up to the point that the public loses interest or release substandard material in a rush to maintain momentum. The record books are, literally, littered with such examples – no shortage of them subsequently hailing from Manchester.

In the Smiths' case, though, precisely the opposite turned out to be true. The completion and release of the LP served to free the group at last to move forward, to start writing songs afresh. They had already introduced one such number at their last show of 1983: 'Barbarism Begins at Home', which would reach a considerably wider audience when they performed it live on *The Tube* in March 1984. It represented a return to the Freak Party beat, especially for Rourke, whose taut, melodic, funky bass line dominated its proceedings.[1] Marr adroitly accompanied him with flexing disco chords while Joyce luxuriated in the freedom to be allowed to stretch out and groove; lest the whole song get carried away onto the dance floor, Morrissey (writing it in public over the course of several live shows, something he was subsequently careful to avoid) supplied grounding lyrics about how 'unruly boys who will not grow up must be taken in hand.' 'Barbarism Begins at Home' represented a break from Smiths 'tradition' – a clear pronounce-ment, from the musical members at least, that they were not averse to dance music, and as the track settled into the live set, it rapidly expanded in length, from four minutes to seven, frequently returning as an encore at Marr's behest. (Around this same time, Marr also played some extremely funky guitar for Mike Pickering's group, Quando Quango, on their Factory single 'Atom Rock'. It marked the first time that Marr met New Order's Bernard Sumner, who produced the single, launching a friendship with long-lasting effects for all concerned.)

Two more new songs were then introduced at the first show in 1984; each had been formulated by Marr on his Gibson 355 in New York, and though they appeared, on the surface at least, to be more conventional Smiths fare, when recorded in March and released to the public in May one in particular revealed a new depth and sophistication to the group – and additionally, a new playfulness. Having toyed once already with Sandie Shaw song titles (turning 'I Don't Need Anything' into 'I Don't Owe You Anything') without anyone noticing, Morrissey decided to do so again, taking another of her failed late '60s singles, 'Heaven Knows I'm Missing Him Now', and replacing the verb and the object with the adjective 'Miserable'. The title served as confirmation to the greater public that he knew their opinion of him and was quite willing to ham it up to drive it home. But it also served as an inside gag with Sandie Shaw. And the best thing about it? Nobody suspected a thing. (This was 1984, after all, and Internet search engines and digital music copying were still very much in the future.)[2]

A similar sense of mischief ran rampant throughout the lyrics, quickly dividing listeners into two camps: those who laughed at the words even as they empathised with them, and those who saw them as confirmation of everything they inherently disliked about the Smiths in general, and Morrissey in particular. The couplet that offered the most universal appeal was the one that pronounced, 'Two lovers entwined pass me by, and heaven knows I'm miserable now,' a feeling that had surely been shared by anyone who had ever experienced a romantic breakup (and, perhaps, many who had not). The one that caused most debate stated, 'I was looking for a job and then I found a job, and heaven knows I'm miserable now.' In a Thatcherite Britain where unemployment – especially among the youth – showed no signs of decline, and attendant teenage poverty was there-fore a constant concern, Morrissey's critics (and there were many) wanted to know how he could object to the idea of work. But Morrissey had already answered that one in 'You've Got Everything Now' and 'Still Ill', and while this latest couplet surely came from his own personal experience (via his unhappy shifts at the Internal Revenue, the Civil Service, and as a hospital porter), it resonated with plenty of other listeners who were, almost daily, engaged in a similar battle between the conflicting demands of job dissatisfaction versus the need to pay the rent. The subsequent chorus – to the extent that the Smiths ever dealt in conventional song structures, this one appeared to come close – only drove the point home: who among the greater public had *not* smiled on a daily basis, for whatever reasons, at people whom they'd much rather kick in the eye?

And yet those who took 'Heaven Knows I'm Miserable Now' as affirmation of Morrissey's permanent state of depression must have missed the subsequent lyrical non sequitur about making

Caligula blush – a tease rendered that much more powerful by the image of Morrissey himself involved in the bedroom escapade. And it would seem certain that he understood as much and duly played it to the hilt, drawing the first-person 'I' out to three syllables in the subsequent line.

It was a lyrical masterpiece, but it would never have carried the same emotional depth without the accompanying arrangement. 'Heaven Knows I'm Miserable Now' represented the first time that Johnny Marr managed to capture that bittersweet sensation of melancholia. ('It's very beautiful, it can fill you up,' he said, describing it as a 'tangible feeling,' as opposed to depression – which was an 'emotion that was just about emptiness.') Recorded at the Fallout Shelter, an Island Records studio in West London, with John Porter again serving as producer, Marr's cascading guitar lines were given the space to breathe, to expand, to fill the song – but without cluttering it, as had always been a danger in the past. In that sense, 'Heaven Knows I'm Miserable Now' was as much Porter's achievement, the producer additionally coaxing a brilliant delivery from Morrissey, full of quavering vibratos and self-referential warbles, and rewarding the singer by ensuring that these vocals were then placed louder in the final mix than ever before – a necessity for all great pop singles.

The fact that a song entitled 'Heaven Knows I'm Miserable Now' could actually be viewed as a pop single was proven upon its release when it rose up the charts to graze (and grace) the top 10. (The ever-higher trajectory had now been maintained through the first four single releases.) A powerful antidote to the sentiments behind the number 1 single the week of its release ('Wake Me Up Before You Go-Go' by Wham!), 'Heaven Knows I'm Miserable Now' also represented one of the few occasions that a Smiths 'cover star' truly reflected the sentiments of the single within. The black-and-white image of erstwhile 'pools' millionaire Viv Nicholson, her platinum-blond hairdo and expensive clothes offset by her naturally hardened expression and the poverty of her surroundings – an otherwise deserted northern terraced street – said everything about getting what you want and ending up miserable regardless.

IN THE MIDDLE of May, the Smiths returned to Ireland for four concerts, including their first in Belfast. It was a matter of pride and principle for them, as a group of Mancunian Irish, that they establish a bond with the land of their fathers (and their mothers), and it was a visit that was greeted by ecstatic audience reactions and quasi-nationalist appreciation in the Irish press. Even before this visit, and based largely on the single show in Dublin the previous year, promoter Denis Desmond had been trying to secure the Smiths as headliners for a festival at Shelbourne Football Club's ground in Dublin, on the premise that it would steal U2's thunder and establish the Smiths as an equivalent or larger act. To this end, the Smiths were offered 15,000 Irish punts, almost five times as much as fellow hit act Aztec Camera (the Style Council, Lloyd Cole and Billy Bragg were also on the proposed bill), along with 50 per cent of all festival profits and merchandising. Ultimately, the Smiths declined the offer, the festival did not happen, and the band returned to Ireland later in the year to play a week's worth of club dates instead.

As the Irish offer intimated, the Smiths had reached a crossroads already in their career. Their relatively overnight fame had propelled them to the point where they could commandeer large sums of money playing to a significant number of people on the European festival circuit. And yet this was a band that had only just emerged from the clubs and was still acclimating itself to concert halls. Comforted by their familiar onstage intimacy, reassured nightly by friendly stage invasions, they had reason to doubt that they were ready for the larger stages. In addition, Morrissey was feeling the immense emotional and physical pressure that came with the reality check of achieving his dream of stardom in such suddenly glaring circumstances.

These competing forces unravelled on a particularly trouble-some visit to Finland for a festival at the beginning of June, with Morrissey succumbing to an attack of tearful depression. More than three years later, in one of his first interviews after Johnny Marr had left the band, he was able to reflect on the incident with unapologetic candour. Citing 'a very horrendous plane journey' as the instigating factor, Morrissey said, 'For some reason the floodgates just opened as they say – and didn't stop for the rest of the day. On the plane, in the airport, in the hotel, at the soundcheck . . . I just couldn't stop.' Confessing to embarrassment at the time, he observed (and not necessarily with any ill feeling) that the rest of the band 'didn't say much . . . They just put their Walkmans on and got out their in-flight magazines.' The Smiths' performance, for which the group's new tour manager, Stuart James, a youthful veteran of the Manchester scene, additionally handled sound duties in the temporary absence of Grant Showbiz, was then rained out midway through. It was a bad day all around.

Circumstances were somewhat more favourable a week later, on Saturday, 10 June, when the Smiths topped the bill at the Jobs for a Change festival in London. The free concert was held within the massive courtyard of the Labour-led Greater London Council, which had been thumbing its metaphorical nose at Thatcher's government in the Houses of Parliament, directly across the River Thames, by constantly updating and publicising, on the side of its building, the ever-rising number of unemployed. The event was not without incident; when the self-explanatory Redskins took to the stage, right-wing skin-heads engaged in their familiar Nazi salute as provocation, provoking a major fracas that sent several people to the hospital. But after further sets by Billy Bragg, Misty in Roots and Mari Wilson – a refreshingly varied bill – the Smiths took the stage as headliners to a crowd estimated at well over 10,000, some of whom scaled the courtyard walls via drainpipes to hang precariously from window ledges in imitation Morrissey stage poses that demonstrated the level of adulation now surrounding the singer. The sterling set they turned in that day (which included Morrissey's proclamation from 'Still Ill' that 'I never had a job, because I never wanted one,' which effectively countered the purpose of the event), when combined with the crowd mania at what was far and away the highest-profile show they had yet played, and to their largest audience, helped confirm the Smiths' status as the people's band.

The group then headed to the other side of the nation for a series of predominantly Scottish dates (after the gruelling experience promoting their album, the Smiths consciously broke their subsequent schedule into regional tours over the course of the year). Stuart James, more of a self-confessed 'Factory type' than a guitar-band aficionado, was quickly learning that such hysteria was merely business as usual: 'If they didn't have a stage invasion, they thought it was a shit gig.' (The invasions were rendered that much easier by the Smiths' contractual insistence on a lack of crowd barriers.)

Sure enough, a stage invasion took place when the Smiths performed at the Glastonbury Festival on 23 June. Far from its subsequent status as an annual carnival for the entire British nation, Glastonbury in 1984 was only just emerging from its long-standing reputation as a hippie gathering while still maintaining its commitment to all musical cultures; the Smiths found themselves playing on a Saturday afternoon bill in between Brass Construction and General Public, their set shortened by the late arrival of pop-reggae band Amazulu and impeded by audience hostility from some quarters. 'It's not something that, quite honestly, I'd like to relive,' said Morrissey later. 'We're very much a live group and it was always very intimate and personal, something we couldn't capture at Glastonbury.'

'We never ever fancied playing a festival,' said Marr. 'We had to be dragged kicking and screaming to do Glastonbury.' Much to All Trade's annoyance, the Smiths cancelled an appearance at the major Roskilde festival in Denmark the following weekend, where they had been advertised low down on a bill that included New Order and Lou Reed but also Johnny Winter and Paul Young. A conscious decision had been made. The Smiths would progress at their own pace, and very much under their own auspices. They would subsequently turn down just about all festival offers, eschewing the annual travelling circus show of mismatched acts performing in variable weather conditions to equally unpredictable audiences, in favour of the security of headlining appearances in an environment of their own choosing.

By RIGHTS, THE release of a quality post-album single should have been enough to allow for time off, if not for good behaviour then certainly for good deeds. But Morrissey and Marr recognised that they had been handed their 'moment,' that they should act on new songs as they wrote them rather than putting them aside for a future album. In this regard they saw the Smiths as a throwback not just to the furious work rate of the first generation punk bands, but to that of Marr's 1960s icons – the original rock groups who frequently stopped into studios between gigs on tour and emerged with historically important 45s.

'Musically I felt quite boundless,' Marr recalled of that immediate period after the first album. Andy Rourke felt much the same way: 'At that time, we felt invincible. We could do anything.' Unlike early days, said Marr of his latest compositions, 'I wasn't looking over my shoulder thinking, "How is this going to sound in the Haçienda?" But "How is this going to sound in our fans' bedrooms?" A lot of that comes with the confidence of [having] the backing of your audience.' In the spring of 1984, he and Angie, successfully reunited after the brief breakup over New Year in New York, had followed Morrissey to London, renting a flat in the genteel Georgian terraces of Nevern Square. (Angie left home in the process.) The Earls Court location was not a great distance from Morrissey's home in Kensington, but it was sufficiently far from the distractions of Central London nightlife that Marr was able to maintain his workaholic lifestyle when not otherwise on the road or in the studio. (Rourke and Joyce, befitting their lower-income status, roomed together in northwest London's less desirable suburb of Willesden.) In a mammoth attempt to compile multiple musical ideas, Marr recorded several instrumental songs onto his Portastudio at the start of June. Morrissey then added enough words to two of those ideas that, in July, when the group went into Jam Studios with John Porter, they formed the basis of the most productive single session of their careers.

Of the two, 'William, It Was Really Nothing', unveiled at the Jobs for a Change festival, had already been pegged as the A-side. It opened with a flamenco-like flourish of competing acoustic guitars (one of which used Nashville tuning, in which the higher-octave strings from a twelve-string guitar replace those on a six-string), an intro as short as the original Radio 1 version of 'This Charming Man.' It then set out to see if it could cram several dozen chord changes, multiple guitar parts both electric and acoustic, and an entire kitchen-sink drama into just two minutes – and succeeded quite marvellously. Lyrically, it conjured up images of the classic 1963 British movie *Billy Liar*, in which Tom Courtenay had played an undertaker's clerk (William Fisher) with a penchant for fantasy/fabrication that somehow failed to deter him from attracting the opposite sex (most notably the sophisticated Julie Christie, for whom the movie served as her big break). Morrissey's immortal line, mid-song – 'Would you like to marry me? And if you like you can buy the ring' – could have been delivered by the foul-mouthed café waitress Rita (played by Gwendolyn Watts), whose determination to capture Fisher in marriage offered a frighteningly vivid reminder of the loveless social contract at the heart of too many young working-class families of that era. But it was Morrissey's additional talent to throw a wrench into his words, and as with 'Girl Afraid', the song seemed to switch gender in the chorus, giving rise to a rumour that the William in question was the singer for the Associates,

Billy Mackenzie, whose friendship Morrissey discussed in print at the time of the single's release. (That Mackenzie later wrote a song entitled 'Stephen, You're Really Something' would suggest that at least one of them saw some truth in that supposition.)

If 'William', like its predecessor 'Heaven Knows I'm Miserable Now,' evinced Morrissey's sense of humour, its B-side, 'Please, Please, Please Let Me Get What I Want' presented him at his most deadly serious. The notion of a newly crowned pop star begging, 'for once in my life, let me get what I want' might once have been laughed out of town, but Morrissey had already established his persona – that odd combination of historical self-doubt masked by hysterical self-belief – to the extent that listeners, even beyond the hard core of Smiths fans, were willing to take him at his word. And as a result, in this song more than most other Smiths songs, it seemed hard to separate the singer from his subject matter.

The lyrics were all the more effective for matching the mood of Marr's lilting arrangement, a 6/8 waltz that the guitarist readily admitted was an attempt to capture a sentimental nostalgia for his childhood Irish holidays. The first time he had presented a ballad in this tempo ('Back to the Old House'), Porter had electrified it and added drums, and it had proven an error. The mistake was not repeated. 'Please, Please, Please Let Me Get What I Want' was augmented by simple electric guitar overdubs that emerged under and around the bridge sections, but an absence of percussion afforded it the feeling of an entirely acoustic performance – serving to spotlight Marr's creative chord structure in the process. The song started with a major seventh, uncommon in most pop music, and ended equally unusually with a mandolin solo that concluded on the dominant chord rather than the tonic, ensuring, by the mathematics of music, that the song – and by extension, its lyric – went 'unresolved.' Would Morrissey get what he wanted? Would the listener? Would they ever?

*   *   *

AMONG THE INSTRUMENTAL demos Marr had recorded at Earls Court in June was one he entitled 'Swamp'. Once the A- and B-sides had been fully realised at Jam Studios by the Smiths as a band, then Marr, Rourke, Joyce and Porter got down to recording it. Morrissey tended only to come in when vocals were required, and by all accounts the words had not yet been fully constructed for this song; his absence allowed the others free rein to indulge their growing experimental tendencies. The session that followed resulted in what would become their most acclaimed song, its unique structure the result of a particularly complex process that requires a detailed telling.

Johnny Marr's writing style, as the two short songs for the initial A- and B-side exemplified, typically saw him picking his way through the strings with his right hand and instinctively moving a finger here and a finger there on his left hand, creating multiple but subtle chord changes in the process, frequently two or more to the measure. 'Swamp' was built around more of a solid, strummed riff, closer to the conventional chord structures of the blues. (It was also built around a groove, as per the unrecorded 'Barbarism Begins at Home'.) This was especially attractive to John Porter, who 'was very into music that didn't have a lot of chord changes,' and who saw an opportunity in 'Swamp' to slow the chord progression down further, to keep the initial F-sharp chord going as long as sixteen bars rather than the original four or eight. Once this idea had been set, and multiple 'ambient' microphones set up at varying distances from the drums to magnify the 'swamp' mood, Porter withdrew to the control room and got the tape running.

The atmosphere in the studio was one of hedonistic self-confidence. 'We used to smoke dope from getting out of bed to going back to bed,' said John Porter. Or as Marr put it, 'It was just like, you're from Manchester, you smoke weed till it comes out of your ears.' Unlike some other people drawn to the drug, the playing members of the Smiths found that they could still make music while stoned. But it wasn't the only substance at hand. Engineer Mark Wallis recalled of the session that followed that 'we were up at least two nights and carried on working through the next day,' and that they were able to do so by constant dabbing at a 'large supply of "fish heads"' – that is, 'really shit speed.' Joyce recalled that they even switched the lightbulbs for red ones to further add to the ambience.

By Porter and Wallis's recollection, they recorded just a couple of takes of 'Swamp' but amassed an entire reel of tape in the process, including at least one fifteen-minute run-through. For the Smiths, the realisation that they had created such an epic groove immediately opened up endless possibilities for overdubs. The first – and most important – addition was the creation of a tremolo effect on the guitars, something that did not exist on the demo. Marr approached it with three reference points in his head. One was essentially generic: the Bo Diddley syncopated shuffle. The others were particular to his childhood: the guitar that ran through Hamilton Bohannon's 'Disco Stomp', from 1975, and the twin guitar groove in the instrumental section of the German band Can's surprise British hit of 1976, 'I Want More'. What the Smiths came away with was something very much of their own creation, and they achieved it by running the initial, dry guitar track back out from the studio desk into three separate Fender Twin Reverb amplifiers, with the vibrato controls on each one set to create a particular 'wobble' effect. Marr and Porter then stood duty at the amps (each miked up individually), adjusting the rotary 'speed' knob by hand to keep in time with the track. When their handiwork went out of sync regardless, Wallis would rewind the tape and punch the pair back in, sometimes for as little as ten seconds at a time. It was a laborious process and worth every painstaking step: the tremolo effect became the song's instant trademark, one of the more recognisable guitar intros in modern history.

To ensure a steady beat, Porter had already programmed a

rhythm track on the LinnDrum, including 'a percussion track with shakers and tambourines and congas and cowbells' – not instruments that Joyce included as part of his regular arsenal. One of these percussion parts was now set to sixteenth beats, and used to 'trigger' a Drawmer noise gate captured from the vibrato guitars, creating what Porter called 'a swirling signal' – a brief digital pulse that balanced the analogue tremolo effect and in the process ensured the track's meticulous rhythm. These multiple guitar parts were then bounced down onto a couple of stereo tracks so that they became their own instrument (this was in part due to logistics; there were only twenty-four tracks available on the tape, after all). At some point the initial fifteen-minute jam was trimmed and edited down to a more manageable length, although given that it was already evident this would not be the typical Smiths song, it was still up at the eight minute mark or so. At that point, recalled Porter, 'we looked at each other and said, "It sounds fucking great, let's keep it like that."'

With the ambitious mood proving contagious, the guitar parts for the song's second of two identifiable sections were now run through a Leslie speaker, typically used for the swirling sound of a Hammond organ. Marr then added some additional top-end lead guitar flourishes, but with his almost inherent aversion to playing solos, they were kept to a minimum. Recognising that the track had latched onto something as futuristic as it was nostalgic, the guitar parts were fed into a new piece of equipment, an AMS DMX 15-80 that was all the rage in studios that could afford it. Marketed as a stereo digital delay, and often referred to additionally for its capabilities as a 'harmoniser', its ability to store what seemed at the time like a magical 1.2 seconds of delay was quickly realised by technicians of the day as a primitive 'sampler' instead, arguably the first of its kind. ('They invented the sampler by mistake,' said Porter of the DMX's British manufacturer Advanced Music Systems.) In this particular example, the brief guitar runs were stored in the DMX, then punched back into the track where needed – a process that, in 1984, seemed nothing less than revolutionary.

Marr's demo had incorporated a slide guitar line, albeit 'a prettier version' than the one that Porter now suggested – which was to play it on the lower strings of the guitar, add a second, harmony track, but then to add a couple of additional notes to each of these tracks by using the AMS harmoniser.[3] Porter recalled that he may purposefully have only recorded the delay rather than the actual note on these digital harmonies so that 'there were these slight anomalies . . . an element of weirdness.' Given that Porter claimed to have played at least one of the slide parts himself, it was perhaps not surprising that he would look back and say, 'I thought that song was as much mine as it was theirs.' Marr, who disputed that Porter played any guitar parts on this song, nonetheless gave him due credit. 'He worked incredibly hard on that song, he pieced together all the sonics. It was like he was piloting the plane on that session, which is what a producer does.'

The final instrumental touch was Marr's relatively simple melody – the high notes heard at the end of each 'verse' – which he played using the electric guitar's natural harmonics. An almost precise replica of the synthesized vibraphone sound heard loudly on Lovebug Starski's 1983 12" 'You've Gotta Believe', this was Marr's nod to Starski as both a distant hip-hop influence and an immediate welcoming presence when the Smiths appeared at Danceteria. Such subtle notations were his way of countering the Smiths' public perception as '60s revivalists and rock purists.

Morrissey, of course, had much to do with this image of the Smiths; his negative proclamations about synthesizers and other studio trickery had sounded suspiciously close to a fatwa. But that was the beauty about the Smiths: that what seemed at times like diametrically opposed forces could find a common musical ground, the resulting combination of which could then appeal to all comers. Morrissey, who was often fulsome in his praise for his band mate's musical compositions, would rarely reveal his true feelings for this, the Smiths' most experimental, club-based track to date. (The song's 96 beats-per-minute tempo was actually much slower than conventional 'dance music', though it was right in the ballpark of most hip-hop.) But he knew that they were working on 'Swamp' and had long been tinkering with prospective lyrics. Porter, as was often his custom, dropped a cassette tape of the eight-minute mix through the singer's letter box on his way home after this lengthy session, and when Morrissey returned to the studio, with his book of prospective lyrics, he delivered his most emotive and personal vocal yet. After borrowing his opening lines from George Eliot's *Middlemarch*, Morrissey met the group's dark dance-floor groove head-on, singing of a nightclub where 'if you'd like to go, you could meet someone who really loves you' – except, of course, that in his case precisely the opposite happens: the protagonist leaves on his/her own, as always, forlorn and suicidal. It may have been mere coincidence, given that it formed part of a longer lyrical theme of resistance to unseen forces, that Morrissey should have chosen this track, with all its digital trickery, to insist, 'I am human and I need to be loved,' but the effect was the same regardless: it sounded as if his very life (or indeed, his death) depended on it. Between the painstaking but euphoric construction of the backing track and the meticulous but cathartic delivery of the vocals, the Smiths had created something quite unlike themselves. As with 'Barbarism Begins at Home', and several other songs the Smiths were working on at the time, the song was awarded a title that had not once been uttered in the actual lyrics: 'How Soon Is Now?'.

THE SMITHS WERE so excited by their new creation that they called up Rough Trade and invited Scott Piering and Geoff Travis to come and hear a rough mix. From Porter's perspective, part of the song's initial attraction was its American vibe. 'I was much more interested in breaking into the American market than they were,' he said of the Smiths. As such, he was keen to get Piering's response: 'I always trusted Scott's sensibilities to a certain extent because he was American and had a slightly different attitude.' Piering, Porter duly recalled, was visibly excited by 'How Soon Is Now?' – and Travis was not. 'He was like, "What are you doing? This isn't the Smiths". 'I remember feeling totally deflated, going home that night thinking, "I really thought we'd got something great here."' Mark Wallis, whose contribution to the session was rewarded with a rare engineer's credit on the record, confirmed that the reaction of 'the business heads' was 'It's not really the Smiths.'

Geoff Travis denied this. 'I remember loving it,' he insisted. 'I can remember going to the studio, I can remember sitting there, listening to it. I can't imagine why my reaction would have been "Well that's quite good." It doesn't make any sense. Maybe I was in a really bad mood that day. It's been known. I'm not right every time.'

This was a key point. It was thanks to Geoff Travis that the Smiths had got a record deal; he had heard something sufficiently exciting in a cassette tape of 'Hand in Glove' to release it as-was. It was thanks to him that the Smiths had had a hit; he had heard 'This Charming Man' being recorded at a Peel session and instantly suggested it as a single. He was now being asked to enthuse about an eight-minute jam – in very rough form – that most certainly was *not* the Smiths as he knew them, and he was facing a studio crew that had been getting by these last few days on equal parts speed and weed. (Travis, by contrast, was close to straight-edge.) If he chose to play it guarded this time around, then that was his right – and to some degree, his manner. 'Maybe I didn't say very much. That's much more likely. In a studio situation, it's very difficult to say much, because it's so intense.'

Certainly, by this point the Smiths were masters of their own domain. Had they wanted to earmark 'How Soon Is Now?' as a single – perhaps the follow-up to 'William' – that was absolutely their prerogative. As it was, there were certainly no objections from Rough Trade to mix it along with the projected A- and B-sides, and the production team subsequently decamped a few days later to Marcus Studios, where Porter, having already bounced the drum parts down to the point where he could no longer mix them in isolation, decided that 'the toms weren't loud enough' and, 'rooting round in the tape store,' unearthed a master recording by the reggae band Aswad. Finding some tom sounds to his satisfaction, he 'dumped it into a sampler, and added it into the drums.' Marcus Studios did not have automation, however, which meant that he and Wallis worked their way through a seven-minute mix with hands on faders at all times. Porter delivered the mix, figuring that his work was done, only to get a call from Geoff Travis a few days later. Morrissey, apparently, did not like the vocals. There was no choice but to go back in and do another mix, from scratch.

And just as well. Somehow, down the line, the Marcus mix of 'How Soon Is Now?' was released in Italy, and it turned out to be not a patch on the final version; as much as anything, the slide guitar was largely inaudible and the vocals not only lacked the warmth of the eventual mix but included a whole section, around five minutes in, where Porter and Wallis had attempted (but failed at) a dub section, over which Morrissey was heard yodelling ineffectively before the faders cut completely so that his quizzical 'OK?' – intended for the producer's ears only – was heard in isolation. (That was the part to which the singer really objected, and understandably so.) All this indicates that until the final mix, 'How Soon Is Now?' might not have been the classic we now know it as (and that Geoff Travis might well have been asked to judge it unfinished).

Porter went into Eden Studios, where he had successfully finished up the Smiths LP a year earlier, and which had an automated desk; there he set about reconstructing the arrangement from the ground up – including a fake fade-out after five minutes – and this time, he pulled it off. This final mix of 'How Soon Is Now?' was handed in to everyone's satisfaction only just in time to be released – as a bonus track for those who bought the 12" version of 'William, It Was Really Nothing'.

Almost as soon as that decision was made and the record hit the shops, everyone involved realised that they had made a mistake. 'William, It Was Really Nothing' was received well enough: it made the top 20 (though it halted the previous steady progress up the charts of each successive single) and there was a temporary frisson of controversy when Morrissey appeared on *Top of the Pops*, live, to strip off his shirt and reveal the words 'Marry Me!' scrawled on his chest in marker pen. 'Please, Please, Please Let Me Get What I Want' was received even better; the unique modal structure of this ballad, its waltz tempo, its brevity, and the inspired use of the mandolin all helped it transcend the Smiths' reputation as a rock band to become ultimately the most frequently covered and widely distributed of all their songs.

But 'How Soon Is Now?' was instantly recognised as something else, something quite beyond anything that the Smiths had yet attempted or released, something beyond what *anyone* had attempted or released; something entirely unique, a piece of music quite unlike any other, it propelled them into a different league entirely. And as 'William' dropped out of the British top 20 almost as quickly as it had entered, there was an awful realisation that it had been wasted.

IT WAS MORRISSEY who came up with a solution: *Hatful of Hollow*, a sixteen-song, budget-priced compilation that gathered up the 1984 non-album singles, the various previous non-album B-sides, and a hodgepodge of the 1983 Peel and Jensen session recordings – presumably those that he thought were better than the versions on the debut LP (which served as a rebuke to John Porter in the process). 'As far as we're concerned, those were the sessions that got us so excited in the first place and apparently it was how a lot of other people discovered us also,' said Morrissey in the official press release. 'We decided to include the extra tracks from our twelve-inch singles for people who didn't have all of those and to make it completely afford-able.' Syntax aside, he had summarised it perfectly.

Other than the fact that it was bookended by the latest single's A-side and B-side, *Hatful of Hollow* appeared to have been sequenced by a roll of the dice. 'How Soon Is Now?' for example, all seven minutes of it, was crammed into the middle of Side 1, in between songs from two different Peel sessions. In that respect, *Hatful of Hollow* had the delightfully random quality of the Who's *Meaty Beaty Big and Bouncy* or, more notably, the Rolling Stones' *Out of Our Heads* – a compilation that had been released similarly early in that band's career, admittedly before the birth of the album as an artistic state-ment.

The risk paid off. As an (unstated, but clearly noted) admis-sion that the debut LP had failed to live up to expectations, *Hatful of Hollow* offered fans a welcome opportunity to own better versions on vinyl. For those who were put off by the very notion of 12" 'bonus' cuts and those who didn't buy singles much to begin with, the compilation of various single tracks on an album was equally appreciated. The gatefold sleeve with the warm picture of the group on the inside (Andy Rourke, to the foreground, with bass in hand, looking very much like the unnamed Cocteau model on the front sleeve) made up to some extent for the rather cold presentation of *The Smiths*. And if the compression of almost thirty minutes of music onto each side was far from an audiophile's delight, that was countered by excellent mastering and a 'Pay no more than £3.99' sticker on the front sleeve. *Hatful of Hollow* was released in the middle of the Christmas market – and quickly became the Smiths' second top 10 UK album of the year.

CHAPTER TWENTY-FOUR

I'd rather be remembered as a big-mouthed failure
than an effete little wimp.
— MORRISSEY, *No. 1*, April 1984

Over the course of 1984, it became increasingly impossible – in the UK at least – to open a newspaper or magazine, or turn on the television or radio, without reading, hearing or seeing Morrissey hold forth in some capacity or another. All of the Smiths were charming and handsome, to use Morrissey's favoured adjectives for song titles, but the rhythm section were not employed to speak to the media, and despite the fact that Johnny Marr joined Morrissey at the early majority of interviews, it was quickly evident who gave better copy – and quickly generated more of it. For while Marr had that timeless look of rock 'n' roll insouciance about him, it was often hidden beneath a fringe or, especially through 1984, round mirrored shades; Morrissey presented his genuinely pretty face unadorned by more than the occasional NHS glasses, his brow fully visible thanks to his rising quiff, and that sense of openness made him a comforting visual prop in teenybopper magazines and on daytime television.

Marr claimed not to mind that the singer soon stole the limelight. 'That was another example of me and Morrissey working in sync,' he said, preferring to see it instead as an ideal division of partnership responsibilities. 'Straight off the bat, when we entered the pop world, Morrissey got in there, and engaged with it, and that took a lot of energy, getting up every day in his place in London to deal with that – the likes of *Smash Hits*, and a David Jensen interview, and this interview and that interview. It was very exciting for him without a doubt and I'm sure he wouldn't have had it any other way. But he went out and brought this energy, and a lot of character and a lot of ideas, and got in the room with all these other pop stars, and just wiped the place out. I was happy to do that on the guitar. We were both like . . . seesawing in a way. I just watched him do that, with awe. Again, it was like a partnership; one of you goes and does that, and one of you goes and does another thing. "All right, see you at teatime, we'll reconvene. I'll busy myself getting the demos together for the next songs and you go slug it out with *Smash Hits*."'

The media attention was so pervasive that there was the inevitable concern of overkill, but if anything, Morrissey took the opposite tack, telling *Jamming!* at the beginning of 1984, 'We want to reach as many people as possible, we've hardly begun.' Citing specific examples of both highbrow and lowbrow contemporary British entertainment shows that he had his eye on, he insisted, 'We think we can do these things and walk away with enormous credibility because we are very strong-willed characters and our belief is very deep-rooted.'

His convictions would quickly be tested – and proved correct. He appeared on *Pop Quiz*, the self-explanatory BBC TV game show, alongside people he'd (presumably) much rather kick in the eye. There, squirming in his seat on a 'team' alongside Alvin Stardust and Kim Wilde, he answered spoon-fed questions about Billy Fury and the Bunnymen, and visibly recoiled at the suggestion that he would come back to appear on the show again. And yet he compensated for his evident embarrassment by sitting down with the *TV-am* morning magazine show and engaging in genuinely intelligent conversation about his opposition to the promotional video. 'It's a complete matter of principle,' he said. 'I think it's pantomime, I think it's trivial, and I really believe the record itself should be all the prop – if prop is the word – that one should need.'

Similarly, he and Marr engaged in a piece of frivolous regional TV exposure by visiting the latter's old primary school, Sacred Heart in Wythenshawe, where the guitarist's considerably younger brother Ian, a pupil there, was ('anonymously') selected to ask them, 'Why do you hold flowers when you sing?' and the producers were so clueless about the phenomenon of the Smiths that they trailed the singer's name as Paul Morressey [sic]. And yet Morrissey still seized the moment to talk above the children's heads and criticise the Catholic school system to which he had returned for the day: 'Lots of the words I write are about school and about the horrible times that I had, and in a strange way it's like revenge on all those horrible teachers that made life miserable for me. So I think it really should be a lesson to all present day teachers that they really do have to treat their pupils with maximum care . . .' Even a ludicrous expedition on an open-top double-decker bus with a group of schoolchildren (this one including Elvis Costello's son) for the TV show *Splat!* paid off once they reached their destination, Kew Gardens, when Johnny Marr picked up his acoustic guitar, Sandie Shaw appeared as if from nowhere to start singing and, sitting cross-legged on the grass, in front of the audience of bemused primary-age kids, the two performed a spine-tingling rendition of 'Jeane'.

It was the same story with the music press. While Morrissey allowed *Smash Hits* and *No. 1* magazines to picture him in soft-focus pinup mode, and contributed to such childish standard fare as 'If I Ruled the World', he also agreed to the latter magazine's suggestion that he sit down in Liverpool with his rival motormouth, Ian McCulloch. The Echo & the Bunnymen singer – surprisingly – admitted to feeling threatened by the Smiths ('they sell more records than we do already,' he said, which was not actually true) and perhaps to book some insurance against Morrissey's own sharp tongue, accompanied his challenger back to Manchester afterward. (Sadly, nothing appeared to come of this potential friendship.)

Ultimately, though Morrissey proved adept at providing filler, he loved nothing so much as to pontificate on serious issues in the music press. 'The focal point for me is loneliness,' he explained to Roger Morton in *Debut*, confirming that he wrote 'for people who wouldn't normally go to concerts, watch television, buy records or listen to the radio.' This was the Morrissey for whom the decision to wear a hearing aid on *Top of the Pops* was inspired by a letter from a deaf fan, and duly interpreted by other acolytes as a statement of solidarity with society's less fortunate, which might explain why, when he next appeared on the show, rather than hide behind his customary contact lenses, he sported standard National Health Service glasses – a simple but powerful act of ordinariness that encouraged count-less teenage viewers to take similarly public pride in their own impaired vision.

Loneliness led to talk about suicide, hardly the typical concern of a newly crowned pop star. 'There's an hour of every single day, a silent hour, where I pray for another world,' he told Jim Shelley in *Blitz*. It was a subject he elaborated upon in some detail in his return to the gay press for an interview with Manchester magazine *Square Peg*. 'I look upon suicide as this incredibly brave thing, having maximum control over one's body,' he said. 'Yet ludicrously suicide has been looked upon as some severe disorder of somebody who doesn't know what s/he's doing. I always saw it as the height of self-awareness and control over one's destiny.' For now this was primarily a conver-sation piece; Morrissey would begin to tackle the issue of suicide in his lyrics over the next year, with inevitably controversial results.

While the feature writers were generally happy to allocate space to such subjects, their first point of reference was typically Morrissey's sexuality. The singer professed surprise at this – 'Simply to concentrate on one small distasteful aspect really belittles everything else we do,' he told *Zigzag* – though the truth was that almost all the songs on the first album seemed to concern sex in some form or another. Inevitably, the subject of his own sexual activities – or rather, the lack of them – was raised in almost every interview: 'I announced that I was celibate . . . so now, journalists telephone me day after day, to see if anything has changed,' he told *Jamming!* towards the end of the year, and he was only half joking. Asked by *Square Peg* whether celibacy was a choice or a dilemma, he said, 'It would take a great deal and something really quite serious to drag me out of it now, I think.' And yet when *Blitz's* Jim Shelley asked whether, 'after seven years of celibacy,' a love affair would have to be sexless, Morrissey responded, 'Not at all . . . Celibacy medallions don't interest me, I'm not after a specially inscribed trophy.'

At least the focus on celibacy diverted attention from what he saw as insinuations about his specific sexual leanings. 'I hate this "festive faggot" thing,' he complained to *NME's* Barney Hoskyns of his public reputation at the start of the year. 'I hate that angle, and it's surprising that the gay press have harped on [it] more than anyone else. I hate it when people talk to me about sex in a trivial way.' He was, therefore, horrified when one of his most important profiles yet, in *Rolling Stone*, for which the journalist Jim Henke was flown to London for the occasion, opened with the assertion that Morrissey 'admits that he's gay but adds that he's also celibate.' Morrissey had admitted to many things over the course of his extended honeymoon with the press, but homosexuality was not one of them, and Henke did not produce a supporting quote from the singer. He did, however, subsequently receive a chastening piece of correspondence from Morrissey, who understood all too well that *Rolling Stone* carried enormous influence across the United States, and that it would take a lifetime of denials to correct an early statement of 'fact' in such a high-profile publication.[1] What Morrissey appeared unable to grasp was that a vast number of American alternative music fans, eager for any voice of authenticity, latched onto that interview as if a key to another world – or at least, another viewpoint. It's no coincidence that in musician-writer Joe Pernice's marvellous novella *Meat Is Murder*, the (heterosexual) high school narrator is remonstrated by his older (homophobic) brother with the following insult: 'God, this music is too fucking miserable for me. Instead of Morrissey, you should listen to Morrison or Clapton . . . And really, how can anybody be gay and celibate at the same time?' (The narrator replies, 'I don't know, Jerry. How do you do it?')

Henke was not the only one at *Rolling Stone* to make a presumption about Morrissey. In the same issue as the interview with the Smiths' singer, Kurt Loder opened his (four-star) review of *The Smiths* with a reference to 'Glad to Be Gay' singer-songwriter Tom Robinson before asserting that Morrissey's lyrics 'probe the daily aching of life in a gay-baiting world,' and the 'sometimes heartless reality of the gay scene.'

The question of Morrissey's sexuality was clearly impossible to ignore – for fans, critics and even friends, some of whom felt that his insistence on presenting himself as a celibate was a cover. 'I knew he was gay from the off,' said Amanda Malone. 'I think that if he said he was gay that would have been OK, and if he'd said he wasn't gay that would have been OK, but when he set himself up as being celibate, that was very silly – because I don't think he was.'

'I think it came from a real exposure to feminist literature about men having feminine sides and sexuality being fluid,' said Liz Naylor of Morrissey's championing of a 'fourth sex,' as in the initial breakthrough *Sounds* interview and periodically thereafter. 'I think it comes from quite a kind of intentional place . . . Those kinds of ideas were interesting intellectually. So the idea of celibacy is an intellectually stimulating experiment . . . But in terms of his own sexuality, what I knew of it wasn't really congruent with what was presented.'

Still, at least one of his band mates insisted otherwise. 'Everything he said during that time, in that regard, he lived,' said Johnny Marr. 'That wasn't posturing. Which may or may not have been bad news to him! But nevertheless, what he was saying was true. There was no one around.' Yet despite Morrissey and Marr spending so much of their working lives together – or at least, as referenced earlier, performing their individual roles within their partnership – they kept very different hours. Marr was a sociable night owl, Morrissey a mostly private day person. And Marr had to admit that, as a romantically secure, heterosexually active young man at the time, he didn't pay personal attention to the emotional impact of Morrissey's statements regarding celibacy, either with regard to the singer himself or the public at large. 'I don't think I was old enough to appreciate the difficulties that some teenagers go through. One can always empathise. But I didn't know it as a syndrome, or part of life. And I think it was a very, very healthy and truly brilliant thing . . . it was totally empowering. And a first. For the singer of a rock band to be saying that was very, very cool.'

It was, and one might have hoped that Morrissey would understand that the occasional misquote or misrepresentation was a token price to pay for so much invaluable free publicity. But he clearly felt otherwise. As well as writing to Henke, in July he wrote to the producers of *Ear Say*, a prestigious British TV show for which he had been interviewed both personally and with Sandie Shaw, to say that he was deeply wounded by [presenter] Nicky Horne describing him as the 'Quentin Crisp of pop.' Many young people in Britain had no idea about Quentin Crisp, and those who did might have considered him merely a queer old British eccentric, someone Morrissey might well have admired. Apparently not. 'Everybody knows the implications behind such a statement,' he wrote, 'implications which Nicky Horne (or anyone else) could never ever seriously justify . . . I could never begin to explain the embarrassment this comment has caused me, and how it has upset other members of the Smiths and our families.'

Morrissey's refusal to declare himself was driven, in large part, by a sensible determination to avoid being pigeonholed or typecast. 'I feel that lyrically I speak for everybody – at least I try to,' he insisted in a(nother) cover story for *Melody Maker*, at the end of a diatribe against Bronski Beat. This act had emerged earlier in 1984 with an openly gay singer, Jimi Somerville, and their hit singles ('Smalltown Boy' and 'Why') were equally transparent discussions of male homosexuality that were heralded by many in both the gay and straight communities as an act of significant bravery. Morrissey was unimpressed. 'As a direct result of my attitude to relationships our audience is split sexually evenly,' he said. 'That's something that pleases me to a mammoth degree. This is why I feel so sad about groups like Bronski Beat who are so steeped in maleness, and quite immediately ostracise 50 per cent of the human race.' In actuality, Bronski Beat had massive appeal with female listeners, and Somerville's stance proved no immediate hindrance to American airplay either. In fact, the stateside success of Bronski Beat, Soft Cell, Culture Club and Frankie Goes to Hollywood, all of whose front men were openly or well known to be gay, suggested that Morrissey had nothing to fear from the assertion of *Rolling Stone* and the insinuation of others except his own personal insistence that they were wrong.

The *Rolling Stone* interview was part of a barrage of high-profile press that accompanied the American release of *The Smiths* in the spring of 1984; recognising that something special was going on in the UK with this band, none of the respected national outlets (including *Creem*, *Musician* and the *New York Times*) wanted to be seen as sitting on the sidelines. While the press attention did not translate into noticeable sales, this was, in part, due to the Smiths themselves, who in a risky but ulti-mately smart move, turned down the opportunity to tour the States 'unless we're really wanted there,' as Morrissey explained to *Musician* that spring, adding, perhaps as a warning to band-mates and fans alike, that 'Endless touring is time-consuming, soul-destroying and it wrecks your health.'[2] And so, in lieu of standing on an American concert stage, Morrissey took to the platform of the press; once he could wrestle Jim Henke away from the subject of his own sexual identity, he used the *Rolling Stone* profile to issue his most outrageous quote yet, and the fact that he supplied an American reference suggested that it was premeditated. 'The entire history of Margaret Thatcher is one of violence and oppression and horror,' he told Henke. 'She's only one person and she can be destroyed. I just pray there is a Sirhan Sirhan somewhere.'

The comment resounded forcefully back to Britain. Even those who privately agreed with him were surprised that Morrissey should state such a view publicly, but he remained unapologetically consistent in his opinion. When the IRA bombed the Grand Hotel in Brighton during the annual Conservative Party Conference, on 12 October 1984, he rejected the notion of sympathy for the five people killed and the dozens who were injured in the attack, insisting instead, in a *Melody Maker* cover story, that 'the sorrow of the Brighton bombing is that Thatcher escaped unscathed. The sorrow is that she's still alive . . . I think that, for once, the IRA were accurate in selecting their targets.' With a nine-date tour of Ireland scheduled for the following month, Morrissey's comment, instantly re-published across all forms of media, necessitated the employment of personal security, especially for the shows in the predominantly Protestant north. Denis Desmond of MCD recommended Jim Connolly, who proved so good at his job that he was subsequently put on the touring payroll as security officer, a protective presence alongside Morrissey throughout the Smiths' career and beyond. (The Irish concerts went off peacefully, although in Dublin, Peter Morrissey, who had moved home to his birthplace, showed up backstage and was refused entry into the dressing room. The Smiths considered it a sacred space and not one for socialising or family reunions.)

Morrissey's comments about the IRA and Thatcher only served to further antagonise the right-wing media, and the *Sun* newspaper (again) sought to enact some revenge, when the brother of Moors Murders victim John Kilbride heard 'Suffer

Little Children' on a jukebox in the summer of 1984 (pride in the album rendition had seen it selected as the B-side to 'Heaven Knows I'm Miserable Now') and accused the Smiths of tasteless sensationalism. The newspaper promptly roped in Anne West, the mother of victim Lesley Anne Downey, for the headline MOORS MUM RAPS MURDER SONG and a powerful quote: 'Whoever wrote the song must be as sick as the killers. It's just blood money.' More so than the child-molesting claims of the previous year, the *Sun*'s latest accusation was entirely unjustified. 'Suffer Little Children', as Scott Piering wrote in a subsequent press release on Smithdom letterhead (the company was now registered at Collier Street, and Piering clearly authorised to represent it), 'was written out of profound emotion by Morrissey, a Mancunian, who feels that the particularly horrendous crime it describes must be borne by the conscience of Manchester, and that it must never be forgotten lest it happen again.' Additionally, Morrissey wrote a long letter to Mr Kilbride and spoke personally with Mrs West, who was so deeply impressed by his sincerity that she withdrew her comments and replaced them with an about turn: 'Morrissey can write a song about my daughter any time he wants.' Some damage had been done by this point: thanks to the *Manchester Evening News* following blindly in the *Sun*'s footsteps, the high-street chain stores Woolworth's and Boots had removed *The Smiths* LP from their shelves, and the Smiths had to pay a (paltry) £400 donation to the Royal Society for the Prevention of Cruelty to Children as some form of penance before either would restock. But greater good had come out of it. Morrissey had been placed in the dock by the *Sun* and accused of being a public enemy – but through his insistence on challenging the charges and stating his case, he had proven himself instead as the people's friend.

CHAPTER TWENTY-FIVE

It's easy to get further and further away from the council estate and you can forget how you felt for twenty-four years before it all happened. You can get quite bedazzled by the lights. Well, we never intend to do that.

— MORRISSEY, *Jamming!*, December 1984

Toward the end of 1984, after less than a year in the British capital, the Smiths all moved back to Manchester. It was a conscious decision, for which Marr took responsibility. The return north was partly born of a need to get away from the capital's rumour mills, its media circus, and the temptation for endless business meetings, but more so of a desire to reconnect with their Manchester friends, their influences, the milieu that had surrounded them growing up. There was a sense that, having made something of themselves on a national level, they could return home with heads held high. There was also the fact that Morrissey and Marr had made enough money to buy houses – in the Manchester suburbs if not yet in Central London. Marr's was half of a vicarage on Bowdon's Marlborough Road, near Altrincham Grammar School, which he and Angie quickly turned into the group's 'engine room' à la Marr's idol Keith Richards, complete with Marr wearing his guitar even in the kitchen, 'all the roadies sleeping on the floor' and a couple of Alsatian dogs for company and security. The hours were late, the mood boisterous, and the vicarage's neighbours no doubt bemused, but it served to give the group an HQ that had been sorely lacking in London, and would have an immediate positive effect on the Smiths' writing and recording.

Morrissey opted for a cul-de-sac in nearby Hale Barns, close to the local tennis grounds and golf course. The detached house he purchased was surprisingly similar in style to the semi-detached on Kings Road that was now consigned to memory, for he installed his mother in the new abode too, from where she took care of business and visitors when he was otherwise engaged in London.[1] He was unabashed about their close relationship, telling *Melody Maker* just a few months later, 'She completely dissects everything that happens. She reads every single interview. She produces long monologues . . . she's very, very much involved in what I do. And hers is the only opinion that I really take remotely seriously.' (Presumably, he did not mean to leave his partner Marr out of this equation.)

In the process of relocating came a realisation that their second album could not afford to sound like the first, flawed as that had been, and neither should it sound like the singles that had followed it, brilliant though they were. For John Porter's greatest skill, it turned out – treating every song as a potential number-one single – was also his greatest drawback, because not all songs required such a commercial approach. The Smiths now saw the need to handle their latest batch of songs as an album, a coherent body of work that would take them to the next level as *artistes*, single sales possibly be damned. To do that, they needed not only to move back to Manchester but also to record in the north again. More so, they needed to take responsibility for the process.

'Perhaps Morrissey had more belief in me than I did myself,' said Marr, who felt that any decision to self-produce an album as the Smiths would ultimately fall on his shoulders. Nonetheless, he said, the decision was made quickly. 'It was just, "All right then, I can do it." So many things didn't need to be discussed for very long because we were on exactly the same page.'

Or as Morrissey put it: 'The whole idea was to control it totally, and without a producer, things were better. We saw things clearer.'

John Porter saw things equally clearly: that he had been fired, and, as far as he was concerned, very much at the behest of Morrissey. At the beginning of their working relationship, the singer had sent him postcards 'thanking me for helping him,' but almost immediately, said Porter, 'he seemed to get suspicious of me. And I think the fact that Johnny and I were so tight and hanging together and smoking piles of dope together . . . we'd become good friends. I think Morrissey felt that I was maybe pushing a wedge between the band.' Aware of this perceived division, he said, 'I really tried to bring Morrissey in to make it a three-way thing. I knew that that would only make it better. And I probably – without voicing it at the time – knew that if I couldn't do that, there would be no future for me anyway.' In a gesture of friendship, Porter even invited Morrissey to his house for dinner, for which his wife, Linda Keith, 'made this *beautiful* vegetarian spread. And he just didn't turn up. He didn't phone, didn't say "I can't make it," just didn't turn up.' Porter's conclusion? 'I don't think Morrissey liked me very much.'

As far as the guitarist was concerned, 'I would have just had [John Porter] produce everything.' Viewed in the light of such a comment, the singer's insistence on dropping Porter at the end of a run of four consecutive top 20 singles, and at the very point that the producer had just laboured over a pair of B-sides that were being hailed as the greatest recordings of the Smiths' career, appeared nothing short of callous.[2] But although Morrissey did not always go about his decisions the right way, his instincts up until then had been largely proven correct, and they were about to be confirmed again when he suggested that they hire Stephen Street, whom the Smiths had met at the Island Records studio when, as in-house engineer, he worked the 'Heaven Knows I'm Miserable Now' session.

Street was twenty-four years old at the time – older than all of the Smiths except Morrissey, but more than a decade younger than John Porter. A capable musician, having played bass in pop/ska band Bim, he'd abandoned the gigging circuit a couple of years earlier to focus on what he realised was his first love, the recording studio. And being part of their generation, subject to the same influences and post-punk experiences, he was already a Smiths fan when he came to work with them. (Indeed, he volunteered for the single session.) 'There was something magical there straightaway,' he said of meeting the band. 'Johnny's guitar playing was obviously fantastic. And there was something about Morrissey. The way he carried himself and the way he generally behaved, you could tell he was getting quite used to this idea of appearing on *Top of the Pops*. There was definitely a star quality emanating from him.'

Street's presence at the Island Records studio had immediately sent alarm bells ringing with Porter. 'As soon as Morrissey came in, he looked at Steve and I thought, "This is it, you're out of a job."' When, at the end of the session, Morrissey asked for the engineer's phone number, and especially when Street was offered belated 'special thanks' on the 'William' sleeve, the writing was on the wall.

'Here was someone who was wide-awake, very enthusiastic, sharp, and obviously very talented,' said Marr in defence of Street's hiring. 'And looked like one of us.' In October, Street was appointed as engineer for the Smiths' second album, and he moved up for a lengthy stay in a Manchester hotel. From there he joined the group on a daily drive in their battered white Mercedes over to Amazon Studios in Kirby, on the outskirts of Liverpool, where Echo & the Bunnymen had recorded much of their hit album *Porcupine*. The sessions were surprisingly routine. By eight o'clock most evenings, Morrissey would be ready to return to Manchester, and because the group was commuting together, as a team, that meant everyone leaving with him. This suited Street just fine; despite his youth, he was not one for Porter's all-night sessions. 'You go through the night, all you end up doing is starting later and later the following day. You don't get any more work done. A ten-hour day, that's enough for me.'

Once they started working together, Street recognised the obvious: that 'part of the reason Morrissey didn't want to work with John Porter is he thought that [Porter] was putting too much emphasis on guitars and not enough on his vocal.' Morrissey and Street quickly became comfortable with each other, in part because Street was willing to jump when Morrissey said he was ready to sing, and to work within the vocalist's confines. 'Nine times out of ten I'd get it in three takes or so,' said Street, though equally often, he would find himself splicing together different lines from different takes to get the best vocal possible. 'It could [even] be words within lines,' he said.

Over the course of the album session, the engineer's inexperience did see him accept one off-key vocal that ultimately prevented the song in question – 'I Want The One I Can't Have' – from becoming an otherwise radio-friendly single. (Morrissey had announced it as their next 45 on the Irish tour at the end of 1984, after the majority of the album had been recorded.) But that in itself was part of the singer's appeal. 'You got a sense of performance from him,' said Street. 'You can't beat that. I'd rather it be slightly sharp or flat and be a performance rather than be note perfect and completely flat in [sense of] delivery.'

As he settled into his working relationship with the band, Street sensed that Marr might now be overcompensating for his previous habits with Porter. 'I always got the feeling that Johnny was being economical,' said Street. 'He wasn't layering just for the sake of layering.'

'We hung a lot of music on the atmosphere,' confirmed Marr, citing the ballad 'Well I Wonder' as a prime example. 'It purposefully has a feeling of suspension in it and is very delicate. I could have put a lot of overdubs on that song, but I left it as it was.' 'Well I Wonder' ended up being based on one simply strummed acoustic guitar (along with drums, bass and textural sound effects), accompanying Morrissey's minimalist, forlorn lyrics, cribbed largely from Elizabeth Smart's novel *By Grand Central Station I Sat Down and Wept* (though none the worse for people eventually discovering as much), and featuring a falsetto vocal finale that sounded so much less forced than past attempts. The sound of rain coming down upon its conclusion was, said Marr, 'the sound of moving back north.' For Marr, the sense of the album they were making was that it was 'done on an industrial estate on a very, very wet Liverpool winter. And we were very druggie. It's druggie music.' The harsh reality of Amazon Studios, however, was that it was not up to standards. Stephen Street ultimately implored the band to move on to a higher-end studio, and subsequent overdubs and mixing and, according to Street, the entire recording of a couple of songs, took place at Ridge Farm Studios in the leafy green belt county of Surrey.[3]

The group had come into Amazon with three songs fully road-tested: the long-standing 'Barbarism Begins at Home', and 'Nowhere Fast' and 'Rusholme Ruffians', both of which they had demoed with John Porter and then recorded with him at a third Peel session in August.[4] It was the rockabilly rhythms of these two newer songs – or what Marr referred to as 'That Sun Records kind of rush' – rather than the funk workout of the older one, that gave the clearest indication of the band's new studio direction. Lyrically, too, that pair helped set the scene for the new album, for Morrissey was evidently determined to move away from the now clichéd Smiths subject matter – his perceived sexual habits (or lack thereof) – while bringing an even closer affinity to the plights and habits, and political targets, of the working classes. In 'Nowhere Fast', he opened the second verse with the assertion, 'I'd like to drop my trousers to the queen/every sensible child will know what I mean.' The wit suggested an element of music hall, that treasured English trait that stretched back from the Smiths' contemporaries Madness to the Kinks and George Formby, the latter of whom Morrissey readily cited in an interview at the time as 'one of the greatest lyricists of all time.' (It also

379

helped pave the way for the theme of the third album.)

'Rusholme Ruffians' was an alliterative ode to the 'fun fairs' of the Smiths' childhood Manchester. While Marr's recollection of such events had been a warm one, of being left alone with his sister to enjoy the pop music blaring from the rides in Wythenshawe Park, Morrissey's was of unprovoked violence, of being head-butted for no reason in Stretford, and since he was the lyricist, it was his memory that prevailed. In the song's opening verse, 'a boy is stabbed and his money is grabbed,' while later on, 'someone falls in love and someone's beaten up,' and a girl considers suicide from the top of the parachute. It was by far Morrissey's longest and most literal lyric to date, and his fascination with violence was notable inasmuch as, while he had his narrator walk home alone, just as he had done in 'How Soon Is Now?', in this case he was buoyed by his experience rather than wanting to die, proclaiming, 'My faith in love is still devout.'[5] Reduced by more than two minutes from the exuberant version demoed with John Porter, 'Rusholme Ruffians' displayed such an obvious doff of the cap to Elvis Presley's '(Marie's the Name) His Latest Flame' that the group would soon include a section of that song in their stage rendition.

By its very title, let alone its lyrics, 'Rusholme Ruffians' played up the sense of the new album as a most northern and physical endeavour. ('I think the way I write is very Northern,' said Morrissey at the time. 'I'm not in the least infected by London or the South.') To this end, it was notable that 'What She Said' – a frenetic under-three-minute attack of buzz-saw guitars and constant drumrolls that announced a previously untapped tension to the Smiths – referenced 'a tattooed boy from Birkenhead,' the Liverpool port just a few miles from Amazon Studios. But the most powerful geographical statement was reserved for the opening line of the opening song, 'The Headmaster Ritual': 'Belligerent ghouls run Manchester schools.'

'The Headmaster Ritual' was essentially a blow-by-blow

account of the daily routine at St Mary's, from Jet Morgan's ludicrously officious inspection of daily uniform to Sweeney's bullying tactics on the playing fields. But despite being set in Manchester, and coming from Morrissey's personal experience, so too was the song to be recognised universally for summarising the emotions of so many within the group's generation. In admitting, 'I wanna go home, I don't want to stay/give up life as a bad mistake,' for example, Morrissey immediately won the sympathy of all those who had dreaded going to school on a daily basis, all who had suffered personally at the hands of aggressive teachers and violent fellow pupils. And yet when he then adapted the opening line in the second verse to spit out the words 'spineless bastards all,' it was the lyrical equivalent of standing up to those bullies. With the rest of the Smiths backing him so confidently – the one-minute introduction featured the most densely layered and yet most dexterous guitar tracks of the entire album, instant vindication of the decision to self-produce – Morrissey was able to switch to a purely phonetic vocal accompaniment, the kind that had sounded farcical in the past but which he now wore as if a second skin. And when the Manchester Education Authority subsequently took public umbrage to 'The Headmaster Ritual', suggesting that they might try to ban the Smiths from playing within their boundaries of Manchester as a result, it served as confirmation that the attack had hit where it hurt – and that, as such, it had been entirely effective.[6]

Morrissey had been accused in the past of clouding his lyrical agenda, of hiding his meaning behind too many metaphors, and if 'The Headmaster Ritual' purposefully opened the second album as an (overdue) statement of absolute clarity, it was nonetheless bested in that regard by the record's unequivocal finale, that for which it was named: the song 'Meat Is Murder'. Vegetarianism itself was far from taboo in 1984, and Morrissey was not alone among his circle in his refusal to eat meat: his mother, Betty; Angie Brown; Grant Showbiz; Sandie Shaw;

the band James; and more recently Marr himself had all made their own commitments to abstain. James, in particular, had caused the Smiths all sorts of amusement by bringing a Calor gas stove on the road and cooking their own meals in the van. (It is perhaps not insignificant that James and Sandie Shaw tried – and failed – to get the Smiths, especially Morrissey, to engage in meditation as a means of dealing with the intense pressure, scrutiny and responsibilities that came with their fame.) By comparison, the Smiths were not even strict lacto-vegetarians: Stuart James had been surprised to find Morrissey eating whole fish on the mid-1984 tours, and Marr had tuna sandwiches on his rider. In addition, collectively they consumed so much milk, cheese and eggs that they could have been sponsored by the factory-farming dairy industry. And they routinely wore animal products. Still, Morrissey had come to see his vegetarianism as a matter not only of pride but principle, and insisted that those around him follow suit. Mike Joyce found the transition easier than did Andy Rourke, but the result of the decree was sufficient solidarity that Morrissey could now sing about his pet crusade with the Smiths not just at his side, but fully behind him.

Having his band's support was crucial. Morrissey knew perfectly well that he ran the risk of alienating at least 90 per cent of his audience with 'Meat Is Murder', and yet it was a risk he was not only willing to take but, in terms of naming the album for it, that he was willing to bet the band's career upon. 'The artist must educate the critic,' Wilde had written, which Morrissey would cite as his most treasured line from his most dependable icon. He set out on the process of educating not just the (Smiths') critics but the public at large without subtlety, without apology, and without guilt; rather, he set out to impose guilt upon the carnivores, even those who were throwing flowers at his feet.

To that end, subsequent charges that 'Meat Is Murder' was dogmatic may have been accurate, but they also missed the point. That point was simple: Meat *is* murder. 'The calf that you carve with a smile?' Murder. 'The turkey you festively slice?' Murder. 'The flesh you so fancifully fry?' Murder. 'It's not "natural," "normal," or kind,' insisted Morrissey, it's 'murder.' To dress the subject matter in more comforting tones would have been the equivalent of dressing the meat of a 'beautiful creature' with tomatoes and lettuce, placing it in a bun, and presenting it to the consumer as something other than what Morrissey believed it to be: murder.

If there was a line in the song that failed to stand up to scrutiny, it was that 'death for no reason is murder.' Death by car crash, or by brain cancer, or in a house fire could be construed as death 'for no reason,' and yet surely not as murder. Then again, Morrissey was not given to outside editing of his words, and for a singer who had traded so far in lyrical obfuscation, the fact that only one line defied logic was noteworthy of itself.

When it came to the music for 'Meat Is Murder', Morrissey had told Marr of both the title and concept in advance and the guitarist duly submitted something atypically flat, ponderous, mechanical and 'nasty' – so much so that it took a while to realise that it had been written in 6/8 time, the rhythm of his nostalgic and melancholic ballads. Morrissey then supplied Stephen Street with a BBC Sound Effects album with mooing cows on it and asked the engineer if he could make it sound like an abattoir. Street, to his personal and professional satisfaction, succeeded by adding other incidental noises to that of the cow and putting them through a reverse echo. That was mixed in alongside the simple guitar chords and Marr's lead piano melody that sounded as if originally intended for a ghost film. The final arrangement was not particularly loud, abrasive, or even harsh. But at more than six minutes in length, 'Meat Is Murder' was as unforgiving of its listeners as Morrissey was of meat-eaters. Even those whose eating habits were profoundly affected upon hearing the song tended to express something of a relief when it concluded.

It was music as propaganda, and as such it would have had no place on a major label. But the Smiths were on Rough

383

Trade, the distribution arm of which was distributing the likes of Crass, Flux of Pink Indians, and other anarchist-punk bands with equally uncompromising messages, and with a number of staff who were vegetarian or vegan as a natural product of their politics and/or lifestyle.[7] News that the label's golden calf was releasing an album with such a militant title was therefore greeted, in some quarters at Collier Street, with genuine excitement. The stakes were raised that much higher when Morrissey then delivered his design for the album cover: an image of an American soldier in Vietnam from the controversial 1968 documentary *In the Year of the Pig*, the album title *Meat Is Murder* inscribed on the soldier's helmet in place of the original motto 'Make War, Not Peace', the picture repeated four times like a Warhol silkscreen. In its simple, two-colour, almost amateur design, it could have been an LP sleeve by any independently distributed political band of the post-punk era. It happened to be by the Smiths, the biggest of them all, and it served as confirmation that for all their mainstream popularity, this was not a group in any mood for compromise.

CHAPTER TWENTY-SIX

To me popular music is still the voice of the working class, collective rage in a way, though seldom angst ridden. But it does really seem like the one sole opportunity for someone from a working class background to step forward and have their say. It's really the last refuge for articulate but penniless humans.

– Morrissey, *NME*, December 1984

At the end of each calendar year in the UK, as the music papers gathered up their critics' and readers polls, John Peel surveyed his Radio 1 listeners for their own favourite songs of the year. As a barometer of mainstream tastes, the 'Festive Fifty' was marginal indeed, which was precisely its point; Peel was, for a generation or more in the UK (and overseas, via the BBC World Service), the arbiter of all that was proper (as opposed to merely popular) about modern music. At the end of 1983, 'This Charming Man' had come second in Peel's Festive Fifty, behind New Order's 'Blue Monday', appropriate confirmation of the two Manchester acts' notable crossover into the pop charts. For 1984, the Smiths came first – with 'How Soon Is Now?'.

Peel's listeners were not the only ones who believed that the Smiths' bonus B-side was in fact the best song of the year. A similar story was unfolding in America, where 'How Soon Is Now?' had proven instantly popular on import, primarily in the alternative dance clubs but also on those radio stations that were already aware of the band. Sire decided to release it as a domestic 12" maxi single, backed with a train-wreck of a 7" edit, and the song 'Girl Afraid'; in the absence of an existing sleeve design, the label approved one that took the gatefold imagery from *Hatful of Hollow* and wrapped it around the outside of the 12". (It was the only Smiths sleeve ever, anywhere, to feature the band on the front.) Meanwhile, Rough Trade's licensee in Holland/Belgium had also decided to cater to the obvious by releasing 'How Soon Is Now?' as a 7" single (this one, mercifully, fading out early rather than being edited to pieces), copies of which soon began showing up in UK stores.

And so, at the start of the New Year, as everyone at Rough Trade sat down to plan the marketing of the biggest album release in the label's history, they became distracted by what they saw as unfinished business. At the precise moment they should have been figuring which of *Meat Is Murder*'s nine songs would make the best single, they decided to release the six-month-old 'How Soon Is Now?' all over again instead, and this time as an A-side.

The Smiths might not have been able to dictate release schedules in other countries; they most certainly had complete control in the UK. But in going along with this decision, they allowed themselves to be sold by the supposed experts, at least one of whom, Scott Piering, had allowed himself to be sold a false bill of goods in turn. Thanks in large part to the Smiths' run of four top 30 hits, Piering had gained permanent access to almost all the various Radio 1 producers, and while some of them still treated Morrissey's voice as if a plague upon its listeners, several had reacted enthusiastically to 'How Soon Is Now?' and indicated that if it was brought to them as an A-side, they would support it. More than one even mentioned it as a 'top three' hit. Piering duly reported such confident assurances as he gathered up advance airplay from the evening shows in anticipation of the Smiths' usual high chart entry.

It didn't happen. The press release to the journalists might have trumpeted 'overwhelming demand' and a need to nullify the 'extortionate price' of the Dutch 7", but the fans weren't buying it, literally. They already owned the song once if not twice (on the 'William' single and *Hatful of Hollow*), and any incentive to purchase it a third time was small indeed, given that the 7" single's B-side, 'Well I Wonder', was to be included on *Meat Is Murder* and that the 12" bonus was a 'mere' instrumental. ('Oscillate Wildly' offered a rare chance for Marr, Joyce and Rourke, average age twenty-one, to experiment with cellos and pianos and baroque textures, and perhaps for the rhythm section to wonder how come Morrissey took his usual co-writing credit regardless of contributing nothing more than the titular pun, while they got none of the proceeds. But for all its majesty, it was always hard to convince the general public that an instrumental was more than a throwaway.) When 'How Soon Is Now?' failed to chart top 20, and an uninspired *Top of the Pops* performance barely nudged it upward, the radio producers backed away from their earlier promises, and Rough Trade, Scott Piering, and to an extent the Smiths themselves were all left looking rather embarrassed by the whole episode. Not even a desperate attempt to promote 'Well I Wonder' to the middle-of-the-road Radio 2 could save the day.

The chaotic history of 'How Soon Is Now?' in the UK was but a reflection of the entire business enterprise surrounding the Smiths. In the weeks leading up to the release of *Meat Is Murder* and 'How Soon Is Now?', a flurry of paperwork between Rough Trade Records and Distribution, All Trade Booking, Appearing Promotions, and Smithdom Ltd indicated not only how deeply devoted the label and agency and various promo divisions were to the Smiths' success, and how hard everyone at Collier Street was working on them, but that the process was stretching these various companies' capabilities to their absolute limits. A major label might have dealt with the pressure by lining up a longer lead time for the album and had its marketing department pull from its previous experiences to plan out the campaign accordingly. Rough Trade not only had no previous experiences of this nature to draw from, it didn't even have a marketing department.

At the start of January, Peter Walmsley, the head of licensing, and Jo Slee, who worked under him, sent Morrissey, at his request, a lengthy breakdown of international achievements to date along with projections for the future. Outside of the UK, *The Smiths* had sold a reasonable 100,000 copies around Europe, Japan and Australia/New Zealand (more than 20,000 of them in Germany, despite the group's cavalier attitude towards touring there) and an additional 50,000 in the States. *Hatful of Hollow* was following relatively fast in its footsteps – more than 25,000 in America already, on import alone – and to the extent that these markets weren't experiencing Smiths fatigue (a genuine concern), Slee and Walmsley were willing to project sales for *Meat Is Murder*, outside of the UK and USA, as high as 250,000. But for this to happen, each territory had similar requirements: a tour, a press day, a photo session and a video. (If they couldn't have the last of these, suggested Rough Trade, maybe the band could release a live 'film.') The memo was exhausting, and Slee recognised as much: 'once one knuckles down to it, one is somewhat overcome by the wealth of information at one's fingertips.'

Domestically meanwhile, Rough Trade UK was also feeling the pressure of increased expectations. Morrissey had trumpeted the lack of promotion as a positive aspect surrounding the debut album's success – the music selling itself – but now he was looking for the sort of visibility commensurate to the Smiths' commercial standing. Rough Trade duly reported that it was looking into TV ads, major installations at key record stores, and fly posters for the upcoming tour (these to be financed by the promoters), though there was still little inclination for advertising in the music press, which tended to publicise the Smiths for free. Again, the feeling from the label was that it could only deliver if the band would do its part to help them, and Rough Trade sent the singer a twenty-seven-bullet-point list of print media requests, some of them broken down into additional sublists of ten or more, which indicated the almost forbidding extent to which the words of Morrissey, in particular, had become so coveted. The question, clearly, was no longer whether the mainstream press would cover the band, but whether the band would do the press, and given the impending tour schedules and the Smiths' admirable habit of popping back into the recording studio every other weekend, that was not entirely certain.

Similarly, Scott Piering reported that 'television is largely there for the asking,' and as proof, he secured the Smiths highly prestigious slots on *The Oxford Road Show* and *The Whistle Test*. It was somewhat easier to book *Granada Reports*, for which the band was forced to stand up to Tony Wilson's typically brash form of questioning, which carried hidden levels of meaning for those who knew of the awkward relationship between the Factory boss/TV presenter and the former Factory acolyte/Smiths singer. Interviewing the group during rehearsals for their upcoming tour in a Chorlton-cum-Hardy basement, Wilson first sat down with the rhythm section, immediately demanding to know if they ever 'get annoyed at the attention given to Morrissey,' and refusing to accept Rourke's insistence that 'he deserves the attention' as a good enough answer. He then castigated the Smiths for being 'a northern group who are traitors 'cause you moved to London,' noting that the move back north was 'about time.' A brief interview with Marr, playing guitar, helped explain some of the method behind the guitarist's technique before Wilson sat cross-legged on the rehearsal-room floor with Morrissey and bantered back and forth. Morrissey, naturally, gave as good as he got. In particular, asked what right he had to 'comment on political and local affairs,' the front man offered one of his more eloquent responses.

'I feel that if popular singers don't say these things, who does? We can't have any faith in playwrights anymore; we can't have any faith in film stars. Young people don't care about those things, they're dying out. And if you say, "What right do you have?", the implication there to me is that popular music is quite a low art, it should be hidden, it can be there but let's not say anything terribly important; let's just, you know, make

390

disco records or whatever. So I really feel that we do have an obligation. And I know that people respect it and they want it and it's working to great effect.'

With all this coverage, the Smiths turned down a repeat visit to *The Tube*; they had grown wary of live television's sound limitations and refused now to perform without lip-syncing, a curious philosophical contradiction given the group's excellent stage reputation. Scott Piering made clear that he was treading warily with the visual medium as a whole. 'TV is particularly draining of their limited energy and time resources,' he wrote. 'I am loathe to change their minds about a particular show because there is a good chance that it will be a disaster in the outcome whether they do it or (worse yet) cancel suddenly before the show.' These were to prove prescient words.

As preparations got further under way for the tour, which was to conclude at London's Royal Albert Hall, a prestigious, histor-ically classical venue only recently (and rarely) added to the rock circuit, Piering found himself frequently attending meetings in official capacity as the Smiths 'management representative.' And yet whenever he tried to secure this standing with the band, he found himself stalled.

'He would sit next to me on a plane,' said Marr, 'and I would know this conversation was coming: "I really need confirma-tion, we need to put this in writing, I'm getting mixed signals."' The personal dynamic between Morrissey and Marr remained closed to outsiders; the pair had moved their initial friendship into what appeared an unshakeable partnership, to the point that if either one put his foot down on an issue – whether it be abandoning a European tour at the airport or refusing to officially appoint a manager – the other would support him out of instinctive solidarity. So while Marr could later claim, 'I wanted Scott as manager,' it was never to the extent of attempting to override Morrissey's reticence. If anything, Piering's insistence on forcing the issue backfired. While Marr acknowledged of the pseudo-manager's inability to secure confir-mation of his status that 'there's someone I liked, being upset,'

he also felt that 'the problem was that they would put themselves in the position where they were being very needy, and
that wasn't good either.'

In September 1984, Piering had received a cheque from
Smithdom for £3,500 – approximately six months' salary at the
old, pre-Smiths, pre-hit record Rough Trade, but barely enough
money to cover the transatlantic phone bills he was now racking
up as American agencies fought for the lucrative rights to book
the Smiths in the States. Unable to secure any further commitment, let alone commission, from the band themselves, Piering
turned to Rough Trade, which agreed (perhaps due to the lack
of a producer taking the same) to put him on a sliding scale
of 'points' for Meat Is Murder.[1] As this would be considered a
promotional expense, to be equally absorbed by the Smiths
prior to the profit split, Rough Trade nonetheless pointed out
that the offer would need to be sent to Smithdom 'in the hope
of their input leading to an agreeable settlement on all sides.'
Smithdom, of course, was registered to the same address as
Scott Piering's promotion company Appearing; he opened its
mail and composed the responses – but only with Morrissey
and Marr's permission. The royalty agreement was never finalised.

In the meantime, the distraction of 'How Soon Is Now?' did
not prevent the various parties from working frantically to
cover all bases to guarantee the success of Meat Is Murder. Five
hundred copies of 'Barbarism Begins at Home' were pressed up
as 12" singles for club DJs (some with an additional 7" edit),
in a unique picture sleeve showing Viv Nicholson at a coal
front, which was about as close as the Smiths came to
commenting on the nearly year-old, increasingly violent and
divisive miners' strike. (Curiously, for all of Morrissey's political
commentary, he had rarely been brought into this debate
publicly. This was a shame. While his aversion to work for the
sake of work stood in stark contrast to the National Union of
Mineworkers' apparent party line and may have contributed to
his silence, it was presumably countered by his open enmity

for the Thatcher government and their draconian attempts to break the country's most militant union. Yet, while the likes of Billy Bragg and others played multiple benefits for the striking miners, the Smiths restricted their political appearances in 1984 to the lone GLC Jobs for a Change festival, for which they were still paid £1,200.)

Additional promotional ideas included an interview between Jon Savage and Morrissey, with the intent of pressing it on vinyl and sending it to European outlets – but although the interview was conducted and edited down to appropriate length, it never saw release. The renowned multimedia American artist Denis Masi, then living in London, whose work dealt with societal power structures, agreed to produce subliminal videos that could be included in London's most prominent shop window, at the HMV store on Oxford Street, which Rough Trade was willing to pay for; this, too, never met with final approval. More successful was the invitation to various fanzine editors to share an afternoon with Morrissey in London – the conversation moderated, with cavalier disregard for the fanzines' independent nature, by the editor of *Melody Maker*. And main-stream journalists were invited to hear *Meat Is Murder* at the Rough Trade offices over 'wine, beer and (ahem) non-meat snacks,' as the press release put it, less than two weeks before the album hit the shops, with the assurance that final review copies would be distributed 'closer to the release date.'

Somehow, it all came off. In the middle of February, *Meat Is Murder* not only entered the British charts at number 1, but in the process it dislodged Bruce Springsteen's *Born in the USA*, the emblematic major-label release of the era. The sales (gold certification for 100,000 upon the day of release) and the number 1 entry position were the stuff of dreams, but much the same had happened to the debut album and it had not carried the same resonance. The more important aspect regarding *Meat Is Murder*'s success, then, was the artistic triumph. *Meat Is Murder* gelled not merely as a collection of tracks, but as an album, in the proper sense of the form(at)

– a coherent musical statement. Scott Piering went so far as to tell *The Whistle Test* host, Mark Ellen, that it was their *Sgt Pepper's*, forcing an embarrassed Johnny Marr to deny such a claim on camera. Even he knew it was not *that* good, though the stylistic leap from *The Smiths* to *Meat Is Murder* was equivalent at least to that made by the Beatles between *A Hard Day's Night* and *Revolver*. Thanks in part to excellent sequencing, the musical vicissitudes proved quite harmonious. The amphetamine rushes ('What She Said' and 'I Want the One I Can't Have') were balanced by a folk ballad ('Well I Wonder'); the rockabilly rumbles ('Rusholme Ruffians' and 'Nowhere Fast') offset by a funk workout ('Barbarism Begins at Home'); and the all-politics-is-personal statements of opposing musical moods ('The Headmaster Ritual' and 'Meat Is Murder') complemented each other as bookends. There was even an official centrepiece, a lengthy, brooding waltz (what Americans sometimes call the 'power ballad') entitled 'That Joke Isn't Funny Anymore' which opened, acoustically, with sufficient space for all four members to stretch out and breathe – encouraging Morrissey, in particular, to turn in one of his finest vocals yet – before concluding with a lengthy, busy coda full of psychedelic guitars that included a fake fade for additional haunting effect. In setting out to make an album that reflected their own cultural values rather than worrying about the contemporary musical climate, the Smiths avoided long-term issues of timeliness; there was little here, musically, apart from a small dose of the era's otherwise pandemic overuse of reverb, to date it to 1984–85. (And even then, 'There's meant to be too much reverb on the guitars,' said Marr. 'It's meant to sound good when you're stoned, and if you're not, then it sounds good too . . .')

As a political statement, *Meat Is Murder* further distinguished itself. In preparing the public for the new album, Morrissey very clearly established the new topics of conversation: his sexual proclivities, while not entirely off limits, were to be replaced by a discussion of terrorism, animal rights, domestic and societal violence, nuclear war, the working class, royalty, famine, Thatcherism – and a bold attempt to link them all together. 'So many groups sell masses and masses of records and don't raise people's level of consciousness in any direction and we find that quite sinful, especially in these serious times,' he explained on *The Whistle Test* in a typical example of setting the political guidelines for the interview to follow. Asked then how he would like people to react to the title of the LP, he appeared quite conciliatory. 'Well, if they eat meat I'd like them to just think about it and just to take it from there really. Because there doesn't really seem to be anything else in modern life that makes people think about this subject really. I think many people are still under the assumption that meat has absolutely nothing whatsoever to do with animals – animals play in fields et cetera and meat is just something that appears on their plate. Which is quite strange because on many, many other issues I think people have become very aware and very enlightened. But on this, this very brutal, barbarous issue . . .' The TV footage quickly switched to a studio lip-sync of the song 'That Joke Isn't Funny Anymore'.

Morrissey would not be silenced. 'Violence towards animals, I think, is also linked to war,' he explained in the trial-by-fanzine *Melody Maker* cover story, explaining the connection between the album's title and its sleeve design. 'I think as long as human beings are so violent towards animals there will be war. It might sound absurd, but if you really think about the situation it all makes sense. Where there's this absolute lack of sensitivity where life is concerned, there will always be war.'

And yet, being Morrissey, he managed to contradict himself almost immediately. 'It seems to me now that when you try to change things in a peaceable manner, you're actually wasting your time and you're laughed out of court. And it seems to me now that as the image of the LP hopefully illustrates, the only way that we can get rid of such things as the meat industry, and other things like nuclear weapons, is by really giving people a taste of their own medicine . . . Personally, I'm an incurably peaceable character. But where does it get you? Nowhere. You *have* to be violent.' (In one of his only comments about the miners' strike, which was soon to end with ignominious defeat for the unions, Morrissey replied to the question 'Do you sympathise with the miners and the way they've been violent?' with the words 'Completely. Just endless sympathy.')

He was walking a thin line (between love and hate) and he knew it. When *Smash Hits*, Britain's biggest-selling pop magazine, put Morrissey on the cover cuddling a kitten, the singer used the interview to justify the tactics of the Animal Liberation Front, which had recently announced that it had poisoned the nation's Mars Bars. (It turned out to be a hoax.) 'Polite demonstration is pointless,' said Morrissey. 'You have to get angry, you have to be violent otherwise what's the point?' This tied into a subsequent discussion in the same interview about the public perception of vegetarianism. 'I can't think of any reason why vegetarians should be considered effeminate,' Morrissey said. 'Why? Because you care about animals? Is that effeminate? Is that a weak trait? It shouldn't be and I think it's a very sad reflection on the human race that it often is.'

This was a key point behind *Meat Is Murder*, and though Morrissey had problems articulating it at times, it gradually seeped through the media and the music and established itself as the message. Morrissey was standing up for the cause of vegetarianism, but not at the cost of testosterone. His insistence that one could become a vegetarian and yet maintain one's militant attitudes proved especially encouraging to a fan base that had been brought up experiencing violence on a daily basis (per 'Barbarism Begins at Home' and 'The Headmaster Ritual') and which could not easily renounce violence as a necessary (and not always a last) resort. But that audience *could* be inspired to think about the necessity (or lack thereof) of eating animals, and instigate a vegetarian diet as a first step towards personal and collective peace.

And that's very much what happened. Despite the fact that the media trod warily around the album's title, a number of Smiths fans digested the *Meat Is Murder* lyrics, read the accompanying interviews, discussed the subject with their friends and/or their families, and made a decision to turn vegetarian. Some of these people eventually relapsed despite their best intentions, but countless others stayed vegetarians in perpetuity.[2] Letters to the band at the time articulated as much; anecdotal evidence over the next several decades confirmed it. In that regard, *Meat Is Murder* was more than just an album that marked a band's musical maturation, or its commercial consolidation. It was an album that, quite literally, changed people's lives.

CHAPTER TWENTY-SEVEN

Q: Why do you want to be a pop star?
A: Well, it doesn't make life worse. That's all that I
can say. You should try it some-day.
  – Morrissey to Tony Wilson *Granada Reports,*
February 1985

At the same New Year session at Ridge Farm at which they'd recorded the instrumental 'Oscillate Wildly', the Smiths had put to tape a riff that Marr had only introduced to Morrissey on the way back down to Surrey from Manchester. Though Marr was trying to emulate the feel of his favourite mid-'60s Stones singles, the rhythm and the style were more stylistically indebted to early rock 'n' roll and rockabilly, the guitarist referencing the Chuck Berry song 'You Can't Catch Me' in particular. Immediately inspired, Morrissey worked up what seemed like a fevered suicide note of sorts, and somehow shoehorned the words into the allotted space. The lyrics were in fact an artful ode to one of his favoured feminist tracts, Virginia Woolf's *A Room of One's Own*, which argued in part that if Shakespeare had had a sister of equal natural intellect, she would have been driven to suicide by her lack of opportunities in Elizabethan England, and the song was titled, accordingly if cryptically, 'Shakespeare's Sister'.

All four Smiths rose to the occasion in the studio, though none more than Mike Joyce, who replicated his agitated performance on 'What She Said' with an equally confident series of tight fills alongside a rapid-fire snare trill. Andy Rourke picked up the cello again, in addition to the bass; and Johnny Marr couldn't help but layer multiple electric and acoustic guitars with the familiar arsenal of accompanying effects. The result, all of 130 seconds long, was a frenetic, frantic rush of blood to the head that would have made a marvellous late addition to *Meat Is Murder* or a perfectly fine B-side. But the Smiths were so genuinely excited by it that they insisted 'Shakespeare's Sister' be released to the public, in the middle of March, in the midst of the UK tour, as an A-side. (The frenzied 'What She Said' was selected as an appropriate flip.)

In fact, the Smiths were *so* enthused by 'Shakespeare's Sister' that they unveiled it on the *Oxford Road Show* the week of *Meat Is Murder*'s release, when they were meant to be performing 'How Soon Is Now?' – a decision that certainly didn't help that particular song's chart progress. To the concern that *neither* of these songs was featured on the new album, the Smiths did not appear unduly worried. They were, it could be argued, following again in the hallowed footsteps of '60s bands like the Beatles, who habitually released new non-album singles (for example, 'Day Tripper'/'We Can Work It Out') the very same week as they released a new album (for example, *Rubber Soul*).

Had 'Shakespeare's Sister' had the trappings of that sort of hit there would have been few complaints. But it didn't. 'I don't think the song was up to the standard required to be a single for the Smiths,' said Stephen Street, who as session engineer did not yet carry the authority to say as much to the band. 'Considering the standards they'd set themselves, I thought it was a little slapdash.' The Smiths had never traded in the typical verse/bridge/chorus/middle-eight format, but their initial run of top 30 hits had all benefited from the song title's frequent refrain. Like half the material on *Meat Is Murder*, however, the title of 'Shakespeare's Sister' never showed up in the lyrics, and the closest it came to any sort of hook was a rather simplistic 'Oh Mama let me go . . .' By contrast, the song that they then returned to the studio to record as the 12" bonus track, 'Stretch Out and Wait', not only had a proper chorus that incorporated the title and a lovely little dip into the minor key as Morrissey sang it, along with a gorgeous, lilting 6/8 arrangement that nonetheless moved just fast enough to avoid the familiar 'ballad' association, it also included Morrissey's finest lyrics yet about the sexual act. They were an update of sorts of the groundbreaking 1961 Goffin-King composition 'Will You Love Me Tomorrow', in which a female protagonist prepares to give her virginity. Morrissey similarly projected the argument of sex-as-nature onto what appeared to be the song's female object: 'Ignore all the codes of the day, let your juvenile impulses sway.'[1] It was one of the clearest, most empathetic and poetic lyrics of his life, one of the band's better arrangements too, and with the Smiths' typical disregard for posterity, it was condemned to relative obscurity.

At Radio 1, the release of yet *another* Smiths 45, only six weeks after the last one had underperformed in the charts, was viewed as too little, too soon. 'Shakespeare's Sister' still made the UK top 30, but not because anybody heard it frequently on the radio, and certainly not because anyone saw them perform it on *Top of the Pops*. For the first time since the Smiths had made the charts, they were not extended the invitation to appear on television's most influential music show. The single was gone almost before it had arrived. Even the Smiths' many foreign licensees had to admit that they could no longer keep up. 'Shakespeare's Sister' was released in but a handful of countries.

This might not have mattered if the Smiths as a whole accepted responsibility for their actions, and the consequential (lack of) results. 'I personally never had a problem that the singles didn't go in the top 20, ever,' insisted Johnny Marr, who has never publicly renounced the choice of single. 'What was important was that we did good, heady stuff.'

Morrissey took an entirely different view, contradicting his partner's casual ethos. 'Shakespeare's Sister' was, said the singer, 'the song of my life. I put everything into that song and I wanted it more than anything else to be a huge success.' When that didn't happen, he looked for people to blame. 'It was blacklisted by the BBC because I denounced the BPI Awards,' he told Danny Kelly of *NME*, who immediately recognised that as a blatant conspiracy theory and demanded some better excuse. 'I think Rough Trade released the record with a monstrous amount of defeatism,' Morrissey then obliged. 'They had no faith in it whatsoever. They didn't service it or market it in any way . . . Rough Trade have done their job and no more. They're bored with the Smiths now. I've seen maximum evidence of this.'

Considering that *Meat Is Murder* had just dislodged Bruce Springsteen from the top of the charts, and without the benefit of an accompanying single, the label, naturally, felt otherwise. 'They were incredibly prolific,' noted Rough Trade's Richard Boon of the Smiths, 'but you saturate your own market to a degree, rather than broadening it, and you can't keep up. And their expectations became increasingly barmy.'

'The band wanted more,' said Rough Trade's Simon Edwards of the Smiths' approach to promotion in 1985. 'They wanted more professionalism, whatever it was. They wanted full-page ads, which we started doing [though] everyone knows mean fuck-all, really. It's an ego thing. So then they have to be in colour. The demands grew.'

The most disputed of these demands was for 'fly-posting' the streets, 'which Geoff Travis thought was a waste of money,' said Mayo Thompson, the group's new label manager at Rough Trade. Thompson, the American-born vocalist of the Red Krayola, loved the inherent creativity of Rough

Trade, but he also understood the importance of business. 'Advertising is ephemeral, but the symbolism is important,' he noted, siding with the Smiths. 'If you market a record without buying advertising, you're going against the grain of the economy. Then there's some philosophical excuse which is convenient for the identity of the self-righteous record company that won't advertise, and you can talk that up into . . . political idealism if you want to, but the price that you pay is that everything is fine – as long as you have enthusiasm.'

Enthusiasm had, at least until now, always been self-evident among staff at the Smiths' label. 'If you talk to people who worked at Rough Trade, they'll say it was the most exciting period of their lives,' said Richard Scott of distribution. 'By a mile. It was so intense.' But now, he felt 'that was suddenly going to come to an end.' In part, he blamed changes in the market: nobody quite knew what the release of *Meat Is Murder* on compact disc portended, for example, and some might claim not to have cared, given that the format was expensive and appeared of interest only for those hi-fidelity buffs who could afford the equipment, not the kind of Smiths fans who still rushed out to buy 7" singles. But for those who were paying attention, it was evident that digital music had arrived, and that there was no turning back. More poignantly, Richard Scott saw the writing on the wall for the company's halcyon days because of its relentless focus on success for the Smiths at all costs. 'The people I was dealing with at the Cartel, and others, were upset . . . that they were going to have to gear up in market areas in which they weren't that interested.' For many of the people working the phones, a job in 'sales' at Rough Trade Distribution had never been about chart positions; it was about the buzz of selling new and exciting independent music into record stores so that people could find it, hear it and buy it. But now, on chart days, said Scott, Travis would arrive first thing, fuming about the Smiths' latest position, demanding to know of Scott and his team,

'Why aren't you on the phone already?' Distribution would have to explain that there were pre-approved days and times of days to call certain wholesalers, and the moment after the chart had been announced was not one of them. Mayo Thompson recalled that by the time he came back to work at Rough Trade for a second stint in 1983, 'distribution was an armed camp and the label was an armed camp and they had an inimical relation to each other. It was like the United States Congress.'

Ultimately, it all came down to the question of whether Rough Trade was incapable of delivering the Smiths the consistent hit singles they deserved, or whether it was, in fact, the other way round. 'Why isn't "Shakespeare's Sister" in the top ten?' asked Richard Boon rhetorically. 'There's a very simple answer to that. It's not a very good record. Why make a point?' (Actually, it *was* a very good record. It just wasn't a very good *single*.)

'They weren't making music that was going to sell twice as much, three times as much,' insisted Simon Edwards. 'The dots were being ticked. You might have ticked that dot a little bit better and that dot a little bit worse. I don't think it would have made that enormous leap to mega-stardom.'

'I think if you listen to the Smiths,' said Travis of the group in 1984–85, 'they're not as populist as the records that are populating the top five. They're too good, they're too clever, they're too left-field. There isn't a lineage to the Smiths that is in the subconsciousness of the British public.' Citing the success of Pigbag and Depeche Mode as evidence that 'the system was in place,' he asked a rhetorical question of his own: 'Would they have had greater singles success anywhere else?'

Seymour Stein certainly didn't think so. 'I was lucky to sign Madonna,' he said of the artist who had become one of the biggest global superstars by 1985. 'She would have happened with anybody. I don't think the Smiths would have happened without Geoff Travis . . . He put his life on the line for them.'

'Rough Trade did what they could for us,' agreed Andy Rourke, saying of record sales, 'if we'd been on Virgin or any other label it would have been the same. But there has to be a fall guy. So if our record didn't enter in the top ten, then somebody got it in the neck.'

'Shakespeare's Sister' was that record. And so, if the single was to be remembered for anything (other than adding to the group's already considerable musical catalogue), it was for officially marking the souring of the relationship with Rough Trade.

FOR THEIR SIX-WEEK tour of England in the spring of 1985, on which every venue but one sold out in advance, the Smiths again invited James along as their support group. The two acts had bonded on the Irish tour, and in his own end-of-year polls, Morrissey had named James his 'Best Act' – no small endorsement considering that they had gone the whole of 1984 without releasing a record. That was to be corrected on the eve of the Smiths tour with a twitchy new single on Factory ('Hymn from a Village'), which won James major press coverage and the interest of every major label in the country – for James had decided that despite their own refusal to compromise commercially, Factory was no longer an appropriate home for them.

Together, the Smiths and James presented something of a united front to the public: single-syllable, common-name bands from Britain's leading musical city, on Britain's two leading independent labels, and ardent vegetarians each, an important point of principle for a tour named Meat Is Murder. As a further sign of solidarity, and as an unpublicised act of continued independent principle on their own part, the Smiths refused to consider the typical record-company 'buy-on' of a support act – by which they could have sold off that opening slot for at least £20,000 – and instead paid James a nominal nightly fee.

The presence of James on the tour had one possibly unintended side effect. The major labels that were showing up in force to secure the opening band's signature on a long-term contract were doing so not necessarily because they understood the group but because they saw James's marketing potential as 'the next Smiths.'[2] As the auction reached astronomical proportions, it could not have been lost on Morrissey in particular that if James were worth £150,000 upfront to MCA (as they claimed to have been offered), then the Smiths, with their proven hit singles and chart-topping albums, had to be worth that much more. In the end, James signed directly to Sire. (They insisted it had nothing to do with the Smiths being on that label in the States.) If they could have seen into the future, James might have wanted to tell the Smiths that they came to regret this decision, that they ended up asking themselves what they ever saw wrong with Factory in the first place. By the time they realised as much, however, it would be too late for both groups.

THERE IS A PERIOD in every successful band's career where it is visibly, audibly, emotionally and viscerally on top of its game – and the Meat Is Murder tour represented that moment for the four-piece Smiths. Last time they'd crisscrossed Britain in earnest, many of the venues had been colleges; now they were playing major theatres, and not just the converted old former Apollo and Gaumont cinemas, but the Royal Albert Hall in London, the Royal Court Theatre in Liverpool and the Palace Theatre in Manchester. (The latter choice of venue was 'to do with history and tradition,' said Marr. 'The Palace is where you went to see the Hollies.')

Each night, the group warmed up backstage to a compila-
tion of Buzzcocks singles; for the audience, the signal for the
band's impending arrival onstage came with the sound of
Prokofiev's 'Dance of the Knights' from the ballet *Romeo and
Juliet*, played at blistering volume. (Introduced in 1984, the
Prokofiev had replaced Cilla Black's 'Love of the Loved'.)
The show, relatively short by some standards, reflected the
group's desire to look forward, not backward: there was no
'This Charming Man' and no 'What Difference Does It Make?'
but as always new and, for much of the tour, unreleased material in place of these obvious hits. Johnny Marr had taken to
using a Gibson Les Paul both in the studio and now onstage
as well: though it was the perennial choice of hard-rock guitar
gods, 'I always had it that I could make the Les Paul cool.'
Rather than engage in power chords or volume for the sake
of volume, he played it much as he would a semi-acoustic,
with a purposefully clean sound that leaned towards the jazz
arena at times, a process aided by Andy Rourke's increasingly
adept playing. (Nonetheless, the use of the Les Paul was, Marr
admitted, considered 'treachery of the highest order' by some
of his indie contemporaries.) The lone special effect was a
mournful guitar slide line played on a foot pedal for 'How
Soon Is Now?' which took on a more desolate air than the
pulsating dance groove of the recorded version. By comparison, 'Hand in Glove' had mutated from the original, roughly
hewn 7" into something of the perfect pop song, the guitar
riff turned into a distinctly simple melody. 'Miserable Lie',
one of a handful of other older songs, had gradually developed
a new introduction of its own. Most of the set, of course,
drew from *Meat Is Murder*, the only one of its nine songs
routinely excluded from the set being the difficult-to-replicate
'Well I Wonder'.[3]

The tour felt like a communal celebration of the Smiths'
success, with stage invasions no longer just routine but
increasingly out of control. Tim Booth of James used the
word 'ecstatic' to describe the audience's reaction to Morrissey

in particular, and in very much the religious sense. 'It was more like coming to see a guru, laying flowers down at his feet.' Given that Booth had a guru already (he and other members of the group had subscribed to a meditation cult called Lifewave, led by a former SAS wireless operator who now called himself Ishvara), Booth knew what he was talking about. So he could see how adulation was taking on frighteningly noncritical proportions. 'Some nights I'd see them not have a not very good gig, or Morrissey look like he was really scared onstage, and be very shy, and then other nights I'd see him when he was clearly having a good time, and enjoying it, and being out there. I could see the variety because I knew him well enough. But it didn't make any difference to the audience: they were just seeing the great Smiths.'

For Booth, it was a shock to find that he could no longer converse with his friend Morrissey in the manner that had still proven possible on the Irish tour. 'He became a prisoner of hotel rooms, and security. And that stuff is really confusing. I remember feeling quite sorry for him, it was just overwhelming.' James looked up to the Smiths: 'We loved them as people, they were just the kindest to us, trying to help us, trying to promote us' – but that didn't mean they wanted to *be* the Smiths. 'We saw what was happening with the Smiths and we purposefully avoided it. It was too scary, too much of a roller coaster. People look from the outside and they think, especially young boys or girls, that you want that level of adoration, but when it comes, at that level, and you're close to it, there aren't that many people who are that desperate to want that . . . I don't think any human beings get through it without being fucked-up to some level.'

The tour's finale, at the Royal Albert Hall, intimated as much. For the audience, the low stage and wide-open space created perfect 'sight lines'; for the performer, there was the sense of being completely exposed, with no wings in which to hide, if even for a moment. For the Smiths in particular, the sense of 'occasion,' especially as the last night of the tour, turned into a distraction. Everybody wanted a ticket, and Rough Trade couldn't oblige, not being the sort of record company that bought up large numbers of seats in advance. The label nonetheless treated it as their own victory parade and put the group under additional promotional pressures. 'There was an awful lot of fuss,' said Marr, 'which is never good when you've got something really important to do. And it sounded lousy on the stage. It was very, very difficult. Morrissey was having a real hard time doing what he does. And I think he had a battle going on.'

'We probably chose the wrong venue,' Morrissey admitted to the audience at the start of the encore. Nonetheless, he then brought out on stage, to join him in singing 'Barbarism', Pete Burns from Dead or Alive. The move was perhaps not a complete surprise: the Smiths singer had frequently expressed an almost fanlike enthusiasm for the vocalist from Liverpool, who had come of age in the same scene as Holly Johnson of Frankie Goes to Hollywood, themselves the biggest hit band in the UK in 1984. More recently, Burns had made a transition from Gothic post-punk to the flamboyant, camp merry-go-round of mid-'80s dance pop; while 'Shakespeare's Sister' struggled to gain a commercial foothold during the March tour, Dead or Alive's 'You Spin Me Round (Like a Record)' spent most of it at number one. The pair had met a few years earlier at a Cramps show, where Morrissey noted that Burns 'looked stunning but he didn't strike me as particularly concerned about *music*. And these things matter.' If so, it didn't matter so much anymore, which made the two singers' subsequent friendship appear, from a distance, an unusual one, hard for purist Smiths fans to accept. As always, Morrissey was unapologetic. 'He's one of the few people I can feel a great affinity with. Namely because he says what he wants to, which, of course, is a national sin within music, especially considering the things he wants to say.' The friendship between Morrissey and Burns would persist and, later in the year, lead to a shared front cover on *Smash Hits*.

Still, during the final encore that night at the Albert Hall, 'Miserable Lie', Morrissey left the stage early, and Marr was forced to beat a hasty retreat himself to console his partner behind closed dressing-room doors. For Marr, this was one of the key moments in the Smiths. Everything about the band peeled away. 'It came right back down to 1982,' said Marr. 'Because '82 was me and him.' ('There was a long old time when it was me and Morrissey, struggling,' he elaborated of that period.) Whatever else the pressures, in 1985, Morrissey and Marr remained unquestionably devoted to each other.

From the public perspective, then, the tour was perceived as a complete and total triumph, confirmation of the Smiths' standing as the most important group in the nation. Privately, it appeared to have pushed Morrissey over a certain edge. The very day after the Albert Hall show, a Sunday at that, when he could (and probably should) have taken a rest away from the band and its various issues, the singer sat down and wrote to Chris Wolfe, his financial point person at Rough Trade. In his letter Morrissey demanded payment for all Smiths sleeves, presumably for their design; queried the label's own list of shared promotional costs; and took them to task for their treatment of the Smiths the previous day, noting that of all Rough Trade employees, only Jo Slee was seen applauding the Smiths at any time. That the label couldn't or wouldn't arrange a post-show party was seen as additional proof that 'Rough Trade are bored with the Smiths success.'

Responding to previous dialogue about the label's tour support (which had been pegged at £5,000 on the assumption that a sold-out tour would turn a profit), he wrote, 'The fact that there is a limit to the costs Rough Trade are willing to share simply shrieks of pettiness. However, we're sorry, and we promise never to go on tour to promote our records again.' And in reply to something in Wolfe's previous correspondence, he concluded:

'Your constant reference to Smiths "management" was amusing. If the Smiths had management I would never need to write these letters.'

The letter was duly passed on to Scott Piering, the Smiths' putative manager, who must have read it and wept.

'IN INTERVIEWS, NOBODY asks me about music,' Morrissey complained in *Jamming!* at the end of 1984 to Jonh Wilde, a music journalist whose adopted last name afforded him a certain commonality with the Smiths' singer. 'Only as the spokesman for a generation, which is quite appealing, but quite strangulating also.' There was something revealing about this, for it was true that Morrissey *had* become the 'spokesman' for his generation: Paul Weller had abdicated the role when he broke up the Jam, Ian McCulloch didn't want it, and Bono couldn't cut it with the British working class. But it wasn't so much that Morrissey was awarded the crown by default as much as that he appeared to actually crave it.

Nowhere was this more apparent than in an interview that ran in *Time Out* in early March 1985. The London listings magazine was hardly the most important media outlet in the nation, and its editorial inattention was confirmed by the lazy headline 'This Charming Man'. The writer, Simon Garfield, however, was sharper (and funnier) than most, given neither to casual hyperbole nor cheap criticism. In a piece that could be praised for balancing personal opinion with professional neutrality, Garfield supplied Morrissey with a platform from which the new generational spokesman showed himself at his cleverest and wittiest – and yet simultaneously revealed a paranoid and vindictive streak.

The former character traits were, of course, the more appealing. Morrissey revelled at the opportunity to explain his lyrics about the queen from 'Nowhere Fast'. 'I despise royalty,' he said. 'The very idea of their existence in these days when people are dying daily because they don't have enough money to operate one radiator in the house, to me is immoral. I've never met anyone who supports royalty, and believe me I've searched. Okay, so there's some deaf and elderly pensioner in Hartlepool who has pictures of Prince Edward pinned on the toilet seat, but I know streams of people who can't wait to get rid of them.'

It was classic Morrissey, conjuring up a comical, even farcical image of northern decrepitude to justify his didactic beliefs – which, as he was right to insist, were hardly those of a small minority. And to the extent that it pitched him yet further against the perceived mainstream, it was a comment inherently connected to his views on Band Aid, the group of wealthy pop stars who had come together at the end of 1984, at the urging of Boomtown Rats front man Bob Geldof, to record a charity single to combat famine in Ethiopia: 'I'm not afraid to say that I think Band Aid was diabolical,' stated Morrissey. 'Or to say that I think Bob Geldof is a nauseating character.' This, in early 1985, was akin to slandering Mother Teresa, and as with his comment about royalty, he followed it with an absurdly witty epigram: 'One can have great concern for the people of Ethiopia, but it's another thing to inflict daily torture on the people of England.' In turn, one could observe that even had the Smiths' music been forgotten as quickly as some of the Band Aid singers, that particular quote would still have lived on in infamy.

This made it all the more disconcerting that Morrissey felt the need to defend himself from similar attacks on his own character. His thoughts on Band Aid were not new; he had been making them ever since the record had been released. But for Geldof to say something negative about Morrissey – as he had done just before the *Time Out* interview – necessitated the application of a different standard. 'It was totally unprovoked,' said Morrissey. 'The fact that Bob Geldof – this religious figure who's saving all these people all over the globe – can make those statements about me and yet he seems quite protected, seems totally unfair. But I'm not bothered about those things . . .' Unprovoked? Unfair? Not bothered? If the reader wasn't so keenly awaiting Morrissey's next character assassination or witticism, he or she might have thrown the magazine aside in disdain.

Sadly, Morrissey was beginning to exhibit a similar suspicion for the world at large. 'People,' he suggested, somewhat amorphously, 'want to throw a blanket over even the slightest mention of the Smiths.' Such a comment would have been laughed out of the court of public opinion had a trial proven necessary, given that it was impossible to *avoid* the Smiths between the group's hectic release schedule, considerable chart success, constant touring, and, yes, *blanket* coverage in the media. And the only evidence that 'the music industry absolutely *detests* the Smiths,' which he insisted was the case, was that Radio 1 did not greet each new single of theirs with as much fervour as it did, say, the latest record by Duran Duran. This was not a bad thing: the Smiths' frequent appearances on *Top of the Pops* needed to be offset by *some* last bastion of establishment resistance. After all, the band's fans worshipped the Smiths largely for their independence – political, musical and ethical – which made it all the more upsetting that Morrissey appeared to be additionally including his record label in his list of perceived enemies: 'We were really their last vestige of hope,' he told Garfield. 'I'm convinced that if The Smiths hadn't occurred, then Rough Trade would have just disappeared.' If any of his other comments could have been taken with a pinch of proverbial salt (in Morrissey's defence, much of what he said in print came across that much more Stalinist than in person, where politeness typically prevailed and one could almost catch him sniggering at his own ridiculousness), this attack appeared to hit below the belt. The notion that a label that had put out so many culturally significant records (several of which had made the national singles or albums chart along the way) would somehow have collapsed without signing the Smiths appeared something of a cheap shot at the company's considerable A&R, marketing and distribution capabilities.

413

If there was any semblance of truth to Morrissey's statement, it was that Rough Trade had now fallen into a very major label trap: it was investing too much of its time and its effort into its biggest-selling act at the expense of the rest of its roster. The success of the Smiths had already seen fellow Mancunians the Fall pack up and move elsewhere, and though Travis and company were investing heavily in the likes of the Woodentops, Microdisney, and Camper Van Beethoven while continuing to release a number of excellent reggae records (though 'reggae is vile,' Morrissey had noted in his 1984 *NME* poll), none of these acts were selling in remotely similar quantities. The label would surely not have 'disappeared' without the Smiths, but at the same time, it could no longer afford to do without them.

CHAPTER TWENTY-EIGHT

Morrissey sang like he was as miserable, terrified and as poorly designed as the rest of us. He captured it perfectly.

— JOE PERNICE, *Meat Is Murder*

America had been waiting for the Smiths. Not just in the literal sense, in that there were some people who had latched onto 'Hand in Glove' when it came out in 1983 and had spent the subsequent twenty-four months eagerly anticipating the announcement of an American tour. But in a less tangible manner, a certain Stateside audience had long been looking for a band like the Smiths to come on the scene and, to use the sense of religious fervour that was often applied around the cult of Morrissey, to save them.

The Anglophile musical tastes of a significant percentage of young Americans were part of a cultural continuum that had begun with the Beatles and the original British Invasion and had continued on through years of hard rock, to the point that the introduction to punk rock and New Wave came for many not through native acts such as the Ramones and Richard Hell but the likes of the Clash and Elvis Costello. Indeed, in large parts of the States, the thriving American punk independent scene was all but ignored for the constant flurry of new musical activity from the UK. This was a bone of significant contention for those American acts who traversed the country on a shoe-string budget through the early 1980s, opening up and then servicing an entire new network of venues, fanzines, radio outlets and record stores. But then, most of these acts were noncommercial by design (R.E.M. being a notable exception), the tag of 'hardcore' adopted by many as an antidote to the era's perceived domination by Reaganites and yuppies.

Those American youth who considered themselves outside of the mainstream but nonetheless wanted some melody in their new music and some flamboyance from their (preferably overseas) idols served as the ideal initial audience for MTV, which launched in 1981 and soon made stars out of image-conscious British acts like Culture Club, the Eurythmics, Adam and the Ants, Duran Duran, A Flock of Seagulls, and so many more. Away from this mainstream so-called Second British Invasion, young Americans with somewhat more esoteric tastes were best able to hear new, independent British music either via the multitude of noncommercial college radio stations or the growing number of commercial 'progressive' and 'new music' stations. College radio could take the credit for leading the true cultural change over the course of the 1980s, eschewing the traditional habit of playlists in favour of individual DJ choices that largely focused on independent releases, including those from the American underground. But it was the increase in commercial stations that most emphatically benefited British bands like the Smiths.

The arrival of this new radio format proved sufficiently organic that it lacked for an official name. (The term 'modern rock' was not recognised as worthy of a distinct *Billboard* chart until 1988, after the Smiths broke up.) At KROQ in Los Angeles, which officially abandoned its stalwarts like the Rolling Stones and Pink Floyd for a diet of solid New Wave in 1982, they called it 'the rock of the '80s.' On Long Island in New York, at WLIR, one of the original East Coast progressive rock stations and one that made a similarly permanent switch that same year, they called it simply 'new music.'

The immediate success of these powerful bicoastal stations quickly inspired others in similar territories to follow suit. In January 1983, 91X in San Diego switched to the 'rock of the '80s' after playing 'Stairway to Heaven' one final, exhausting time. That spring, the owners of the *Boston Phoenix* weekly arts paper bought a minor local station, Y102, which had been successfully broadcasting New Wave music twenty-four hours a day for the past year, and boosted it into the highly influential station WFNX. Unlike college radio's free-form tradition, the 'new music' stations created their 'own top forty and played the same songs sixty to seventy times a week,' said Matt Pinfield, who appeared as a DJ on the (New) Jersey Shore's 'new music' station WHTG (which switched from adult contemporary in 1984), maintained a college radio show, and also DJ'd several nights a week in the local clubs, where 7" singles by British bands – sought out on import at local independent record stores – frequently filled the dance floor.

As this 'new music' format gathered momentum, it discovered its niche: melodic British bands (the word 'postmodern' was more likely to be used in the States than 'post-punk') that had been picked up by American major labels but had not been overly hyped by them, and which could cultivate a live reputation away from MTV's image-conscious affiliations. To the extent that one could line up the leading acts musically, U2 stood at one end of this spectrum, Depeche Mode at the other, and the Cure, Echo & the Bunnymen and New Order filled some of the more prominent positions in between. When the Smiths came along, it was as if they had been tailor made to appeal right across this spectrum. As a four-piece guitar band that eschewed the use of synthesizers, they were instantly credible with U2 and Bunnymen fans. As an act that proved immediately popular on the 'alternative' American dance floor, they appealed to New Order and Depeche Mode acolytes. And as a band whose lyrics spoke vividly about (sub)urban alienation, sexual confusion, teenage angst, economic inopportunity, domestic violence, educational disappointments and personal dysfunctionality, it turned out that, geographical origins be damned, they connected with an entire generation of American adolescents, for whom such subject matter was universal. 'The stories of provincial England resonated somehow, impossibly, with my agonised adolescence in provincial Montana with all its hicks and jocks and repressed, meddling adults,' said Colin Meloy, then a 'clumsy and shy' fifteen-year-old, who would go on to front the Decemberists, just one of many major American acts influenced by the Smiths. For him, 'the carnival idyll of "Rusholme Ruffians" could be the Last Chance Stampede and Fair with all its wheeling rides, desperate teens and drunken toughs; the brute in "The Headmaster Ritual" was my moustached, short-shorted gym teacher Mr Trenary.'

Throw in the fact that the Smiths initially put off touring America, that their 'second' album, *Hatful of Hollow*, was available only as an import, as were so many of their additional singles, and that they had not even been seen on the fringes of MTV (having made no videos), there was an almost mystical element of intrigue about the Smiths. Indeed, their music was frequently exchanged among fans on home-copied cassette tapes, while videotape bootlegs of their *Old Grey Whistle Test* performance from Derby in late 1983 could be found on sale at import record stores on St Mark's Place in New York City.

Within all this, it was no coincidence that the Smiths shared the same corporate umbrella as so many of their (supposed) British peers in the States. Alone among the American majors, Warner Bros Records enjoyed a reputation for putting music first, which meant that even as the company was making its money from the likes of Van Halen, Foreigner, Prince and Rod Stewart in the early 1980s, it created an environment whereby less commercial groups were allowed to develop at their own pace. Specifically, Warner Bros distinguished itself by establishing and funding an 'alternative marketing' department. For the Smiths, whether it was club promotion with the dance mixes of 'This Charming Man' or the push to college and other radio of 'What Difference Does It Make?' (which made the top

75 of 1984 at both KROQ and 91X), money was made available to connect the band with its potential audience. The 50,000 sales of the debut album may have been an absolute drop in the Atlantic Ocean compared to the 4,000,000 copies sold that same year by British duo Tears for Fears, but they were enough to confirm the existence of a following. And when 'How Soon Is Now?' was released domestically as an A-side, on the strength of alternative dance-floor reaction to its import B-side, that foothold proved pivotal: driven by overwhelmingly positive listener reaction, it rose on the college and commercial new-music radio charts like the proverbial bullet. The week that *Meat Is Murder* topped the British album charts, 'How Soon Is Now?' did likewise in the States on the highly influential CMJ (College Music Journal) retail charts. The song could additionally be found at number 3 on both CMJ's 'Progressive Radio' 100 *and* its combined 'College/Non-Commercial' airplay chart.

Singles in the UK, as the Smiths knew all too well, tended to come and go in a matter of weeks. In the States, they built over the course of many months. (Depeche Mode's 'People Are People' came out on Sire in the summer of '84; it eventually made the American top 20 a full year later, the first such hit by any of the key British 'new music' acts.) So, once it became apparent that 'How Soon Is Now?' had serious potential, the Smiths' point person at Warner, Steven Baker, took the song to Jeff Ayeroff, recently appointed as head of creative services, a position most labels had established since the advent of MTV. Ayeroff listened, loved it, and decided to make a video.

It wasn't that Warner Bros didn't know the Smiths were opposed to videos. It was that, frankly, they didn't give a damn. 'How Soon Is Now?' had the makings of a crossover hit, and if producing a promotional video would help it cross over further, so be it; from the perspective of a label that may have prided itself on its musical reputation but which was foremost concerned with selling records, this decision no more required the consent of the band than did the inclusion of the single on *Meat Is Murder* (Side 2, Track 1) or using that inclusion as the album's main advertising tag.

Ayeroff hired a director, Paula Grief, who in turn employed a female model to act (and dance) appropriately disaffected and alienated, and spliced that footage in with chimney-smoke imagery – 'collapsing buildings in Cleveland,' as Johnny Marr came to view it – that was presumably intended to illustrate the band's industrial Manchester roots. Grief then further edited in grainy live footage – home video shot by Grant Showbiz from the side of the stage in Leicester in early 1984. To what extent the group knew about this was never fully established: Showbiz said that he was neither consulted nor paid for it, the band was to act as if stunned by the video's very existence, and Piering, who would have been the obvious person to have supplied the footage, claimed that the video was made without the group's permission.[1] Regardless, the finished video offered a fair interpretation of, and visual accompaniment to, the song in question; in fact, given some of the videos that were then hitting the market – overblown stage performances or tacky narrative interpretations, intercut with what were perceived at the time as hi-tech edits but have subsequently come to look excruciatingly out-dated – the use of proper film (and Super 8) gave 'How Soon Is Now?' an impressive realist edge. Delivered to the media with a major push, it secured reasonable coverage on MTV and other cable video outlets, gaining the Smiths further fans, many of whom duly bought *Meat Is Murder*, which quickly showed up in the lower reaches of the album charts. By any measure, the Smiths now had some seriously credible traction in America.

As a result, when it came time to tour the States, it became apparent that the Smiths could afford to bypass the clubs and appear directly in American theatres. To this end, both Mike Hinc and Scott Piering had entertained eager approaches from all the major American agencies, and though Piering did not agree with the choice, ATB awarded the subcontract to Ian Copeland of Frontier Booking International, FBI for short.

Copeland had made his name on the American success of his brother Stewart's band the Police. He had then established his credibility by taking on R.E.M. while they were still unsigned. In 1984, R.E.M.'s second album, *Reckoning*, had matched its debut in sales, helping solidify the group's standing as America's great alternative hope. Their unapologetically independent stance, refusal to compromise for radio or MTV play, wilfully obtuse album covers, and, most important, consistent touring, all made FBI a natural home for the Smiths, too, given that they shared so many of these attributes. Copeland duly booked the Smiths on a tour through the month of June that focused on the Anglo-centric East and West Coasts, especially those areas with prominent alternative commercial radio stations, plus Toronto, Chicago and Detroit. The theatres in question typically ranged from 2,500 seats on the East Coast up to 4,400 on the West Coast (and many more in Toronto), but the level of anticipation surrounding the Smiths immediately allowed for second nights to be added in New York and Los Angeles – and even for a show at Irvine Meadows in Southern California, where the Smiths would be playing to as many as 10,000 people and earning over $50,000. Indeed, it was a mark of the Smiths' already fanatical following that these were many of the same theatres that the chart-topping, multiplatinum Tears for Fears were playing during the same month.

The Smiths' sudden entry into the big leagues (as well as Copeland's oversized personality) became evident when the agent received the group's stage requirements and concluded that they 'would seem to describe a Ping-Pong table compared to the stages on this tour.' But he didn't take into account the Smiths' fixed sense of proportion. 'The band always wanted to maintain that sense of being in proximity to each other,' said John Featherstone. 'There was a relatively compressed sweet spot where everyone wanted to be. We never had a wider stage opening than forty feet.'

As the tour grew closer, the lack of an authoritative

management figure became a much greater issue of concern. Scott Piering had experience of touring the States dating back to Bob Marley and Third World, but because he had neither the time nor the capacity to tackle the logistical intricacies for the Smiths, he recommended the group hire a long-term professional acquaintance, top tour accountant Hector Lizardi, who planned to maximise the band's revenue by having local promoters supply the PA and lights for every venue. The group's crew, having developed a specific stage presence for the Smiths, preferred the more expensive option of renting their own equipment for the entire tour and having it trucked from city to city. Piering sent Morrissey press cuttings about Lizardi, noting, 'Unlike *anyone* you now work with, he is not out of his depth and is not a gold-digger.' (Paranoia in the Smiths camp, evidently, was no longer confined to the singer.) In classic Smiths fashion, days and then weeks passed with no decision. Tickets went on sale; concerts sold out. Promoters, agents and de facto management alike began to pull their hair out.

The likelihood of the tour going ahead as planned was dealt a further blow when, in early May, Morrissey stood up an interviewer from *People*, arguably America's most prominent magazine, with readership in the thirty-million range. Rough Trade's good-natured and eternally patient press officer, Pat Bellis, had brought the journalist up to Manchester for the occasion, only to spend the entire day sitting in the Britannia Hotel while frantic phone calls were made to London and Phil Powell dispatched from Marr's house in Bowdon to Morrissey's at Hale Barns to try to locate the singer. (Naturally, there was no reply.) The next day Bellis, professionally embarrassed by the experience, sat down to express her disappointment. 'Morrissey,' she pleaded in writing, 'all I ask is that if you do not want to do an interview or whatever, please, please just say so or even if you change your mind at the last minute to telephone someone to let them know what is going on – it is then our job to make the excuses on your behalf, which although that is hardly a pleasant task in itself, is far better than leaving people sitting around waiting for your arrival.' As with Piering's fears about television, Bellis concluded, 'I am now more than ever concerned about arranging interviews or press for you as I can never be sure that you will turn up,' and signed off by sheepishly apologising for the need to vent. Nonetheless, the *People* magazine interview was rescheduled, Morrissey showed up this time, and a two-page spread appeared in the midst of the American tour. The journalist, Fred Hauptfuhrer, turned out to be a major fan, and the piece, other than references to Morrissey's close relationship with his live-in mother (who 'thinks all her son needs to make life complete is a good woman'), was complimentary in the extreme, with no mention of his maltreatment first time around. Pop stars, Hauptfuhrer probably knew from experience, could get away with such behaviour. Journalists could not.

WITH THE FATE of the American tour still uncertain, in the middle of May 1985, the Smiths visited Italy and Spain for the first time. The two territories were among the more problematic in Europe, the former susceptible to unscrupulous promoters, the latter still recovering from four decades of military dictatorship. At Heathrow Airport, Rough Trade employees personally begged the group to fulfill a promise to appear on an Italian TV show; Jo Slee, as European licensing representative, then joined the Smiths on the plane to Italy in part to ensure it took place and in part to foster relations with Rough Trade's new licensee there, Virgin. The visit got off to a bad start when the band rejected the Mediterranean-style hotel that the promoters had booked, complete with tile floors and traditional furniture and insisted on a generic, American-style hotel instead. (They moved to the Sheraton, nearer the airport.) The concert at the Tendastrisce turned out almost par for the course – it took place in a large circuslike tent rather than the theatre everyone thought they were playing – but went off extremely well nonetheless, with the Italian audience engaging in stage invasions and frequently pulling Morrissey's microphone out from its cable.

It was when the group showed up for the TV show the next day that things went badly awry. From Virgin's perspective, it was the prestigious equivalent of *Top of the Pops*. From that of a northern European band not used to the gaudy nature of Italian television, it was not even close. 'The stage set was ridiculous,' said Andy Rourke. 'There were kites and fake decaying pillars.' After attending rehearsals, they decided not to perform. 'Morrissey said "I'm not going to humiliate myself." He stormed out, we stormed out.'

Again, Johnny Marr backed his partner's decision to bail on their commitments. 'The easy option would have been to do it,' said Marr. 'It took some real insight and perception to go, "I don't want to be seen doing this." I'm really glad [Morrissey] saved my bacon. Sometimes he took one for the team.'

That was not how the record company saw it. Virgin disowned the Smiths for the foreseeable future and its new licensing relationship with Rough Trade was badly damaged too. 'And there was never any sort of apology,' said Richard Boon, who called it 'a very significant incident' and one that gave Rough Trade 'the reputation of unreliability across the board.' Stuart James, meanwhile, as tour manager, was 'annoyed that I hadn't been let in on the discontent initially. It would have been a lot easier to say, "We're not doing it" instead of getting all the way there and even doing a bit of a run-through and then cancelling at the very last minute.'

The next day, as the group sat around in the hotel lobby preparing to fly to Spain, a disappointed Jo Slee vented at Mike Joyce that if she wasn't going to be allowed to do her job properly, she might as well quit. '"Well, if it's not you, it's just going to be someone else,"' she recalled Joyce saying, concluding for her own part, 'Coming from the drummer, that told me everything I needed to know . . . Dealing with them was like going up the down escalator all the time and they seemed to take every excuse to sabotage what Rough Trade were doing.' Slee flew back to England to quit licensing for production, where she could work alongside Richard Boon; she took over handling the Smiths' artwork, dealing directly with Morrissey, with whom she developed a close association. The Smiths flew on to Barcelona for a successful club show that was also filmed for television. They then moved on to the Spanish capital, Madrid, on 18 May, for a major outdoor concert at Paseo de Camoens, sponsored by Madrid Town Hall to celebrate the holiday for the local patron saint; this concert too was being filmed for television.

Unbeknownst to many people surrounding the band, the Smiths had just hired a lawyer, Alexis Grower of Seifert Sedley Williams, who, on 16 May, after the group had left for Europe, wrote to Scott Piering, care of Smithdom, announcing his appointment. He had, he wrote, 'today dispatched letters to Rough Trade and telexed Sire in accordance with my instructions.' Those instructions were the equivalent of a nuclear bomb dropping on Collier Street: as it was later noted by the label, 'the Smiths had "by way of letter from the Artists' solicitors"' dated 16 May, contended that their original agreement from 1 June 1983 had been terminated.' In other words, the Smiths were announcing their intent to leave Rough Trade, effective immediately.

The letter from Grower to Piering further clarified that the solicitor was in direct contact with Ian Copeland regarding the American merchandising deals and dealing with a third party to ensure proper tour accounting, which marked the end of any association with Lizardi. In closing, he wrote, 'If there are any matters which you wish to discuss with me and which I am able to discuss with you bearing in mind the confidentiality of my Clients' instructions I will be happy to speak to you.' It was difficult for Piering not to read all this as his formal firing, and he decided to get on a plane and fly to Spain to confront the band about it: 'I was their conscience, and they had to deal with it.'

426

Mike Hinc also flew out to Madrid, in large part to try to keep Piering and the band apart. (Peter Walmsley, Rough Trade's head of licensing, additionally came out to Spain; whether or not he had yet received Grower's letter announcing the band's proposed termination of its contract, he chose not to make a scene of it.) In recent months, while each maintained his loyalty to the greater cause (formerly Rough Trade, now the Smiths), Hinc and Piering had been at constant logger-heads. Hinc's distrust of Piering reached its nadir when he saw that one of their conversations was being recorded; Piering later told Johnny Rogan that he taped it because he felt he could not trust the agent to keep his word to begin with. Matters were hardly helped by a familiar conflict of allegiances. Johnny Marr liked Scott Piering but not Mike Hinc; for Morrissey, it was the other way around. Morrissey won the day. When the Smiths arrived at their Madrid hotel, they found Piering waiting for them, asleep in the lobby. They quickly changed hotels. While Piering spent the waking day trying to secure some form of meeting, the band did its best to avoid him. Piering recalled to Rogan: 'I hung out and didn't pressurise them. I let them know I was there, made myself available and had a few words with them, but they just didn't deal with it.' Eventually, Mike Hinc took Piering aside for a necessary 'talk' about the group's decision. 'I don't think our friendship ever recovered from that,' said Hinc.

'I hated him for three or four years afterwards,' confirmed Piering of Hinc; the erstwhile caretaker manager treated himself to a week's holiday in Madrid as part of his post-Smiths recovery process before returning to London, where he none-theless continued his role as their plugger. Before all that, he attended the concert in Madrid, held outdoors in front of several thousand at the end of the vast Paseo de Camoens Boulevard, which came off almost perfectly despite the day's behind-the-scenes machinations. (The TV footage remains the only quality video souvenir of the entire *Meat Is Murder* tour.) This proved just as well, for the next day, minus Hinc,

Piering and Walmsley, the Smiths moved on to San Sebastian for a Sunday-night concert. There it turned out that the venue had been supplied with the wrong equipment rider. Stuart James again found himself frozen out of the dialogue; after a frustrating soundcheck, 'the crew went beyond me and went straight to the band and said, "We can't do the gig."' The Smiths returned to their hotel, and James stayed with the crew at the venue, which came under attack from disgruntled fans waiting outside, once it was announced that the concert had been cancelled. In the meantime, back at the hotel, the press, who had been quickly alerted by the promoters, cornered the group to explain themselves. 'It all got very nasty,' said James. 'We weren't being blackmailed into doing the gig, but we weren't really being given any assistance, either. All the band wanted to do was get the hell out.' The police arrived to deal with the crowd disturbances, and there was talk of the crew being arrested; the promoters ultimately defused that scenario, but with contact between venue and hotel restricted, the group resorted to making phone calls to the British consulate. Eventually, band and crew alike were allowed to leave and caught a dawn flight home from Bilbao. The next day, Stuart James called Mike Hinc to resign as tour manager. He was told that he couldn't; the band had already fired him. The American tour was now two weeks away.

IT IS SYMPTOMATIC of the lack of communication even within the very heart of the Smiths that there should have been so much confusion regarding Scott Piering's dismissal. 'Maybe he pushed too hard for that Italian television performance . . . maybe that became something that he got wrong,' surmised Marr. As far as he recalled events, 'No one said, "Scott's out,"' which would suggest that he either didn't know about, didn't understand the implications of, or ultimately forgot about the solicitor's letter sent on his and Morrissey's behalf while the group was in Europe.[2] 'For whatever reasons,' said Marr of Piering in 2011, 'he withdrew.'

This was evidently not the case, and there were those within the group who wished that Piering had in fact been allowed to officially assume the managerial role. 'Scott did a lot of work for us that was not recognised, in my eyes,' said Andy Rourke. (Among other things, Piering had called into question the financial fairness of the Smiths' internal business arrangements.) 'I would say that for at least a year, a year and a half, he did manage us. And never got any recognition, never got paid. He put his heart and soul into it. I think he never got any thanks for it. I think he busted his balls to try and do everything for us.'

'I loved Scott,' said lighting director John Featherstone, who recalled that Piering's office 'was almost like our clubhouse when we were in London. I think Scott is due a lot of credit and probably more credit than he gets, for really stepping into the breach and fulfilling the role of manager.' For Featherstone, that was about more than just business; it was about artistic integrity, too. 'He could say to me, "That's a great idea but I saw the Velvet Underground do it, and it didn't work."'

As the stakes had grown ever higher around the Smiths, Piering may not always have been the music industry's notion of the ideal manager. 'Scott wasn't on the ball all the time,' said Grant Showbiz. 'He was overdriven. He would be doing too much stuff for too little money for too much of the time.'

Johnny Marr offered similar memories: 'He was no saint. He would be late for things. He was often quite flustered.' And this was true. If it was something of a surprise to Steven Baker at Warner Bros (for whom 'Scott was the band's manager as far as I was concerned') that Piering never flew to America to plan the campaign for *Meat Is Murder*, it was more of a shock when Piering occasionally told him that he'd have to cut their phone calls short because they were costing him too much money. And Piering's ill-fated efforts to organise the *Meat Is Murder* American tour had been marked by increasingly desperate communication methods that were quite at odds with the more measured presentations and reasoned language used by other staffers when communicating with Morrissey – or indeed, that from Morrissey himself. Of course, the very fact that Morrissey went over Piering's head to deal directly with everyone else at Rough Trade only exemplified the supposed manager's impotence. Geoff Travis, curiously, said that Piering 'never really represented himself to me as their manager. [Within] the conventional parameters of what a manager would do, I don't really remember anything coming from [Scott] towards us. Nothing like "You've got to spend more money" or "We need full-page ads." None of that.' For those issues, Travis would talk directly with Morrissey – who 'pretty much got what he wanted all the time.'

By taking on the role under such circumstances, Piering was always operating from a position of weakness in regard to his relationship with Morrissey – and he knew as much. 'The last thing he wanted you to be was clinging,' Piering told Rogan. 'As soon as people were clinging [Morrissey would] shun them. He'd get you in that position where you'd try to say, "What about *me*? What about *my* role?" And he'd make you feel embarrassed for doing it. It was a very clever psychological manoeuvre.'

The managerial uncertainties were not rendered easier by the fact that Joe Moss had been quietly but firmly insisting on payment for the money he had fronted the group, a total of £6,000, including the cost of the PA. Moss found it hard to understand how his protégé, Johnny Marr, could not negotiate a second signature on a cheque for such a relatively trifling amount, and to the extent that he harboured disappointment with a group he had successfully managed and mentored for eighteen months, it was directed not at the singer – 'I never expected anything from him' – but the guitarist, whom he had employed and housed in addition to professional management for which he was not even seeking commission.

All this paints an unpleasant picture, especially so long after the event. The reality of the situation in 1985 was that Morrissey, having never owned a chequebook before the Smiths (because he never had enough money to need one), was now generating vast sums of income as a very public icon – and yet he was a highly private individual of infamously poor social skills, who had chosen to buy a house for and then move back in with a fiercely protective mother who was vocal in her own assertion that the music industry was 'full of sharks.' The reality, equally, was that Johnny Marr was only twenty-one, and despite the fact that he had the people skills his partner may have lacked, was only marginally more experienced in business, and living the life of a newly minted rock star at full throttle. He pushed the band to record new singles before new albums had even been released; he agreed to touring schedules that gave little time for recuperation in between. He did not eat properly, let alone sleep. Nocturnal by nature, he was also given to partying hard, and while that was never at the expense of his creativity, he did not allow himself time to sit back, accumulate, regenerate, and make sensible, sober, conscious decisions about the band's business setup. Besides, to do so would mean confronting Morrissey, and his unwillingness to do so over the hiring and firing of managers was in line with his refusal to do so over the split of the band's internal profits – and which was met with similar regret years down the line.

'We were very foolish,' said Marr a quarter of a century later. 'We made many mistakes. We made some mistakes that we shouldn't have made throughout our career.' One of those, he said, concerned the role of Piering: 'Scott should have managed us.'

The Smiths' ongoing manager 'problems' looked particularly ridiculous given that they'd had, not once but twice now (with Moss and Piering), much better qualified and more experienced representation than either of their primary independent peers. After all, Rob Gretton had grown up as just another Wythenshawe bootboy/Bowie kid turned punk turned local club DJ, but that didn't stop him successfully managing the band that became Joy Division (and then New Order). As for

Depeche Mode, they didn't even *have* a manager; they entrusted Daniel Miller, despite the potential appearance of conflict of interest based on his dual role as their record label, to advise them on all important business decisions.

It's not so much ironic that of these three significant British independent bands of the era, on the three largest and most significant independent labels, all operating on 50–50 profit splits, it was the band that had signed a binding contract – the Smiths with Rough Trade – that decided to move on. It's more that it's hard to imagine under what moral or legal basis Morrissey and Marr thought that they could terminate the Rough Trade agreement. Having begged for the chance to sign with Britain's leading independent label, they had been rewarded with a number 2 and a number 1 album (with an additional compilation making the top 10) and, including the Sandie Shaw collaboration, a run of seven consecutive top 30 hits after their initial introductory release. Neither New Order nor Depeche Mode (nor, for that matter, the Cure, the Bunnymen, or even U2) could boast anything like such a consistent combined run of successes so early in their career. Admittedly, sales were more modest in other countries, where Rough Trade dealt with a multitude of licensees of varying degrees of efficiency, and a major label might have been able to make more of the band in this regard, but the Smiths were hardly putting in the necessary legwork overseas to encourage anyone to push harder on their behalf.

The actual contract with Rough Trade was technically messy, what with all its handwritten queries and addendums, but the one aspect never in dispute was the initial three-year term. Even had the band (or its lawyer) believed that *Hatful of Hollow* somehow fulfilled their initial obligations of three albums (which was not the case, given that the contract specified 'previously unrecorded material'), Rough Trade would still have had the option to renew the deal for another year (and another one after that). And for its own part, the label had no interest in letting the group go.

'I couldn't think what we had done wrong. If I had thought that we had failed them I would have said, maybe, "Good luck to you guys," but I thought, "Not only have we done a good job, but we have done above and beyond what anyone else would have done in terms of time and commitment."' After attempting (unsuccessfully) to resolve the issue internally, Rough Trade initiated legal proceedings in early July to protect their investment, seeking an injunction preventing the Smiths from delivering their recordings to any other label but Rough Trade. In the meantime, everyday business with the Smiths continued apace. 'It's a farce,' said Travis of the process at the time, citing the comedy movies that had been such a part of Morrissey's upbringing. 'It's like a *Carry On* film – except the lawyers are involved! That was normal Smiths life, like a *Carry On* film.'

CHAPTER TWENTY-NINE

Most music reminds people of when they first heard it, but the music of the Smiths – this is what we were.
– MATT MILLER, *All Men Have Secrets*

The Smiths were the most perfect idea I'd ever heard. Or seen.
– MARK SPITZ, *How Soon Is Never?*

A few days after he was fired, Stuart James was asked to resume his role as tour manager, at higher wages, and travel to America with the band. On Concorde. By the time they transferred airports in New York to connect with a domestic flight to Chicago, where the tour was to commence, the crew had beaten them there by conventional jetliner. While the group decamped to the Aragon Ballroom for rehearsals, Stuart James and his new production manager, Mark Gosling, who had been loaned from All Trade in the wake of the Lizardi fiasco, holed up at the Ambassador Hotel, as made famous by both *The Blues Brothers* and *North by Northwest*, to belatedly and furiously 'advance' a tour that was now all but sold out. The crew had won its fight to rent PA and lights in Chicago and truck them around America. The band had won its own battle to install James on tour as opening act, despite the fact that their friends had yet to release a record in the States. Shortly before the tour was due to commence, James pulled out: their guru, Ishvara, had announced that he would be coming to Manchester (all the way from Basingstoke) to lead a retreat, and 'that was more important than doing an American tour with the Smiths,' said Tim Booth. Only later down the line would he recognise Lifewave as 'the standard archetypal cult.' Morrissey, however, was 'so upset' by the news of James's cancellation that 'he went AWOL for a day and a half and said he wasn't going to do the American tour,' recalled Booth. 'Geoff Travis called us at one point and asked if we knew where he was.' In the meantime, a call went out to Billy Bragg, whose 'Between the Wars' EP had just gone top 20 in the UK. He was winding up some American dates of his own and was able to join the Smiths through the first half of the tour. Morrissey asked for (and succeeded in getting) drag queens to open for the Smiths, lip-syncing in cabaret style where Bragg could not perform; the reaction was as hostile as one might have expected.

Into this chaos stepped a new manager. Matthew Sztumpf was gainfully employed looking after Madness, whose transition from cheery ska-pop band to sensitive political troubadours had proven so complete that they had just about lost their original audience – though not before running up an impressive catalogue of UK top 10 hits, and a couple of American crossover singles that gave Sztumpf experience in dealing with that country's labels, agents and media from a position of temporary power. Given that Madness comprised seven strong and demanding personalities, Sztumpf had every reason to believe that he could manage the four within the Smiths. By all accounts, he acquitted himself perfectly well.

Despite the fact that it would have been his job to handle the record company, Sztumpf was unable to prevent Morrissey from a rare case of voluntary confrontation backstage at the opening show in Chicago, where, Steven Baker from Warner Bros. recalled, 'he was totally blunt and told me what he thought' about the label's handling of 'How Soon Is Now?'. Morrissey repeated his complaints the next day in Detroit when he sat down with *Creem* magazine and turned what should have been a victory speech regarding the band's American reception into a vindictive one instead.

'I feel we were signed originally as a gesture of *hipdom* on [Sire's] part, and that was really it,' he told Dave DiMartino. 'And they had no intentions of the Smiths ever meaning anything on a mass level. And they still don't. And they've made several marketing *disasters* which have really been quite crippling to us in personal ways.' There was the 'abhorrent sleeve' for 'How Soon Is Now?' There was the complaint that 'they released the album *Meat Is Murder* with the track "How Soon Is Now?" unlisted, without printing the lyrics,' which was true of the LP, initially marketed with a sticker advertising the bonus addition of 'How Soon Is Now?'. And there was the additional assertion that 'they released the cassette without the track "That Joke Isn't Funny Anymore",' which was entirely false.

Morrissey reserved his greatest ire for the promo clip. 'It had absolutely nothing to do with the Smiths – but quite naturally we were swamped with letters from very distressed American friends saying, "Why on earth did you make this foul video?" And of course it must be understood that Sire made that video, and we saw the video and we said to Sire, "You can't *possibly* release this . . . this degrading video." And they said, "Well, maybe you shouldn't really be on our label."'

Such a conversation, in more general terms, might possibly have taken place; it was not beyond an American record company boss to let an English group know, typically via their manager, that if they weren't willing to sell themselves then maybe the label should not be spending money on them. And it was ironic that Morrissey's major complaint about Rough Trade, a lack of apparent promotion, had now been flipped with regard to Sire. Still, 'I felt like I fucked up,' allowed Baker, who took responsibility for some of these decisions. 'I'm sure it was a big deal to them. As a marketing person you're supposed to listen to the group and represent their interests in the company and make sure that things aren't done that don't represent them properly. I think I was just so happy that the label was interested enough to make a video . . .' When the *Creem* story was eventually published – fortuitously, perhaps, after the tour had concluded – Baker took the comments in the spirit of what he now understood to be the 'compelling . . . drama' surrounding the Smiths, all of which 'translated that this was a group that was seriously independent in every possible way' and therefore contributed to audience fanaticism, which in turn fed back into record sales: 'If he wasn't giving those quotes to the press, if he wasn't being who he is, it wouldn't be the Smiths.'[1]

'We took an adversarial position towards the American record company,' confirmed Marr, 'and with good reason. Because people would show up and quite obviously didn't understand the group, and didn't care very much. And we felt like it was so much lip service.' Like Morrissey, Marr was frustrated that 'the video didn't look like how we were really representing ourselves,' though he subsequently allowed that it 'was incredibly ahead of its time.' But he was more frustrated 'that they had tagged "How Soon Is Now?" onto *Meat Is Murder* . . . We felt on that issue that even if we were wrong, we were the artists and it was our prerogative to not put it on. The fact that they rode roughshod over us, we felt, patronised us and pulled rank. That really did infuriate me. We had sequenced that album very, very carefully. We felt it was really tacky and that it messed with art.' Sire was only acting in a time-honoured American label manner (*none* of the Beatles' first half-dozen albums came out with the original British running order, and Sire had just compiled a Depeche Mode album out of bits and pieces to capitalise on that band's growing success), but that mattered little to him at the time. 'It was all very well them coming to a show and telling us how much they loved us but when it came to a standoff, they just said, "Deal with it. We've done it."'

As with many of the issues that riled the Smiths, time would temper some of the anger. 'We didn't understand that it was about the market,' Marr was ultimately able to admit, 'and really our arguments were purely aesthetic and we couldn't argue about the market because we didn't know about the market . . . Years and years later, I know that people are vegetarian because "How Soon Is Now?" had been snagged on the front. I would have preferred they had not done it. But a lot of good did come from it, thankfully.'

But back in the summer of 1985, the Smiths were so infuriated that Morrissey had Stuart James call Seymour Stein and tell him he was off the guest list in New York.

THE SMITHS' RELATIONSHIP with their Stateside audience, on the other hand, immediately exceeded even their wildest expectations. Although other British groups enjoyed a hysterical welcome in America through the 1980s, something about these particular four lads extended that much further into a certain American psyche. Fans at the American shows didn't just cheer, clap, and holler. They actually screamed. Billy Bragg noticed immediately how 'there was a kind of Beatlemania going on that I'd never seen before,' and that included the American tour he had undertaken with the Bunnymen the previous year. The same with FBI booking agent Steve Ferguson, who at the Beacon Theater in New York was 'amazed on so many levels by the intensity of the fans.' He called it 'like watching history in the making,' citing 'this tidal wave' of fans invading the stage, 'just worshipping and hanging on every syllable that Morrissey would sing. They were clearly different than just another English band coming from overseas. It was such a unique situation. I'd never seen people behave like that before. It was boys *and* girls. This was like going to church for them and Morrissey was the Messiah and people were just losing their shit.'

'Morrissey's lyrics were universal,' noted Andy Rourke of the singer's appeal in America. 'They talked about what nobody else in the music industry was expressing at those times. He said what everybody was feeling. The kids in America have to go to college, they're ripped away from their home. Sure, there are lonely people there and people who don't fit. And that was the main thing, that Morrissey's lyrics spoke to those lonely people, those misfits.'

'Particularly at that time, what he was doing was so different to what everyone else was doing,' said Billy Bragg, whose ongoing inclusion of 'Jeane' in his set saw the Smiths reclaim it by the time they hit Boston. 'The only other person I could ever think of who'd done that before was Bowie, when he was going through his androgynous phase. And I think some of the responses to the Smiths were about the same sort of level as people responded to Bowie when he first broke. Morrissey's presence somehow allowed you to do things that you wouldn't otherwise be allowed to do. There was something vaguely transgressive about Mozzer.' To this end, Morrissey's quote in *Rolling Stone* the previous year in which he said, 'I don't know anybody who is absolutely, exclusively heterosexual, it limits people's potential in so many areas,' appeared to have had a direct and positive impact on the Smiths' potential audience and his own reception.

'I was always so proud of our gender politics, and our Politics with a capital P,' said Marr. 'And as we got bigger, I became more proud, but none more so than when we went to America, where it really flew in the face of the mainstream. It was weird to call a number-one album *Meat Is Murder* in England, but in America in the mid-'80s it was really something.'

If the Smiths, especially Morrissey, appeared exotic to the American fans, the reaction was no less profound in reverse. John Featherstone recalled collective astonishment when they made it to the San Diego Open Air Theater and looked out on the audience: 'It was like being on Planet Beautiful,' he said of the Southern Californians, whose behaviour was similarly alien to a band of working-class Mancunian Irish from poor backgrounds. 'Americans know how to do many things. They don't know how to do dark and northern. Watching the way that someone Californian tries to be dark and northern, it has an underlying exuberance to it which doesn't have years of depressed economy and decline [as an] undercurrent to it.'

It helped that, artistically, the group was absolutely on fire. 'Everybody was talking up the Smiths all the time, nobody was talking them down,' said Mike Hinc, who was present for the Los Angeles shows. 'But when they got there, they had the goods, and they delivered.' From his perspective, 'It was the guitar that cracked it for America. Morrissey is critical to the band in all countries in all stages, but what opened the door to America was the guitar work.'

'I felt from the minute I got there in America, it was difficult for me because I assumed they weren't going to understand my approach to the guitar,' said Johnny Marr. 'I felt under such incredible pressure in America. I was being heralded as the biggest thing, but I never played solos. And I didn't play conventional rock guitar.' His fears proved unfounded. 'From the very first American show, it worked out. The Americans loved it.'

Indeed, the shows were phenomenal, running to an hour and a half, with the 'Barbarism Begins at Home' encore frequently stretched to a twelve-minute funk workout as (some of) the crowd danced alongside the band onstage. Audiences seemed to know every song, from 'Hand in Glove' through the *Hatful of Hollow* import cuts, down to every last word of *Meat Is Murder*. Even 'Shakespeare's Sister' elicited screams of recognition, in part because it had been included as a B-side on the 7" of 'How Soon Is Now?' – the song that, more so than any other, caused immediate frenzy in the mostly seated venues.

That the group reached a zenith on this tour may have been because it was operating as a team. The core crew – Showbiz, Featherstone, Powell, Hallam and Barton – had been with the Smiths almost two years already. Security officer Jim Connolly, whose role became increasingly important in the bigger venues with their attendant frenzy, had earned Morrissey's trust. Matthew Sztumpf appeared to operate as a manager should, staying out of the band's way while making sure that the top echelon of business was taken care of; Stuart James had been through enough to have earned the group's respect while understanding their needs; Mark Gosling brought a professionalism to the production that ensured the shows ran on time, that the travelling American PA crew was encouraged to permit the stage invasions despite fear of damage to their equipment, and that the complete ban on meat backstage extended even to the heavy-duty union crews that governed venues like the Beacon Theater, where Andy Warhol was among the many celebrities to witness the band from the seats out front.

Given that Morrissey had been such a student of American music in general, the New York scene in particular, his sudden godlike status would have been expected to have had a profound effect on his psyche. But despite the tour running efficiently, there was a lack of experienced counsel in this regard. 'I think Morrissey needed the most looking after, and perversely, I think he didn't feel like he needed looking after,' said Grant Showbiz, who had more experience of touring America than anyone else in the inner circle. 'That joy at his own company and belief in the way he did things meant that he needed more help taking advice on things like . . . how to relax. How to keep himself healthy. How to express the after-show . . . I sometimes used to think, "What is Morrissey doing now, as we are shouting loudly in a room with drink and people who want to talk to us and tell us we're wonderful, what is Morrissey doing now? Is it all being internalised, is he asleep, is he reading a book?"' The problem was that nobody really knew. The rest of the Smiths entourage was too busy having fun.

'That whole tour was head-turning,' said Andy Rourke. 'England is such a small place and people have a small mentality. So to be thrown into America and have all this adoration . . . Fame is a strange thing and everyone handles it different. Between us band members, we never talked about it. For me, I launched myself into drugs and drink. I don't know what Morrissey launched himself into: hot chocolate and Oscar Wilde books? We were young kids . . . I was twenty-one when I went to America. And there's no handbook for handling fame. No instructions.'

'You come out of the '80s in the UK, and you've come up from some council estate in Manchester and someone wants to send you off business-class on some jet to New York, you're going to make the most of it, aren't you?' said Mark Gosling. 'The Brits abroad have always been like that.' With quality cocaine in plentiful and inexpensive supply, Gosling found himself 'roped into a role as the supplier of things that kept everyone going.'[2] The three playing members, and most of the crew, were enjoying the rock 'n' roll aspect of touring America; Morrissey was coping with the adulation aspect on his own.

'When the sticks went down and the microphone went off, Mozzer kept himself to himself,' said Mike Joyce. 'Maybe we should have dragged him out a bit more. He did have some friends, but nobody else would know them. Very arty. I felt very inadequate, as if they couldn't wait to get away and talk about great authors! Andy felt that way too. Johnny maybe less so.'

'Everyone loves getting caught up in that "Here he was off on his own, and then the other three were sitting around . . ."' challenged Marr, who cited the example of he and Morrissey heading off to buy records whilst on tour as evidence that it was otherwise. 'That is just bollocks. You can't do that for five years when you're best friends. Morrissey and Angie spent a lot of time going round together, especially on the American tours. They had their own relationship, which I was and am very proud of. He and I would go and do stuff together. He wasn't entirely isolated. There were times when he wanted to be, and that's when we let him be like that. You do whatever your friend wants.' In Toronto, for example, when the theatre was within a giant theme park, the singer was sufficiently relaxed to take in the fair rides after soundcheck alongside Billy Bragg. In 1985 in America, the pressures upon Morrissey seemed to be easily outweighed by the rewards.

The American tour was short by many standards, and wisely avoided areas in which ticket sales may have been slower and reactions less hysterical. As it turned out, 'How Soon Is Now?' did not cross over into the pop charts. And *Meat Is Murder* had peaked on the American album charts just before the group arrived, stalling outside the top 100, though that still represented a significant achievement for a British band that was coming up through the alternative channels. And over the course of the tour the relationship with the record company was repaired as well. On the West Coast, Lenny Waronker came down to meet Johnny Marr at soundcheck and talk production techniques, and Seymour Stein demonstrated his allegiance (and lack of hard feelings about the New York snub) by flying out to LA, jumping about in the front rows at the Palladium, and taking Morrissey out for a high-profile power dinner at the Ivy, where Paul Simon was brought over from an adjacent table to meet Sire's latest star. The tour concluded with that vast crowd at Irvine Meadows Amphitheater and a greater stage invasion than usual that led to the longest-ever encore of 'Barbarism Begins at Home' – a full fifteen minutes. It was the last time the Smiths would play that song.

The tour proved additionally memorable for the fact that, on 20 June, in San Francisco, Johnny Marr and Angie Brown got married in a civil ceremony. Andy Rourke, Marr's longest-standing friend within the Smiths' entourage, served as witness, and with no show that night, the Smiths threw a major wedding party for the couple at the Westin Miyaka. 'It was a nice day,' said Rourke. 'But it was just weird. It didn't seem real.' For those who knew Johnny and Angie to have been made for each other, the question was never 'if' but 'when'. That the couple chose to formalise their commitment almost six thousand miles from their families in Manchester perhaps said more about their entwined devotion to the family that was the Smiths than any disharmony with their blood relatives back home.

A couple of weeks later, back in Britain, Morrissey tried to put the whole American experience into words for Eleanor Levy at *Record Mirror*. 'It was very hysterical, very wild, very passionate, very moving. All those things people never believe! It was really quite stunning, even for me, to see it happen. We went over there I think, with quite a humble nature and we didn't expect any fanatical fervour or uncontrollable hysteria. Therefore, when it happened I was rendered speechless.' From his time living in Colorado as an anonymous social inadequate, Morrissey had firsthand experience of the blandest, most crass elements of American pop culture, politics, and everyday living. Now, from the vantage point of the touring icon, it all looked very different. 'Meeting the people there was an extraordinary eye opener because one is fed all these fixed impressions of the American music buying public and they didn't turn out to be that way. They turned out to be rational, incredibly sensitive poetic human beings.'

CHAPTER THIRTY

Don't forget I'm still only twenty-one. I really do believe that Johnny Marr and The Smiths have many many years ahead of them and plenty of surprises in store. I can never see myself working with anybody else.

– JOHNNY MARR, *Melody Maker*, August 1985

The Smiths didn't need to release a new record. They'd already put out two singles and an album in 1985 and were still barely halfway through the year. But the concert at the Oxford Apollo in March 1985 had been recorded and broadcast by the Radio 1 evening show, and even by the exacting standards of the Smiths, it was a particularly high-quality recording of a band that was now known as one of the best live acts in the world. Plans were duly made – even before the Smiths went to America and got yet better onstage – to release a live EP from the concert, led by and named for 'Meat Is Murder', which had developed into a high point of the live set.

Live EPs had something of a noble tradition in the UK. They were often used as limited-edition giveaways to assure strong first-week sales of a single or an album (as had helped the Jam go straight to number 1 with 'Going Underground'), and sometimes to showcase a new band in its best light (as per Eddie & the Hot Rods and their 'Live at the Marquee' series). Occasionally they became major hits in their own right: the Specials had gone to the top of the charts with a live EP in 1980, a perfect confluence of circumstances that saw a group still very much on the rise leading its release with a markedly different version of an album track ('Too Much Too Young'), then following it with no fewer than four previously unreleased cover versions.

The Smiths' scenario was quite different, though: they were out of stockpiled new material, not given to playing other people's songs, and no longer the new band in town or radio favorites. A live EP would, by its very nature, require Smiths fans to repurchase songs they mostly already owned in studio formats; many additionally already had the Oxford concert on cassette from the BBC broadcast. Throw in the fact that 'Meat Is Murder' was almost six minutes long, morally challenging and commercially untenable, and they were setting themselves up for a major fall. That might explain why, despite having a catalogue number assigned and multiple test pressings ordered in both 7" and 12" formats, 'Meat Is Murder' was dropped as the lead track at the last minute. In its place, the studio version of 'That Joke Isn't Funny Anymore' became the A-side instead.[1] 'Something from the LP should be released because I think they're too good to be buried,' Morrissey had said back when 'Shakespeare's Sister' came out (which was of course the perfect moment to act on this belief), but although it was unquestionably one of the finest compositions and strongest productions in the band's entire canon, 'That Joke Isn't Funny Anymore' was just as long as, and barely more commercial than 'Meat Is Murder'. The Smiths were merely swapping the frying pan for the fire.

To make it a more palatable length, the single version of 'That Joke Isn't Funny Anymore' did away with the song's instrumental reprise, which eliminated much of the majesty but did nothing to make it more radio-friendly. And in the process of switching out a live song for a studio one, they second-guessed their original intent. Though it was always a long shot, a live EP, properly designed and promoted accordingly, would have made for an interesting concept if not necessarily a chart hit, and could just have won over the loyal Smiths fans and served its artistic purpose. A four-month-old album track backed by various live versions of familiar songs smacked of something else entirely, and was unlikely to be snapped up by any but the most fanatic of all Smiths fans; its only real hope of success was in gaining massive airplay, which Geoff Travis tried – in vain – to convince Morrissey was unlikely.

'That was the biggest argument I ever had,' said Travis. 'Because I just said, "It's not a single." And Morrissey said, "It is a single." And I said, "It's not a single, and if we put it out, it won't do very well, and then all you'll do is blame us."' 'That Joke Isn't Funny Anymore' barely scraped into the top 50. It was the Smiths' first flop. 'And did we get any recognition?' asked Travis somewhat rhetorically long after the event. 'No, of course not.'

From Rough Trade's perspective, there was a cost factor to this. Singles were not cheap to promote to begin with, and Morrissey's increasing demands for advertising and, in this case, his insistence on fly-postering, meant that 'That Joke Isn't Funny Anymore' may have ended up being a financial setback for label and band alike without generating the additional *Meat Is Murder* sales to compensate. But there was also a loss of prestige – both externally, in terms of the Smiths and their public perception as a hit singles act, and internally, in terms of the final collapse of what had started out as such a mutually respectful relationship. 'I remember feeling very disillusioned about losing that argument,' said Travis. 'I just felt that showed that Morrissey was losing the plot.'

It probably did not help the Smiths that they released 'That Joke Isn't Funny Anymore' the week before Live Aid, which took place in London and Philadelphia on Saturday, 13 July. The largest musical charity event in global history, Live Aid had the unintended consequence of either launching, reviving or merely accelerating the careers of a number of its performers – including U2, who would now permanently leave behind any semblance of cult status. The Smiths were not invited to appear at Live Aid: Morrissey's comments about the event's organiser, Bob Geldof, and the Band Aid single that had preceded it, had made sure of that. The Smiths *were*, however, invited to appear on Terry Wogan's talk show the following Friday, 19 July. At a point at which British TV was just beginning to experiment with the idea of regular musical guests in such a format, the offer carried enormous promotional clout: the *Wogan* show was a phenomenon, with more viewers than *Top of the Pops* (which with 'That Joke Isn't Funny Anymore' the Smiths missed out on for the second single in a row), and though the genial Irish host had made his name as a housewives' favourite on Radio 2, far away from Smiths fans, he was not particularly disliked by the youth. Appearing on his show was something of a risk on the part of the Smiths, but a calculated one – and an additional opportunity to remind a massively distracted record-buying public that Live Aid hadn't had a monopoly on great British talent.

It was also something of a coup on the part of Scott Piering. However, the group's 'plugger' appeared to have forgotten his own written warning from earlier in the year. For, while three of the Smiths dutifully showed up on the BBC set that Friday afternoon, Morrissey did not. Nor could he be found. It was left to a highly embarrassed Matthew Sztumpf, clearly wondering what he had gotten himself into, to attempt to placate the initially puzzled and then increasingly angry BBC producers. 'That was the low point of my career,' he told Johnny Rogan. (It was also the last straw for Sztumpf, and his final involvement with the Smiths – for the time being.) 'The embarrassment was having the members of the band and myself sitting in the studio waiting for him, and the lack of consideration Morrissey had for us. The least he could have done was tell his band!' This was pertinent. On previous occasions when Morrissey had bailed on a group commitment it had been in tandem with the group, and they understood and even agreed with his reasons. In this case, it was an arbitrary decision – and they did not know why he had made it. In public, 'we closed ranks and backed him up,' said Johnny Marr, who ultimately presumed that Morrissey had decided, 'It was just not something that we should appear on.' All the same, he said, 'It would have been nice to have been told that Morrissey was not going to be there and that we didn't need to go there. That aspect of it caused a little crack in my resolve.'

The fact that 'That Joke Isn't Funny Anymore' had been released in the midst of legal action between the band and its label had introduced a degree of paranoia, with each side second-guessing the other's tactics. Certainly, it was beyond coincidence that in the wake of the Wogan no-show and the single's chart failure, the music papers were suddenly full of speculation that the Smiths were about to leave Rough Trade for a major label. The rumours gained traction for a couple of weeks and then appeared to conclude when Johnny Marr was featured for the first time as *Melody Maker* cover star and announced, 'The next collection of Smiths songs' – though he did not mention an album – 'will definitely come out on Rough Trade and I'm pleased to be able to say that.'

ACROSS LONDON, AT Manchester Square, EMI's new managing director, David Munns, read of the unrest in the music papers and decided to act on it. Munns had spent most of his professional life at EMI, but the last five years of it in Canada, away from the day-to-day buzz of signing and breaking British acts at the premier British major label. He had come home to find that while EMI had maintained its market share, thanks largely to the phenomenal success of Duran Duran, it was *still* known throughout the industry, as he put it, as the label that 'wouldn't protect the creative juices of a band named the Sex Pistols.' The news items in the music papers trumpeting the discord between the Smiths and Rough Trade was therefore music to his ears.

'Without this being an A&R decision, I thought that if we could sign the Smiths it would go a long way towards restoring our credibility,' said Munns. 'It was exactly the sort of act that, if you could put it on the EMI label, would mitigate some of that Pistols thing. And there are not many acts that have any kind of name or reputation that come on the market very often.' That EMI had put them in the studio back in 1982 only to 'pass' on them was irrelevant to his thought process – both because Munns knew nothing about it and because there was no proof that the Smiths would ever have become a 'name' act had they signed to EMI back then.

From Munns's perspective, the relationship between the Smiths and Travis had already soured; it was therefore entirely appropriate for him to make enquiries as to their availability. 'I started ringing Alexis Grower,' said Munns, 'and I rang him all the time – every two weeks. Every time I had a spare minute, I said, "I want to sign the Smiths, are they out of their deal?"' For now, given that Rough Trade had initiated its own protective proceedings in the wake of Grower's challenge to their contract, the answer was no. But Munns was not used to taking that for an answer. 'I kept saying, "You make sure you tell Morrissey that EMI is calling all the time."'

AFTER A SEVEN-MONTH absence, by far the longest since they had formed, the Smiths returned to the recording studio in August 1985. They initially decamped to Drone in Manchester, scene of those original EMI demos, to record at least one of the songs that had been worked up at soundcheck back on the English tour. By the time they were done with it, 'The Boy with the Thorn in His Side' sounded, to their ears, close to perfect. In positively contrarian Smiths fashion, they decided that this eight-track demo should become their next single. Only when they booked time to record its B-sides at RAK Studios in London did they transfer the 8-track to 24-track and 'carried on doing some overdubs on it,' said Stephen Street, a process that served to give the single some professional polish while preserving the simplicity and enthusiasm of the initial performance.[2]

This was key to the Smiths' statement of intent. Things had gotten complicated of late on all fronts, but it had been especially evident in the density of the three singles since 'William'. It was time to strip things back, to rediscover the lightness of touch that had made that song, among others, so instantly appealing. It was therefore a compliment that the acoustic guitar arrangement at the heart of 'The Boy with the Thorn in His Side' should be likened to West African 'highlife' music, even though that had not been Johnny Marr's original intent. (He had been trying to emulate Nile Rodgers of Chic.) It was a delight to hear a marimba, even if it was essentially percussive. It was a relief to hear the bass more relaxed than in the past, yet playing an even more important role in the arrangement. And it was especially pleasing that Morrissey's vocals should sound so delightfully yearning as they danced their way around a melody that managed to be simultaneously upbeat and yet melancholic. In all this, it was no coincidence that the single carried the credit 'Produced by Morrissey/Marr' as opposed to 'Produced by the Smiths'. The 'Shakespeare's Sister' session had seen all four members of the band at the mixing board, each with hands on the faders of their own given instrument, a time-honoured recipe for failure. 'After that session,' recalled Stephen Street, 'Johnny said he wanted to have control.'

The RAK session proved exceptionally productive. In addition to cleaning up 'The Boy with the Thorn in His Side', the Smiths recorded and mixed its B-sides: 'Rubber Ring', another song rehearsed during the spring tour soundchecks, and 'Asleep', a ballad that, for the first time, featured Morrissey and Marr alone. This same session then additionally produced the bulk of what would turn out to be the next Smiths single, 'Bigmouth Strikes Again', similarly worked up at the soundchecks in March. Initially inspired by the Rolling Stones' 'Jumping Jack Flash', the final recording of 'Bigmouth' proved considerably more restrained, dominated initially by multitracked acoustic guitars and audacious for the fact that it consisted of but a single verse followed by multiple choruses and a guitar interlude. Breaking with a self-imposed ban on outsiders, the Smiths invited Kirsty MacColl (she of Billy Bragg's 'A New England' crossover success and married to producer Steve Lillywhite) to sing backing vocals, and even employed a trumpet player on yet another new number, 'Frankly, Mr Shankly', which included four words that summed up Morrissey's lyrical manifesto at the time: 'fame, fame, fatal fame.'

The tendency of the rock star to sing about his chosen career in the spotlight as if a plight or a burden has always been an inherently dangerous one. John Lennon just about pulled it off in 1969 with 'The Ballad of John and Yoko', setting the way for Ian Hunter of Mott the Hoople to do likewise with the self-referential songs 'All the Way from Memphis' and 'Ballad of Mott the Hoople' (and his book, *Diary of a Rock 'n' Roll Star*). But it was an easy trait to overdo, as the Clash discovered when praise for the anti-corporate 'Complete Control' turned into criticism for the self-mythologising 'Clash City Rockers'.

Morrissey brilliantly distinguished himself from these icons by presenting himself as the subject matter of his songs, over the course of three singles and a couple of B-sides, without ever naming himself as such. He had started the dialogue with 'That Joke Isn't Funny Anymore', a thinly disguised attack on the music press. 'I was just so completely tired of all the same old journalistic questions and people trying, you know, this contest of wit, trying to drag me down and prove that I was a complete fake,' he told *Melody Maker* upon its release. In this context, the line 'kick them when they fall down' was self-evident, but to someone who didn't read the interviews, it could as easily have applied to school bullies. Morrissey's public confessional continued with the new single, 'The Boy with the Thorn in His Side': as he told Liverpudlian actress Margi Clarke on *The Tube* shortly after its release, 'The thorn is the music industry and all these people who would just never believe anything I said, tried to get rid of me, wouldn't play the records.' Knowing as much, the words 'how can they see the love in our eyes and still they don't believe us' clearly applied to the (misunderstood) Smiths – unless, as with 'Hand in Glove' and its similar refrain 'no, it's not like any other love/this one's different because it's us,' the listener applied it to his or her own personal life, in which case it resonated no less powerfully. As for the following single, 'Bigmouth Strikes Again', there appeared less reason to question whether Morrissey was singing about himself, given the title and the reference to Joan of Arc's 'hearing aid', Morrissey's famous prop. The supposition became, in part, that Morrissey was comparing himself to the historic martyr – and that only he could get away with it. But again, that need not be the only point of reference.[3] Who had *not* hurt the one they loved by saying something like (as per the words in 'Bigmouth') 'You should be bludgeoned in your bed,' only to feel such remorse as to conclude 'I have no right to take my place in the human race'?

'Bigmouth Strikes Again' was saved from hubris by its humour: 'I would call it a parody if *that* sounded less like self-celebration, which it definitely wasn't,' said Morrissey himself two years later. 'It was just a really funny song.' So too, up to a point, was 'Frankly, Mr Shankly' which, given Morrissey's issues with his record company at the time of its writing and unveiling, was widely taken to be an attack on Geoff Travis. (The choice of pseudonym may have been a random rhyme. Then again, the name Shankly in the UK was widely associated with the manager of the incredibly successful 1970s Liverpool Football Club; a comparison to Travis as the public leader of the dominant Rough Trade label was inevitably invited.) Under the circumstances of their self-imposed battle with Rough Trade, lines like 'I want to leave, you will not miss me, I want to go down in musical history' appear almost uncommonly direct, the closest Morrissey the singer had yet come to singing about Morrissey the singer. As for the final words, calling the Shankly character 'a flatulent pain in the arse' appeared positively unpleasant on paper, but given its music-hall arrangement, it came across as something closer to comedy.

Fortunately, Morrissey's ego was not so evident in 'Rubber Ring', which, until its last verse, glorified not the saga of the singer but rather the power of his songs to, quite literally, save lives: the lyric 'they were the only ones who ever stood by you' was very close to the words Morrissey had used in many an interview to describe other artists. Now that his own band's words and music appeared capable of doing likewise for thousands of similarly troubled youths, Morrissey felt confident enough to project himself, in the final verse of 'Rubber Ring', into the 'corner of your room,' to ask, 'Can you hear me?' and then to request, 'When you're dancing and laughing and finally living, hear my voice in your head and think of me kindly.' The conclusion might well have been that the subject (the singer) had helped bring its object (the listener) through the fraught difficulties of adolescence into a happy adulthood. But a tape sample that was played over the song's coda – 'You are sleeping, you do not want to believe' – suggested something more sinister, and the track that it then segued into on the 12" single, 'Asleep', furthered the notion of impending darkness.

Morrissey had discussed mortality already at length in interviews. And he had touched on it several times throughout *Meat Is Murder*, with the schoolboy of 'The Headmaster Ritual' who wants to 'give up life as a bad mistake,' the schoolgirl in 'Rusholme Ruffians' who asks, 'How quickly would I die if I jumped from the top of the parachutes?', the female character in 'What She Said' who is 'hoping for an early death,' and the narrator in 'That Joke Isn't Funny Anymore' who admits that their 'only desire is to die.' He had then taken full aim at suicide on 'Shakespeare's Sister', where 'the rocks below, say, "Throw your white [or skinny] body down!"' He was to make two more references to premature death in songs that were written in the summer of 1985, even though they would not be heard by the general public until well into the following year.

But nowhere did he address death by suicide quite so determinedly as on 'Asleep', arguably the most graceful, eloquent and dignified song on the subject ever recorded by a popular rock band. Part of its success came down to its composers' willingness to abandon the rock tradition and instead embrace a classical format: it was no coincidence that a song that opened with the words 'Sing me to sleep' should be arranged as a nocturne, the name given for solo piano pieces associated with the night. The piano part in question was almost identical to that recorded back at Shelley Rohde's house in 1982 and tacked on to the end of the original 'Suffer Little Children' demo, Marr playing the purposefully haunting chords and melody with the quietly stated determination of a diligent student, over which a harsh wind from a BBC *Sound Effects* album accentuated the air of doom. Morrissey's lyrics, once more to his credit, managed to avoid all mention of the word death, let alone any means of attaining it, but it was hard not to construe them as a suicide note all the same – not with lines like 'Deep in the cell of my heart, I want to go' and 'I don't want to wake up on my own anymore.' It was a painful admission of a failure at living and loving from someone who could only conclude 'there is a better world,' signing off by singing 'bye-bye' as a music box morosely faded out the song to 'Auld Lang Syne', a tune associated not only with New Year's celebrations but funerals and other farewells.

A year later Morrissey volunteered the fact that six people 'who were alarmingly dedicated to the Smiths' had taken their

lives. ('Their friends and parents wrote to me after they'd died.')
And a few months after that *NME*, in a special news story about
the growing number of youth suicides on both sides of the
Atlantic, additionally reported 'two recent instances of young
people who wrote to [Morrissey] on a daily basis and afterwards
killed themselves.' Understandably, Morrissey was then asked to
explain himself. He remained customarily unapologetic – and
yet appropriately sympathetic. 'I don't want to be a nurse,' he
told Martin Aston about his role in the wake of this news. 'I'd
rather say, in essence, well, the despair you feel is true, and it's
common. Not enormously common, but common.' Further ques-
tioned as to whether, 'in the case of two Smiths fans who killed
themselves, who took your words very seriously,' he felt 'a sense
of achievement in touching them,' he had the courage to reply
in the affirmative. 'Yes, because quite largely people in such
situations are untouchable by the human race, and nothing makes
sense to them. So I think it is quite remarkable.' All the same,
it was perhaps a shame that 'Rubber Ring' should have preceded
'Asleep' on vinyl, because the youthful Morrissey who had so
frequently entertained suicidal thoughts had been saved by pop
music, and perhaps now stood in the position of saving Smiths'
fans who gravitated to the band for the very reason that he wrote
such personal, unique lyrics. As it stood on the 12" single,
however, the optimistic endorsement on 'Rubber Ring' of those
'songs that saved your life' was quickly followed (and countered)
by the pessimistic request on 'Asleep' to put an end to it.[4]

Either way, the eight-minute piece of music signified a
marvellous maturity in the work of the Smiths. The inclusion
of found sound and odd samples, the use of the piano as lead
instrument, and the absence of other familiar instruments all
reflected an experimental edge far removed from public perception of the Smiths as a four-piece rock 'n' roll group. The
decision to then blend the two songs into each other as part
of a joint narrative was something that the Beatles had only
dared try in the latter stages of their storied career. Unfortunately,
only those who bought the 12" (on which 'Rubber Ring' served

as the bonus cut) heard it that way; when the tracks were subsequently included on compilations, they were separated by other songs, as if a bad influence on each other.

MORRISSEY AND MARR would look back on that summer of 1985 with particular fondness. The rigours of a major British and European tour behind them, the (perceived) problems with Rough Trade kept at the distance that separated Manchester from London, they found time to hang out with each other much as they had when the Smiths first started. They wrote a considerable amount of new material together, face to face at Marr's place in Bowdon, and it would prove some of their most critically acclaimed and enduring. They also embarked, at Morrissey's suggestion, on a mission for Marr, now that he had the money, to re-purchase all the singles he had swapped or permanently loaned before becoming successful. At one point they drove from Manchester to Brighton and back just to acquire a copy of the 1973 single 'Good Grief Christina' by Chicory Tip. It was a combination of rock star self-indulgence and pure fandom, fuelled by an impenetrable friendship, and the hours spent together helped explain why each would continue to back the other for as long as they could see ahead.

There was never any shortage of issues to discuss, especially when the conversation came back around to the Smiths. Morrissey had been instinctively correct about so many things regarding the marketplace, the public, and his own role at the heart of it all, but when he had justified the Smiths' decision to 'bypass the whole video market' because 'I think it's something that's going to die very quickly,' he had got it wrong. By mid-1985, it was evident that videos were as much a part of modern promotion as a picture sleeve, a poster or an advertisement, and every bit as desirable. The question for most acts was less about turning down the opportunity than about making the most of it. So to the valid argument that videos in the early days of MTV distracted from the music, the response now needed to be in the form of an artistic statement that complemented said music. R.E.M. had finally understood as much: after initially turning their back on the format, and for very similar reasons as the Smiths, three members of the group had declared official disinterest and handed the reins over to the group's artistic director, singer Michael Stipe, who had set about making short films that, even if they didn't receive much play, satisfied demands for some form of video while maintaining the group's visual integrity. The Smiths could have done something very similar, especially given Morrissey's proven skills with the record sleeves, but having only just told *Melody Maker,* 'We'll never make a video as long as we live,' he had left himself no room for manoeuvre.

Johnny Marr had willingly stood by his partner on this issue. 'I thought all the videos that I was seeing were awful and I couldn't imagine us doing one of those videos,' he said. At the same time, he admitted, 'I didn't have in mind an alternative.' He and Morrissey had effectively lost their argument with 'How Soon Is Now?' when Sire had made a video regardless, and lost it again when it had clearly helped sales. Now came the news that the American label, invigorated by the success of the tour, wanted to release 'The Boy with the Thorn in His Side' domestically, this time with the appropriate artwork and with the intent of making some sort of success out of it. The Smiths had long complained that Sire did not release their UK non-album singles. Here was a chance for everyone to make good – but for that to truly happen, Sire needed some form of a promotional video.

And so, under enormous pressure, the Smiths finally succumbed. They agreed to make a clip, but only if the crew came to *them,* while they were in the studio at RAK working on the new album, and bought a case of wine along so the group could drown their compromise. Their refusal to meet the project even close to halfway (quite literally: 'I will move three feet,' said Johnny Marr of his willingness to engage the camera) left open the opportunity to blame the other side if it didn't turn out well.

And it did not. 'They still managed to make us look like twats,' said Johnny Marr. He was right: the video, such as it could be called one, was an embarrassment. Compared to the clip for 'This Charming Man', shot for and by *The Tube* two years earlier, it felt like a step back several years. Both videos had been made in a closed room, with the band playing direct to camera, but the earlier one had captured a look, a style, a feel, and a sense of purpose. The new one suggested a complete lack of creativity on the part of the director (Ken O'Neill) and band alike. (It also intimated a total lack of budget.) If there was a lesson to be learned, it was surely that the Smiths needed to step up and get creatively involved in the video process rather than leaving it to others. The lesson they took away was the opposite: that videos remained a waste of time and money. They were therefore thrilled when 'The Boy with the Thorn in His Side' charted just high enough for them to be invited to appear on *Top of the Pops* again, in person.[5] Yet it was hard to say how much it helped them. 'The Boy with the Thorn in His Side' was a beautiful song and, one would have thought, a commercial one too; with its experimental B-sides, it formed by far their strongest statement since the 'William'/'Please, Please, Please'/'How Soon Is Now?' trifecta. But it was only a modest hit.

IN 1983, ECHO & the Bunnymen had undertaken an unusual tour of Britain that had seen them venture to village halls on the Scottish Isles of Skye and Lewis. For their Scottish tour of September 1985, the Smiths went one better: all the way to Lerwick, in the Shetland Islands, the northernmost point of the British Isles. For their support act, they brought along another group from Manchester, Easterhouse, whose guitarist Ivor Perry was Morrissey's former Kings Road neighbour. Perry had moved out to a tower block in Hulme, a dad already at the age of twenty-one and, with his brother Andy, had formed the band originally called In Easterhouse, after an infamous Glasgow housing estate. The Perry brothers were working-class youth who read up on their politics and were interested in changing the world – through music if possible, but in the case of Andy Perry, who was a member of the Revolutionary Communist Party, by other means if necessary. After Perry, converted to the Smiths by 'Hand In Glove', had brought Morrissey a demo of his group, Easterhouse were invited to open for the Smiths at Dingwalls in 1983, where they presumed to have played a passable show until 'Morrissey leaped on waving flowers over his head, wearing a silver blouse unbuttoned, and metamorphosed into this superstar performer,' recalled Ivor Perry. 'We were so outclassed as a group.'

Morrissey and Perry grew close, the guitarist frequently coming over to Kings Road to hang out. 'He was very interested in how I fitted into the world,' said Perry. 'And how I fitted into the music, and what I thought of his music, and he was very complimentary of our music.' Specifically, the pair bonded over literature, Morrissey loaning Perry his copies of *Last Exit to Brooklyn* and *The Female Eunuch*. 'We read,' said Ivor Perry. 'It was what bound us together. It wasn't just, "I want to be a rock star." There was more to it than that.'

Now, two years later, Easterhouse had just ended a short and unpleasant relationship with a major label and were relieved to find themselves among like-minded souls on Rough Trade. It was a shock, then, to find out that the Smiths viewed their world differently. 'It was suddenly, "We're carrying the can for all these whack groups on Rough Trade,"' said Perry. 'But there's always been whack groups on Rough Trade. Surely their idea is to put out loads of records that will sell five hundred, and let the bands flourish or not.'

Record-company travails did not stop the Smiths granting Access All Areas passes to Geoff Travis, Scott Piering, Martha

DeFoe and almost forty others – a number that reflected not only the increased demands on the Smiths' entourage but also the band's desire to consider certain people as part of the family. Among them were Fred Hood, drummer with major-label signees the Impossible Dreamers, whose new single 'August Avenue' came with a big sticker on the picture sleeve announcing Johnny Marr's credit as producer, and a long-standing female Japanese fan who went by the name of Oska, as in Wilde, and who became something of a Morrissey confidante, often sitting with him on the tour bus.

In so many ways the seven-date tour presented the Smiths at their very best. It took in the famous sweat box and sprung floor of the Glasgow Barrowlands, which many in attendance (including Geoff Travis) considered to be the finest Smiths' show ever; Easterhouse manager John Barratt spoke of Morrissey that night 'being up there with Jagger' and of the Smiths making U2 look 'weedy' by comparison. At the other end of the tour, the Clickimin Centre in Lerwick saw the Smiths play to an audience of seven hundred people that included pretty much every young person in the town, regardless of their musical tastes (most of which, apparently, veered towards hard rock). The shows also took in the Edinburgh Playhouse – a theatre in the vein of those they had recently played in Manchester and Liverpool – and what was advertised as the 'largest sports centre in Europe,' the Magnum Leisure Centre in Irvine. Morrissey was in particularly vivacious form throughout, perhaps enjoying the tour's relative distance from the media spotlight; it was probably no coincidence that he chose Lerwick for the rare treat of drinking with the entire entourage in the hotel bar through the night. Unlike James (whose debut single, 'What's the World', the Smiths began performing on the Scottish tour, their first onstage cover version since 1982), Easterhouse could party as hard as the Smiths. At an end-of-tour celebration in Inverness, the champagne flowed, and Perry and Marr ruffled each other's feathers, as they had done all the way back at Dingwalls. It could not have gone unnoticed that

Easterhouse's lone single on London Records featured guitar playing not dissimilar to that of Johnny Marr; the Smiths' influence upon their generation was becoming increasingly apparent.

Part of the onstage confidence and offstage exuberance may have come down to the fact that the recording sessions at RAK had already produced such a wealth of wonderful new material. Throughout the tour, and often back to back, the Smiths performed not only the new single, 'The Boy with the Thorn in His Side', but fully complete renditions of 'Frankly, Mr Shankly' and 'Bigmouth Strikes Again'.[6] The Smiths additionally used the tour to introduce a verse of Elvis's 'His Latest Flame' into 'Rusholme Ruffians', and Morrissey frequently introduced 'Nowhere Fast' with a put-down of Prince Charles and Princess Diana's child, Prince William. The singer, it appeared evident, had no interest in toning down his attacks on the royal family.

CHAPTER THIRTY-ONE

I never really like to say, I never really like to pin it down. Do you understand that? I mean, there's someone in Huddersfield who might have a fascinating, fiery explanation, and then I go and shatter it by saying it's about greyhound racing. Their life collapses.

– MORRISSEY on lyrics, *Record Mirror*,
February 1987

Throughout the saga of the Smiths, only one central figure to the story was able to demonstrate an ability to manage the personalities of both Morrissey and Marr equally, to be appreciated by each of them equally, and to survive with his reputation unscathed, at least until the band broke up. That person was Stephen Street, credited as their recording engineer though unofficially recognised as their co-producer through three of their four studio albums.

'Street was straight down the middle,' said Johnny Marr, 'totally partisan' in his relationships with the group members, a viewpoint confirmed by Andy Rourke, who stated, 'Stephen was very attentive to everybody, and that's why we all loved him.' These playing members had had no qualms with John Porter, either, but Porter had nonetheless been unable to secure the trust of Morrissey. By succeeding in this regard, Street revealed not only his considerable talents as an engineer, but the people skills necessary to satisfy, support and motivate the most difficult of artists.

'You've got to be very attentive to Morrissey,' said Street.

'You've got to make him feel that he's special, and I did, because he *is* special. I didn't have to fake it. When the guy came in to do his work, he was brilliant. I was very keen on making sure that everything that Morrissey wanted, to make him happy in the studio, I would do.' But Street applied the same philosophy to the other members too. 'When it's their point in the recording where it's important, I try to make each person really, *really* feel as if they're the most important thing in the band at that point.'

This impartiality was noticed beyond the four musicians. Grant Showbiz, himself an active producer in between Smiths tours, observed, 'Stephen could balance up Johnny and Morrissey in a studio managerial way better than John Porter.' And Geoff Travis lamented how one of the major disappointments of the Smiths is 'that they didn't find a manager that managed to get a balance in a way that Stephen Street did between the two of them – or the four of them.' The ongoing lack of permanent management was to hover menacingly throughout the group's continued recording career, but Street expressly forbade it from intruding on the actual sessions. 'Why should I get involved in the business side of things?' he asked. 'All I wanted to make sure was that I was just making as good as possible a record.'

Street's selfless attitude had already produced results with *Meat Is Murder*. When the session at RAK studios in August 1985 proved equally rewarding, he took the initiative to ask Johnny Marr, directly, if he could get a royalty. Typically, this was not something requested by a mere engineer, but by now Street recognised, 'I was making some key decisions towards how the records sounded.' Marr and Morrissey evidently agreed; after conferring for a few minutes they granted his request, and the paperwork confirming Street's single percentage point was subsequently completed and signed, something that not many people around the Smiths (including the rhythm section) were ever able to claim.

Suitably encouraged, Street returned to work on the new

album – tentatively titled *Margaret on the Guillotine*, though Morrissey later substituted the stark image of Thatcher's execution for *The Queen Is Dead* – with increased vigour.[1] From Street's perspective, the sessions – which got under way in earnest, after the Scottish tour, at Jacob's in Farnham, Surrey – were 'a happy time,' which perhaps also reflected Marr's understanding of Street as an ideal collaborator. 'The closest we got to a relaxed presence was Stephen Street,' he said, 'because even though it was a real roller-coaster ride making the records with us, he had enough of a sense of himself. He was able to get out there in the stratosphere with us mentally, but he was always very, very grounded.' For Marr's own part, however, the new album was to prove a markedly different experience: 'I was so completely immersed in *The Queen Is Dead*,' he recalled. 'The other band members will agree that you couldn't be as immersed in that as I was.'

They did. Mike Joyce told Johnny Rogan of the sessions, 'Johnny became insular and detached from myself and Andy. He was taking on a lot and wanted to do it himself. I remember him not wanting us around for a while.' Fred Hood, Marr's friend in the Impossible Dreamers (and Grant Showbiz's future musical partner in the hit act Moodswings), observed that he'd 'never seen anyone so under pressure as Johnny was when they were doing *The Queen Is Dead*. Johnny was writing all the songs, then arranging for Morrissey to get to the studio when nobody else was there, such were Morrissey's stipulations. And Johnny was beginning to have a good time outside of that . . . he was beginning to enjoy being in more normal musicianly surroundings. The Smiths were abnormal because they were hermetically sealed.' Distracted perhaps by the group's lack of management, which meant that he was not only assuming the task of administering the various studio bookings but frequently being called away to phone calls or discussing business with Morrissey, Marr's main motivation was nonetheless that of the twenty-one-year-old wunderkind who had only just told *Melody Maker* in their cover story on him: 'I just look at what we have done and it all seems so tiny and we still have the universe to go.'

Jacob's, one of Britain's premier facilities at the time, was set in a Georgian mansion with a sizeable swimming pool and in-house catering; its two separate studios included a former drawing room and a converted stables, and its residences included a cottage where Marr holed himself up with demo equipment that, when not in the main studio, he used to complete some compositions and start others from scratch. He would get up around lunchtime, start work, and then 'drive myself and drive myself' through the day and way into the night. In fact, he had become almost completely nocturnal by this point. 'It was the only way I could get any peace and quiet.'

Morrissey's daytime hours, meanwhile, suited Stephen Street, who, by having the singer to himself, managed to secure additional vocal takes from the singer. 'Sometimes I would make out it was my fault, that there was a problem with a compressor or whatever. I'd just find a way of getting a good vocal performance out of him, and I think he appreciated that when he listened back to the record at the end of it all. I often got a postcard from him afterwards, congratulating me on my efforts and saying, "Well done and thank you."'

The first song to be worked up at Jacob's was 'I Know It's Over', which Morrissey and Marr had written in Bowdon over the summer (alongside 'Frankly, Mr Shankly') and which had already been recorded as an instrumental demo at RAK. When Morrissey delivered his vocals at Jacob's, as was often the case it was without sharing them with the group in advance: Marr described watching Morrissey's delivery as 'one of the highlights of my life.' Continuing the morbid theme that ran through so much of his work in 1985, 'I Know It's Over' opened with the memorable line 'Mother, I can feel the soil falling over my head,' which had to be presumed as metaphorical given the narrator's lucidity through the rest of the song, bemoaning his romantic isolation in the face of (supposedly) contented married couples, and who was further humiliated by questions hurled at him, presumably by the object of desire, along the lines of, 'If you're so funny, then why are you on your own tonight?' In whatever way this song may have been personal to Morrissey, the listener was welcome to project this series of questions instead towards anyone he or she had ever disliked or envied.

It was the third of the summer's co-compositions that would prove the most endearing and enduring. Written in a minor key, and played several frets up with a capo, allowing for those higher, almost flamenco-like frequencies that were so familiar to Smiths fans, 'There Is a Light That Never Goes Out' opened with an intro lifted from both Marvin Gaye's 'Hitch Hike' and the Velvet Underground's 'There She Goes Again'. Over Marr's comparatively uncluttered chords (barely five of them, all easily figured and fingered), Morrissey projected himself back into the passenger seat of 'This Charming Man', but this time as an already infatuated if apparently unconsummated romantic partner. As the verses unravelled, there were hints at an unhappy home life to which the passenger had no desire to return, and an almost tangible sense of longing for the driver, including a beautifully illustrated example of missed opportunity: 'But then a strange fear gripped me and I just couldn't ask.' Every word was perfectly situated, forming the spine of a narrative without fleshing out the body too much, and it was all in thrall to the chorus, the narrator's willingness to be struck by an oncoming bus or truck: 'to die by your side/such a heavenly way to die.' In those few words, Morrissey somehow summed up the thoughts of all those who had ever loved and lost or never loved at all; they were to become among the most commonly quoted of all Smiths lyrics.[2] The song's title itself was then left to stand alone, repeated frequently during the outro but never fully explained. (Years later, an earlier recording would emerge with a slightly different vocal, which concluded, 'There is a light in your eyes and it never goes out,' offering an elucidation that was never actually required.)

As a pure love song, 'There Is a Light That Never Goes Out'

was rendered that much more potent by its rare reliance on compositional convention: intro, verse, verse, quick bridge, chorus, verse, verse, quick bridge, chorus, outro, fade. This seeming simplicity would have counted for nothing, however, without Marr's regal chord structure, Morrissey's devotional lyrics, and a studio arrangement that cast aside any attempt at pretence or protest and dived headfirst instead into all the classic pop-ballad production techniques. A tearjerking string accompaniment introduced itself on the first chorus (performed on the Emulator, a state-of-the-art sample keyboard of its time, the strings were essentially authentic but fell digitally short of a full orchestra's occasional overkill), and an Emulator flute melody (with a touch of delay) on the third verse, the strings and flute then combining and counterpointing over the traditional instrumentation during the lengthy outro. The Brill Building-era songwriting partnerships and the mid-'60s Svengali producers alike would have been proud.

A modest amount of detective work would subsequently reveal that the first verse of 'There Is a Light That Never Goes Out' borrowed a line from the movie *Saturday Night and Sunday Morning* ('Why don't you take me where it's lively and there's plenty of people?') and that the second used a couple from the New York Dolls' 'Lonely Planet Boy' ('How could you be drivin' down by my home when you know I ain't got one?'), but it really didn't matter; as Oscar Wilde biographer Arthur Ransome wrote of his own subject, 'He stole freely, but often mounted other men's jewels so well that they are better in his work than in their own.' In fact, Morrissey chose to confront accusations of his plagiarism head-on, and with almost giddy delight, on another song, the purposefully misspelled 'Cemetry Gates'. Over another simple acoustic chord sequence and recognisable song structure (ABBCBCA), Morrissey offered a nostalgic recollection of his graveyard wanderings at Manchester's Southern Cemetery with Linder and others, before allowing his protagonists to have at each other with their literary idols. 'Keats and Yeats are on your side,' sang

Morrissey, but 'Wilde is on mine,' acknowledging at last in lyric his most frequently cited influence. Deliberately misquoting Shakespeare, and inventing an alliterative nonsensical quotation of his own, Morrissey's words were a tumbling torrent of a tease, defying the odds in maintaining some semblance of melody as they danced in and around Marr's busy guitar work.[3] 'If you must write prose poems, the words you use should be your own,' he sang with impressive conviction for a line so disingenuous. It was a work of almost impossible self-confidence, a gleeful poke in the eye of his detractors – and a sublime piece of music to boot. Recording it, recalled Stephen Street, 'the vibe was just wonderful.'

Morrissey's impishness and impudence was additionally evident in 'Vicar in a Tutu', and it's of no small import that this song became a last-minute replacement for a sombre ballad entitled 'Unlovable'. When the latter showed up as the B-side to 'Bigmouth', it was rightly dismissed as a very rare case of the Smiths underperforming musically and conforming to lyrical cliché; had it been included on *The Queen Is Dead*, it would have served the additional dispurpose of tipping the album over to the dark side. (The inclusion of a lumbering 6/8 ballad, 'Never Had No One Ever', though full of menace and to become much loved by Smiths fans in concert, already threatened that emotional balance.) In its place, 'Vicar in a Tutu', set to a spaghetti rockabilly skiffle riff enforced by Mike Joyce's syncopated snare rolls, offered lighthearted relief, and yet it was saved from pure comedy by Morrissey's underlying empathy for the cross-dressing clergyman ('He's not strange, he just wants to live his life this way') and his antipathy for religious structure to begin with (literally so, his narrator 'lifting some lead off the roof of the Holy Name Church' as the song opens). It was throwaway popular music of the highest order, and became one of Morrissey's favourite Smiths songs.

In somewhat similar fashion, Morrissey took the role of the quintessentially fey Englishman, acting all embarrassed and shocked by bodily parts and their recreational/procreational functions (think Michael Crawford in the theatrical romp *No Sex Please, We're British* and the equally enduring TV comedy *Some Mothers Do 'Ave 'Em*) for 'Some Girls Are Bigger Than Others', a simple statement of biological fact that Morrissey nonetheless presented as if a revelation. Refusing to capitalise on its opening tease (other than conjuring up the image of a camp Mark Antony), it served as an unexpectedly lighthearted conclusion, very much at odds with 'Suffer Little Children' and 'Meat Is Murder' on the preceding albums. But it also served as a deliberate juxtaposition to *The Queen Is Dead*'s opening song and title track, the number that has come to be revered as quite possibly the Smiths' greatest studio performance.[4]

That title had been lingering in the air since America, where Morrissey had ad-libbed it at the end of 'Barbarism Begins at Home'. Once Marr learned that it was to be used for a Smiths song, he took the phrase as overdue opportunity to combine the violent guitar work of Detroit's highly politicised MC5 with the minimalist repetitiveness of New York's apolitical Velvet Underground, specifically their 1969 outtake 'I Can't Stand It', which had been released post-breakup on the album *VU* within the past year. As with 'How Soon Is Now?', the song 'The Queen Is Dead' ultimately bore little outward sign of these influences, and as with that other confirmed Smiths studio classic, it came together through a series of fortuitous experiments resulting from a lengthy studio jam. 'Sometimes you can go into the studio and you can play for a whole day and nothing will happen,' said Andy Rourke. 'That day the magic happened and we came up with this amazing song that became the theme of the whole album.'

'The Queen Is Dead' was propelled by the Smiths' rhythm section at their most inspired, Joyce holding the beat with a ferocity born of his punk days but a finesse that could only have been acquired with the Smiths, and Rourke discovering a rumbling, rising-octave bass line that anchored the track and gave it the vital element of danger. Once the initial backing track jam had been recorded, Marr delivered his most savage guitar performance to date, heavy on the wah-wah pedal, returning to the control room 'shaking' at his own intensity. As the group settled down to listen back, they noticed that the pedal had been left open when Marr had thrust the guitar back on its stand, producing a ghostly harmonic that the guitarist now rushed back to capture on tape, opening and closing the pedal in time with the music. The effect was kept throughout the song, providing an ambience that subtly but crucially distinguished it from just another flat-out rock performance.

Upon Morrissey's request, 'The Queen Is Dead' opened with the sound of actress Cicely Courtneidge singing 'Take Me Back to Dear Old Blighty' from the 1962 kitchen-sink drama *The L-Shaped Room*.[5] Though the novel and movie were set in a boarding house of that postwar era in West London, the song in question dated from World War I, and thereby conjured up images of some ancient and venerable Britain that Smiths fans would never have known and certainly no longer have recognised. This alone made it a perfect sample for the conflicted feelings that Morrissey (and so many of his listeners) held towards their home nation, but those who had seen the movie – and that naturally included the singer – would have been able to gather much more of relevance from the scene in question. Coming together in their landlady's room on Christmas Day, the tenants of the boarding house represented the outcasts of late '50s/early '60s British society, all engaged in a daily battle to survive against an institutionalised nation whose past glories meant little with regard to their own present lives. Their numbers included a pregnant Frenchwoman (for which role actress Leslie Caron was nominated for an Oscar); a couple of prostitutes (one played with especial vigour by the erstwhile *Coronation Street* and 'Shakespeare's Sister' cover star Pat Phoenix, whom Morrissey interviewed in 1985 for *Blitz* magazine); a failed male writer; a young African; the tempestuous landlady and her lover man; and Courtneidge herself as an

Meat Is Murder, a bold album title for a chart act, inspired many listeners to vegetarianism. 'As long as human beings are so violent towards animals there will be war,' Morrissey elaborated of the cover art.

Morrissey as idol at the London Palladium, October 1986.
'I always thought being famous was the only thing worth doing in life,
and anything else was just perfunctory.'

At the 'From Manchester With Love' benefit at the Royal Court Theatre in
Liverpool, 8 February 1986. 'When the time came to actually mount the stage,
it was almost as if this strange forceful character completely took over,'
said Morrissey. 'I actually stayed in the wings almost.'

Geoff Travis, founder of Rough Trade and the Smiths' A&R man throughout their career.

The Smiths' road crew, backstage in Phoenix, Arizona, on 31 August 1986. John Featherstone and Phil Powell are in the foreground. Grant Showbiz is at the back of the right-hand row.

Stephen Street in the studio in the 1980s. Street engineered or co-produced three of the four Smiths studio LPs and many of their hit singles.

John Porter, with occasional Smiths engineer Kenny Jones, in the 1980s. Porter produced the Smiths' first LP and most of their biggest hit singles.

The five-piece Smiths relax on the American tour of 1986, which was cut short after twenty-four dates. 'We were always OK when we were working,' said Andy Rourke. 'But when we had time off it got messy.'

Johnny Marr, Andy Rourke and Stuart James, the Smiths' longest-serving tour manager, at the Blarney Stone in Ireland, November 1984.

Angie Brown, Johnny Marr's life partner. The pair were married in June 1985 in San Francisco, on the Smiths' first American tour.

Morrissey, Andy Rourke, Craig Gannon (playing his third gig), Johnny Marr:
The five-piece Smiths at the G-Mex Centre in Manchester, 9 July 1986.

The Smiths as a quartet again, outside Albert Finney (Senior)'s
betting shop in early 1987 – 'looking for all the world as if they
belonged in *Saturday Night and Sunday Morning*'.

The iron bridge across the railway tracks to Kings Road remains as it was –
except for extensive graffiti added since the 1980s, almost every last word
of which lovingly quotes a lyric by the most famous St Mary's 'old boy' of all.

aged stage girl, and a lesbian at that, a revelation that, even in 1962 could only be rendered in a movie by the confession that 'it takes all sorts, dear.' In this, the 'Take Me Back to Dear Old Blighty' sing-along suggested an additionally subtle hint at the album title's intended double entendre. For while 'The Queen Is Dead' would be taken at face value as wishful thinking on Morrissey's part with regard to the British monarch (understandably so, given the line 'Her Very Lowness with her head in a sling, oh it sounds like a wonderful thing'), its roots lay in a lengthy, disturbingly decadent chapter of that same name from one of Morrissey's favourite books, Hubert Selby's 1964 novel *Last Exit to Brooklyn,* which followed the travails of a transvestite hooker, her friends, and their attempts to drink, drug and seduce a group of avowedly heterosexual street toughs.

In sending the album artwork to Jo Slee at Rough Trade, Morrissey wrote, tongue somewhat in cheek, 'It's about the death of a panto queen . . . yes, it's autobiographical,' but later elaborated to the press, with rare candour, that 'there's the safety net in the song that the "old queen" is me . . .' Camp references aside, Morrissey packed more of substance into 'The Queen Is Dead' than anything else in the Smiths' canon. The rolling visual narrative depicted a rain-swept Britain numbed by its subservience to royalty and religion, to alcohol and drugs, a place where a companion is invited for a walk to talk about precious things like 'love and law and' not poetry but 'poverty' – a place where, ultimately, 'life is very long, when you're lonely.'

'The song is certainly a kind of general observation on the state of the nation,' Morrissey admitted after its release. Britain was halfway through its second term under Thatcher at the song's point of composition, and the headlines made grim reading for those who, like the Smiths, had been brought up working-class. The miners had been defeated, and with them the power of the unions; unemployment had reached catastrophic levels in vast swathes of the country, and the governmental policy to shift from a manufacturing society to a consumer-based one saw minimum-wage labour replace former job security for those who could even find the work. Multiculturalism, sexual permissiveness, gay rights and progressive education were all under attack. Locally elected left-wing councils were being abolished, spending on the welfare state reduced, government-owned industries privatised, council property sold off to those tenants who could afford it, and though neither the resultant wealth in the hands of the few nor the poverty endured by the masses was restricted to one part of England, still the party line in terms of parliamentary representation that ran across the middle of the country certainly appeared to suggest as much. 'The Queen Is Dead' made almost no reference to any of this, and yet it somehow acknowledged all of it, and that was no small achievement.

In his essay 'The Smiths and the Challenges of Thatcherism', Joseph Brooker offered some interesting parallels between Morrissey and Thatcher. 'Both drew on their backgrounds in England's regions to articulate their creeds. Both arrived in the centre of public attention with a messianic sense of purpose, determined to scourge established institutions. Both were provincial puritans, possessed of a zeal and self-belief that could reach absurd heights and inspire fanaticism in others. Their clarity of purpose and image lent themselves to caricature, which was one sign of their success. Both were defining figures of the 1980s.' This was fair comment, and it offered the unstated understanding not only that powerful political music typically arrives as a direct reaction to daunting political times, but that in Thatcher, Morrissey benefited from having someone as obstinate and unforgiving as himself to rail against. Yet Brooker also noted their defining difference: that while Thatcher was 'notoriously, almost inhumanly devoid of humour,' Morrissey was 'among the wittiest stars pop has produced.' It was this that helped distinguish the Smiths from almost all of their political peers (Easterhouse included), and nowhere more so than on 'The Queen Is Dead'. If one of Morrissey's most audacious lines was to imagine a cross-dressing Prince Charles on the cover of the *Daily Mail*, it was outdone by the verse in which, replicating an incident from 1982, Morrissey's character breaks into Buckingham Palace – with the incongruous combination of 'a sponge and a rusty spanner' – to confront the queen.[6] 'Eh, I know you, and you cannot sing,' he quotes the monarch as saying (a clever touch by which Morrissey the songwriter acknowledges and promotes his infamy), to which he responds, 'That's nothing, you should hear me play piano.' One almost expects to hear the familiar cymbal-crashing acknowledgement of a punch line.

If it was ultimately true that 'The Queen Is Dead' did not match the political fury of the Smiths' punk rock predecessors such as the Sex Pistols' 'God Save the Queen', it was partly because it was too witty for that, too clever, too poetic. Wisely, Stephen Street recommended editing (rather than fading out) the final recording; by removing just over a minute of the group's outro jam, he saved it from overkill and ensured that the opening track to the Smiths' third album would set the highest of possible standards for the rest of the record to (hopefully) follow.

WITH THIS, THE album should have been finished. But Street had been experimenting with digital recording on *The Queen Is Dead*, and when it came time to mix 'Frankly, Mr Shankly', he discovered 'a huge dropout' on the tape, which the machine manufacturer, tape manufacturer and studio all blamed on one another.[7] 'Ultimately, we had to re-record the whole song. And getting the enthusiasm from everyone all over again was not easy.' The last to record his part, as always, was Morrissey, which rendered it somewhat ironic that when time ran out at Jacob's, Johnny Marr chose to do the vocals with John Porter instead. The guitarist and the former Smiths producer had maintained their friendship over the past year and a half; specifically, as the process of recording *The Queen Is Dead*

477

exacted a steadily increasing toll on Marr, the youth had come to rely on his elder for advice. Porter recorded Morrissey's vocals, a perfectly fine performance that verified the producer's own professionalism, at Wessex Studios, where the singer threw in a parting shot at the Shankly/Travis character as the group hit its final chord, growling, 'Give us yer money.'

It was a subject evidently on everyone's minds, for Porter and Marr then recorded a track the guitarist had been working up at home, built around a mid-tempo blues-based riff that paid slight homage to 'How Soon Is Now?'. 'Morrissey didn't want to sign onto it,' recalled Porter, and with the rhythm section not present for the Wessex session, Joyce's parts were played by LinnDrums, a poor imitation for the human spirit. The instrumental was subsequently credited to Marr only, saved for a future Smiths B-side, and entitled 'Money Changes Everything'.

Precisely. *The Queen Is Dead* was now complete, but its release was not yet sanctioned – not on Rough Trade, and not even *to* Rough Trade. On 20 December, the label was granted an injunction requiring that the master tapes be delivered at last – to its solicitors. The injunction was delivered personally on Morrissey.

CHAPTER THIRTY-TWO

There is a *lot* of worth in the Eighties. This generation is very honourable and valorous and quite a
brave generation, certainly compared to the decadence
of the late Sixties.
    – JOHNNY MARR, *Melody Maker*, August 1985

The new year of 1986 saw the launch of a new British political movement: Red Wedge, spearheaded by Billy Bragg to coalesce the era's left-wing musicians. Identifying the enemy was easy: Thatcherism. Figuring out an alternative to support and promote was that much harder: many musicians were inherently wary of aligning themselves with a Labour Party that had proven tragically out of touch with changes in the nation's working class and its youth, a disconnect widely blamed for the ease with which Thatcher had been reelected in 1983. Bragg believed in being more proactive than that, and formed a tentative liaison between Red Wedge and Labour, which appeared to have been reinvigorated under the new leadership of Neil Kinnock, in the hopes of influencing policy. 'All of us, myself included, were learning how to do politics as we went along,' said Bragg. 'Our first impulse was to get out there and bring people together and try and focus people's anger and solidarity, as we'd done in the miners' strike.' A nationwide Red Wedge tour in early 1986 served, then, as something of a travelling left-wing Live Aid, an attempt to present a united front of high-profile musical voices to the people in the midst of what Bragg's last minor hit had rather forlornly labelled 'Days Like These'. The tour was anchored by Bragg, the Style Council, the Communards (featuring Jimi Somerville, recently split from Bronski Beat), soul singer Junior Giscombe, reggae singer Lorna Gee and, as DJ, the Specials' gap-toothed songwriter Jerry Dammers. Lloyd Cole, Tom Robinson, Madness, and Prefab Sprout all performed along the way.

Bragg was understandably keen to get the Smiths involved too, and was thrilled when Johnny Marr and Andy Rourke joined him onstage in Manchester on 25 January for one of his songs ('A Lover Sings'), one of theirs ('Back to the Old House') and one by the Rolling Stones ('The Last Time'). 'Johnny was the one I always thought understood the sociopolitical role of what we were doing,' said Bragg. 'He didn't see it as just being in the Smiths, he saw it as being in the Smiths *during the miners' strike*, or during the years of Margaret Thatcher.'

Marr and Rourke travelled on with the tour to Birmingham, after which show the guitarist called up Morrissey and Joyce and begged them to drive up to Newcastle, where the four-piece Smiths duly appeared, unannounced, performing four songs on the Style Council's equipment, and stealing the show.[1] After that, they went home. They had expressed their solidarity, though subsequently they confessed to some ambivalence. For Marr, 'The Red Wedge gig at Newcastle City Hall was one of the best things we ever did,' though not necessarily for political reasons. 'The atmosphere around the other bands on that tour was really shitty. They treated me and Andy pretty scrappily.' The arrival of Morrissey and Joyce therefore became a case of '*my* mates showed up and shut everybody up. I always felt very proud of us when there were other bands knocking about because I felt that we were the best.' Morrissey, meanwhile, confessed, 'I wasn't terribly impassioned by the gesture.' His cynicism regarding party politics was confirmed when he followed up by saying, 'I can't really see anything especially useful in Neil Kinnock. I don't feel any alliance with him, but if one must vote, this is where I feel the black X should go.'

A week later, the Smiths played another political benefit, alongside New Order, the Fall and John Cooper Clarke, on behalf of the beleaguered Liverpool City Council; its youthful, outspoken, confrontational and persistently well-dressed Marxist-Trotskyite deputy leader Derek Hatton had developed a profile to rival that of the Greater London Council's leader, Ken Livingstone, and was facing similar obliteration. (The GLC had just been abolished by Act of Parliament.) The concert at the Liverpool Royal Court, titled 'From Manchester with Love', was organised by Tony Wilson as an important gesture of friendship and unity from one rival city to another in the face of their common enemy. As Marr pointed out to Martin Aston in 2011, 'By definition, if you were an indie group, you were against the government. And if you had a voice, you had to shout up for your own generation.' On this occasion, the Smiths played a full set, introducing several songs from *The Queen Is Dead* for the first time, but again, they came away disenchanted: Hatton and his cronies had demanded that the bands join them for a grandstanding finale, and the Smiths had resisted, forcefully. ('Nobody tells me when and what to play,' said Marr.) Via their music, and their mouthpiece Morrissey, the Smiths would continue to take a political position, but as perennial outsiders, they would shirk other benefits and causes until the very end of their career.[2]

Marr had additional motives for taking Rourke on the Red Wedge dates: to 'keep an eye on him.' Rourke's drug problem, it turned out, had been getting steadily worse over the course of the Smiths' success: as the bass player succinctly put it, 'I got money, so my heroin addiction got bigger.' By the point of recording *The Queen Is Dead*, it was a problem that should no longer have been ignored – except that the group had no manager to attend to such issues; Rourke's best friend, Johnny Marr, was becoming sick through overwork and poor sustenance himself; and his other ally, Mike Joyce, felt unable to discuss the issue. ('You want your mate to be all right,' said Joyce, 'but you don't know the right steps to take.')

Morrissey, as far as these three were concerned, knew nothing about Rourke's habit – in part because the bass player did such a good job of keeping it hidden, but also because the singer rarely socialised with the rhythm section. In his widely circulated *Time Out* interview earlier in 1985, Morrissey had declared, 'I'm not a rock 'n' roll character. I despise drugs, I despise cigarettes, I'm celibate and I live a very serene lifestyle.' Many Morrissey fans took this as a manifesto of sorts, against which the other Smiths' affinity for alcohol, cannabis/marijuana, and casual indulgence of other substances was always going to look like a contradiction. (Morrissey's own fondness for a drink somehow escaped inspection.) For a member of the Smiths to use heroin would have been perceived by Morrissey as a betrayal of his audience's trust – and would likely have endangered the group's respect within the musical community, where the drug was so frowned upon that the band New Model Army had taken to wearing T-shirts emblazoned with ONLY STUPID BASTARDS USE HEROIN. In fact, the scourge of heroin among British youth was such that the health authorities had taken to placing full-page ads in the music papers detailing the drug's adverse effects. The previous spring, during the *Melody Maker* trial-by-fanzine editors, Morrissey was asked specifically if he would be 'taking part' in 'the anti-heroin crusade in pop.' He responded that he had officially declined. 'I think people get into drugs simply because they want to,' he declared. 'I don't believe people who say "I'm trapped, I can't stop this." It's a lot of bosh really.'

If Rourke had read that piece, he would surely have wished he could have explained to Morrissey that it was not as simple as that. 'I had this monkey on my back and I wanted to shake it off,' he said. 'I wanted rid of it.' During the recording of *The Queen Is Dead*, in deepest suburban Surrey, he tried going cold turkey. 'At some points I hadn't slept for nearly two weeks, because

I was withdrawing from heroin. I couldn't sleep. The only thing that saved me was going in the studio and playing these songs.' Ironically, he delivered some of his best performances during this period: neither 'The Queen Is Dead' nor 'Cemetry Gates' would have sounded anything so effective without his contribution. 'When Andy was required to be in the studio he was fantastic, and his bass playing on that record was brilliant,' said Stephen Street, who was able to look back and conclude, 'If he was on [heroin], I was completely oblivious to it.'

'I couldn't tell anybody about it,' said Rourke. 'OK, I'm sure the rest of the band members knew. But I didn't complain. I couldn't say, "I'm going cold turkey here, I'm withdrawing." I had to suffer in silence.' He did well enough that Morrissey as well as Street remained unaware of his addiction; Marr and Joyce, who knew about it, remained unsure how to deal with it. After all, said Marr, 'he took care of business. He never goofed off. He never let me down. So my opinion of his lifestyle was just my opinion.' Or, as John Featherstone, a self-confessed 'control freak' who eschewed hard drugs, put it, 'With all the best intentions but in hindsight with poor execution, everyone validated it by ignoring it.'

And so it continued. At times during *The Queen Is Dead* sessions when the call proved too powerful, Rourke would take the shuttle from Heathrow to Manchester, the one place he knew where to score, spend £200 or so on heroin, and fly back again the same day. As the New Year dawned, and with *The Queen Is Dead* held up in litigation, the typically hectic work schedule by which Rourke was saved from his own worst enemy – himself – was found lacking. Hence Marr's invitation to come on the Red Wedge tour, a period that Rourke could only recall as 'a really low point in my life.'

It was about to get lower. The Smiths had lined up three shows in Ireland. Rourke, unwilling to take heroin into another country and determined not to score once there, visited a Harley Street doctor, who loaded the bass player up with valium and sleeping pills. The problem, said Rourke, 'was that I'd take a load of valium to ease the withdrawals from the heroin, and then I'd get so wasted on the valium that I'd forget I'd taken the valium and I'd take some more, and then I'd go onstage.' By his own admission, by the time he played at the Dublin National Stadium on 10 February, only forty-eight hours after the Liverpool show, he was 'wobbly.'

Much was subsequently made about Rourke's performance that night. To the extent that he was below par, he was not cited as such in reviews. The group played its full set, including two encores, and the crowd reacted much as would be expected for an honorary Irish band. But it was not their best show. There was one specific mishap, when Rourke played 'Cemetry Gates' (only its second public airing) a full tone higher than it had been recorded, creating such confusion that Johnny Marr stopped playing until he could figure out the problem and adjust his capo accordingly. The explanation was relatively simple: ever since the early days when the band had tuned up to accommodate Morrissey's vocal range, Rourke typically had two basses on hand, one in concert E, one in F-sharp. In Dublin, Rourke was sufficiently with it to play 'Cemetry Gates' note for note; he was sufficiently out of it not to notice that he was using the wrong guitar. There was an additional delay after 'What She Said', at which Marr resorted to playing the song 'Walk Away Renée' on guitar to keep the crowd entertained. Then there was something of a backstage postmortem at which Rourke was well and truly blamed for the mistakes. The following two nights' Irish concerts – one a hotel ballroom in Dundalk, the other a major headliner in Belfast – were completed successfully; the latter show was, without question, magnificent. In fact, tour manager Stuart James said that he was 'oblivious all the way through' to Rourke's habit. 'They all used to have a smoke. Maybe I just thought he was stoned. But certainly not on heroin. He looked fine. He was eating OK.' Regarding the mishaps in Dublin, and the subsequent reaction, 'I was thinking "Bloody hell, that's a bit tight, considering the amount of shows we've done."'

James's comments only served to confirm the extent to

which the Smiths were extraordinarily self-contained in their decision-making process, and the extent to which they kept secrets even from other members of their inner circle – not just Stuart James but Stephen Street, for example. Nonetheless, with Morrissey now aware of Rourke's habit, the bassist was summarily fired on the group's return to Manchester. He discovered as much, he said, when he found a note on his car outside his new home in Altrincham. 'I woke up and there was what I thought was a parking ticket. But my car was parked in the driveway. There was an envelope with a postcard from Morrissey. It said, "Andy, you have left the Smiths. Good luck and good bye."' He never found out who placed it there: Morrissey, he said, 'wouldn't have had the balls.' That night, he recalled, he went over to visit Johnny Marr, his best friend and his talisman, 'and cried in his arms.'

THE DECISION TO fire Rourke had been executed callously by Morrissey. But it had not been taken lightly by the others. If carrying Rourke around the world with his addiction had not worked to cure it, the hope was that by dropping him – by expelling him from the one thing that he needed more than the drug – he would be jolted into sobriety. Precisely the opposite happened. Barely two weeks after being thrown out of the Smiths, Rourke drove to Oldham to make a purchase of heroin. Fortunately – as it turned out – his dealer was under surveillance: 'the doors went down, twenty policemen came in,' Rourke recalled, and he was arrested for possession. The news travelled, via *News at Ten* and *Granada Reports* (though oddly, not via the music press), as far as Majorca, and the public shame of being busted for hard drugs and the threat of jail time proved effective where the quiet ejection from his band had not: it was enough to convince Rourke to get clean.

It appeared, however, that he was too late. Johnny Marr briefly hosted Andy Rourke at his house during this period as his friend, but as the band's musical director he was determined that the Smiths would not slow down. Despite the fact that the release of *The Queen Is Dead* remained in legal limbo, the group was pressing forward with the understanding that the situation would have to be resolved sooner rather than later. Plans were already afoot to return to America, and for a much longer tour this time. Marr got on with the process of hiring a new bass player.

He didn't look far. Si Wolstencroft told him about Craig Gannon, a Salford boy with whom he had just completed a tour as part of the Colourfield. Gannon was all of nineteen years old, a talented prodigy along the lines of Marr himself at that age. He was as diffident as Steven Morrissey had been at that age. He wore a quiff better than most of the Smiths. Prior to the Colourfield, he had been in Aztec Camera, with whom he had toured large venues in the States, opening for Elvis Costello, and had also played with the Bluebells, who had enjoyed a top 10 hit in 1984 with 'Young at Heart'. His guitar-playing credentials were, evidently, impeccable. Marr invited Gannon over to Marlborough Road for an evening, where they talked about their various professional experiences and mutual respect for Roddy Frame.[3] Gannon, as a young professional touring musician, had heard little of the Smiths other than what he had caught on the radio, and did not, prior to listening to *The Queen Is Dead* tapes in Marr's home studio, consider himself a fan. Marr ended the evening by explaining that they were letting Andy Rourke leave due to 'problems,' and that Gannon was welcome to join the band – as bass player.

This would have made sense – but for the fact that Gannon had, by his own admission, 'never played the bass.' Whether Marr had seriously considered the implications of this invitation or merely acted on a whim would prove hard to ascertain; the circumstances surrounding Gannon's inclusion into the Smiths were to shift over time. Gannon recalled that at this point he neither accepted nor declined the offer, though he stayed over for drinks, and once Mike Joyce came over to join them, he and Marr got the guitars out finally and found that their playing styles were compatible. They left it that they would get together again soon, and the call duly came for Gannon to join Marr, Joyce and driver Phil Powell for a meeting with Morrissey, at his new flat in London. He did so, and the process proved remarkably smooth. 'I got on with Morrissey really well, got on with everyone, got back in the car, and Johnny said, "That's it, you're a Smith. As much a Smith as me, Mike and Morrissey."' The crew then booked into the Portobello Hotel in London's Notting Hill for a few days to get to know one another better. Gannon still hadn't been auditioned.[4]

IN 1895, THE Cadogan Hotel on Sloane Street had served as the scene for Oscar Wilde's arrest on charges of 'gross indecency' after his libel case against the Marquess of Queensbury broke down. It may have been pure coincidence that Morrissey chose Cadogan Square, just around the corner, as his new London address, but it added a certain cachet to his credentials once Morrissey realised that he desperately needed – in a very fundamental sense, and despite Marr's stated fondness for their northern roots – a residence that validated his reputation. Just as with his previous London home on Campden Hill Road, his fashionable new address in the heart of Chelsea was soon to play host to interviewers – though this time only for the more favoured of journalists. 'If I couldn't have really beautiful furniture I'd sleep in a shoebox,' he told one as he showed him around.

As revealed by this comment, and by the address itself (and by the fact that the Cheshire house with his mother remained very much intact), Morrissey was hardly hurting for money. But that did not mean he was willing to give up the fight with Rough Trade. The label's successful injunction indicated that the recording contract had held up to initial legal inspection; Geoff Travis recalled, 'The lawyers were quite proud of it when it was eventually waved around in court.' But given its multiple scribbles and lack of specificity, it was always possible that a further challenge would find in the Smiths' favour, and Rough Trade could ill afford such a conclusion. The company had even drawn up an in-house study, 'The Effects on Rough Trade and the Cartel of Ending Our Relationship with the Smiths', which only confirmed what everyone already knew: that the band's departure would be catastrophic, not merely to the Rough Trade label but to the entire independent distribution network, which had come to rely on the group's constant (though modest) hit singles to sell other independent records into the high-street chains.

Somewhere down the line, in a fit of intoxicated late-night frustration, Johnny Marr had decided that he would retrieve the tapes on behalf of the group. He and Phil Powell set off from Bowdon in the early hours of a harsh wintry morning, and made it to Jacob's around music-business breakfast time; Powell stayed in the driver's seat with the engine running, and Marr went in search of the tape cupboard. He was confronted by a bemused studio manager, who had no intention of releasing the tapes until they were fully paid for. Marr and Powell drove the two hundred miles north somewhat chastened by their own false optimism.

Desperate to break the legal deadlock, Morrissey and Marr turned once more to Matthew Sztumpf. The Madness manager had been left in the lurch after the previous year's American tour, but at least he had been paid for it, and, aware that the group had not hired anyone else in his absence, he agreed to address the Rough Trade situation with a firm view to keeping the managerial job this time. Under pressure from Morrissey, he even agreed to move his management business away from Madness's own offices and into a neutral space. The group could have used Sztumpf to additionally address Andy Rourke's problems, securing him some professional medical help, and also to suggest how to approach Rourke's replacement, especially with regard to payment. But the Smiths viewed internal band issues as just that, and appeared to entrust Sztumpf with little more than negotiating their way out of the Rough Trade mess.

There was, in reality, little to negotiate. Rough Trade was not set up to pay royalties on anything other than a profit share, which benefited the Smiths over a fixed royalty anyway. The list of acceptable 'costs' could certainly be better defined, and more upfront money secured for the Smiths as per a traditional contract, but that was about it. Ultimately, the most important issue for Morrissey and Marr was the term itself, which currently ran to five studio albums, of which the Smiths had completed only three. A standoff ensued, but Rough Trade blinked first, and agreed to shorten the contract by one album. With that, each side could declare victory and move forward.

While the exhausting, months-long process was officially handled by the lawyers and managers, Jo Slee had maintained unofficial contact with Morrissey throughout: 'I'd tell him where we were up to on our side, and he would tell me about where they were up to on theirs.' When the Smiths' lawyer continued to 'raise further objections,' which Rough Trade considered 'a smokescreen,' it became apparent that if an agreement were not finalised now, the album might have been put back until *after* the summer. 'I phoned Morrissey and told him about the further objections and he said that he appreciated all we had done and that my calls had helped keep him sane in the bad times,' Slee told Neil Taylor in *Document and Eyewitness*. 'We all went home and about 11 o'clock that night Morrissey rang back very angry and very determined: "Please can someone . . . bring the contract over tomorrow morning and we'll sign."'

Geoff Travis was in America at the time. Peter Walmsley, head of licensing, brought the contract over instead. 'It was probably the first time Morrissey had properly acknowledged me,' Walmsley told Taylor. 'The whole thing had been a silly argument. It was not only soul-destroying but it put the whole company at risk.'

From Rough Trade's positive spin on the proceedings, they still had the Smiths, and for two more albums, of which they already knew *The Queen Is Dead* to be a classic. It was time to get to work. Although Geoff Travis hoped for 'There Is a Light That Never Goes Out' as a single (it had been announced as such on the Irish tour), Marr pushed equally hard for 'Bigmouth Strikes Again', not merely because it was the original choice back in the autumn but because it sent a stronger, more authoritative musical message. As ever, the Smiths won the fight, and what was surely their most commercial song was to remain forever 'buried' on an album. (Then again, the 'failure' to release what might well have become their biggest-ever hit prevented them from the perception of 'selling out' and perhaps losing their hard-core following as a result.)

One thing was certain – that after just one more studio album, the Smiths would be free from their commitment to Rough Trade. The call finally came in to David Munns at EMI: Morrissey is ready to talk.

SHORTLY AFTER HIS drug bust, a decision was made to reinstate Andy Rourke. As Morrissey put it, with no acknowledgement of how he had fired the bass player, 'his leaving seemed more wrong than his staying.'⁵ There was no absolute guarantee that Rourke had or could wean himself off heroin, and he had not gone into any sort of clinic to do so. (Rather, he had just 'gone abroad' for a couple of weeks.) But there did appear to finally be willpower, which, combined with the existing *desire* to quit, was partially good reason to welcome him back. There was also the very genuine fear of what might happen to Rourke if they continued to abandon him to his own vices; after his arrest, none of them wanted the next news item about their 'former' bassist to be that of a fatal overdose, with all the attendant guilt it would bring. (The fact that Rourke did not inject heroin but smoked it made such a catastrophic scenario unlikely for the time being, but a descent into needles and true junkie status had to be considered a very real possibility.) Most important, though, they simply couldn't imagine the

Smiths with another bass player; Rourke may have been the quietest member, he may have been the most subservient, but his contributions had proven absolutely imperative to the group's success. And in so many ways, he had served as the group's rock and its soul, emotional terms that double as musical genres, and understandably so.

A news item in the April 19 edition of *Melody Maker* belatedly announcing Rourke's departure 'after their recent tour of Ireland' (which had taken place two full months earlier), noted, 'No explanation for his decision was offered by Rough Trade' and that 'Rourke's replacement is Craig Gannon, a session musician who has formerly played with Aztec Camera.' In the typical fashion of British music press gossip, enough aspects of this statement were accurate for the false ones to be taken as truth too. The fact was that by the time this item hit the papers, Rourke had already been reinstated and Gannon hired as a second guitarist instead; the public statement in *Melody Maker* that Gannon was to play bass might explain why it has become perceived fact that he was only offered the role of second guitarist as some sort of consolation prize. It was true that Marr had initially approached Gannon as a bassist, but by the time of the meeting with Morrissey in London, Gannon was absolutely certain that he was being considered as a guitarist instead – the only role that would make sense for him – and that when he attended his first rehearsal with the group, at Mike Joyce's house in Altrincham, it was with guitar in hand, especially as he didn't own a bass. Johnny Marr himself stated, only that summer, 'It was when we got back from [Ireland] that I realised I wanted to get another guitar player in,' which would suggest that he did not hire Gannon for that role as a mere after-thought. And certainly the Smiths were far too mercurial, and Morrissey far too focused on finances, to offer anyone an equal share of anything (including the limelight) based on the idea of it being some sort of consolation prize.

In reality, *The Queen Is Dead* was more musically complex than the albums that preceded it, and it was becoming increasingly difficult for Marr to emulate all his various parts onstage; in fact, as a result of his focus on the complex arrangements, his guitar often sounded quieter in concert than audiences might have expected. Marr, of course, was much loved for this finesse, but the thought of being able to bounce off of a second guitarist, to flesh out the live sound without simply relying on volume, had certainly become an appealing one.

But the decision was not properly thought through. How was Gannon to fit in, for example, onstage, where the Smiths had always been perfectly symmetrical? And as a supposed fifth member, how was he to be paid? Would Marr and Morrissey reduce their own share of proceeds to 35 per cent each, affording Gannon the same 10 per cent as the rhythm section? Would Rourke and Joyce be asked to take an even lesser share to accommodate him? Or would Gannon be put on a flat wage, like a crew member? Did he need a contract confirming this, and should such a contract clearly express that he had no claim on songwriting? Within weeks of his first rehearsal, Gannon was recording a hit single as a member of the Smiths. Like the rhythm section alongside him, he had no clear idea how he was being recompensed.

EAGER TO MAKE up for lost time and afford *The Queen Is Dead* the maximum possible attention, Rough Trade and its licensees moved into promotional overdrive. To that end, Morrissey and Marr embarked, for the first time, on a visit to America, decamping to Los Angeles for several days with Rough Trade publicist Pat Bellis and current 'manager' Matthew Sztumpf in attendance. Given the group's renewed focus on the States, Sztumpf suggested that they meet with a business friend of his, Ken Friedman.

Friedman was a tall, confident, garrulous, twenty-five-year-old Californian who, like Scott Piering before him, had started out promoting concerts in San Francisco. Specifically, in handling

U2's first show there in 1981, he had befriended that band's manager, Paul McGuinness, who encouraged Friedman to follow a similar path. The spring of 1986 found him the highly successful American representative already for Simple Minds, UB40 and Shriekback. Of these, Simple Minds were far and away the most popular in America, having just launched into the commercial stratosphere with the number 1 American single 'Don't You (Forget About Me)' via its use as theme song for the hit John Hughes movie *The Breakfast Club*. The benefits of a musical tie-in with Hollywood were nothing new, of course, but the mid-1980s represented a moment when the two entertainment industries came to fully recognise the potential of cross-promotion, especially once it became apparent that the thirtysomething writer/director/producer John Hughes had somehow tapped the emotional zeitgeist of the current American teenage generation, or at least the part of it that went to see movies in droves and bought the associated soundtracks.

This relationship was not always welcomed by the fans of bands – like the Smiths – who felt that 'their' music, which was already catching on more rapidly than they might have liked due to exposure on MTV and the increasing popularity of college and new-music radio, was being misappropriated by the mainstream via Hughes's hit films. *The Breakfast Club* offered a good example: a comedy of sorts, it told the story of five disparate high school students who spend the day in detention and ultimately find commonality. The denouement comes when the 'basket case' character (played by Ally Sheedy) – an outsider, dressed in black, wearing baseball boots, certainly the only one of the five who looked like they might have been a fan of the Smiths or similar acts – is given a makeover by the 'princess' character (Molly Ringwald), turning her into a conventionally pretty girl by which she suddenly becomes the object of desire for the 'athlete' (Emilio Estevez). There is a clearly stated assumption that only by conforming like this to accepted mainstream values could the so-called basket case find so-called happiness.

In the wake of *The Breakfast Club's* runaway success, Hughes – a committed music fan – ensured that the soundtracks for his next two movies, *Weird Science* and *Pretty in Pink*, were heavily loaded with appropriately teen-friendly but somewhat left-of-centre New Wave. *Pretty in Pink* was in fact named for a five-year-old song by the Psychedelic Furs, the British post-punk group whose modest success had seemed like a worthy goal for Mike Joyce back when he joined the Smiths. Molly Ringwald assumed the role this time of a poor high school girl, Andie, who works in a hip Chicago record store, Trax. Her best male friend is Duckie (Jon Cryer), himself a witty, alternative, Smiths type of guy, whose long-standing romantic yearning for Andie has always gone unrequited; she favours rich preppy Blane (Andrew McCarthy) instead. Duckie's rejection is demonstrated in a scene where he lies, forlorn, in his rundown bedroom, listening to 'Please, Please, Please Let Me Get What I Want'. (It was not the only major piece of product placement for the band in *Pretty in Pink*; the Smiths were given their own section in the record racks at Trax, with a colour poster of them from 1984 placed prominently on the stockroom door.) There is no denouement, no justice for Duckie: it is still sensitive rich guy Blane who gets together with Andie at the high school prom.[6] To what extent any of the Smiths, especially the avid movie-watcher Morrissey, followed these nuances may never have been asked of them; it was probably enough at the point that Morrissey and Marr landed in Los Angeles, in the spring of 1986, that both the *Pretty in Pink* movie and its soundtrack were riding high in the charts (the latter on its way to a million-plus sales), and that the Smiths were winning new fans without having to do anything for it. Nor were they alone: the *Pretty in Pink* soundtrack, on which 'Please, Please, Please Let Me Get What I Want' served as the final song, additionally included New Order and Echo & the Bunnymen as well as the Psychedelic Furs. Their scene was bursting wide open.

Sztumpf called on Friedman with the view that perhaps the American could represent the Smiths in the States while

Sztumpf concentrated on the European side of their business. Friedman, with the American industry very much at his fingertips, had every reason to be intrigued by the highly credible (and teasingly commercial) possible addition to his roster. 'I wasn't like a groupie,' he recalled of his exposure to the Smiths at this point. 'I didn't know every song. I knew enough to know that they could have been huge. I knew the Smiths had that same formula that every great rock group has. That Peter Buck and Michael Stipe had, and Mick and Keith. It's the faggy poetic lead singer and the cigarette-smoking, drug-taking, model-shagging guitar player. I thought, "These guys have that formula but they're both so over the top." Johnny believes everything he reads about the Stones and the Who and Eric Clapton so he takes as many drugs as he reckons all these guys did. And Morrissey is the master manipulator of the press: he's gay but he says he's celibate, he takes it even further than Mick Jagger did, or Freddie Mercury. So I knew these guys were going to be huge – and in LA, they already were huge.'

Friedman and Marr shared similar personalities, and it was no surprise that they immediately hit it off, the former taking the latter on a tour of the musical landmarks of the city's famed Laurel Canyon singer-songwriter scene. Marr then suggested Friedman meet with Morrissey, too, and after sharing an introductory drink at the hotel bar, those two went off on their own cultural tour of the city, this one taking in the famed Duck Soup bookstore and various Hollywood stars' residences. Friedman got on well with Morrissey, too: 'The fact that I wasn't obsessed with him helped. Once he opened up, the campier he got, the more he wanted to know about old Hollywood, specifically Gloria Swanson and Marilyn Monroe. It was all divas.' By the end of the visit, Friedman was being touted as manager.

'Ken was a big thinker and an ambitious person,' said Marr. 'And saw that we could be big in the States, without a doubt. And he had some success, and he was young, too, and he was kind of maverick, and he was a very charming guy.'

Shortly after returning to the UK, Matthew Sztumpf was let go. ('I wasn't there long enough for royalties to be commissioned,' he told Johnny Rogan, 'so I just billed them for my services. I'd fulfilled my purpose, but they paid me, and I enjoyed it while it lasted.') Marr claimed that Sztumpf's firing was not his decision. 'I really liked Matthew. I remember being really embarrassed, it being really awkward. This mild-mannered guy was really unhappy about it. He came to me and demanded "Why?" And I just said, "I can't tell you." I didn't know he was going to be hired and I didn't know he was going to be fired.' If Marr was becoming increasingly frustrated by his partner's capricious business decisions, he was still not willing to stand up to him on them – but in Ken Friedman, he now saw the potential for someone who could properly assume the difficult role of Smiths manager, and he intended to pursue this one to fruition.

CHAPTER THIRTY-THREE

This image of a typical Smiths fanatic being a creased and semi-crippled youth is s-l-i-g-h-t-l-y over-stretched . . . it's not really true at all. Smiths concerts are really quite violent things – we even have people breaking their legs and backs. If the audience was a collection of withering prunes those things wouldn't happen.

– Morrissey, *i-D*, October 1987

Time away from the public eye turned out to be the best thing possible for the Smiths. While a constant presence is always a good thing for a *new* band, a substantial break indicates a major group's confidence that it is no longer only as good as its last hit, but as good now as its long-term reputation. And for all the fuss about hit singles and lack thereof, the Smiths' reputation was still very much intact, as proven by the emphatic manner in which they ran away with the *NME* Readers' Poll (Britain's most prestigious) for 1985. Some fifteen months after appearing on the *Oxford Road Show*, the Smiths' return to the live TV studio on the BBC's *Whistle Test* on 24 May 1986, promoting their first single release in eight months and additionally unveiling the Smiths as a five-piece, served as the very definition of the term 'eagerly awaited'.

In its own way, their performance that night of 'Bigmouth Strikes Again' (and, later in the show, 'Vicar in a Tutu') proved as powerful as that of 'This Charming Man' on *Top of the Pops* in 1983, when a young Noel Gallagher had watched Johnny Marr and had his future decided for him by the experience.

This time around, it was the turn of Andy Bell, who would join Gallagher in Oasis after many years in his own band, Ride, and Bernard Butler, who would co-lead the very Smiths-influenced group Suede. Butler videotaped the performance that night and watched it relentlessly, studying Marr's technique in particular: 'So many people thrash on the guitar, but his wrist is moving really gently,' he noted of how Marr tamed the typically masculine Gibson Les Paul guitar while Gannon, sandwiched between Rourke and Morrissey, fleshed out the sound on Marr's Rickenbacker. All five members, even Mike Joyce, sported the casual rocker uniform of jackets and blue jeans, though Morrissey, with a tie done up to his collar and the hearing aid reaffixed to his left ear had more the air of an overgrown schoolboy – until he began moving, at which point he came across as the consummate performer his fans knew him to be. Lights poured down on the group from every direction but in front. In all regards, the Smiths looked and sounded more like a major rock band than ever before. And, depending on perspective, they looked and sounded better for it too.

Confidence in the new lineup had already been instilled at a long-overdue recording session earlier in the month, for which John Porter had returned as producer. This decision came as a shock and a disappointment at the time to Stephen Street, who knew he had just made a brilliant album with the band and could only conclude that maybe he was 'slightly more Morrissey's choice than Johnny's choice to make records with.' Marr had been pleased with Porter's work finishing off 'Frankly, Mr Shankly' on short notice, and the pair had been working together again that spring on the new Billy Bragg album, Marr's most serious bout of 'moonlighting' to date, although not anything that Morrissey appeared to mind. (When Marr played his set piece 'Walk Away Renée' in the studio, Bragg begged to record it and, rather than sing a cover version, wrote a spoken-word treatise that night about a youthful infatuation that finally ended when 'she cut her hair and I stopped loving her.' It was a line that bore all the hallmarks of a Morrissey classic and would be remembered as one of Bragg's finest lyrics.) But whether stated or not, the decision best reflected the understanding that while Street was an outstanding engineer who had enabled the Smiths to make the grade as an albums act, Porter was a phenomenal producer who had delivered them five UK top 30 singles in a row, and their most requested songs in America. This was no small matter given that they wanted to concentrate on their most emphatic and potentially commercial anthem to date.

The chord structure for that song, 'Panic', was lifted right off of 'Metal Guru', the T. Rex single so beloved by Marr and Morrissey upon its release in 1972, back when John Porter was highly present on the glam scene himself as part of Roxy Music. The words, as always, had come together later in the day. Specifically, they were influenced by the events surrounding the Chernobyl disaster of 26 April, when a Russian nuclear reactor had exploded and caught fire, and in typically secretive Soviet fashion, news of the catastrophe had been muzzled until a radioactive cloud caused alarm bells to ring, quite literally, at a nuclear plant in Sweden, 1,100 kilometres away, two days later. Smiths legend had it that when Morrissey and Marr first heard Radio 1 report on the disaster, at the latter's house (presumably on 28 April), the DJ Steve Wright followed up immediately with 'I'm Your Man' by Wham!, a choice so blatantly incongruous that Morrissey finally had lyrical motivation for a song title he'd been kicking around for months. The anecdote might well be true, though 'I'm Your Man' had been off the charts for several months already, and Morrissey hardly needed further provocation to attack Wright, whose highly ranked afternoon show treated *all* popular music as secondary to his madcap party format. (Scott Piering had reported, a year earlier, that both Wright and his producer 'have openly expressed dislike of the Smiths in general.') What really mattered about this anecdote was that Smiths fans had a backstory to a song that conjured up the image of an unnamed crisis unfolding through a roll call of British cities: London, Birmingham, Leeds,

Carlisle, and later the rhythmic tumble of 'Dublin, Dundee, Humberside.' In fact, only when he came up with the solution – 'Burn down the disco/hang the blessed DJ' – did Morrissey appear to clarify the problem: that 'the music they constantly play says nothing to me about my life.' From there it was obvious that he had found his hook and he hung the remainder of the song on it: 'Hang the DJ,' repeated almost ad infinitum. It was *Margaret on the Guillotine* in half as many syllables, and just as powerful.

'Panic' came together with great ease in the studio. Despite Porter recalling that Gannon 'diplomatically stayed out of the way,' the teenager nonetheless played some of the key riffs on the recording. That was true too of the B-side, 'The Draize Train' – the third (and, it would turn out, final) Smiths instrumental, for which Morrissey declined to write words because 'I thought it was the weakest thing Johnny had ever done.' John Porter had always noted that his main creative contention with the Smiths singer was their markedly differing opinions of American black music, rhythm & blues in particular, and if it therefore offended Porter to produce a song that called to burn down the disco, he (and Marr?) may quietly have sought satisfaction in recording a bonus B-side that presaged the shifting mood on many an underground British dance floor. At the Haçienda, Mike Pickering's Friday night residency, 'Nude', now prominently featured an American variation on disco, 'house music', which had begun to make its presence felt with a new generation of Thatcher's bastard children who felt that rock music said nothing to them about *their* lives. 'The Draize Train' was vari-speeded upward to precisely the same tempo as this early house music – 120 beats per minute – and alongside its various synthetic keyboard sounds that appeared to render this more than mere coincidence, initially included an additional pulse that could have made it a genuine contender for the Haçienda dance floor. Curiously, this effect was ultimately jettisoned for an entirely different sound, one that was equally close to its composer's heart and much more pervasive in the mainstream at the time, that of electric guitar 'noodling' – as close as Marr had yet come to filling out the vocal-free spaces in a Smiths composition with solos.

THE FIRST MEETING between Morrissey and EMI's David Munns took place on 'a Sunday afternoon for tea at a very out-of-the-way little country hotel in Oxfordshire somewhere,' recalled Munns. The pair had spoken on the phone briefly a couple of times by now, and enough negotiating had taken place with Alexis Grower for Munns to know that EMI was in the lead for the group's signature. Morrissey and Marr were impressed both by EMI's financial offer (in the mid-six-figure range per album, though for a major label 'it wasn't an incredible amount of money,' said Munns) and also their degree of commitment, which was for four albums, 'firm.' This was one more even than Rough Trade had built into their contract and represented an enormous degree of faith on EMI's behalf in the Smiths' long-term commercial viability: 'No one had ever signed an act for four albums firm before,' said Munns. It also raised precisely the same problem the band had had with its current label – that they would be locked into a long-term deal even if it soured. Nobody seemed to question that aspect.

Certainly, there were some business concerns. Though Geoff Travis had calculated that the 50–50 profit split (75–25 overseas) was equivalent to 'about 21 to 22 per cent royalty,' almost double the standard 12 per cent rate and beyond even that of proven superstars, Munns believed that it came in significantly lower than that, and felt that by offering the Smiths a conventional but consistently high royalty rate, it would prove more beneficial for the band in terms of stability. He could also dangle the assurance that the Smiths would never have to endure Rough Trade's cash-flow problems. 'EMI is a public company,' he was able to tell Morrissey. 'You can audit our accounts. Whatever arguments you may hear about us, there is no question that EMI doesn't have the money to pay your royalties.'

There were aesthetic concerns, too, and for these, Munns brought in A&R man Nick Gatfield, who had recently quit his job as saxophonist with Dexys Midnight Runners, largely in frustration at front man Kevin Rowland's mercurial nature. As a musician, Gatfield could communicate with Morrissey and Marr in a manner that Munns could not, though Gatfield recognised immediately, from his own experience, the delicate nature of the various relationships. The Smiths 'were obviously the most important band in the country at the time,' he said. 'They were the darlings of the indie scene; the idea of coming to a major was not something I would consider an easy sell, though I think they recognised at the time that their career opportunities might have peaked at Rough Trade and that they needed to be on a bigger platform. That was the premise, and we were very careful about how we couched that, because for Morrissey, particularly, it wasn't necessarily about cash, it wasn't necessarily about worldwide support. He wanted to be left alone, and I think he had that luxury at Rough Trade. Johnny, on the other hand, was a more commercial animal, just a much more approachable character. You could take him down the pub and have a drink, have a bit of a laugh. Be much more upfront in regard to where we could go, what we could do with the project.' Marr's conviviality was interpreted by Gatfield as him having 'bigger aspirations of rock stardom than Morrissey did.'

'To be fair,' said Marr years later, 'you get excited about the prospect that "OK, now we can go and be on the same label as the Beatles." We were seduced, and a lot of it was just wanderlust. It wasn't thought through, it wasn't personal, it wasn't sinister, it was almost like a novelty. It certainly wasn't for the money.' For Morrissey, however, and despite Gatfield's belief, money had almost everything to do with it. 'We have to move to EMI for financial reasons,' he insisted just a few months later. 'It's not that we want *more*, but just that we want *some*. We've made lots of records which have done really well and we've never seen any money for them. And we've never *ever* made a penny on tours which have always been really successful.' This plea of poverty seemed somewhat at odds with Morrissey's multiple residences, and the general air of wealth that surrounded the Smiths as a thriving business enterprise.[1] All the same, 'Most of our focus was on wooing Morrissey,' said Gatfield, 'as the more difficult one to convince that the move was right.'

That wooing had now paid off, and the conversation came down to, quite literally, the choice of label. Munns ordered up from the pressing plant actual labels of every single imprint within the corporation and sent them to the singer. 'And two days later I heard back: "I want to be on HMV."' One could almost have predicted as much: more than merely the name of a prominent Oxford Street record store, this was the label of 'His Master's Voice', as it had originally become known for using the 'Nipper' image of a dog listening to a nineteenth-century gramophone. When first revamped as a label in 1955, HMV utilised (and therefore authenticated) the word 'POP' as its catalogue number prefix; a year later, HMV released Elvis Presley's first UK single. Morrissey recollected it as the home to Paul Jones, Johnny Leyton, and literally 'hundreds' of other records from the 1960s. The only problem was that HMV was now a classical music label. 'A huge fight ensued, because the classical people went mad,' said Munns. 'I said, "Who cares? Too bad. We're not going to stand in the way of this just because of the guys in the classical division thinking Morrissey is not highbrow enough to be on the HMV label. In the end they would have to climb down." Somehow or other I got to talk to Morrissey and say, "It's fine, you can be on the HMV label. Let's make a deal." And we did.'

'Bigmouth Strikes Again' was not quite the hit that everyone had hoped it would be. Airplay, as always, was something of a problem, the group refused to make a video, and they weren't invited to appear on *Top of the Pops*. In fairness to fans, it was known that the A-side was going to appear on the forthcoming album, and the B-sides were not amongst the Smiths' best; under the circumstances, its top 30 status was something of a reassurance. Of far more importance was reaction to *The Queen Is Dead* upon its release in June, and in this regard, it did not disappoint. The size and positioning of the reviews, not just in the music papers but in the broadsheet newspapers and monthly magazines alike, saw the crowning of the Smiths as Britain's premier rock act. Amongst the enthusiasts was Nick Kent, the rock journalist whose decadent Stones-Dolls chic in the pre-punk music scene had made him an early music press celebrity and earned Morrissey and Marr's approbation as a result, only for him to run afoul of the band when he exposed more than they would have preferred in a cover story for *The Face* the previous year.[2] Clearly harbouring no sore feelings, Kent almost fell over himself in superlatives while reviewing the album for *Melody Maker*: 'This group is the one crucial hope left in evoking a radical restructuring of what pop could – nay, should – essentially be moving towards . . . *The Queen Is Dead*, England in ruins, but here, in the marrow of this extraordinary music, something precious and innately honourable flourishes.'

He was right. Debut album *The Smiths* had delivered a number of great songs not necessarily performed or produced to the best of their ability, and without a natural shape or substance. *Meat Is Murder* had corrected these errors and succeeded in its mission to declare the band's political and musical independence, but to a fault; its lack of accompanying hit singles would ultimately affect its long-term reputation. By comparison, *The Queen Is Dead* appeared perfect, a step forward in every aspect, with no accompanying loss of credibility. It offered every available musical mood, every shade of light, and every touch of texture. It was additionally enhanced by its visual presentation: the cover shot of a prostrate Alain Delon from the 1964 French film *L'Insoumis*, while of little instant recognition to the Smiths' audience, subtly summed up the lyrical imagery of various songs, and the particular two-colour combination, a greyish-green for the photograph superimposed with a luscious pink for the type-setting, set a similarly appropriate tone. (The Delon image also harked back to that of another French actor, Jean Morais, on 'This Charming Man' and thereby to the Smiths' original glory.) The simplicity of the back cover – song titles in pink on green – was almost regal. And the use of a gatefold sleeve, the first for a Smiths studio LP, served as an endorsement of the group's importance, their status as a major act.

On one side of the gatefold was printed, as always with a Smiths album, the lyrics; on the other was a band photograph. It had been taken the previous December, exactly a week before the injunction was served on the finished album (and before Gannon joined), by Stephen Wright, a Smiths fan and budding professional who had sent photographs of the group in concert to Rough Trade and been rewarded with this surprise commission. The locations for the shoot included Manchester Victoria Station and the Arndale Centre, but the one that it was to be remembered for took place, at Morrissey's instigation, outside the Salford Lads Club. Eighty years after being established, the club seemed something of an anachronism of a bygone Britain – which was partly why Morrissey had suggested it, of course – and had fallen on hard times; there were those who would view the finished pictures, in which the group posed against iron gates and graffiti-splattered brick walls, and conclude that the Lads Club had gone out of business. The almost comically archetypal cold drizzle on the afternoon of the shoot furthered the atmosphere of northern depression, forcing Johnny Marr, looking haggard from hard work, to huddle into his clothes in an attempt to stay warm. Mike Joyce, meanwhile, cigarette burning at his waist, stared down at Wright's camera with casual intensity while Rourke practised his own artistic habit, one much beloved by rock photographers, of looking slightly askew from the lens. They were a good-looking band, the Smiths, but it was Morrissey who appeared most beautiful that day, and most at ease with proceedings, wearing an expensive cardigan by fashionable designers Body Map and an impenetrably enigmatic expression that Wright later likened to that of the Mona Lisa. Although the Smiths were not themselves Salford boys, the picture nonetheless seemed to sum up everything that Morrissey, in particular, wanted to say about his band in a single northern image – especially as he was afforded the additional bonus of the neighbourhood's Coronation Street signage next to that of the Salford Lads Club. In years to come, after the club initially disavowed any connection with the photograph due to the album's anti-monarchy sentiments, it welcomed the steady stream of Smiths fans as potential allies, eventually establishing a 'Smiths Room' – a shrine in which fans were invited to pin up their own re-creations of the famous photograph and leave written notes as tributes. Among them would be Morrissey's postcard to the photographer: 'A sweeter set of pictures were never taken.'[3]

The Salford Lads Club was not the only organisation to assail the Smiths for *The Queen Is Dead*. The tabloid media rose to the bait and once again accused the Smiths of being 'sick' for their choice of title and lead track. In such a divided Britain as 1986, this served as only greater endorsement for Smiths fans – and other leftists who rallied instinctively to their side. Ironically given its title, the reaction to and success of the album – it made number 2 on the British charts, and stayed around longer than *Meat Is Murder* – would herald what has been widely referred to, including by the Smiths themselves, as their 'imperial' phase.

This was evidenced with the release of the single 'Panic', unveiled to the public on 5 July on a special 'Eurotube' extravaganza, for which the Smiths again braved the live studio performance, and this time in front of an audience. All of them were wearing formal jackets again, Morrissey's clothing considerably more fashionable now than the ladies' blouses and torn jeans of old; Marr and Rourke both wore shades indoors, and the bassist unveiled a new peroxide look. They opened with

'There Is a Light That Never Goes Out', clear recognition of its popularity as an album cut and credibility as a live song, and returned later in the show to announce the campaign to 'Hang the DJ' with the addition of a professional child actor masquerading as an old-fashioned schoolboy in shorts and blazer, wearing a hearing aid and singing along with Morrissey in the chorus.[4] The schoolboy was something of a distraction, but he was not the only one. The group themselves were frequently blocked from the camera lens by young men dancing to the Smiths atop of each other's shoulders. And therein lay the group's new dichotomy: with imperialism comes an army.

It would be simplistic, a lie even, to suggest that the Smiths' audience changed overnight in 1986. Despite the fact that the Smiths' core crowd was presumed to be that of students, loners and depressives, the sexually confused and socially inadequate, still the presence of Johnny Marr as guitar hero (even a decidedly postmodern one) and the s(t)olid sight of the down-to-earth rhythm section, Mike Joyce and Andy Rourke – and to a certain degree, Morrissey's additional persona as someone very attuned to the underbelly of working-class life – ensured that the group had always had a following of what had come to be known, though not exactly in the manner that the Salford Club had originally used it, as 'lads'. One such fan, Stuart Deabill, viewed himself at the time he encountered the Smiths as 'a fully fledged teenage Chelsea casual, going the length and breadth of the country following the team . . . and getting caught up in all that,' meaning the violence that was part of the routine for a lot of young male travelling football fans. Old enough to have been into the Jam but too young to have seen enough of them, Deabill was initially attracted to the Smiths by the sight of Marr's Rickenbacker, but then the first album came out, and 'I realised I had more in common with Morrissey than I thought, with the lyrics of love lost (or not found), and ventured deeper into reading all the old interviews and discovering a mind-set, something quite alien but totally unique.' As Deabill vocalised his passion for the Smiths, and Morrissey in particular, 'The train journeys with my football pals were littered with [comments like], "You still wanking off over that miserable northern poof?"' Confident in his own status, Deabill brushed off the taunts: 'I used to thrive on it, as it stood me out from the crowd!' Instead, Deabill teamed up with a couple of like-minded friends and followed the Smiths around the UK, taking in the Irish tour of '86 and the mainland Scottish dates in '85, where they feared that their London accents and rival football allegiances might cause problems, but were instead embraced as fellow Smiths fans by similarly hardened football casuals from Edinburgh and Glasgow. (They were also welcomed by the group, whose warm attitude towards fans rewarded and simultaneously reinforced their loyalty.)

Phil Gatenby, an ardent fan of Manchester City, likewise travelling around the country to follow his team during the 1980s, found himself attracted to all aspects of the band. Musically and visually, it was the performance on *The Tube* of 'This Charming Man' that won him over, especially that line 'I would go out tonight, but I haven't got a stitch to wear.' (Gatenby later started a football fanzine, *This Charming Fan*, and later still, put together tourist guidebooks on *Morrissey's Manchester* and started the Manchester Music Tours.) He heard 'Reel Around the Fountain' for the first time on his twenty-first birthday, in the midst of an affair with a woman in her mid-thirties; for him, the line 'It's time the tale were told, of how you took a child and you made him old' had nothing to do with paedophilia. When he moved back to Manchester from his childhood home of Coventry, primarily because of his football allegiances, 'I literally knew just two people . . . It was a case of going to a club and standing on my own and going home alone.' Combined with the fact that his older brother had turned him on to the kitchen-sink dramas of the late '50s and early '60s, it was as if the Smiths had been tailor made for him. 'I didn't become a fan and say, "I need to fit this mould." I was in that mould and they came out and sang for the people who were in that mould.' Like Deabill, Gatenby had to endure a certain amount of ribbing on the terraces for his fandom. 'If you wore the Smiths shirt at the football it was either "Nice one, mate," or "You poof – where's your daffodils?"' And like Deabill, he endured the abuse with pride.

That sense of otherness, even among the lads who could hold their own in a fight, was about to change. In the three years since the Smiths had formed, English football had reached its nadir, the territorial violence that had been growing on the terraces for the last fifteen years combining with the decaying state of fifty- to one-hundred-year-old grounds to deadly results. In May 1985, at a major match in the Yorkshire textile city of Bradford, an ancient wooden stand (with copious combustibles having accumulated underneath over the years) caught fire; fifty-six people were killed in the inferno. Just weeks later, travelling Liverpool thugs at the European Cup Final in Belgium attacked rival and neutral supporters on the terraces and of those trying to escape the assault, thirty-nine were crushed to death when a wall collapsed under the pressure. English clubs were banned from Europe indefinitely, with Liverpool extended an additional three-year ban. Thatcher declared her own war on the hooligan culture, calling for national identity cards and encouraging football grounds to erect impenetrable fencing around the playing areas.

In what was truly the English game's darkest hour, the 1986 World Cup Finals offered a slight ray of hope. Held in Mexico through the month of June, too far away for most of the violence-seekers to travel and cause mayhem, they saw the England team reach the quarterfinals for the first time since 1970, losing out to the eventual winners, Argentina. Scotland also qualified for the finals that year, and as a result, normal life in Britain pretty much ceased to exist for the month as people gathered around their television screens to watch live transmissions from the other side of the world at various odd times of the day and night. Though few bands dared tour during a World Cup, the Smiths included, *The Queen Is Dead* was released in the very middle of the tournament and in its subtle theme of (decaying) British Empire, served as an unofficial soundtrack. The reference to a Mr Shankly (as the Scottish-born manager of England's most prominent, and currently most discredited club) was just one of many coincidental reasons for this association – though when the tabloids reported the band's anti-monarchy sentiments, it fed into the prejudices of the far-right-wing nationalists who had maintained a significant presence on (and typically recruited from) the terraces throughout the game's decline. The confluence of these circum-stances, and then the unveiling of the anthemic single 'Panic', ensured that the Smiths now meant something very different to the vast majority of young male football fans from when the Deabills and Gatenbys of their world had been ridiculed for their love of the band. All of a sudden, and regardless of whether they fully understood them, the Smiths became the band for these people to see.

The Smiths encountered this shift in audience during the handful of British shows they played in the middle of July. After a typically rowdy opening night at the Glasgow Barrowlands, the second concert in Newcastle saw the group met by rare hostility from a violent minority; it was assumed, though it was always difficult to prove, that they were *Sun* readers who had come to express their loyalty to the queen. By various accounts, Morrissey was heckled, had pints of both beer and piss thrown at him, and was additionally spat upon throughout. He held on as long as he could, only storming off during the final encore of 'Hand in Glove' when phlegm caught him in the eye. The Smiths had enjoyed a long and profitable relationship with the city of Newcastle; apart from their headlining performances, they had visited *The Tube*'s studios three times and only just raised the roof at the City Hall during the Red Wedge tour. It appeared in this case that their audience was not just changing but that it had been infiltrated, creating a pressure the Smiths had never had to deal with before.

Two nights later, attention turned to an entirely different set of rivalries as the Smiths performed at Manchester's Festival of the Tenth Summer, in honour of the pivotal shows by the Sex Pistols at the Free Trade Hall a decade earlier. The week-long 'festival', the brainchild of Tony Wilson, featured ten events 'to celebrate Manchester,' from an art show (featuring Peter Saville's designs, naturally) to a fashion show (held at the Haçienda of course); a photography exhibition (by Kevin Cummins); and a book (put together by Richard Boon with Cath Carroll and Liz Naylor). All these helped confirm Manchester's significantly improved cultural status in the years since it had been written off as a dying postindustrial wasteland – and that nothing spoke to Manchester's national standing as much as its music. Concerts across a variety of venues included the bands James, Easterhouse, the Jazz Defektors, the Durutti Column, Andrew Berry's new group the Weeds, and Factory's new signings the Happy Mondays, a rambunctious group of hedonistic hoodlums from the city's north side whose first single for the label, 'Freaky Dancin'', suggested that the intent of Johnny Marr and Andy Rourke's group Freak Party had lived on elsewhere within the city's music scene.

The festival culminated on 19 July with a massive concert at the G-Mex Centre: the recent revamping of the former Manchester Central Railway Station, which had lain dormant since 1969, was itself significant in the city's gradual turnaround. The Smiths headlined alongside New Order and the Fall, Pete Shelley and John Cooper Clarke, A Certain Ratio and the Worst, and Wayne Fontana and the Mindbenders (the only act on the bill to have topped the American charts). Sandie Shaw and Orchestral Manoeuvres in the Dark, for their connections with the Smiths and Factory respectively, performed as honorary Mancunians. It was the culmination of much that the Smiths had set out to achieve and much that Morrissey could not have dared dream of back when he attended those two famed Sex Pistols shows a decade earlier, or back when he was considered the outsider even in a scene full of outsiders, back when Tony Wilson didn't reply to his letters and Rob Gretton thought his band was 'shit.' That band, the Smiths, were now the biggest noise in Manchester, and Manchester itself was making some of the biggest noise in England, and that ought to have made it a night to savour. But though they acquitted themselves admirably in a vast hangar that had been purpose-built for exhibitions, not concerts, Morrissey remained typically uncomfortable about the concept. 'I didn't really feel any sense of unity or celebration,' said Morrissey. 'Certainly not backstage . . . Nobody put their arms around me and said, "Isn't this wonderful?"'

It wasn't for lack of trying. Ruth Polsky had made the journey over to see several of her American acquisitions in one place and at one time, and by the singer's own admission, approached Morrissey seeking a hug. As he later wrote to his close friend and Polsky's former employee Amanda Malone, he refused. The non-encounter was to be his last vision of her. (Polsky was killed that September by a runaway taxi outside a Manhattan club where she was promoting a show.)[5] The relationship between the pair had been tainted by Polsky's aggressive attempt to secure the Smiths' management, and as far as Morrissey was concerned, she was too promiscuous for comfort. But Morrissey's reluctance to excuse supporters for their character traits meant that he was steadily alienating those who, like Polsky, had been highly generous to the Smiths: Cath Carroll recalled Morrissey turning his back on her at the Red Wedge show, still smarting from an incident regarding an (unpublished) negative write-up by Liz Naylor almost three years after the event, yet only months after Carroll's own latest positive Smiths review in *NME*. All the same, Morrissey wrote to Tony Wilson after the G-Mex event, stating, 'The Smiths need a manager' and asking if he knew of 'any handsome bastard willing to tackle haughty and unmanagable [sic] swines such as we?' If he was personally beseeching Wilson to apply for the position, the Factory and Haçienda founder chose not to follow up on it.[6]

To balance the forbidding scale (and ticket price) of the G-Mex event, the Smiths played their own show at Salford University the following evening. Salford was hardly lacking for prodigal sons: Mark E. Smith, Tony Wilson, John Cooper Clarke, Bernard Sumner and Peter Hook were just a few of the G-Mex show's luminaries to hail from there, yet Salford hosted few concerts of its own due to a lack of viable venues and an unstated concern about the rival metropolis' reputation, which was seemingly borne out for the Smiths by an audience comprised of rowdy male youths who made the most of the rare occasion, stripping off their shirts, clambering on one another's shoulders, and throwing themselves about the ill-equipped university hall with total abandon. 'The atmosphere was such that if somebody lit a cigarette lighter, the place would have exploded,' said Phil Gatenby. 'There was part of you worried that you were going to get your head kicked in by these hooligans, but at the same time these hooligans were singing and acknowledging very effeminate songs.'

Notably, the crowd followed almost every Smiths song with the same chant of territorial support for their home city: 'Sal-ford, Sal-ford.' It was partly a provocation to fans from neighbouring Manchester and may have been connected to the group's visual appropriation of their own Salford Lads Club. And it made for a volatile mood. 'At a football match you're all in your own pen, so though there's tension you know it's not going to kick off inside,' said Gatenby. 'But this was tension at a gig. We're all here for the same reason but you've got this Salford element that's waiting for someone to shout "Eccles" or "Gorton" and then it would all kick off.'

In the end it fell to Morrissey to respond: just before 'The Queen Is Dead' he feyly proclaimed his own neighbourhood: 'Stret-ford, Stret-ford.' From anyone else that night it would have led to a fight; from the star of the show, it successfully defused tensions. Having ripped off his 'Hang the DJ' shirt (emblazoned with the image of DJ Steve Wright), Morrissey concluded the show stripped to the waist, leaping around as furiously as any of the teenagers who had now clambered onto the stage in dozens and who were prevented from overrunning the singer less by the phalanx of security kneeling nervously in front of them than by their own apparent respect. The evening ended with Johnny Marr standing atop the drum riser during a frenzied finale of 'Hand in Glove', and Craig Gannon playing on resolutely from in front of it, almost buried by the fans but loving 'the vibe': Aztec Camera, the Bluebells and the Colourfield had never seen anything like this. Phil Gatenby, having been separated from his friends, 'ended up dancing with this lad, bare-chested and muscled, and at the line "I'll probably never see you again," we actually hugged each other!'

For Gatenby, who had always been around such lads, the Salford show was possibly the best that the Smiths had ever played – and there were those in the band who felt much the same way. The frail boys and girls who had bought into the sensitivity of the Smiths found themselves, in the thrust of the newly energised five-piece and its increasingly aggressive following, being forced, once again in their lives, to the back of the crowd.

CHAPTER THIRTY-FOUR

I like to wear sunglasses, I play guitar in a hip group
and I'm skinny, with dark hair. Sounds perfect to me!
– JOHNNY MARR, *Record Mirror*, June 1986

The Smiths were making up now for lost time. In June 1986,
before *The Queen Is Dead* had been released, let alone
'Panic', the group *again* returned to the studio, again with John
Porter. Their new focus song, 'Ask' maintained the simplicity
of 'Panic', from its title through to its uncomplicated musical
structure, but otherwise offered an immediate counterpoint to
that song's voluminous, fast-paced approach, and would prove
all the more rewarding for the change in mood. Singing in a
somewhat higher key than usual, Morrissey opened 'Ask' with
an acknowledgement of shyness and coyness, later referring to
a pen-pal youth spent 'writing frightening verse to a buck-tooth
girl in Luxembourg,' a classic example of his confessional style
combining with his exaggerated wit, all while singing about a
subject to which his audience could relate. Kirsty MacColl
returned to contribute backing vocals. On 'Bigmouth Strikes
Again', the group had substituted her voice at the last moment
for the high-pitched, digitally harmonised Morrissey vocal,
which had afforded that song a particularly unique sound. This
time around, especially given the inherent femininity of 'Ask',

MacColl's understated accompaniment fit perfectly. Behind the two vocalists, the twin guitars of Marr and Gannon maintained a warm, semiacoustic accompaniment. Profoundly commercial without seeming to advertise itself as such, 'Ask' was an obvious single.

With 'Panic' and 'Ask', the Smiths would take a solid step towards solving their 'video' conundrum. Mayo Thompson at Rough Trade, figuring that 'the only way we're going to pull this off is with someone they cannot refuse because of his reputation,' approached Derek Jarman, the controversial British director of *Jubilee*, *The Tempest*, and the soon-to-be-released *Caravaggio*, with the idea of making not a video but a 'film'. This was more than mere semantics: rather than shoot the group in performance or repose, Jarman would be left alone to provide an uninterrupted accompaniment to 'The Queen Is Dead', 'There Is a Light That Never Goes Out' and 'Panic'.[1] (He later made an additional film for 'Ask'.) It wasn't an especially original idea, as Thompson well knew: Jarman himself had done precisely the same thing for three songs from Marianne Faithfull's acclaimed 1979 album, *Broken English*, in the pre-video era. Still, Jarman's fast-cut style, veering between the literal (grainy shots in various urban locales, with beautiful individual boys, girls, women, and men as visual ciphers) and the impressionistic (colourful crowns, roses, guitars), served up a hefty dose of visual credibility for the band, although whether it was 'great art' or not remained a matter of debate. After being unveiled at the Edinburgh Festival in August, Jarman's fourteen-minute film was given its television premier on BBC2's *Rock Around the Clock* in September and subsequently shown in cinemas alongside the Alex Cox biopic *Sid and Nancy*.

As part of their stockpiling of new songs, the Smiths had recorded the rambunctious 'Sweet and Tender Hooligan' during the 'Panic' sessions, and at Jam Studios for 'Ask', they added a mid-tempo quasi-rockabilly number entitled 'Is It Really So Strange?', which Morrissey and Marr had written face-to-face during their recent trip to Los Angeles. Neither song was finished to the band's satisfaction; the B-side to 'Ask' featured instead, and for the first time, a cover version. This was at Morrissey's suggestion, and understandably so; having recently endured a couple of instrumental B-sides over which he didn't feel sufficiently inspired to write words, he may have figured that if he wasn't going to claim a royalty, he might as well sing someone else's tune entirely. He chose, not surprisingly, a song from his childhood: 'Golden Lights' by Twinkle. The arrangement was very much a product of its time, 1965, but the subject matter – fame, fame, fatal fame – said plenty to Morrissey about his situation, especially as Twinkle was perhaps the only female pop star of that era to have written her own material. Marr and Gannon, gamely, played acoustic guitars and mandolins in a bossa nova style, and Kirsty MacColl again accompanied Morrissey on vocals. Rourke and Joyce were not included. Porter played bass, and once more programmed the rhythm on the LinnDrums, something he had also done with Marr's two most recent B-side instrumentals, much though it jarred with familiar Smiths sensibilities.

Morrissey's misgivings aside, there were those who had heard one of those instrumentals, 'Money Changes Everything', as crying out for a vocal. Prominent among them was Bryan Ferry, in the midst of recording a new album when the track crossed his path (quite possibly sent to him by Warner Bros Music with the idea in mind), and who quickly sought and received permission to write an accompanying lyric. If Morrissey feared that the first Smiths track not to feature his name as a co-composer might now show up with that of a 1970s idol in his place, he had further cause for concern when Ferry's group concluded, after much trial and error, that they couldn't possibly emulate Marr's handiwork and invited the guitarist in to re-record it himself.

Marr had already made a small name for himself as a ready and able guest musician. But his previous studio appearances had all been on behalf of friends (Everything but the Girl, Quando Quango, Billy Bragg) who were nominally part of an

520

alternative/independent scene. Bryan Ferry, on the other hand, especially in 1986, represented commercial pop music at its most sophisticated and slick. Additionally, Marr had only recently bad-mouthed Ferry, in his *Melody Maker* cover interview, for his performance at Live Aid, complaining that Ferry 'used the event for personal gain'. Nonetheless, Marr accepted the invitation.

The subsequent collaboration, renamed 'The Right Stuff', fulfilled Smiths fans' worst fears, emerging as either a caricature or archetype (depending on taste) of mid-'80s mid-tempo glossy pop-rock. That it was (finally) released in the immediate wake of the Smiths' breakup, with an appropriately lavish and hollow video (in which Marr appeared, alongside many dancing female models), would do little to improve the guitarist's credibility at that point with disappointed Smiths fans. In the spring of 1986, however, the collaboration seemed most important for another relationship Marr developed in the studio. Like Johnny Marr, Ferry's bass player Guy Pratt was a highly prodigious young musician, encyclopaedic in his knowledge of pop culture, an outgoing character of considerable wit and panache, and given to excessive self-indulgence in the name of rock 'n' roll hedonism. A South Londoner raised on the Who, Pratt had extricated himself from the mod revival's cul-de-sac to play with the likes of Womack & Womack, Icehouse and Robert Palmer (as well as Ferry), developing the haircut and the fashion sense – and indeed, the bass-playing style – to go with it. 'I loved that shiny techno pop thing, and I was really into being a good funky player,' he said. In short, he had missed out on the Smiths, which meant that witnessing Marr at work in the studio – 'this amazing orchestral rock 'n' roll player' – was nothing less than a revelation. 'He wasn't bound up in tradition, and he wasn't into boxes with flashy lights. He knew how to get the exact tremolo sound of an old Fender Twin. And that really wasn't what was happening at the time at all. He was the real deal. In a way, he made me feel ashamed, that I had lost touch in something.' The pair became instant best friends, aided by the fact that Pratt's steady girlfriend, Caroline Stirling, hit it off equally well with Angie, who was much the same age. The Marrs had recently moved back to London, in part because the Bowdon house had become overly popular with all sorts of visiting vagabonds and hangers-on, but also because Marr, like Morrissey before him, was feeling claustrophobic in Manchester and, it would be fair to say, sought some of the opportunities available to someone of his professional reputation. The Marrs were invited by Kirsty MacColl to use her vacant flat just off Holland Park Road (Marr took to calling her his 'Electric Landlady'), and along with Pratt and his girlfriend, they soon added MacColl and husband Steve Lillywhite to a network that also included the Rolling Stones' Ron Wood, with whom Marr would visit and play guitar, fulfilling another childhood dream.

Meanwhile, with the American tour looming very large on the near horizon, it appeared increasingly likely that Andy Rourke's recent drug arrest would prevent him receiving a work visa. The Smiths were again faced with the prospect of a substitute bassist and again, Marr did not shop around; he offered his new friend Guy Pratt the part-time job instead. Pratt recalled the invitation as demonstrating Marr's own capacity for a quotable turn of phrase: 'Guy, how do you fancy coming to the States to play punk rock and fall over?' Pratt duly showed up for the tour rehearsals, at a luxurious farmhouse near Gatwick Airport – to find that he was being taught by none other than Andy Rourke. 'If I can't play the bass lines,' figured the temporarily exiled Smith, 'I want whoever else plays them to do it right.'

'We were all laughing about it that night; craziness ensued until dawn,' said Marr. 'Andy can't have felt any long-term threat, or he would have been too sad to do it. And nobody would have been callous enough to make him do it.'

'It felt fantastic,' Pratt recalled of his new assignment. 'I was very cocky. I turned up not feeling daunted at all.' He was astute enough, however, to notice that 'the dynamic of the band was Johnny and Andy. I thought as long as those two were cool everything else was cool.' As such, he was under no illusions about being hired for anything longer than the American tour – unlike Craig Gannon, the fully fledged fifth Smith. Pratt lacked the new boy's down-to-earth northern sensibility and matching haircut (Andrew Berry came to Sussex to give Pratt a suitable Smiths bob), but he had something that Gannon lacked: the confidence of personality by which he could hold his own within such a tightly knit unit.[2] That confidence occasionally overextended itself, as when he hammered on Morrissey's door in coke-fuelled enthusiasm one early morning at the farmhouse, mistaking it for Marr's room instead – and his failure to connect with the singer was partly why he suspected all along that the chance to join the Smiths, if only for one tour, was 'too good to be true.' After the last day of rehearsals Andy Rourke heard, to his considerable surprise, that his visa had come through. He would be going to America after all.[3] It was just as well: the addition of Craig Gannon presented enough of a shift in the group's previously emphatic lineup without audiences being subjected to a session bass player (even one of Pratt's calibre) in place of the real thing.

Pratt received the news from Mark Fenwick, Bryan Ferry's manager, who, in the wake of Marr's appearance on his client's album, put his name forward for the same job with the Smiths. Fenwick was of particularly well-bred stock (his family owned and operated the department store of the same name), and though he took meetings with the group and was assigned some American preproduction tasks in consideration of a fuller appointment, Morrissey and Marr recognised that his world-view, and that of his company EG Management, was too far removed from the down-to-earth sensibilities of the Smiths. Like Matthew Sztumpf before him, and Ken Friedman waiting in the wings across the Atlantic, he was not invited into the negotiations with EMI, which were busy being finalised by Alexis Grower. In the midst of all the chaos of tour preparations, the concern about Andy Rourke's availability and auditions with Guy Pratt, the acclimatisation of Craig Gannon, and the high-profile warm-up dates in the UK and all the attendant aggravation, that contract was delivered to Morrissey and Marr on the very eve of the tour and 'signed and sent off from the airport,' said Marr. The Smiths left England as a Rough Trade band licensed to Sire in the States. They arrived in America in the knowledge that their future, so they thought, lay with EMI.

THE WEEK BEFORE the band arrived in America, *The Queen Is Dead* shot up twenty places in the charts there to become the Smiths' first top 100 album. That achievement was rendered all the more impressive by the fact that, although 'The Boy with the Thorn in His Side' had been something of a dance hit, Sire had not released another official single in advance of *The Queen Is Dead*. (It seemed pointless without a video.) They promoted the album the old-fashioned way instead, investing in the group's evident strengths: their live reputation, their credibility with the press, and their popularity at college and 'new music'/'modern rock' radio. ('Bigmouth Strikes Again', 'The Queen Is Dead', 'There Is a Light That Never Goes Out' and then 'Panic', which the label released as a 12" 3-track single at the end of the tour, all showed up on a number of stations' end-of-1986 lists for most-played songs.) In the meantime, 'Please, Please, Please Let Me Get What I Want' appeared to be taking on a life of its own, thanks to its inclusion not only on the bestselling *Pretty in Pink* soundtrack but in yet another John Hughes hit film, the outright comedy *Ferris Bueller's Day Off*, this time as an instrumental performed by British band the Dream Academy.[4] Thanks in no small part to the patronisation of Hughes, the 'jocks' – the approximate American counterpart to the football fans in England – began showing up to the Smiths' concerts in packs.

The Smiths continued to voice complaints in America about a lack of commercial-rock airplay, the absence of hit singles, and an album chart position they saw as incommensurate with their ticket sales; it was the familiar charge from foreign bands who didn't understand that in America it was possible to be a cult act on a scale of perceived stardom. That the Smiths were in fact following the classic American upward trajectory can be verified by comparing their progress with the two major rock groups of their generation who would stay together and go on to multiplatinum global stardom. When U2, who played America consistently, had promoted their third album, *War*, in 1983, their tour concluded at Pier 84 in New York; when America's own alternative/independent heroes, R.E.M., who likewise toured America almost without a break, had released *their* third album, *Fables of the Reconstruction*, in 1985, they moved up to New York's 6,000-capacity Radio City Music Hall. The Smiths in 1986, similarly promoting a third studio album but on only their second American tour, were able to book *both* these New York venues – and sell both out. (They were even treated to the sight of Mick Jagger dancing at the side of the stage at Pier 84.) Outside Boston, they played the 15,000-capacity Great Woods Amphitheater (or 'shed', as such vast outdoor arenas, with additional lawn space, were commonly known in the States). Their profile was equally high on the West Coast: the 1986 tour included two sold-out shows at the 6,000-seat Los Angeles Universal Amphitheater, and saw a return to the previously conquered open-air locations in San Diego and Irving Meadows. It remained no coincidence that these were the same markets serviced by the leading commercial 'new music' radio stations; generally speaking, the Smiths sold considerably fewer tickets on their initial ventures north into Canada's Ottawa, London and Montreal; south to Miami, New Orleans and Houston; and as far into the American heartland as Phoenix, Dallas and even Nashville.

All told, the tour was to last a full seven weeks and involve playing to well over 100,000 people – far and away the longest, most prestigious and, depending on final figures, either lucrative or costly run the group had ever embarked upon. As such, it needed to run like a well-oiled machine – and for that, the Smiths needed both an experienced band manager in an office and an equally experienced tour manager on the road. They had neither. The first, of course, was by choice – though it was evidently not a smart one. The second was a direct result of Stuart James leaving the fold after the Irish tour. He did not fall out with the group; in fact, James would later live with the Marrs in Bowdon. But he did not consider tour managing his natural vocation and, given the constant pressure, opted to return to the recording studio. His replacement for the American tour was Sophie Ridley, who had worked her way up the tour production ranks and came with ample qualifications but had never worked with the Smiths prior to the UK warm-up shows.

Relations got off to a bad start at the production rehearsals in London, Ontario, where neither the right equipment nor the crew's pay cheques showed up. Rather than take their problems to Ridley, the proper chain of command, or perhaps because she was unable to satisfy their complaints, the crew descended on Johnny Marr, who for his part appeared equally incapable of either relinquishing or delegating such responsibilities. After a heated standoff – the crew had grown in size to include several newly hired hands – Marr had to call Warner Bros to say, 'We are not going to play a note until these guys have . . . their wages in advance, and the staging is right.' While the label had put some financial tour support into a dedicated account (to be repaid at the end of the tour, should it turn a profit), it was not required to deal with production specifics or crew payments. The fact that the conversation so quickly became skewed like this reflected Marr's belief that 'the tour manager we had was very, very weak,' though as he also noted, 'I don't know if anyone could have been up to it.'

Andy Rourke was more sympathetic to Ridley's plight. 'She was put in this unfortunate position to manage the unmanageable band,' he said, noting that she had the additional task of handling his prescription medications. 'She was like my nurse-maid, babysitter – she had a lot on her plate and she did what she could.' At Warner Bros, Steven Baker was positively enthusiastic: 'Sophie was the greatest,' he said. 'She was like this great energy. Sophie was like the manager for me.'

If it was Ridley's difficult challenge to try to corral a famously contrary band that had no higher authority than its two leading musicians, it was Craig Gannon's near impossible task to try to fit in both professionally and personally with this group. The tour party commenced, in Ontario, in something of an ominous manner when the Smiths' rhythm section decided that Gannon should celebrate his twentieth birthday by downing a cognac for every one of those years. 'We nearly fucking killed him,' said Rourke. 'I went to his room the next day and it had all been taped off. He'd done this projectile vomit everywhere.' Gannon's first North American show with the band took place that same night, and in the way of rock 'n' roll on the grand American scale, the tour promptly rolled on as it had begun. 'It got pretty chaotic with the drinking with everybody except Morrissey,' Gannon admitted. Or as Mike Joyce himself adroitly put it, 'Bar Morrissey, we were certainly burning it at both ends. And in the middle.'

Despite the excesses, Gannon admirably fulfilled his onstage role, which was to play a multitude of highly complicated guitar parts, on a variety of guitars, and allow Johnny Marr the physical and musical space to expand upon that. Marr noted that 'cometh the hour, he did exactly what he was meant to do.' Andy Rourke considered the appointment a success on all fronts: 'I don't think anyone else could have pulled it off,' he said of the new addition, noting that 'Craig was this meek and mild guy but also massively talented. He looked cool as well. He made it look effortless. He'd wake up every morning with this perfect quiff.'

'It felt really comfortable,' confirmed Gannon. 'I didn't feel like a spare part or that I didn't deserve to be there. I felt like I was a part of this band and I didn't feel out of place. Being young and foolish, you think, "This might be permanent." Well it *was* supposed to be permanent.'

Nonetheless, those just outside of the group, even as they complimented his playing, saw Gannon cause a notable shift in the Smiths' previously tight dynamics. Mike Hinc, who had known Gannon since he was with Aztec Camera, said that 'to be the fifth member of that band would have been a nightmare for anyone, and Craig was just . . . he was an ingénue. Lovely kid but an ingénue.'

'It must have been an incredibly difficult position to be in,' said John Featherstone. Having helped produce a forty-foot re-creation of *The Queen Is Dead* album cover as a backdrop for the tour, Featherstone was still wrestling with the placement of Gannon onstage. 'He just stood at the bottom of a couple of steps leading up to the drum riser. And I think it was in no small part due to Craig's reserved style, he just kind of stood there almost as if – as one person uncharitably said – he looked like he'd been left behind by the opening band.'

'Craig Gannon was a brilliant idea on Johnny's part, and I thought he really worked well,' said Grant Showbiz. 'In essence, Craig Gannon is the subtlest of guitar players. His remit was just to play what Johnny had played on record, and he did it very, very well. Musically he didn't tread on anyone's toes.' All the same, 'he was on to a loser from day one trying to join the gang at such a late stage. And being a slightly diffident, shy sort of guy, he wasn't going to jump in with us. He probably drank a little too much alcohol to overcompensate for that. But onstage he was just what they needed, because he *didn't* rock out. The person who was rocking out was Johnny.'

This was true. Though it was something he disputed as the kneejerk reaction of long-term fans to the addition of a second guitarist, it is hard to deny that Marr developed a rock-star persona in 1986. The case can absolutely be made that, if it's what he wanted for himself, then as the most talented young guitarist of his generation he had every right to strap on his Gibson Les Paul and pull some familiar guitar-hero poses onstage, to stand aloft on the drum risers if desired, to start jamming with members of the Rolling Stones during his spare time, to appear on Bryan Ferry's records, to wear Yohji Yamamoto suits, to get drunk on champagne cocktails and Rémy Martin and get high on marijuana and, if he desired, cocaine – especially as the last of these, on an American tour, was almost impossible to avoid. ('They put it out with the deli tray basically,' quipped Andy Rourke. 'You get your cheeses, your olives, and there's your mound of cocaine.') The drug has always been tempting for touring bands and their crews because it allows them to maintain their post-concert high, to stay up all night and keep drinking and talking, to feel good about themselves and their place in the world. But because cocaine is essentially an ego drug, it is the sworn enemy of musical subtlety. (In an interview with Simon Goddard for an *Uncut* magazine special about *The Queen Is Dead*, Marr offered a retrospective view on substance abuse: 'too much has been made of this partying thing over the years. Yes, on tour, absolutely. Copious amounts. But in the studio, I was really together. Cocaine has always been a disaster for people's music, and alcohol ain't too clever, either. But smoking pot till it came out of me ears I never had a problem with. Pot, hash, was really good for the sounds, and I think you can hear that. But it's not like I was sprawled all over the mixing desk. That just wasn't the case.') And in America in 1986, with Craig Gannon on board to fulfill the rhythm role, there is no doubt that Johnny Marr lost much of his performing sensitivity.

The changes were minor at first, but once the tour reached California, they became more pronounced. On 'Please, Please, Please Let Me Get What I Want', for example, the concluding mandolin part, played with a wistful flamenco flourish on record, was performed as heavy-handed, high-pitched notes on electric guitar. On 'How Soon Is Now?' while Gannon played the tremolo rhythm part, Marr's solo guitar tinkles, tucked away in the recorded mix, became a central constant. For 'The Boy with the Thorn in His Side', on which Marr had previously played only the chord changes in semiacoustic fashion onstage, he now performed the lead melody as a high-pitched electric solo that ran roughshod over verses and choruses alike. The bottleneck slide guitar line on 'Panic' was mixed higher than on record. And so on. The American audiences, raised on guitar heroes, lapped it all up, not knowing that they were acting as enablers.

It can be stated as fact that all rock bands who aspire to greatness must learn to meet the demands of bigger audiences, which can mean employing additional musicians (as the Smiths had done with Craig Gannon), video projections (as they could have done with the Derek Jarman films), and/or special effects (which the Smiths wisely opted to avoid entirely).[5] It can also mean simply turning up the volume, puffing out one's chest, and moving about the stage more emphatically, which the Smiths did as a matter of course. The lengthy American tour rendered them more polished, more professional, more athletic and anthemic, and this was arguably necessary and therefore positive, to a degree. The rest of the band was performing largely to the peak of its potential, and a number of songs, of varying musical moods ('The Queen Is Dead', 'Heaven Knows I'm Miserable Now', 'There Is a Light That Never Goes Out', 'I Know It's Over') were no more aggressive and yet all the better for the additional guitarist. Johnny Marr recalled 'weeks of killer shows.' Grant Showbiz called the concerts 'incendiary.' Craig Gannon noted that 'it was just chaos in America,' especially compared to his previous experience touring the same venues with Aztec Camera. 'I don't know what it was: whether Morrissey whipping them into a frenzy, or just the charisma coming off the stage or the power coming off the stage.' And certainly, audiences did not forget them in a hurry. All the same, this was a drastically different Smiths from the one that had unveiled its five-piece self with impressive grace on the *Whistle Test* just a couple of months earlier, and largely unrecognisable from the four-piece that had stormed through Scotland the previous autumn. Suggestions that the Smiths were turning into the Rolling Stones were not as lazy as the band subsequently claimed them to be. The lineup, after all, now matched that of the classic Stones quintet – and the hedonistic lifestyle seemed not that far behind.

This much became evident once the group decamped to the Le Parc Hotel in Los Angeles for ten days, the first five of them without a concert to perform. 'We were always OK when we were working,' said Andy Rourke. 'But when we had time off it got messy.' While Morrissey used the time to visit his relatives in Colorado, the others invited wives and girlfriends over to join them. As a twenty-first birthday present for Guy Pratt's girlfriend Caroline Stirling, and something of a compensatory gift for Pratt not making it into the band after all, Johnny Marr flew the couple over to join the festivities. John Porter also came out for a week; Mike Hinc arranged a visit to his American girlfriend to coincide. The British band Eighth Wonder was staying at the same hotel, and various Smiths were distracted by the sight of vocalist Patsy Kensit, well known in the UK as a child actress and model before her teenage pop career, sunbathing topless. Guy Pratt introduced his friend Steve Dagger, the streetwise manager of both Eighth Wonder and Spandau Ballet, to Johnny Marr as yet another candidate for the vacant position surrounding the Smiths; Ken Friedman, though he resided in LA, was off on tour with Simple Minds at the time and had to trust that his standing with Morrissey and Marr could survive his absence.

John Porter had every reason to feel fully satisfied with his own (renewed) standing in the Smiths camp. 'Panic' had just become the group's first top 20 hit in two years, very nearly making the top 10. (Unavailable to perform on *Top of the Pops*, the Derek Jarman film was used in the Smiths' absence, much to their delight.) Porter was now looking forward to finishing off 'Ask,' which he considered another classic in the making, albeit with a difficult final mix ahead of him. 'There were five of these picking guitar parts, playing the whole way through,' he recalled. 'And in the middle it was all going to disappear into a kind of wash – and you could hear seagulls. It was very complicated but I had it all written down. I had this map of where stuff would be and what was going to happen.' In the meantime, he had 'tossed off' a rough mix for the band to listen to on their travels. In Los Angeles, as he recalled, Morrissey told him that he didn't like the mix. 'I said, "Well I haven't mixed it yet." Which shows how much communication there was between everybody! And he said, "Oh, well I've asked Steve Lillywhite to mix it." I was like "Oh . . . that's . . . he can't mix . . . this is our great creation."'

It was equally evident of the Smiths' communication process that Steve Lillywhite recalled that the approach 'came from Johnny, not Moz . . . I had never met Moz,' while Marr insisted that the idea 'definitely didn't come from me.' (Geoff Travis owned up: 'I'm sure that was us [who] got Steve Lillywhite involved.') Regardless, Porter had expected that the mix would necessitate several hands on an automated desk and was disappointed to discover that Lillywhite mixed it on his home studio in Ealing, using Marc Wallis, Porter's former assistant who had helped make 'How Soon Is Now?' such a masterpiece. Wallis recalled, 'We had no automation at Steve's studio, so we set it up in sections, all hands-on, proper old-fashioned mixing. It was just a day's work. Wasn't a big deal.' Lillywhite confirmed as much: 'Considering how big they were and the opportunity I could have had, I should have booked a proper studio and done it properly. But I did it in my own home studio by hand. And actually it turned out pretty good.'

It did. Though famous at the time for producing the arena rock of U2 and Simple Minds, Lillywhite had come up through the post-punk ranks with the likes of Siouxsie & the Banshees, XTC and the Chameleons, and his mix of 'Ask' was perfectly restrained. All the same, he said, 'I do remember Johnny saying he loved the mix but that the middle bit with the seagulls wasn't how he'd envisaged it. But I don't know what his vision was for that.' Which was precisely John Porter's objection. Porter was similarly perturbed to hear that 'Golden Lights' had been farmed out to Stephen Street, who inexplicably sent Morrissey's voice through a flange effect and buried the bossa nova guitars, rendering the song every bit as atypical as any of the similarly LinnDrum-accompanied instrumentals and, by general consensus, the only true disaster in the band's entire catalogue. The Smiths had never previously recused themselves from the final mixes of a single and would not make the same mistake again.

Porter was not the only unhappy Englishman in Los Angeles. Geoff Travis had heard through the grapevine about the EMI deal and, rather than keep talking through lawyers, decided to confront the group about it in person. He got his chance at the soundcheck at Irvine Meadows. Steven Baker from Warner Bros was with him, backstage, where he recalled 'the band walking by, the question being popped, and somebody turning around and affirming it.' Travis may have taken this casual affirmation in stride; after such a long and protracted battle with the band for their loyalty, it probably seemed par for the course that, just as everything seemed to be progressing perfectly, the group would sign to EMI regardless. Steven Baker, however, by nature a mild-mannered man, expressed his feelings by punching the backstage wall in frustration – an act that caught Johnny Marr by surprise and gave him cause to wonder whether EMI's American executives would prove similarly passionate about the band.

The Smiths, said Baker of his reaction, 'certainly have a right to their feeling as to what Sire/Warner Brothers/Rough Trade were doing for them, and what they needed to do next to survive as a group. If the deal's up, they get to do what they want. And if they didn't think we deserved to resign them, that's their business. But you can still have your feelings about a group. And that goes beyond whether they can sell any records or not. It's just the pleasure of working with a band, and the band then saying, "We want to get a divorce." I normally take things in stride, but that really pissed me off.'

Seymour Stein, when the news reached him, was apoplectic

– until it appeared that when the Smiths had renegotiated their contract with Rough Trade, reducing the term by one album, the label did not do likewise with Sire, to the American company's possible benefit. 'In the process of making this deal I discovered that there was one extra album owed to Sire,' confirmed EMI's David Munns. 'So the idea was that we would sign this four-album deal but the first album would not include North America and they would give it to Seymour. But I said, "No give it to me, and I will licence it to Seymour." They agreed but they didn't tell Seymour. So when this all came out, Seymour was very upset. He was yelling down the phone at me but that was too bad. He didn't want to get his last album through EMI. I just told him to fuck off.' It was probably mere coincidence, but *The Queen Is Dead* peaked in America at number 70, the same week that the American label found out the band had jumped ship.

Most of this was beyond the Smiths' purview while in California. Of greater immediate concern was the breakdown in trust and communication between the band and Sophie Ridley. Mike Hinc ended up staying on the road to try to mitigate the remaining dates – of which there were many. The fact that Johnny Marr and Hinc did not get along made the agent's task that much harder.

Understandably, given so much chaos and confusion, Craig Gannon retreated further into his shell. His girlfriend, the first truly serious relationship of his life, had come over to join him in Los Angeles, and the pair made a point of going to the beach on their own. Once the tour resumed its travels, heading across the Southwest and then the Deep South, Gannon found himself distanced from Marr, who was seen to snap at the new recruit. Marr confirmed that he and Craig 'did have a couple of fallouts,' but that they were because 'he damaged a hotel room. That wasn't a sacking offence, but it pissed me off.'

Frightened of flying at the best of times, Gannon increasingly opted to travel overnight on the crew bus, further isolating himself. (This also gave him the opportunity to join some of the crew in eating steak, away from the band's no-meat policy.) Gannon's gradual disappearing act reached an almost inevitable conclusion when he was inadvertently left behind in New Orleans, something only ascertained when the entourage checked in at the airport. (Mike Hinc stayed behind to travel up to Tampa-St Petersburg with him on a later flight.) The previous night, the group had played a small university auditorium in New Orleans, where the promoter would later recall two specific and dramatically conflicting memories of the backstage scene prior to the show: his doing cocaine with Johnny Marr in his office, and then watching Mike Hinc have to physically accompany an exhausted Morrissey on to the stage to perform. ('The amount of time it took to get Morrissey onstage was getting longer and longer,' said Grant Showbiz. 'There was this great game he'd play of wanting to be asked fifteen times, if it'd been fourteen the night before. Johnny was like "Let's Rock!" and Mozzer'd be "Well, somebody's gotta ask me another seven times."')

In short, the wheels had come off the tour.

'The schedule we had was unrealistic, it would break any man,' said Andy Rourke. 'We were all tired. And when you get tired you lean on things like drink and drugs. We were all becoming crazy. We were going insane. But nobody was telling the other person that they were going insane. So everybody was going quietly insane on their own. And then there came a breaking point.'

'It wasn't just "I'm tired,"' said Marr. 'Everyone was very upset. When there's too much alcohol and drugs around, things get very melodramatic.'

Following the show in St Petersburg, there were only four concerts left: Miami, Atlanta, Nashville, and the sold-out finale at New York's Radio City Music Hall, one of the most magnificent seated venues in America and an opportunity for the Smiths to end the tour in triumph. For Morrissey and Marr, the only ones making the decisions, it may as well have been a hundred shows; they simply couldn't see that far ahead.

'We were just burned out,' recalled Marr. 'Burned, burned

out. And that's all there was to it. Looking at it philosophically, we were in a position to deliver on performances and tour at a certain level, but again, the perennial issue: not having management meant that we didn't have the support setup to get us through it. It's amazing that we got as far through that tour as we did. Because when you've got the right tour manager, and input from the record company, it's very hard. But when you don't have the right tour manager, and no input from the record company, and you're inexperienced, and young at that level, with no guidance, things are going to give. And where guidance would have come in, would have been: "First off, go to bed now." "No, really, we've got to stop and get some food." "Stop drinking so much." "Hey, look, that guy's feeling a little bit sensitive, turn the music down, chill out, and watch a movie on the bus." Just those things that you know from a bit of maturity . . . But we were all pretty headstrong, and the thing is . . . young guys don't look after themselves very well. And they definitely don't look after *each other* very well.'

'You can only ever get in debt with sleep; you can never get in credit,' observed John Featherstone, who agreed with Marr's assertion that 'the degree of exhaustion was largely to do with lack of management.' As Featherstone saw things, 'There's a natural tension between the promotion folks pushing – and the band's management pushing back. From a PR person's perspective, their metrics of success is that if you can get the band on the phone, on the radio, on TV, 24/7, then you're doing your job. And a lot of the pushback comes from management. There was none of that pushback going on. I remember them doing [publicity] stuff at all ridiculous hours of day and night.'

And just as there was no one to push back against label demands, there was no one to push them forward to the end of the tour, to cancel all remaining interviews if need be, promise them a holiday when they got back, offer all sorts of bonuses and incentives, but to let them know that *these four shows* mattered. As Featherstone put it, 'It turned into "It's just four more shows, it's no big deal."'

'We weren't seeing the complete picture there,' admitted Marr, years later. All he knew at the time was, 'I didn't want to complete the tour.' By his own confession, he had driven himself to complete and total sickness. It had never been uncommon for him to throw up before taking to the stage out of pure nervous energy, but in America he had then taken to consuming alcohol during the gigs, on an empty stomach. It was, he explained, partly out of a 'want to calm the nerves down, partly out of relief at the end of the shows. Because from the halfway point, I was just really relieved. So by the end of them, the crowd had worked me up, the event had worked me up, and I'd worked myself up so much.' Marr later figured he was downing at least a bottle of Rémy Martin a night, and the post-show party typically continued through all hours back at the hotel. Though he was hardly alone in his indulgences (Rourke confessed to drinking equal amounts of Rémy, and Gannon admitted that he and the rhythm section typically closed out the bar every night), the others were not carrying Marr's weight of responsibility. Andy Rourke recalled being brought to Johnny's room at one point by Angie, to find his friend 'in bits on the bed, feeling really ill, dead upset.' Rourke worried that Marr was having 'a nervous breakdown' but, much like the others with regard to his own heroin problems, 'didn't know what to do.' Angie, apparently, did, and Marr increasingly came to rely on her for sustenance and support, and even for elements of tour management. 'She had a credit card and good sense, and she was on the case.'

Morrissey, though he avoided the worst of his playing part-ners' excesses ('I never heard the word [cocaine] mentioned,' he insisted in 1989 of the Smiths on tour), was not beyond the occasional bout of hedonism himself. There were frequent visits to the hotel bar, the rare sight of him smoking a cigarette, and a drunken onstage conversation with Marr where the pair admitted they didn't know what song they were playing. And Morrissey, hampered already by the fact his preferred lifestyle was at odds with that of the rock 'n' roll tour, was under no less public, personal and professional pressure than Marr. He had become a demigod in the States to rival his 'spokesman' reputation in the UK, and he had done his best to live up to expectations, throwing himself across the stage like a dervish every night, exalting in the acclaim but simultaneously working for it; he'd challenged security when they wouldn't let kids up to dance or to the front of the hall, sometimes physically; he'd conducted more interviews than made sense, and all without any real attention or assistance from anyone but his security man, Jim Connolly.[6] When Marr declared his inability to continue the tour, Morrissey was not able, and perhaps not willing, to convince him otherwise.

'Normally you could give Morrissey a reason to continue,' said Mike Hinc, 'like, "There's four sold-out shows, and huge lawsuits if we don't play them without reason." Morrissey would usually say, "Let's do it." But none of the band wanted to do it. The wives certainly didn't want to do it.' (Hinc, like many involved in the touring process, was not enthused by the group's partners coming on the road.) 'There was just no one [who] wanted to go on to do it. Someone, somewhere said they weren't going to make any money from the tour . . . nobody knew at that time because it was something in process and the figures hadn't been done. Because of that, it was a case of, if they weren't going to make any money why should they continue? And there was the question of why had they done all this? Whether those reasons were chemical, alcohol or just sheer fatigue I don't know; the energy had run out of the door.'

The final decision was made by Morrissey and Marr at the group's hotel in Tampa, Florida, the day after the St Petersburg show. Everyone else in the entourage was excluded from this conversation. John Featherstone recalled 'sitting on the beach at St Petersburg with Grant [Showbiz] and Phil [Powell], just not wanting to go back to the hotel. Because stuff was going on and we didn't really understand it; it really felt like there was some very serious stuff going on here. It was just incredibly uncomfortable. We had lost the model of the old forum, of everyone sitting down and saying, "How do we figure this out?"

There was this strange dynamic that changed in the end with the addition of Craig, from my perspective. [He] tipped the balance of the band more towards Mike and Andy's type of "lads out for a laugh," and less in terms of the balance of Johnny and Morrissey's higher goals – without judgement to Mike and Andy. I think what happened there was, that tended to fragment and fracture the band more than it had done in the past. I don't blame Craig for that; it's not his fault, it's just a factor of him being around. Certainly the way I recall it, there was a tendency for Mike and Andy and Craig to hang out, and Johnny to be on his own a bit, and Morrissey to be on his own a bit – rather than it be a gang of four of them.' It was something of a familiar rock 'n' roll story: the communication that had seemed so natural when everyone travelled together in a Renault splitter van had disappeared amid a world of limousines, air shuttles, private hotel rooms – and additional musicians. As a result, said Featherstone, 'It almost felt like Johnny and Morrissey were daring each other not to play Radio City.'

'I wish we'd played it,' said Marr of the show's intended finale many years later. 'For the significance. Because we were conquering everywhere else, and it would have been another great story to tell.' At the time, he admitted, 'I don't think I personally recognised the significance of playing Radio City, and it's almost news to me that there were other gigs after Florida. Because we ended the tour in Florida.'

While Morrissey and Marr were coming to this conclusion, out on the beach Andy Rourke went for a paddle in the ocean to cool off – only to return to the shore screaming. Initially he thought he'd stood on some glass, given the jarring pain and the fact that when he went to the shower on the beach, he saw blood spurting out of his ankle in rhythm with his pulse. Then he was told that he'd been stung by a stingray, and advised to seek emergency treatment immediately; if the stinger was embedded in his leg, he was told, it could kill. He recalled the agony: 'The pain went up my leg, then up both legs, then it hit my balls, and it felt like I'd been punched in the balls.

Then it went up, and my heart started beating fast and when it hit my head . . . I thought I was going to die.'

Mike Hinc helped rush Rourke to the hospital, where the vagaries of the American medical system meant that, without insurance details or a credit card immediately at hand (the bass player had travelled in his swimsuit) he was left to fend for himself with the pain until someone else came from the hotel with the paperwork. Once the insurance issues were finally settled, Rourke was given a tetanus shot, and his foot placed in a bowl of warm water, assured that it would draw out the sting in half an hour; he was understandably frustrated not to have been given such straightforward advice an hour earlier. It all seemed a perversely typical bout of drama to accompany the one that was taking place back at the hotel – until the doctor on duty told Rourke not to stand on his injured foot for a few days for any length of time, and Mike Hinc immediately asked for official medical documentation to that effect. The Smiths now had a viable reason – albeit an excuse – to cancel the final four dates. 'And that's what we used for the insurance company,' recalled Hinc. 'That's why nobody got sued for it.'

Following Morrissey and Marr's closed-door decision, the Smiths and the close members of the crew, equal parts relieved to have ended the tour at last and disappointed not to have finished it as intended, chose to deal with their exhaustion by contributing further to it: they had the drinking session to end all drinking sessions. Andy Rourke, already doped up on pain-killers, experienced hallucinations and he eventually hit the beach, valium in hand, to watch the sun come up with his old school friend Phil Powell. The pair were woken by Jim Connolly many hours later, badly sunburned already, to be informed that their plane was leaving in a matter of minutes. The Smiths, all nursing horrendous hangovers, boarded a Concorde flight from Miami back to London.[7] New York's Radio City Music Hall, along with the cities of Miami, Atlanta and Nashville, would have to wait until next time.

CHAPTER THIRTY-FIVE

Q: What are you driven by?
A: Hate largely. This will sound almost unpleasant but *distaste for normality*. I've never really liked normal people and it's true to this day. I don't like normal situations. I get palpitations. I don't know what to do.
                                    – MORRISSEY to Paul du Noyer, Q,
                                                    August 1987

At the start of 1985, when *NME* readers had voted the Smiths as Best Band, proclaimed Johnny Marr the Best Instrumentalist, and Morrissey and Marr the Best Songwriters, the papers' critics took a very different view of the year's stars. Their collective poll hailed Bobby Womack's *Poet 2* as best album of the year, Womack & Womack's 'Love Wars' as Best Single, and demonstrated further high regard for American R&B over British independent rock in ranking additional records by James Ingram, Prince and the Staple Singers all above the Smiths. The disparity at *NME* represented a significant standoff in the culture wars that took place through the early 1980s, accelerated by the onslaught of so many style magazines that reported from nightclubs worldwide and celebrated the music of the global dance floor, and it showed no signs of calming down as the decade wore on. As Len Brown, employed at the leading weekly for most of the Smiths' career, later wrote in his book *Meetings with Morrissey*, 'battle lines were drawn between those who felt the paper should continue to give the readers their fix of Morrissey and those who thought it was time for

NME to set a new agenda, embracing the diverse forms of black American music that were increasingly dominating the charts and the London club scene.' This music in question ran the gamut from New York hip-hop and electro to DC Go-Go and Chicago house, with plenty of underground funk and slick R&B from around the rest of the country. As such, when 'Panic' was released, it was considered a provocation by those who already felt antagonistic towards the Smiths and what they saw as the group's persistent championing of a dying genre, rock music. Paolo Hewitt, a leader of *NME*'s 'soul boy' brigade, critiqued the lyrics on face value. 'If Morrissey wants to have a go at Radio 1 and Steve Wright, then fine,' he wrote. 'When he starts using words like disco and DJ, with all the attendant imagery that brings up for what is a predominantly white audience, he is being imprecise and offensive.'

He had a point: Morrissey had made no explicit mention of the radio in his song, and his lyrics could therefore be construed as reviving the racist and homophobic 'Disco Sucks' campaign of late 1970s America. Of course Morrissey was anything but homophobic and, given his professed love of Motown and his leftist values, it was assumed he was no racist, either. For British Smiths fans, the 'disco' of 'Panic' was generally presumed to mean the long-standing city centre meat market, which suggested exclusivity by demanding patrons wear a tie, or at least to 'dress smart,' but where drinks were overpriced, fights routine, and both the disc jockeys and the commercial top 40 music that they played was almost embarrassingly disconnected from the neighbouring streets. Then again, when the Smiths performed 'Panic' to nearly 15,000 mostly white American college kids, outdoors in the suburbs of Massachusetts, such reference points, vaguely stated in the first place, were easy to misconstrue.

As it turned out, *NME* was not close to being the *New Morrissey Express* of some cynics' insistence; it put the Smiths on the cover just four times in five years. It was fellow IPC publication *Melody Maker* – long considered the most traditional of the music weeklies – that made frequent cover stars of the Smiths, and it was for yet another such feature that journalist Frank Owen was flown to Cleveland, early in the American tour, to interview Morrissey 'on the road.' Owen was, like Morrissey, a Mancunian of working-class Irish stock. He had come of age alongside Morrissey in the city's thriving post-punk environment, and had played in the band Manicured Noise, of which Morrissey had been a fan. A devotee from childhood of disco, reggae and soul, and already a keen proponent of house music, Owen sought in his feature to establish the connection between punk rock, gay clubs, discos, black music, the Smiths, the DJ and 'Panic'. Given the hastily written nature of the British music weeklies, he failed to pull it off successfully. Verbally, however, he gave it his best shot. After an initial back-and-forth about Morrissey's 'no sex' agenda (Owen dared suggest in writing that in years to come, Morrissey would be into 'fisting and water sports'), he raised an accusation recently made by Scritti Politti's Green Gartside, that 'the Smiths and their ilk were racist.'

Morrissey not only took the bait, he swallowed it hook, line and potential career sinker. 'Reggae . . . is to me the most racist music in the entire world,' he was quoted as responding in part. This was no more true of a genre that admittedly had its share of black nationalist Rastafarians than it was true of rock music, which likewise had its share of white supremacists performing under the Oi! banner in Britain and infiltrating the hardcore scene in America. Not content to leave it there, Morrissey went on to express how much he detested the 'black modern music' of Motown descendants Stevie Wonder, Janet Jackson and Diana Ross, stating, per the lyrics to 'Panic', that 'in essence this music doesn't say anything whatsoever.'

Owen claimed to understand this thinking. 'When NME and Melody Maker started putting black acts on the cover,' he recalled, 'there was a huge backlash to it. I used to get letters all the time. And it wasn't explicitly "We don't want blacks on the cover," it was more like "This is our scene and what do blacks have to do with it?'" And so, in his *Melody Maker* feature, as a response to Morrissey's own response, Owen tried to answer that question: 'What it says can't necessarily be verbalised easily,' he wrote. 'It doesn't seek to change the world like rock music by speaking grand truths about politics, sex and the human condition. It works at a much more subtle level – at the level of the body and the shared abandon of the dancefloor. It won't change the world, but it's been said it may well change the way you walk through the world.' Within a year or two, as acid house exploded (the kindling lit on the Haçienda dance floor) and the rave movement emerged in its wake, a large section of British youth would come to share Owen's sentiment, the Smiths' Johnny Marr and New Order's Bernard Sumner among them. In the summer of 1986, though, Morrissey was still the voice of his generation, which was perhaps why he then dared issue the most ludicrous comment yet of a continually outspoken career: 'Obviously to get on *Top of the Pops* these days, one has to be, by law, black,' which he followed up with an equally ridiculous claim of personal persecution. 'The last LP ended up at number two and we were still told by radio that nobody wanted to listen to The Smiths in the daytime. Is that not a conspiracy?' As a simple point of fact, the Smiths were on *Top of the Pops,* in absentia, the very week before Morrissey and Owen conducted this interview. And while it was true that the Smiths were treated cautiously as a pop act with regard to daytime airplay on Radio 1, they received all due attention and respect as a rock band across the BBC's many channels, with televised concerts, in-studio performances, on-air interviews, radio sessions and unedited Derek Jarman premieres.

Even the singer's attempt to restore proceedings mid-interview sounded suspect. 'My favourite record of all time is "Third Finger, Left Hand" by Martha and the Vandellas,' he said, citing a (black) Motown single from 1966, 'which can lift me from the most doom-laden depression.' And yet this was as stereotypically romantic, conventionally sexist, and thereby nonfeminist a song as had ever been written. It would have said nothing about Morrissey's life when it came out, and said even less about his life and that of his fans twenty years later. He was in essence employing a double standard, based on what Owen correctly referred to as a 'nostalgia . . . that afflicts the whole indie scene.' A subsequent debate about the use of technology in music, especially the rhythm of rap, revealed what could only be described as Morrissey's Luddite attitude: 'Hi-tech can't be liberating. It'll kill us all. You'll be strangulated by the cords of your compact disc.'

As it turned out, Owen wasn't particularly put out by Morrissey's comments in defence of 'Panic'. 'I never thought Morrissey was a racist,' he said. 'I always thought it was just a big put-on, that it was just a way to wind people up, the same way that punks wore swastikas.' Morrissey's subsequent, considerable anger over the published interview, Owen felt, was inspired by the section that followed, in which the journalist tried to engage the singer in a walk down Manchester's gay punk disco memory lane. 'Morrissey is the biggest closet gay queen on the planet,' said Owen, 'and he felt that I was trying to "out" him by bringing this up. But that wasn't the point. The point was that if you were a punk rocker in Manchester, you couldn't go to straight clubs 'cause you'd get the shit kicked out of you. So there was a very close relationship between the gay scene and the punk scene. Like the Ranch . . . it was essentially an old gay club, like one of those cowboy gay clubs. That's why it was called the Ranch – it had saddles for seats.'

On this issue, Morrissey did *not* take the bait. 'The gay scene in Manchester,' he said, 'was a little bit heavy for me. I was a delicate bloom.' If he wanted to play coy, that was his prerogative, although with Thatcherite policies coming down increasingly hard on homosexuality, many other artists had decided to 'come out' in response.[1] As Len Brown wrote, 'It was a time when everyone – artists and journalists – seemed to be asking the question (politically and sexually) "Whose Side Are You On?" To which Morrissey insisted on being individual . . . a card-carrying member of nothing but his own cult of personality.' Worse than that, in this *Melody Maker* feature, he appeared to be projecting some prejudices of his own. When the interview was published, it caused, understandably, a more heated and visceral reaction than any previous Smiths feature. Some *Melody Maker* readers vowed to boycott the band's music; over at *NME*, Morrissey's comments appeared to confirm the 'soul boy' brigade's worst suspicions. There were, nonetheless, those who believed that Morrissey had been quoted out of context; their numbers included the singer himself. 'He called up *Melody Maker*, said that I had invented those quotes, and they were going to sue us for libel,' said Owen. 'So I said, "Fine, here's the tapes." We gave them to *Melody Maker*'s lawyers – and of course he never sued.'

THE 'RACIST' CHARGES were not the only ones being hurled at the Smiths. The same week that *Melody Maker* published its controversial interview – and in a way it served as a useful distraction – the music papers also revealed that the Smiths had signed to EMI. Rough Trade initially feigned surprise: 'We knew they were talking to EMI but no one told us that papers have been signed,' claimed Rough Trade/Smiths press officer Pat Bellis; 'The contracts have been signed,' crowed EMI in response. As the story unfolded over the next couple of weeks, it became apparent that everyone involved in the deal – including the Smiths – was perfectly aware that Rough Trade still had a fourth studio album due under contract, and that Geoff Travis had no intention of giving it up. When EMI offered what it arrogantly called 'an amount that would exceed monies that Rough Trade could possibly hope to recover from the record's release,' he merely dug in his heels. The knowledge that he could prevent EMI from releasing a Smiths record anytime soon helped mildly soften the blow caused by their defection.

There was, nonetheless, a palpable disappointment felt

across the national music scene that Britain's biggest independent label had lost its most credible band to Britain's largest major record company. It signified, for many, a sense of disloyalty and avarice on the band's part, an acknowledgement that everyone had their price. (Travis certainly felt as much: he accused the band of 'excessive greed.') And of course it threw the future of the independent music scene into doubt, especially as no other act appeared to be waiting in the wings to assume the Smiths' mantle. This had been somewhat confirmed in the spring, when *NME* (ironically, given some of its writers' opinions on such music) had decided to revisit the British independent scene five years after the groundbreaking *C81* only to discover that it had turned in on itself, creating a musical ghetto. And that the Smiths had much to do with it.

In fairness, not all the groups on the *NME*'s C86 promotional cassette were influenced by the Smiths, and of those that were, not all were influenced *only* by the Smiths, but still it had to be said: the Bodines, the Pastels, the Close Lobsters and the Shop Assistants, to name but four, all opened their songs with gently strummed, semiacoustic, slightly reverbed guitar riffs as if in apparent tribute to the Smiths' early run of hit singles, before giving way to vocals that were purposefully restrained and borderline tuneless, as if exaggerating the original Morrissey style. The one obvious difference from the Smiths circa 1984 was the gleeful amateurism that ran through the C86 roster. This approach proved so readily identifiable that C86 became shorthand for a new sound of 'shambling' guitar bands.

The divide between independent and major was further emphasised by the success of the Housemartins, the nearest the Smiths had to any sort of new competition in 1986. By taking a more professional approach in the studio than the C86 acts, the four-piece band from Hull scored a top 3 single the same month *The Queen Is Dead* was released: an up-tempo, guitar-based flip-off to normality entitled 'Happy Hour' that sounded alarmingly similar to 'I Want the One I Can't Have'.

The Housemartins made light of their provincial roots (they named their debut album *London 0, Hull 4*), dressed down in what looked like their dads' cardigans (making 1983-era Morrissey look positively dandy by comparison) and were more avowedly political than the Smiths: they refused to support Red Wedge unless Labour made a campaign promise to nationalise the music industry. In this, they were arguably more hypocritical than the Smiths as well, for while their label, Go! Discs, which had made its name with Billy Bragg, presented itself as an independent, it was both funded and distributed by Polygram. The Housemartins' significant success in the singles charts only clarified for Morrissey his displeasure with Rough Trade, and his belief that EMI would surely do a better job of rewarding the Smiths with similarly high placements.

All of this made it that much more important for the Smiths to remain in the musical vanguard. Johnny Marr seemed little worried by the proposition. 'The *C86* scene,' he said, 'the clichéd indie vibe, didn't sound anything like what we actually sounded like at the time. It sounded like some weird Xerox of what we were supposed to sound like two years earlier. It might have our instrumentation, but it just didn't have the darkness. Or the heaviness. I was trying to get further and further away from that.' The question was how the Smiths intended to do so. Would they turn into a major rock band (as per 'Panic'), embrace commercial pop (as per 'Ask', which would also make the top 20 upon its release in October), or become more experimental? Was it possible to manage all three?

In striving to maintain their musical momentum, the Smiths continued to bounce between John Porter and Stephen Street, a seesaw relationship that reached a farcical apotheosis at the start of October, when the group booked several days at Mayfair Studios in Primrose Hill and split them between the two producers. Porter came in first to handle 'You Just Haven't Earned It Yet, Baby', a joyously commercial pop song that was, so Morrissey later claimed, a direct quotation from Geoff Travis. (This was unfortunate, and not only because Travis did not use the word 'baby'. It typecast a lyric that would otherwise have allowed multiple interpretations.) Throughout a song that owed plenty to the Clash's 'London Calling', Marr and Gannon delivered a cascade of jangling guitars that were as effervescent as anything the Smiths had recorded – or that John Porter had produced for them. His final mix positively shimmered with clarity, and given the song's atypically orthodox structure and classic mid-song breakdown and build back up, it sounded like an obvious hit single – assuming that the Smiths wanted to return to, or follow, pop formula.

The recordings that Stephen Street then worked on were not so obviously designed for airplay consideration, and yet were more faithful to the essence of the Smiths; in this, the Mayfair session ably revealed the true difference in the two producers' styles. The songs 'Half a Person' and 'London' (for which Street received his first co-production credit) were, in fact, of a lyrical pair, dealing as they did with the journey south to a capital city and a prospective better life. The former, finalised between Morrissey and Marr on the stairs in the studio, was written in the first person and contained a largely autobiographical declamation – 'sixteen, clumsy and shy, I went to London and I booked myself in at the YWCA' – that nonetheless resonated globally. 'London' was written in the second person, with Morrissey asking the protagonist, about to board a train to Euston: 'Do you think you've made the right decision this time?' It conjured up the climax to *Billy Liar*, wherein William Fisher had promised to take a similar journey with his alluring Julie Christie girlfriend, only to cowardly disembark at the last moment – except that in the Smiths' case, the young man stays on board, and it is his girlfriend who remains on the platform, hoping for his eventual return but already knowing better.

The story of the young man taking his future in his hands in a strange and forbidding London was as old as Dick Whittington, of course, but the impressively vivid lyrics took on new light at a time when the economically depressed northern English cities (and pit villages) were experiencing a mass exodus of unemployed youths heading to the capital – easy prey for drugs, prostitution and crime, and often to be found sleeping rough and begging in the streets. Accordingly, 'London' served as one of the more aggressive and abrasive of Smiths songs, launched with a squeal of a train whistle feedback after which Marr held down the dirty Stooges-style riff while Gannon provided the jangled overdubs using Nashville tuning. By comparison, 'Half a Person' appeared more sympathetic to the narrator's migration in its comfortable mid-tempo, a deliciously sweet arrangement helped along considerably by Gannon and Marr recording their guitars in tandem.

Stephen Street took a liking to Gannon. 'I got on fine with him, I think he was a really nice guy,' he said. 'When we did "Half a Person", he had an acoustic, Johnny had one, I had 'em left and right in the speakers and it sounded great, and I thought everything was hunky dory. He kept his head down, just got on with it, did his job.' The feeling was mutual. 'I felt like I clicked with him straightaway,' said Gannon of Street. 'I just thought he was a really decent person. He made me feel dead comfortable.'

As they were packing up on the last day, Street complimented Gannon's guitar work to Johnny Marr. 'Between you and me,' Marr responded, 'Craig's not going to be around very much longer.'

CHAPTER THIRTY-SIX

I'm not really out to have an easy time. To make a contribution is more important to me, a significant contribution. One that's provocative, not necessarily in an irksome way. To be provocative doesn't always mean to be violent or revolutionary, but really to make people think that at least if you hate or you adore the Smiths, that they stand on their own. That's all.

    – MORRISSEY, Piccadilly Radio, November 1986

It remained the five-piece Smiths for the British tour through the second half of October; James Maker's new band, Raymonde, unsigned and highly hyped as a 'new Smiths' (much like the band James the previous year) came along as the support act. Marr still wore his suits, still flexed the Gibson Les Paul, still occasionally overdid it on 'How Soon Is Now?'. Morrissey was seen to take the stage in sunglasses himself on occasion. But whether by accident or design, a change in heart or the change in audience, the worst of the musical excesses were mostly tamed in the UK without sacrificing the best of the athleticism. It was still difficult for some of the long-term fans to accept the new Smiths as so much bigger and bolder an act than the old one, but others understood that the circumstances now seemed to demand it of them. Besides, the Smiths remained musically adventurous when it came to the set list, which varied from night to night and included the unreleased songs 'London' and 'Is It Really So Strange?' at almost every show.

It was, all the same, an odd jaunt, due largely to the aggressive new crowd that had first made itself known in the warm-up shows in the summer. 'Your band reaches this tipping point, where they go from being this undiscovered jewel that people feel like sharing to this bandwagon that people feel like.they want to jump on, and everyone has their own agenda for wanting to jump on it,' noted John Featherstone, who could observe as much from his vantage point at the light board. 'And I feel the edginess of Smiths gigs was somehow used as a resting place for some of the people that had enjoyed some of the borderline violence and aggression of the Clash and a lot of their contemporaries, and they were looking for places they could go to crowd surf, balcony jump, stage dive. Certainly I remember looking at some of these audiences, the gigs at St Austell, Gloucester and Newport, and thinking, "What the hell is going on?"'

It was at the Newport show, on 19 October, that an accident long waiting to happen finally occurred. Morrissey was holding out his hand as ever to members of the front row reaching up to him when he was pulled from the stage and disappeared into the audience. Retrieved and taken backstage for treatment, he was reputedly advised by the on-site doctor not to continue with the show. Grant Showbiz came on to apologise on behalf of the band and received a bottle in his face for his troubles; he was taken to the hospital while the crowd rioted, the police were called and six people were arrested. Newport was a tough Welsh city rapidly losing its dock and ironworks jobs, and Smiths fans were always excitable by nature, but this (over)reaction (arguably on both sides) seemed to represent a breach in the long-standing trust between group and audience. The same in Preston, just outside Manchester, towards the end of the tour, when Morrissey was hit in the head with an object after the opening number, and the set cut short as he was rushed to the hospital for treatment. While this crowd did not riot, there remained considerable confusion about what had actually transpired. The group (and their agent) were certain that Morrissey had been hit with a sharpened 50-pence piece and that it was the work of right-wing troublemakers.

But there were those in the crowd who believed that it was the drumstick that Johnny Marr routinely used to beat the guitar with at the beginning of 'The Queen Is Dead', and which they said he had thrown into the crowd himself. Either way, the show's cancellation – and that of the following night's show in nearby Llandudno, Wales, while Morrissey recovered – meant that three of the short tour's thirteen concerts had been adversely affected. That was not an encouraging average.

And yet the audience aggression was not an entirely negative experience. At most concerts, it served to whip the group up into their own frenzy. At this particular point in the UK, it would be hard to imagine any band that could have matched the Smiths for energy or vitality, or indeed for volume: Rourke and Joyce, in particular, had turned into one of the finest rhythm sections in rock. Craig Gannon contributed to the group's increasingly powerful onstage presence; offstage, however, he had by his own admission retreated 'into my shell.' He had already sensed that the writing was on the wall regarding his future. 'I started feeling like a bit of an outsider,' he said. 'I didn't feel comfortable anymore.' His personal life was in trouble, and he saw that 'as the most important thing to me at the time,' but spending time with his partner 'distanced me a little bit more from the band.' It was, he said, and this despite having what appeared to be, from the outside at least, one of the coveted jobs in the music world, 'a pretty bad period in my life. I was probably a bit depressed at the time, and that made it even harder to speak to people.' Gannon figured he must have gone days at a time without even talking to anyone, and this on a sold-out tour.

For Marr, the tour had many moments of discomfort, brought on by the audience aggression, the abandoned and cancelled gigs, the personality problems with Gannon, and continued exhaustion brought on by self-abuse: the hedonism didn't cease just because the band was now back in Britain. He had grown used to dealing with it all as (ab)normal life in the Smiths – until his reaction to one such moment of drama caught him

555

by surprise. 'Before I left the hotel one day for a gig that felt ominous, a little voice in my head said, "Well, it isn't that things are impossible. There is actually a solution. If you can't take any more of the drama and frustrations, there is actually a solution."' The words sound like that of someone contemplating suicide, the subject so frequently addressed by Morrissey in song. But Marr was hardly the type to consider taking his own life. The thought that had entered his mind was what many would have considered professional suicide instead: leaving, or ending, the Smiths. The problem with this solution to his problems, he said, was that 'when you start seeing things in a job or a relationship that you start not liking, you can't unsee them.' All of a sudden – and it *was* sudden – the question for him was no longer one of whether he would leave the Smiths, but when.

His band mates and audience alike remained blissfully unaware of this subtle but pivotal shift in his attitude. And certainly, it all came (back) together for the three shows in London: one at the Kilburn National Ballroom, which was recorded by the BBC, another at the Brixton Academy, and one in between at the esteemed London Palladium. On a basic level, the Palladium show satisfied the desire to play formal seated theatres as well as standing-only venues, for the Smiths to prove that they could excel in either format. And it was the London Palladium that had seen the birth of Beatlemania, back in October 1963, just days before Johnny Marr was born. There was no claim to similar importance in the Smiths' appropriation of the venue, rather an unstated acknowledgement that here was where history was made. It didn't harm the Smiths' personal reputation that they opened their concert at such a regal venue with 'The Queen Is Dead', either, Morrissey waving a placard around with those words on it as if Manchester's very own Joey Ramone. Interestingly, the audience that night verified John Featherstone's observation that 'there's almost a requirement to behave that is sometimes imposed by the building itself.' As at Nottingham's seated Royal Concert Hall earlier in the tour, where the stage invasion for 'Bigmouth' was so good-natured that it was allowed to continue unimpeded for once, the Smiths fans treated the plush velvet confines of the Palladium with respect. Which is not to say that they were restrained. Smiths fans were never restrained. Except by force.

The tour concluded at the Free Trade Hall in Manchester on 30 October. The G-Mex show in the summer had been difficult, for all the obvious reasons of size and scope; the Free Trade show, their second visit to the historically important venue, was everything they had hoped for. A banner was placed at Morrissey's feet that read WELCOME HOME, acknowledgement from the fans on how the Smiths were now perceived in Manchester. Morrissey in turn recognised the tribute. The Smiths opened the show that night with 'Ask', closed with 'Bigmouth Strikes Again', and in between, played seventeen other songs from across their four-year career. Minutes after the concert finished, Johnny Marr turned twenty-three. It was to be his last birthday as a member of the Smiths.

THE SMITHS DID not agree to participate in an anti-Apartheid benefit to appease the charges against Morrissey of racism; they had lined it up before the controversial *Melody Maker* story had hit the stands. But the announcement of the concert, to take place at the Brixton Academy just two weeks after the UK tour's conclusion, with the Fall in the opening slot, did go some way to remind critics and fans alike that this was a group that had typically worn its leftist politics on its sleeve. This would also serve as the third concert alongside Mark E. Smith's ever-changing lineups within the year, a proper gesture of professional respect for a group that had been so influential on the music scene, within Manchester and beyond. The fact that Si Wolstencroft had joined the Fall earlier in the year played no small part in the growing friendship between the groups, though the drummer was the first to admit that it was 'crazy,' given his reasons for turning down the job with the Smiths, that he would end up somehow surviving in the Fall for the following decade.

When fans arrived at the Brixton Academy on the night of 14 November, however, those who hadn't heard the last-minute announcement on local radio were shocked to discover that the Smiths would not be performing, and that this time it was not Morrissey who had been taken ill. A few nights before the concert, Johnny Marr had been out in Manchester with Mike Joyce and his girlfriend. Marr was driving – without a licence. This was illegal, if not unusual: though Phil Powell was his official driver – and Angie his unofficial one – Marr was, as we have already surmised, frequently to be found behind the wheel. But Marr had also been drinking: tequila and wine, a deadly mix. After dropping Joyce off at his house on nearby Springfield Road, Marr returned to the Vicarage, which lay on a narrow road, close to a difficult intersection, a route that involved a couple of dangerous bends. He was listening to a cassette tape of his latest home demos, and when it flipped sides and a new track started up just as he arrived at his house, he decided to take a spin around the block to hear it one more time, at euphoric volume. 'I popped my foot down,' he recalled, 'and I just hit this bend really fast, and I bounced from one side of the bend to another. The car literally went off the ground, I hit this high old Victorian stone wall, whacked off the wall, and then bounced – and just as it was about to turn over [the car] landed on its side and then bounced again on the road, went straight down, and the front end of the car came right up.'

His BMW was not just wrecked; it was accordioned. 'You would not believe someone could survive that,' said Marr. 'I had no idea how I ended up with my legs or my chest.' With the adrenaline rush that comes from danger, Marr was able to extricate himself, run home in his severely damaged Yamamoto suit, and get help from Phil and Angie to clear and explain away the wreck. (The subsequent press announcement had it that Angie was alongside him in the car; she was not.) Amazingly, his injuries were comparatively minimal, requiring little more than a fitted neck brace and a period of recuperation. The day after the accident, Marr was called into the local police station, where he should have been charged on several counts. The policeman, it turned out, was a Smiths fan and a budding guitarist. He let Marr go.

Near-death experiences have a habit of redirecting ongoing lives. Two years after R.E.M.'s drummer Bill Berry suffered an aneurysm onstage, in 1995, he quit what was by then one of the world's top two or three bands, choosing to become a hay farmer, leaving behind a trio that quickly likened itself to a 'three-legged dog.' Marr wasn't looking that far ahead as he realised that he was 'very lucky to be alive.' But all the same, 'I changed after that,' he admitted. 'I just really got my act together. And got my attitude together. And my disposition. The car crash – it wasn't just about behaviour behind the wheel, drinking and all of that. It was like an epiphany.' The long-term repercussions would only slowly become apparent. The short-term effect was much more pronounced: a feeling of total clarity and purpose. 'It absolutely reset me in such a fabulous way,' he said. One of the first things he did was to mend the damaged relationship with journalist Nick Kent, putting in a call before it was even announced that the Brixton Academy show would have to be cancelled.

One thing he did *not* do was take a break. 'There was a level of exhaustion that Johnny never really caught up from,' said John Featherstone. 'I don't think he ever really, being the workaholic, driven guy that he is, allowed himself to really recover all the way from his accident.' Marr denied that this was an issue for him, but either way, before the month was out, and still wearing the neck brace, he booked the Smiths into Trident Studios in London to record another new song, 'Shoplifters of the World Unite', which he now favoured as a much darker choice of single over the eminently commercial 'You Just Haven't Earned It Yet, Baby'. That he and

Morrissey might, in the process, be risking once more the Smiths' run of hits did not occur to him as much as did making the right artistic choice. 'I would do a single, and then almost pathologically, not care about it once it had been released,' he said. 'At all. Just purely the fact that it exists, and people who are interested can hear it and judge it and like it or not, is the job done for me. That may be negligence on my part, or cavalier, or puritanical, which is the way I am.' Stephen Street was not available at such short notice, and so for the first time, Marr decided to produce a Smiths track – and take sole credit – himself. He was happy to be aided in his quest by a highly capable engineer, Alan Moulder. He was less pleased to find out that the Trident studio that the Smiths were booked into was not the famous room used by the Beatles, David Bowie and Lou Reed, but the adjoining 'jingle' room. The Smiths had to wait for the secretaries to leave so they could set up the drums in reception – 'and not because it had great acoustics.'

When 'Shoplifters' was released, there were observations that it was attempting to emulate 'How Soon Is Now?' but Marr claimed otherwise. 'It's just what I was playing at the time. It's rhythmical and it's mid-tempo and it's swampy, but I would never have been so gauche as to try and re-create any of our songs.' As far as he was concerned, 'the vocal was the best part of it.' And it was true, Morrissey gave a particularly strong performance, even harmonising with himself in the absence of a Kirsty MacColl or any digital effects. Though the title and chorus appeared to be yet another in Morrissey's long list of provocative calls for attention (and publicity), Morrissey explained that he was referring to shoplifting purely in the 'spiritual' sense and left it at that. It was a murky summation for a murky song that featured the surprising exaltation of a twin guitar solo, in the style of Thin Lizzy, right where one might otherwise have expected a third verse to come in. Though barely fifteen seconds in length, and more melodic than it was dexterous, the solo was to be considered by some as sacrilege, which would only serve to increase Marr's concern that he was being typecast in the Smiths.

The Smiths returned to their original four-piece lineup with this session. Given the personal dynamics over recent weeks, Craig Gannon was not unduly surprised to find that he had been fired. Given the chaotic state of the band, it might not even have been a shock that nobody called to tell him as much, that he heard the news from a friend in Easterhouse. But it was to serve as a disappointment, once his departure finally broke in the media, when he was bad-mouthed in public. 'His involvement, recording wise has hardly been anything at all,' Rough Trade's Pat Bellis was quoted as saying to the music press. 'He just didn't seem very interested and there were times when he didn't turn up for rehearsals.' A simple statement from the band confirming his departure and expressing thanks for his contribution would surely have sufficed.

'At the time,' said Marr, who was to find himself in a public spat with Gannon that ought to have been avoidable, 'I viewed his behaviour as not . . . taking the opportunity that we were oh-so-kindly offering. I wasn't able to see what a difficult position he was in. He was on a real hiding to nothing and looking back on it, he handled it really well. What was he going to do, sit down in between me and Morrissey and say, "I think you should do things differently"? He played great, and he played appropriately – which is another way of saying that he played great.' Six months after Gannon left, Marr was, in fact, able to take greater responsibility for his own (in)actions: 'I began to get very complacent in my own guitar playing,' he admitted as justification for trimming back the lineup.

Gannon had no contractual claims on the Smiths. But he did have a right to expect payment for his work thus far: £30,000 was the amount he believed to have been agreed, a decent annual salary in the UK in 1986 but not an overwhelming sum of money for a few months in the music business, considering the level of the tours he had undertaken and the successful, hit-producing studio work for which he had been offered no

561

other compensation. As Gannon settled back down in Salford, praying that his next musical project would be less stressful, he began to wonder when he would get the cheque.

JUST BEFORE THE rescheduled anti-Apartheid benefit at Brixton Academy, in early December, the Smiths recorded a fourth Radio 1 session for John Peel. They were able to finagle John Porter as their producer once again; despite the possibility that Porter may have been frustrated by the band's treatment of him, he liked them too much to ever refuse to work with them. The session featured the two new B-sides, 'London' and 'Half a Person', and the two songs that had been left unfinished earlier in the year, 'Sweet and Tender Hooligan' and 'Is It Really So Strange?'. All four versions were tribute to both Porter and the group's ability to record successfully in haste when circumstances demanded. They were, in fact, so good that they led to suggestions that the band might have brought in their own master tracks for the latter two songs in a deliberate attempt to secure finished versions; it appears to have been no coincidence that they ended up purchasing both 'Sweet and Tender Hooligan' and 'Is It Really So Strange?' from the BBC and using them for a future B-side. In addition, Craig Gannon was certain that he recognised his guitar work on 'Is It Really So Strange?'[1] In the meantime, the Smiths' enduring popularity with Peel listeners, three years after they broke into the big-time, was confirmed when 'There Is a Light That Never Goes Out' topped his 1986 Festive Fifty. If ever a Smiths song appealed to all comers, this would appear to have been the one.

It was a much rejuvenated Smiths that took to the stage for the rescheduled anti-Apartheid benefit at the Brixton Academy on Friday, 12 December. The reasons were many, including Marr's renewed sense of clarity, the enforced rest after the heavy touring schedule, the invigorating recent recording sessions, a considerably changed-up set list and, it had to be said, the return of the group to its original four-piece lineup: minus Gannon to play rhythm guitar, Marr was forced to reassume that role himself and all but abandon the solo work, and he – and the band – were all the better for it. The set list unveiled 'Shoplifters of the World Unite' as the 'new single,' and made a point of similarly including 'Some Girls Are Bigger Than Others', the only song from *The Queen Is Dead* not to have been previously performed in concert. 'This Night Has Opened My Eyes' and 'William, It Was Really Nothing' were recalled to the set after a long absence; so too was 'Miserable Lie', forming a medley with 'London'. During 'Still Ill', Johnny Marr, having abandoned the formal Yamamoto suits for more casual wear, broke with his traditional stage position (from which he would interact with Morrissey and exchange musical cues with Mike Joyce), and came over to stand by his old friend Andy Rourke. Morrissey joined them, and for the next minute or two, the three front members of the Smiths, performing on one of London's larger stages, were huddled tightly together like a support band at the Rock Garden. They never looked happier. For 'The Queen Is Dead', Morrissey's placard was changed to read TWO LIGHT ALES PLEASE. The possibilities for future slogans appeared endless.

The final encore recalled back to the set the group's first single, 'Hand in Glove', which had been absent from the last British tour. Morrissey, wearing a Smiths T-shirt as had become his rite during the past year, bounced about the stage as if he were one of the fans who had, as ever, earlier clambered on board for their fifteen seconds of fame and camaraderie. Marr, cigarette hanging from his lips as had become his own prop throughout 1986, reenacted that familiar dance of mutual appreciation with his partner as the song reached its climax, while Joyce and Rourke hammered out the beat with an intensity that demonstrated that for them, at least, the tribulations of the year's difficult touring had proven to be something of a musical asset. The sense of collective euphoria might explain why Morrissey extended the finale with an additional twenty seconds of purely guttural excitement – all of which made it only that much more poignant that the last lines he would ever sing in concert as a member of the Smiths were 'I'll probably never see you again.'

CHAPTER THIRTY-SEVEN

Within the Smiths the reason it worked so well was that everybody knew their place and their capabilities and each other's position. It was such a tight unit and nobody it seemed could penetrate The Smiths' little secret private world. On the occasion that somebody did break through the mould everything fell in twenty-five different directions.

— MORRISSEY, *NME*,
February 1988

There was no need to rush, and yet there was no attempt to slow down. If anything, Johnny Marr's car crash appeared to have increased his work rate, or at least his determination to get things done *now*, as if time might run out. The very day after the Brixton Academy show, he assembled the band and John Porter at Paul Weller's Solid Bond Studios in Marble Arch to record yet another new song, 'Sheila Take a Bow'. Morrissey did not show – and one could understand as much; a front man is entitled to a day off after putting in as much energy as he had the previous night. Then again, Morrissey had invited Sandie Shaw along to sing backing vocals, and for that reason alone he might have either made the effort to attend or called his heroine to offer his apologies. He did neither, and Shaw was left to deal with Marr, who, she recalled, 'now wore the haggard look of a man tired of making excuses for his ill-mannered play friend.' The session was abandoned.

Johnny and Angie hosted Guy Pratt and his girlfriend, Caroline, for New Year, after which they treated Pratt to a whistle-stop twenty-four-hour jaunt to Rome for his twenty-fifth birthday; there they got sufficiently wrecked on grappa that they took apart a hotel room, behaviour Marr had frowned upon in Craig Gannon. Almost immediately upon return, the band was back with John Porter at Matrix Studios, where they had recorded much of *The Smiths* and their initial collaboration with Sandie Shaw, in another attempt at the new song. This time, Morrissey showed up. As did Shaw, only to find that 'Sheila Take a Bow' had been pitched so high that the only harmony she could supply was lower than the lead. She likened the outcome to Nancy and Frank Sinatra's 'Something Stupid', which was not, perhaps, the negative connotation for fans that it appeared to be for her.[1] Either way, the group scrapped almost the entire session and booked in with Stephen Street, instead, at yet another London studio, Good Earth, owned by Bowie's producer Tony Visconti. This was apt inasmuch as 'Sheila Take a Bow' revived the glam beat that had been such a success with 'Panic' and lifted almost the exact words of a Bowie song for the key line 'throw your homework onto the fire.'[2]

That was not all that the final version lifted. From the original session with John Porter, Johnny Marr took a high-pitched sliding guitar effect that sounded something like an air horn, placed under the down beat of the chorus – but without his friend's permission or acknowledgement. Porter had himself 'flown' parts in to the BBC sessions from his private recordings with the Smiths, and even stolen parts outright, as with the tom-tom sounds on 'How Soon Is Now?'. As such, he had no real grounds for complaint – except that, he claimed (and it was 'just to save time, there was no ego involved'), it was *he* who had played the original slide part. Porter's unhappiness upon hearing the final Stephen Street version therefore joined his growing list of grievances addressed at the Smiths: 'You don't even credit me with playing these things in the first place. You've used the arrangement I've cobbled together. Then you add insult to injury by using my guitar part – and not even mentioning it to me, asking me if I'd like a session fee or anything.' The opportunity to work with the band again never arose. 'It was a sad ending,' he admitted.

Such incidents could be put down to the exuberance of young musicians who didn't fully understand the protocol involved in the recording process. As with so much else surrounding the Smiths, it would have been the responsibility of a manager to ensure that if dual producers were employed, their feathers weren't ruffled in the process. As the New Year dawned, it appeared that the Smiths – or at least Morrissey and Marr doing business as the Smiths – had finally settled that long-standing problem. They appointed Ken Friedman as their manager.

Though Friedman had missed the band's Californian dates, he had been over for the final Brixton Academy show, by which time his employment had just about been confirmed. A crucial incentive for the band was his willingness to move to London to open an office, in the Nomis Building, a music-business office-rehearsal complex behind Olympia in West London, from where he would manage both the Smiths and UB40. (The Birmingham reggae group lacked the Smiths' credibility, perhaps, but sold more records around the world – and were equally difficult clients, being an eight-piece group that included siblings and insisted on unanimity for decision-making.) Nonetheless, 'it took a long time for them to say I was the manager,' said Friedman. 'I had to come over a couple of times. I remember having meetings at Morrissey's flat in Cadogan Square. I remember leaving, saying to Johnny, "I've got to get back, am I hired or not hired?" And Johnny saying, "I *think* you are."' Once the decision was finally made, Morrissey appeared to be fully on board: 'It did seem for once in our lives,' the singer said a few months later, 'that everything was going to be ironed out and the future was quite solid.'

However, Friedman immediately fell into the trap that snared almost anyone who came into close contact with the Smiths. As Andy Rourke noted, 'People always warmed to Johnny first and then me and Mike, and I think Morrissey always saw that as "This isn't working because this guy isn't communicating with me.'" Sure enough, 'Johnny and I became mates very quickly,' said Friedman. 'So Morrissey would speak to me through Johnny and vice versa. So I never had a communication with Morrissey until later, because Johnny would pass it on and it was effortless.'

Friedman's first act was to make the rounds of the Smiths' business partners. Geoff Travis warned him that the Smiths were 'unmanageable' and that he was 'wasting his time,' which, said Friedman, only 'made me want to do it more.' As far as the new manager could read the band's relations with Travis, 'Johnny hated him, and Morrissey had a real love-hate relationship with him. Geoff would perhaps paint a picture of how close they were. But Geoff could never get Morrissey on the phone.' (Then again, could anyone?) Travis, who said that Friedman 'turned out to be nice' but 'fell into the either/or camp too quickly,' agreed with part of this: 'I wish I had had more access to Johnny during those years. But it wasn't the nature of the relationship. I think with the wisdom of hindsight, I would probably make an effort to put more time into Johnny. But I thought he was pretty happy to be playing the role that he was playing.' (Marr confirmed as much: 'I never felt neglected. Or disrespected, in any way.') Travis also noted that by the time Friedman came on board 'the relationship had definitely changed. It had cooled.' The group's fourth – and final – studio album for the label 'was pretty much made without us.'

One thing, however, remained clear: it would be coming out on Rough Trade. As if to rub EMI's face in this fact, Rough Trade solicited the Smiths' permission to release another compilation, *The World Won't Listen*, comprising A- and B-sides all the way back to 'Shakespeare's Sister'. Given that many of these tracks had appeared on albums (including, as if recognition of the single that should have been, 'There Is a Light That Never Goes Out'), the compilation was not as altruistic as its predecessor *Hatful of Hollow*; in fact, of the sixteen tracks squeezed onto one piece of vinyl, only 'You Just Haven't Earned It Yet,

Baby' was otherwise unavailable, and in the era before digital copying, this didn't sit well with Smiths fans who felt compelled to buy the album just for that one song. Regardless, the compilation became another bestseller for the band, again peaking at number 2 in the UK. The sleeve used two early 1960s photographs by the Hamburg photographer and former Beatles stylist Jürgen Vollmer. The one on the front depicted four older teenage boys looking off to the side and the back, all the better to showcase their greased 'DA' haircuts; the one on the reverse showed four unknown teenage girls at a fairground, in equally uniform bobs and fringes, staring detachedly out and down almost as if at the boys on the other side. It was an artful juxtaposition of images very true to the group's own, and perhaps because it veered away from the traditional solo cult figure, served as many people's favourite Smiths cover of them all.

The success of the recent singles, and then of *The World Won't Listen*, certainly reinforced the popularity of the Smiths for EMI, who were otherwise required to wait to claim their prize. Friedman sat down with Nick Gatfield ('I knew and liked him') and David Munns ('quite a scary guy'), and quickly realised his limitations. Munns, said Friedman, 'just wanted me to deliver this one thing – a meeting – and I couldn't deliver it. They didn't want to meet him at all.' In the States, Friedman talked with both Seymour Stein and Steven Baker, each of whom he already knew, and they quickly informed him, as they had Munns, that they still had a claim to future Smiths albums. They asked Friedman to clear up this issue.

Morrissey and Marr were equally confused on this front, and even more frustrated that they had not yet received the monies they had expected from the first – and, until they were fully free from Rough Trade, the only – EMI advance, which appeared to have been eaten up by the lawyer's bills. ('Neither Morrissey nor myself has yet seen a penny,' said Marr in an interview with *NME*'s Danny Kelly in February, six months after signing.) All of which necessitated that Friedman sit down with Alexis Grower to get some answers. But the Smiths were no longer using Grower's services, which might explain why, when they met, 'he was very unapologetic,' said Friedman. 'He didn't care that he'd fallen out with the band; he was very kind of arrogant. He literally sat there in a tracksuit with his feet up on the desk, not making eye contact, and then whisking me out of there after eight minutes and ending the meeting. I guess he felt disrespected by the band and was taking it out on me, but it really was one of the more awkward meetings of my life.'

There was little, then, that Friedman could do to change anything with any of the three key record companies (or to earn himself commissions) – though it did not go un-noticed that, shortly after he assumed the management role, Pat Bellis handed in her notice at Rough Trade following what was reported as an 'altercation' with Friedman. The new manager considered both Bellis and Jo Slee – who 'was always at Morrissey's house, cutting things out, doing artwork' – as 'fag hags, in love with him, enamoured with him, whatever he did they loved.' (Johnny Marr had his own issues with Jo Slee, especially at this juncture: 'It was quite evident to me, Mike and Andy that she was besotted with Morrissey, and missing what the Smiths was. It was all about Morrissey for her.') With regard to the press office, Friedman felt that 'they were biased, never objective. They were on Morrissey's side, not Johnny's. Or the record company's side, not the Smiths'.' Bellis's comments regarding the EMI deal and Gannon's firing were evidence of this. Friedman hired Mariella Frostrup, an independent publicist with major clients. Friedman's intent in changing this scenario, he explained to Morrissey, was to get someone who 'will do the best thing for the group. Not fall in love with you, not work for Geoff Travis, not get in the middle of an EMI versus Rough Trade thing. So Morrissey agreed. We did interviews and he liked Mariella Frostrup the best.' Frostrup was an independent publicist who later became a major TV presenter. 'I'm not sure how long that lasted,' noted Friedman.

With regard to the publishing, there was no desire for change – Warner Bros Music was the top British publisher through the

1980s and beyond, officious and effective – other than for Friedman to increase the advances, something that had nobody had sought to do until this point. 'I don't recall being asked for additional monies,' said managing director Peter Reichert, who had viewed Scott Piering only as the band's plugger (albeit a 'great' one). 'That's unusual. That's why you need a manager. A manager will say "Hang on, I know Warner Brothers are holding quarter of a million quid for you boys, let me go and get it." And they could have had it earlier, it made no difference to me. Maybe they didn't need it.'

As the situation with the EMI advances, the lack of pressure on Warner Bros Music, the confusion over tour profits and the distribution of band income all made clear, the Smiths' finances were a mess. It was in the hope of clearing all this up that Friedman switched the Smiths' accountancy firm, hiring U2's accountants, O. J. (Oz) Kilkenny, located in Soho Square. This was more than a minor reassignment: good music business accountants not only take care of the day-to-day business of banking cheques and paying bills but also put money aside for taxes, which they keep to a minimum thanks to long-term investment planning and short-term loopholes. Marr would prove grateful for the change, staying with Kilkenny in perpetuity. But Friedman would find that he had still not solved the problem of getting the Smiths to pay their bills. 'I had to run after them to sign cheques all the time. I'd get Johnny to sign something, then I'd run after Morrissey and he'd just weasel out. I'd be sitting with him and I'd turn 'round and he'd be gone. It wasn't fun at all.' The account from which these bills were paid, he said, 'was not Smithdom.'

Friedman then suggested that Morrissey and Marr reconsider the distribution of royalties. The new manager had learned of the inequities almost as soon as he had assumed the reins. 'Mike's dad was calling, saying, "You tell Morrissey and Johnny that they need to honour their commitments." Lecturing me.' Friedman, as ever, went to U2's Paul McGuinness for advice. What he was told was simple: Give them an equal share. That, Friedman knew, was never going to happen: 'Johnny would have done it, he wanted it to be a group. Morrissey would have just hired two other people.' The new manager's suggestion was either to secure the rhythm section 10 per cent of everything, including publishing, or to at least get them paid directly by the label so that there could be no suggestions of impropriety. 'Johnny said, "Yeah, great idea!"' recalled Friedman. 'And Morrissey said, "Excuse me," and I never heard from him again [about it].'

That left just about one area in which Friedman felt he could properly influence the group's future: touring. As far as the new manager was concerned, the Smiths had barely scratched the surface of their global potential. And if they wanted to capitalise on this popularity, he figured, they needed a more powerful agency than All Trade Booking. 'The problem with Mike Hinc,' he said, 'was that he never stood up to the group. At all. He never said, "*You must do this.*"' From Friedman's perspective, the Smiths needed to be with Wasted Talent, whose founder Ian Flooks (had) represented not just Friedman's own clients Simple Minds but also U2, the Clash, Talking Heads, R.E.M., the Pretenders and the Eurythmics. This was such a significant crop of big-money acts that it enabled Flooks to effectively control the European festival circuit, which the Smiths had wilfully ignored based on early bad experiences with billing. If they went with Wasted Talent, so they were now assured, they would be booked no lower than second on the bill to one of Flooks's headliners. A handful of such appearances at the major European festivals and they wouldn't have to worry about the petty Continental club dates that had been the bane of their earlier existence. Plus, Flooks had no problem with them staying with Ian Copeland in the States, who was eager to get the Smiths back over to pick up where they had left off the previous summer. Then they could start looking at the continents they had yet to visit but where they had a fanatical following, from Asia to Australasia to South America. Marr, said Friedman, seemed more than amenable to the change, and reported back that Morrissey would also go along with it. 'So I sacked Hinc,' said Friedman. 'It was hard, it always is. He was their mate. But I felt I needed strong people around us to be able to convince the group to do things. And Flooks was the best agent out there.'

'Ken spent three months telling me how good it would be when he got to manage them,' said Hinc, 'and then when he got to manage them the first thing he did was to sack me.' As far as Hinc was concerned, this said everything he needed to know about Friedman's credibility.[3] In the end, which Hinc was to find perfectly ironic, Wasted Talent only booked the Smiths into one show – the San Remo Festival in Italy, a 'playback' (i.e., lip-synced) performance for national television. It involved appearing on a rotating stage alongside many of the pop acts the Smiths claimed to detest, in which there were definite echoes of the disastrous previous visit to Italy two years earlier; this time, perhaps as an act of good faith for Friedman, they went ahead with the 'performance'. But they were not exactly impressed by it.

Neither, in retrospect, was their new manager. 'They should not have done San Remo, it was not cool,' Friedman admitted, claiming that he was 'pressured' into it, which was exactly how the group had felt in so many similar scenarios over the last four years. 'Being American, I didn't know how uncool it was. That it was really very pop. The Smiths were the least likely group to do it.' And yet, he maintained of the weeklong stay, which included lavish record-company dinners and various red-carpet affairs, 'It was fun, and Morrissey came out of his shell. He socialised with other pop stars.' Those included the Pet Shop Boys, Style Council and Spandau Ballet, though when Friedman unwittingly tried to introduce Morrissey to his nemesis Bob Geldof, he witnessed the singer's fear of confrontation for himself. Friedman recalled that he and Marr tried to make the most of Morrissey's rare socialising to get him to indulge in some of the vices that tended to find their way to pop stars, with but limited success. The San Remo Festival marked the last time the four Smiths stood onstage together outside the UK.

CHAPTER THIRTY-EIGHT

Q: Can you ever see yourself writing any songs with anyone else other than Johnny Marr?
A: Not really. I don't really think about that; it doesn't really seem necessary. I'm perfectly happy.
   – MORRISSEY to Mark Radcliffe, Piccadilly Radio,
November 1986

Morrissey's my best friend.
   – JOHNNY MARR, *NME*,
February 1987

The New Year of 1987 saw a new look to the Smiths. Gone were the designer suits and casual New Wave jackets, the shades and peroxide crops; gone too was the Gibson Les Paul, that totem of rock stardom that Marr had used for two solid-bodied years. All four members now sported a similar Andrew Berry haircut – a tightly shorn quiff – to match, as best as possible, the cover shot of Elvis Presley on the 'Shoplifters' single, taken by the King's own hairdresser all the way back in 1955. (In a moment of inspired marketing, Rough Trade had shipped copies of the single inside a plastic bag emblazoned with the image of Elvis on one side and the word 'shoplifter' on the other. It helped the single continue the Smiths' renewed run of top 20 UK hits.) It was in this manner that they appeared on *Top of the Pops* promoting the single in February, Johnny Marr back on a Gretsch, Morrissey wearing denim jeans and jacket over a T-shirt of the Presley image, suggestively swivelling his hips per early Elvis. This back-to-basics image was reinforced with a memorable cover shot by Lawrence Watson for *NME* a couple of weeks later, for which they posed outside Albert

Finney (Senior)'s betting shop in Salford, looking for all the world – especially given the paper's astute use of a sepia duotone – as if they belonged in *Saturday Night and Sunday Morning*.

The cover story interview itself was conducted not with Morrissey but Johnny Marr, who additionally took on the role of Smiths spokesman in interviews with *Hot Press* and *The Face*. The singer was left with the decidedly unglamorous *Record Mirror*. 'I don't court publicity,' Morrissey had insisted to Mark Radcliffe on Manchester's Piccadilly Radio back in November, at the end of a British tour in which his onstage injuries had been reported in the tabloids. 'I honestly don't care if people don't want to interview me for another twenty years.' An exaggeration, perhaps, but Morrissey did seem somewhat chastened, if not fully silenced, by his overreaching sound bites the previous summer to Frank Owen. Comparing his comments in *Record Mirror* with those of Marr in *NME* the same week made for fascinating reading, especially given that they were asked essentially the same questions. About EMI, Marr was anything but apologetic when it came to the financial incentive: 'I'm not going to get defensive about it – why should I? Obviously the money's part of the reason we signed . . .' On this same subject, Morrissey was supremely modest: 'It's a very touchy issue and let's say I'd rather just get on with it rather than dissect it.' About Rourke's drug habit (which had only just become a matter of public record a full year after he'd been evicted and then reinstated), Marr denied nothing and explained everything, whereas Morrissey offered, 'I don't really know that it's my place to speak on Andy's behalf, because it is quite personal.' On the success of the Housemartins, who had just enjoyed the number 1 Christmas single, it was the singer who was positively charitable: 'I'd rather have them in that position than anybody else.' Marr laughed them off the front pages. 'If they really *are* our closest rivals it's no wonder I'm so confident about The Smiths!'

It would be fair to say that Marr approached the Smiths' new album from a different standpoint from the others. 'I had this new clarity and a sort of passion, but a healthy objectivity, I think,' he said later, 'because I knew that if things went bad, I'd decided inside myself that I had a life without the group. I had no idea what that life was, and it was giving up everything, but there was an answer.' This could be interpreted as advance knowledge that he was making his last Smiths album, but he insisted that was not yet the case; if anything, like the others, he had every reason to hope that, especially with the new manager and the looming switch to EMI, and given the group's impressive return to commercial form, things would continue to move upward and onward. But he was determined to no longer assume the weight of the world on his shoulders, or to make himself sick with overwork as had been the case with *The Queen Is Dead*. Equally, he was adamant that the Smiths progress musically. In revamping the 'Panic' groove, 'Sheila Take a Bow' had certainly *not* lived up to these intentions, which was partially why it did not show up on the subsequent album. Another new song recorded at the same session, 'Girlfriend in a Coma', did do so, however, and the Smiths' first task of duty once they moved into Wool Hall Studios near Bath, in March, far enough from London that they couldn't be easily distracted, was to complete the song that would turn out to be their follow-up A-side.

It would also turn out to be their shortest, their softest, and certainly among their most sublime. Marr would make a lot of the fact that it was inspired, musically, by 'Young, Gifted and Black', the 1970 reggae hit for Bob and Marcia, so frequently referencing how much he and Morrissey 'adored it', that it seemed as if he was deliberately trying to counter the singer's recently pronounced hatred of the genre. The reggae reference was patently apparent in the original recording from Good Earth, and it was a shame that this arrangement could not have been kept, as it was the only recorded evidence of the band (or at least Johnny Marr) delving into a Jamaican groove. Still, the subsequent acoustic rhythm guitar, acoustic picking and electric high-life flourishes gave the Wool Hall master a lightness at deliberate odds with its cruelly hilarious lyrics, which offered an extreme take on the ancient pop culture of 'death songs' such as 'Tell Laura I Love Her' and 'Leader of the Pack'. The addition of Emulator strings afforded extra drama in what passed for a chorus, while Morrissey's confession that 'there were times when I could have murdered her' offered a conscious throwback to the sentiment of 'Bigmouth Strikes Again'. As an exercise in 'levity,' in all senses of that word, 'Girlfriend in a Coma' was one of the Smiths' greatest triumphs.

Strangeways, Here We Come, as the new album would be titled ('Because,' said Morrissey, 'the way things are going, I wouldn't be surprised if I was in prison twelve months from now'), was to mark the first time in the Smiths' career that so much material was finalised in the studio. It was also to be the last time. As a result, there were those close to the band who posited that if the Smiths could have played a few shows around its recording, the fire that smouldered deep within them would have been rekindled and the subsequent split potentially averted. It's a good theory, even if it must remain hypothetical. But it has to be countered by the band members' insistence that the mood at Wool Hall was overwhelmingly positive. 'I think it had the best atmosphere of any album that we'd recorded,' said Mike Joyce, 'because by that time we were old hands: we'd finally honed the recording technique.'

'We'd record two, three songs a day then have big playback sessions till three or four in the morning, drinking crates of beer,' recalled Rourke. Indeed, drinking was no less restrained than ever, other substances continued to abound, and post-recording hours were relieved by performing the greatest hits of the hilarious *This Is Spinal Tap* fake rock documentary; even Stephen Street was brought into the proceedings. (Morrissey, who kept to his daytime hours, was not.)

The argument against playing more live dates also had to take into account that neither Morrissey nor Marr, both worn out from their experiences in 1986, were desperately keen to resume touring, and that even had they been willing to test

579

new material via some low-key performances, Wasted Talent was none so equipped as All Trade to hastily set up a series of club dates or Scottish village halls. It was, in fact, a deliberate policy that the new songs be largely formulated in the studio rather than at soundcheck or in concert – a means by which the group sought to change things up – but the process was inherently challenging. Once 'Sheila Take a Bow' was released in April, that would make ten songs that the Smiths had recorded and released since *The Queen Is Dead*. The self-imposed pressure to release an album a year (what Stephen Street likened to the annual 'fashion house collection') now meant that they were going to have to come up with their *second* new album of material in less than twelve months. This would have been difficult enough even under the best of circumstances – an invigorated partnership of Morrissey and Marr sitting down for old-fashioned writing sessions in Bowdon, for example – but it soon became apparent to all concerned that while Marr had completed some instrumental demos, and while he had distributed some of them to Morrissey, the pair had ceased writing face-to-face. 'I was aware that these songs had not been written, they hadn't worked them together,' said Stephen Street. 'It was a case of, "Try this, is that key OK? Fine, is this speed OK?" You could tell that this was the first time that they were all coming in together.'

For the most part, the new approach paid off. (And it was new only for the Smiths; many groups write in the studio as a matter of course, especially as they get older and take more time off from one another). It was hard to imagine 'Death of a Disco Dancer', for example, being constructed anywhere other than in the studio. A lengthy jam on one repeated chord pattern (loosely based on the Beatles' 'Dear Prudence'), it turned into something of a free-for-all at the three-minute mark, once the vocals had made their point (namely, as per the misunderstood intent of 'Panic', that the English disco was a deadly environment). Mike Joyce laid claim to one of his finest Smiths contributions, providing something of a shattering conclusion late in the song as he erupted – methodically, without showing off – around the kit. Morrissey subsequently returned to the studio to record his first-ever instrumental overdub, a cascade of piano keys that were just tuneful enough to maintain some semblance of melody but abrasive enough to contribute to the song's sense of foreboding. Marr topped it off with an Emulator drone. As he had done with the previous album's major statement, Street wisely edited a minute out during the mixing processes.

'A Rush and a Push and the Land Is Ours' exuded a similar sense of creativity, not least because it was the first Smiths song (other than 'Asleep') to omit the guitar, for which its placement as *Strangeways*'s opening track would serve to purposefully confound expectations. Constructed around an upbeat piano riff, loaded with Street and Morrissey's favoured 'reverse echoes', rounded out with Emulator flutes and marimbas, and including a syncopated Emulator piano part similar to the digital piano riffs of contemporaneous ground-breaking house and techno classics (listen to Rhythm Is Rhythm's 'Strings of Life', also from 1987, for evidence), it presented the Smiths' opening address on the group's broadest of musical envelopes.

The song title was taken directly from the writings of Oscar Wilde's mother, who had published it, under the pen name Speranza, in the Irish newspaper *The Nation* at the time of the Potato Famine. 'One bold, one decisive move,' she had written. 'One instant to take breath, and then a rising: a rush, a charge from North, South, East and West upon the English garrison, and *the land is ours* . . .'[1] But if Morrissey was hoping to inspire a similar united uprising against the modern English garrison, it would prove too late: Thatcher was elected to a third term as prime minister in the period between the song's recording and its release. (So much for Red Wedge.) Besides, the song itself did not expound much upon its title; rather, the lyrics quickly diverged into the first of *Strangeways*'s many songs about failed love.

The best of these, at least from the point of studio

arrangements, was 'Last Night I Dreamt That Somebody Loved Me', which both Morrissey and Marr would repeatedly claim as their favourite Smiths song of all. Morrissey had spoken the previous November of wanting 'to do some very searing ballads,' and Marr had made it clear of his determination to progress musically; the merger of a hefty ambient piano mood piece with a dramatic 3/4 ballad subsequently satisfied both demands, calling up in the process just about every piece of studio sophistication in the Smiths' arsenal: *BBC Sound Effects* albums, vast Emulator orchestras, deep resounding sampled bass notes, arpeggiated keyboard melodies balanced against those of the guitar, syncopated drum inflections, and an exploratory guitar solo deep in the mix at the song's conclusion. It was hardly surprising to discover that the song was worked on, steadily, for two weeks or more at Wool Hall, and that it was largely finished before Morrissey came in to deliver his vocals, which, despite the title suggesting a repeat of his long-standing formula, served instead as his final word on the subject – at least within the Smiths. Simon Goddard referred to it, fairly enough, as the 'shattering hopeless resignation that this merciless solitude is the protagonist's life sentence,' and concluded that 'Morrissey's voice is all the more affecting for its lack of hysteria, baring his soul with an almost unbearable reconciled sincerity.'

Strangeways was certainly not all high drama. 'Stop Me If You Think You've Heard This One Before', as its playful title inadvertently suggested, brought back the melodic guitar formula that had served the early Smiths so very well, from the use of hand-picked arpeggios to the dropping of kitchen knives on open strings. But it was more artfully arranged than its predecessors, as was 'Paint a Vulgar Picture', which, though it was essentially the sound of the unadorned four-piece band, would have sounded too sophisticated on any of the previous albums – in part because it included a clearly defined guitar solo, although not without ironic recognition of this fact; the

582

drums even dropped out to highlight rhythmic handclaps as accompaniment to this rare break with tradition.

Similarly, while 'Unhappy Birthday' retreated to the semi-acoustic guitars and straightforward band performances of many earlier Smiths songs, the addition of an effects-heavy electric guitar and harmonium distinguished it from previous albums. 'It's still introspective,' observed Johnny Marr, 'but there's a wistfulness to it. There's a carefree aspect to it.' That latter attribute lay behind the original intent of 'I Started Something I Couldn't Finish', which, it was not surprising to discover, given its almost juvenile glam-rock rhythm, had begun life as a jam during the 'Sheila' session. Augmented by hammy horn blasts from the Emulator, and with a digital snare beat for additional glitter-band feel (Marr offered that Sparks's 'Amateur Hour' was his actual inspiration), it included all kinds of guitar bursts, drum breakouts and special effects, and concluded with the rare sound of Morrissey in the booth: 'OK, Stephen, shall we do that again?' (The answer, evidently, was 'no need.') Given its exuberance, it came as something of a surprise to discover that the song had provoked one of the only studio arguments in the group's entire recording career, when Stephen Street took a rough cassette mix to Morrissey's adjoining cottage only to return with the news that Morrissey didn't like the arrangement. 'Fuck him,' Marr shouted. 'He can think of something then.' It was, said Street, 'the only time I ever really saw Johnny flash,' and if he took that as a sign that tensions were beginning to bubble to the surface, it was equally a mark of the partnership's long-standing harmony, for there were few bands whose members didn't occasionally erupt at each other in the studio as part of the familiar creative push and pull.

All along, the plan was for the undisputed epic, 'Last Night I Dreamt That Somebody Loved Me', to conclude the album – until a more poignant song popped up from nowhere at almost the very last moment, when Marr decided to dust off an old auto-harp sitting around at Wool Hall. 'It again was

one of those things where I was just playing how I felt,' said
Marr. 'There's a melancholy in there, but it wasn't weighed
down by any other instrumentation.' Using a familiar chord
pattern, such as the one that had informed 'Ask', Marr hit
on something magical, and recorded it immediately. Street
remembered that in this particular case, Morrissey was present
in the studio and quickly asked for a cassette. When he
returned to sing his vocals (eventually augmented by a
restrained bass line and little else other than vocal harmonies), it was as if he had found in its simple structure the
potential for a true torch song, another of the 'searing ballads'
he was so keen to perform. He called it 'I Won't Share You',
and the others recalled that as he sang it, shivers shot down
their spines. For aside from the beauty of his performance,
the manner in which he once more so deftly matched his
songwriting partner's musical motif, it raised the question:
who was he not willing to share?

CHAPTER THIRTY-NINE

Q: What are your defence mechanisms?
A: Sudden illness. It never fails.
> – Morrissey to Andrew Male, Mojo,
> April 2006

All the no-shows and blowouts that happened, particularly over the last two years of the band, were a very significant factor in my decision to quit the band and a huge factor in my no longer feeling the same friendship with Morrissey.
> – Johnny Marr, March 2011

The majority of major rock bands demand to be left alone while recording an album. Tours can be pencilled in for further down the line, and the occasional business meeting held with management over dinner, perhaps, but otherwise the artist typically desires peace and privacy to focus on his or her art. The Smiths, however, were too famously hyperactive, and too infamously disorganised, for this to ever be a possibility. Though they didn't enter Wool Hall Studios until they had wrapped up the promotion for 'Shoplifters of the World Unite' and *The World Won't Listen*, they did not manage to complete the album before promotion kicked in for 'Sheila Take a Bow'. (The option to delay the single until they were done with *Strangeways* appeared not to have been taken into consideration.) Significantly, at the end of March, right in the middle of the session, Sire unveiled its own double album compilation, *Louder Than Bombs*, comprising everything the Smiths had not released on an American studio album.[1]

It was an astonishing body of work: twenty-four songs in all, going as far back as the single version of 'Hand in Glove' and coming right up to date with 'Sheila Take a Bow'. That the sequencing appeared random was part of its charm: it careened from ballad to rocker, from early Peel session to latter-day glam anthem, all with the unpredictable rush of a future iPod set to shuffle. Given the quality and quantity – and the scope – of the material, it could lay claim to being the finest of all Smiths records released during the band's career. Sire certainly thought so – which was why the label once again approached the thorny issue of a promotional video.

'We were limited in airplay because there were only so many (radio) stations that were playing the Smiths, and only so many that were set up to play artists like the Smiths,' said Steven Baker of Warner Bros. On the other hand, 'MTV was interested in the Smiths, so that was part of our frustration. Here's a company that's an important part of the marketing of the groups, but we couldn't deliver to them the video that other alternative groups were making.' Over the last couple of years, MTV had play-listed the likes of Lloyd Cole, the Woodentops and Pete Shelley – all considerably less significant to the station's audience than the Smiths. In late 1986, New Order, the Smiths' equally obstinate Mancunian counterparts, had allowed the artist Robert Largo to direct a video for their single 'Bizarre Love Triangle', and the fast-cut, colourful result had broken through in America in a way that the claustrophobic Derek Jarman Smiths videos simply could not. Also the previous year, MTV had launched a weekly Sunday-night 'alternative music' show, *120 Minutes*, which, especially for those who lived in remote areas without access to alternative radio, immediately developed a fanatical following; again, the Smiths were obvious contenders for focused rotation. 'Anytime the Smiths got one video spin on *120 Minutes* or one play on KROQ it turned into immediate reaction,' said Baker of the Smiths' fanatical appeal. 'Anything we got was worth a hundred times what some other band might have gotten.' Now, with 'Sheila Take a Bow', an anthemic single that was to be featured as the second song on *Louder Than Bombs*, Sire/Warner Bros pushed once more.

The label recommended to Ken Friedman that the band work with a young female director, Tamra Davis, who described herself as 'the director that companies hired to get the video out of somebody that would never make a video.' In this capacity, Davis had already delivered videos to Warner Bros for Depeche Mode and New Order. 'I always came to it that I was a big fan, and that I worked with bands that I loved. My work was not big and commercial, it was more artist-inspired.' Of the Smiths, she declared the same impossible devotion as did hundreds of thousands of others: 'I was the biggest fan in the world.' For the Anglophile Davis, this was a dream assignment.

For Friedman, it made sense too. As he attempted to line up tours – one of the European summer festivals and another of the American sheds – on the back of *Louder Than Bombs*, he found Morrissey, in particular, resistant to the idea. 'It's true, if I'd nodded, a world tour would have happened,' the singer admitted less than a year later. 'But I wasn't prepared to become that stale pop baggage, simply checking in and checking out, not knowing where I was or what clothes I was wearing, and quite ritually standing onstage singing.' This was frustrating not only because touring was the manner by which rock bands were typically expected to promote their records, and not only because the Smiths were so incredibly good onstage, but because Friedman wanted to show that he could line up a tour of America that would prove lucrative, and absent the drama that had caused the 1986 tour to run out of steam. Yet the more he had come back to Wool Hall with reduced schedules and increased financial projections, the more he appeared to be irritating one of his clients. Stephen Street recalled 'Ken trying to have meetings with Johnny and Morrissey to plan out what they were going to do, as any manager would want to do when they finish an album, and you could just tell Morrissey was not interested.' Friedman himself recollected Morrissey saying to him, 'I'm in the studio trying to create art and you're here trying to talk business with me. It's messing me up. I can't do both. Get out.' With time running out to confirm live dates, a video or two became all the more important.

Davis was flown over to England, with the clear message from Warner Bros that, as she recalled it, 'the band really has to support this record and participate in the video, and if they mess up they're going to have to pay for it,' meaning that the entire cost would be added to the Smiths' account with the label. Davis and Friedman went down to Bath and stayed in a house near Wool Hall. 'The plan,' said Davis, was that 'we would spend a few days with them, get them familiar and comfortable with me. This was why I loved doing music video, because I always came at it with my heart: "What do *you* want to do?"'

That question was never going to be easily answered by someone as mercurial as Morrissey. 'It was this very bizarre thing. I spent two, three days with him, sitting in his bedroom, sitting on his bed, and I had this feeling, "Is he really crazy and odd, or is he just trying to convince me?" I couldn't work it out if it was an act or not.' This was becoming an increasing concern around the singer, as those who knew him better than Davis worried that his affectations were taking over his true instincts. All the same, Davis found what she presumed was common ground. 'We bonded on our love of old Hollywood and glamour.' A decision was reached: as well as handheld footage that she had shot around the studio in Bath, she would film the band in proper performance mode in London (none of the halfway measures of 'The Boy with the Thorn in His Side') and 'intercut it with old Hollywood movies.' But even as she made those plans, she remained confused by her subject. 'I definitely found this disassociation between what he was doing and what the band was doing.' Morrissey's daytime life-style and the other members' nocturnal habits were testing the limits of their mutual work time; Street observed that they often didn't start recording until the afternoon, which 'Morrissey found a little bit annoying, having to sit around waiting for things to happen.'

At the very beginning of April, as mixing got under way at Wool Hall, Johnny Marr, Mike Joyce and Andy Rourke arrived for the video shoot at a soundstage in Battersea, South London, on schedule. Morrissey – you can guess – did not. At first it was presumed, or at least hoped, that he might just be running fashionably late, but given that Morrissey was the diurnal member of the group, this seemed unlikely. In the meantime, the production crew of cameramen, sound operators, caterers and various technicians and assistants stood around aimlessly, totting up a bill that ran into thousands of pounds per hour.

Davis was panic-stricken, Friedman furious, both aware not only of the considerable cost of the production but also its importance to the relationship with the American label and the industry at large. Without the promo clip, Morrissey's demands for greater exposure in America would be greatly hampered, and the label's enthusiasm for the group in general perhaps equally damaged. (And Sire, it had now been determined, certainly did have additional Smiths albums under contract; the effort they were putting into *Louder Than Bombs* suggested that it intended to make the most of them.) With Johnny Marr unable to offer any explanation, the three of them descended on Cadogan Square.

'Somehow we know he's there,' recalled Davis. 'But he won't open the door. And Johnny is saying, "We cannot be a band if this is how you're going to act. Come on outside right now, we've got to do this, we're responsible for this video, it's costing us money." I remember very distinctly that I had no idea if Morrissey was standing behind that door laughing at the three of us pleading with him, or crying, also being upset. Because he was making this sound, like a cough. I didn't know. My heart was broken. Tears were running down my face. You're breaking up the band? Don't do this. Ken was trying to hold it all together. I'm crying so hard. Johnny was like, "That's it. The band is over. Ken, it's over." And he walks away.'

Time and again over the years, Marr had instinctively protected Morrissey when his partner had failed to show, circling the wagons over issues like the Wogan nonappearance, studio absences and abrupt European tour cancellations. On this occasion, he could not do so. 'For me to be treated just like everyone else meant that . . . why should I back you up? Because you're treating me like a camera guy I've never met.' The three of them headed off to the Portobello Hotel to get 'absolutely hammered,' as Davis described it, a process that was accelerated and exasperated by the presence there of New Order, who were headlining the Brixton Academy themselves that week.

In the wake of the following day's hangover, Marr did not break up the Smiths. But he had reached the end of his emotional tether. The disharmony went some way to explaining their somewhat subdued performance on *The Tube* the following Friday, 10 April, where they introduced 'Sheila Take a Bow' alongside 'Shoplifters of the World Unite'. It was to be their last live performance.

In the days before or after *The Tube*, Marr insisted on a meeting with Morrissey, at the latter's flat, to discuss their future. It was Morrissey who delivered an ultimatum: Ken Friedman had to go. The singer and the new manager had grown extremely exasperated with each other over recent weeks, and it was impossible not to conclude that Morrissey's video no-show had been his way of expressing displeasure. That there were cheaper and more politic ways of doing so should have been obvious, but no longer mattered.

Friedman had, it was fair to say, operated like the proverbial 'bull in a china shop' since taking over the Smiths, replacing the group's long-standing booking agent and press officer as well as their accountants all in a matter of mere weeks. 'We could always have done with someone more mellow,' observed Marr, citing the examples of Scott Piering, Joe Moss and Matthew Sztumpf – but then none of *those* managers had satisfied Morrissey either. And Friedman insisted that he had not made the changes purely for the sake of it, but with the clear intention of elevating the Smiths to the level they deserved. (Besides, it was not he who had decided that they needed to leave Rough Trade for EMI, the most dramatic shift of all.)

The only possible conclusion was that Morrissey did not want to be managed. This was the understanding that Marr took away from his summit with his partner: Morrissey, Marr recalled, suggested that 'things should go back to the way they were, which was that I was running it. And I just wasn't prepared to accept that responsibility. Finding a bass player and a drummer, and a lead singer, and then the lighting guy and getting a record deal, and writing the music and producing the records, I could do. But managing one of the biggest bands in the world, and dealing with agents, dealing with lawyers, renegotiating big record contracts, getting the band around eight-week tours – and it was only going to get even bigger – was something that not only was I not prepared to do, but I didn't have the capabilities to do, even if I wanted to do it. I've never met anyone who thinks that the twenty-three-year-old guitar player of a really big band should be the manager.'

Yet Morrissey felt a similar weight of responsibility. 'There were so many creative ideas that came from my head and no one else's,' he explained a decade later. 'Apart from singing, creating vocal melodies and lyrics, and titles, and record sleeves, and doing interviews, there was always more to consider. Most of the pressure fell on my shoulders.' If Marr was absolutely insistent on delegating some of his long-standing (and long-suffering) responsibilities, Morrissey felt equally adamant that he could *not* do likewise; his were the tasks demanded of the Artist.

The pair, then, had reached an impasse. Though Marr accepted that Friedman would have to go if he and Morrissey were to stay together, he refused to carry out the execution. 'I couldn't bring myself to do it because . . . It wasn't my decision. Again. And it was another person I liked. And particularly because of what happened with the video. I'd already had Ken's fury and all the phone calls from everybody, the money it was going to cost us. I just wasn't prepared to go through another massive breakup with someone I'd just spent weeks hanging out with. Too tough.'

Marr suggested, instead, that he and Morrissey get an annulment, in the hope of seeing 'a massive weight off his and my shoulders.' By becoming separate business entities, ran Marr's way of thinking, they could appoint their own managers (Friedman recalled that they were already looking for separate lawyers), make their own financial decisions, be responsible for their own actions, and still make music together as the Smiths. Morrissey could not contemplate all of this being conducive to the notion of the Smiths as a functioning band, let alone Morrissey and Marr as a creative partnership, which might be why, in the immediate aftermath of Marr's eventual departure, while promoting the release of *Strangeways, Here We Come*, the singer would observe, 'It was brewing for a long time, and although many people didn't realise it, I certainly did. It was less of a blow, really . . . not terribly surprising.'

Andy Rourke and Mike Joyce, however, remained in the dark. As far as they were concerned, they were finishing off the best album of their career, and the most recent costly no-show was just that: the latest in a long line of them. The Smiths came together again to perform 'Sheila Take a Bow' to tape on *Top of the Pops* on Thursday, 23 April, their rockabilly look abandoned now for casual jeans, with Johnny Marr in a beret, playing on a stage pumped with dry ice and decorated with balloons to an audience wearing party hats as if it were the Christmas season. In this crass presentation, it was almost a return to the group's introduction on the show with 'This Charming Man' just three and a half years earlier, and the Smiths looked both as incongruous and as comfortable as they always had in this format. (In fact, they would prove sufficiently happy with the performance to include it on an eventual compilation in place of the 'official' American video that Tamra Davis apologetically cobbled together for Warner Bros from non-concurrent live footage.) The following week, 'Sheila Take a Bow' rose to number 10 in the charts, a position the Smiths had only previously achieved with 'Heaven Knows I'm Miserable Now'. *Louder Than Bombs* had just launched itself straight into the American top 100, *The World Won't Listen* was still riding high in the UK, and the prestigious *South Bank Show* was in the middle of producing a documentary about them. Though they may not yet have known it for certain, the Smiths had chosen what was quite possibly the peak of their career to make their last public performance.

INCREASINGLY EXASPERATED, JOHNNY Marr called an emergency meeting of the Smiths at Geales, an upscale fish-and-chips restaurant in Notting Hill. There, he laid out his immediate concerns: he had been invited to play on the Talking Heads' new album, which was being produced by Steve Lillywhite; Bryan Ferry was gearing up to release his album *Bête Noire*, featuring 'The Right Stuff' as the lead UK single, and had asked to involve Marr in its promotion. Marr planned to say yes to both of these opportunities, and others that were coming his way. He saw neither the need to seek permission nor make apologies for doing so, especially given the roadblocks he felt Morrissey was putting in the way of the Smiths' career. But first off, he wanted to take a proper holiday, something he hadn't allowed himself in the five hectic years – almost to the day – since he had knocked on Morrissey's door.

The others heard all this as Marr's resignation speech. 'Let's just do one more album,' suggested Mike Joyce, as a knee-jerk reaction. It was, he later admitted, 'probably the worst thing I could have said.'

Morrissey's reaction was more circumspect. 'One night, we had a conversation about it,' he said, recalling these discussions a few months later, 'and he was saying, "I think it's about time" and "I've had enough" and I was saying, "Yeah, I understand," but I didn't really mean it. I didn't think that he'd completely pull the plug.'

'I don't remember if I said that I was going to leave the band or not,' Marr said years later of that summit, acknowledging the conflicting memories of it. 'But I said that we needed a break, and that we needed to rethink what we were doing. Because I wanted to do other things, and one of them was to go away for a couple of weeks. We'd just done a record that I thought was the best thing we'd ever done. And we didn't have a tour on the horizon, and it just seemed like a really smart move. They could have sat there and listened to me being re-enthusiastic about a reinvention of my life, and their lives. Or they could have heard me say those words as "This is the end, I want out, I'm not coming back." Which is what they did.' Andy Rourke's typically droll pronouncement that 'we actually broke up in a chippy' confirmed that they heard it the latter way.

'The Smiths broke down because of strain,' said Morrissey, not long after the breakup. 'I think Johnny simply had enough of the intensified pressure and wanted to play music . . . He just really wanted to play music and get on with it. That's why the Smiths ended.'

Marr would not have denied this, but, confirming Morrissey's original supposition of the meeting, neither was he yet certain that he wanted to leave. 'I loved the way we worked,' he said, 'which was me and Stephen Street with the band's input, but I also really loved the idea of working with Steve Lillywhite with the Talking Heads.' His insistence on spending a few days in Paris on what would turn out to be that group's final album together appeared only to open a chasm of what he called 'insecurity and paranoia,' which naturally fed back on him. 'The more they insinuated that I was being disloyal, the more I got upset about that insinuation, and then communication broke down. It really pissed me off to be talked to like I was about to be treacherous.'

Morrissey would deny that he, for one, was unsupportive of

Marr's musical side ventures. 'I was *always* the *only* person who encouraged him to do extracurricular activities,' he insisted just a few months later, though by that point he had claimed that he knew nothing of the Talking Heads session until after the fact, which seemed highly unlikely. Either way, it was Marr's recollection that in the wake of the Geales meeting, the other Smiths came back to him with a demand of their own: that they record B-sides for 'Girlfriend in a Coma' – and now, before Marr took his break. The group had always functioned best as a cohesive unit in the studio, more so than on tour, and there may have been a hope that a relaxed B-sides session would renew the team spirit. There might also have been the supposition that Marr, who was typically so eager to record that he had recently done so while in a neck brace, would welcome the opportunity to ensure that everything was lined up for the album. But while the need for B-sides was genuine (unlike *The Queen Is Dead*, there were no tracks left over), the urgency was forced: the release of the single was still months away. Besides, Marr's well was dry; he had no new material to offer. In addition, just like the last album, the process of recording and mixing *Strangeways, Here We Come* had left him exhausted, which was all the more reason he wanted a holiday. The only reason he could see that the band was insisting on doing the B-sides now was out of a fear that he wouldn't return to them – which he took as a provocation. And in coming to him as a united front, it was evident that something had taken place that would never previously have been suspected: collusion between Morrissey and the rhythm section.

Andy Rourke and Johnny Marr had been best friends for a decade now, through thick and thin, through fame (for both of them) and fortune (for one of them), through sickness, drug addiction, and in good spirits, if not always in health. Yet somehow, they had stopped communicating. 'Some of it was my fault,' said Marr, 'because I'd got too far away from him. And my relationship with Morrissey got even more exclusive. But Andy created some of that by getting very, very distant because of his drug issue. Years later I realised that his role in the band, my friendship with him, in being part of my roots, and in a way my refuge, was no longer there.' He was left to wonder whether 'had me and Andy not got so estranged, things wouldn't have got to such a boiling point.'

Rourke agreed. The bass player noted that the subsequent split 'was a culmination of a lot of things: the pressure of us not having a manager, the musical direction that Morrissey wanted to take was different from the one that Johnny wanted to take.' In particular, though, he said, 'the solidarity that we had in '83, '84 had gradually been knocked down by outside pressures, and I think had we still had that, the band would have carried on, but we weren't communicating with each other as well as we should have been doing.'

Rourke was not an instigator. His personality was to go with the flow. And if the flow of his continued musical career depended on siding with his new best friend, Mike Joyce, alongside Morrissey – rather than with his original but perhaps now former best friend, Johnny Marr – then that would have been his natural path of least resistance. More curious, especially considering what would transpire down the line, was Mike Joyce's decision to side with Morrissey, in effect taking over Marr's role in the band while Marr was still *in* the band. This shift would become clear when Marr succumbed to pressure – but unwillingly, which hardly helped proceedings – and agreed to spend a week in the middle of May recording B-sides at his friend Fred Hood's studio, the Cathouse in Streatham, South London, with Grant Showbiz producing. On the first day, Marr recalled, Mike Joyce came up to him to announce that they would be recording Cilla Black's 'Work Is a Four-Letter Word' from the critically panned 1968 hit movie of the same name.

'That doesn't happen,' said Marr. 'No slight on Mike. I'm sure he was only doing what he thought was right. He was given the arrow and he stuck it in.' As far as Marr was concerned, the only person who could advise him what to record would be Morrissey, 'who would have suggested it in exactly the right way.' That, said Marr, 'was the first part of that problem. The second part of it is the actual song.' The very notion of covering 'some silly Cilla Black song' was anathema to Marr's forward-looking agenda (especially after the disastrous Twinkle cover). In addition, he took 'Work Is a Four-Letter Word' at face value and 'as a very pointed sort of choice.'

The lyrics bore out his concern. They could, at that point in time, have been written directly from Morrissey's hand to Marr's ears, perhaps none more so than the lines 'If you stay I'll stay right beside you and my love may help to remind you to forget that work is a four-letter word.' But if Morrissey intended any of that to be a signal of his devotion, Marr took it, instead, as an insult. 'I defy anyone to think that my dedication and hard work was ever in question. No way. So you expect me to go along with that, not just perform it and produce it, but actually take that shit? That I've been anything other than driven, to an insane degree? My back just went up.'

Grant Showbiz was thrilled at finally being able to record his main employers. From his vantage point at the mixing board on tour, he had heard many a Smiths song come together at soundcheck and imagined it sounding different on record. 'With that ego you have as a producer, I thought, "I know this band really well, if I could just get the chance to get in there and show my mettle we could create beauty and wonder."' Instead, he found himself trying to wrestle a couple of finished mixes out of five different songs (including a cover version of Elvis Presley's 'A Fool Such As I' and two incomplete and formulaic instrumentals) attempted over a weeklong session that felt a lot longer. Though he insisted that it wasn't '*that* awful a time,' it was still the first occasion he had seen Morrissey and Marr snap at each other: 'To suddenly see this entity fighting itself was very peculiar.' On one occasion Morrissey got drunk, stumbling around with a bottle, insisting, 'Let's go do this song.' Marr shouted back at him, 'What song? We haven't *got* a bloody song.' Showbiz had often hung out in the studio with the

Smiths; it was the first time he had ever seen them dysfunctional. Nonetheless, like Street before him, the fact that he didn't know any more about the state of their relationship than what boiled over in public indicated the extent to which the group continued to close ranks – even in front of one of its very closest confidants.

In hindsight, Showbiz realised, 'Johnny's nature and drive to hold the Smiths together and make it work was fighting a complete disillusionment in the whole thing. He was drowning, not waving.' Marr himself saw of the session that 'it very much came down to a standoff that was three against one. I was sleeping under the mixing desk, trying to get stuff finished, songs I didn't like. And then the three of them would convene and come in together, en masse. That was the first time that had happened, and that was a statement – and that added to me feeling really alienated. I was feeling very unloved.'

For those who knew neither of Marr's determination to move away from such music nor of Morrissey's message to him via the lyrics, 'Work Is a Four-Letter Word' came across a faithful rendition of an archetypal piece of '60s cinematic melodrama; saved from the pointless trickery of 'Golden Lights', it was Smiths lite, perhaps, and a throwback to the jangly sound of old, but it had the air of the easygoing, mildly throwaway cover version that adorned many a major band's B-side. The session's lone surviving original composition, 'I Keep Mine Hidden', turned out to be the last of the Morrissey-Marr songwriting partnership, and in that sense, an apt follow-on from 'I Won't Share You', although it would ultimately precede the album track into the record shops. Two minutes of Madness-meets-the-Kinks, knees-up, upright piano, guitar, bass, and drums, with Morrissey playing the whistling milkman at the front end, it was rightly considered the Smiths' ultimate music-hall statement. It could have been a perfect pub sing-along, perhaps an encore performance at the London Palladium. It would never get the chance. In the lyrics, somewhat buried in a mix ultimately handed to Stephen Street, Morrissey confessed to his repressed personality: 'Hate love and war, force emotions to the fore, but not for me of course, of course, I keep mine hidden.' The object of his affections, however, was either praised or accused (or perhaps simply informed) of the opposite trait.

It was true that Marr wore his emotions very much on his sleeve, and that didn't always make him an easy person to be around. 'I'm not saying by any means that throughout the band, that I was never a pain in the arse,' he admitted. 'I'm sure I was. I'm sure they had to put up with stuff from me.' But at the Cathouse, he felt that he was being subjected to passive-aggressive behaviour that did nothing to convince him to stay with the Smiths after his holiday.

All the same, Showbiz left the session relatively optimistic. 'There were wonderful and amazing moments in it and it wasn't an incredible grind. There would be that kind of antagonism and then everyone would be back in the mould.' As far as he was concerned, 'you could quite easily have expected that band to go off and rejoin up in a few weeks' time.'

In a normal scenario, he would have been right. But Marr saw it differently. 'The last night I was in the band,' which was the last night at the Cathouse, 'I turned to Andy and said, "You know the way this is going to end?" and he looked up and said, "Yeah, I do." And I took that as approval. And it was outside of being in the Smiths. It was just two people who knew each other very well.'

Morrissey was not present in the studio that day, 22 May, which was his twenty-eighth birthday – and his last, as he might have suspected by then, as a member of the Smiths. The following week, Marr and his wife flew out to Los Angeles, where *Louder Than Bombs* had just peaked at number 62, the Smiths' highest chart position yet, on its way to being certified gold for sales of 500,000 copies – without the benefit of a proper video, let alone a single live date. In the absence of any other necessary activity, Morrissey took a holiday in the same location. The partners and best friends of the last five years did not see each other while in the City of Angels. They would not see each other for many years to come.

IF ANYBODY AT Rough Trade suspected anything was amiss, they certainly weren't about to publicise as much. The label went ahead and scheduled 'Girlfriend in a Coma' for release in early August, and *Strangeways, Here We Come* for late September, the first Smiths studio album to be released in the busy end-of-year season. Morrissey, as ever, put together the artwork: *East of Eden* actor Richard Davalos on the album, and for the single, Shelagh Delaney, who had also been featured on *Louder Than Bombs* and who was widely presumed to have been the subject of 'Sheila Take a Bow' (not that Morrissey's lyrics were so direct as that). Notably, the sleeve for 'Girlfriend in a Coma' contained the additional credit 'Love and Thanks to Angie Marr'. This was the first printed acknowledgment of her integral role – with Johnny, with Morrissey, and with the band as a whole – and it suggested that someone knew they were running short of opportunities. Still, while in Los Angeles, Johnny Marr stopped in at KROQ, where the Smiths were nothing short of gods, and offered no hint of strife. 'I haven't seen him for a week and I really miss him,' he said of Morrissey, which, if it wasn't an outright lie, deserved some sort of action upon his return to demonstrate as much. For his own part, Morrissey gave a major interview to the new monthly music magazine *Q*, in which he appeared perfectly relaxed and confident, although his confession that the thrill of live performance had 'totally, totally gone . . . and I don't really know what to do about it' came as a surprise to those who knew him to say that he only truly became himself onstage. Perhaps this comment, like Johnny Marr's, demonstrated a desire to paper over a chasm.

While much of the *Q* interview was taken up with his usual aphorisms on daily life, Morrissey appeared inflamed about the fallout with Ken Friedman. 'He lasted five and a half weeks,' said the singer. 'And he's not going to go down without a hideous great big dirty fight. It's very depressing for instance to think that he is going to fight for fifteen per cent of every-thing we earn for the next twelve months. He's not going to get it but fighting him off is going to cost an enormous amount of money and physical hardship.' Friedman had had little oppor-tunity to commission a group that had consciously signed its major-label deal in between managers (and apparently paid a price for it, literally, in terms of legal fees) and who had not played a show under his jurisdiction. But he would have had a legal claim on the royalties for *Strangeways*, which had been recorded during his brief period in charge. He ultimately settled for a one-off payment, largely at Johnny Marr's insistence that Morrissey, as he recalled, is 'going to make your life miserable, just give it up.'

Friedman's stint with UB40 had already come to a similarly chaotic premature demise when the group's bassist, Earl Falconer, was charged in the driving death of his brother, the group's sound engineer and dub producer, a problem that put Andy Rourke's drug bust in very minor perspective. As UB40 took a sabbatical, Friedman closed up his office and returned to California. The other Smiths were concerned that Marr had fallen under Friedman's spell and that the choice of Los Angeles as a vacation destination was a first step towards relocating in the rock capital. On the second fear, they were right: he did, in fact, move there for a while, the following year. On the first, however, they were wrong: while Marr was in California, Friedman was in Nepal, trying to clear his head in high altitude. When he returned and Marr explained what had happened to the Smiths, Friedman offered him sound advice based on how he had seen the Police handle their own breakup: 'Don't make an announcement. There's no upside. The press will not let the truth get in the way of a good story. They will write what-ever story they want. If you say anything, what's the point? Except getting it off your chest. In which case, write it down and throw it away.' In the meantime, Friedman lined up a meeting with the president of Capitol, Marr's future American record company. Marr, uncharacteristically, failed to show: presumably, there was nothing he felt he could say for himself that the label would want to hear.

Once he and Morrissey were back in Britain, they let July pass by with no attempt at formulating either an exit strategy or a continued game plan. Andy Rourke and Mike Joyce saw each other all the time, as usual, but there was almost no other communication. And there was nobody in a position to communicate for them. Everyone had taken sides, including the crew, the agents, the managers, the record companies. It didn't take long for word to spread around Manchester that Morrissey and Marr weren't talking.

Bizarrely – and this has to appear as confirmation of the north-south divide, even within the politically correct music business – that word failed to reach the offices of the London music papers. It was only when the *NME* stringer Dave Haslam, a long-term Smiths fan, a journalist, a Haçienda club DJ and close friend with Andrew Berry and, by extension, part of Johnny Marr's circle, was on a phone call pitching ideas to features editor Danny Kelly in late July, that the news finally travelled to the capital. 'I'm not a cutthroat journalist,' said Haslam, who only two years earlier had been one of the fanzine editors 'moderated' by the *Melody Maker* editor for their collective interview with Morrissey. 'I'm not the kind of person who's going to ring up the *NME* and say "I've got a scoop." I just remember a conversation where I said, "You do know that Johnny Marr is not working with Morrissey anymore and the general implication seems to be that they're not going to be working together again in the future?" And he said, "I didn't."'

This was all the more surprising given that *NME* had only recently published an interview with the Cradle, the new Manchester band put together by former Easterhouse guitarist Ivor Perry, who had grown frustrated with his brother's over-politicisation of that band, and none other than Craig Gannon.

A discussion about Gannon's time with the Smiths quickly turned to his nonpayment for that role, and manager John Barratt was forced to interrupt before anyone said anything legally damaging, accidentally letting on in the process that 'the Smiths are going through great personal turmoil.' Nobody appeared to pick up on it.

For his part, Danny Kelly had conducted both of NME's last two cover stories on the Smiths, one with Morrissey, the more recent one with Marr, and may have felt that he knew them as well as anyone in the press. One would like to believe he was enough of a fan that he did not want to see the group break up. But his first loyalties appeared to be not so much to his musical tastes or even that of the paper's readers as much as to his own pursuit of the big story. For their 1 August edition, NME trumpeted the rumour 'Smiths to Split?' on the cover. Inside, on page 3, the paper used the same three words but minus the question mark, as if a statement of fact. Kelly's uncredited news story was hardly the height of music journalism, but neither was it a total lie. It may have been true that Marr was fed up with 'the singer acting the self-centred star,' though the guitarist was not the type to put it that way in public. And it may equally have been correct to state that Morrissey was 'not pleased with the company that Marr is keeping,' but neither would the singer have put it so bluntly. The assertion about Marr 'interrupting Smiths recording sessions to fly to the States to record with Talking Heads, and using Rough Trade money to pay for the trip' was a damaging fabrication. And the revelation that Marr was 'acting the guitar hero' by 'playing on albums by Keith Richard, Bobby Womack and Bryan Ferry' [sic] was tabloid hysteria worthy only of the Sun: the first two collaborations never emerged (Marr had joined Womack on playing with Ron Wood in private), and the third should have been old news already, given that the Smiths had conducted a world tour and recorded one album and three additional singles in the time since Marr had recorded with Ferry. But taken together, it was enough to fan the flames of controversy. Unable to contact any members of the band, Kelly quoted Mike Joyce's girlfriend instead ('he doesn't want to talk about that' she had reputedly told *NME* on the phone, inadvertently giving the game away). And they eventually got an official denial from Morrissey, through Rough Trade, which nonetheless had the hollow ring of desperation: 'Whoever says the Smiths have split shall be severely spanked by me with a wet plimsoll.'

When *NME* hit the stands, Johnny Marr, his paranoia now rampant, concluded that the story had been planted as a further provocation, and 'I just couldn't work out any way that that could have got to the newspaper without it coming from one of the other three.' The fact that it might, if only inadvertently, have come from someone in his *own* camp never occurred to him. Rather than call Morrissey to ask as much, or to clear the air, or even to confirm his departure before making it public; failing to heed Ken Friedman's advice; too impetuous to call anyone else to talk him out of it, Johnny Marr picked up the phone, dialed *NME*, and confirmed the rumours.

He did so calmly, countering Kelly's hyperbolic claims one by one, and then, concisely, offering an explanation for his departure. 'There are things I want to do, musically, that there is just not scope for in The Smiths.' The infamous 'musical differences'? asked Kelly. 'I've got absolutely *no* problem with what The Smiths are doing,' Marr replied. 'The stuff we've just done for the new album is great, the best we've ever done. I'm really proud of it. But there are things that I want to do that can only happen outside of The Smiths.' Any fan with any sort of brain, reading as much, would have felt compelled to ask: why was it not possible to do both?

The same evening that the paper was published, Janice Long had the honour of unveiling 'Girlfriend in a Coma' on Radio 1. She preceded this exclusive with the announcement that the Smiths had split up.

CHAPTER FORTY

It was a special musical relationship. And those are few and far between. For Johnny and I, it won't come again. I think he knows that and I know it. The Smiths had the best of Johnny and me. Those were definitely *the* days.

　　　　　　　　– Morrissey, *Select*, July 1991

I think my life has turned out as it was meant to be. And I would suggest that Morrissey's has too. Absolutely. I really would.

　　　　　　　　– Johnny Marr, March 2011

After recording seven albums in less than four years, releasing countless non-album singles in between, and almost coming apart at the seams after a chaotic world tour, the biggest band in Britain announced that they were taking three months off from one another. It was September 1966, and that band was the Beatles. John Lennon acted in a movie; Paul McCartney made music for a movie; George Harrison went to India to study with Ravi Shankar; and Ringo Starr stayed home. The press had a field day speculating on their likely breakup and noted that the Monkees were selling more records anyway. But when the 'trial separation' ended, the Beatles quickly reunited. 'I didn't meet anyone else I liked,' said Paul McCartney. They spent the next three years making some of the greatest records in the history of popular music.

Could the Smiths have benefited similarly from such an officially sanctioned sabbatical? Those close to the group certainly thought so. 'If they'd only just let Johnny go on holiday for three months, they'd still be playing,' said Geoff Travis almost a quarter of a century later. With equally lengthy hindsight, Grant Showbiz was able to observe of his fateful production session with the band, 'It has to be said that cancelling those sessions and giving [Johnny Marr] a break would have been the answer.' John Featherstone saw the problem as, 'There wasn't anybody saying, "Hey, it's OK to take a break. It's OK to slow down." All the band had done was record, do live shows, record, do live shows . . . Nobody had connected the dots that you could do something else.'

Other bands *had* connected those dots, and not just the Beatles twenty years earlier. The Smiths' American counterparts, R.E.M., had recognised from the outset that, hard as they worked (an album a year for six years straight, plus much more consistent touring than the Smiths), they each had a life outside of the band. For their hyperactive guitarist, Peter Buck, that meant playing with other musicians at every opportunity; not on the scale of Johnny Marr's A-List requests, perhaps, but moonlighting all the same. He was given that crucial leeway in large part because the rest of his group, but especially singer, lyricist, college generation idol and Buck's cofounder in the band, Michael Stipe, had enough self-confidence to know that his guitarist would return, happier and healthier as a result. It's the tragedy of the Smiths that Morrissey appeared to lack such self-assurance to allow his partner similarly free rein. But it's an equal tragedy – at least for fans who wanted to see them stick together – that Marr couldn't play the Peter Buck role so well. As Ken Friedman, who would later attract U2 and Michael Stipe as investors in his New York restaurant, observed, 'Johnny is such a good guitar player. Johnny's better than [U2's] the Edge, he's better than anybody, but Johnny's ego is too big to take a back seat to any lead singer. I blame Morrissey for ninety-eight per cent of the Smiths breaking up, but Johnny should have known how to just let Morrissey be the lead singer. Just be the guitar player. Johnny wanted to be the equal, and it's never really that way. Michael Stipe and Peter Buck aren't really equal.'

Perhaps not; perhaps the reference point should be Keith

Richards and Mick Jagger. Though this pair would ultimately come to be seen as sharing equal power, responsibility and credibility in the Rolling Stones, that was not an immediate observation on the part of the fans, or even within the group. It was not until a power struggle throughout the late 1980s, more than a quarter of a century after they had formed, that Richards was able to demonstrate his unequivocal importance, and only after waging a war of words in the press with his childhood friend and releasing a more positively received solo album than Jagger's. Marr, evidently, did not have the patience for such a long marriage.

Morrissey seemed to understand as much. 'When he left,' he said of Marr not long after the event, 'he wanted to make a name for himself, which he did. He wanted to be recognised as Johnny Marr. He was no longer satisfied with a secondary role of living in my shadow. He knew that if he stayed in the group he would always be the guitarist. That wasn't enough for him anymore.'

Of course, it's easy to point the finger at the real problem in this failure of communication and empathy, the inability to trust each other to take time away from each other: the lack of management. U2 and R.E.M. each had managers on board from the beginning, trusted individuals, who not only maintained professional relations with record companies and ensured smooth travels on tour but could run interference between members when relations ran sour, and could rally the troops when the occasion demanded. Johnny Marr was eventually able to admit that calling *NME* to confirm his departure from the Smiths 'was one of the many things that would have been handled better had we had an objective, guiding, wiser head around us. Like Joe [Moss].' (One of Marr's first acts upon leaving was to settle the Smiths' debt with Moss.) But Morrissey would never put sufficient trust in any qualified manager for long enough to let one offer such guidance. As such, he had only himself to blame when there was nobody around to talk Marr into staying.

Marr had little time for all the what-ifs and if-onlys. 'I think the band needed to split when they split,' he said; the most he was willing to offer was, 'Had we carried on, we would have split in the next year anyway.' His reasoning came down not merely to the nature of the Smiths' musical direction, which was clearly coming into conflict, but the very essence of what had made the Smiths unique: the personalities. 'As people we're just too different. I have my way of doing things and he has his.' Marr considered himself 'a studio musician who gets dragged onstage.' Morrissey, he said, 'knows he's a performer.'[1]

If so, it took the singer a while to realise as much: more than two years passed between the last Smiths concert and the first Morrissey solo show. In the immediate aftermath of the Smiths' breakup, Morrissey could not agree with his former partner that they had ended at the right time. 'The Smiths were almost like a painting,' he explained eloquently to Len Brown in *NME* while the dust was still settling. 'Every month you'd add a little bit here and a little bit there . . . but it wasn't quite complete and it was whipped away. And I find it quite hard to adapt to that.' Time only somewhat repaired the wound: 'I feel a complete sense of hopelessness about the demise of the Smiths,' he said in 1991. As late as 2004, talking to *Mojo* after seven years without a record release, he still insisted that he 'was absolutely horrified' when the Smiths finished, but at least he was now able to laugh about it as he said so. 'I've had the time to get over it,' he continued, 'and I've had excessive counselling and I've picked up the pieces of my life and I'm marching on into . . . the abyss.'

The regret nonetheless remained (and especially for the underpaid rhythm section) that the Smiths did not stay together long enough to properly capitalise on their credibility. They were still on an upward trajectory at the time they broke up, as proven by the fact that *Strangeways, Here We Come* sold just as well in the UK as its predecessors, and that much better in the States, where it would become their highest-charting (and second gold) album despite the absence of almost any valid promotional tool. In terms of American acceptance, the Smiths were right behind Depeche Mode and the Cure (who each went on to multiplatinum albums and stadium concerts), having already charged ahead of Echo & the Bunnymen and New Order; they were almost in lockstep with U2 and R.E.M. at similar points in their American careers. Had they been able to weather the storms that appear to challenge every rock group's stability after five years' constant hard work and the wanderlust that inherently calls out to its creative forces, they would surely have reaped the results.

'They could have been one of the biggest bands in the world,' said Ken Friedman, who was hardly alone in expressing this opinion, and as the band's final manager, was able to offer an inside perspective on their failure to realise as much. 'I'm not convinced Morrissey didn't want it. I think he was afraid of it. Morrissey is lazy. Morrissey doesn't deal in reality. He won't deal with the fact that you should pay people, or if you say you're going to do it, you should do it. Morrissey loves money as much as anyone I know, but he just isn't willing to do the work.'

Others considered that the Smiths had already achieved everything that was coming their way. 'Did they fail?' asked Billy Bragg. 'Or did they stay true to what they believed in? I see that they did what they set out to do – which was to set the world on fire. What they didn't set out to do was become the new Pink Floyd.'

'The success would have been staggering and the trajectory would have been so clichédly brilliant if they'd *had* great management,' said Grant Showbiz. 'But the fact that they didn't and it still happened . . . The fact that the booking agency wasn't that great, and the record label weren't that brilliant, and Mozzer and Johnny *didn't* know as much as they thought they knew – and thank God they didn't know and thank God they thought they knew, because they took us to that brilliant place. What I always like is that the success of it is built completely on the brilliance of the music. And maybe some of the interviews. The Smiths is a miracle from beginning to end.

That Johnny found Morrissey and that Morrissey had that loner thing but somehow was pulled into it all by Johnny and went along with it. And then stayed long enough to do all that. It's the perfect story, because they made these incredible records. Maybe five years is good for a band?'

Maybe it is. Indeed, for every R.E.M. and U2 who, with the right organisation behind them, can slow down sufficiently to ensure their longevity, there are bands (typically British) like the Jam and the Clash who release a torrent of brilliant work in a blazing stream of exhaustive glory and fall apart after five or six years as a result. The Smiths joined that very short list of truly great groups who never embarrassed themselves either by persisting together into mediocrity, or by subsequently reuniting. By that, their musical reputation would remain intact.

It was almost not so. The 8 August *NME* story that trailed the words '"Why I Quit" by Johnny Marr' on its front cover also carried a rushed statement from 'the Smiths' via Rough Trade, one that was not approved by the band's founding member. 'The Smiths announce that Johnny Marr has left the group. However they would like to confirm that other guitarists are being considered to replace him.'

Even all these years later, it is difficult to comprehend what could have been going through the remaining Smiths' minds when they made this announcement – let alone that they then acted upon it. Leaving aside, for the moment, the highly thorny issues of creativity and credibility at stake by continuing without Marr, the essential question remains: why the hurry? Not only was *Strangeways* about to hit the shops, and presumably take care of audience demand for most of the following year, but it had been preceded by such a flurry of singles activity that both Rough Trade and Sire had released bestselling compilations of this material in the spring. The market was once again saturated; there was simply no need to flood it with further new music. The only logical reason for the Smiths – as led by Morrissey, and without Marr – to keep going at that immediate point in time would have been to tour the new album, but that was never mentioned to prospective guitarists; besides, Morrissey had all but announced his retirement from the stage in his *Q* cover story that month, when he stated, 'I no longer feel that it's something I want to continue doing.'

The excuse offered at the time, at least to the 'replacement' who made it as far as the recording studio, was that there was a desire to record B-sides for subsequent *Strangeways* singles, but, even were that the reason, there was still not a *need*: the Smiths typically only took two singles from an album at most, and there were plenty of alternate versions sitting around to satisfy whatever demand might exist to fill out the last 12". Why risk everything and change the lineup for a final 'bonus' track?

The guitarist who made it to the studio was, perhaps not surprisingly, Ivor Perry. After a barrage of phone calls from Jo Slee, acting as Morrissey's point person in the absence of an official manager, Perry went to see Morrissey in Cadogan Square. There, he recalled Morrissey telling him, 'I don't think the Smiths should end,' to which Perry recalled responding: 'I think they should end. There's no way you can have a rock group where I replace Johnny Marr. It won't be authentic. I'm not an idiot and I don't play like him.' Morrissey, he said, replied, 'It's not set in stone but if you do a couple of B-sides I've got, you'll get paid quite handsomely.' Perry said he received additional pressure from Geoff Travis; whether this was in a genuine quest for potential Smiths B-sides, or whether Travis (and Slee) were operating under the illusion that Rough Trade would continue to record and release either a Smiths or post-Smiths group, was never fully explained. Ultimately, Perry acquiesced. 'I was intrigued by how it would sound,' he said, justifying it to himself as 'artistically challenging and interesting.' After raiding his considerable stockpile of material, he attended a session in August, just as Marr's departure from the Smiths hit the music press, at the Power Plant.

The producer at that session was Stephen Street. Like the Smiths themselves, Street viewed *Strangeways* as his 'favourite' album. ('I'd got better at my job, they'd got better at their jobs, and I just thought we'd made a fine-sounding record.') He was also among several Smiths insiders to express amazement at the announcement of their breakup: 'I really thought it was just a bit of a tiff, and they'd be back together within a year.' Knowing, however, that the Power Plant session was 'an attempt to keep the Smiths going with a new guitar player,' Street's reasons for participating as producer were as difficult to understand as those of the three remaining Smiths. 'I said, "Obviously I want to help out but I hope Johnny doesn't hate me for doing this."' He ought to have known Marr's response, and that it would serve to establish the previously unconfirmed supposition that Street had been Morrissey's man all along.[2]

Morrissey, Rourke and Joyce should have known too that, in going ahead with a new guitarist already, they were ensuring that any last possible vestige of goodwill that still existed between themselves and Johnny Marr, any hope that some time away from the band would convince their guitarist to rethink his future, was about to be thoroughly eradicated. It was, to put it crudely, an ill-thought-out 'revenge fuck' – and it had the same effect as such actions often do in a troubled romance. 'I was really, really hurt,' said Marr. 'To be replaced so quickly by your friends, before you've even had a chance to change your mind, was the end of it.'

It turned out to be the end of it anyway. For one thing, Johnny Marr had no intention of letting the others use the name of the Smiths, which he co-owned. For another, the session was a disaster. Despite Perry being impressed by Morrissey's ability to rearrange his music – 'He went, "The verse is the chorus, the chorus is the verse, and the middle eight is the start,"' – the chemistry was not there. Street and Perry already knew that they didn't like each other, from a failed attempt by Street to produce Easterhouse for Rough Trade; this was far from the productive relationship Street had enjoyed with Johnny Marr. After two days, Morrissey abandoned the session and returned to Manchester. He left it to Mike Joyce to inform Perry. As one of the Smiths' greatest fans, Joyce had stepped into the prospective position of musical director in large part because he had no intention of letting his favourite group (and with it his career) grind to a halt without giving it everything he had. But he did not relish telling one of Morrissey's own friends that Morrissey had fired him. Perry, predictably, was outraged not to be informed in person. 'I was aware of his relationships with other people where he doesn't like conflict, he just cuts people out. And we were good friends. So I wrote him a harsh letter. He really was trying to keep the Smiths going, and he hadn't been straight with me.'

They never spoke again. (Nor was Perry paid.) But Morrissey did reply. Perry summarised his letter as saying: 'Your tunes were too good to be B-sides. It was just time to move on.' Morrissey had been giving a series of interviews promoting *Strangeways, Here We Come* in which he had been pushed by the press to justify continuing in Marr's absence, and he had given it his best shot. 'There's certain things I don't have any specific control over and I really can't stop them happening, like Johnny's departure,' he told Chris Heath of *Smash Hits*, assuring him, 'the few people who've stepped forward for the job have been very good, very interesting and certainly possible so it's just a matter of making a slight mathematical calculation.' When an incredulous Dylan Jones from *i-D* (the magazine that had conducted the very first Smiths interview) insisted that Johnny Marr was 'half of the creative team,' Morrissey tried to comfort him: 'I know, and it's distressing, but it's not the Smiths' funeral by any means.'

But it was. On Friday, 4 September, Mike Joyce released a statement saying he had 'fulfilled his role' with the Smiths. The next day, Pat Bellis, having resumed her role as Morrissey's spokesperson (despite the fact that it conflicted with her job as press officer both for the Smiths and for Rough Trade itself), announced that the singer had now confirmed what Marr's lawyers would have ensured anyway: the end of the Smiths. When the news made the following week's music press, it should have put an end to the previous month of rumours and denials, yet it was accompanied by all kinds of fresh inaccuracies: that Joyce and Rourke had gone over to Marr's musical side, and that 'the auditions to replace Johnny were never taken really seriously.' But one central element proved entirely correct: Stephen Street had stepped up to write songs with Morrissey, who would be recording under his own name for EMI. Other than the speed of it all (again, why the rush for Morrissey to record what was, for him, a third album's worth of material in just eighteen months?), this made sense; it was, perhaps, how things were meant to pan out. With Street on bass, the singer was to turn for guitar work – at the suggestion of Geoff Travis, who proved unable to relinquish involvement – to Vini Reilly, the Wythenshawe boy and Durutti Column recording artist who had first come to attention on the cover of that 1977 Ed Banger and the Nosebleeds single, wearing a blazer from Johnny Marr's secondary school. It was odd how the world turned. But turn it did. Morrissey's debut album would be finished before Christmas.

Marr, meanwhile, followed up on almost all the opportunities that came his way. After participating in the Talking Heads session (he appeared on four songs on the album *Naked*), there was the Bryan Ferry single to promote. Chrissie Hynde then invited him to join the Pretenders, and Matt Johnson, figuring that it was now 'the perfect moment,' invited him to join The The; he agreed to both, even though for a while it meant literally going from one band's recording session to the other's in the same day. (He may have resisted the responsibility of leading another band, but he could not resist the temptation to work too hard.)[3] In September 1987, though, before he started on these new ventures, Marr returned to the States and hung out on the Echo & the Bunnymen/New Order co-headlining tour.

Both of these northern English groups were going through their own personal turmoil, which they handled in markedly different ways from the Smiths. Ian McCulloch would leave Echo & the Bunnymen in 1988; in this group's case, an equal distribution of income did not save a band from its personality clashes. Once it was evident that he was not coming back immediately, the remaining Bunnymen allowed themselves to be talked into auditioning replacement singers by their record company, WEA; the subsequent album was laughed all the way into the remainder bins. McCulloch would eventually rejoin the group after a couple of poorly received solo albums, but it could never be the same; the legacy had been irrevocably damaged.

New Order decided *not* to announce a split when they took a well-needed break from one another in 1989, thirteen years after the original members first played together. Instead, with no set date (or even a firm agreement) on when to return to the band, they took on side projects, the most prominent of which saw Bernard Sumner team up with Johnny Marr to form Electronic. In the short period since the Smiths had split, the indie guitar riff had met the rave dance groove on the Haçienda dance floor and produced what Factory Records' Happy Mondays labelled 'Madchester' – a hedonistic, bacchanal state of mind(altering drugs) that pulled the Stone Roses, the group put together by Si Wolstencroft's old college friends John Squire and Ian Brown, along in its wake. As Madchester became the capital for a new generation of club-going, ecstasy-popping indie kids, the supposedly gloom-laden, guitar-based music of the Smiths suddenly sounded very old-fashioned. Electronic, though, did not, and 'Getting Away with It', as sung by Neil Tennant of the Pet Shop Boys, secured Marr his first American top 40 hit.[4]

But all this was in the future. In the autumn months of 1987, both Morrissey and Marr were going through periods of great unhappiness and uncertainty. 'He knows that at the end of the Smiths I was in a very, very depressed state – and that possibly the fact that he broke up the Smiths could have killed me,'

Morrissey told the *Observer* fifteen years later, still hurting. He was right, which was why Marr had asked Grant Showbiz to visit Morrissey in Cadogan Square. 'There was genuine concern about where Morrissey's head was at,' said Showbiz. 'I can recall no conversations about what had happened, and just a series of delightful aphorisms, and tea. Logic dictates that if he was depressed then Johnny was showing some concern. But it was also "I'm backing off this, I'm not doing this."'

Sandie Shaw, in her memoir, also talked of visiting Morrissey around the time of the breakup, where 'he looked dishevelled and worry-laden.' Determined 'not to take sides as I did not want to alienate Johnny,' she nonetheless found her former suitor 'exasperating.' 'From where I was standing, all Morrissey's problems started with himself – his insecurities and the way they made him behave. He seemed never to have learnt the art of friendship, and I felt desperately sad for him, imprisoned in his self-imposed solitude.'

For his part, Johnny Marr insisted that throughout the year-long breakup process, 'I always felt incredibly clearheaded. And focused and relaxed.' Grant Showbiz confirmed that 'when I spoke to Johnny directly after it happened, he was so happy. You could just feel like this weight had been lifted. There wasn't any sadness about it at all. At the time I probably felt sadder about it than he did.' All the same, Marr was heartbroken that the Smiths had tried to carry on so quickly without him, and equally upset that he was depicted as the villain in the story, as the man who had broken up Britain's best band. This media perception would last for years; one of the reasons Marr engaged in so much side work (as opposed to starting his own project) was in an attempt to avoid the attentions of the press.[5] 'A lot of people turned their back on Johnny at that point,' noted John Featherstone, who stayed with Marr in Bowdon after the split, in large part to support his friend while holding out hope for a poetic ending to the Smiths. 'Morrissey could have, with perfect movie-script irony, knocked on Johnny's door rather than the other way 'round like it was at the beginning, and said, just, "Hey, thanks for everything." Or, "Can we just talk about this?" Or, "What can we do to make this move forward?" I remember sitting there going, "He's going to show up. He's going to knock on the door.'"

He didn't. But in the midst of this period of bitterly frozen relations, it was nonetheless Morrissey who sought to break the ice. He called Johnny Marr on the phone and suggested the Smiths play a farewell gig, at the Royal Albert Hall. Marr declined.

Morrissey continued to hold out the olive branch – or the prospect of one – as he conducted interviews for his first album on EMI, provocatively entitled *Viva Hate*, released in the spring of 1988 and yielding the top 10 singles he had always suspected would have been the Smiths' by right had they too been signed to a major label. 'I would be totally in favour of a reunion,' he told *NME*'s Len Brown in February. 'As soon as anybody wants to come back to the fold and make records I will be there!' The rhythm section, otherwise engaged at the time with Sinéad O'Connor, would heed his call later in the year, and so would Craig Gannon, the three of them joining Morrissey and Stephen Street to record several songs, two of which would make the UK top 10. When, on 22 December, 1988, Morrissey finally stepped onto a stage again, playing a concert in Wolverhampton that granted free entry to those wearing Smiths or Morrissey T-shirts, the musicians appearing alongside him were Mike Joyce, Andy Rourke and Craig Gannon. Morrissey wore a Smiths T-shirt himself, and came onstage to the sound of Prokofiev. Apart from Morrissey solo material, the group played three latter-day Smiths songs, carefully choosing ones that their former band had never performed in concert.[6] With stage invasions taking place throughout, it appeared like a happy reunion of the Smiths in all but Marr and name. But it was not to be. Mike Joyce, Andy Rourke and Craig Gannon were by then already in the process of taking both Morrissey and Johnny Marr to court for disputed and/or unpaid royalties.

*   *   *

THERE ARE TWO great tragedies surrounding the release of *Strangeways, Here We Come.* (Other than the fact that it was the Smiths' last album, of course.) One is that none of the songs was ever afforded the opportunity to develop onstage, at least not as performed by the Smiths. The other is that nobody but the group's inner circle ever had the luxury of listening to the album without knowing that it was the Smiths' swan song. That knowledge sullied the experience for many. Short of a controlled scientific experiment with a new generation of historically uninformed Smiths fans, nobody will ever be able to offer a completely neutral perspective.

The individual Smiths' eternal insistence that it was their finest work has occasionally seemed like a retroactive defence against obvious inclinations to hear it as the work of a band on the brink of breaking up. But that decision had not yet been made when Morrissey told *Melody Maker,* in the summer of 1987 that '*Strangeways* perfects every lyrical and musical notion The Smiths have ever had . . . It's far and away the best record we've ever made.' Sonically, at least, he was not wrong. The progression in production values from *The Smiths* – even from *The Queen Is Dead* – was emphatic. 'Death of a Disco Dancer' and 'Last Night I Dreamt That Somebody Loved Me' were studio masterpieces. The delicacy of 'Girlfriend in a Coma' and 'Unhappy Birthday' reflected Marr's assertion that 'there's air in that record.' The ambitious arrangements of 'Stop Me If You Think You've Heard This One Before', 'Paint a Vulgar Picture' and 'I Started Something I Couldn't Finish' failed to underscore their playfully direct sense of purpose. And few could dispute that 'I Won't Share You' captured a beautiful sense of mutual melancholy in both words and music. The band had every right to feel proud of themselves.

But that's not to say it's what the fans wanted to hear. *Strangeways* sounded too *much* like a group that was experimenting in the studio and not enough like a group that had previously recorded as if their every breath depended upon it. There was nothing in its grooves with the urgency of 'The

Queen Is Dead', just as there was nothing with the melody of 'There Is a Light That Never Goes Out'. Nothing to match the funk of 'Barbarism Begins at Home' – or the fury of 'What She Said'. The general problem with *Strangeways* – one that was rarely noted at the time – was that the album did not properly coalesce *as* an album. *The Smiths*, for all its complicated recording history, was still a series of songs enjoined by their leitmotif of social and sexual desperation and isolation. *Meat Is Murder* was an album about violence – domestic, institutional, social, genocidal. *The Queen Is Dead* was, in enough places to render it conceptual, a flamboyantly witty eulogy to a collapsing empire. *Strangeways* had no such unifying theme. Even the album cover – and title – felt disconnected from the music. *Strangeways* was ultimately a series of disparate songs collected together on a single long-playing record. And not even that long: barely thirty-seven minutes at a time when the compact disc was increasingly pushing albums towards the hour mark. This might explain why, in the absence of an eleventh finished song to take its place, the group included 'Death at One's Elbow', a conventional and uninspired rockabilly stomp quietly tucked into the penultimate position, as if in the hope that nobody might notice it there. The Smiths had often released tracks that some of their fans did not like; that, in a way, was a mark of their ambition and appeal. But until now, at least on album, the Smiths had never been guilty of releasing anything *inconsequential*.

Regarding the lack of unifying theme, it might not be too strong to suggest that Morrissey's words on *Strangeways* said nothing to the fans about their lives. To his credit, the singer was trying to write more by way of narrative, and songs such as 'Stop Me If You Think You've Heard This One Before' and 'I Started Something I Couldn't Finish' were positively intriguing in that respect. (It was entirely possible to read the latter as a summary of Oscar Wilde's seduction of the young Lord Douglas, which would explain its placement immediately after the song named for Lady Wilde's writings.) But for all the wicked humour of 'Girlfriend in a Coma' and the wrought personal confession that was 'Last Night I Dreamt That Somebody Loved Me', *Strangeways* found Morrissey trading, uncommonly so, in absolute negativity. 'Paint a Vulgar Picture,' for example, asked the fans to join him in condemning the music business' rapacious greed, which was a little strong coming from someone who had just abandoned the independent sector and whose personal avarice was now a poorly kept secret; his use of the words 'sycophantic slags,' even if intended ironically, saw him bordering on a sexism he had always so pointedly opposed. As for 'Unhappy Birthday', for the first time in what had always been a bitterly humorous lyrical balancing act, he appeared to have crossed the line into outright spite.

'Death of a Disco Dancer', meanwhile, though one of the album's genuine musical leaps, was to prove quickly outdated. Morrissey's cry, 'If you think peace is a common goal, that goes to show how little you know,' may have been true of the British meat-market discos of old, but as the rave generation took to flooding the nation's nightclubs in smiley-face T-shirts, popping pills that led them to hug complete strangers, it came to seem oddly archaic.

Inevitably, it was 'I Won't Share You' that proved subject to the greatest posthumous scrutiny. Morrissey was rarely so taste-less as to name his lyrical subjects (which was why his attacks on music-business figures were so distasteful), and the presence of a female character in the lyrics helped diffuse the obvious suggestion that it was addressed to Johnny Marr. But between the title and its follow-on lines like 'With the drive, the ambi-tion, and the zeal I feel this is my time,' it was hard not to hear it as a closing statement to his partner of five years. Quizzed about it in public, Marr would typically respond, defensively, 'I'm not anyone's to share,' but pushed to recognise that the lyric might not have needed a response as much as an acknow-ledgement, he was more giving: 'That's the intrigue about that song, isn't it? Only one person knows. But I do feel like . . . Thank you. Thank you for that. If it is true, thank you.'

Ultimately, the most sincere way to praise *Strangeways, Here*

We Come was to acknowledge it as a transitional album. It was the sound of a group escaping the formula that had made it successful, displaying occasional flashes of brilliance and inspiration on its way to an undetermined future destination. The next Smiths album would have placed *Strangeways* in full and proper context – but of course that next album never arrived.

STRANGEWAYS, HERE WE Come rose to number 2 in the British charts, the fourth of the six Smiths albums on Rough Trade to do so. (It would become five out of seven a year later, when Morrissey compiled the live album *Rank* from the BBC's tapes of the Kilburn National show.) To promote 'Girlfriend in a Coma', a video was hastily put together by Tim Broad that featured Morrissey, and only Morrissey, singing in close-up over a backdrop of scenes from 1963's *The Leather Boys*, one of his favourite movies. It was as if, the group having collapsed around him, Morrissey – the man who had railed against the promotional video for four solid years, who had wheedled his way out of making them, who had criticised those made without him, who had cost himself tens of thousands of dollars in royalties and contributed to the breakup of his band by failing to show for the most recent of them – could turn his back on his career principles now that he was Morrissey, the solo artist. The record, it was worth remembering, was by the Smiths.

The same with the next single. The intent had been to release 'Stop Me If You Think You've Heard This One Before', probably the most commercial song on *Strangeways* after 'Girlfriend', but a deadly shooting spree in an England that was not familiar with them caused it to be dropped at the last moment due to its use of the phrase 'mass murder.' It was replaced with 'I Started Something I Couldn't Finish' – and the same video.[7] Tim Broad shot it on Sunday 18 October, bringing together a dozen Morrissey 'apostles' and lookalikes (quiffs, Smiths T-shirts, NHS glasses), along with their idol, on a bicycle tour around various Smiths-related Mancunian landmarks (in the rain, of course): rundown Hulme council flats, the Salford Lads Club, boarded-up Coronation Street, Victoria Station, and the Albert Finney bookmakers in Salford. Again, the other Smiths were heard but not seen.

'Girlfriend in a Coma' proved a significant hit; it was as sweet a song (musically, if not lyrically) as the Smiths ever presented to mainstream radio. 'I Started Something I Couldn't Finish' struggled for similar acceptance; it didn't have quite the same swing as the intended 'Stop Me If You Think You've Heard This One Before,' although the unearthing of the Troy Tate production of 'Pretty Girls Make Graves,' complete with cello, served as a modest incentive to hard-core fans. With support from Morrissey, who said that 'if there was yet another opportunity to infest the airwaves I thought it should be done,' Rough Trade then broke with all Smiths tradition and released a third single from the album right on its heels. What anyone hoped to prove, other than that the Smiths could release five singles in a calendar year, or that Morrissey could finally put Billy Fury on the front of a Smiths sleeve, was never clarified. Neither was the choice of song: 'Last Night I Dreamt That Somebody Loved Me' may have been their great studio epic, but it was hardly the sound of Christmas cheer, and no video was produced to offer any other message. The instrumental piano introduction was edited out; the B-sides drew on old Peel sessions. Under the circumstances, the fact that it scraped into the top 30 had to be construed as a success. It was the Smiths' seventeenth single in four and a half years. It was the last to be released under that name for just as long.

As Morrissey and his dozen apostles packed up their bicycles on the evening of Sunday, 18 October, a last supper of sorts took place in the form of the ITV *South Bank Show* on the Smiths. It was an appropriate form of highbrow recognition for the band, given that it was the airing of the *South Bank Show*'s Leiber and Stoller episode back in February 1982 that had led Marr to Morrissey's door in the first place. In that sense, the reverential treatment should have been considered a triumph;

sadly, it had to be viewed instead as a swan song. There was no reference to the split except in the host's pre-amble and a hastily reedited final five minutes; otherwise, the group was perceived and presented instead as a fully functioning unit. Several of the Smiths' closer friends or allies were brought in to provide perspective, including John Peel, Nick Kent, Sandie Shaw and Jon Savage. The singer himself, though he had no part in the editing, nonetheless dominated proceedings; interviewed primarily at a desk laden with books (and also in an armchair, wearing a rugby shirt), he appeared the very personification of the intellectual pop star. In his conversation and confidence, his presentation and wit, this was a man absolutely on top of his game, dedicated to his craft, in love with his career, and clearly harbouring no idea that it was about to come crashing down around him. (Johnny Marr, sporting the tight quiff from early in the New Year, seemed somewhat more animated, even antagonistic in his own interview; Mike Joyce provided the kind of good-natured banter that, as always, sounded better than it looked written down; Andy Rourke was nowhere to be seen.) It was as if Morrissey's whole life had been leading up to this moment, when this 'child from the ugly new houses,' as 'Paint a Vulgar Picture' had put it, this working-class son of Irish immigrants, this lapsed Catholic, secondary modern dropout, this celibate/asexual/gay social recluse and former candidate for suicidal tendencies could finally demonstrate his greatness on a stage worthy of the acclaim.

The producers' choice of closing statement, in their eventual acknowledgement of the Smiths split, saw Morrissey return to a theme and a theory he had frequently tested over the years: 'The way I see the whole spectrum of pop music is that it is slowly being laid to rest, in every conceivable way . . . So with the Smiths, I do really think it is true, I think this is really the end of the story. Ultimately, popular music will end. That must be obvious to almost everybody. And I think the ashes are all about us, if we could but notice them.' At which he gave that winsome smile of his. Even in this farewell, he was able to provide inspiration, if not for quite the reason he might have hoped; a pair of teenage best friends from Colchester, Damon Albarn and Graham Coxon, Smiths fans both, sat down to watch the show in eager anticipation but found themselves offended by Morrissey's insistence that 'the Smiths were the last group of any importance,' as Albarn interpreted it. He walked home that night, hatching plans, insistent that 'No one is going to tell me that pop music is finished.' Albarn and Coxon would soon form the band Blur, signing to an independent that was itself signed to EMI, and with Stephen Street as their producer, eventually led a 'Britpop' movement that, over the course of the 1990s, took the Smiths 'indie' aesthetic (minus its femininity, tragically) to the top of the charts; there, pitted against the Manchester group Oasis, who Johnny Marr brought to the attention of his post-Smiths management in the first place, they even made it onto the national news.

Other than Morrissey himself, the star of the *South Bank Show* was Linder, Morrissey's mentor, muse and eternal comrade in feminism and art. She painted a perfectly pleasant picture of her now decade-long friendship with Morrissey, of afternoon walks with him through Southern Cemetery, nights on the periphery of the Manchester dance floor, and daytimes spent with their noses pressed up against high-street glass, 'looking through a store window at somebody.'

'He'd say, "Do you think they're really happy?" and I'd say, "I think so, I hope so." And he'd say, "Could I ever be like that?" But no, of course not, he could never be happy.' At this Linder laughed. 'I pray to God that one day he's happy – but it's taking a long time coming.'

ACKNOWLEDGEMENTS

I t was only when I started in on the actual process of writing this book that I realised just how much I had been asking of my subjects. When I wrote my first two biographies, on Echo & the Bunnymen and R.E.M., in the late 1980s, the process seemed relatively easy. I didn't grasp at the time that this was in part because the two groups were very much ongoing entities, sufficiently secure in one another's company as to only tell me about each other what they would want to hear about themselves, and young enough not to be especially protective of their legacies or to have left behind any especially bad memories. When I later wrote an enormous biography about Keith Moon, a necessarily complicated and controversial character, I was more determined to write an unadulterated account of his life, and I had the vantage point of history at my heels. But I also had on my side the (sad) fact that my subject had been dead for twenty years – and people who might not have spoken freely about him in the immediate aftermath of his demise felt that they could do so that long after his passing, in certain knowledge that he would not return to this world to punish them for it.

With the Smiths, the process is that much more complicated.

(For one thing, thankfully, nobody within the band has passed on.) While hindsight absolutely has its advantages, and while the passing of time has only elevated the Smiths' musical legacy, it has not been as kind to their personal relationships with one another. In fact, the quarter century since the group's breakup has seen all kinds of unfortunate recriminations – to the point where many stories about the group concentrate on the negatives first, specifically the court case that has made it hard, perhaps even impossible, for four or five certain individuals to ever fully resume their former friendships. Those individuals have every right to be guarded about their personal story, and suspicious of anybody looking to come and tell it (yet again), especially in a format over which they have no editorial control.

So while I offer my thanks to *everyone* who allowed me to interview them, and all of whom did so with the full understanding that they would have no say whatsoever over the final words, I must offer special thanks to both Johnny Marr and Andy Rourke for allowing me to talk with them on several occasions, across a period of two years or more, without ever putting any limits or conditions on our conversations. I don't take their cooperation lightly, and I hope that the finished book repays some of their trust. I also hope that they, as with all my interviewees, understand that the author of a biography like this is inevitably caught between trying to tell the story as it actually happened, and telling it with the benefit of the subjects' hindsight. In this regard, Johnny Marr's personality looms especially large. While it has retained its intensity and enthusiasm, and while his work ethic continues to inspire and occasionally frighten, he is now a teetotal, marathon running, vegan Buddhist. His perspective on the band's history twenty-five to thirty years on, understandably, proved different from how he lived it at the time, and he appeared fully aware of this dichotomy. In quoting him throughout this book, I have tried to allow him the occasional opportunity to suggest how things could or should have been handled while ensuring that at no point are events rewritten as taking place in a different manner from how they did. I trust that I have gotten the balance right.

One of the great joys of undertaking this particular project was the opportunity to renew old acquaintances and friendships. As a teenage fanzine editor in London, I was in and out of Rough Trade on a weekly, often daily, basis from 1978 onward; as an aspiring musician in the very early 1980s, I met several of the producers, musicians and A&R men featured in this story long before they themselves met the Smiths; as a music journalist and magazine editor in my late teens and early twenties, I got to know many of the media and industry figures and was privy to much of this story, if only very occasionally an even minor part of it; as a resident of the United States since the late 1980s, I have also gotten to know many of the important American characters and, additionally and crucially, I hope, developed an understanding of the American music scene. All this may have made it somewhat easier for me to secure the cooperation of my interviewees, but it also raised the stakes regarding any contradictory perspectives or less-than-savoury recollections. My loyalty in all these cases has been, first and foremost, to the finished biography, its accuracy and its fairness. I have dared to presume that those whose names crop up in this story, whether as walk-on characters or major players, have developed thick skins along the way and will recognise that none of us, as the author freely admits for his own part, have lived our lives perfectly – especially in the furious, unscripted and often hedonistic environment of the music industry. Thank you for cooperating and trusting.

With only one exception, the interviews themselves were entirely pleasurable. Most were conducted in person, and in a multitude of locations that ranged from personal homes to public houses, private members' clubs to public cafés, restaurants to record-company offices. They were also conducted by phone, by Skype, and, where absolutely necessary, by e-mail. Research is generally the 'fun' part of the biography process, and can easily be extended ad infinitum if one is not careful. At some point, the writer has to get on with the process of writing, regardless of whether he has gathered up every last kernel of information or possible participation. To that end, I returned to many of my subjects by e-mail time and again over the period of writing this book, driving several to distraction I don't doubt. While I make no apology for pushing as hard as I did in my quest for accuracy, I do recognise that I occasionally tested the limits of my subjects' patience.

Thank you for your time and your memories and your perception and perspective: Amanda Malone, Andrew Berry, Andy Rourke, Barry Finnegan, Bill Anstee, Billy Bragg, Bobby Durkin, Cath Carroll, Chris Nagle, Craig Gannon, Dale Hibbert, Dave Harper, Dave Haslam, David Jensen, David Munns, David Pringle, Frank Owen, Geoff Travis, Grant Showbiz, Guy Ainsworth, Guy Pratt, Hugh Stanley-Clarke, Ivor Perry, James Maker, Joe Moss, John Featherstone, John Porter, Johnny Marr, Ken Friedman, Kevin Kennedy, Liz Naylor, Marc Wallis, Mark Gosling, Matt Johnson, Matt Pinfield, Mayo Thompson, Mike Hinc, Mike Pickering, Mike Williams, Nick Gatfield, Nick Hobbs, Paul Whiting, Paul Whittall, Peter Reichert, Peter Wright, Phil Fletcher, Phil Gatenby, Richard Boon, Richard Scott, Seymour Stein, Simon Edwards, Simon Wolstencroft, Stephen Adshead, Stephen Duffy, Stephen Street, Stephen Wright, Steve Diggle, Steve Ferguson, Steve Lillywhite, Steven Baker, Stuart James, Tamra Davis, Tim Booth, Wayne Barrett.

As noted in the introduction, the names of Morrissey and Mike Joyce are missing from the above list. For a multitude of reasons, I did not especially expect Morrissey's cooperation, although I certainly requested it several times; I would like to thank those of his assistants and managers who ensured that my correspondence reached him. Mike Joyce's refusal to participate came as more of a surprise, given that he was the only member of the Smiths, coming into this book, with whom I thought I had an ongoing friendship. I had perhaps relied on this too much, and apologise if he felt that I took his cooperation for granted. We did have the opportunity to talk, and I respect his reasons for not participating. I'd like to offer both him and Morrissey my gratitude for their contribution to popular culture; I trust that comes across in the text.

I am grateful to Howard Devoto, Jo Slee, Martha DeFoe, James Henke, Gordon Charlton, Alexis Grower, Martin Haxby, Phil Cowie, Ian Chambers, Brian Grantham and Damian Morgan for engaging in correspondence and/or returning phone calls.

Thanks to Lindsay Hutton, Moz Murray, Oliver Wilson, Hilary Piering, John Cooper, Michael Knowles, David Whitehead, Robin Hurley, Eric Zohn, Tom Ferrie, Michael Pagnotta and Robert Cochrane for various degrees of research assistance. There are dozens more I could add to this list, including various professional artist managers, assistants and publicists. To start down that line would be to risk offending those I would inevitably leave out. I appreciate all your work.

I am eternally grateful to Jeni de Haart for providing me with an open-ended residential base in South London as well as for being such a great friend. A massive thanks to Tom Hingley and Kelly Wood-Hingley for hosting me in Manchester – and to Tom for the additional hours of stimulating political conversation late at night *and* at the local swimming pool at seven in the morning! Thanks to John and Jamie for doing so on an earlier visit. Thanks to my mother, Ruth Fletcher, for letting me use her house in Beverley as an office when I might have arrived professing to a family visit instead, and for dropping and/or picking me up many a time at the local train station for my commutes to London and Manchester.

Help and assistance, warmth and friendship, was extended by Matthew Norman at Manchester District Music Archive (mdmarchive.co.uk), Leslie Holmes at Salford Lads Club, and Simon Parker at various locations and at various times over the years in Manchester and beyond. Additional thanks to David Groves for use of his London premises and resources.

An extra credit to Andrew Berry for providing me with a Central London 'office' underneath his hair salon, Viva, while I was running around town on my typically frazzled trips back home – and this without any previous contact between us. He remains, to the end, the hairdresser on fire.

Thank you to the Zen Mountain Monastery in my home hamlet of Mount Tremper for providing a compassionate environment, and to the various Smiths fans among the monastics and other residents for their encouraging and enthusiastic conversations.

Though nobody should be surprised by the number of Smiths websites, we ought to be extraordinarily impressed by the depth of some of them. This book would have been that much harder to complete accurately without having these resources at my fingertips: vulgarpicture.com, plunderingdesire.com, morrissey-scans.tumblr.com, smithsrecycle.blogspot.com, motorcycleau-pairboy.com, foreverill.com, and the late passionsjustlikemine.com. My thanks to Jason from Plundering Desire, Stephane from Passions Just Like Mine, and Flavio from Vulgar Picture for their unconditional help in additional research via e-mail.

I would be lost without the existence of bricks-and-mortar libraries. As Morrissey would presumably agree, there is nothing to match the sensation of picking up a hundred-year-old, limited-edition, hand-printed biography of Oscar Wilde by André Gide from the local library (Woodstock, in this case), free of charge despite the fact that such a book has a high resale value. Likewise I spent several glorious days at the Manchester City Library on Deansgate, lost in old political pamphlets and case studies from industrial-era Manchester. As always, I made frequent visits to the New York Public Library for the Performing Arts at Lincoln Center in Manhattan: while it is possible to find most published Smiths articles online these days, there is no better way to attain context than by reading through the actual music papers of the time. I again made full use of my local Mid-Hudson Libraries, and am specifically grateful to everyone at the Phoenicia Library for being such a damn cool group of people. Unfortunately, in the midst of researching this book, the Phoenicia Library was destroyed by a fire; happily, the library found new rental space immediately, and a series of community benefits have helped raise money to add to the insurance payments and ensure proper rebuilding (and restocking) in the near future. Our public libraries engage in so much more than merely the loaning of books; they are an essential part of our commitment to educate and inform and leave a legacy to future generations; please support them however you can.

I am especially grateful to my agent, Mike Harriot, at Folio Literary Agency for his calm and professional consideration throughout this process; it helped that he is such a Smiths fan. Thank you to Caspian Dennis at Abner Stein as well. With this book, I have developed new professional and personal relationships with my editors, Jason Arthur and Tom Avery at William Heinemann in London, and Suzanne O'Neill at Crown in New York. I'd like to thank them for their encouragement and patience, and I trust that these relationships will grow and prosper, as with other staff at both publishing houses with whom I am just becoming acquainted.

A special acknowledgement to Chris Charlesworth and Johnny Rogan for their understanding and their support. And friendship.

Finally, family. My deadlines have never made it easy on my wife and kids; I would like to believe that this one proved some- what less fraught. The passing of time means that I no longer pull all-nighters – although I do occasionally get out of bed in the *middle* of the night, when the idea on how to open a new chapter suddenly seizes me and won't let go. So, my love to Posie for putting up with me as always (and for transcribing some of the early interviews); we've come a long way since the Melody dancefloor. Props to Campbell for being a real live emotional teenager. And as for little Noel, the process of researching and writing this book was made so much more enjoyable by having a budding guitarist in the family. Watching a six-year-old learn his way around multiple tunings, capo positionings, picking styles and passing chords made writing about the Smiths' music that much more fun. And to that point, Johnny Marr's fear – that by the end of this process, I would never want to listen to a Smiths song again – has been proven ill founded. If anything, I have gained fresh and additional appreciation for the multiple layers of complexities and subtleties that went into their words and music. Thanks to everyone who helped make it happen.

BIBLIOGRAPHY

Books

Axon, William E. A., and John Heywood, ed. *Annals of Manchester, A Chronological Record from the Earliest of Times to 1885.* Manchester: Deansgate and Ridgefield, 1887.

Belford, Barbara. *Oscar Wilde: A Certain Genius.* New York: Random House, 2000.

Benson, Richard, ed. *Nightfever: Club Writing in The Face 1980–1997.* London: Boxtree, 1997.

Bracewell, Michael. *England Is Mine: Pop Life in Albion from Wilde to Goldie.* London: Flamingo, 1998.

Brown, Len. *Meetings with Morrissey.* London: Omnibus Press, 2009.

Campbell, Sean, and Colin Coulter, eds. *Why Pamper Life's Complexities? Essays on the Smiths.* Manchester: Manchester University Press, 2010.

Carman, Richard. *Johnny Marr: The Smiths & the Art of Gun-Slinging.* Church Stretton: Independent Music Press, 2006.

Covington, Peter. *Success in Sociology.* Oxford: OUP, 2008.

Cronin, Jill, and Frank Rhodes. *Ardwick.* Stroud: Tempus Publishing, 2002.

Cummins, Kevin; Gavin Martin, contributor. *Manchester:*

Looking for the Light through the Pouring Rain. London: Faber and Faber, 2009.

Deakin, Derrick, ed. *Wythenshawe: The Story of a Garden City*. Chichester: Phillimore, 1989.

Delaney, Shelagh. *A Taste of Honey: A Play*. New York: Grove Press, 1959.

De Tocqueville, Alexis. *Journeys to England and Ireland*. New Haven: Yale University Press, 1958.

Douglas, Lord Alfred Bruce. *Oscar Wilde and Myself*. New York: Duffield, 1914.

Dunphy, Eamon. *U2: The Unforgettable Fire*. New York: Warner Books, 1987.

Ellman, Richard. *Four Dubliners*. New York: George Brazilier, 1988.

_____. *Oscar Wilde*. New York: Alfred A. Knopf, 1988.

Gallagher, Tom, and Michael Campbell and Murdo Gillies. *The Smiths: All Men Have Secrets*. London: Virgin, 1995.

Gatenby, Phil. *Morrissey's Manchester: The Essential Smiths Tour*. Manchester: Empire, 2009.

Gide, André. *Oscar Wilde: A Study from the French*. Oxford: The Holywell Press, 1905.

Goddard, Simon. *Mozipedia: The Encyclopedia of Morrissey and the Smiths*. New York: Penguin, 2010.

_____. *The Smiths: Songs That Saved Your Life*. London: Reynolds & Hearn, 2006.

Gould, Jonathan. *Can't Buy Me Love: The Beatles, Britain, and America*. New York: Harmony, 2007.

Harris, Frank. *Oscar Wilde: His Life and Confessions*. New York: Horizon Press, 1974.

Haslam, Dave. *Manchester, England: The Story of the Pop Cult City*. London: Fourth Estate, 1999.

Holland, Merlin (introduction). *The Real Trial of Oscar Wilde*. New York: HarperCollins, 2003.

Hopps, Gavin. *Morrissey: The Pageant of his Bleeding Heart*. London: Continuum, 2009.

637

Hunt, Tristram. *Marx's General: The Revolutionary Life of Friedrich Engels*. New York: Metropolitan, 2009.

Kureishi, Hanif, and Jon Savage. *The Faber Book of Pop*. London: Faber and Faber, 1996.

Maker, James. *Autofellatio*. Kindle Edition, 2010.

Manchester City Council. *Manchester: 50 Years of Change*. UK: Bernan Assoc, 1995.

McKenna, Neil. *The Secret Life of Oscar Wilde*. New York: Basic Books, 2005.

Morrissey. *New York Dolls*. Manchester: Babylon, 1981.

———. *James Dean Is Not Dead*. Manchester: Babylon, 1983.

———. *Exit Smiling*. Manchester: Babylon, 1998.

Nolan, David. *I Swear I Was There: The Gig that Changed The World*. Manchester: Independent Music Press, 2006.

O'Tuathaigh, M. A. G. *The Irish in Nineteenth Century Britain: Problems of Integration*. As part of *The Irish in the Victorian City*. London: Croom Helm, 1985.

Parkinson-Bailey, John J. *Manchester: an Architectural History*. Manchester: Manchester University Press, 2000.

Pearson, Hesketh. *Oscar Wilde: His Life and Wit*. New York: Harper, 1946.

Pevsner, Nikolaus. *Lancashire, The Industrial and Commercial South*. London: Penguin, 1969.

Pratt, Guy. *My Bass and Other Animals*. London: Orion, 2007.

Ransome, Arthur. *Oscar Wilde: A Critical Study*. New York: Haskell House, 1971.

Reynolds, Simon and Press, Joy. *The Sex Revolts: Gender, Rebellion and Rock 'n' Roll*. Cambridge: Harvard University Press, 1996.

Roach, Martin. *The Right to Imagination & Madness: An Essential Collection of Candid Interviews with Top UK Alternative Songwriters*. London: Independent Music Press, 1994.

Robb, John. *The North Will Rise Again. Manchester Music City 1976–1996*. London: Aurum, 2009.

Robertson, John. *Morrissey: In His Own Words*. London:

Omnibus, 1988.

Rogan, Johnny. *Morrissey & Marr: The Severed Alliance*. London: Omnibus, 1992.

_____. *The Smiths: The Visual Documentary*. London: Omnibus, 1994.

Shaw, George Bernard. *Memories of Wilde*. New York: Horizon Press, 1974.

Shaw, Sandie. *The World at My Feet: A Personal Adventure*. London: HarperCollins, 1991.

Simpson, Mark. *Saint Morrissey*. UK: SAF, 2004.

Slee, Jo. *Peepholism. Into the Art of Morrissey*. London: Sidgwick and Jackson, 1994.

Southey, Robert. *Colloquies on the Progress and Prospects of Society*. London: John Murray, 1829.

Spitz, Bob. *The Beatles: The Biography*. New York: Little, Brown, 2005.

Sterling, Linder; Morrissey, contributor. *Linder Works 1976-2006*. Zurich: JRP Ringler, 2006.

Swift, Roger. *The Irish in the Victorian City*. London: Croom Helm, 1985.

Taylor, Neil. *Document and Eyewitness: An Intimate History of Rough Trade*. London: Orion, 2010.

Wild, Peter, ed. *Paint a Vulgar Picture: Fiction Inspired by the Smiths*. London: Serpent's Tail, 2009.

Williams, Emlyn. *Beyond Belief*. London: Pan, 1968.

Woodcock, George. *Oscar Wilde: The Double Image*. Montreal: Black Rose Books, 1989.

Young, Rob. *Rough Trade*. London: Black Dog, 2006.

Periodicals

Albert, Billy. 'The Smiths on Tour 1982–86.' *Record Collector* (UK), January 2011.

Aston, Martin. *Oor* (Holland), November 1986, as reprinted in *Q Special Edition: The Inside Story of the Smiths & Morrissey* (UK), May 2004.

_____. 'Northern Alliance.' *Mojo* (UK), April 2011.

Bailie, Stuart. 'The Boy in the Bubble.' *Record Mirror* (UK), 14 February 1987.

Barber, Lynn. 'The Man with the Thorn In His Side.' *The Observer* (UK), 15 September 2002.

Bell, Max. 'Bigmouth Strikes Again.' *No. 1* (UK), 28 June 1986.

Berens, Jessica. 'Spirit in the Dark.' *Spin* (US), September 1986.

Birch, Ian. 'The Morrissey Collection.' *Smash Hits* (UK), 21 June– 4 July 1984.

Black, Bill. 'Keep Young and Beautiful.' *Sounds* (UK), 19 November 1983.

Black, Johnny. 'No Time Like The First Time.' *Mojo*, June 2004.

Boon, Richard. 'Morrisey.' *The Catalogue* (UK), September 1998.

Boyd, Brian. 'Paddy English Man.' *Irish Times* (Ireland), 20 November 1999.

Bracewell, Michael. 'One Man Melodrama.' *ES* (UK), June 1992.

Brown, James. 'It's That Man Again.' *NME* (UK), 11 February 1989.

Brown, Len. 'Born to be Wilde' and 'Stop Me If You Think You've Heard This One Before.' *NME*, 13 and 20 February 1988.

Cameron, Keith. 'Who's the Daddy?' *Mojo*, May 2004

Carroll, Cath. 'Crisp Tunes and Salted Lyrics.' *NME*, 14 May 1983.

Cavanagh, David, 'We're Home.' *Select* (UK), July 1991.

_____. 'The Good Lieutenants.' *Select*, April 1993.

_____. 'Nothing to Declare But Their Genius.' *Q*, January 1994.

Cooper, Mark. 'Flowers of Romance.' *No. 1*, February 1984.

Cranna, Ian. 'A Friendship Made IN Heaven.' *Smash Hits*, 22 October 1985.

Deevoy, Adrian. 'Flower Power.' *International Musician* (UK), October 1983.

_____. 'Morrissey: Solo Artist of the Year.' *GQ* (UK), October 2005.

De Martino, Dave. 'We'll Meat Again.' *Creem* (US), May 1985.

Dessau, Bruce. *Oor*, February 1987.

Dorrell, David. 'The Smiths Hunt.' *NME*, 24 September 1983.

Du Noyer, Paul. 'Goons and Philistines.' *The Hit* (US), October 1985.

_____. 'Oh, Such Drama!' *Q* (UK), August 1987.

Fielder, Hugh. 'Scratch'N'Smiths.' *Sounds*, February 1984.

Fricke, David. 'Keeping Up With The Smiths.' *Rolling Stone* (US), 9 October 1986.

Garfield, Simon. 'This Charming Man.' *Time Out* (UK), March 7–13 1985.

Goddard, Simon. 'Crowning Glory.' *Uncut* (UK), January 2006.

Graham, Ron. 'These Charming Men.' *City Life* (UK), April 1984.

Harris, John. 'Trouble at Mill.' *Mojo*, April 2001.

Harrison, Andrew. 'The Band that Dreams it Never Broke Up.' *Word* (UK), June 2004.

_____. 'Home Thoughts from Abroad.' *Word*, May 2003.

Hauptfuhrer, Frank. 'Roll Over Bob Dylan and tell Madonna the News.' *People* (US), 24 June 1985.

Heath, Chris. 'Morrissey.' *Smash Hits*, August 26, 1987.

Henke, James. 'Oscar! Oscar! Great Britain goes Wilde for the "fourth gender" Smiths.' *Rolling Stone*, 7 June 1984

Hibbert, Tom. 'Meat Is Murder!' *Smash Hits*, 31 January 1985.

Hoskyns, Barney. 'These Disarming Men.' *NME*, 4 February 1984.

Hughes, Andy. 'The Smiths Strange Ways Have Found Us.' *Creem*, July 1987.

Johnson, David. 'Haircuts.' *The Face* (UK), p.6, early 1984.

Jones, Allan. 'The Blue Romantics,' *Melody Maker*, 3 March 1984.

_____. 'Johnny Guitar.' *Melody Maker*, 14 April 1984.

_____ et al. 'Trial by Jury.' *Melody Maker*, 16 March 1985.

Jones, Dylan. Mr Smith: 'All Mouth and Trousers?' *i-D* (UK), October 1987.

K, Graham. 'Strictly Shrubwise.' *Record Mirror* (UK), November 1983.

Kelly, Danny. 'The Further Thoughts of Chairman Mo.' *NME*, June 8, 1985.

_____. 'Exile on Mainstream.' *NME*, 14 February 1987.

Kemp, Mark. 'Wake Me When It's Over.' *Select*, July 1991.

_____. 'Morrissey and the Art of Self-Obsession.' *Option* (US), May/June 1991.

Kent, Nick. 'Dreamer in the Real World.' *The Face*, May 1985.

_____. 'The Band with the Thorn in its Side.' The Face, April 1987.

King, Emily. 'Fuck Morrissey, Here's Linder.' *032c* (Germany), Issue 11, Summer 2006.

Kopf, Biba. 'A Suitable Case for Treatment.' *NME*, 22–29 December 1984.

Leboff, Gary. 'Goodbye Cruel World.' *Melody Maker*, 26 September 1987.

Levy, Eleanor. 'Fake.' *Record Mirror*, 3 August 1985.

_____. Johnny Marr. *Record Mirror*, 14 June 1986.

Loder, Kurt. 'The Smiths.' *Rolling Stone*, 7 June 1984.

MacKenzie, Suzie. 'After the Affair.' *The Guardian*, 2 August 1997.

McCormick, Neil. 'All Men Have Secrets.' *Hot Press* (Ireland), 8 May 1984.

McCulloch, Dave. 'Out To Crunch.' *Sounds*, 14 May 1983.

_____. 'Handsome Devils.' *Sounds*, 4 June 1983.

McIlhenny, Barry. 'Strumming for the Smiths.' *Melody Maker*, 3 August 1985.

Miles, Catherine. 'Morrissey of the Smiths.' *'HIM'* and *'Gay Reporter'* (UK), August 1983.

Morley, Paul. Live review. *NME*, 3 June 1978.

_____. 'Wilde Child.' *Blitz*, April 1988.

Morrissey, Steve. 'A Fabulous Adventure . . . A True Story.' *Kids Stuff* (UK), Issue 7, January 1978.

_____. 'Whatever Happened To the New York Dolls.' *Kids Stuff*, c. 1978.

Morrissey, Steven. 'New York Dolls.' *The Next Big Thing*, issue 8, 1978.

_____. 'Manchester Slips Under,' 'Re-Introducing Sparks,' 'James Dean is Not Dead.' *The Next Big Thing*, issue 9/10, late 1979.

_____. Live reviews. *Record Mirror*, 29 March, 5 April, 10 May 1980; 18 July, 22 August 1981.

_____. 'Portrait of the Artist as a Consumer.' *NME*, September 1983.

_____. 'Sandie Shaw.' *Sounds*, 24 December 1983.

_____. 'Linder.' *Interview* (US), April 2010.

_____. 'Singles.' *Melody Maker*, August 1984.

Morton, Roger. 'Far from the Madding Crowd.' *Debut* (UK), Undated, 1984.

Nine, Jennifer. 'The Importance of Being Morrissey.' *Melody Maker*, 9 August 1997.

Nolan, Paul. 'I've Got Something To Get off my Chest.' *Hot Press*, 30 June 2008.

O'Brien, Lucy. 'Youth Suicide.' *NME*, 8 November 1986.

Oldfield, Jim. 'Moors Mum Raps Murder Song.' *The Sun*, 4 September 1984.

Owen, Frank. 'Home Thoughts from Abroad.' *Melody Maker*, 27 September 1986.

Pye, Ian. 'Magnificent Obsessions.' *Melody Maker*, 26 November 1983.

_____. 'A Hard Day's Misery.' *Melody Maker*, 3 November 1984.

_____. 'Some Mothers Do 'Ave 'Em.' *NME*, 7 June 1986.

Reynolds, Simon. 'Songs of Love and Hate.' *Melody Maker*, 12 and 19 March 1988.

Rimmer, Dave. 'Hits and Myths.' *Smash Hits*, 16 February 1984.

Samuels, Tim, and Juliet Gellatley. 'Meat Is Murder.' *Greenscene* (UK), Issue 6, 1989.

Savage, Jon. 'The Enemy Within.' *Mojo*, April 2011.

Shaw, William. 'Glad All Over.' *Zigzag* (UK), February 1984.

Shelley, Jim. 'The Smiths: Manchester Haçienda.' *NME*, 26 March 1983.

_____. 'Soul on Fire.' *Blitz*, May 1984.

Simpson, Dave. 'Manchester's Answer to the A-Bomb.' *Uncut*, August 1998.

Strikes, Andy. 'Morrissey Dancing.' *Record Mirror*, 11 February 1984.

Swayne, Karen. 'If I Ruled The World.' *No. 1*, 7 January 1984.

Thrills, Adrian. 'Onto a Shaw Thing.' *NME*, April 1984.

Trakin, Roy. 'The Smiths'. *Musician* (US), June 1984.

Unknown. Page 1 story on Whit Walks. *Manchester Evening News* (UK). 22 May 1959;

Unknown. 'Dogs join in a Massive Comb-Out for Boy.' *Manchester Evening News*, p.8, 25 November 1963.

Unknown. Page 10 story on search for missing girl. *Manchester Evening News*. 31 December 1964.

Unknown. 'Item 38 – The Smiths.' *i-D*. February 1983.

Unknown. 'The Smiths.' *The Underground* (UK), issue 2, 1983.

Unknown. 'The Smiths: Manhattan Sound.' City Fun (UK), issue 13, spring 1983.

Unknown. '"Ban Child-Sex Pop Song Plea to Beeb."' *The Sun* (UK), 5 September 1983.

Unknown. Interview CD. *Ask Me, Ask Me, Ask Me*, January, 1984.

Unknown. 'Blind Date.' *No. 1*, 28 April 1984.

Unknown. 'Morrissey.' *Square Peg* (UK), 1984.

Unknown. '20 Questions.' *Star Hits* (US), 1985.

Unknown. 'Smiths Sign to EMI.' *NME*, 27 September 1986.

Unknown. News item, page 3. *Melody Maker*, 4 October 1986.

Unknown. *Hot Press*, March 1987.

Unknown. 'Smiths To Split.' *NME*, 1 August 1987.

Unknown. 'Marr Speaks.' *NME*, 8 August 1987.

Unknown. 'Marr Quits.' *Melody Maker*, 8 August 1987.

Unknown. 'Goodbye, Smiths.' *NME*, 12 September 1987.

Unknown. 'Smiths Split!' *Melody Maker*, 12 September 1987.

Unknown. Billy Duffy interview. *Spin*, September 1989.

Unknown. 'Morrissey Misery over Court Verdict.' *BBC News*. 6 November 1998. Archived at http://news.bbc.co.uk/2/hi/uk_news/209224.stm

Unknown. 'Choirmaster jailed for indecent assault.' *BBC News*, 27 March 2002. Archived at http://news.bbc.co.uk/2/hi/uk_news/england/1896961.stm

Various. 'The Smiths: Q Special Edition: The Inside Story of The Smiths & Morrissey.' *Q*, May 2004.

Various. 'Q/Mojo Special Edition: Morrissey and the Story of Manchester.' *Q/Mojo*, April 2006.

Various. 'The Queen is Dead Anniversary Issue.' *Mojo*, April 2011.

Van Poznack, Elissa. 'Morrissey.' *The Face*, July, 1984.

Wilde, Jonh. 'The Smiths.' *Jamming!* (UK) January 1984.

_____. 'Morrissey's Year.' *Jamming!*, December 1984.

Worrall, Frank. 'The Cradle Snatchers.' *Melody Maker*, 3 September 1983.

Radio

BBC Radio 1, David Jensen interview with Morrissey, 4 July 1983.

BBC Radio 1, Roundtable, Morrissey reviews singles with Paul Weller, 9 December 1983.

BBC Radio 1, Roundtable, Morrissey reviews singles with Sandie Shaw, undated early 1984.

BBC Radio 2, Russell Brand interview with Morrissey, 2 December 2006.

BBC Radio London, Morrissey interview, 17 September 1983.

Piccadilly Radio, Morrissey interview with Mark Radcliffe, 30 November 1986.

Television/DVD/Film

Brit Girls. Morrissey interview with Len Brown, Channel 4, 13 December 1997.

Culture Show, The. Morrissey interview BBC2, December 2006.

Datarun. Morrissey and Marr interview, ITV, 7 April 1984.

Do It Yourself: The Story of Rough Trade. BBC4, March 2009.

Granada Reports, Granada Television, 21 February 1985.

Importance of Being Morrissey, The. Directed by Tina Flintoff, Ricky Kelehar, Channel 4, June 2003.

Inside The Smiths. Rourke and Joyce interviews. Directed and produced by Stephen Petricco/Mark Standley, MVD Visual, 2007.

Les Enfants du Rock. Interview with Morrissey and Marr, 18 May 1984.

MTV. Interview with Morrissey (unedited tapes), conducted 5 April 1985.

Oxford Road Show. Morrissey interview. BBC2, 22 March 1985

Pebble Mill At One, BBC1. Morrissey interview. 21 February 1985.

Pop Quiz. BBC1, early 1984.

South Bank Show, The. The Smiths: From Start To Finish. Produced & directed by Tony Knox. ITV, 18 October 1987.

Splat. Morrissey and Marr interview, Charlie's Bus, TV-AM, 16 June 1984.

The Rise and Fall of the Smiths. Smiths documentary. BBC, 1999.

These Things Take Time. Smiths documentary, ITV, 2002.

The Tube, Geoff Travis interview, Smiths performance, 4 November 1983.

The Tube, Morrissey interview with Tony Fletcher, 27 January 1984.

The Tube, Morrissey interview with Margi Clarke, 25 October 1985.

TV-am, Morrissey interview with Paul Gambaccini, early 1984.

Whistle Test, Morrissey and Marr interview with Mark Ellen, BBC2, 12 February 1985.

World In Action, Hulme Crescents, 1978. Retrieved from http://youtu.be/S1qpf9hogI0

Wrestle With Russell, Morrissey interview with Russell Brand, bonus DVD with *Years of Refusal*, February 2009.

Zane Lowe Meets Morrissey. MTV, February 2009.

INTERVIEW SOURCES

All interview quotes are from the author's own interviews, except as follows. The sources are listed in order of first reference. Full citations for the source can be found in the bibliography section.

Introduction
Brown, *Melody Maker*, February 1988; Pye, *Melody Maker*, November 1984; Savage, *Mojo*, April 2011; *BBC News*, November 1998.
Chapter 2
Kopf, *NME*, December 1984; Hoskyns, *NME*, February 1984.
Chapter 3
Oxford Road Show, March 1985; Rogan, *The Severed Alliance*, p. 43; McCormick, *Hot Press*, May 1984; McKenzie, *The Guardian*, August 1997; Black, *Sounds*, November 1983; Morrissey: *In His Own Words*, p.33; *Brit Girls*, December 1997; Graham, *City Life*, Spring 1984; Morrissey, *Sounds*, December 1983; Lowe, *MTV*, February 2009; Barber, *Observer*, September 2002; Roach, *The Right to Imagination & Madness, p. 311*; Boyd, *Irish Times*, November 1999; *South Bank Show*, October 1987.

Chapter 4

Oxford Road Show, March 1985; Bracewell, *ES*, June 1992; Birch, *Smash Hits*, July 1984; Rogan, *The Severed Alliance*, pp.58, 71; *Greenscene*, 1989; Goddard, *Mozipedia*, pp. 482–3; K, *Record Mirror*, November 1983.

Chapter 5

Nolan, *Hot Press*, July 2008; Rogan, *The Severed Alliance*, p.65; Kemp, *Select*, July 1991; Goddard, *Mozipedia*, pp. 287–88; Brown, *Meetings With Morrissey*, p.54; Morley, *Blitz*, April 1988; Boyd, *Irish Times*, November 1999.

Chapter 6

Staugs.org/reaction.htm; Cummins, *Looking for the Light*, p.149; Robb, *The North Will Rise Again*, p.53.

Chapter 7

Morley, *Blitz*, April 1988; Robb, *The North Will Rise Again*, pp.58–59; King, *032c*, 2006; Rogan, *A Visual Documentary*, pp.21, 22, 24, 25; Boyd, *Irish Times*, 1999; Jones, *i-D*, 1987; Jones, *Melody Maker*, March 1984; Brown, *Meetings With Morrissey*, p.63.

Chapter 8

Spin, September 1989, p.66; Cummins, *Looking for the Light*, p.150; Brown, *NME*, February 1988.

Chapter 9

Rogan, *The Severed Alliance*, p. 69.

Chapter 10

Morley, *Blitz*, 1988; Jensen, Radio 1, July 1983; Sterling, *Works*, 2006; *South Bank Show*, Oct 1987; Morrissey, *Interview*, April 2010; Rogan, *The Severed Alliance*, p.107; Pye, *Melody Maker*, November 1984; Van Poznack, *The Face*, July 1984; Rimmer, *Smash Hits*, 1984.

Chapter 11

Robb, *The North Will Rise Again*, p.193.

Chapter 12

Jensen, *Radio 1*, July 1983; Robb, *The North Will Rise Again*, p.195; Morrissey, *In His Own Words*, p. 48; MTV Interview, April 1985; Black, *Sounds*, November, 1983; Deevoy, *GQ*, October 2005.

Chapter 13
Rogan, *The Visual Documentary*, pp. 36–38; *The Rise and Fall of the Smiths*, BBC, 2001; Rogan, *The Severed Alliance*. p.147; *The Underground*, issue 2, 1983; Black, *Mojo*, June 2004.

Chapter 14
Black, *Mojo*, June 2004; Goddard, *Mozipedia*, p. 154.

Chapter 17
Goddard, *Songs That Saved Your Life*, p.58; Campbell, ed., *Why Pamper Life's Complexities?*, p.119.

Chapter 18
Inside The Smiths, 2007; Deevoy, *International Musician*, October 1983.

Chapter 19
The Rise and Fall of the Smiths, BBC, 2001.

Chapter 20
Harrison, *The Word*, 2004.

Chapter 22
Wilde, *Jamming!*, December 1984; Pye, *Melody Maker*, November 1983; Strikes, *Record Mirror*, February 1984.

Chapter 23
Heath, *Smash Hits*, August 1987; Rogan, *The Visual Documentary*, p.74.

Chapter 24
Wilde, *Jamming!*, January 1984; Pop Quiz, BBC, 1984; *TV-am*, 1984; Datarun, April 1984; Unknown, 'Blind Date' *No. 1*, April 28, 1984; Morton, *Debut*, 1984; Shelley, *Blitz*, May 1984; Unknown, *Square Peg*, 1984; Shaw, *Zigzag*, February 1984; Wilde, *Jamming!*, December 1984; Hoskyns, *NME*, February 1984; Henke, *Rolling Stone*, June 1984; Trakin, *Musician*, June 1984.

Chapter 25
Jones et al, *Melody Maker*, March 1985; Knopf, *NME*, December 1984.

Chapter 27
Kelly, *NME*, June, 1985; Levy, *Record Mirror*, August 1985; Jones, *Melody Maker*, March 1985; Wilde, *Jamming!*, December 1984; Garfield, *Time Out*, March 1985.

Chapter 28
http://stereogum.com/113481/meat_is_murder_turns_25/top-stories/; Taylor, *Document & Eyewitness*, p.285; Rogan, *The Severed Alliance*, pp.235, 232; Kent, *The Face*, May 1985; Hauptfuhrer, *People*, June 1985.

Chapter 29
De Martino, *Creem*, May 1985; Levy, *Record Mirror*, August 1985.

Chapter 30
Jones, *Melody Maker*, March 1985; Rogan, *The Severed Alliance*, p.239; Clarke, Margi. *The Tube*, October 25, 1985; Leboff, *Melody Maker*, September 1987; Pye, *NME*, June 1986; Aston, *Oor*, November 1986; Fletcher, *The Tube*, January 1984; Pye, *Melody Maker*, November 1984; Rogan, *The Visual Documentary*, p.122.

Chapter 31
Bailie, *Record Mirror*, February 1987; Rogan, *The Severed Alliance*, p.242; Goddard, *Uncut*, January 2007; Unknown, *Melody Maker*, August 1985; Dessau, *Oor*, February 1987.

Chapter 32
Goddard, *Mozipedia* p.345; Pye, *NME*, June 1986; Aston, *Mojo*, April 2011; *Inside The Smiths*, 2007; Taylor, *Document & Eyewitness*, pp. 288–289; Bell, *No. 1*, June 1986.

Chapter 33
Various, *Mojo*, April 2011; Brown, *NME*, February 1988.

Chapter 34
Kent, *The Face*, April 1987; Unknown, *Hot Press*, March 1987.

Chapter 35
Owen, *Melody Maker*, September 1986.

Chapter 38
Kelly, *NME*, February 1987; Bailie, *Record Mirror*, February 1987; Radcliffe, *Piccadilly Radio*, November 1986; Leboff, *Melody Maker*, September 1987; *Inside the Smiths*, 2007.

Chapter 39
Nine, *Melody Maker*, August 1997; Jones, *i-D*, October 1987; *Inside the Smiths*, 2007; *The Importance of Being Morrissey*, 2002; Rogan, *The Severed Alliance*, p.286; Reynolds, *Melody Maker*,

March 1988; Goddard, *Mozipedia*, p.296; Du Noyer, *Q*, September 1987; Unknown, *NME*, August 1, 8, 1987.

Chapter 40

Gould, *Can't Buy Me Love*, p.371; Brown, *NME*, February 1988; Kemp, *Select*, July 1991; Cameron, *Mojo*, May 2004; Heath, *Smash Hits*, August 1987; Jones, *i-D*, October 1987; *South Bank Show*, October 1987; Cavanagh, *Select*, July 1991.

NOTES

Introduction

1 As a comparison, during the same period at the beginning of their recording career, the Beatles recorded eighty-six original Lennon-McCartney compositions, and though their repertoire was significantly boosted by cover versions and George Harrison compositions, it's worth remembering how much quicker the recording process in the 1960s was – and how many years the Beatles had been together before signing a record deal.

2 Among British pop and rock stars, only Sir Cliff Richard has enjoyed a similarly high profile with any equal claims to celibacy, though in Cliff's case, this was not publicly stated throughout much of his long career.

3 Johnny Marr, however, proved none so reticent. Asked at a major awards show in March 2012, yet again, about a Smiths reformation, he responded, 'If this government steps down, then I'll reform the band.'

4 Not unconnected to knowledge of my own impending biography, Rogan and his publishers opted to update *Morrissey and Marr: The Severed Alliance* with a '20th Anniversary Edition' in 2012, adding almost 200 pages of

content to the original, and publishing it just in advance of *A Light That Never Goes Out*. At the time of going to press, I have not read Rogan's revised book, but my initial point, regarding my motivation and intent with my biography, still holds.

Chapter 1

1   According to Roger Swift's book *The Irish in the Victorian City*, the Irish-born immigrants in Manchester already accounted for one-fifth of the population by the year 1834.

Chapter 2

1   MacColl, a folklorist whose communist leanings put him under the watch of MI5 for a while, and who would later sire the singer Kirsty MacColl, composed that song for a locally based play of his own, *Landscape with Chimneys*, and therefore found it natural to specify Salford in the lyrics, too; but protests from the City Council at being associated with a 'Dirty Old Town' resulted in the proper name being replaced by the adjective 'smoky.'

Chapter 3

1   From Harper Street to Queen's Square and later Kings Road, Steven Morrissey grew up in what was then known as the Municipal Borough of Stretford, which bordered the western side of the City of Manchester and the southern edge of the City of Salford. Old Trafford was one of many neighbourhoods inside Stretford; Moss Side officially existed only within Manchester itself, though the Morrissey family laid claim to it given how close they lived to the Stretford-Manchester border. As a result of the Local Government Act of 1972, the relationship between Trafford and Stretford was reversed: the Municipal Borough of Stretford was abolished and instead swallowed up inside the newly established Metropolitan Borough of Trafford, one of sixteen such boroughs (the Cities of Salford and Manchester among them) that formed the equally new Metropolitan County of Greater Manchester.

The new Metropolitan Borough of Trafford additionally absorbed, from the County of Cheshire, the Municipal Boroughs of Sale and Altrincham, and the Urban Districts of Bowdon and Hale – names that become familiar later on in the Smiths story. The Marr family's subsequent home in Wythenshawe stood outside the Metropolitan County of Greater Manchester, but inside the City of Manchester.

2   By 1978, the six doctors in the Hulme medical practice were prescribing some 250,000 tranquillisers a month.

Chapter 4

1   Officially, the Tripartite System that had been in place since 1944 supported three formats: grammar schools, technical schools and secondary moderns. In reality, few technical schools were ever built, and so the system came down to a simple process of (unintended) elimination.

2   Margaret Clitherow was arrested for harbouring priests, which was a capital crime, but she was executed for refusing to enter a plea to this charge, which was also a capital crime. (She claimed that she saw no crime to plead against.) Queen Elizabeth later wrote to the people of York to apologise for the execution of a woman.

3   In 1984, Morrissey told *Smash Hits* that 'a day rarely passes when I don't listen to *The Importance of Being Earnest*. I have it on tape.' A major TV documentary in 2002, for which he provided unusually close access, was entitled *The Importance of Being Morrissey*.

4   It was pure coincidence that the week I finished writing this chapter, an essay on Wilde ('Deceptive Picture', puta- tively about the variations in Dorian Gray manuscripts) appeared in *The New Yorker*, 8 August 2011, penned by Alex Ross, the magazine's modern music critic. Ross's finding confirmed my own writings. Most interesting was his observation, as a liberated (indeed, married) gay man of the twenty-first century, that 'as recently as the late eighties, you could still find bookish young people coming

to terms with their sexuality by way of reading Wilde.'
He was talking about himself, but he could have been
referring to Morrissey a decade earlier.

Chapter 5

1   Graham Pink later became famous as a persecuted 'whistle-
blower' after he revealed the appalling standards of care
in his local NHS hospital.

Chapter 6

1   What can only be described as a propaganda film,
produced by the City of Manchester in 1946, attempting
to sell the attractions of Wythenshawe in comparison to
the hardships of Hulme, made much of the fact that 270
tons of solid soot and dirt had been recorded in Hulme
in one year (and 450 pounds in Ancoats); by contrast,
Wythenshawe had 'only' 120 tons. The film, *A City
Speaks*, on show at the Museum of Science and Industry
in Manchester, is fascinating for its stereotyping: while a
clipped BBC voice sells the virtues of the new estates,
and an almost indecipherable Mancunian from Hulme
initially expresses his doubts but is swiftly convinced, the
reel homes in on the very caricature of a poverty-stricken
old lady huddled in her Hulme slum with a cup of tea,
juxtaposed with a beautiful young wife enjoying her
outdoor garden in Wythenshawe. Certainly, there were
positives behind the process of slum clearance and forced
relocations, and the Maher family appeared to benefit
from them. All the same, it is worth recounting the
memories of Jack Kirwan in *Annals of Ardwick*, an inde-
pendently-published pamphlet unearthed at the
Manchester City Library. Kirwan had the job of physically
removing one such old lady from her Hulme home during
what he called 'the great destruction,' the period when
both the Morrisseys and Mahers were relocated. 'As I
arrived in the morning, at the agreed time, she was there
waiting, with all her possessions neatly wrapped and
packed up. The house and the rooms were spotless. I

knew instantly that, regardless of poverty, she had maintained the standard so essential to working class values. She was crying constantly and the situation made me feel helpless. She had been born in the house and had never lived anywhere else, had brought up a family there and all her life and memories were there. I attempted to console her the only way I could, and told her that she would have better facilities where she was going, although I knew it was too late for her to start again in new surroundings and among strangers . . . I moved her to the high rise block in Bagnall Court, Northenden and I was told later she had died within a fortnight.'

2   Fletcher and Duffy both recalled a letter in a music paper from Morrissey, with his full address, seeking petitioners to get the New York Dolls *Whistle Test* appearance re-aired on the BBC, and that they wrote to him offering their support. I have not seen this letter.

3   Marr has recalled that his very first show was Rod Stewart at the Belle Vue, near his old home in Ardwick Green, on the Tonight's the Night tour, where he met Britt Ekland at the mixing desk. 'I thought every gig I would go to from then on I would meet a famous actress.' That show was November 1976; the Wythenshawe Forum Slaughter & the Dogs concert is generally agreed to have taken place in August.

4   The story has also been told that it was Rourke who was wearing the Neil Young badge; at this point in time neither man seems quite sure anymore.

Chapter 7

1   'The first year or so we didn't really have that much contact,' said Rourke of his mother's abrupt departure. 'And then she invited us all over for some holiday. Because the guy she worked for, Joe, who became her partner for twenty-five years after that, he was away working, and she had this big villa in Son Vida in Majorca with a swimming pool. She invited all four of us down for the week.

And we did a lot of talking about stuff and she explained her reasons, and why she left. And things have been fine since then.' Andy's younger brother John later moved to Majorca himself, where he died, aged twenty-four, after the Smiths broke up, from 'drugs and alcoholism.' Andy was at his brother's bedside at his passing alongside their father Michael.

2   Durkin prefaced that observation by saying, 'Andy won't mind me telling you this.'

3   There is no evidence that he managed to make it inside the club; the drinking age was eighteen at the time in New York, and strictly enforced.

4   In the 2000s, the image was purchased by the Tate.

5   Morrissey's typically cruel but hilarious observations merit further discussion. Despite the fact that punk was considered a working-class revolt, still it came under common attack from those at the *very* bottom of Britain's clearly defined social strata. 'The whole idea that punk was a street music was bollocks,' said journalist Frank Owen, who was raised in Manchester and played in the band Manicured Noise at the time. 'The street kids were the Perry kids, the football hooligans, the kids with the jumbo cords and the Stanley knives, they were the street kids living in the council estates. The kids who were punks were more likely to be upper-working-class, their dads had good jobs in the factories, they had a little bit of money . . . The whole idea that it was lumpen proletariat on the council estate, that was bullshit. Those kids hated punks.' It's for this reason that Slaughter & the Dogs, generally written out of punk history for being the kind of uncouth yobs to whom Owen refers, are so important: their second single, 'Where Have All the Bootboys Gone' glorified the very culture that most punks, theoretically, opposed.

6   On the cover of the Nosebleeds single, Vini Reilly wore a borrowed St Augustine's school blazer, compulsory wear at the time for Johnny Marr and Andy Rourke.

7   It's been reported that Morrissey also sang with the Nosebleeds in April, at a Rabid Records night that included Slaughter & the Dogs, Jilted John and John Cooper Clarke. If so, the Nosebleeds went unbilled. They did not go unbilled at the Ritz, where their name appeared on a poster, contradicting Morrissey's later assertion in *The North Will Rise Again* that it was Duffy's venture, under a different name, and only mistakenly reviewed in *NME* as the Nosebleeds.

8   This was much kinder than a subsequent observation by Morley, printed in *Mojo*, June 2004, and elsewhere, that 'Morrissey was always laughed at in Manchester . . . he was the village idiot.'

Chapter 8

1   Morrissey has repeatedly tried to play down his involvement with the Wythenshawe punk scene. 'Local history has me down as an ex-member of Slaughter & the Dogs or the Nosebleeds, which is ridiculous,' he told John Robb for *The North Will Rise Again*. Members of those bands are under no illusions regarding his membership, however short-term it may have been.

Chapter 9

1   The couple was still together, married with children, more than thirty-two years later.

2   Robertson suffered a premature, alcohol-related death.

Chapter 10

1   'I suffered greatly from depression,' said Morrissey on the documentary *The Importance of Being Morrissey*. 'It was very serious when I was a teenager and when I was in the Smiths, so I took prescribed drugs for a long time.'

2   I assure readers that I was customarily guilty of the same throughout the 1980s.

3   When the Nosebleeds broke up for good, drummer Phillip 'Toby' Tomanov promptly joined Ludus. Morrissey was sure to give him a personal shout-out in his first Ludus review.

4 Upon *Exit Smiling*'s eventual publication, in Morrissey's original typed manuscript, complete with handwritten corrections, Morrissey issued a statement asking fans not to buy it, giving the clear impression that he had never wanted *any* of the three books to be published, at any point, and dating their composition back to the 1970s, which seems unlikely. His disowning of the books raises the question as to why he sent the manuscripts to a publisher to begin with; his letters to Tony Wilson suggest that he was in fact desperate for some form of literary recognition.

5 Boon remains adamant about this cassette, and Johnny Marr has expressed his belief in its existence, though there doesn't appear to be a song with the title 'Wake up Johnny' in Bessie Smith's catalogue.

Chapter 11

1 'Papa's Got a Brand New Pigbag' spent some seventy weeks on the indie top 50 and eventually, a solid year after its release, crashed into the top 3 on the national charts, a major achievement for its primary distributor, Rough Trade.

2 Among those to show up at Wolstencroft's house was someone dressed exactly like Malcolm McDowell in *A Clockwork Orange* (bootleg tapes of which had been doing the rounds thanks to the commercialisation of home VHS machines), down to 'the eyelashes, the baseball bat, the jockstrap' as Rourke recalled it. The droog's name was Ian Brown, and he had been the singer in a band at South Trafford College called the Patrol, alongside Wolstencroft and guitarist John Squire.

3 Generally spelled in Smiths literature as 'Decibel', it actually had a French spelling due to its owner, Philippe Delcloque. The former Mill eventually became the location for one of Manchester's preeminent post-rave nightclubs, Sankeys Soap.

4 Marr has often talked about this session as having taken place on New Year's Eve, knowing that the studio would

otherwise be empty. Dale Hibbert was frequently recording bands overnight, without the owner's knowledge, as a means of improving his engineering skills. Though the session may have taken place in winter, it was almost certainly not on New Year's Eve.

5 Anyone who has heard the Jam's early 1982 chart-topper 'Precious' knows that this is no idle aside.

6 The riots did not surprise Morrissey at all. 'Manchester is destroyed,' he wrote to his friend Lindsay Hutton. 'But still, isn't it nice to know that the Royal Wedding is almost upon us? If Charles is so concerned, let him get married in Moss Side or Toxteth.'

7 Eighth Day mutated into a still-thriving health-food store on Oxford Road. The expression also mutated, around the late 1980s, into 'And on the Eighth Day, God created Manchester.'

8 To any argument that Morrissey and Marr's meeting was not quite as magical as legend would have it, given that they had been formally introduced four years earlier at the Patti Smith concert, it should be noted that Leiber and Stoller had spoken on the phone prior to *their* first meeting, and that Leiber's appearance at Stoller's door was far from unexpected.

9 Steve Pomfret's role has certainly been downplayed over the years. Habitually, Marr has given the impression that he had made the journey to Kings Road on his own. To this author, Marr talked about how 'Steve and I knocked on the door, and Steve Pomfret literally did take several steps back to the gate and said good-bye. He didn't come in the house with me.' In rare interviews, specifically with Johnny Rogan, Pomfret has given no cause for doubt that he was in fact part of the conversation upstairs in Morrissey's room, just as he formed part of the Smiths' initial rehearsals.

Chapter 12

1 In fact, he had said, 'I schtip to funk,' meaning that he

screwed to it, which one might have thought a positive referral. However, in a much later edition of *The Face*, in which the magazine's Manchester stringer, David Johnson, wrote up Swing in its own right, and by which point the Smiths were happening, Johnson was willing to rewrite the intent as 'meaning the music was only fit for screwing to.'

2   A silent, minute-long clip of the finale can be found on the Internet.

Chapter 13

1   An edited version of 'Suffer Little Children' that has long done the rounds on the Internet is sadly lacking these elements; the author has heard the complete mix and indeed the individual multitracks.

2   In the interest of disclosure, the author, who was involved at this point in releasing records for the Belfast band Rudi, stayed on Mike Joyce's floor in March 1982, after Rudi had opened for the Jam at the Manchester Apollo that night. Curiously, Morrissey and Mike Joyce were both guests of the Irish band; if they met and conversed that night it has never been publicly recollected.

3   Though it's tempting to think the Smiths might have waited to make the EMI tape before playing anything to Factory, Hibbert is adamant that he recalled Morrissey and Marr making an appointment with Tony Wilson, and making it equally clear that he was not invited.

4   Further disclaimer: I was in a band of my own at the time, Apocalypse, which was courted by EMI during exactly the same period. This band was, likewise, afforded demo time in early 1983, and after much prevarication, eventually signed to the label, by an A&R manager working under Hugh Stanley-Clarke. The advance was no more than the Smiths received for signing to Rough Trade, though the author's group had an indie hit, radio and TV exposure and national touring under its belt. However, at that point, the paths certainly diverged: it

was not until the end of 1983, many months later, that the author's group was finally put into the recording studio to make a single. Ironically, this turned out to be the lavish residential facility Jacob's, where the Smiths recorded *The Queen Is Dead*, though the expensive studio did not contribute to a better record and, with momentum stalled in the interim, the group broke up shortly after it was released. During that same twelve-month period, the Smiths signed to Rough Trade, released two singles, one of which was a hit, recorded their debut album (twice), recorded four BBC radio sessions, appeared on television and on the front covers of the music papers, and made it to New York as the hippest band in the UK. The perennial question – What would have happened to the Smiths had they signed to EMI in 1983? – can perhaps be answered by the author's own experience of sudden stasis. And the equally perennial question – Did the Smiths do the right thing by forging their path on an independent label? – appears purely rhetorical.

Chapter 14

1   The single sleeve noted that it was recorded in March, but by all accounts the recording date was actually 27 February. Other history books state that 'Hand in Glove' was first played live at the Haçienda. But allowing that the Manhattan Sound gig the week before was intended as a warm-up, and that no set lists survive, it seems a reasonable assumption that it had in fact been unveiled at the earlier gig.

Chapter 15

1   To further confuse matters, while allowing that Rourke was on Marr's shoulder throughout the exchange, Travis recalled Joe Moss being present as well – and Moss was as certain of the fact that he was at Rough Trade that day as Rourke and Marr were insistent that he was not. 'He had to be forced to listen to it and he listened to it there and then while we were there,' recalled Moss of Geoff Travis.

'He did like it. We said quite cockily that if he wasn't going to put it out, we were going to put it out.'

In 1988, in an interview with Richard Boon for independent distribution magazine *The Catalogue*, Morrissey delivered a humorous description of the first meeting, in which he inserted *himself* into the escapade to London: 'We waited for hours to then be told Geoff couldn't see us, so Johnny said, "Who is Geoff Travis?" and someone pointed to a looming figure swarming down a corridor and Johnny raced after him and forced him to listen.' The indentation at the top of this page should perhaps be made clearer.

This, then, is the biographer's curse – that there is no such thing as fact when it comes to individual memories. That is why, as Tony Wilson (played by Steve Coogan) said in the movie *24 Hour Party People*, when confronted with the legend or the truth, always print the legend.

2   The reviewer, Jim Shelley, was subsequently thanked on the debut album's sleeve credits.

Chapter 17

1   The original citing of Rough Trade Distribution, which was not actually crossed out, was to be upheld legally in 1989 when the company went bankrupt, causing chaos over ownership of the Smiths' catalogue, which, it turned out, did not actually belong to the label.

2   In 'Childhood, Sexuality and the Smiths', an essay that forms part of *Why Pamper Life's Complexities?*, Sheila Whiteley, a self-proclaimed Smiths fan, devotes several thousand words to analysing these songs and reflecting on this incident and trying desperately to draw a positive conclusion, but still admits, 'Clearly, there is no empirical evidence to help interpretation.'

3   The first of these lines was a rewrite of one of anarcho-punk band Crass's: 'Do they owe us a living? Of course they fucking do.' The second was one of Morrissey's favourite ripostes, and would form the centrepiece of a future Smiths

single. Taken together, they were quite majestic. The 'iron bridge' referred to in the song, like other lines, appears to come from Viv Nicholson's *Spend, Spend, Spend* but was widely presumed by Smiths fans to reference the one that crossed the railway tracks from King's Road to St. Mary's.

4　Oscar Wilde, in correspondence with his close friend André Gide, had referred to his prison warden as 'quite a charming man,' though the influence on Morrissey may have been entirely subliminal.

Chapter 18

1　In *The Smiths: Songs That Saved Your Life*, Simon Goddard points out that the bootleg mixes of the Troy Tate album available online are considerably inferior to the final mixes, which this author has not heard.

2　This certainly makes more sense than the story that has typically been reported – that Porter had been cold-called by Geoff Travis, barely a week before he met the band at the BBC session, with a view to remixing the Smiths album. Not only would this have stretched coincidence to its limits, but it would have negated the need for the Smiths to approach Porter in the BBC canteen and introduce themselves in order for him to switch sessions.

3　Ever the optimist when it came to the Smiths, Morrissey assured listeners that it would be out in a month 'because I think the time is right.'

4　At some point Porter did get his wish. A 'Single Remix' – of the London session – was ultimately issued after the band's breakup. It sounds muddier than the original mix.

5　While completing this chapter, the author heard the multi-tracks for 'This Charming Man'. Marr's multiple guitar parts represent, not surprisingly, a true *tour de force*, all the more astonishing for the guitar player's youth; in addition to the various riffs and arpeggiated solos recorded onto different tracks, there are acoustic guitars and plenty of backwards reverb that add (hidden) volumes to the overall mix. Morrissey's vocals, draped in reverb though they may be, are equally impressive. Rourke's bass part reveals yet greater melody and dexterity than was audibly apparent on the final mix, while the bleed of the otherwise finished song through the isolated drum tracks confirms that Joyce recorded his drums at the end of the session.

Chapter 19

1 Given Travis's working relationship with Stein, it's entirely possible that the deal was agreed and the paperwork generated throughout the summer, based on the buzz surrounding the Smiths, and then signed and sealed after Stein saw the group in the flesh.

2 In Britain at the time, a little over 6 per cent of all record sales went direct to the Mechanical Copyright Protection Society by law; these royalties were then fed through to the composers via their publishers.

3 Marr was at pains to point out to the author that the money did not go exclusively into his own pocket. 'The first thing I did when I got publishing, was bought Mike a kit, bought Andy his amp, and Angie a ring. And I got myself a Rickenbacker. Morrissey had done the deal too so he didn't need me to buy him anything!'

Chapter 20

1 This shift in priorities caused enormous turmoil within Rough Trade. Richard Scott recalled that Geoff Travis had told him upon signing the Smiths that he viewed Morrissey as 'the next Boy George,' which Scott took as a commercial ambition rather than perhaps a cultural observation. 'That locked everything into clear perspective,' said Scott. 'That what I thought we'd been trying to achieve actually wasn't the case at all. That he had a completely different agenda. That suddenly it had to do with money and chart success.' The degree to which this had opened up a schism in the company was evident the day that summer that I arrived at Rough Trade's Blenheim Crescent offices to

interview Geoff Travis for *The Tube*'s segment on the label only to find him in a screaming match with various of the label's other major players. Travis was sufficiently put off balance that he initially insisted someone else be interviewed for the television show in his place; he eventually calmed down and sat for the interview, delivering precisely the sort of comments that were causing the internal fighting. 'Rough Trade wants to be successful in the most mainstream possible sense,' he said on camera, adding, 'I am very sick that we have lost groups who are as good as Scritti and Aztec to other majors . . . But we always had a moral problem because I never felt I could sign a group to a six-album contract without knowing that I had the resources to compete in the marketplace properly.' His conclusion? A prescient one: 'I think what's really been proved is that in a majority of artists' cases, they'll always take the money.'

2   In May 1983, just as the Smiths released 'Hand in Glove', Rough Trade had secured its first top 40 hit in the unlikely form of Robert Wyatt's 'Shipbuilding', a song written by Elvis Costello about the previous year's Falklands War, and released by Wyatt to coincide with the general election that returned the Thatcher government to power, largely on the back of the military victory in the Falklands.

3   It was at the Venue, on 15 September, that I first saw the Smiths in concert, thanks in part to the persistent urging of Scott Piering. It was immediately evident that something special was afoot, not least in the presence of a substantial following, many of whom were carrying flowers. I refer readers to Len Brown's book *Meetings with Morrissey* for a truly evocative first-person account of that show, his own first exposure to the Smiths, and how it profoundly affected him.

Chapter 21

1   Though it's often been stated that Morrissey chose the

667

hotel based on its bygone popularity with his idol James Dean, the Iroquois was in fact *the* rock 'n' roll hotel of choice by promoters in a city that lacked for affordable rooms. Its nonpaying guests, the cockroaches, were a familiar aspect of New York domesticity at the time.

Chapter 22

1   Time failed to heal Morrissey's perception of Porter's production. *The Sound of the Smiths*, a 2008 compilation of the band's singles with a few more classics thrown in to fill out the CD, swapped out the 7" release for the Peel version, supposedly at Morrissey's insistence.

2   The interview at the Haçienda was conducted by the author, and YouTube clips confirm the perils of a television show conducting an outside broadcast from a nightclub in real time. The front-of-house volume was meant to be muted on the Factory All-Stars, who were performing onstage at the time, once our interview got under way on the balcony. For some reason it didn't happen, resulting in Morrissey and I shouting at each other over the noise in an attempt to hear each other. TV viewers at home had no such problems, given the position of our microphones, except perhaps to wonder why the interviewer had stalled for ten seconds before starting the interview. Now they might know. Unfortunately, I can offer no similar excuses for the equally frazzled interview with Tony Wilson, Peter Hook and Paul Morley, except to suggest that as a nineteen-year-old fanzine editor dropped into the world of live television, I was evidently out of my depth. It was fun while it lasted, however.

3   When the Smiths were coaxed back to Europe, for a major German TV show, the three playing members and Sandie Shaw turned in a wonderful lip-sync performance of 'Hand in Glove' for the show *Formal Eins*, which replicated the 1960s sets of shows like *Ready Steady Go!* and Germany's own *Beat Club*.

Chapter 23

1 Marr claimed it had been written by him and Morrissey in the summer of 1983. Rourke did not receive a writing credit for what was widely considered his finest bass line.

2 In interviews for this book, Geoff Travis said it was the first he had ever heard of it.

3 John Porter, whose ability to conjure up subtle studio tricks was seemingly endless, recalled that one of these AMS-derived tracks may have added a harmonised note on both a major third and an octave above, the other on a major third *below* as well as an octave above.

Chapter 24

1 A year later, Morrissey was still smarting over Henke's apparent error. It was 'news to me,' he told Dave DiMartino of *Creem*, going on immediately to say that 'it had an absolutely adverse effect on our chances in America . . . And obviously Sire backed away immediately.' None of this was borne out by the evidence, and of all American labels that might have had an issue with gay artists, one would have hoped that Sire would have been the least concerned.

2 Contrary to accounts published elsewhere, no American Smiths tour was announced or advertised in 1984. Certainly the band did not abandon an American tour at the London airport, which would have had high-profile repercussions; that only happened with the European tour-in-progress earlier in 1984.

Chapter 25

1 As one of the many indicators of how irregular was the Smiths' business setup, various employees from Rough Trade and All Trade pitched in at Campden Hill Road to help Morrissey pack and move.

2 Without a producer earning one or two percentage 'points', as John Porter had done, there would also be more profit for Rough Trade to split with the band.

3 Though he was employed strictly as an engineer, Street brought to the studio a musical reference point: Lloyd Cole & the Commotions' debut album, *Rattlesnakes*, produced by Paul Hardiman, which hit the stores just as the Smiths hit the studio. 'I saw that as the standard that had to be achieved,' said Street. 'From a sound point of view. And also because it was in the same kind of terrain: really good, delicate guitar playing.'

4 Contrary to other accounts, 'Rusholme Ruffians' and 'Nowhere Fast' were not recorded in the same session at Jam as the 'William, It Was Really Nothing' single. As for the Peel session, which would be Porter's last session with the Smiths for the time being, the group also performed 'William' and 'How Soon Is Now?'. To successfully replicate the latter in the confines of an eight-hour BBC session, Porter cheated, bringing in the multitracks and transferring the tremolo guitar part (and maybe some others) onto the BBC tapes. The Smiths were fortunate to have a producer who also worked for the BBC and could get away with this.

5 Simon Goddard traced this line, as with many others in the song, to lyrics by the British comedienne/singer/actress Victoria Wood, namely her songs 'Fourteen Again' and 'Funny How Things Turn Out'.

6 In 1984, Rough Trade distributed an album by Flux of Pink Indians entitled *The Fucking Cunts Treat Us Like Pricks*. It made number 2 on the independent charts. By comparison, distributing and promoting *Meat Is Murder* was a cakewalk.

Chapter 26

1 These were scheduled to rise from 0.5 to 2 per cent, to the point where if the album sold 250,000 copies in the UK, Piering would be in for a £22,600 bonus.

2 As readers might have surmised, I count myself among these people. While I can't credit *Meat Is Murder* as the sole reason for my becoming a vegetarian, or even as the

final impetus (that one involved a fireman on a skiing holiday), it was arguably the most significant influence on a lifestyle change that, in my case, proved permanent. Let me put it this way: I would certainly not have turned vegetarian (and subsequently vegan) at that point in time had the Smiths not made *Meat Is Murder*. I know that I am but one of thousands of people whose lives were changed similarly and, quite apart from the music, I thank the Smiths for taking that stand, helping instigate the debate, and for positively impacting upon my life.

Chapter 27

1 The version released in the States later that year carried different lyrics from the British one – replacing the opening line 'on the high-rise estates' with 'all the lies that you make up.'

2 I say this in some part from experience. I attended the show at the Oxford Apollo – one of the most thrilling concerts I've ever witnessed. I knew many of the younger A&R people around this time, and one of them had brought her boss to see James; memory recalls that it was the label that almost signed the group. The A&R head took us aside after their set and, in all seriousness, asked us to explain the appeal of the two bands, because he could not understand it for himself.

3 'Well I Wonder' was in fact the only song from the Smiths' first three albums never to be performed live.

Chapter 28

1 Piering did, however, film the group in Super 8 in Ireland in November 1984, right at the point that Sire was putting together this video. It can't be discounted that his footage didn't make the cut and he ended up sending over Showbiz's footage instead.

2 Marr has been careful never to name Grower in the same sentence as the lawyer whom he has described as a 'shark.' He has also not been able to explain how Grower came to represent the Smiths in the first place: 'Alexis Grower

didn't come in from my side of things,' he told me in 2011. 'I'd never heard of him before.'

Chapter 29

1 Morrissey additionally tried to use this interview to gain revenge on Jim Henke of *Rolling Stone* by outing Henke in turn. 'The journalist who wrote it . . . is himself very steeped, he's a very strong voice in the gay movement in New York, I think it was just wishful thinking on his part,' said Morrissey, perhaps not knowing that music journalists at rival magazines might actually be friends. DiMartino felt compelled to come to Henke's defence, closing out his article by noting, 'You should be told that the *Rolling Stone* writer who wrote that statement is *not* very steeped, *not* a strong voice in the gay movement in New York, and it *wasn't* just wishful thinking on his part.'

2 On return from the States, Gosling's role continued. 'With Andy and Mike it started to get a bit more serious. They were trying to see me, catch up with me, to keep on sorting stuff out for them.' And then, suddenly, all contact stopped. 'There are forces within any band. Who knows what Moz thought of it all? Who knows whether Johnny might have decided at the end that it was all a bit too much?' Gosling was not hired for their next tour. 'It's one of those lessons you learn in life and the next time someone tries to put you in that role you say, "No thanks."'

Chapter 30

1 The live 'Meat Is Murder' became the B-side to the 7", marking this as the first Smiths single to use the generally rare 3/4 (or 6/8) ballad tempo for both sides. 'Nowhere Fast', 'Stretch Out and Wait' and 'Shakespeare's Sister' were included in its place on the 12". Original 12" test pressings that included 'Miserable Lie', which had changed significantly in concert over the years, and 'William, It Was Really Nothing', became some of the more valuable pieces of Smiths memorabilia.

2　The single sleeve noted that the record was 'Recorded in Manchester'. There was no mention of RAK.

3　It was not the only reference point. In Patti Smith's 'Kimberly', the song that had influenced 'The Hand That Rocks the Cradle', the singer referenced a 'flame' and compared herself to Joan of Arc.

4　'Rubber Ring' was Morrissey's specific term for the Smiths' music, as it applied to their fans.

5　When a Smiths compilation DVD was released in 1992, it was the *Top of the Pops* performance of 'The Boy with the Thorn in His Side' that was included, not the promotional video.

6　'Asleep' was played in Inverness, but only because the small venue had been unable to remove a piano from the stage and Marr decided to take advantage of it; Rourke and Joyce provided rudimentary bass and drums.

Chapter 31

1　'Margaret on the Guillotine' was later resurrected by Morrissey as a song title for his debut solo LP.

2　Asked if the song 'There Is A Light That Never Goes Out' was 'written about your relationship' with Johnny Marr, by Adrian Deevoy in GQ Magazine in 2005, Morrissey explicitly replied, 'It wasn't and it isn't.' In his own interview with the author, Marr nonetheless sang the lyric 'driving in your car' when explaining that, despite his lack of a license, 'I used to drive me and Morrissey around.'

3　As with 'Bigmouth Strikes Again', 'Cemetry Gates' used nonstandard tuning to help achieve its particular resonance.

4　Among respected British critics, Simon Goddard called it their 'greatest singular recording' in his book *The Smiths: Songs That Saved Your Life*; John Harris referred to it as their 'single greatest achievement' in *Mojo* in April 2011; and Jon Savage labelled it 'The Smiths' mature masterpiece' in the *Guardian* in December 2010.

5   The movie segment and the song itself were segued by the sampling of a Mike Joyce tom-tom roll on a primitive sampler of the era (the Window).

6   On July 9 1982, in a highly embarrassing breach of security, thirty-one-year-old Michael Fagan broke into Buckingham Palace and entered the Queen's bedroom, where she was sleeping alone. He subsequently spent six months in a mental institution.

7   The emergence of a rudimentary recording of this song, complete with the trumpet but few other overdubs, should not be taken as an untruth on Street's account, merely as evidence that the song certainly existed at some point in unbroken form.

Chapter 32

1   I attended this show. I'm not sure what I was doing in Newcastle, other than that I had ties with many of the people involved in Red Wedge and an affinity for that city based on my previous work for *The Tube*. As such, I was well aware that the Smiths were to be playing (unannounced); whether that factored into my decision to make the journey, or only became evident once I was in the venue, I cannot say.

2   Derek Hatton was expelled from the Labour Party later in 1986 for his membership in the Marxist-Trotskyite Militant Tendency, which the Party had outlawed in 1982, in a visible attempt to move further towards the centre.

3   Aztec Camera was no longer any sort of musical threat to the Smiths. After leaving Rough Trade for WEA, Frame recorded the overly produced album *Knife* with Dire Straits guitarist Mark Knopfler at the helm, and embarked on a British tour of seated venues; the American support slot with Elvis Costello was equally indicative of attempts to market Frame as 'adult-oriented rock.' His was a textbook case of the dangers of leaving a credible independent label for the lure of major-label waters.

4   Gannon had not auditioned for anyone since joining Aztec

Camera at age sixteen. That said, it was still surprising that he was hired with so little discussion.

5 Morrissey has denied writing the note that was left on Rourke's car. Rourke remains absolutely insistent that he received it.

6 It is fascinating, even reassuring, to note that Hughes originally intended for Duckie to win Andie's heart at the prom, but test audiences – perhaps evincing mainstream Hollywood expectations – recoiled at the idea. A different ending was subsequently filmed, against Hughes's wishes. Actor Andrew McCarthy, having shaved his head in the interim to appear in a play, was forced to don a wig for the scene.

Chapter 33

1 The notion that the Smiths did not see 'any money' from their record sales is, frankly, preposterous. Had that been the case, they would have been able to walk from Rough Trade after the first album for non-payment of royalties. Geoff Travis, noting the various 'houses and cars' acquired by various Smiths, said of the royalty cheques that went out from Rough Trade, 'I don't think they were seven figures but they were significant.' Even Sandie Shaw noted in her autobiography 'the big dollop of royalties I received from Rough Trade' – and that for merely singing on one minor hit single, 'Hand In Glove'.

2 *The Face* feature opened with 'manager' Scott Piering asking to see the story before it went to press, disturbed that Kent had interviewed several former Morrissey associates, including 'at least one sworn enemy.' Though the galleys were indeed sent to Piering, the story was still littered with inexcusable inaccuracies: the singer's name was misspelled throughout as Morrisey. Still, the piece was best remembered for Johnny Marr's final quote about his friend: 'I think he needs a good humping.'

3 Thanks to the arrival of Leslie Holmes, who hailed from Yorkshire and had a more open attitude, the Lads Club has gone on to host many concerts by famous groups,

and been used as a venue for talks and seminars and radio shows. A major fund-raising campaign in the twenty-first century saw Morrissey lead the way with a generous donation. Though Coronation Street is mostly boarded up and the surrounding area, with its new estates, bears little relation to that of late Victorian, industrial Salford, from the upper rooms of the Lads Club one can still see the gasworks of Ewan MacColl's 'Dirty Old Town'.

4 While recording 'Panic' at Livingston Studios in North London, John Porter had recruited the local primary-school choir to give the single some juvenile authenticity to match its rebellious nature; this also served as a nostalgic throwback to the days of T. Rex-era glam, when primary-age schoolchildren, like Marr, Rourke, and Joyce, formed a significant part of the audience.

5 Despite his harsh posthumous comments, the 1987 single 'Shoplifters of the World Unite' was 'dedicated to Ruth Polsky.'

6 Tony Wilson's dedication to the cause of Manchester music above all else was apparent in a letter he wrote to the G-Mex coordinators in advance of the Tenth Summer concert complaining about their minimal contribution towards better acoustics for the event. 'I know now that the sound on Sat July 19th will not be as good as it should be; just how disastrous, remains to be seen. Manchester, a city with great pop music, SHOULD have a fine large scale, pop venue. Your insistence, at this, the first pop concert in the dear old station, to pocket all but one thousand pounds of your full fee, and not to invest in the future of the building by supporting our efforts at acoustic treatment, does a disservice to the space, and does a disservice to Manchester.'

Chapter 34

1 Jarman did not meet with the band about the film other than to be introduced to them backstage at the G-Mex concert, where Marr was busy vomiting at the time due to pre-show nerves.

2   Pratt recalled his astonishment that the Smiths drank champagne cocktails – and that Rourke, despite coming off heroin, was 'doling out a lot of prescription drugs.'

3   His case had been put off until November, and so he had not yet been found guilty of a drug offence. He was ultimately given a two-year suspended sentence for possession of heroin.

4   The Dream Academy had initially released their version of the Smiths song as a B-side on Blanco y Negro, Geoff Travis's other label.

5   Simon Goddard deserves the credit for positing the idea of using the Jarman films as touring backdrops.

6   Recordings of the Irvine Meadows concert of 28 August, at which the Smiths played to 15,000 fans, have him screaming at security, 'Jesus Christ, don't be so stupid!' while Johnny Marr calls them 'Neanderthal fucking idiots.' Other reports of that night have suggested that kids in the audience were high on angel dust and thereby charged security without fear. At the Greek Theater in San Francisco, meanwhile, the audience hysteria saw fans clambering over the tour bus and helicopters called in.

7   Craig Gannon recalled that Morrissey was not with them on Concorde, suggesting that he might have returned to Colorado.

Chapter 35

1   The parliamentarian backlash against homosexual permissiveness began in earnest in 1986, with 'An act to refrain local authorities from promoting homosexuality' introduced in the House of Lords. The following year, Clause 28 was successfully amended to the Local Government Bill. It stated that a local authority 'shall not intentionally promote homosexuality or publish material with the intention of promoting homosexuality' or 'promote the teaching in any maintained school of the acceptability of homosexuality as a pretended family relationship.'

Chapter 36

1   The original demo for 'Is It Really So Strange?'

has subsequently become available, and it can be confirmed that the two versions are precisely the same tempo. As for 'Sweet and Tender Hooligan', the original Porter recording has not surfaced to allow for such a comparison.

Chapter 37

1 The recording completed with Porter eventually emerged, many years later, without Shaw's vocals, and with a sitar-like introduction, played by Porter on the Emulator.

2 The David Bowie song 'Kooks' on *Hunky Dory* includes the line 'If the homework brings you down, then we'll throw it on the fire.'

3 Morrissey, on the other hand, would demonstrate his own loyalty to Hinc by returning to the agent as a solo artist.

Chapter 38

1 For publishing Speranza's words, the *Nation's* editor, Gavan Duffy, was charged with sedition. At his trial, Lady Wilde stood up and took responsibility. 'I am the culprit. I wrote the offending article.' Perhaps because of her status, she was not charged.

Chapter 39

1 The one exception was 'The Draize Train', which was also absent from *The World Won't Listen*. The reason was never made clear.

Chapter 40

1 'I don't perform,' Morrissey insisted years later during an interview, correcting Russell Brand, then a radio host and consummate Smiths fan and not yet a world-famous actor and Morrissey compadre. 'Seals perform, unfortunately.' Morrissey said that he preferred the term 'appear live.'

2 The next time they met – 'Quite a long time later,' said Street – Marr 'was a bit cold towards me, to be honest with you. I just thought, "Well he's obviously felt I've thrown in my hat on that side of the fence, as it were."' The pair would eventually rebuild those fences and work together on the remastering of the Smiths catalogue in the 2000s.

3 Marr played on The The's album *Mindbomb* and the

Pretenders' single 'Windows of the World', neither of which were released until 1989. He also toured with The The as a full member, and subsequently played on the act's 1993 album, *Dusk*, as well.

4 The guitar riff for 'How Soon Is Now?', as sampled by British act Soho for their indie-dance single 'Hippy Chick', made it into the American charts later in 1990. As the legal co-writers of the single, it gave Morrissey-Marr as composers, and the Smiths as a group, though Marr was the only one actually sampled, their only American top 20 credit.

5 It followed Marr anyway. Matt Johnson noted to the author that, 'in some ways I suppose The The became a bit of a shelter in a storm for him as he was getting a huge amount of grief from certain elements in the music press, specifically the *NME*, who really resented the fact he'd just killed the goose that was laying their golden eggs.' Johnson recalled that Danny Kelly, 'would do his utmost to undermine Johnny's move from the Smiths to The The at every opportunity . . . This post-Smiths atmosphere became really poisonous and I remember Johnny actually apologising to me for bringing all this negativity with him. It wasn't his fault, of course, though he used to get quite down about it. I just told him to simply stop reading the music papers.'

6 Those three songs: 'Stop Me If You Think You've Heard This One Before', 'Death at One's Elbow' and 'Sweet and Tender Hooligan'.

7 The Smiths' instinct regarding the commercial appeal of 'Stop Me If You Think You've Heard This One Before' was confirmed a full twenty years later, when the club DJ/producer Mark Ronson took a version of it to number 2 in the British charts, as sung by Daniel Merriweather. Entitled simply 'Stop Me' and including a brief refrain from the Supremes' Motown classic 'You Keep Me Hanging On' for its finale, this was to be the highest-charting Morrissey-Marr composition in the UK.

PICTURE CREDITS

Plate section 1

'The Smiths' Manchester' by John Gilkes (www.johngilkesmapart.co.uk)

'Queen's Square, Hulme' and 'Brierly Avenue, Ardwick' courtesy of Manchester Libraries, Information and Archives, Manchester City Council

'Kings Road, Stretford' and 'Churchstone Walk, Wythenshawe' © Tony Fletcher

'The Smiths at Manhattan Sound' © Rick Stonell

'The Smiths at Manchester Central Railway Station' © Paul Slattery

'Morrissey and Johnny Marr' and 'Andy Rourke and Mike Joyce' © Paul Cox (www.paulcoxphotos.com)

'Without Doubt we are incurable Sandie Shaw fans' and 'The Smiths in concert, early 1984' © Paul Slattery

'The Smiths in 1984'© Barry Plummer

'Johnny Marr with Billy Bragg' © Stephen Wright (www.smithsphotos.com)

Plate section 2

'Morrissey as idol' © Barry Plummer

'At the "From Manchester With Love" benefit' © Steve Double (www.double-whammy.com)

'Geoff Travis' © Getty images, courtesy of the Estate of Keith Morris (www.keithmorrisphoto.co.uk)

'The Smiths' road crew'© John Featherstone

'John Porter' © John Porter

'Angie Brown' and 'Johnny Marr, Andy Rourke and Stuart James' © Stuart 'Jammer' James

'The five-piece Smiths at the G-Mex Centre' © Ian Tilton (www.iantilton.net)

'The Smiths as a quartet again' © Lawrence Watson. Courtesy of Retna, Ltd.

'The iron bridge across the railway tracks' © Tony Fletcher

INDEX

(in subentries, the following initials represent members of the Smiths: AR = Andy Rourke; JM = Johnny Marr; MJ = Mike Joyce; SPM = Steven Patrick Morrissey)

693